150 YEARS OF BASEBALL

Contributing Writers

Stephen Hanks

Perry Barber
Allen Barra
Thomas W. Gilbert
Joe Glickman
Owen Kean
Berry Stainback

Photo Researcher

Mark Rucker

PUBLICATIONS
INTERNATIONAL,
LTD.

ISBN 1-56173-090-4

Library of Congress Catalog Card Number: 89-61429

Contributors

Stephen Hanks (essays for The 1920s to The 1980s, captions) is Vice President and Editor of Phenom Publishing, Inc., a New York-based sports magazine publishing company. Mr. Hanks has also written about baseball for many national publications, including *Esquire, SPORT, Inside Sports,* and *The Village Voice.*

Mark Rucker (photo researcher) is a free-lance artist, designer, and picture editor. Living now in Saratoga Springs, New York, he was raised in Colorado and born in Chicago's south side, so he is a White Sox fan. He provides images for *The National Pastime* magazine, and his most notable work to date is the co-authored *The Babe: A Life in Pictures.*

Perry Barber (umpire essays) is one of the nation's few professional women baseball umpires. Ms. Barber works in various leagues around the United States and has umpired major league exhibition games in Florida and Japan. She currently writes a monthly column for *Referee Magazine.*

Allen Barra (The 1950s) is a Brooklyn-based free-lance writer who is a regular contributor to *The Village Voice,* writing about baseball, football, and boxing. Mr. Barra has also written two books on football and contributes to many national publications, including *Sports Illustrated, American Film,* and *Esquire,* writing on sports, film, and music.

Thomas W. Gilbert (The Early Years, The Turn of the Century, essays for The Early Years and The Turn of the Century, and captions) is a writer and artist living in Brooklyn, NY, and has been a history buff all of his adult life. He is a member of the Society for American Baseball Research (SABR) and is a contributing baseball writer for Phenom Publishing in New York.

Joe Glickman (The 1970s and The 1980s) is a Brooklyn-based free-lance writer who has written baseball articles for Phenom Publishing and contributed to *The Village Voice* and many New York-area publications.

Owen Kean (The 1920s and The 1930s) is a Brooklyn-based free-lance writer. He is a contributor to Phenom Publishing's baseball magazine and was formerly an editor for *Sports, Inc.* magazine.

Berry Stainback (The 1940s and The 1960s) co-authored *Snake,* the best-selling autobiography of former pro football quarterback Ken Stabler. Mr. Stainback has also collaborated on the autobiographies of baseball legends Joe Pepitone, Earl Weaver, and Frank Robinson. He is a former editor of *SPORT*.

Picture credits

Arizona Historical Society Library: pp. 105, 120. **Associated Press Photos. Bob Barton:** p. 433. **The Bostonian Society:** p. 215. **Boston Public Library:** p. 31. **George Brace Collection:** pp. 81, 97, 121, 137, 255, 307. **Dennis Brearly Collection:** pp. 193, 227, 251. **William Broderick:** pp. 178, 206, 214. **Bronx County Historical Society Collection:** p. 165. **Brooklyn Museum:** p. 191. **Carnegie Library:** pp. 95, 107, 117, 199. **Thomas Carwile:** pp. 132, 140, 142, 147, 158, 171, 176, 191, 210, 215. **Chicago Historical Society:** pp.

117, 129, 209. **Cincinnati Historical Society:** pp. 73, 252-253, 281. **Nancy Crampton:** p. 442. **Ken Felden:** pp. 36, 50, 54, 57, 61-62, 65, 67-69, 71, 75-76, 82, 84, 89, 95-96, 103-104, 106, 109, 112-113, 118, 121, 128-129, 133, 139, 146, 153, 157, 164-165, 173, 179, 182, 191-192, 200, 213-214, 218, 220, 225, 228, 232, 240-242, 250, 254, 260, 319, 386, 427. **Bruce Garland:** pp. 19, 151, 216, 249. **Dennis Goldstein:** cover, pp. 27, 63, 78, 83, 90, 92, 110, 114, 126, 148-149, 159, 163, 199, 209, 214. **Barry Halper:** cover, pp. 13, 143, 149, 155, 175, 192, 208, 214-215, 235, 244, 258. **Walter Handelman:** p. 30. **John Holway:** p. 249. **John Kashmanian:** pp. 8, 11, 21, 24, 31, 33, 41, 69, 81, 96, 133. **Keystone-Mast Collection:** pp. 145, 231. **Library of Congress:** pp. 9-10, 17, 19, 110, 184. **Lew Lipset:** pp. 30, 47. **William Loughman:** pp. 109, 131, 133. **Ace Marchant:** p. 93. **Michael Mumby:** pp. 169, 223, 229, 235, 241, 243, 247, 256, 259, 261, 263, 263, 265, 273. **National Archives:** pp. 142, 150. **National Baseball Library, Cooperstown, NY:** pp. 5-6, 8-9, 11, 15, 17, 24, 26-29, 32, 34-36, 46, 48, 51-53, 55-56, 58-60, 62, 65-67, 70-75, 77-80, 83, 85-91, 93-95, 97-103, 105-109, 111, 113-116, 119-122, 124-125, 127-139, 141, 143-146, 148-154, 156-163, 165-175, 177, 179, 180-182, 184-187, 190, 193, 195-197, 199-200, 202-205, 207-209, 211, 213-219, 221, 224-225, 227-234, 239-243, 245-246, 248-251, 253, 255, 257, 259, 261, 263-275, 278-284, 287, 289-294, 296-302, 305-307, 309-319, 323-337, 340-347, 349-351, 353-363, 365-369, 371-373, 375-377, 379-383, 385, 387-392, 394-395, 397-402, 405-408, 410-411, 413, 415-425, 427, 429-433, 435-439, 441-445, 449-453, 455, 457, 460-463, 465, 471, 473, 480, 483, 498. **NBL/Tom Heitz:** pp. 488-489, 490. **Anthony Neste:** cover, pp. 396, 426, 434, 439, 451, 465-466, 470, 474, 487, 494-495. **New York Library:** pp. 10, 16, 21, 32, 41, 44, 53. **Oberlin College Archives:** p. 57. **Ohio Historical Society:** p. 23. **TV Sports Mailbag:** cover, pp. 160, 168, 188-189, 192, 194, 197, 202, 205-206, 211, 219-220, 222-223, 225-227, 229, 231, 235-238, 245, 247, 251-254, 256-262, 266, 269, 271, 273, 275-279, 281, 283, 285-288, 290-291, 294, 297-299, 301-305, 307-315, 317-321, 323-329, 331-333, 335, 337-339, 341, 343-345, 347-348, 350-352, 355, 357, 359, 361, 363-387, 389, 396, 398, 400-401, 403-405, 409-412, 414, 416-420, 423-425, 428-431, 433-434, 437, 439-441, 443-446, 449, 451, 453-459, 461, 463-466, 468-470, 472-473, 475-479, 481-485, 487-489, 491, 493, 495, 497, 499. **Michael Pozini:** pp. 433, 457-459, 467, 474, 479, 481, 483, 489, 492-493, 496, 498. **Patrick Quinn/Sports Collectors Store:** pp. 81, 98, 116, 121, 183, 197-198, 238, 287. **Fred Roe:** p. 419. **Doug Ropp:** p. 427. **Mark Rucker:** pp. 4-7, 9-23, 25-26, 28-29, 31, 33-34, 37-39, 41-43, 45-47, 49-50, 52-56, 58-61, 63-70, 72, 75, 79, 82, 86, 88, 92, 99-101, 103, 105, 111, 113, 117, 123, 126, 131, 135, 137, 139, 143, 147, 147, 165, 179, 181, 184-185, 219, 287, 348, 441. **Bruce L. Schwartzman:** pp. 401, 414, 448, 451, 453-454, 456, 460, 471, 478-479, 481, 487, 491-492, 497. **Carl Seid:** p. 183. **John Spalding:** pp. 190-191, 207, 209, 223-224, 226, 274, 279. **David Sutton:** p. 376. **John Thorn:** pp. 84, 121, 239, 244, 246, 273, 275, 305, 308, 317, 335, 439. **United Press International Photos. UPI/Bettmann Newsphotos:** pp. 136, 138. **Western Reserve Historical Society:** p. 105. **Robert White:** p. 147. **Bob Wood:** p. 129. **Bryan Yablonsky:** pp. 393-394, 408, 447, 450, 455, 459-460, 476, 481, 486, 491, 497.

Special acknowledgment to Patricia Kelly and the staff of the National Baseball Library at the National Baseball Hall of Fame, Cooperstown, NY.

CONTENTS

The Early Years **4**

According to legend, Abner Doubleday laid out the first baseball diamond in Cooperstown, NY, in 1839. In fact, the first game was played on June 19, 1846, following the rules and principles of baseball created by Alexander Joy Cartwright.

The Turn of the Century **44**

The National League withstood challenges by new leagues but ultimately prevailed. Baseball tinkered with the rules, trying to maintain a balance in offense and defense. The long-range trend, however, was toward pitching dominance.

The 1900s **76**

The 1900s saw the emergence of Ban Johnson's American League and a period of unprecedented peace and prosperity in baseball. The 20th century opened with a drastic rule change; for the first time, a foul ball was counted as a strike.

The 1910s **108**

Ty Cobb was one of the few hitters to succeed in the decade, as pitchers such as Walter Johnson and Grover Cleveland Alexander dominated. And baseball's growing gambling-related corruption culminated in the 1919 Black Sox scandal.

The 1920s **140**

America in the "Roaring '20s" encountered a new chapter in baseball, emphasizing home runs and potent offenses, authored by Babe Ruth. The Bambino's slugging ability and charming personality caught the public's eye as no player ever had.

The 1930s **188**

With the country enduring the torment of the Depression, baseball was knocked off its competitive balance. By 1939, however, bolstered by stars like Joe DiMaggio and Ted Williams, gate receipts reached new highs.

The 1940s **236**

Night games, televised games, and World War II would prompt more changes in the game during the 1940s than in any decade since the 1880s. No other milestone matched in importance that of Jackie Robinson breaking the color barrier.

The 1950s **284**

Baseball had troubles in the 1950s. Less people went to deteriorating stadiums, which couldn't accommodate cars and were far away from the suburbs; fans instead watched games on TV. The game was dominated by a few teams, most notably the Yankees.

The 1960s **338**

Baseball expanded in the 1960s — with more teams and more games — leading to a wider audience. Expansion brought new ballparks and Astroturf. There were more black and Hispanic players; by 1969, there were 13 blacks and Hispanics among the 18 .300 hitters.

The 1970s **392**

The name of the game was speed in the 1970s. Baseball enjoyed increased popularity due to hustling offense, colorful superstars, and exciting pennant races. And, in 1973, the A.L. introduced the designated hitter.

The 1980s **446**

In the 1980s, such words as free agent, arbitration, and collusion became a part of the lexicon. Several stars joined the million-dollar-per-year club. Improved conditioning spawned athletes who were bigger, stronger, and faster.

Index **500**

THE EARLY YEARS

According to legend, Abner Doubleday laid out the first baseball diamond in Cooperstown, NY, in 1839. In fact, the first game was played on June 19, 1846, following the rules and principles of baseball created by Alexander Joy Cartwright.

A photo found in a Princeton College class album from 1861 (page 4) could be the earliest photo of a baseball game. Cricket is played on the left and baseball on the right. Alexander Joy Cartwright (page 5, top left) is the "Father of Baseball." An 1845 reward of merit (page 5, top right) features a scene of an early base and ball game. An 1832 woodcut (page 5, bottom) depicts another base and ball game.

THE
EARLY YEARS

Baseball as we know it began in 1846 on the Elysian Fields in Hoboken, NJ — where two teams of New Yorkers, the Knickerbockers and the New York Nine, played the first formal match under a code of 20 rules written by Alexander Joy Cartwright. These rules are the foundation upon which baseball developed, over the course of a century and a half, into our modern game.

There is, however, a far better known account of how baseball began. As the story goes, young Abner Doubleday founded baseball when he laid out the first diamond in Farmer Phinney's lot in Cooperstown, NY, in 1839. Supposedly, Doubleday invented the force-out and was the first to limit the number of players to nine; he then spent his teens and early 20s as a sort of baseball Johnny Appleseed, spreading the game across the country, until interrupted by the Civil War.

This tale has served as the official story of baseball since the Mills Commission thrust it upon the public in 1907. The only problem is that it is completely false. General Doubleday attended West Point in 1839; there is no proof that he ever even visited Cooperstown. Not only did Doubleday himself not claim to have invented baseball, but throughout his life he never showed more than an ordinary interest in the game.

The reason for the fabrication of the Doubleday story has nothing to do with Doubleday personally and everything to do with American politics in the early 1900s. At that time a public debate raged over whether baseball was a purely American creation, the view argued by Albert Spalding, or whether it was a descendant of British games such as rounders, which was the opinion of sportswriter Henry Chadwick.

Cartwright and the Knickerbockers had apparently been forgotten. Though Spalding agreed with Chadwick in private, he felt that for patriotic reasons Americans needed to believe that their national pastime was completely their own.

As a public relations maneuver, Spalding arranged for a rigged blue-ribbon commission to name Doubleday as the father of baseball. A well-known Civil War hero (who had fired the first shot at Fort Sumter in 1861), Doubleday was ideal for Spalding's purpose. Chadwick never took the matter very seriously, later dismissing it as "a joke between Albert and myself." Nevertheless, the Doubleday myth lives on. While it was designed to appeal to the nationalism of our great-grandparents, today it is the element of nostalgia for baseball's phony rural beginnings that we find appealing. In the words of Harold Peterson, "Abner Doubleday didn't invent baseball; baseball invented Abner Doubleday."

Alexander Joy Cartwright did not invent the rules of baseball from nothing; bat-and-ball games are as old as Anglo-Saxon culture, if not older. Forerunners of baseball, with names like old cats, stoolball, and goalball, were played in Great Britain and the empire hundreds of years before 1846. These games were broadly similar to modern baseball; they featured pitching, hitting, and rounding a certain number of bases in order to score runs. Like modern baseball, they were structured according to outs and innings.

In goalball and stoolball, which originated in the Easter festivities of medieval England and parts of the European continent, stools (or equivalent objects) were

This is a token for the 1858 Pioneer Base Ball Club of Springfield, MA.

ALEXANDER CARTWRIGHT

Alexander Joy Cartwright, who gave the world its 20 original baseball rules, is a dim and distant figure in baseball history; most details of his early life are unknown. We don't even know what kind of a baseball player he was. Perhaps not so surprisingly, his surviving pictures often show him formally dressed, as if about to umpire a game (as he was often called upon to do) or attend a Knickerbocker Base Ball Club banquet.

Cartwright was working for a New York City bank when he first joined the club in the mid-1840s. The club may have been related to a volunteer fire company of a similar name, as the volunteer fire company movement was an important civic cause of the time and was Cartwright's other passion.

In 1849 (three years after the first baseball game) Cartwright traveled to San Francisco by wagon train, taking with him an old Knickerbocker baseball. According to his fragmentary diary, Cartwright amused himself by teaching his game to people he met at stopping points along the journey west. There probably were western Indians playing New York-style baseball before it was even heard of in Boston or Chicago; there is no doubt that it was played earlier in Hawaii. Not happy in California, Cartwright sent for his family. He loaded up a ship with various goods and set out to sell them in the Hawaiian Islands. There he settled and stayed until his death in 1892.

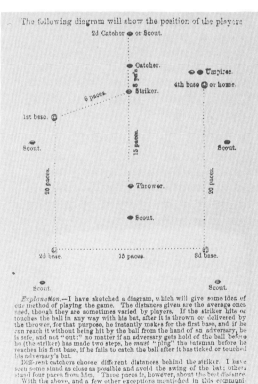

Explanation.—I have sketched a diagram, which will give some idea of our method of playing the game. The distances given are the average ones used, though they are sometimes varied by players. If the striker hits or touches the ball in any way with his bat, after it is thrown or delivered by the thrower, for that purpose, he instantly makes for the first base, and if he can reach it without being hit by the ball from the hand of an adversary, he is safe, and not "out;" no matter if an adversary gets hold of the ball before he (the striker) has made two steps, he *must* "plug" the bateman before he reaches his first base, if he fails to catch the ball after it has ticked or touched his adversary's bat.

Different catchers choose different distances behind the striker. I have seen some stand as close as possible and avoid the swing of the bat; others stand four paces from him. Three paces is, however, about the best distance.

With the above, and a few other exceptions mentioned in this communication, our rules of the game are similar to those of the Putnam Club.

The New York Active Base Ball Club (top) is shown in a ambrotype picture taken sometime between 1856 and 1863. An 1857 diagram (bottom right) from Porter's Spirit of the Time *describes "soaking" the batter by hitting him with the ball. A woodcut (bottom left) from 1820 shows a group of children playing an early base and ball game.*

THE EARLY YEARS

used as bases. In old cats the number of bases depended on the number of players on a side: In one old cat there is one base; in two old cats there are two, and so on. The old English game of rounders, which is played mainly by children throughout Great Britain and her former colonies, is closely akin to these primitive games.

The word "baseball" itself has a long history. In memoirs published in England in 1700, a certain Reverend Wilson protested the widespread playing of "baseball" on Sundays. Written accounts mention games of "base" being enjoyed by George Washington's Revolutionary soldiers at Valley Forge.

Of course, not all games called baseball were the same. Baseball before Cartwright was not one game, but a family of related games, with each locality practicing its own particular variety. In the mid-19th century, some of these games developed formal rules and were played by adults in organized clubs. One example is Philadelphia's town ball, which employed a very dead ball and stakes arranged in a square configuration instead of bases in a diamond. Town ball clubs formed in Philadelphia and nearby Camden, NJ, as early as 1831.

The Massachusetts (or New England) game, which was closely related to town ball, featured 60-foot base paths and also used wooden stakes for bases. It was obviously a high-scoring affair: One out constituted a half inning, and the game ended when one side scored 75 "tallies" or runs. In 1858, there were enough clubs competing in the Boston area to form a league, the Massachusetts Association of Base Ball Players, with a constitution and a common code of rules.

For a time, town ball and the Massachusetts game threatened to rival Cartwright's New York game for national supremacy. But by the end of the Civil War, just as Philadelphia and Boston were outstripped economically by New York City's commercial power, town ball and its Massachusetts cousin were abandoned in favor of the rapidly expanding New York games.

Today, variant forms of baseball have not disappeared. Softball, stickball, and myriad baseball-type games of the playground remain extremely popular. Some of these retain archaic elements, such as throwing the ball at a baserunner in order to put him out. This practice was known in town ball as "soaking."

Ever since the 1840s, however, these games have been outside the mainstream of organized baseball. The history of baseball as a sport in the modern sense — with organized leagues playing under standardized rules, schedules, and record-keeping procedures — begins with Alexander Cartwright.

In the early 1840s, Cartwright's game was not a very impressive sight. A group of young men would meet on occasional mornings to play ball on a vacant spot of land near Madison Avenue and 27th Street in Manhattan. There were no formal matches, rules, or uniforms — nothing to distinguish Alexander Cartwright and his friends from any other group of city-dwellers enjoying a little exercise with a bat and a ball.

In 1845, however, Cartwright and his associates took the first step toward formal organization by establishing the Knickerbocker Base Ball Club, with the intention of sponsoring games among its members. Although little is known

This whiskey flask with a baseball motif is from the 19th century.

HENRY CHADWICK

Born in England in 1824, Henry Chadwick came to the United States at age 13. He played and reported on cricket, then a professional sport in America, until 1856 — when he fell in love with the new American game and devoted himself to a lifelong publicity campaign on its behalf.

Starting in 1857, Chadwick covered baseball for the *New York Times,* the *World, Herald, Evening Telegram,* and other dailies across the country. In 1858, he became the baseball editor of the influential *New York Clipper.*

Personally an austere and hard-working man, Chadwick fought to rid baseball of alcoholism, gambling-related corruption, and other bad influences. In 1876, he convinced the National League to ban all open pool-selling (then the most popular form of baseball betting) from its ballparks.

Chadwick was more than baseball's unofficial conscience; he also played an important official role as chairman of the rules committee for the old National Association of Base Ball Players. There he guided the game through the rules changes and controversies of the turbulent 1850s and 1860s, baseball's difficult adolescence. Baseball owes to Chadwick the first box score (1859), the first rule book and scorecard (1858), and virtually all of its fundamental statistics. He edited *Beadle's Dime Base Ball Player* (an annual guide) from 1860 to 1881 and the original *Spalding Guides* from 1888 to 1908.

A tintype (top) illustrates the 1859 Atwater Base Ball Club of Westfield, MA. The Lowell Base Ball Club (middle left) of Boston were the champions of New England. The "On the Fly" tobacco label (middle right) from the 1860s features a baseball vignette. This ticket (bottom) is for the American Academy of Music's ball for the Philadelphia Athletics Base Ball Club, held on February 22, 1866.

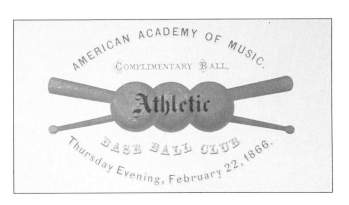

9

THE EARLY YEARS

about the club's membership beyond their surnames, club rules required not only that players be strictly amateur, but that they have the "reputation of a gentleman."

The spirit of these original rules seems to be that of the emerging urban professional and middle class, with its pretensions to aristocratic manners. One section of the Knickerbocker constitution argues for the "respectability" of recreation, something that would have been a given for true members of the Anglophile American upper classes. Most Knickerbockers seem to have been white-collar workers from New York's financial district.

Whoever they were, the Knickerbockers were the first to play baseball according to Alexander Cartwright's rules, which were adopted by the club on September 23, 1845. These rules established a diamond, bound by four flat bases 90 feet apart. They set precedents in such areas as the definition of fair and foul, the foul third-strike rule, the pitcher's balk rule, force-outs and tag-outs, three outs to a side and three strikes to an out, and nine men on a side. Cartwright's game would be easily recognizable to today's fans as baseball; the main differences between his rules and ours are that games were decided when one side scored 21 runs (instead of after nine innings), a fly ball could be caught on one bounce for an out, and pitching was underhand.

As baseball rapidly grew more and more popular in New York City, the Knickerbockers moved their games to the open spaces and well-maintained cricket grounds of Hoboken, a short ferry ride across the Hudson from Barclay Street in lower Manhattan.

By 1846, other clubs modeled on the Knickerbockers had begun to spring up. One of them, the so-called "New York Nine," was the visiting team in the first interclub match in baseball history. It was held on June 19, 1846; Alexander Cartwright served as umpire. To anyone who has ever competed in this most difficult of sports, it will seem poetic justice that the visitors thrashed his Knickerbockers in four innings 23-1.

Baseball changed more in the 22 years between 1846 and 1868 than in its entire history since. Beginning as a game played by no more than a few hundred members of some casual clubs, by the end of that period baseball was being played by everybody — children, rank amateurs, and bona fide athletes performing before paying crowds.

A Star Club tobacco label (top) from the 1860s features a baseball scene in Cuba. The champion of Missouri in 1867, the Union Base Ball Club of St. Louis (bottom), had a march composed in its honor.

THE WRIGHT BROTHERS

The Wright brothers George (left) and Harry.

Harry Wright was born in England, the son of cricket player Sam Wright. After his father emigrated to the United States to work as the cricket professional at the St. George Cricket Club on Staten Island, Harry switched to the American game and played with the original New York Knickerbockers. Later he managed the first openly professional team, the Cincinnati Red Stockings, to their miraculous 57-0 season of 1869. While with the Reds, Harry was the first to use coaches' hand signals.

Harry's younger (American-born) brother George was the better player. The first to play deep in the hole like today's shortstops, he pioneered defensive play at the position. George joined his brother's Reds and became their biggest star. During the 52 games he played for the '69 Reds, George batted .518, crushed 59 home runs, and scored 339 runs.

Taking the name Red Stockings with them, the Wrights moved to Boston in 1871, putting together that city's entry in the new National Association. From 1872 to 1875, they won four straight pennants. Boston's domination was so great that it eventually killed fan interest in the Association. Winning continued to follow George around; he won three more pennants in the National League, two as Boston's shortstop and a third as manager of Providence.

Both of baseball's Wright brothers were elected to the Hall of Fame, George in 1937 and Harry in 1953.

KNICKERBOCKER NINE,
1864.

The Excelsiors Base Ball Club of Brooklyn gave bronze pins (middle) to its players in 1860. The 1864 Knickerbocker Nine (top) of Albany, NY, unite for a photo. The 1864 New York Mutual Nine (bottom) and other clubs paid their star players, though the clubs were still technically amateur. Players were often paid through sinecure or no-show jobs.

MUTUAL NINE, 1864.

THE EARLY YEARS

The speed of baseball's geographical expansion was astonishing. Baseball was born in New York City in the 1840s, grew up in New York and Brooklyn in the 1850s, and rapidly spread across the United States in the 1860s. Shortly after the end of the Civil War, baseball as our "national pastime" was already a cliché.

But before baseball was to belong to the nation, it had to be taken away from such gentlemen, however self-styled, as Cartwright and his friends.

The Knickerbocker Base Ball Club was formed on the model of an English cricket club, and it attempted to rule over baseball in the same way that the Marylebone Cricket Club did in cricket. Cricket was the single greatest influence on the founders of baseball, inspiring the standardization of its rules and scoring methods, the form of matches between clubs, and even its early ideals of amateurism and gentlemanly behavior.

The Knickerbockers took these ideals seriously. Their rules provided for monetary fines for players who swore or showed poor sportsmanship. Umpires were treated with a respect that seems almost comical today. At a time when rules were few and sometime vague, the umpire had great power, at times performing the functions of a modern commissioner, league president, and rules committee on the spot. The umpire of the 1840s cut a dignified figure, standing off the first base line with one foot on a short stool, wearing a long coat, high silk hat, and a cane. The only other official present was the scorer, who sat near the catcher at a table that also served as a bar. Much like cricket at that time, baseball Knickerbocker-style was as much a social occasion as an athletic one. Competition among the early clubs in the giving of lavish postgame banquets became such a distraction from the games that the practice was legislated against at the 1859 national convention.

In baseball as in cricket, the purpose of amateurism and its associated values was the exclusion of those considered socially inferior. However, as baseball spread beyond the Knickerbockers and their circle to New Yorkers and Brooklynites of all classes, this kind of exclusivity became more and more unworkable.

The first formal baseball authority was the annual Knickerbocker club meeting, which determined rules changes and guidelines for matches. This gave way first to Knickerbocker-sponsored meetings of the New York clubs and then, in 1857, to the first national convention, an institution that elected officials to oversee the game. Democracy spelled the end of the Knickerbockers' power; by the time of the second national convention in 1858, none of the six officials elected was a Knickerbocker.

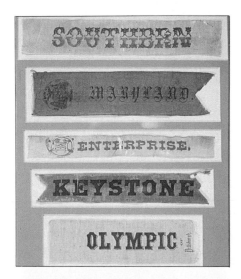

These silk ribbons (top) were won on a tour by 1860s baseball clubs. This brass statuette (bottom) dates back to the 1860s.

JAMES CREIGHTON

Pitcher Jim Creighton was the greatest star of the late 1850s and early 1860s, an era when Brooklyn and New York comprised the baseball world. His underhand fastball was the best anyone had ever seen, and he made the Excelsiors nearly invincible.

A larger-than-life figure, Creighton was the star attraction on the Excelsiors' famous barnstorming tour through western New York, Canada, and the middle Atlantic region. Actually, it was more like a triumphal march. Paying their own way like true amateurs, the Excelsiors would come to town, defeat the local all-star nine by an outlandish score like 54-14 and 50-9, and then enjoy their opponents' hospitality.

Creighton was the pitcher usually selected to represent Brooklyn in the various all-star games against New York. In the *Clipper* Silver Ball game in 1861, Creighton beat New York 18-6 and contributed at the plate too, scoring two runs.

Personally, Creighton seems to have been given a special respect by his fellow ballplayers; this was evident from the reaction to his shocking sudden death at the age of 21, which came as a result of internal injuries suffered while swinging a bat. His grief-stricken friends buried him in Brooklyn's Greenwood Cemetery under a marble pillar upon which was carved a pair of bats, cap, base, and score book.

*This 1865 picture (top) of Massachusetts ball at Boston Common is the only
known photo of this form of the game while in progress. It was a stereoscopic
photo that when looked at through a special viewer gave the impression of 3-D;
this type of photography was popular in the 1850s and 1860s. The Philadelphia
Athletics team (bottom) was founded in 1860; this is the 1865 team.*

THE EARLY YEARS

In the 1850s, baseball crossed the East River to Brooklyn, where the Atlantics, Eckfords, Excelsiors, and other clubs were born. They soon became the equals of the top New York clubs such as the Knickerbockers, Gothams, and Empires. A lively intercity rivalry sprang up and further stimulated the development of the game, especially pitching. Though pitchers of the late 1850s still threw underhand, they were learning to throw harder and harder. And much like a modern amateur team that employs a "ringer" or two at key positions, many teams of the 1850s found that if they wanted to stay competitive they had to hire a star pitcher or shortstop.

For instance, the Brooklyn Excelsiors of the late 1850s and early 1860s, who originally called themselves the "Knickerbockers of Brooklyn," professed strict amateurism. But this didn't stop them from raiding a rival club for Jim Creighton, the Dwight Gooden of his day (minus the curveball, which hadn't been invented yet), whose unhittable fastball propelled them to the top of the baseball world.

In 1860, the Excelsiors, who later that year became the consensus world champs, made a historic barnstorming tour across the Northeast. Led by Creighton and their captain, J.B. Leggett, the Excelsiors defeated 15 straight local all-star teams from western New York state to Philadelphia and Baltimore. These matches drew crowds as large as 3,000 or more and greatly popularized the game. Brooklyn clubs continued their domination during the Civil War, with the Eckfords of Greenpoint (later part of Brooklyn) winning championships in 1862 and '63, and the Atlantics winning in 1864 and '65.

Baseball began to be covered in the newspapers in 1853. A series of articles in the *Mercury* describes two contests between the Knickerbockers and the Gothams; the Knickerbockers won both, 21-12 and 21-14 (21 runs still decided a game).

That year the Eagle club was formed in New York and in 1854, the Eagles, Gothams, and Knickerbockers agreed to hold interclub matches under a modified version of Cartwright's rules. During the summer of '54, these three teams played closely fought series that captured the imagination of the press and public.

In 1854 and '55, many new clubs sprang up in New York and Brooklyn, including the Empires, Eckfords, Excelsiors (originally called the "Jolly Young Bachelors"), Putnams, Unions, Atlantics, and many others. Some of the new clubs represented unions or trade associations and were made up of working people. For example, the Eckfords were "shipwrights and mechanics" from the shipyards of

The Rockingham Base Ball Club of Portsmouth, NH, strikes a pose in 1867.

DICKEY PEARCE

Dickey Pearce's professional record is not very impressive: He hit .206 and .172 in two years in the National League with St. Louis and .256 over five years in the National Association with three teams. Of course, you have to consider that when the National League was founded, Pearce was 45 years old — and still playing shortstop; he played a total of five games at other positions in his professional career.

Pearce was not only the best defensive shortstop of the amateur era, but (together with George Wright) he invented the position as it is played today. When he started with the Brooklyn Atlantics in the early 1850s, the shortstop was used as an extra outfielder and universal cut-off man, much like the short-center fielder in softball. It was the Brooklyn-born Pearce who first saw the possibilities of playing it as an infield position.

Pearce was an offensive innovator too; at 5'3" he had to be. Famous for his ability to get on base, Pearce invented the bunt and later the "fair-foul" hit, which was perfected by Ross Barnes.

Pearce was the anchor of the Brooklyn Atlantic dynasty of the 1860s. In the biggest game of his career he faced the Cincinnati Reds' George Wright, his rival for greatest shortstop of the 19th century, and had the key hit in the Atlantics' 11th-inning rally that ended the Reds' amazing 79-game unbeaten streak.

This game (top) was played at Amherst College, MA, in 1868. The Keystone Base Ball Club (bottom) of Philadelphia in 1865 was one of many teams throughout the nation. The New Yorkers who fought in the Civil War spread the game throughout the country.

The Keystone Base Ball Club, Philadelphia, 1865

One of the notable clubs of that date

THE EARLY YEARS

Greenpoint (now Brooklyn). Still, at this time the season consisted of no more than a few dozen formal matches played by five or six major clubs.

In 1857, 16 ballclubs from the vicinity of New York and Brooklyn held a convention that was not under direct Knickerbocker control. They adopted a set of rules written by Henry Chadwick. These rules were more or less the same as Cartwright's, except that games were now to be played until nine innings instead of 21 runs.

Formalized under the name the "National Association of Base Ball Players" or the "Association" for short, the convention attracted 26 clubs in 1858. A rules committee was formed that presented rules changes to the membership annually.

The highlight of 1858 was a best two-out-of-three all-star series between New York and Brooklyn. Since there were no enclosed ballparks then, and a large crowd was expected, the opening game was held at the Fashion Race Course, a horse racing track near Flushing (now Queens). For the first time an admission was charged — 50 cents. The *New York Tribune* describes a Coney Island atmosphere outside the spectator stands, complete with three-card monte games, "guess your weight" machines, and much open gambling. A crowd numbering in the low thousands saw Brooklyn and its stars J.B. Leggett and Peter O'Brien lose to New York and Harry Wright 22-18.

Brooklyn dropped the series two to one, but regular season results show that the baseball balance of power had now shifted to Brooklyn. Of the top five teams in the 1858 regular season — the Atlantics, Empires, Eckfords, Excelsiors, and Putnams — all but the Empires were from Brooklyn.

Curry Klunk played for the Baltics of Wheeling, WV, in 1867.

The national convention of 1859 hosted 49 clubs; in 1860 there were 62, including teams from New Jersey, Boston, Detroit, Baltimore, and Washington, D.C. The 1860 convention issued a new, more detailed set of rules that provided for the umpire to call strikes as a warning to batters who tried to tire out a pitcher by refusing to swing.

Because of the war, attendance at the national convention dwindled to 28 clubs in 1861. However, development of the game did not come to a halt. In 1861, the *New York Clipper* newspaper offered a silver ball to the winner of a series of matches between New York and Brooklyn all-star teams. It was won by a Brooklyn squad loaded with stars from the Atlantics, including Dickey Pearce, Al Reach, and Creighton.

The 1862 convention instructed umpires to call balls as well as strikes, but only for the purpose of preventing delay, as in some kinds of modern slow-pitch softball. In 1863, the pitcher was restricted to a 12-foot by three-foot box (in 1867 it was changed to six-feet by six-feet). This zone is the origin of the expression "to hit one back through the box."

The Atlantics were champions in 1864, going 19-0. This was the start of baseball's first dynasty. The Atlantics remained undefeated until early in '66 and were champions of baseball for most of the next five years.

In 1865, men were home from the war and baseball picked up

ROSS BARNES

Although many old-timers put Ross Barnes on their all-time greatest list, his record is often denigrated today because of the fact that he went into decline soon after the National League abolished the "fair-foul" hit. Before 1877, any ball that bounced first in fair territory was fair, no matter where it went afterward. This is the reason that pictures from the time often show the third and first baseman hugging the lines. Barnes and other hitters perfected the art of bunting or slapping the ball so that it would roll far into foul territory or take a big bounce into the stands for a ground-rule hit.

Barnes and George Wright (Boston's double-play combination as well) set the table for the great Red Stocking lineup in the days of the National Association. It is difficult to stand out for a team that hit .295, .308, .323, .327, and .326 in its five years in the league, but Barnes outhit his team every year, batting .378, .404, 402, .339, and .372. He and Wright batted one-two and scored runs in droves; Barnes scored 126 runs in 60 games in 1873 and 116 runs in 78 games in 1875, and for his N.A. career he crossed the plate an incredible 462 times in 266 games.

Barnes was one of the "Big Four" whose controversial defection to Chicago hastened the birth of the National League. There, he won the N.L.'s first batting title by hitting .429 in 1876, exceeding the runner-up by 60 points and scoring 126 runs in 66 games. He also hit the league's first home run.

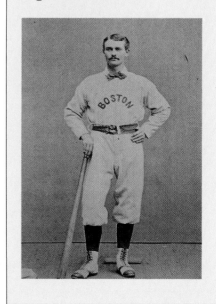

16

CHAMPIONS OF AMERICA.

The 1865 Brooklyn Atlantics (top) were declared the nation's champions. The spread of baseball led to a decline of dominance by clubs from Brooklyn. The Philadelphia Athletics' clubhouse (left) in 1865 was the quarters of the Olympic Town Ball Club, organized in 1833. The Atlantics-Athletics match (bottom) was illustrated in Harper's Weekly November 18, 1865.

THE EARLY YEARS

where it had left off, with more and more clubs playing matches that drew thousands of fans. In a match billed as being for the "Championship of the United States," 20,000 fans at the newly renovated Elysian Fields in Hoboken saw the Atlantics beat the New York Mutuals 13-12.

The number of runs scored in games between the better clubs was beginning to drop. This statistic and the frequent controversies over pitching rules, especially those governing the pitching distance and pitchers' motions, indicate that pitchers were illegally using sidearm deliveries. And more and more they were ignoring the rule prohibiting pitchers from "jerking" or snapping their wrists to put spin on the ball. Chadwick, baseball's leading authority at the time, wrote in favor of relaxing limitations on the pitcher, arguing that lower-scoring games were more "scientific."

Rules against professionalism were also being bent, broken, and just plain ignored during this period. Most of the big stars, the Creightons, Reaches, Cummings,

This tintype pictures a mascot of an early team.

and Joe Starts, moved from club to club as teams outbid each other for their services. In 1866, the Gothams went the way of the moribund Knickerbockers when five of the irregular players were hired away by other clubs. Not coincidentally perhaps, 1865 also saw the first major game-fixing scandal, when the Mutuals handed the Eckfords 11 runs in an inning filled with outlandish errors. Three Mutuals were suspended from the amateur Association, but reappeared within a few years.

In January 1865, the Atlantics and Gothams gave new meaning to the phrase "baseball fever" when they played a series of games on ice skates. The games were played on public skating ponds in Hoboken and Brooklyn, at least one of which was actually a ballpark that was converted for winter use as a rink.

At the 1866 convention, 202 clubs were represented, including notable newcomers the Philadelphia Athletics and the Washington Nationals. Yet another so-called world championship match was set for Philadelphia between the Athletics and the Brooklyn Atlantics. Eight thousand tickets quickly sold for 25 cents each, and by game day some were being scalped for as much as $5. Betting and, no doubt, drinking were vigorous. Eventually, the frenzied crowd became uncontrollable, spilling out onto the field and forcing cancellation of the game. The games were relocated to Brooklyn's Union grounds, where the Atlantics took two out of three by scores of 27-13, 12-31, and 34-24.

Tickets for the third game sold for $1 at the gate. How much money was that in the 1860s? Consider that ten years later an average factory worker made $1.25 a day. This means that general admission spectators at this game were probably paying somewhere between two days' and one week's pay — several hundred dollars in today's money — for a ticket.

Two of the better clubs in 1867 were the Irvingtons of Irvington, NJ, and the Unions of Morrisania (now the Bronx). The Unions won the championship by defeating a colorful Atlantic team featuring Charlie Pabor, an eccentric who while in training only ate chicken; Dickey Pearce; Joe Start;

WILLIAM "CANDY" CUMMINGS

Candy Cummings (left) poses with an 1869 Brooklyn teammate.

William Cummings, a skinny 5'9", 120-pound righthander who pitched from the late 1860s until the early days of the National League, always claimed to be the inventor of the curveball. If Cummings didn't throw the first curve, he certainly threw the first one that lots of opposing batters had ever seen. Playing for the Brooklyn Excelsiors against Harvard in 1867, Cummings and his pitch drew a crowd of skeptical onlookers, including members of the Harvard Physics Department, who denied that such a thing as a pitch that curved was possible. As Cummings later recalled, "I curved them to death."

Nicknamed "Candy," Cummings went 33-20 for the Mutuals in 1872. Throughout the season, disbelieving hitters asked umpires to check Cummings' baseballs, but the umpires never found anything suspicious. He pitched for Hartford in 1876, the first year of the National League, winning 16 and losing eight with five shutouts and a 1.67 ERA.

Facing St. Louis in his first National League start, Cummings showed how helpless big league batters could be when his sharp-breaking deuce was on: 24 of the 27 St. Louis outs came on pop-ups, 21 to the catcher and three to Cummings himself.

Only a year later, Cummings' style of pitching suddenly became obsolete when pitchers were allowed to throw from a higher arm angle. Cummings couldn't adjust, and he retired after finishing his last season 5-14.

FRANK LESLIE'S
ILLUSTRATED
NEWSPAPER

Entered according to the Act of Congress in the year 1866, by FRANK LESLIE, in the Clerk's Office of the District Court for the Southern District of New York.

No. 564—Vol. XXII.]   NEW YORK, JULY 21, 1866.   [PRICE 10 CENTS. $4 00 YEARLY 13 WEEKS $1 00

The management (left) of the amateur Association had to oversee 202 clubs in 1866. This color baseball panorama (bottom left) was printed in the late 1860s. An advertisement for a Boston printing house (bottom right), also from the 1860s, contains wisdom that extends beyond baseball.

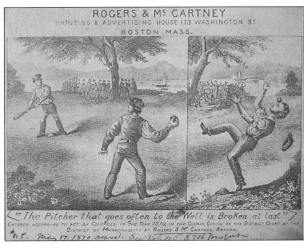

19

THE EARLY YEARS

George Zettlein; and the owner of a great nickname, Bob "Death to Flying Things" Ferguson, one of the period's great outfielders.

At this time any game could be advertised as being for the world championship, because the term had no universal definition. To the extent that there were legitimate champions, they were determined by consensus, much as boxing and college football titles are decided today. There were often competing claims to the same title, and the only generally accepted way to win the championship was to defeat the incumbent champion.

In 1868, however, the *New York Clipper* attempted to create standard criteria for determining the best team and the best players.

The newspaper offered a gold medal to the player with the best statistics at each position, and a gold ball to the winner of a best two-out-of-three series between the top clubs. Unfortunately, the '68 season ended without the two best teams, the Athletics and Mutuals, agreeing to play a decisive game.

During this time the amateur Association was repeatedly forced to change or refine its rules in order to maintain competitive balance, as the players found ways to circumvent them. Innovative forms of trickery and outright cheating from the 1860s include Bob Ferguson's habit of blocking baserunners when the umpire wasn't looking and the tactics of a Philadelphia pitcher who confused baserunners by interrupting his motion to scoop up a handful of dirt from the ground. It was this kind of creativity that has given us the exasperatingly complex modern balk rule.

A tremendous amount of "contract-jumping" occurred in 1868 by players who were still technically considered amateur. An example of how jaded baseball had become about professionalism is that a stern Henry Chadwick strongly attacked the jumpers for their dis-

This season's pass was for the 1877 Allegheny club of Pittsburgh.

loyalty but never mentioned their violation of the amateur ethic. Finally, the amateur Association institutionalized its own hypocrisy on the question of professionalism by establishing new "classifications" for ballplayers and teams. No one had to be told that the upper classification was, in effect, the pros.

By 1869, the unwieldy amateur Association, which now consisted of hundreds of clubs ranging from fully amateur to semipro to fully professional, was seriously weakened by scandal and internal conflict. It didn't take much of a blow to finish it off completely, and that blow was delivered by the Cincinnati Reds.

The Reds, short for Red Stockings, were founded by Cincinnati

THE ATLANTICS VERSUS THE REDS

On June 14, 1870, the openly professional Cincinnati Reds came to Brooklyn's Union grounds to take on the greatest team of the amateur era, the Brooklyn Atlantics.

A year to the day earlier, the Reds came to Brooklyn as an obscure western club and gained

their first national notoriety by defeating the New York Mutuals 4-2. Since then, the Reds hadn't lost a single game.

In the 1870 game, the Reds scored in the first inning on singles by George Wright, Doug Allison, and Harry Wright, and made it 3-0 in the third. Their star pitcher Asa Brainard held Dickey Pearce, Joe Start, and the other powerful Atlantic hitters until the fourth, when he allowed

two runs on a throwing error by third baseman Fred Waterman. Now it was Atlantic fireballer George Zettlein's turn to hold the Reds, as Brooklyn took the lead with two more scores in the sixth. But the Reds had not gone 79-0 over two seasons without being able to come back; the lead changed hands again in the next inning. The score was tied in the bottom of the eighth after Brooklyn's Charles Smith tagged up on a sacrifice fly by slugging first baseman Start and scored on a close play at the plate.

In the thrilling 11th, the Reds went ahead 7-5, but Brooklyn staged a desperate one-out rally to win the game 8-7.

Modern writers sometimes depict this game as a temporary victory for a doomed era, struggling Camelot-like to turn back the tide of professionalism. But it was not perceived that way by fans of the time, who knew well that, "amateur" in name or not, the Atlantics weren't playing for nothing either.

This woodcut is the only known scene of the Red Stockings vs. Atlantics match.

The 1868 Pastimes of Baltimore (bottom) featured pitching star Bobby Mathews, who is seated second from the left. He compiled a 132-111 record pitching for five years in the National Association and a 166-138 record while hurling for ten seasons in the National League. This rare 1868 baseball newspaper (top left) was in existence for only nine months. The 1867 Troy Haymakers (top right) assemble for a photo.

THE EARLY YEARS

lawyer and entrepreneur Aaron Champion. He held the very modern view that success in baseball would be good for the city and good for business. And Champion went about assembling a winning baseball team in a very businesslike way. In 1868, he built new baseball grounds, hired the best baseball mind in the country (Harry Wright) as player/manager, and openly set out to buy as many of the *Clipper* gold medalists as possible.

He didn't get all of them, but by 1869 his lineup could pass for an amateur Association all-star team. Included were third baseman Fred Waterman from the Mutuals, center fielder Harry Wright from the Nationals, shortstop George Wright from the Unions, pitcher Asa Brainard from the Excelsiors, right fielder Cal McVey from the Actives of Indianapolis, and both second baseman Charlie Sweasy and left fielder Andy Leonard from the Irvingtons. Only first baseman Charlie Gould was from Cincinnati.

With this kind of personnel playing under Harry Wright's brand of discipline and teamwork, the Reds set out on a national tour and won every game. One surprised Eastern powerhouse after another went down to defeat. Streaks of all kinds have always had a unique appeal to baseball fans, and the Reds' winning streak captured the imagination of the whole country. They traveled over 11,000 miles (by train), played before more than 200,000 people, and finished 57-0 for the season. They won 22 games in 1870 before their first loss.

It didn't take long for other clubs to follow the Reds' lead, and by late 1870 the better players were gravitating to a small number of high-paying teams. By 1871, the baseball world was irreconcilably divided between the amateur and semipro teams.

The 1869 Reds were neither the first to pay their players nor the first to admit it. What made the Reds unique was their strong organization and their aggressiveness.

This is a membership card for the Maryland Base Ball Club of Baltimore in 1868.

They weren't content to hire a star or two; they went after a star for every position in the lineup. The Reds were more like a corporation than an amateur athletic club and they treated their players as employees. They put all of them under contract and paid top dollar. Annual salaries ranged from George Wright's $1,400 to $600 for the utility player. In return they demanded that the players train hard, play hard, and stay in shape. Most importantly, the Reds were successful. During their season and a half of utter domination over the rest of baseball, the Cincinnati Reds paved the way for the first professional league, the National Association, by making professionalism respectable.

The 1869 season began where the previous season had left off, with arguments over whether the Mutuals or Athletics were the 1868 world champions and therefore

THE 1871 WHITE STOCKINGS AND THE FIRE

Late in 1871, the National Association's first season, two teams were fighting it out for the championship. Chicago had the best record at 17-8, with Philadelphia just behind at 17-9. The National Association championship, however, was determined not by won-lost record, but by most season series won, a season series being best-three-out-of-five. This meant that Chicago and Philadelphia were actually tied with four season series won apiece.

On October 8 and 9, the Great Fire devastated the city of Chicago, taking with it the White Stockings ballpark, equipment, and uniforms. The city's economy was so badly damaged that it was unable to field a professional franchise again until 1874.

More immediately, the fire deprived Chicago of their important remaining home games against Troy and rival Philadelphia. Nevertheless, the White Stockings vowed to finish the rest of the season in one great Eastern road trip.

After bad weather repeatedly prevented Chicago and Philadelphia from completing their series, the league decreed a one-game playoff for the championship, to take place in Brooklyn on October 30.

The White Stockings arrived tired, broke, and dressed in a motley assortment of uniform parts borrowed from other teams. Some were unable to find caps. Their play was ragged too. But even after being shut down through eight by Philadelphia pitcher Dick McBride, the plucky White Stockings never quit. They lost the championship, but averted a shutout by scoring in their final at-bat to lose 6-1.

The 1871 White Stockings, hosted by the Troy Haymakers, wore an assortment of borrowed garb.

ATLANTIC BASE BALL CLUB OF BROOKLYN.													
PLAYERS	P	1	2	3	4	5	6	7	8	9	10		R.
1 Pearce, S. S													
2 Smith, 3rd B.													
3 Start, 1st B.													
4 Chapman, L. F.													
5 Ferguson, C.													
6 Zettlein, P.													
7 Hall, C. F.													
8 Pike, 2nd B.													
9 McDonald, R F													
TOTAL		0	0	0	2	0	2	0	1	0	0	5	8

RED STOCKINGS BASE BALL CLUB OF CINCINNATI.													
PLAYERS.	P	1	2	3	4	5	6	7	8	9	10		R.
1 G. Wright, S. S.													
2 Gould, 1st B.													
3 Waterman, 3rd B.													
4 Allison, C.													
5 H. Wright, C. F.													
6 Leonard, L. F.													
7 Brainard, P.													
8 Sweasy, 2nd B.													
9 McVey, R. F.													
TOTAL													

The 1869 Cleveland Forest City Base Ball Team (top) had five professional players, with Deacon White, seated at far right, the highest paid at $125 a month. Harry Wright's 1869 Cincinnati Red Stockings (bottom left) look dashing in a woodcut that appeared in Frank Leslie's Illustrated Newspaper. *A scorecard (bottom right) of the July 14, 1870, Atlantics vs. Red Stockings game tells the fateful story.*

entitled to the *Clipper* gold ball. After a string of easy victories against weaker western opponents that served as a kind of spring training, the year-old Reds came to the Union grounds in Brooklyn to face the Mutuals. In a contest that was defensively very well played for the time, the Reds won 4-2 behind pitcher Asa Brainard. The game created something of a sensation because the Reds did not commit either a wild pitch or a passed ball, and first baseman Charlie "Bushel Basket" Gould made 12 putouts without an error. These were still the days before gloves of any kind; all the players, including the catcher, fielded with their bare hands.

The Reds also showed the Mutuals one of the trick plays that was becoming their trademark: With men on first and second, Brainard intentionally dropped a fly ball and fired it to the third baseman, who turned the double play. In another version, with a man on first base, the Reds catcher would drop a third strike. According to

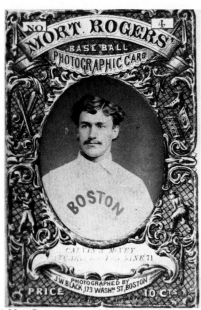

A Mort Rogers scorecard for the 1871 Boston Red Stockings featured Cal McVey, who batted .419 that season.

the rules of the time this compelled the batter to run to first, and the catcher would turn the double play second to first. The rule book eventually caught up with both of these maneuvers.

The Reds added three more wins in the next three days against the Atlantics, Eckfords, and Irvingtons. After sweeping the three principal Philadelphia teams — the Athletics with Al Reach and Levi Meyerle, the Olympics, and the Keystones — the Reds became a national phenomenon. In Washington, D.C., they were invited to the White House by President Ulysses S. Grant, who saw them defeat the Nationals and Washington Olympics to run their unbeaten streak against major Eastern opponents to nine.

The Reds' success caused yet another national controversy over the championship. According to custom, the championship belonged to whomever first defeated the previous champion twice in a row. Therefore, the New York papers claimed that it had remained with the Mutuals (who had only lost once to the Reds) until their second loss to the Eckfords on July 29. Cincinnati papers argued that while the Reds may not have won the championship technically, they were proven to be the best team.

In July of 1869, the Mutuals announced that they had adopted a strict Reds-style code of conduct and a system of penalties for such offenses as coming late to practice. The year ended with the credibility of the Association championship as poor as ever. The gold ball had changed hands several times among various Eastern teams, but there was no doubt in anyone's mind that the 57-0 Reds were the class of the field.

Public confidence in the Association generally was at an all-time low. The 1869 season was marred by many minor gambling scandals and charges of what was euphemistically called "indifferent play." Journalists sarcastically termed phony upsets "wondrous" or "inexplicable" and sometimes went as far as to speculate openly that games had been fixed.

In 1870, the Reds carried their unbeaten streak back to Brooklyn, where they were defeated for the first time by the Atlantics on June

ORATOR JIM O'ROURKE

Considered versatile even for an era when rosters were small and players had to be generalists, Jim O'Rourke was recruited for the National Association's Boston Red Sox by Harry Wright, who saw O'Rourke in amateur ball in his native Connecticut and was impressed that he could play catcher, shortstop, and third base equally well. O'Rourke was also a fine cricket player and was one of the stars of Harry Wright's English tour of 1874.

Called Orator because of his eloquence with the language, O'Rourke came into his own in the early days of the National League. Given a regular position at last, he was the league's finest right fielder for a decade. He had a great throwing arm. Pregame distance throwing contests were popular in the 1860s and 1870s; during one of them, O'Rourke made the second-longest throw ever before 1880— 365 feet. For the decade of the 1870s, O'Rourke hit .331 and had the highest seasonal RBI total, 62 in 1879.

He left Boston in 1879 and went on to have a 19-year major league career, playing outfield, catcher, and third base mainly with Buffalo and the New York Giants. He had a career .310 average, and for his time O'Rourke had good power; he slugged .422 lifetime and led the N.L. in home runs with six in 1880, and triples with 16 in 1885.

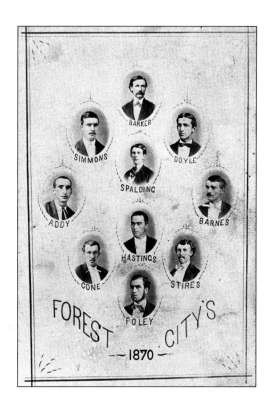

FOREST CITY'S
—1870—

Baseball fashions (top left) were quite formal, as shown in this print from the New York Clipper. Al Reach is in an Athletics uniform. The Rockford, IL, Forest City club (top right) featured Al Spalding and Ross Barnes. In 1867, this club upset the mighty Washington Nationals, creating an outburst of regional pride in the Midwest. An 1876 cigar-box label (bottom) shows a scene of the Boston Red Stockings and the Philadelphia Athletics playing on tour in England.

THE EARLY YEARS

14. Although the Reds continued to win nearly all of their games, their fortunes declined rapidly. Without the attraction of the amazing unbeaten streak, attendance plummeted, even at home in Cincinnati.

Other clubs, such as the Chicago White Stockings, nick-named the "$18,000 Nine," were now fielding all-salaried teams. Chicago had its own all-star team of sorts, including Levi Meyerle, former Troy Haymaker Bill Craver, and four former Eckfords; they put the last nails in the Reds' coffin when they beat them twice, on September 7 and October 13, 1870. Soon after the season the Reds went bankrupt and disbanded permanently.

The battle between amateurs and pros came to a head in early 1871, at a bitter amateur Associa-tion meeting that ended with the amateur teams walking out for good. Representatives of the remaining ten pro teams met at a New York City bar on St. Patrick's Day of that year to form the "National Association of Profes-sional Base Ball Players," or National Association for short. All but one of the teams, the Eckfords, agreed to pay the $10 entry fee for the 1871 season. The original National Association clubs were: the Philadelphia Athletics; the Troy, NY, Haymakers; the Wash-ington Olympics; the New York Mutuals; the Boston Red Stock-ings; the Rockford Forest Cities; the Cleveland Forest Cities; the Chicago White Stockings; and, joining a little later, the Ft. Wayne, IN, Kekiongas.

The National Association was the first baseball organization that resembled a league in the modern sense. Hoping to avoid the errors of the amateur Association, the National Association set up a cen-tral authority in the form of a league president and other officers who were more powerful than those of the Association. It estab-lished clear criteria for the league championship; each team was to play a best three-of-five series against every other club, with the winner of the most series being given the championship, which for the first time was called the "pen-nant."

In the long run, however, this limited structure proved not nearly strong enough and the league proved too fragile to survive. With-in five years, the National Associa-tion was overcome by the same instability and corruption that killed its predecessor.

Long Levi Meyerle was the first batting champion, hitting .492 for the 1871 N.A. Philadelphia Athletics.

Like the Association, the National Association had no sched-ule. As long as teams played the required number of series, they could play an unlimited number of "exhibition" games (with league or nonleague opponents) during the season. In fact, some teams played more exhibition games than official games, and fans were often con-fused about which games were which. The National Association president lacked the authority to deal with contract-jumping or "revolving"; because the league had no basic agreement with the players, they were bound only by the terms of their contracts with the individual clubs. On their own, and often on the day of the game, the clubs decided how to divide up gate receipts, who was to serve as

KING KELLY

Mike "King" Kelly was one of baseball's first superstars.

Though he had no better than above-average speed, Kelly ter-rorized defenses with his aggres-sion on the base paths. He was one of the first to show that the stolen base could be an important offensive weapon; in 1887, the first year that stolen bases were counted, Kelly stole 87, even though he was past his prime. He perfected the art of sliding, inventing the "fadeaway" slide. Playing for Chicago in the glori-ous 1880s, Kelly hit .354, .288, and .388 from 1884 to 1886 and led the National League in runs scored with 120, 124, and 155.

The King was famous for his quick-wittedness and trickery, and he personally caused the N.L. to rewrite many of its rules. One of his specialties was run-ning from first to third base directly across the diamond when the umpire had run to the outfield to follow an extra-base hit. Once he was sitting out a game on the bench when an opposing batter hit a foul fly out of reach of the catcher but right toward Kelly. Perfectly in accor-dance with the rules of the time, which allowed for instant player substitutions upon a verbal announcement, he shouted "Kelly now catching" and grabbed the ball for the out.

Tired of trying to curb Kelly's late-night drinking and other nonbaseball pursuits, Chicago horrified its fans by selling him to Boston in 1887 for the huge amount of $10,000.

A book of baseball rules (top) was published in 1872. Teams played baseball more uniformly as the rules were standardized. The Troy Haymakers of 1871 (bottom) were 15-15. Lip Pike, standing in the middle, hit .351 and scored 42 runs, while Clipper Flynn, standing far right, hit .311 and scored 44 runs.

THE EARLY YEARS

umpire (umpires were still unpaid volunteers), and what players were eligible to play. In one case, Chicago refused to play Troy for an entire year in a dispute over the status of a former White Stocking on the Haymakers. Nor could the league president take any action against the persistent problems of gambling, drinking, and rowdiness at the parks, which damaged the league's public image.

The financial backers of the National Association clubs never achieved anything comparable to the complete control over their league that the National League owners later exercised. A sign of the owners' weakness was the election of a player, Bob Ferguson, to the National Association presidency in 1872. The owners didn't turn much of a profit either. Boston, one of the strongest clubs, lost $3,000 in 1872 and made about $4,000 in 1873, but paid its players totals of $16,700 and $14,900. In terms of profits, the National Association club owners probably finished no higher than third, after the bookmakers (no records available) and the players.

The National Association had one other major problem: the Boston Red Stockings. The Red Sox hired Harry Wright as manager in 1871, and he reunited the nucleus of the great old Cincinnati team: George Wright to play shortstop, Cal McVey at catcher, Charlie Gould at first, and Wright himself in center field. He later added Ross Barnes and pitcher Al Spalding from Rockford. Wright's team dominated the National Association almost as completely as the Reds had dominated the last days of the Association, running away with four of the league's five pennant races. Except for the 1871 race, which was close because of a season-long injury to George Wright, the only suspense for National Association fans was in waiting to see the size of the Red Sox' margin of victory.

Armed with a blistering fastball (that could knock Boston catchers out of the game) and a good change-up, Spalding was a major contributor to Boston's success. He compiled a record of 207-56 in five years. In 1875, he opened the season with 20 straight wins, a tie, and then four more victories for a streak of 25 games pitched without a loss. The 1875 Red Sox finished the year 71-8, 15 games ahead of the Philadelphia Athletics. Four of the National Association's top five hitters were from Boston, eight of the top 20. Most of the other clubs never became competitive with Boston; in 1875 several teams dropped out of the league during the season and only two of the nine finishers were above .500. Overall, in the five-year history of the National Association, 25 different clubs came and went.

During the political struggles of the late 1860s and early 1870s that created and then later destroyed the National Association, which was baseball's first experiment with the league format, the game continued to develop on the field.

JAMES "PUD" GALVIN

A contemporary of Old Hoss Radbourn, Pud Galvin was another great workhorse pitcher of the 1880s. Active in the National League between 1879 and 1892, Galvin pitched more innings (5,941⅓) than anyone in history except for Cy Young. He is sixth all-time in wins (361), second in losses (310), second in complete games (639), and ninth in shutouts (57). Though small (5'8" and 190 pounds), Galvin had a powerful fastball and terrific control; in his 14-year career he struck out 1,799 and walked only 744.

Galvin went 46-29 for Buffalo in 1883, with a 2.72 ERA and a league-leading five shutouts. Together with Radbourn, Charlie Buffinton, and Mickey Welch, Galvin was a major contributor to 1884 — the year of the pitcher. An unprecedented seven no-hitters were pitched in the three major leagues that season, and league ERAs plummeted to 2.98 in the N.L., 3.24 in the A.A., and 2.99 in the Union Association.

Galvin's peak year was 1884. For the season, he went 46-22 with four ties; he had a 1.99 ERA and 12 shutouts. He completed 71 of his 72 starts and led the league in innings pitched with 636. And in one magnificent series with Detroit, Galvin was as close to perfect as a pitcher has ever been. Pitching three games of the four-game set, Galvin threw two shutouts, one a no-hitter, and lost the third game, 1-0. For the whole series, he pitched 39 innings and allowed one run, for a 0.92 ERA. His usually excellent control was flawless: 36 strikeouts and not a single walk.

This game was played at Wesleyan University, Middletown, CT, in 1874.

NEW YORK FASHIONS
FOR MARCH 1870.
Published by E. BUTTERICK & CO., 589 Broadway

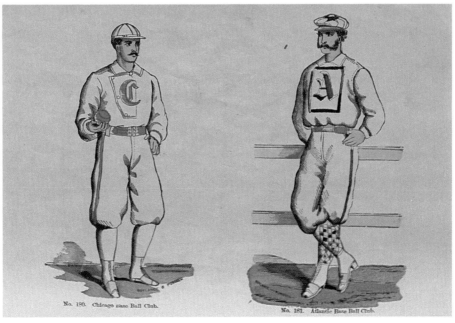

No. 180. Chicago Base Ball Club.

No. 181. Atlantic Base Ball Club.

An 1870 New York fashion magazine (top) displayed the latest attire for the player who wanted to be in vogue. Peck & Snyder's 1875 Sporting Goods catalog (bottom) displays the uniforms for the National Association Chicago White Stockings and Brooklyn Atlantics. Chicago was 30-37 that year, while Brooklyn was 2-42.

THE EARLY YEARS

Most of the action in National Association baseball was in the infield. The Cincinnati Reds-turned-Boston Red Sox proved that a tight, sure-handed infield was the key to winning. With the ball relatively dead, doubles and triples were much rarer than in today's game. Though a few parks were enclosed, and others sometimes put overflow crowds behind ropes strung in the outfield, hitting home runs over these barriers was very difficult. When they did occur, as in the case of Charlie Gould's widely reported "home run with the bases full" against Chicago in 1871, home runs were treated as curiosities. The base on balls was also rare and was considered as an error by the pitcher rather than as an offensive weapon.

After the 1875 season, the National Association was swamped by problems on and off the field. The combination of the league's instability, yearly scandals, and off-season contract musical chairs gave such owners as Chicago's William Hulbert the opportunity to blame everything on the players and to lay the groundwork for a new league that would answer only to the owners.

In many ways, modern baseball is a product of the events of the seven years between 1876 and 1883. In 1876, the first modern league, the National League, was founded; in 1882, baseball experienced its first interleague war; and in 1883, baseball first experimented with the two-league format, which we have today.

Modern baseball's concentrated ownership structure and its poor labor relations can also be traced back to this period. When a band of owners left the moribund National Association to form the National League in 1876, it meant the end of the players' influence and ultimately their freedom. The

George Wright of Boston batted .353 in five seasons of N.A. ball from 1871 to '75; he hit .256 in seven years of N.L. ball.

new league was a monopoly, tightly controlled by the owners. Like any monopoly, the National League operated by excluding competitors, and in 1882 this resulted in a scenario that would repeat itself in the 20th century. When there were enough potential baseball owners and baseball cities that had been expelled or denied franchises by the National League, the outsiders formed a rival major league, the American Association. Next came all-out war, with the new league raiding the old for players and undercutting its ticket prices. Unlike many of the later conflicts, this one was short-lived, ending with a cease-fire in the form of the 1883 National Agreement. The two leagues made peace and scheduled the first annual World Series between two major leagues.

This period also saw the greatest advances since the 1860s in the game on the field. Basestealing became a more important element of offense. Players began to use catcher's equipment and primitive fielding gloves in the late 1870s, allowing catchers to stay directly behind home plate at all times and greatly reducing the number of unearned runs that were scored. The days of the common 35-10 score were over; teams of the early 1880s averaged about six runs for each side per game. But the most drastic changes were in pitching. As Henry Chadwick had urged, pitchers were allowed in 1881 to throw sidearm and beginning with the 1884 season, overhand. These were not small adjustments for the players; each rules change forced many veteran players to retire from the game.

The National League came out of William Hulbert's machinations

DEACON WHITE

Jim White — called "Deacon" because he didn't drink, smoke, or gamble — was a pioneer of modern catching on the field and an early activist in the players' union movement off the field.

White was Cleveland and Boston's catcher in the bare-handed days of the National Association, where he hit .347 and where he caught Al Spalding from 1873 to 1875. In the late 1870s, White developed a rudimentary catcher's glove and mask, which enabled him to become the first catcher to play directly behind the plate as modern catchers do. Not coincidentally, White was an early master of the curveball, which he taught to many of his pitchers. He was also the first to see the value of offering a proper target.

White had his best offensive year with pennant-winning Boston in 1877, leading the National League in batting (.387), slugging (.545), triples (11), and RBI (49). In a 14-year career he hit .303 and slugged .382.

White's main involvement with the players' union movement began in 1887, when Detroit sold him and shortstop Jack Rowe to Pittsburgh for $7,000. Vowing that "no man is going to sell my carcass unless I get half," White refused to report. Instead, he and Rowe bought the Buffalo franchise in the minor league International Association. Organized baseball then moved to prevent White and Rowe from playing for their own team. The resulting bitter stand-off greatly polarized the players and owners and contributed to the Players' League revolt in 1890.

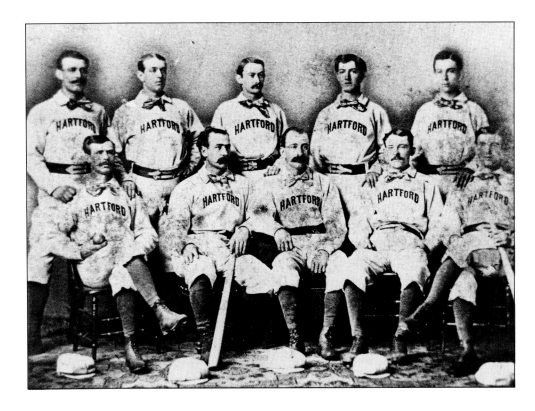

An 1870s advertisement (top right) reveals that bats were made of different woods. The 1875 Hartford (top left) club featured Candy Cummings, standing in the center. Cummings claimed to have invented the curveball about 1864 or '65, saying that he noticed the curving flight of clam shells that he was tossing on the beach. The Boston Red Stockings (bottom) were the N.A. champions in 1872, plus they had "permanent" wooden grandstands.

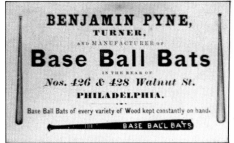

BENJAMIN PYNE,
TURNER,
AND MANUFACTURER OF
Base Ball Bats
IN THE REAR OF
Nos. 426 & 428 Walnut St.
PHILADELPHIA.
Base Ball Bats of every variety of Wood kept constantly on hand.
BASE BALL BATS

ATHLETICS   BOSTON
1. George Hall 2. George Bechtel 3. Wm Craven   7. Jim White 8. Al Spaulding 9. George Wright
4. Adrian (baby) Anson 5. Ezra Sutton 6. — Clapp   11. Harry Wright 10. — McVey 16. Andy Leonard
12. — Fishler 13. —Force 14. —Eggler 15. Dick McBride 17. Jim O'Rouke 18. — Barnes 19. Shaffer

GRAND STAND BOSTON BASEBALL GROUNDS 1872

THE EARLY YEARS

against the tottering National Association in 1875. Infuriated by the Davy Force case, Hulbert decided to fight fire with fire. He secretly signed four members of the champion Boston Red Sox: Al Spalding, Ross Barnes, Cal McVey, and Deacon White, along with Philadelphia's Cap Anson, to contracts for the 1876 season.

Under National Association rules, a player who signed with another club during the season was technically subject to expulsion. When word of the signings leaked out and created an uproar, Hulbert and Spalding came up with the idea of a new league in order to head off any punitive action by the National Association. Hulbert marshaled support for his new league by cleverly playing on the universal desire for baseball reform and on the dissatisfaction that prominent figures in baseball had with the National Association. These individuals included Harry Wright, who felt the National Association was dominated by Philadelphia interests; Henry Chadwick, who had railed for years against its instability and corruption; and owners in the western cities of Louisville, St. Louis, and Cincinnati, who resented the Eastern Establishment. A general meeting was held on February 2, 1876, in New York City, where Hulbert and the westerners presented delegates from Boston, Hartford, New York City, and Philadelphia with a 13-point National League constitution as a fait accompli. After a surprisingly short debate, the Easterners agreed to join, and the National Association for all practical purposes was dead.

The National League constitution was designed to transfer all league authority to the owners, to prevent the coming and going of franchises, to discourage gambling-related corruption, and to end labor-management conflict. As it turned out, it would be far more successful on the first count than the final three.

The new league's antigambling stance was completely ineffectual. Ironically, the league's high standards and competitive parity appealed to gamblers as well as to fans. Better-regulated competition was both easier to follow and easier to bet on. And as owner exploitation of the players led to declining salaries in the late 1870s, the players became easier targets for exploitation by gamblers for their game-fixing schemes. The Louisville affair of 1877 hurt the young league's reputation badly, and it proved to be only one of many such scandals.

As intended, the National League's tough policy toward players put an end to most contract-jumping, but it led to problems that made the National Association look like the picture of labor-management harmony — some of these problems have continued to the present day. The reserve clause and the National League's other collusive practices gave the founders of the rival American Association a powerful weapon to use against Hulbert's monopoly. The National League had attempted to protect its status as the sole major league by creating an umbrella organization to oversee all professional leagues and to

Cal McVey hit .362 in his five years in the National Association, including .382 for the 1874 Boston Red Stockings.

WILLIAM HULBERT

Chicagoan William Hulbert founded the National League almost single-handedly and ruled over it as his personal kingdom until his death in 1892.

He served as league president every year except for the league's first, 1876, when he gave the job to Morgan Bulkeley. As it turned out, this maneuver cost Hulbert his place in the Hall of Fame. Before the Hall opened in 1939, a committee was chosen to induct baseball's "pioneering executives." The committee had clearly not done its research, ignoring Hulbert and picking Bulkeley on the basis of having been the N.L.'s first president.

Hulbert was an example of the new breed of businessmen owners who came into baseball in the 1870s. Unlike many of the uninvolved "backers" of nominally amateur clubs of the 1860s, Hulbert was no gentleman promoter. He was in the game to win and to make a profit.

While owner of the White Stockings in the National Association, Hulbert grew tired of the N.A.'s infighting, weakness, and what he saw as its coddling of spoiled ballplayers. Hulbert's National League and its owners wielded unprecedented power and held on to it so tightly that baseball's subsequent history has been punctuated by player rebellions, strikes, and lawsuits pitting players against management.

On the other hand, Hulbert's league is still around, which is more than can be said for many other of history's would-be major leagues.

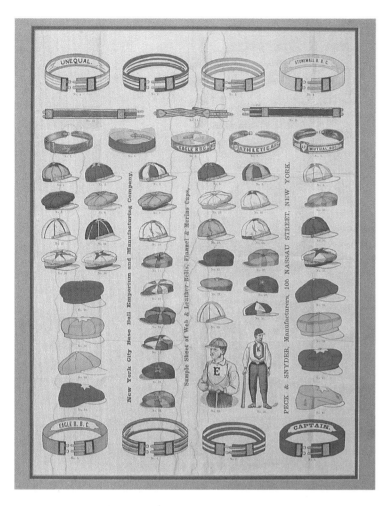

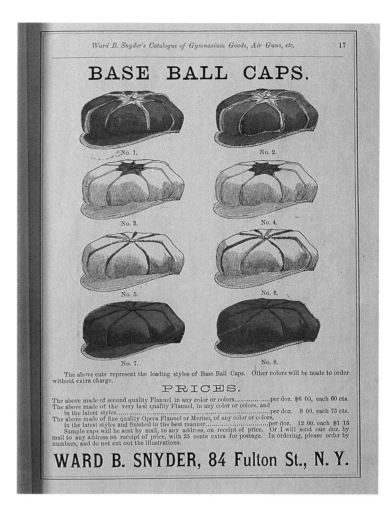

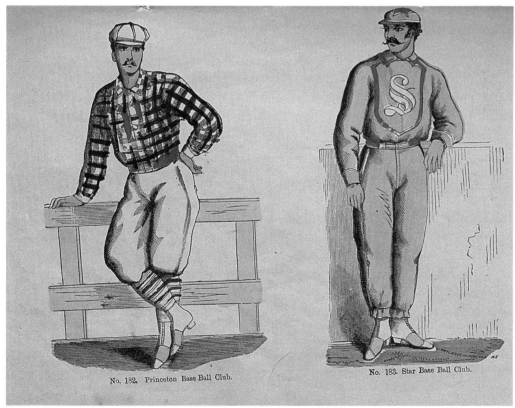

No. 182. Princeton Base Ball Club.

No. 183. Star Base Ball Club.

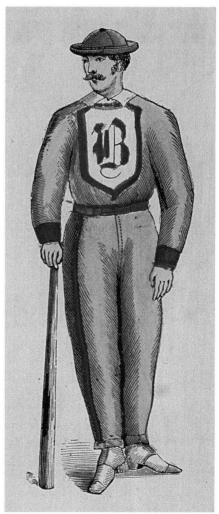

An 1875 poster (top left) displays the merchandise of Peck & Snyder, the "New York City Base Ball Emporium." This page from the 1875 Peck & Snyder's Sporting Goods catalog (top right) presents the style of baseball caps of the day. The catalog also had uniforms for amateur teams (bottom left) and "New Styles" (bottom right) for the asking.

THE EARLY YEARS

enforce the distinction between the majors and the minors, which in this era was often more semantic than real. Nevertheless, in 1881 a coalition from outside organized baseball — made up of financial speculators, brewery owners, and would-be club owners from Brooklyn, St. Louis, Pittsburgh, Cincinnati, Columbus, Philadelphia, and New York — formed the American Association. This new league, modeled closely on the National League, allowed both beer to be sold at its parks and Sunday games, and had 25-cent ticket prices, half the National League price.

For 1881, the American Association tried to hire only those non-reserved National League players whose contracts were up; by 1883, bitterness between the leagues erupted into all-out mutual raiding of rosters. When the new league gained the upper hand by offering players contracts without the infamous reserve clause, the National League was forced to reconcile for peace.

As part of the peace treaty, the American Association sold out the players by agreeing to a new reserve clause and promising to respect all National League contracts. Under the agreement, the relationship between the two leagues was essentially the same as that between today's two major leagues. This new order lasted for exactly one season. In 1884, a new league, the Union Association, fought the next battle in the monopoly wars that were to occupy baseball for the next two decades.

1871

On May 4, 1871, the first National Association game took place when the Fort Wayne Kekiongas defeated Cleveland 2-0. Catcher Deacon White of the Forest Citys, who later went on to have

Frank Flint of the 1877 Covington, KY, Stars.

a 14-year career in the National League, got the first hit, a double.

The pennant race of 1871 was close throughout the season, with Chicago and New York running neck and neck until the Mutuals faded in July. Both Boston and Philadelphia then came on and the three teams finished within a couple of games of each other. What came next was a controversy worthy of the old Association and a bad omen for the National Association's future. When Philadelphia challenged the results of two early losses to Rockford, saying that one of Rockford's players had been ineligible, the league awarded the games to the Athletics as forfeits. These two games gave Philadelphia the best yearly record only because the league refused to take similar action in a similar case involving a loss by Boston to Washington. Some blamed undue Philadelphia influence in the league offices for this apparent inconsistency.

1872

In 1872, the minimum number of games for a complete season series was raised from three to five apiece, making the season (officially, at least) a minimum of 50 games long. At 39-8 Boston finished 7 1/2 games ahead of Philadelphia and far ahead of the rest of the 11-team field, which included five noncompetitive clubs who had only paid their $10 admission fee in order to collect their share of the gate in

PETE BROWNING

The original "Louisville Slugger" (after whom the bat was named), Pete Browning was born, played, and died in Louisville, KY. In his eight years with Louisville in the American Association, 1882 to '89, the mighty Browning was the league's top power hitter, winning two batting titles and leading the league in slugging once. In his 13-year career, Browning hit .400 once, .330 eight times, and .300 11 times. In the days when home runs were rare, Browning slugged over .500 four times. His lifetime batting average of .343 is tenth best in history, third best for righthanded hitters.

Browning had a reputation for clowning and drinking. His problems may have been related to a lifelong ear disease that rendered him at times partially or totally deaf. Browning's behavior ranged from the eccentric to the self-destructive. Like Joe Jackson, the only other of baseball's top ten batters who is not in the Hall of Fame, Browning collected bats (at one time as many as 200) and gave them names.

Browning's hearing disability was definitely responsible for his poor defensive play. While playing second base early in his career, he was deemed a laughingstock because of his fear of incoming baserunners. But that fear was justified; on several occasions he was spiked by sliding runners that he never heard coming. Things only got worse when he was moved to the outfield, where hearing the sound of the ball on the bat is an essential part of fly-ball judgment.

Baseball's first dynasty was the Boston Red Stockings, a virtual all-star team of the early 1870s. The Red Stockings ran away with the National Association pennant from 1872 to '75. This 1871 photo features the stars of that great early team. Pitcher Al Spalding (center) won 207 of the team's 227 wins from 1871 to '75. Below Spalding is manager/outfielder Harry Wright, and continuing clockwise from bottom left is catcher Cal McVey, third baseman Harry Shaer, second baseman Sam Jackson, shortstop Ross Barnes, outfielder Dave Birdsall, outfielder Fred Cone, and first baseman Charlie Gould.

THE EARLY YEARS

games against the contenders. Only six of the 11 teams finished the season. Because of the National Association's minimal standards, this scenario repeated itself throughout the next four years.

The better teams played many proficient and lower-scoring games, including Boston's 4-2 defeat of the Mutuals on May 11. But games such as the May 20 contest between the Athletics and Baltimore showed the consequences of the league's lax umpiring standards and its inability to control either player or fan behavior on the field. The game was delayed for several hours while the two teams squabbled over the selection of an umpire. By National Association rules, each team had veto power, and this often resulted in a standoff. When a young amateur ballplayer from Baltimore was finally selected, he was abused and intimidated by the Athletics players throughout the game. This caused the home crowd to protest every call; then during a lengthy argu-

A 1910s Mail Pouch tobacco advertisement features an 1870s baseball scene.

ment in the eighth inning, a Baltimore player successfully pulled the hidden-ball trick on an Athletic baserunner who had assumed wrongly that the umpire had called time out. At this, the Athletics refused to continue, and the game ended with angry fans mobbing the playing field. The league later ordered the game replayed from the beginning.

1873

Nine teams, including five of the six 1872 finishers, started the 1873 season, but only seven were still there at the end. With the additions of Deacon White and outfielder Orator O'Rourke, Boston won 43 games and lost 16, coming in 4 games ahead of the newly formed Philadelphia White Stockings, who had acquired star pitcher George Zettlein and hired away five players from their cross-town rivals, the Athletics.

Brooklyn's Union Grounds, the premier ballpark of the time and the site of many National Association games, had a facility for handling baseball betting on the premises and set aside a special section of the stands for gambling fans.

In an 1873 game between Baltimore and the Mutuals, league president Ferguson, who was serving as umpire, got into an argument with the Mutuals catcher, grabbed a bat, and broke the backstop's arm in two places. A policeman who was sitting in the stands tried to arrest Ferguson, but his victim refused to press charges.

1874

Although Boston won as usual in 1874, the eight clubs who made up the league were unusually competitive. The full championship season had been lengthened to 70 games, ten against each opponent. While no National Association team yet had ever actually played the officially required minimum, this year four of the teams managed to play over 50.

There were several more game-fixing scandals in '74. In a game between the revived Chicago White Stockings and the Mutuals, New York pitcher Bobby Mathews left the mound in the fifth inning, complaining of an illness. Many fans and reporters smelled a rat and accused Mathews and three

ALBERT SPALDING

Albert Spalding was the first professional pitcher to win more than 200 games in his career. He retired at age 26 because he found that he could make far more money outside baseball than in it.

Spalding first became famous at 17 when he pitched little Rockford, IL, to a victory over the Washington Nationals. He was a mainstay of the great National Association Boston Red Sox dynasty of 1871 to '75, compiling yearly records of 20-10, 37-8, 41-15, 52-18, and 57-5 for a career winning percentage of .787. He also hit .320 in 1,445 at-bats. He pitched only a little more than one season in the National League, going 48-13 with a 1.78 ERA, again, attaining a .787 winning percentage.

But early on, Spalding had seen the commercial possibilities of the growing national pastime; he retired to found the Spalding Sporting Goods Company. He made use of his friendship with N.L. president William Hulbert (whom Spalding had advised during the planning of the National League) by becoming the official supplier of league baseballs. Soon, Spalding's sporting goods empire made him a millionaire.

In 1890, loyal to the league that he had helped create and ever the capitalist, Spalding was the point man in the National League's fierce suppression of the Players' League revolt, falsifying attendance figures for the press and successfully undermining the new league's financial backing.

The Brooklyn Atlantics (top left) of the National Association were 17-37 in 1873. Manager Al Reach's 1874 Philadelphia Athletics (top right) pose before a trip to England in this print from the cover of The Daily Graphic *newspaper of July 13, 1874. Pitcher James Dickson McBride was 33-22 in 1874. The* Daily Graphic *woodcut (bottom) pictures the opening game of the 1874 season. A "daisy cutter" is a hard-hit grounder.*

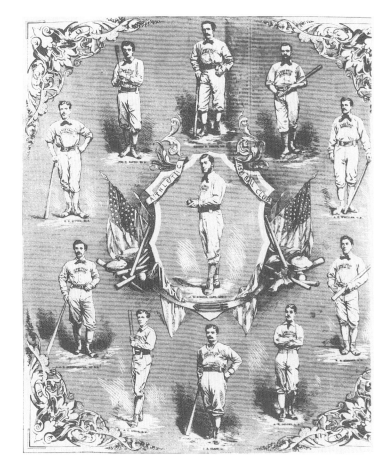

THE EARLY YEARS

other Mutuals of conspiring to throw the game. When the furor refused to die down, Mutual management felt it necessary to produce a doctor's note to prove that Mathews was really ill. In another case, the league unsuccessfully attempted to cover up a number of charges of crooked play made by respected umpire Billy McLean. McLean testified that at various times during the 1874 season, he had overheard players discuss game-fixing plots that were either planned or already under way. After his testimony became public, one player was expelled from the league, only to be reinstated the following year.

In July, the Boston Red Sox and Philadelphia Athletics made the first European baseball tour, to Great Britain and Ireland. The teams played 14 games, stopping at Liverpool, Manchester, London, Sheffield, and Dublin. The baseball games were a mixed success, but British fans were interested to see the Americans defeat several of the best cricket clubs at their own game. At this time there were still enough former cricketers (like the Wrights) among the American pros that a competent cricket 11 could easily be assembled from a group of two or three dozen baseball players.

1875

The eight 1874 clubs returned in 1875, and they were joined by five weaklings who finished the season a combined 18-101. Boston turned in its finest season (71-8) and finished 15 games ahead of the second-place Athletics. By this time even Boston fans were becoming bored with their team's success.

In 1875, the National Association wrote its own death sentence when it offended influential Chicago owner William Hulbert. Hulbert considered himself the injured

This Home Favorite cigar-box label was printed about 1878.

party in the National Association's most celebrated contract-jumping episode, the Davy Force case in 1875. Force, a shortstop with Chicago in 1874, had signed contracts with both Philadelphia and Chicago for the '75 season. The two teams took the matter to the Association, which first decided in favor of Chicago but later, after a Philadelphia partisan was elected league president, reversed itself. Soon Hulbert was assembling political and financial support for a new league.

1876

The National League used a round-robin scheme for the 1876 season, but starting with 1877, the clubs operated under a regular schedule drawn up by the league. The eight National League clubs in 1876 were: Chicago, St. Louis, Hartford, Louisville, Philadelphia, Cincinnati, Boston, and New York.

The first game in National League history was played on April 22, 1876, in Philadelphia between the White Stockings and the Athletics. Veteran George Wright was the first batter and grounded to short. Boston's Orator O'Rourke made the first National League hit, a single, and Boston won 6-5.

With the core of Boston's great National Association team and Cap Anson from the Athletics, player/manager Al Spalding guided the White Stockings to a 52-14

THE BIGGEST INNING EVER

Both the National League and the American League modern (post-1900) records for most runs scored in a single inning were set in a 13-month period between 1952 and '53. In May of 1952, Brooklyn scored 15 runs in the first inning against Cincinnati; in June of '53, Boston put 17 men across the plate in the seventh inning of a game against Detroit.

But the all-time record biggest inning occurred on September 6, 1883, when Cap Anson's fearsome Chicago White Stockings, winners of the National League pennant three years in a row, scored 18 runs on 18 hits and 29 total bases in one inning versus Detroit.

Up 8-3 before their half of the seventh, the Stockings batted around without making an out, and the score then stood at 15-3. Third baseman Ed Williamson, one of eight Chicago batters to collect three or more hits that day, singled in two more runs and knocked the poor Detroit starter out of the box. In those days, there were no reserve players, so instead of heading for the showers, he changed places with the right fielder.

The next man up homered; two successive doubles made the score 20-3. After an RBI single by right fielder Billy Sunday, both speedy Chicago outfielders Abner Dalrymple and George Gore made outs. One error and five runs later, Detroit retired Sunday on its third attempt of the inning. The final score was 26-6.

This card of Cap Anson is in the 1887 N-28 Allen & Ginter tobacco trading issue.

The first-known photo of blacks playing baseball (top) shows a game at the Rochester House of Refuge in 1875. The blacks were wearing the solid-color caps while whites were wearing the striped, multicolored caps. The 1876 Chicago White Stockings (bottom) were the first N.L. champs. Ross Barnes hit .429, an average due at least partly because of "fair-foul" hits. A ball was fair if it hit the ground first in fair territory, no matter where it rolled afterward. He bounced these fair-fouls far into foul territory.

ANSON   GLENN   A.G. SPALDING   BARNES   BIELASKI

ADDY   PETERS

ANDRUS   JAS. WHITE   McVEY   HINES

THE
EARLY
YEARS

record and won the first National League pennant hands down. Chicago was paced by batting champion Ross Barnes' .429 average and Spalding's 47-13 and 1.75 ERA pitching. Chicago hit .337 and slugged .416 as a team; no other club hit over .271 or slugged over .342. The White Stockings scored 624 runs, 2.6 times more than last-place Cincinnati's total of 238. All of the top five RBI men in 1876 were White Stockings. The season ended with a strong Hartford club putting together a nine-game winning streak, but they finished tied for second with St. Louis, 6 games out.

1877

In 1877, Hulbert, who had been the power behind the scenes all along, was named National League president. After he ordered the expulsion of the clubs from the league's two biggest cities, New York and Philadelphia, only six teams started the season.

The first minor leagues, the International Association and the League Alliance, were formed in 1877. Candy Cummings served as the first International Association president.

The problem of gambling's influence on baseball refused to go away. Few fans of the mid-1870s took the National League's antigambling rules seriously, and for good reason. Though perhaps a little more discreet, gambling was still going on as usual at National League ballparks and charges of game-fixing were as common as ever. When the league admitted the crooked Mutuals in 1876, it had sent out the message that baseball would continue to say one thing and do another on this issue.

But the Louisville scandal of 1877 struck a serious blow to baseball's integrity, and the league was compelled to take action. Behind

ace pitcher Jim Devlin, the Louisville Grays were well on their way to clinching the 1877 pennant, when they suffered a very suspicious-looking losing streak that in the end gave the flag to Harry Wright's surprised Red Sox. During a road trip, club officials noticed heavy telegraph traffic to and from some of their players, in particular utility player Al Nichols. They insisted that he open all of his wires and discovered evidence that gamblers were paying George Hall, Bill Craver, Jim Devlin, and Nichols to throw games. All four were banished from baseball for life.

For years afterward, Craver and Devlin, a close friend of league president Hulbert, begged for reinstatement. It never came. Devlin finally gave up hope and joined the Philadelphia Police Department; Craver also took up a career in law enforcement with the Troy police.

Though the league's handling of the Louisville scandal bolstered its prestige in the long run, the scandal's immediate repercussions caused both Louisville and St. Louis, who had secretly hired the four guilty players for the 1878 season before the scandal, to drop out of the league.

Boston's Deacon White led the National League in batting at .387. McVey and Anson hit .368

Lee Richmond pitched the first perfect game in National League history, as he hurled Worcester over Cleveland 1-0 on June 12, 1880.

and .337 respectively for Chicago, which fell to fifth place. Big factors in Chicago's decline were the loss of Al Spalding as a pitcher (he played first base before retiring the following year) and the collapse of Ross Barnes, who hit only .272.

1878

Boston won the 1878 pennant fair and square, behind a one-man show by Tommy Bond, who led the league in winning percentage at .678, wins with 40, innings with 533, and shutouts with nine. He completed 57 of the 59 games he pitched. Boston went 41-19 despite hitting only .241 and finishing fourth in runs. The Red Sox added good defense to their great pitching, fielding .914, the only team over .900.

Indianapolis, Milwaukee, and Providence joined the National League in 1878; Louisville, St. Louis, and Hartford dropped out. It was a year of illustrious rookies, including outfielder King Kelly of Cincinnati, Milwaukee catcher Charlie Bennett, and pitcher "The Only" Nolan, the only gate attraction of 24-36 Indianapolis.

During the 1878-79 off-season, President Hulbert proposed a salary-cap system that would limit each club's payroll and set maximum salaries for each position. The idea was abandoned when it became clear that most National League clubs intended to evade the limitations.

1879

The league returned to eight teams in 1879, and it remained at that number, with few exceptions, until 1962. The teams in '79 were: Providence, Boston, Buffalo, Chicago, Cincinnati, Cleveland, Syracuse, and Troy, and they finished in that order. Providence shortstop/manager George Wright, 32 and in his last year as a regular player, led all league shortstops in putouts and assists, and fielded .924, second only to Davy Force of Buffalo. Other Providence stars were outfielder Orator O'Rourke, who hit .348; outfielder Paul Hines, who led the league in hits; and 47-17 pitcher Monte Ward, who led the league in wins, winning percentage, and strikeouts.

Among the other teams, Cap Anson hit .396 for fourth-place Chicago, and Boston's Charlie

After a two-year reign as N.L. champs, Boston in 1879 (top) finished in second place behind Providence. Red Stockings manager Harry Wright is pictured in the foreground. A cigar-box label (bottom left) from 1880 depicts "Our Nine." Tintypes (bottom right) were common for players of the 1880s.

THE
EARLY
YEARS

Jones hit an amazing nine home runs, the highest one-year mark of the 1870s. Jones also led the National League in total homers for the decade with 18. Only 58 home runs were hit by all of the National League teams put together in 1879.

1880

In 1880, the National League reduced the number of balls required for a base on balls to eight (two years later, it was changed again, to seven). This was the first in a series of rules changes that baseball experimented with in this period, as it tried to maintain a proper balance between offense and defense.

Most of the changes were in the pitching rules. In 1881, pitchers were allowed to throw sidearm, making pitching both more effective and more stressful on the arm. As pitching deliveries rose higher and higher in the late 1870s and the 1880s, the idea of the pitcher as an every-day player was becoming obsolete. Teams of the 1880s began to carry one or more "change," or backup, pitchers. To help the hitters, the pitching distance was lengthened from 45 feet

to 50 feet, where it stayed until it was moved to 60 feet, six inches (the present distance) in 1893.

The National League achieved a measure of stability in 1880, with the only new club being Worcester, MA, which replaced Syracuse. This year debuted the National League's first dynasty: Cap Anson's mighty Chicago White Sox, who won three pennants in a row between 1880 and 1882. Led by player/manager Anson, who hit .337, and speedsters George Gore (.360), Abner Dalrymple (.330), and King Kelly (.291), Chicago led the National League in 1880 in batting (.279) and slugging (.360). Pitchers Fred Goldsmith and curveballer Larry Corcoran (who held the major league record for career no-hitters with three until Cy Young matched him) went 21-3 and 43-14 respectively. At 67-17, the White Sox finished 15 games ahead of Providence.

1881

Chicago's domination continued in 1881 as Anson led the league in batting (.399), RBI (82), and total bases (175) and his team led the league in hitting at .295. Corcoran and Goldsmith finished with ERAs of 1.95 and 1.75, good enough for the Sox to beat out perennial also-ran Providence and their ace pitcher Old Hoss Radbourn, who went 25-11 with a 2.43 ERA in '81. Chicago was 56-28, while Providence finished at 47-37.

Cincinnati withdrew from the league after the 1880 season in a dispute over its policies of playing Sunday baseball and allowing beer at the ballpark.

1882

In 1882, the new American Association, under its aggressive president Denny McKnight, opened for business. Initially, the league had little success in wooing National League players away from their teams, but it drew well anyway because of the 25-cent admission and because it took advantage of the tremendous population areas that the National League had neglected.

A former National League club, Cincinnati, with pitcher Will White and second baseman Bid McPhee, won the first A.A. pennant, finishing 55-25 with a .264 team batting average. White's major-league caliber pitching overwhelmed the rest of a relatively weak field; White went 40-12, and his 1.54 ERA was mostly responsible for Cincinnati's league-leading 1.67 team ERA; no other Association team had an ERA of under 2.08. Aside from McPhee, the American Association discovered several young future stars in 1882, such as Charles Comiskey and the original "Louisville Slugger," Pete Browning.

Chicago was the National League champion for the third season in a row in '82. Cap Anson finished second in the league in hitting to Buffalo's Dan Brouthers, .362 to .368 respectively. The White Stockings were 55-29, while Providence was 52-32.

1883

Under the National Agreement of 1883, all existing major and minor leagues promised to respect each other's contracts and, in the case of the two major leagues, their 14-player reserve lists as well. Virtually every club made a profit in 1883, and baseball's new prosperity proved that there were plenty of major league players — and plenty of fans — to go around.

Boston won the National League pennant in 1883, behind the hitting of Jack Burdock and Ezra Sutton and the pitching of Jim Whitney. Propelled by the speed and power combination of Harry Stovey, Philadelphia won in the Association. Stovey hit .352 with a league-leading 110 runs scored and 14 home runs; he was one of only two men in the entire American Association that year to reach double figures in homers.

This Home Run Cigar box label from the early 1880s is typical of how tobacco companies used baseball settings to promote their products.

Providence (top) finished 3 games out of first in 1882. Old Hoss Radbourn was the motivation behind their finish, going 31-19 with a 2.09 ERA. Joe Start, nicknamed "Old Reliable," led the club's offense by batting .329 and scoring 58 runs. This game (bottom) was pictured at Bates College, ME, in 1882.

THE **TURN** OF THE **CENTURY**

The National League withstood challenges
by new leagues but ultimately prevailed.
Baseball tinkered with the rules, trying
to maintain a balance in offense and
defense. The long-range trend, however,
was toward pitching dominance.

Phillies shortstop Art Irwin tags out teammate Al Maul (page 44) in an 1887 photo. Buck Ewing of the 1890 Players' League New York team (top) is pictured in a woodcut published in Leslie's Weekly.

THE TURN OF THE CENTURY

During the mid-1880s to the end of the century, baseball on the field was fundamentally the same game that is played in the major leagues today. Beginning in 1884, pitching was permanently freed from all restrictions on the angle of delivery; during the late 1880s and early 1890s, pitchers perfected the art of overhand pitching. As they did so, league ERAs hovered around 3.00 until 1893 when, after four straight years in which the National League's ERA declined, the pitching distance was lengthened to 60 feet six inches, where it remains today.

In 1884, baseball adopted the two major league World Series format that was to prove lasting and successful. It has stood unchanged in baseball since 1903 and has been often imitated by other professional sports.

The two-league format was not an immediate success, however; only one year after the National Agreement between the National League and the American Association, major league baseball's equilibrium was again upset. Throughout the next two decades the major league baseball monopoly came under constant attack — from within by the players' union movement and from without by new would-be major leagues. The American Association-National League conflict of 1882 and '83 was only the first of five baseball wars that defined the last quarter of the 19th century. These "Monopoly Wars" were: the American Association war, the Union Association war, the Players' League war, the second American Association war, and the American League war.

The first American Association war set the pattern for all those that followed, with the exception of the Players' League war. A number of owners formed a new league made up of new franchises or exist-ing minor league clubs, declared major league status, and attempted to gain credibility with the public by raiding existing major league rosters for big-name stars. When the time came for peace, the National League would either absorb the new league and take in its stronger franchises, or agree to a "peaceful coexistence," during which the National League would bide its time and gradually under-mine the new league. It was not until the 20th century that the National League completely aban-doned its goal of being the one and only major league. To each new league, except the American League, peaceful coexistence with the National League meant death.

For the players, each war brought increased competition for their services, leading to salary increases and weakening of the reserve clause; each settlement meant a return to artificially low salaries and subjection once again to the reserve clause. Twice during intervals of peace in this period, in 1885 and 1892, the National League imposed maximum player salary caps.

The Union Association war is a classic case. Like the American Association, the new league's main weapon against the baseball estab-lishment was to exploit player resentment of the reserve clause.

An 1886 trade card portrays the lot of a catcher and an umpire.

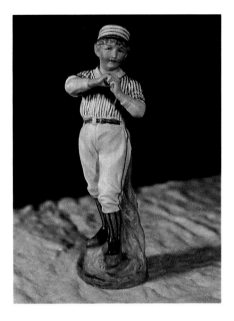

Fred Dunlap (top left) was the Union Association's brightest star in 1884, leading that league in hits (185), homers (13), runs scored (160), and batting average (.412); he returned to the N.L. and never again batted above .274 for a season. Bisque figures such as this one (top right) were manufactured in Germany in the 1880s and exported for the United States market. The earliest spring training photo known (bottom) was taken in Hot Springs, AK, probably during the 1887 or 1888 preseason.

47

THE TURN OF THE CENTURY

Ultimately, however, the Union Association proved just as willing as the American Association had been to sell out the players for a piece of the major league pie.

The force behind the Union Association was Henry Lucas, a flamboyant St. Louis railroad millionaire with a passion for baseball. Lucas' wealth and drive attracted other owners to the Union Association cause and got the league off the ground for the 1884 season. Unfortunately, these qualities were also responsible for the Union Association's downfall a year later. Lucas' team was the St. Louis Maroons, which he had provided with stars like second baseman Fred Dunlap from Cleveland and hard-throwing pitcher Charlie Sweeney from Providence, as well as a palatial ballpark that seated 10,000. The Maroons utterly dominated the Union Association's one and only season. They finished 94-19, 21 games ahead of second-place Cincinnati and 61 games ahead of last-place Kansas City. Attendance

was poor throughout the league; even St. Louis fans preferred to watch the fourth-place A.A. St. Louis Browns, who at least were in a pennant race.

The National League and the American Association played hard-ball with Lucas' upstarts. By threatening to blacklist players who jumped contracts to join the U.A., they had prevented player defections on the scale of those of the American Association war in 1882. At the urging of the N.L., the American Association expanded into Toledo, Indianapolis, Richmond, Washington, and Brooklyn, thereby depriving the Unions of all or part of several potential markets. With Union franchises folding left and right in the late summer, the final blow came when N.L. representative Al Spalding offered Lucas a deal: publicly renounce his opposition to the reserve clause and pay compensation for the players he had hired away from the other two leagues, and he would be allowed to enter his Maroons into the National League. Lucas accepted, effectively dooming the Union Association, but after two years of losing money trying to compete for fans with Chris Von der Ahe's St. Louis Browns A.A. dynasty, Lucas quit and left baseball for good.

In 1885, the N.L. and A.A. instituted a salary maximum of $2,000 per player. This enraged the players, since salaries had risen as high as three or four times that amount. The players decided to do

A medal for '87 Boston's top base-runner.

something for themselves about the salary cap and other grievances, including "modification" of the hated reserve clause. They formed the first players' union, the Brotherhood (the word "union" had leftist overtones in the late 19th century) of Professional Base Ball Players.

At this time it seems to have been generally accepted by the players, the fans, and the press that the reserve clause (which covered five players when it began in 1879, 11 players in 1883, and the whole roster by 1887) was unfair, immoral, and probably illegal. Only the owners saw it as their absolute right. In the many legal challenges of the 1880s and 1890s, contracts containing the reserve clause were overturned in court on the grounds that they lacked "equity" — because they compelled players to give up something for nothing. Nevertheless, most players felt that a limited reserve clause was neces-

CAP ANSON

No player was ever so identified with his team as Adrian Anson was with the Chicago White Stockings. Anson played for Chicago from 1876, its first

National League season, to 1897, its 22nd year in the N.L. He played for so long that he was known by three different nicknames: "Baby," from his continual complaining to umpires early in his career; "Cap," short for Captain, later on; and finally "Pop," when he managed the team from 1879 to 1898. For years after the respected Anson left the team, the White Stockings were known as the "Orphans."

Anson played every position on the diamond in his long career, but mainly first base, where he was a fine fielder. A contact hitter with good power, Anson hit .352 in his five years in the National Association (from 1871

to '75, when he played for Rockford and Philadelphia) and .334 for his 22 years in the N.L. He was the leader of the White Stockings' first great dynasty, the team of 1880 to '86, during which time he won five pennants.

Anson won three batting titles, hitting .396 in 1879, .399 in 1881, and .344 in 1888. He hit over .300 20 times, including his final season when he batted .302.

Anson's managerial career with Chicago came to an end after a series of colorful conflicts with Chicago owner Al Spalding. He tried managing the New York Giants in 1898, but his heart wasn't in it and he quit baseball altogether, 22 games into the season.

A cartoon from the New York Daily Graphic *shows that public opinion generally was on John Ward and the players' side.*

SLAVERY DAYS AGAIN.

THE ANNUAL BASE BALL AUCTION—"GOING! GOING! GONE!! FOR $12,000."

THE TURN OF THE CENTURY

sary for the game's stability. They were willing to concede some of their legal and moral rights for the good of the game as long as the owners didn't abuse their power.

But throughout the 1880s and 1890s, as they have throughout major league history, the owners did just that. They used the reserve clause to trade or release a player, or cut a player's salary arbitrarily. The reserve clause even enabled individual 19th-century owners to blacklist players from baseball for life. Current writers sometimes see the blacklist mechanism as a stabilizing influence on the game or as a way that baseball was able to rid itself of dishonest players. But imagine the consequences of putting that kind of power into the hands of owners who were less responsible than today's owners.

By 1889, the Brotherhood and its leader, Columbia-educated lawyer and player Monte Ward, had given up trying to negotiate with the owners, having gotten little response beyond being called

Charlie Comiskey managed the Players' League Chicago team.

"anarchists" and other insults. The year before, the owners had agreed under public pressure to eliminate salary caps but then, after waiting until Ward was en route to Europe by boat and unreachable for weeks, went back on their word and reinstated the salary cap at $2,500. The furious players wanted to strike but when Ward returned, his reaction was not to get mad but to get even.

After quietly assembling financial backing for a new league, Ward issued to Spalding and the owners an ultimatum: Take back the salary cap and give players some say over trades, or the players would revolt and form a Players' League for the upcoming 1890 season. The owners said no.

The Players' League came very close to succeeding. It was at least as well-financed as the A.A. and U.A. had been, and the P.L. attracted far more major league players — about 80 percent of the National League players, including most of the bigger stars. Initially, union loyalty among the players ran high: When Spalding offered King Kelly the huge sum of $10,000 to jump from the Players' League, he was shocked to be turned down. Ward had set up a stable, cooperative structure in which teams sent two delegates each to a league governing body that divided profits according to a formula between players and investors. And the league won the support of the fans; the P.L. put seven of its eight franchises right in National League cities and, for the most part, outdrew them.

Spalding's strategy for the owners was to destroy the confidence of the Players' League investors, who Spalding knew were in baseball for the same reason he was — to sell tickets and make money. After only limited success with a program of attempting to bribe the players into betraying their backers, he concentrated on a campaign of public disinformation and propaganda against the P.L. Accusing them of leftist sympathies wasn't enough; the players were supported by many prominent voices in the press. So Spalding went after the sporting press with moneybags. He silenced *Sporting Life* by buying it. He muted *The Sporting News* by having its largest advertisers threaten to pull out.

MONTE WARD

Pitcher/shortstop/lawyer/union activist John Montgomery Ward was one of the most versatile men in baseball history, on or off the field.

Joining Providence in 1878 as an 18-year-old rookie pitcher, Ward got the most out of his skinny (5'9", 165 pounds) frame, winning 22 games and losing 13 with a league-leading 1.51 ERA. Ward didn't have much natural stuff, but in 1879 he overpowered N.L. hitters with an excellent curve and amazing control. Pitching the Grays to the pennant, he threw 587 innings, striking out 239 and walking only 36. His record for the season was 47-17 with a 2.15 ERA. At the end of his short pitching career, Ward was 161-101 with the fourth-best lifetime ERA in major league history: 2.10.

Ward declined as a pitcher in the early 1880s and was traded to the Giants in 1883 as a utility player. When some players might have retired, Ward worked hard to make himself into a good hitter and was the team's starting shortstop on the 1888 and 1889 pennant-winners. In 1887, he led the National League in stolen bases with 111; he also hit .338.

In the off-seasons, Ward studied at Columbia University, and in 1887 he earned both a bachelor's in Political Science and a law degree. Using his legal training to fight for the rights of his fellow players (most of whom earned far less than Ward), he helped form the first players' union. Ward retired in 1884 at age 34 to practice law full time.

RUSIE'S DELIVERY.

MEEKIN AFTER DELIVERY.

CAPTAIN DAVIS AT BAT.

THE OPENING OF THE BASE-BALL SEASON—THE GIANTS AT PLAY.
PHOTOGRAPHS BY HEMMENT.

New York Giants Amos Rusie, Jouette Meekin, and George Davis (top) are pictured in an 1895 photo. In 1894, Rusie was 36-13 with a 2.78 ERA, and Meekin was 36-10 with a 3.70 ERA, as the Giants finished second; in '95, Rusie fell to 22-21 with a 3.73 ERA, and Meekin dropped to 16-11 with a 5.11 ERA, while the Giants plunged to ninth. A travel poster (bottom) displays Al Spalding's 1888-89 tour to Australia.

THE TURN OF THE CENTURY

Even if he couldn't win the hearts and minds of the fans or the press, Spalding knew where to worry the Players' League backers: at the gate. He discounted tickets and held promotions and give-aways. If that wasn't sufficient, he faked attendance figures. When confronted with evidence that the N.L. attendance totals were dishonest, Spalding blandly asserted that the P.L.'s were too.

With hindsight it is clear that Spalding and his friends almost lost their war with the Players' League. The P.L. outdrew the N.L. in 1890 by 100,000; that year the New York Giants would have failed in mid-season if Spalding hadn't personally put $80,000 into the club. Privately, other N.L. owners admitted that they were on the edge. The truth is that both sides were losing money, but in public Spalding and his fellow owners presented a united front and bluffed the P.L. into thinking that they were willing to lose any amount of money. Ultimately, before the 1891 season, the P.L. backers blinked first. The National League and the American Association invited the players back and, as a conciliatory gesture, they put the salary cap regulations and the reserve clause (now called the "option to renew") into euphemistic language. The players had learned, as Monte Ward put it, that "baseball is a business, not simply a sport."

The two major leagues' triumph in 1891 was a costly one. With three major leagues and 24 teams competing for the same fans, and with all the ticket giveaways and price-cutting, the 1890 season was a financial disaster for everybody — but especially for the American Association, which had never fully recovered from its war with the N.L. or its ill-advised expansion during the U.A. war in 1884. In the aftermath of the P.L.

war, the National League saw its opportunity to regain sole possession of the baseball monopoly. Ignoring their agreement with the Association that each league would get its own players back from the P.L., the N.L. began to outbid the A.A. for all returning personnel. The second American Association war was on; the Association severed relations with the National League and tried to fight back, but this time the A.A. was too weak. After the 1891 season, Columbus and Louisville folded, and the rest of the A.A. owners were forced to accept either consolidation or a buy-out from the N.L.; they chose the latter. From 1892 until 1899, a new 12-team N.L. had the major league baseball monopoly all to itself.

In spite of this eight-year peace, the monopoly wars were not yet over; the forces were gathering for one more attempt to loosen the N.L.'s tenacious grip on baseball. In 1885, some owners who were veterans of the Union Association war had formed a new minor league called the Western League. In the early 1890s they were joined by A.A. interests who had been left

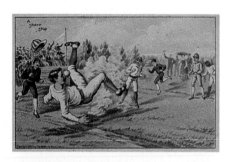

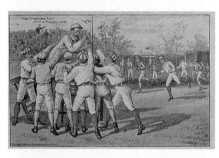

Trade cards, such as these three from 1887, were illustrated with comic but realistic scenes.

Curt Welch snatched home and $15,000.

The best-of-seven 1886 World Series was one of the few exciting postseason series of the 19th century. It was decided on what is probably the only ending that can top a bottom-of-the-ninth game-winning homer: an extra-inning World Series-winning steal of home.

Part of the drama came from the rivalry between the American Association and the N.L. Both had something to prove; Chicago wanted to back up its frequent boasts of National League superiority and St. Louis wanted to win legitimacy for the A.A. Attracted by the added excitement of a winner-take-all (of the gate receipts) format, fans made the '86 Series the most popular of all. The games drew from 5,000 to 10,000 fans each.

St. Louis managed to survive its two biggest obstacles, three Chicago home games and the pitching of John Clarkson, by going 1-2 in Chicago and beating Clarkson 8-5 behind Dave Foutz in Game Four at St. Louis. There, Comiskey's Browns enjoyed one of baseball's greatest home-field advantages, thanks to their menacing fans, and St. Louis pounded out 11 hits to win Game Five, going ahead three games to two.

Game Six matched the two teams' aces, Clarkson and Bob Caruthers. Behind 3-0 after seven innings, the Browns tied it up in the eighth. After Curt Welch then singled, he advanced to third on an error and a one-out sacrifice bunt by Yank Robinson. Welch then stole home as King Kelly bobbled a pitch in the dirt. The play was known as the "$15,000 Slide" after the approximate amount of the Browns' winnings.

Charles Comiskey (top left) scored 994 runs in 13 seasons as a player and had a
.607 winning percentage (which is third all time) in 11 years as a manager. King
Kelly (top right) led the N.L. in doubles three times and averaged more than 30 a
season from 1881 to 1889. Jack Clements (bottom left) was a lefty catcher for the
Philadelphia Phillies from 1885 to 1897. A tintype (bottom right) from 1887
pictures Charlie Buffinton, a star pitcher for N.L. Boston and Philadelphia. In
1884, Buffinton won a career-high 48 games, starting 67 and completing 63.

THE TURN OF THE CENTURY

out of the 1892 consolidation. Finally — after the N.L. dropped Baltimore, Louisville, Washington, and Cleveland in 1899 — the Western League seized its chance. It put teams in the disenfranchised cities and in 1900 declared itself to be a new major league under a new name: the American League.

During the wars and experiments with various league structures that took place between 1884 and 1899, baseball itself was also changing. For the most part these changes were more fine-tuning than profound or revolutionary alterations of the game.

From 1880 to 1889 baseball tinkered with the rules governing balls and strikes, decreasing the number of balls required for a walk from nine to eight in 1880, to seven in 1881, to six in 1884, to five in 1887, and conclusively to four in 1889. The number of strikes for a strikeout was increased to four as a one-year experiment in 1887, and in 1894 a foul bunt (and in 1895 a held foul tip) was ruled a strike; ordinary fouls were not counted as strikes until 1901 in the National League, 1903 in the American.

These adjustments were made to offset advantages that arose in either offense and defense, often themselves caused by other rules changes. Beginning in 1887, for example, batters were no longer allowed to call for a "high ball" or a "low ball" as they wished, and the modern strike zone was implemented. In order to lessen the negative effect of this change on hitters, they were given the extra strike. The results showed that the second change was far more significant than the first; the N.L. ERA shot up from 3.31 to 4.05, the A.A. ERA from 3.45 to 4.29. The next season the fourth strike was taken away and ERAs came back down: to 2.83 in the N.L. and 3.06 in the A.A.

The long-range trend was toward domination by pitchers. Overhand pitching was both more effective and harder on the arm; beginning in the late 1880s, teams began to assemble rudimentary pitching staffs rather than rely on an every-day pitcher. Unlike the early 1880s, when more than a two-man staff was an extreme rarity, in 1889 six of the eight N.L. teams carried four pitchers and the other two teams carried three. Each season during the 1880s batters found themselves facing fresher and fresher arms and the effect on offense was obvious; the advent of the pitching rotation was around the corner.

To respond to the upper hand gained by defense, in 1893 the N.L. moved pitchers back to 60 feet six inches from home plate and, by establishing the pitching rubber, eliminated the practice of running up or stepping to deliver the ball. The immediate effect was drastic: after N.L. ERAs of 3.60, 3.34, and 3.28 from 1890 to '92, ERAs rose to 4.66, 5.32, and 4.78 in 1893 to '95 respectively. Over time however, pitchers adjusted to the extra distance surprisingly well and by 1898 and 1899 ERAs were again below 4.00.

A fan has a chromo lithograph of a baseball scene (top). An 1884 Brooklyn scorecard (bottom).

In the 1880s, catching was just as important as it is today but much more physically demanding. This explains why Buck Ewing, the decade's greatest catcher, rarely played a full season and took frequent rests at other positions. Ewing caught only 636 games in his 17-year career, playing 253 games at first base and 235 in the outfield. Ewing's 1893 season gives some idea of the punishing effect that catching in those days had on offensive production. With Cleveland that year, Ewing played almost exclusively in the outfield and, at age 33, turned in his best season at the plate. He hit .344 with 28 doubles, 15 triples, and 47 stolen bases. He scored and drove in more than 100 runs for the only time in his career.

But even when he was playing behind the plate, Ewing was a good hitter, batting .300 in six of his seven seasons with the Giants and ten times overall. He slugged a respectable .455 for his career and was in double figures in triples 11 times. Ewing had 336 lifetime stolen bases.

Besides being the best-hitting catcher of his day, Ewing was considered the ideal defensive receiver. Contemporaries said that his throws to second base arrived as if they had been handed to the second baseman. He often threw from a crouch and picked off straying base-runners.

Ewing deserves some of the credit for the great New York Giants pitching staffs of the 1880s. When the first vote was taken to elect old-timers to the Hall of Fame in 1939, Ewing finished tied for first with Cap Anson.

Posed for this classic photo (left) are Boston Beaneaters stars Billy Nash at the left and Hoss Radbourn. Nash was the on-field leader of a team known for its slick teamwork at bat and in the field. Using a primitive glove so thin that a modern player might use it at the plate, Nash fielded over .900 four times and led National League third basemen in fielding three times. By the late 1880s, Radbourn was on the downside of a Hall of Fame career. One of baseball's legendary iron men on the mound, "Old Hoss" completed 489 games in 12 seasons and between 1883 and '84 won an incredible 109 games for Providence. The Nebraska Indians (bottom) posed for this shot in 1892.

THE TURN OF THE CENTURY

One thing that didn't change in this period was the relative unimportance of the home run. While enclosed wooden ballparks were being constructed through the 1880s and 1890s, the fences were too far and the baseballs too dead to make the home run much more of a factor than it had been in the late 1870s.

Without home runs and with pitchers mostly in control of the game, the 1880s and 1890s fostered much offensive innovation, which for the most part consisted of such dead-ball strategies as bunting, basestealing, and the hit-and-run. The two teams leading the way were the early 1890s Boston Beaneaters of Tommy McCarthy, Hugh Duffy, and Billy Nash, who perfected the hit-and-run and invented runner-to-batter signals, and the mid-1890s Baltimore Orioles of Ned Hanlon, John McGraw, and Hughie Jennings, who invented the "Baltimore chop."

The stolen base was first officially counted in 1887, probably indicating its growing importance in the game. The role of the stolen base at this time was roughly comparable to its role in baseball today; typically players led the National League in stolen bases in the late 1880s to early 1890s with totals ranging between the 60s and the low 100s.

Off the field, baseball continued to suffer occasional scandals, though for the most part they involved drinking and violence rather than the gambling-related corruption that was so rampant in the 1860s and 1870s.

The late 1880s brought another, quieter scandal: the drawing of the color line. While black players had been few and often badly treated before this time, there had been no formal exclusion. Notable black players included major league catcher Moses Walker and his

Moses Fleetwood Walker with Toledo in 1884.

brother Welday, who played for American Association Toledo, and minor league stars Frank Grant, Bud Fowler, and George Stovey, most, if not all, of whom had the ability to play at the major-league level. The International League was sometimes derisively called the "Colored League" because of its relative tolerance of blacks. But the increasingly open racism and pro-segregationist sentiment of late 1880s America naturally affected baseball too.

In an 1883 exhibition game, the White Stockings' Cap Anson, who was openly intolerant, had attempted to intimidate Toledo into benching Moses Walker by threatening not to play. But Toledo refused and the game eventually went on. Anson was even made to look a little ridiculous in press accounts of the incident. But by 1887 times had changed. Anson refused to play George Stovey's Newark club in a similar situation, and this time he got his way; Stovey was benched. Shortly afterward, the International League announced that it was outlawing the signing of black players. Since several clubs relied on their black players, the ban was not enforced right away. But when Moses Walker retired two years later, he was the last black in the establishment's major and minor leagues and remained so until Jackie Robinson in the 1940s.

1884

There were three major leagues in 1884 and 34 major league teams, the highest number in history. This included two teams in Boston, Chicago, Cleveland, Indianapolis, and New York City;

A rowdy, hustling St. Louis team with lots of speed and line-drive power in the lineup, verbally and physically aggressive — maybe too aggressive for some people's taste. Sound familiar? No, it's not the Gas House Gang of the 1930s, it's little Arlie Latham and the bad Browns.

The American Association Browns of the 1880s believed in the power of verbal intimidation of their opponents. Often, when the Browns were at bat, their third baseman, Latham (called "The Freshest Man on Earth"), would roam up and down the baselines screaming at the opposing pitcher. Umpires got the same treatment. (Ultimately the league had to institute the coach's box to stop him.) When Latham or another Brown would be fined by the league, St. Louis owner Chris Von der Ahe would cheerfully pay up.

Latham could play too. He was the most prolific run-scorer of the time. In the 11 years between 1884 and 1894, Latham averaged 117 runs scored a season with a peak of 163 in 1887. Though only a .269 lifetime hitter, he was a stolen base threat (179 steals between 1887 and 1895) and he had some power; three times he hit in double figures in triples.

Latham was the soul of a team that won four A.A. pennants in a row between 1885 and 1888 and proved that A.A. baseball was major-league caliber by defeating Cap Anson's White Stockings in the 1886 World Series.

An Oberlin, OH, Base Ball Club team photo (top) pictures the last blacks to play in the major leagues until Jackie Robinson broke the color line in 1947. Moses Fleetwood Walker, seated far left, and his brother Welday Walker, standing third from left, both played for Toledo of the American Association in 1884. "Fleet," a catcher, played 42 games and scored 23 runs while hitting .263; he was good enough to have the fifth highest batting average among the 24 catchers listed in the A.A. that season, but he never played another major league game. This Lorillard & Co. tobacco poster (left) pictures "Representatives of Professional Base Ball in America."

three teams were in Cincinnati, Kansas City, Philadelphia, Pittsburgh, and St. Louis.

Historically, dramatic expansion has upset the balance of the game in favor of the hitters (as in 1961), but 1884 was the first of two years of dominant pitching. N.L. Buffalo's Pud Galvin, N.L. Chicago's Larry Corcoran, and five other pitchers threw no-hitters that year, an all-time record. Ten major league pitchers — and *two teams* — turned in ERAs under 2.00. Overall, league ERAs dropped to 2.98 in the National League, 3.24 in the American Association and 2.99 in the Union Association. National League batters hit .247 and slugged .340; A.A. batters hit .240 and slugged .325; and U.A. batters hit .245 and slugged a minuscule .316. Six Union Association teams slugged under .300.

Not surprisingly, the heroes of all three pennant races were pitchers. In the N.L., Boston was nip and tuck early in the season with the Providence Grays, who had won the 1879 pennant and finished second in 1880, '81, and '82. The Grays were known for their outstanding pitchers, including Monte Ward and Old Hoss Radbourn, who had gone 25-11 in '80, 31-19 in '81, and 49-25 in '83. But when 1884 began, Providence manager Frank Bancroft infuriated Radbourn by giving the number-one starter's job to Charlie Sweeney, a hard-throw-

New York Giants pitcher Tim Keefe in 1886.

ing 20-year-old righthander. As the pennant race wore on, Sweeney's constant drinking became intolerable. When Bancroft finally discovered Sweeney indulging between innings of a game that he was pitching, he released Sweeney and gave Radbourn his old job back.

As for Radbourn, the veteran publicly promised to deliver a pennant, singlehandedly if necessary. And, almost singlehandedly, he did. He pitched 35 of the season's final 37 games and finished with a league-high 60 victories against only 12 losses. He led the N.L. in ERA at 1.38 and struck out 441 men in 678⅔ innings. The 1884 National League race ended in a Providence rout, as Boston and ace pitcher Charlie Buffinton dropped to 10½ games behind on the last day of the season.

In the American Association, manager Jim Mutrie's New York Mets won their only pennant in 1884 behind ace Tim Keefe, who went 37-19 with a 2.29 ERA (after 1883, when he was 47-27 and completed all 68 of his starts). The Mets had a good lineup that featured first baseman Dave Orr, who hit .354, and third baseman Dude Esterbrook, who hit .314. But the Mets were shut out of baseball's first World Series, losing all three games to Providence in three days. The games, all of which took place at New York City's original Polo Grounds (located just north of Central Park between Lenox and Fifth avenues), drew only 3,100. The fans must have known something that the Mets didn't: Radbourn defeated Keefe easily in the first two games, allowing a total of seven hits and three runs, and he was nine runs ahead in the sixth inning of the third game when Keefe, now umpiring on his off-day, put the Mets out of their misery by calling the game on account of afternoon "darkness."

The 1884 Union Association season was a race in name only, with St. Louis winning 94 of its 113 games. Along the way St. Louis compiled a team ERA of 1.95, smacked 24 percent of the 12-team league's home runs, hit 21 percent of its doubles, and scored 18 percent of its runs.

It was the year of the pitcher, but it was also the year of the weakling. Because of runaway expansion caused by the Union Associa-

HUGH DUFFY

Hugh Duffy was one of the mainstays of the great Boston National League teams of 1891 to '93 and 1897 and '98. He hit for average (.328 lifetime), including 12 .300 seasons, and ran the bases well, stealing 599 bases in his 16 full seasons.

But the surprising thing about the 5'7", 168-pound outfielder was his power and consistent RBI production. Duffy led the National League in home runs twice, in 1894 and 1897, and he hit 80 home runs for the decade, more than anybody. Between 1889 and 1899, Duffy scored or drove in 100 runs 17 times. He also had the most RBI of any hitter in the decade: 1,085.

The rest of Duffy's career is dwarfed, however, by his historic 1894 season. He hit .438, the highest single-season batting average ever achieved, and led the N.L. in slugging at .679. He made 236 hits, the 19th best ever. Duffy led the league in doubles with 50, home runs with 18, and RBI with 145. (Unfortunately for Duffy, there was no triple crown award in the 1890s, so for him it was just a great year.) He also scored 160 runs, stole 49 bases, and hit 13 triples. He had two five-hit games and an incredible 12 four-hit games.

Retiring in 1906, Duffy went on to manage four different teams until 1922. He was elected to the Hall of Fame in 1945.

Hoss Radbourn (top left) was 162-87 from 1883 to '86, accumulating 245 complete games in that four-year span. A charcoal portrait (top right) depicts an 1880s ballplayer from the Clinton, NY, club. The 1884 New York Gothams (bottom) finished in fifth place with a 62-50 record. Monte Ward is standing far left; Buck Ewing is standing far right.

tion war, each league contained players and whole teams that did not deserve the label "major league"; many probably couldn't have competed in the high minors. Twelve of the 34 teams in the three major leagues finished more than 40 games out of first place. Some of the worst were: N.L. Detroit, which batted .208 as a team and finished 28-84; 12-51 A.A. Washington; and four Union Association teams: St. Paul, Altoona (PA), Milwaukee, and Wilmington (DE), which won a combined 18 games on the 1884 season.

1885

In 1885, baseball was back down to a manageable 16 teams and two major leagues, but pitchers were still learning the advantages of the newly legalized overhand delivery, and it was another pitchers' year. The National League ERA dropped to 2.82 and the Association's remained at 3.24. Numerous pitchers had career years, including N.L. New York's Mickey Welch (44-11, 1.66 ERA), A.A. St. Louis' "Parisian" Bob Caruthers (40-13, 2.07 ERA), and John Clarkson (53-16, 1.85 ERA). Clarkson led Cap Anson's rejuvenated Chicago club to the N.L. pennant over the Giants of first baseman and batting champion Roger Connor (.371) and the league's top catcher, Buck Ewing (.304).

The years 1885 and 1886 represent the second phase of the great Chicago dynasty of the 1880s. Behind Clarkson, who won 35 games in '86, both clubs finished second in the N.L. in team ERA at 2.23 and 2.54. But the key to Chicago's success was its versatile offense. Anson had 17 home runs and 261 RBI over the two seasons, and second baseman Fred Pfeffer had 166 RBI. In the outfield, the White Stockings had a very modern-looking combination of

speed and power, including Abner Dalrymple, daring King Kelly, George Gore (who averaged one run scored per game for his career), and Billy Sunday, one of the era's fastest sprinters in or out of baseball. They helped the Chicago offense score 834 runs in 1885, 143 more than second-place New York and more than twice last-place St. Louis' total of 390.

The second World Series matched Chicago against Charlie Comiskey and his A.A. pennant-winning St. Louis Browns, who at 79-33 had run away and finished 16 games ahead of Cincinnati. Though lacking a dominant hitter or much team power (no Brown finished in the top five in the league in batting, slugging, home runs, or total bases), St. Louis ran, hustled, and bench-jockeyed their way to 677 runs, second in the A.A. only to Harry Stovey and Philadelphia's 764. St. Louis' real strength was the pitching of Caruthers and Dave Foutz (33-14, 2.63 ERA), who were mainly responsible for the Browns' league-low 2.43 ERA and 461 runs allowed.

At that time, the World Series format was left up to the two pennant-winners, and in 1885 they decided on a seven-game series, with games to be held in Chicago, St. Louis, Pittsburgh, and Cincinnati. The series was a disorderly affair, marked by fan rowdiness and disputes between the players over the umpiring of Dan Sullivan,

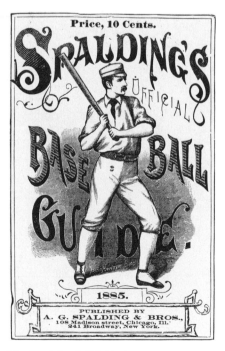

A Spalding's Baseball Guide from 1885.

NED HANLON

Like many great managers, Ned Hanlon's playing career wasn't very impressive. At age 32, he discovered that he was better at managing.

In the 1880s and 1890s, the manager's job included that of today's general manager — running the team off the field and finding players either through trade or scouting. Hanlon proved to be a shrewd judge of talent, bringing Baltimore up from 12th place in 1892 to eighth in 1893 and finally to a pennant in 1894, by signing John McGraw, Heinie Reitz, Joe Kelley, Dan Brouthers, Hughie Jennings, and Willie Keeler. With this nucleus, Hanlon won the N.L. pennant three years in a row between 1894 and 1896. A slightly remodeled version of the same team won for Hanlon in Brooklyn in 1899 and 1900.

On the field, Hanlon ran a smart, overachieving offense that relied on working sophisticated variations of the prevalent dead-ball strategies of the day: the sacrifice, the stolen base, and the hit-and-run. The Orioles played as a team on defense as well, perfecting a system of outfield relay throws and infield backups. The Orioles also played mean, dirty baseball, using everything from tricks like switching live balls for dead when the opposition was batting to calculated physical intimidation of the umpire.

Most of Hanlon's tactics went out with Babe Ruth and the home run era, but some of the spirit of Hanlon's managerial philosophy lives on today.

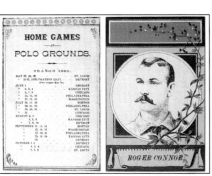

A cartoon from an 1887 Puck *magazine (top left) predicted how second sackers could get some spring into their game. An 1886 trade card (top middle) shows a "centerfielder" in action. George Gore (top right) averaged 119 runs scored between 1883 and '86. An 1886 Giants scorecard (second row left) features Roger Connor, who batted .318 in an 18-year career and hit 233 triples, the fifth highest amount in baseball history. Mickey Welch (second row middle), pictured on this 1886 Giants scorecard, was a top-quality hurler who averaged 36 wins a season from 1883 to '86 for New York. He pitched 13 years and ended his career with a 311-207 record and 525 complete games, fifth on the all-time list. This woodcut (bottom) is from* Harper's Weekly *August 22, 1885.*

THE TURN OF THE CENTURY

who was removed after the irate Browns walked off the field in the sixth inning of the second game. The games drew poorly, especially after the fourth game, and the series was finally called off in the eighth inning of Game Seven, with both teams having three victories. A dispute over whether the second game should be ruled a tie or a forfeit to Chicago was never resolved and two teams split the $1,000 prize money.

1886

This was the last hurrah for Chicago, which after the season sold King Kelly to Boston (he was followed there in 1888 by John Clarkson). In 1886, Anson's wrecking crew led the league in doubles and triples, and scored 900 runs; six of the remaining seven N.L. teams scored fewer than 700. But 1886 was the second of four straight pennant-winning seasons for a new St. Louis Browns dynasty.

The St. Louis style of baseball also included nonstop verbal abuse of the opposition and baiting of the umpire. This irritated fellow players and the sporting press alike, but it worked, both by unnerving opponents and by intimidating umpires with the

From 1885 to '89, John Clarkson was 208-93.

veiled threat of violence by an incited St. Louis crowd. The Browns won their four pennants by margins of 16, 12, 14, and 6½ games. Joining Caruthers and Dave Foutz was Silver King, who went 34-11 (3.78 ERA) in 1887 and 45-21 (1.64 ERA) in 1888. On offense, the team was powered in 1886 by Arlie Latham, who scored 152 runs, and Caruthers, who played the outfield between starts and hit .334.

Fans eagerly awaited a St. Louis-Chicago rematch, and the seven-game 1886 World Series drew an unprecedented 43,000 fans. The acrimonious 1885 series had ended with Cap Anson stating that the Browns would be a fifth-place club in the National League; Bob Caruthers angrily responded with a $1,000 bet on their next meeting. Before the 1886 games began, however, Al Spalding insisted on a winner-take-all format. So instead of $1,000, there was a gate of between $13,000 and $14,000 riding on the Series.

Chicago took two of the first three in Chicago, with Clarkson winning 6-0 and 11-4; the only loss came in Game Two when St. Louis scored 12 runs on two Tip O'Neill home runs and 13 Chicago errors, and Caruthers pitched a two-hit shutout. Pitching his third game in four days, John Clarkson lost 8-5 in St. Louis. By Game Six, which took place the next day, both teams' pitchers were exhausted. Chicago put outfielder Jimmy Ryan on the mound (he had pitched only 23⅓ innings the whole season), and he lost 10-3 to St. Louis' number-three pitcher, Nat Hudson. Then, in a thrilling, extra-inning game, Bob Caruthers beat Clarkson in Game Seven 4-3 and won for the Browns their only world championship.

1887

In 1887, the Browns hit .307 as a team; emerging star outfielder Tip O'Neill became one of only two men in the decade to reach the .400 mark in batting, hitting .435 and slugging a league-leading 14 homers and 357 total bases. The stolen base became an official stat in 1887, and Browns' Arlie Latham and player/manager Comiskey were second and third in the A.A. (behind Cincinnati's Hugh Nichol) with 129 and 117. The new fourth strike rule in 1887 devastated pitching. The National League ERA

ED DELAHANTY

One of five brothers who played major league baseball, big (6'2", 180 pounds) Ed Delahanty was a .345 lifetime hitter, fourth on the all-time list. He hit .400 twice and was one of the best hitters for average in an era of gaudy batting averages.

Playing left field and first base for National League Philadelphia for 12 of his 16 big league seasons, Delahanty was also the premier power hitter of the 1890s; for the decade he averaged .354 with 226 hits, ten home runs, and 131 RBI a season. While home run totals of ten to 15 look small today, to Delahanty's contemporaries he had unheard of power. Delahanty led the league in doubles five times and reached double figures in triples ten times, hitting 21 three-baggers in 1892. He slugged .504 for his career, which is a rare feat even today, and slugged over .500 in eight seasons. Delahanty scored or drove in 100 runs 17 times.

Like several of his fellow players, Delahanty had a severe drinking problem; in 1903, this led to his being suspended from A.L. Washington indefinitely. Then, while on his way home by train from Detroit, he had a few too many and was put off the train in Niagara, Ontario, for pulling some of the more sober passengers out of their sleeping berths in the middle of the night. For some reason, Delahanty decided to try to follow the train on foot across a drawbridge, fell into the Niagara river, and drowned.

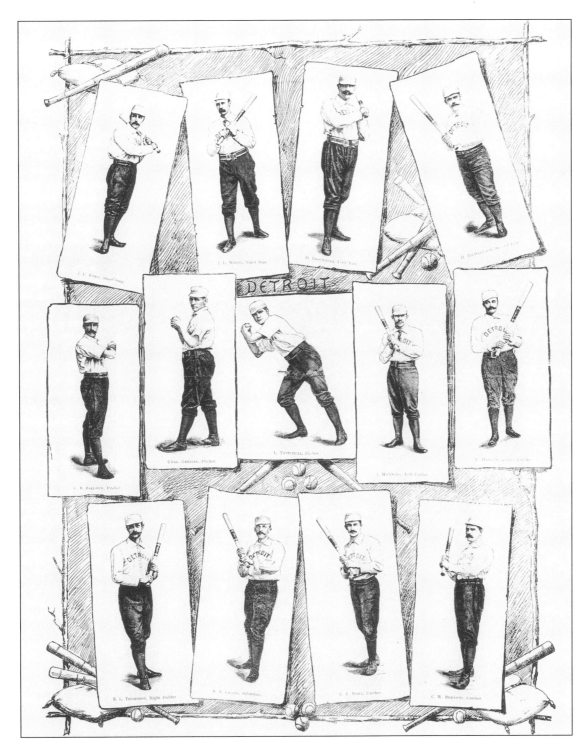

The 1886 Detroit Wolverines (top) finished second in the National League. They were led by Dan Brouthers, top row third from left, who tied for the league lead in homers; outfielder Hardy Richardson, top row far right, who led the league in hits and tied Brouthers in homers; and pitcher Lady Baldwin, second row far left, who led the league in wins with 42. The 1886 N.L. champion Chicago White Stockings (left) were led by Cap Anson, standing in the middle; John Clarkson, seated second from right; and King Kelly, standing far right, Anson led the league with 147 runs batted in, Clarkson compiled a 35-17 record with a 2.41 ERA, and Kelly batted a league-high .388, as Chicago finished at 90-34.

THE TURN OF THE CENTURY

rose from 3.31 to 4.05, the Association's from 3.45 to 4.29. The N.L. batting average went up 18 points and the A.A.'s 30. Strikeouts declined from 4,315 to 2,837 in the National League and from 4,730 to 3,075 in the Association. Individual batters benefited even more; Pete Browning joined O'Neill in the .400 club by hitting .402. And with more strikes to play with, hitters began to swing for the fences; Billy O'Brien led the N.L. in home runs with 19 and O'Neill led the A.A. with 14. In 1886 the two league-leaders had hit 11 and 7 homers.

The heaviest hitters of them all were the Detroit Wolverines, who scored 969 runs and led the major leagues with a .436 slugging average. Led by batting champ Sam Thompson's .372 batting average and 166 RBI, Detroit had three players in double figures in homers, two with over 100 RBI, and the league's three top run-scorers: first baseman Dan Brouthers at 153, shortstop Jack Rowe at 135, and super-sub Hardy Richardson at 131.

This mighty offense was built in a series of outright purchases by Detroit owner Frederick Stearns, who is estimated to have spent $25,000 between 1885 and 1887. He started by buying the entire Indianapolis team, who had compiled an .880 winning percentage in the Western League in 1885; included was Hall of Famer Thompson, who hit .331 lifetime and either scored or drove in 100 runs in a season 18 times in his 15-year career. After picking up lefthanded pitcher "Lady" Baldwin, Stearns bought the core of the powerful Buffalo offense, known as the "Big Four": Brouthers, Deacon White, Richardson, and Rowe.

With Baldwin going 42-13 with a 2.24 ERA in 1886, the Wolverines barely missed beating out Chicago for the N.L. pennant after taking it

Clockwise from upper left, Mickey Welch, Monte Ward, Roger Connor, and Tim Keefe in 1887.

down to the final series of the season. But in 1887, in spite of a nagging arm injury to Baldwin, Detroit went 79-45 and finished first by 3 1/2 games over Philadelphia.

The St. Louis Browns hitters had their finest year in 1887, scoring 1,131 runs and batting .307 as a team. But their only real power hitter to compare with the Detroit sluggers was Tip O'Neill. As the 1887 World Series approached, the Browns announced publicly that they were going to steal their way to the world championship, pointing out that Detroit's best defensive catcher, Charlie Bennett, was playing with severely injured hands and could hardly throw.

The 1887 Series was played in ten cities and lasted 15 games. Apparently this was two games too many for the fans; the final contests drew only 371 and 659 fans. But long before then, Detroit had proven its superiority by outslugging, outpitching, and even out-stealing (40-30) the Browns. Bennett played most of the games and held St. Louis' top basestealer Arlie Latham to one stolen base. Detroit outscored St. Louis 73 to 54 and took the Series 10-5.

1888
With a return to the three-strike strikeout in 1888, pitchers regained their supremacy. The St. Louis Browns won their fourth and final pennant on the strength of a team ERA of 2.09 and Tip O'Neill's slugging, even though Von der Ahe, disappointed with the outcome at the 1887 Series, had sold off pitchers Bob Caruthers and Dave Foutz to Brooklyn and outfielder Curt Welch to Philadelphia before the season started.

WEE WILLIE KEELER

Brooklyn-born Wee Willie Keeler certainly lived up to his nickname; at 5'4 1/2" and 140 pounds, he was one of the smallest major leaguers ever. Naturally, Keeler couldn't keep up with the sluggers of his time. So he invented a unique personal style that he himself summed up best by saying, "I hit 'em where they ain't." Keeler couldn't — or wouldn't — take 'em; he walked almost as rarely as he struck out. But by using the lightest bat of his time and by choking halfway up the bat, Keeler would swing late, slapping at the ball and driving it through the infield. He prided himself on his ability to make contact with the hardest fastball.

The leadoff man for the Orioles, Keeler scored 100 runs eight times and scored 140 or more five times. He collected 200 hits for eight straight years, an all-time record. For his time he was a good but not great base-stealer; he stole 495 bases in his 19-year career with peaks of 67 and 64 in the late 1890s.

It is as a hitter for average that Keeler is best remembered. He hit .345 lifetime, fifth all-time, and hit .300 or better in his first 14 years. In 1897 and '98, Keeler won back-to-back batting titles, hitting .432 and .379, and in 1897 he set the National League record by hitting in 44 consecutive games.

Keeler was one of the outstanding hitters for average in his time and the catalyst for one of history's greatest offensive teams.

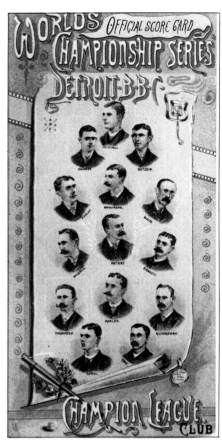

Detroit (top right) won the world championship in 1887 behind Sam Thompson, fifth row far left, who drove in 166 runs. The Sphinx (top left) doesn't look very impressed, and neither were the Arab people, when Chicago White Stockings owner Albert Spalding, who is in the center wearing a pith helmet, brought his team and an "All-American" squad of major leaguers to Egypt as part of his 1888 to '89 world tour. Spalding was seeking to spread the gospel of baseball — and his sporting goods business — via a series of exhibition games. The tour was a mixed success. In Italy, for example, Spalding failed in an attempt to arrange a photo opportunity with the Pope and angered Italians by offering $5,000 to rent the Colosseum for a game. Some bewildered natives regarded the baseball stars as though they were, as one player said, "so many escaped inmates." Spalding's intrepid baseball missionaries drew converts in the English-speaking world, however, especially in places familiar with the British sports of cricket and rounders, such as Australia (bottom). Although Spalding committed a public gaffe by touching the Prince of Wales on the shoulder during a game at Kensington Oval Cricket grounds, baseball was moderately well received in England. The tour's visit to Australia drew 10,000 spectators for the opening game in Melbourne, where the local press praised baseball's "enterprising spirit." Some speculated that the American game might someday be popular "Down Under," as, indeed, it has become—a century later.

THE TURN OF THE CENTURY

Comiskey still had Silver King (45-21, 1.64 ERA) and found Nat Hudson (25-10, 2.54 ERA) to pick up the slack, and the Browns went to the World Series to face a new National League powerhouse: the New York Giants. Managed by Jim Mutrie, the Giants had a strong offense made up of slugging first baseman Roger Connor, Monte Ward (now a shortstop), Orator O'Rourke in left, and Buck Ewing at catcher. But the 1888 team was carried by its two pitching stars Tim Keefe and Mickey Welch, who were responsible for 61 of the team's 84 victories. New York led the N.L. in fewest runs allowed (479) and shutouts (19), and had a major-league leading 1.96 ERA.

Mutrie had managed the 1884 American Association pennant-winning New York Mets but switched the next year to the Giants. Through a bit of intrigue he was able to take with him the Mets' star pitcher Keefe. In the 1880s and 1890s, owners were allowed to hold stock in more than one major league team; this led to situations where owners shifted talent to the stronger of their two clubs, often rendering the weaker club completely noncompetitive. This was the case with the Mets and Giants, whose common ownership plotted to have Mutrie secretly release Keefe and then resign himself. Mutrie then invited Keefe on a vacation to Bermuda, where he would be incommunicado for the ten-day waiting period that was required before a player could be signed by a new team. At the end of the trip, Mutrie formally joined the Giants and signed Keefe to a N.L. contract before the Mets fans or the American Association authorities knew what had hit them. This maneuver strained relations between the two leagues, but in the end Keefe stayed in the N.L.

In June, the New Yorkers were stuck in fourth place, but on June 22, Keefe began a 19-game winning streak during which he struck out 152 and walked 32, holding opponents to a .199 batting average. On the Fourth of July, the Giants were in second place behind Detroit and in late July they passed Detroit for good, finishing 9 games in front.

Keefe defeated Silver King three times in the World Series, going 4-0 and allowing only 19 hits in 36 innings. New York won the world championship 6-4.

1889

The Giants repeated in 1889, but this time the hitters were the team's main strength. Connor hit .317 with 13 homers and led the league with 130 RBI, right fielder Mike Tiernan hit .335 with 11 homers, and three other Giant regulars hit over .300. As a team New York scored 935 runs, batted .282, and slugged .394, all league highs. But all that hitting was needed as they barely squeaked by Boston — which had bought Detroit stars Brouthers, Richardson, and Bennett — on the final day of the season when Boston's ace John Clarkson lost to Pittsburgh.

In the Association, St. Louis was dethroned by Brooklyn with the help of former Brown Bob Caruthers, who led the A.A. with 40 wins, and pitcher-turned-first-baseman Dave Foutz, who drove in 113 runs. In the first New York-Brooklyn World Series, Brooklyn won three of the first four games and then proceeded to drop five straight and the series. Giants pitcher Ned "Cannonball" Crane won three and lost one.

The back cover of an 1888 tobacco album.

BILLY HAMILTON

The best offense of the slugging early 1890s belonged to Philadelphia, who had the National League's two best RBI men in Ed Delahanty and Sam Thompson.

More often than not, the man they were driving in was "Sliding" Billy Hamilton.

Hamilton was the prototypical leadoff man. He hit .344 lifetime, eighth on the all-time list, and led the N.L. in hitting twice; he hit .300 or better 12 years in a row. Hamilton was the fastest man in the game and he stole 937 bases lifetime, the record that Lou Brock broke. He led the league in stolen bases seven times, stealing more than 100 bases three times. In an era of free-swingers, Hamilton knew how to get on base; he led the league in walks five times, walking more than 100 times in five seasons.

He led the league in runs scored four times and scored 100 or more runs 11 times, including ten years in a row.

Moving to Boston in 1896, Hamilton helped to revive the Beaneaters dynasty, playing on both the 1897 and '98 pennant winners and scoring 262 runs over the two seasons. Hamilton's finest season came in 1894 with Philadelphia, when he hit .399, stole 99 bases (including seven in one game) and set the all-time record for runs scored in a single season, with 196; he has one other season (1895 when he scored 166 runs) in the all-time top ten.

Dummy Hoy (top left) scored more than 100 runs eight seasons in his 14-year career. Billy Sunday (top middle) retired after his finest season in 1890 at the age of 28 when he discovered that his greatest talents lay in another line of work: evangelism. Jake Beckley (top right) drove in 104 runs a season between 1890 and 1895 for Pittsburgh. An action shot (middle) during pregame warmups shows the Polo Grounds in New York in the early 1890s. Tim Keefe (bottom left), shown in a rare action shot in 1892, was 20-16 in '92, his last 20-win season. He ended his career with a 344-225 record and a 2.62 ERA. Billy Nash of Boston (bottom right), depicted on an 1889 Duke Tobacco premium cabinet card, scored 84 runs, drove in 76 runs, and stole 26 bases in '89.

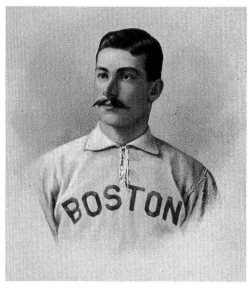

THE TURN OF THE CENTURY

1890

After looking at the Players' League rosters in 1890, it is easy to see why most fans regarded the P.L. as the only major league. Most N.L. personnel and many of the A.A. players had joined the Players' League; some came over as whole teams. Clearly, even though the players ultimately lost their fight in the boardrooms and at the negotiating table, they would never have lost on the field.

Pennant-winning Boston, for example, had Dan Brouthers (who hit .345), Billy Nash, King Kelly, Hoss Radbourn, and three other players from the 1889 Boston National League team. The New York P.L. entry must also have looked very familiar to the fans, with Roger Connor, who hit .372 and led the P.L. in homers with 13; Orator O'Rourke, who hit .360; Buck Ewing; Tim Keefe; and four other 1889 regulars.

One of the few 1889 A.A. teams to remain intact was Brooklyn, but instead of jumping to the Players' League, they joined the N.L. and won the '90 pennant over a weakened field, going 86-43 and scoring 884 runs. Their hitting stars were Oyster Burns, who hit 13 home runs and had 128 RBI, and Dave Foutz, who hit .303 and drove in 98. But when Brooklyn met a faceless Louisville team in the so-called World Series of 1890, the fans stayed away in droves. With attendance figures of 1,050, 1,000, 600, and 300 for the final four games, the Series was called off for lack of interest. The result, fittingly, was inconclusive: Brooklyn three wins, Louisville three wins, and one tie.

Always considered the inferior league, the American Association was so weakened by the events of 1890 that it was no longer thought of as a major league by the fans. Baltimore and Kansas City dropped out and were replaced by weak entries from Rochester, Syracuse, and Toledo, who finished the 1891 season a combined 52½ games out of first place. The A.A. Brooklyn club that had formed to replace the 1889 pennant-winners (now in the N.L.) folded in August. Boston won the last American Association pennant in 1891, but no World Series was played and the Association collapsed completely before the 1892 season. P.L. Boston's star third baseman in 1890, Billy Nash, followed King Kelly across town to Frank Selee's Boston Beaneaters.

1891

In 1891, the Beaneaters won the first of three straight National League pennants to become the first dynasty of the 1890s. In a decade usually thought of as belonging to the Baltimore Orioles, Boston had the best overall record, 869-508, and the most pennants, four. The 1891 pitching staff of John Clarkson and Kid Nichols led the N.L. in ERA at 2.76, complete games with 126, and fewest walks with 364. Boston had an all-star infield of Billy Nash at third, Tom Tucker at first, Herman Long at shortstop, and Joe Quinn at second. Veteran Charlie Bennett did the catching. Boston led the new 12-team league in offense, scoring 847 runs and using what Monte Ward called "teamwork at the bat": stealing bases, the hit-and-run, and a variety of other trick plays on the base paths. Aside from shortstop Long, who hit ten home runs, Boston's only bona fide power hitter was the speed and power combination of outfielder Harry Stovey, who finished second in the N.L. in homers with 16, second in slugging at .498, and fifth in stolen bases with 57.

An 1890 McLaughlin Home Baseball Game box lid.

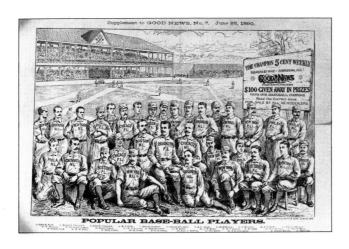

The players and manager of an 1890s women's team (top left) pose for a picture. The White Stockings won two pennants in 1885 and '86 then dumped an "old" King Kelly (top right). He averaged 96 runs scored, a .308 batting average, 26 doubles, and 68 RBI over the next five years; Chicago did not win another pennant until 1906. The "bleachers" are full for this Players' League match (middle) between New York and Pittsburgh. New York was managed by Buck Ewing and featured first baseman Roger Connor, who hit .372 with 13 homers and 103 RBI. Pittsburgh was managed by Ned Hanlon and starred first baseman Jake Beckley, who hit .324 with ten homers and 120 RBI. A print from Good News (bottom) in 1890 features National League and Players' League stars.

THE TURN OF THE CENTURY

A presentation pin (top) for the '94 N.L. champion Orioles. An 1894 Giants candy box (bottom).

1892

In 1892, Boston added outfielder Tommy McCarthy and pitcher Jack Stivetts, who replaced the fading Clarkson. Control pitcher Nichols, who won without a curve or a good fastball, became Boston's ace; he won 35 and lost 16 with a 2.83 ERA in 1892 and went 33-13 with a 3.52 ERA in 1893. For his career with Boston, Nichols had a .700 winning percentage. From the defunct Boston A.A. franchise, the Beaneaters acquired center fielder Hugh Duffy, who along with Tommy McCarthy made up the "Heavenly Twins." Duffy hit .301 in 1892 and .363 in '93, but he came into his own in '94, when he had a triple-crown year that any of today's power hitters would gladly take: He hit .438 and led the league in homers with 18, RBI with 145, doubles with 50, slugging at .679, and total bases with 366.

Boston became the first National League team to win 100 games, going 102-48 and finishing 8½ games over Cleveland and ERA leader Cy Young, who went 36-11. In lieu of a World Series, the N.L. tried a split-season format that was dropped the next year. In a six-game series, first-half winner Boston demolished second-half winner Cleveland 5-0 with one tie.

1893

With the pitching distance changed to the modern 60 feet six inches, the 1893 season was the beginning of a long period of heavy offense. Boston hit .290 and scored 1,008 runs, but incredibly, neither of these led the league. Pittsburgh hit .299; Cleveland, with Jesse Burkett, hit .300; and Philadelphia led the N.L. in batting at .301, slugging at .430, and home runs with 79. Philadelphia's big guns were Sam Thompson, who hit .370 and drove in 126 runs; Billy Hamilton, who

led the league in hitting at .380; and big Ed Delahanty, who hit .368 and led the league in home runs (19), RBI (146), slugging (.583), and total bases (347).

1894

This was the high-water-mark season for slugging in the overhand-pitching era. The league ERA rose to 5.32. Only one team, the New York Giants, had an ERA of under 4.00; only two teams were under 5.00. Boston led the hit parade, topping the N.L. in runs scored (1,222), doubles (272), home runs (103), and slugging (.484), while batting .331 as a team. But all of this wasn't enough to overcome their mediocre pitching.

Hitting .300 as a team was nothing special in 1894; eight teams did it, led by Philadelphia at .349 and Baltimore at .343.

In 1894, Ned Hanlon's Orioles won the first of three straight pennants and the first pennant of any kind for Baltimore, which had been represented in various professional leagues since 1872. Relatively unsung except for first baseman Dan Brouthers, the Orioles went from a 60-70 record and eighth place in 1893 to 89-39, 3 games ahead of New York, in '94. Out of the running for much of the early part of the season, the Orioles put on a June charge and battled league-leading Boston all summer.

AMOS RUSIE

Amos Rusie, the "Hoosier Thunderbolt," was the Nolan Ryan of the 1890s. He was fast — striking out more than 300 men three times and leading the N.L. in strikeouts in 1890, '91, '93, '94, and '95 — and he was wild. Rusie walked 1,716 men in his ten-year career, and he led the league in five different seasons.

Walking a lot of batters didn't stop Rusie from winning, though. Except for his rookie season, he won 20 games or more every year, including winning 30 three times. He led the N.L. in ERA twice and finished with a career record of 243-160.

Rusie made the transition to the new 60-foot, six-inch pitching distance almost effortlessly; he was 32-28 with a 2.88 ERA in 1892, and his ERA rose by only 0.35 to 3.23 in 1893 after the pitching distance was changed, while the National League ERA jumped by 1.38. The rule change didn't take away from Rusie's durability either; in 1893 he went 29-18 and led the league in starts with 52 and complete games with 50. He also led the league in innings pitched with 482, shutouts with four, strikeouts with 208, and walks with 218.

At the end of the 1895 season, Giants owner Andrew Freedman arbitrarily deducted $200 from Rusie's paycheck on the pretext of some vague infraction. When Rusie refused to play in '96 until he got his money, Freedman wouldn't back down. Finally Rusie sat out the entire season and played in 1897 only when the rest of the N.L. owners chipped in and paid Rusie the salary he had missed during the holdout.

Herman Long (top left) scored more than 100 runs every season from 1891 to 1896. Tommy McCarthy (top right) together with Hugh Duffy made up the "Heavenly Twins" for Boston. McCarthy scored an average of 109 runs a season in his four years with the Beaneaters. This photo of the Page Fence Giants (middle) dates back to 1895. Dan Brouthers (bottom left) led the N.L in slugging each season from 1881 to '86. An 1892 scorecard (bottom middle) features Chicago manager/first baseman Cap Anson. Jimmy Ryan (bottom right), an outfielder for Chicago, scored 100 runs eight times in his 18-year career.

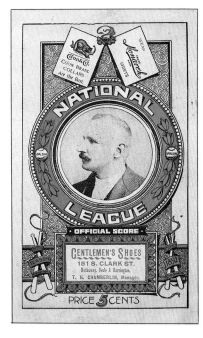

THE TURN OF THE CENTURY

Finally, Baltimore put Boston away but had to fend off a 12-1 streak by New York and their ace pitchers Amos Rusie, the N.L. ERA leader at 2.78, and Jouett Meekin, who went 36-10 with a 3.70 ERA.

Baltimore lacked a dominant pitching ace, and throughout the mid-1890s their pitching was fragile. Nevertheless with Sadie McMahon, Kid Gleason, and a patchwork of such veterans as Tony Mullane and Duke Esper, the Orioles were second in pitching to the New York Giants in 1894. The '94 Orioles relied on a well-balanced lineup that contained eight .300 hitters, led by Joe Kelley at .393 and Wee Willie Keeler at .371; five 100 RBI men; and two of the top three in the N.L. in runs scored. Young third baseman John McGraw batted .340 and stole 78 bases, second only to Philadelphia's Billy Hamilton (99).

The Orioles were known at least as much for their profanity and dirty, sometimes brutal, style as for their hitting. Hanlon taught willing pupils like McGraw the arts of blocking baserunners, interfering with opposing catchers, and abusing and spiking umpires.

But Hanlon was also a master of tactics and on-field discipline. Hanlon's team bewildered defenses with plays like the two-base sacrifice, usually worked by McGraw and Keeler; with McGraw on first, Keeler would place a bunt so that it had to be fielded by the third baseman and McGraw, off with the pitch, would make third easily while the opposing infielders scratched their heads. Hanlon's teams used these tactics to lead the N.L. in runs in 1896 and finish second in runs in 1895 and '97. The success of the Orioles style of play made them the model for baseball offenses until the home run era.

By 1894, baseball was facing up to the problem of maintaining fan interest in a one-league, 12-team pennant race, a problem that ultimately was never solved. That year the N.L. tried the Temple Cup. This was an award to be given to the winner of a best four-out-of-seven postseason series between the first- and second-place clubs. The problem with this kind of series is that the pennant winner has nothing to gain and everything to lose. The Orioles discovered this when they were defeated 4-0 by the New York Giants in the first Temple Cup, and New York fans spent the off-season proclaiming loudly that their team was the real champion. The Temple Cup series were also often anticlimactic following a close pennant race, and after 1897 they were ended.

1895

With their pitching thinner than usual because of McMahon's sore arm, the Orioles floundered for the first few months of 1895. But they rallied in mid-season and overtook Cleveland behind a rested McMahon, who went 10-4 with a 2.94 ERA down the stretch, and rookie Bill Hoffer, who finished 30-7 with a 3.21 ERA. The Baltimore offense was second only to Philadelphia's, which featured Sam Thompson (who hit .392 with 18 homers and 165 RBI) and Ed Delahanty, the National League's best one-two punch.

An early catcher's mitt from an 1890s ad.

1896

McGraw missed much of 1896 with typhoid fever and once again the Orioles started slowly. But in August and September they caught fire, led by newly acquired first baseman "Dirty" Jack Doyle, who hit .345; Hughie Jennings, who hit .398 and batted in 121 runs; and

The mid-1890s Baltimore Orioles (top left) of Willie Keeler and John McGraw, standing, and Joe Kelley and Hughie Jennings, seated, were experts at manufacturing runs. Louis Sockalexis (top right), the first American Indian in the major leagues, played with Cleveland from 1897 to '99. The Cincinnati Red Stockings (bottom) received a hero's welcome in Wilmington, OH, on August 16, 1897. Buck Ewing's Reds finished third in the N.L. in '97 with a 92-60 record.

THE TURN OF THE CENTURY

pitchers Billy Hoffer and George Hemming, who finished first and second in the N.L. in winning percentage. And once again, Patsy Tebeau's Cleveland Spiders finished second, this time 9½ games behind. Cy Young was fifth in the league with a 3.24 ERA, and the Cleveland offense was sparked by Cupid Childs, who hit .355 with 106 RBI, and Jesse Burkett, who led the league in batting at .410.

1897

In 1897 and 1898, a rebuilt Boston club took the N.L. pennant back from Baltimore. They still had Kid Nichols, Jack Stivetts, and the nucleus of their great offense from the early 1890s: Hugh Duffy, Bobby Lowe, and Herman Long. But slick-fielding Fred Tenney had taken over at first, and in 1896, Selee added outfielders Billy Hamilton and Chick Stahl, third baseman Jimmy Collins, and young catcher Marty Bergen. With Nichols leading the N.L. in wins in 1897 with 30, Collins and Duffy driving in 261 runs between them, and leadoff man Hamilton scoring a league-high 152 runs, the Beaneaters caught Baltimore with a 17-1 July, and the two teams stayed within one game of each other for 28 days in August and September. The pennant race was finally settled in an end-of-season three-game series in Baltimore, with Kid Nichols winning the decisive game 19-10.

1898

Boston won the pennant in 1898 by 6 games over Baltimore. Kid Nichols won 29 and lost 12 with a 2.13 ERA, third-best in the N.L. Jimmy Collins hit .328, slugged 15 home runs, and drove in 111 runs. Boston hit .290 as a team, surpassed only by Baltimore's .302 average.

The late 1890s was a dreary period for baseball. Attendance declined each year, both because of a general economic depression that was related to the Spanish-American War and because of the inherent lack of interest in the 12-team format. In 1897, for example, last-place St. Louis went 29-102 and finished 63½ games out of the running. The National League cellar was very deep; there were six teams ahead of St. Louis in the standings who were below .500 on the season. In 1898, both Washington and St. Louis lost over 100 games and eight teams finished 20 or more games out of first. Naturally, it was difficult to attract fans under these circumstances, and by 1898 and '99, many N.L. clubs — even good teams like Baltimore — were close to bankruptcy.

1899

In 1899, Ned Hanlon had seen the handwriting on the wall for the weaker franchises and put together a group of investors who bought stock in both the Baltimore and Brooklyn clubs. Hanlon then installed John McGraw as manager of faltering Baltimore and moved to Brooklyn, taking with him most of the stars of the old Baltimore dynasty, including Keeler, Kelley, and Jennings. It was in Brooklyn that Hanlon won the 1899 pennant, going 101-47 and beating second-place Boston by 8 games. The last year of the century was the ninth straight year that the National League pennant was won by a team managed by either Frank Selee or Ned Hanlon.

THE 1899 CLEVELAND SPIDERS

The late 1890s National League had some of the worst major league teams in history, including 39-111 St. Louis in 1898 and 38-93 Louisville in 1896. But the absolute worst of all was the 1899 Cleveland Spiders.

Once a pennant contender and featuring such stars as Jesse Burkett and Cy Young, the Spiders fell victim to the evils of what was then called "syndicated baseball" — two clubs with common ownership. When Cleveland owner Frank Robison bought the St. Louis Browns, he decided that St. Louis, a bigger city with legalized Sunday baseball, was a better market. Before the 1899 season, he cannibalized the Spiders, moving Burkett, Young, Patsy Tebeau, Cupid Childs, and Bobby Wallace to St. Louis.

Cleveland was left with a mix of over-the-hill incompetents and young nonprospects. The result was a season that embarrassed the N.L. and was part of the reason that Cleveland and three other franchises were dropped from the league in 1899, indirectly leading to the formation of the A.L.

The Spiders went 11-102 on the road, but improved to 9-32 with the home-field advantage. Nevertheless, the Spiders played the last half of the season on the road because of understandably poor home attendance. They finished last in the N.L. in batting, slugging, doubles, triples, home runs, ERA, runs allowed, and runs scored. The Spiders ended the season 84 games behind pennant-winning Brooklyn.

The 1898 Spiders featured (left to right) Cy Young, George Bristow, and Jesse Burkett and went 81-68. With Young and Burkett gone, Cleveland went 20-134 in '99; the Spiders won one game and lost 40 in their last 41 contests.

In 1900, at the age of 30, Kid Nichols (top left) became the youngest pitcher ever to win 300 games. Nichols won 30 or more games seven seasons in a row from 1891 to 1897. His 360 career victories place him seventh on the all-time win list. Jesse Burkett (top right) was a lifetime .341 hitter and one of the top leadoff men of his era, scoring more than 100 runs in nine seasons and a peak of 160 in 1896. The 1899 transfer of Burkett, Patsy Tabeau, Cy Young, and Cupid Childs from Cleveland to St. Louis was one of the most infamous abuses of "syndicate baseball."

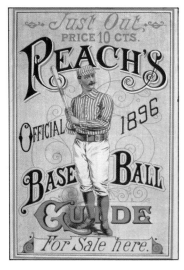

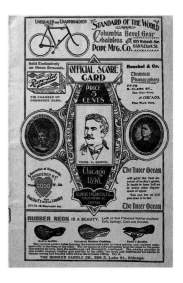

An 1896 advertising poster (middle left) promoted the new Reach Baseball Guide. An 1898 Police Gazette poster (middle center) features the managers of the National League clubs. Chicago manager Tom Burns, featured on an 1898 scorecard (middle right), replaced Cap Anson in '98 after Anson had been the White Stockings skipper for the previous 19 years. Beaneaters first baseman Fred Tenney (bottom left) was a solid-hitting player for 11 seasons with Boston. Jack Glasscock (bottom right) was a steady shortstop for 17 years, averaging 94 runs scored between 1884 and 1893.

THE 1900s

The 1900s saw the emergence of Ban Johnson's American League and a period of unprecedented peace and prosperity in baseball. The 20th century opened with a drastic rule change; for the first time, a foul ball was counted as a strike.

Nap Lajoie (page 76), shown on a large silk made in 1907, was partially responsible for the acceptance of the American League when he had a great season in the A.L. in 1901. Ban Johnson (page 77, top) leaves the American League office after serving as the A.L.'s president for 27 years. This scorecard (page 77, bottom) is from the 1901 A.L. Milwaukee franchise.

THE 1900s

The first decade of the 20th century saw the last of the major "Monopoly Wars" and the beginning of a period of unprecedented peace and prosperity in baseball. After 1903 — when the National League and the American League laid down arms and agreed to live together in a two-league format and to play the first modern World Series — there were no major interleague wars until 1913 and no more franchise shifts until 1953. With the nation's economy recovered from the war-related depression of the late 1890s, attendance skyrocketed.

Major league bats were peaceful, too. The versatile and exciting "run-and-gun" offensive style of the 1890s, which produced a generation of terrorized pitchers and hundreds of batting records that still stand, came to an abrupt halt with the adoption of the foul-strike rule by the N.L. in 1901 and the A.L. in 1903. Batting averages and ERAs plummeted. The 1900s were the heyday of dead ball, a plodding, one-run-at-a-time style of play.

In a larger sense, the American League arose from the same causes that produced the American Association, the Union Association, and the Players' League: the dissatisfaction of major league caliber cities, owners, and players who were denied entry into the National League or oppressed by its collusive and authoritarian practices. But the more immediate inspiration was Ban Johnson — a shrewd former sportswriter and president of the minor Western League — who had been carefully gathering economic backing and making plans for the most successful assault yet on National League supremacy. After the 1900 season, he was ready and announced that the Western League was claiming major league status under the name of the American League. For the 1900 season, the A.L. operated franchises in Chicago, Detroit, Cleveland, Milwaukee, Indianapolis, Kansas City, Minneapolis, and Buffalo.

Johnson had timed his move well; in 1900, the National League was at an historic weak point. Attendance was down because of the economy and because the one-league, 12-team structure was simply boring. The National League ownership was deeply divided between a faction led by Chicago's Jim Hart — including Brooklyn's Charles Ebbets, Philadelphia's John Rogers, and Pittsburgh's Barney Dreyfuss — and a faction led by New York Giants owner Andrew Freedman and including Arthur Soden of Boston, Frank and Stanley Robison of St. Louis, and John Brush of Cincinnati.

The conflict between these two factions came to a head over the election of the National League president in 1901. Freedman supported incumbent Nick Young; the opposition nominated Al Spalding. Naturally, the vote was 4-4, and it

Wee Willie Keeler hit .333 from 1900 to 1906.

BAN JOHNSON

Ban Johnson took on the National League monopoly and won.

Johnson's baseball career began when he was a crusading sportswriter in Cincinnati. There he waged a one-man campaign for reform of the National League in the mid-1880s. When Charles Comiskey was recruiting for his new Western League in 1893, he asked Johnson if he wanted to try to do something about baseball's problems himself. The 29-year-old Johnson agreed, became the league's president, and immediately began to formulate plans to gain major league status for the new league; this was accomplished when the Western League became the American League in 1901.

Johnson was autocratic, high-handed, and a fierce guardian of baseball's integrity. One of his first acts as A.L. president was to issue the edict that "clean ball is the main plank in the American League platform. There must be no profanity on the ball field. The umpires are agents of the League and must be treated with respect." If today extreme verbal abuse of umpires is grounds for ejection, physical abuse is almost unthinkable, and it is taken for granted that all umpires' decisions are final, the reason is Johnson's reforms of the early 1900s.

Expansion into the modern, two-league format would have been impossible without Johnson, whom Branch Rickey once called "a supersalesman of ideas."

"Iron Man" Joe McGinnity (left) averaged 384 innings pitched in his first six seasons; he won 57 games in his first two major league years. Boston shortstop Herman Long (top right) led the National League in homers in 1900 with 12. An original painting by Mark Rucker (bottom right) depicts an early baseball poster.

THE 1900s

remained dead-locked through 25 ballots. Finally, when Freedman and his friends walked out, Spalding was named president. Freedman's response was to go to New York Supreme Court, where a judge granted a permanent injunction against Spalding.

Because of this infighting, the National League was left essentially leaderless for the most critical year in its history. With the expiration of the National Agreement in 1901, the A.L. began to raid N.L. rosters, grabbing such stars as Nap Lajoie. The National League fought the Lajoie signing in the state courts and won, but Johnson merely transferred him to Cleveland and kept him out of the state of Pennsylvania. A series of related lawsuits backfired on the N.L., as judges repeatedly overturned contracts based on the reserve clause, for the same reasons that they had done so in the 1880s and 1890s.

By 1902, all the old National League tricks, such as trying to bribe defecting players back into the fold and offering the stronger A.L. clubs entry into the N.L., had failed. The American League was holding the line and — after dropping its weaker teams in Indianapolis, Kansas City, Minneapolis, and Buffalo and replacing them with Philadelphia, Boston, Baltimore, and Washington — was making its owners happy with large profits. After Spalding resigned and Freedman gave up and left baseball, the N.L.'s new president, Harry Pulliam, reconciled for peace. Before the 1903 season, the two leagues agreed to respect each other's contracts and operate under a single three-man commission that would include the two league presidents and Garry Herrman of Cincinnati. A close friend of Herrman, Ban Johnson immediately became the real power behind the National Commission.

Pittsburgh pitcher Deacon Phillippe notched five 20-win seasons between 1899 and 1905.

Fans welcomed a return to the two-league system and attendance soared to nearly 50 million between 1901 and 1909. Whereas a crowd of 4,000 or 5,000 was unusually large in the 1890s, teams of the 1900s averaged more than that. The biggest drawing card of the era, John McGraw's New York Giants, drew almost one million fans in 1908, or over 10,000 per game. The World Series was also a big hit. The eight-game 1903 Series drew over 100,000 fans; the seven-game 1909 Series drew one and a half times that. This prosperity enabled clubs of the 1900s to build the first really permanent ballparks, steel and concrete affairs that one-by-one replaced the old wooden parks. The first example was Philadelphia's Shibe Park in 1909, which seated 30,000-plus fans in three decks. Later that season, 23,000-seat Forbes Field opened in Pittsburgh and wooden League Park in Cleveland and Sportsman's Park in St. Louis were renovated in steel and concrete.

For the players, the new era brought a return to the reserve clause and business as usual. But the new National Commission was too smart, at least at first, to polarize the players by anything so inflammatory as a salary cap. Players of the 1900s were paid fairly well compared to the 1890s and were treated with the kind of mostly benevolent paternalism that has characterized the more peaceful chapters in 20th-century baseball labor relations. Through judicious co-opting of the leadership of the weak players' union, the Players' Protective Association, Johnson and the owners were able to avoid significant labor trouble for a decade.

The 20th century opened with a drastic rule change. For the first time, in 1901 in the National League and in 1903 in both

JIMMY COLLINS

Considered the finest third baseman of his time, Jimmy Collins played from 1895 to 1908, also acting as manager of A.L. Boston from 1901 to 1906. Collins won two pennants as a player with the great N.L. Boston Beaneaters of the late 1890s and two more as player/manager of the new American League Boston club in 1903 and 1904.

Collins hit .294 and slugged .408 lifetime with 194 career stolen bases. He hit .300 or better five times. He had his best season with the Beaneaters in 1898, when he led the National League in home runs with 15, hit .328, and both scored and drove in more than 100 runs.

But Collins was elected to the Hall of Fame more on his glove than on his bat. Playing in the bunt-crazed 1890s and 1900s, he was universally considered to be death on bunts. One observer described him charging a bunt with a "swoop like a chicken hawk," fielding the ball and firing to first with accuracy from any angle. On one occasion, the old Orioles decided to test Collins; starting with John McGraw and Wee Willie Keeler (both masters of the bunt), each of the first four men in the batting order bunted up the third base line. Collins threw every one out at first.

From 1897 to 1903, Collins had most defensive records for third basemen all to himself. He led the league in putouts four times, assists four times, double plays three times, total chances per game twice, and fielding average twice.

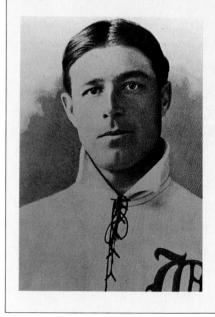

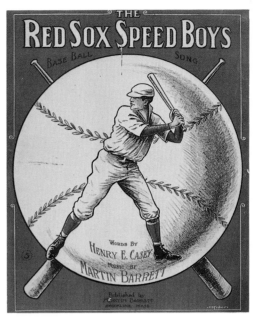

The White Sox March *(top left) was published in 1907 to celebrate the '06 world champion Pale Hose. This sheet music (top right) was for the Red Sox in the mid-1900s, even though Boston finished at or near the bottom of the league in stolen bases during that time. The 1900 Detroit Tigers (bottom) and other American League teams played baseball on par with N.L. teams, although the A.L. was considered a minor league.*

THE 1900s

leagues, a foul ball was counted as a strike. This caused the single greatest change in the way baseball was played until Babe Ruth and the home run era. ERAs dropped all the way below the levels of 1880s baseball; a British journalist once described baseball as a game in which "the odds against (the batter) are so great that our English love of fair play is offended." From 1893 to 1899, the National League ERA had been above 4.00 every year except for 1898 and 1899, when it fell to 3.60 and 3.85. 1904, however, was the first of six consecutive years that neither league's ERA rose above 2.99.

The 1900s produced a generation of individual pitchers at least as dominant as the pitchers of the 1960s, another historic low point in hitting. The Gibsons, Koufaxes, and Marichals of the 1900s were: Christy Mathewson, who averaged a 29-14 record and a 1.97 ERA per year for the decade; Cy Young, who averaged a 27-15 record and a 2.12 ERA per year; and Three-Finger Brown, who averaged a 29-13 record and a 1.63 ERA. These pitchers and their contemporaries rewrote the all-time record book permanently.

Defense — aided by bigger gloves, better-maintained fields, and advances in catchers' equipment such as shin-guards — also improved. While defensive improvement has been a constant throughout baseball history, the 1900s were a time of particularly rapid advances in fielding. From 1893, when the modern pitching distance was established, to 1899, the overall National League fielding average climbed 11 points, from .931 to .942. But from 1900 to 1908 it climbed 19 points, from .942 to .961.

The 1900s' decline in offense was across-the-board and affected every hitting category, even home

runs. Not that home runs had ever been a very important part of offense in the 1890s; in 1894, the average National League club hit only 52 homers and in 1895 only 40. But these would have been high figures in the dead-ball era; National League clubs averaged 22 home runs in 1904 and 23 in 1905.

Batting averages and slugging averages fell even more. In 1893, National League batting champion Billy Hamilton hit .380 and top slugger Ed Delahanty slugged .583. From 1894 to 1899, the National League leaders compiled batting averages of .438, .423, .410, .432, .379, and .408; leading slugging averages in those years were .679, .654, .631, .578, .494, and .585. Honus Wagner, the dominant hitter of the 1900s, led the league in batting average in 1903 at .355, in 1904 at .349, in 1906 at .339, in 1907 at .350, in 1908 at .354, and in 1909 at .339. With the exception of 1908, none of these performances would have been good enough to make the top five a decade earlier. League-leading slugging performances of the 1900s declined even more than batting averages, by 50 to 100 points as compared to the 1890s.

The unfortunate batters of the 1900s were left with few ways to score runs beyond the hit-and-run, the bunt, and the stolen base. These strategies had all been developed in the slugging 1890s, but in the more conservative 1900s they were applied very differently. Instead of using the hit-and-run to aggressively exploit the weaknesses in opposing defenses as Frank Selee and Ned Hanlon had done, it became primarily a way to play for one run and to stay out of the dou-

This baseball design is from 1907.

JOHN McGRAW

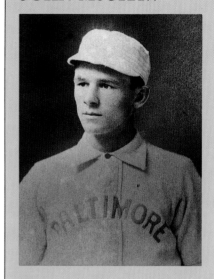

John McGraw was an aggressive, hustling player who would look for any edge — even an illegal one — to win. Just as aggressive as a manager, he was demanding and hard on players, opponents and umpires alike. On both sides of the foul lines, McGraw was successful.

Some of McGraw's hardness came from a brutal childhood in upstate New York. By age 18, McGraw was playing third base for the Baltimore Orioles and was the prime pupil of Ned Hanlon, the first great modern manager. McGraw learned his lessons so well, going on to a 33-year managerial career in which he won ten pennants and three World Series, that his career as a player was often overlooked. In 16 years, mostly with the Orioles of the 1890s, McGraw batted .334, including nine straight years above .300. He played a great defensive third base and was a run-scoring machine; he got on base (twice leading the N.L. in walks), stole 436 bases in his career, and scored more than 100 runs five times. In 1898 and '99, McGraw led the league in runs scored with 143 and 140.

There were two sides to McGraw the manager: the terror of umpires and league presidents who was fined and suspended numerous times for violent behavior on the field, and the kind and generous man who inspired tremendous loyalty among his players and who, in one of baseball's oddest couples, was the lifelong best friend of mild-mannered, college-educated Christy Mathewson.

The popular actor/singer DeWolf Hopper (left) made the poem Casey at the Bat his personal trademark, reciting it more than 10,000 times. He first decided to deliver the poem as a monologue between acts of a comic opera. The poem's author, Ernest Thayer, was an amateur writer and poet who never took his creation very seriously; feeling that it wasn't very good, he published it in the San Francisco Examiner on June 3, 1888, under a pseudonym (years passed before he bothered to reveal himself). No one paid any attention to it until two months later in Chicago, when Hopper delivered the poem. Attending that night were members of the Chicago White Stockings and the New York Giants. In his memoirs, Hopper said "when I dropped my voice to a B flat, I remember seeing (Giants catcher) Buck Ewing's gallant mustachio give a single nervous twitch. And as the house, after a moment of startled silence, grasped the anticlimactic denouement, it shouted its glee." Even after Casey became a nationwide hit, Thayer never asserted his copyright privileges or asked for any part of Hopper's profits. Big Ed Walsh (bottom left) of the White Sox became one of the dominant hurlers of the decade. Cy Young (bottom right) moved to the Red Sox in 1901 and led the A.L. in wins for three consecutive seasons.

the 1900s were much more evenly distributed within the pitching staff than in previous decades, contributing to the trend toward pitching dominance. For example, in the 1890s seasonal leaders in games pitched typically were in the low to mid-50s, with a high of 75 games pitched by Wild Bill Hutchinson in 1892. Only once (in 1897) did a pitcher lead the league with fewer than 50 games. But in the 1900s it happened five times. The typical leader in games pitched was in the high 40s, with the single-season high being Christy Mathewson's 56 in 1908. Adding to the hitters' woes was the development of the spitball, which — along with related trick pitches such as the shine ball, emery ball, and mud ball — was perfectly legal until 1920.

It's no wonder that in 1904 Honus Wagner called for help for his beleaguered fellow major league hitters. The answer, Wagner said, was to eliminate the foul-strike rule, move pitchers three feet farther back from the plate so that "the spitball wouldn't break so well" and reduce the number of balls required for a walk to three.

1900

The year 1900 was the last hurrah for many of the stars of the

A 1900 Harvard baseball mug.

ble play. Instead of a means of getting on base, the bunt was used more and more exclusively as a sacrifice.

The dominant offensive weapon of the 1900s was the stolen base; this decade is remembered today as a time of running offenses and such great individual base-stealers as Ty Cobb and Honus Wagner. Compared to later decades, there was a lot of base-stealing in the 1900s, but even this element of offense declined as compared to the 1890s.

As if pitchers of the 1900s didn't have enough of an advantage over hitters, in this decade managers began to rely less and less on a single pitching ace, and more and more on efficient three- or four-man rotations. This was a gradual process, but pitchers' workloads in

late 19th century, including manager Ned Hanlon, one of the principal architects of 1890s baseball. After winning the 1900 pennant with a record of 82-54, 4½ games ahead of Pittsburgh (where young Honus Wagner led the league in hitting at .381 and drove in 100 runs while playing five different positions), Hanlon would never win another pennant in seven years of managing. It was also the last championship season for many of the old Orioles, who now wore the Brooklyn uniform. When Hanlon left Baltimore for Brooklyn after 1898, he had taken along most of the starting lineup: Dan McGann, Wee Willie Keeler, Joe Kelley, and Hughie Jennings. After new Baltimore manager John McGraw finished a surprising fourth place in

1903 WORLD SERIES

In the first modern World Series in 1903, Jimmy Collins and the A.L. champion Boston Pilgrims were not considered much of a match against the great Pittsburgh dynasty, which was in its prime, but limped into the series with ace Sam Leever limited by a sore shoulder to ten ineffective

innings and number-three starter Ed Doheny out of action. The great Honus Wagner was hobbled by a leg injury; he hit only .222 and led all fielders with six errors. The burden fell on Pittsburgh pitcher Deacon Phillippe, who put on a heroic performance, pitching five complete games in ten days to keep his team alive until Game Eight.

More than 16,000 watched in Boston as Phillippe beat Cy Young in the opener 7-3, behind Jimmy Sebring's seventh-inning home run. The next day, Boston's Bill Dineen struck out 11 and beat Leever (who didn't make it out of the second inning) 3-1. On one day of rest, Phillippe won Game Three 4-2, as Pittsburgh doubled four times off Long Tom Hughes. Phillippe then won Game Four, although he tired by the end. He allowed three runs in the ninth, and Boston had the tying run on second when he got out of the jam.

The Pirates were now up three games to one, but their pitching was fatally thin, and Boston won the next four straight. Young beat Brickyard Kennedy 11-2 in Game Five. Dineen beat Leever 6-3 in Game Six. Young beat Phillippe 7-3 in Game Seven. And in Game Eight, Dineen beat Phillippe 3-0.

The Boston bench looks on during the first modern World Series. By defeating Pittsburgh five games to three, the Pilgrims gave the American League legitimacy in the eyes of the public.

Hughie Jennings (top) watches one of his Tigers during sliding drills. Jennings became Detroit's manager in 1907 and brought the Tigers three straight A.L. pennants. Outfielder Mike Donlin (bottom), called "Turkey" because of his showmanship and love of fancy clothes, was a free spirit who played with six different teams in his 12-year career. Everywhere he went the fans loved him, but Donlin had a way of wearing out his welcome with managers by staying out all night, getting arrested for assault, and generally showing more interest in his girlfriends than in his profession. Donlin hit .333 for his career and was an aggressive outfielder and baserunner. After he married Mable Hite, a popular actress of the 1900s, he bounced back and forth between baseball and appearing on stage in his wife's hit act. In between, he did jail time in Baltimore. Donlin died at age 55 in — where else? — Hollywood, CA, where he spent the last few years of his life playing bit parts in motion pictures.

THE 1900s

'99 with only the talent that Hanlon hadn't thought worth pirating, Hanlon went back and corrected his oversight. He took second baseman Gene DeMontreville, outfielder Jimmy Sheckard, and pitchers Frank Kitson and "Iron Man" Joe McGinnity. The Iron Man put Brooklyn over the top in 1900 with a league-leading 45 games, 347 innings pitched, and 29 wins against only nine losses.

Brooklyn's veteran hitters led the National League in 1900 in runs (816) and produced numbers that in the coming dead-ball era would soon be all but unreachable: a .293 team batting average, .383 slugging average, and 274 stolen bases. Keeler led the team in hitting at .368 and stolen bases with 41. Joe Kelley placed fourth in the N.L. in slugging.

Led by Honus Wagner, the next generation of greats was beginning to be heard from. The great Nap Lajoie settled in for his first season as a starting second

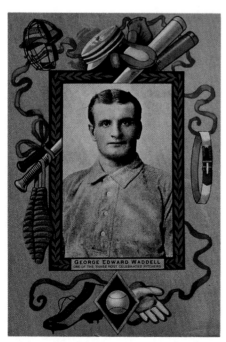

Rube Waddell in 1905.

86

baseman, a position he would dominate for the next 17 years. And in his first full season, Rube Waddell won the National League ERA title at 2.37 and led the league in strikeouts with 130.

1901

In 1901, the American League played its first season as a major league, after having hired more than 100 of the National League's regular players. Ban Johnson's strategy was to stay away from N.L. players who were under multiyear contracts but to refuse to honor either the National League's salary cap or its reserve clause. A.L. Boston landed third baseman Jimmy Collins with a $1,600 raise; he was followed by fellow Beaneaters Buck Freeman, Chick Stahl, and pitcher Ted Lewis. With the help of Cy Young — who was hired away from St. Louis and went 33-10 with five shutouts and a league-best 1.62 ERA — player/manager Collins and his Boston Pilgrims (later called the Red Sox) led most of the way in 1901, only losing out to Chicago in the final few weeks. Freeman was second in the league in batting at .345, slugging at .527, homers with 12, and RBI with 114.

Owner Charles Comiskey put together a running ballclub in Chicago that stole a league-leading 280 bases, led by first baseman Frank Isbell's 52. With the same personnel, pitcher/manager Clark Griffith had won the pennant the year before, when the American League was still technically a minor league. On the strength of Griffith's .774 winning percentage and 24-7 (2.67 ERA) record and Roy Patterson's 20-16 (3.37 ERA) performance, Chicago led the American League in team ERA at 2.98 and allowed fewer runs, 631, than any other team except Boston.

Napoleon Lajoie moved across town from the Phillies to the new Philadelphia A.L. club in 1901, taking with him thousands of fans. Here Lajoie had one of the great seasons of the 20th century, batting .422, slugging .635, driving in 125 runs, scoring 145 runs, and hitting 13 home runs and 48 doubles. All were league-leading figures. Former Brooklyn third baseman Lave Cross hit .331 and outfielder Socks Seybold hit .333 with 90 RBI.

NAPOLEON LAJOIE

Napoleon Lajoie, called "Nap" or sometimes "Larry" (by people who couldn't pronounce his last name), was one of the best-hitting second basemen of all time.

Playing 2,036 games at second over his 21-year career, mostly with N.L. Philadelphia and A.L. Cleveland, Lajoie hit .339 and slugged .466 lifetime. He hit .300 or better in 16 seasons and slugged over .500 nine times, including a string of six straight seasons from 1899 to 1904. In all his 21 years, though, he never played on a championship team.

Lajoie's best season came in the American League's first year, 1901, and he deserves a great deal of the credit for the new league's immediate credibility with the fans. Lajoie made Connie Mack's Athletics the top team in Philadelphia by hitting .422, still the post-1900 record for a single season, and slugging .635. He also led the league in homers (with 14) and four other principal offensive categories. When Lajoie moved to Cleveland in 1902, his tremendous popularity made that franchise a success.

Lajoie was a notorious bad-ball hitter with little strike-zone judgment. He walked only 516 times in two decades, but he hit the dead baseball of his time as hard as anybody. He was a quick, sure-handed fielder, although he wasn't fast. Lajoie stole a total of 395 bases in his career, with totals in his prime of between ten and 20 for a season.

Elmer Flick (top left) of Cleveland led the A.L. in triples, batting average, and slugging average in 1905. The American League leader in batting (.376), slugging (.590), and doubles (43) in 1902, Ed Delahanty (bottom left) drowned at Niagara Falls in July 1903. Jake Beckley (top right) led the National League in doubles in 1901 with 39. In 1905 for Cincinnati, Cy Seymour (bottom right) had a career year, leading the league in doubles (40), triples (21), base hits (219), average (.377), and slugging average (.559).

John McGraw returned to the major leagues as manager of a new Baltimore club that was finally out from under the thumb of Ned Hanlon and his Brooklyn syndicate. The Orioles featured Mike Donlin (who hit .341), future Hall of Fame catcher Roger Bresnahan, and McGraw himself, who led the team in hitting at .352 and stole 25 bases in only 69 games. McGraw was able to steal Joe McGinnity back from Hanlon, and the Iron Man was a one-man pitching staff, going 26-20 with a 3.56 ERA and leading the league in games (48), complete games (39), and innings pitched (382).

A relatively intact Pittsburgh team won the National League pennant in 1901 by 7½ games over Lajoie-less Philadelphia and 9½ games over Brooklyn without McGinnity. Pittsburgh's big guns were Honus Wagner and Fred Clarke, two players they had stolen from Louisville the year before in another syndicate arrangement, thus earning their nickname "Pirates." Wagner hit .353 and led the league in RBI with 126 and stolen bases with 49. Although he was still used by player/manager Clarke as a fill-in at five or six positions in 1901, for the first time in his career Wagner played the majority of his games at shortstop. Clarke manned left field and hit .324 with 60 RBI. Pittsburgh led the N.L. in team ERA at 2.58 behind aces Deacon Phillippe and Jack Chesbro, who won 43 games between them. The 1901 Pirates, who brought Pittsburgh its first pennant in 20 years of major league representation, were the first of four pennant-winning teams from the smoky city in the 1900s, including three in a row between 1901 and 1903. Besides Clarke and Wagner, the Pirates were loaded with young talent, such as speedy first baseman Kitty Bransfield, outfield-

er Ginger Beaumont (who averaged 116 runs scored per season between 1900 and 1903 and led the N.L. in hits four times), and third baseman Tommy Leach.

At the bottom of the N.L. second division, New York Giants rookie Christy Mathewson showed the first indication that the trade of veteran Amos Rusie for Mathewson might be about to pay off; he went 20-17 with a 2.41 ERA. And in his first full season, "Wahoo Sam" Crawford of last-place Cincinnati hit .330, slugged .528, and led the league in home runs with 16.

Three-time .400-hitter and 19th-century great Jesse Burkett won his last batting title in 1901, hitting .382 for fourth-place St. Louis, with a league-leading 139 runs scored.

1902

In 1902 the American League and the National League were still

Frank Merriwell's exploits in 1902.

at war, and the chief battleground became the Baltimore Orioles franchise. In 1901, a determined Ban Johnson had declared war on baseball rowdyism, especially the brand of umpire intimidation and abuse that had been John McGraw's trademark in the National League. With the equally willful McGraw now in the A.L., it was only a matter of time before the two collided head-on over this issue. Round one took place two weeks into the 1901 season, when Johnson suspended McGraw for five days for his verbal outbursts at umpires in a series against Philadelphia. Early in the 1902 season, McGraw began to get the feeling that Johnson was mak-

HONUS WAGNER

Honus Wagner, who played with Louisville from 1897 to '99 and then — thanks to syndicate baseball — was moved to Pittsburgh, where he played until 1917, was one of the great stars of the dead-ball era (or any other era). Along with Ty Cobb and Napoleon Lajoie, Wagner was a member of a baseball triumvirate that controlled the game in the low-scoring, pitching-dominated days before Babe Ruth.

Considering that the 1900s were the low point in hitting in the 20th century, it is amazing that Wagner was able to finish his career with a lifetime batting average of .329 and a slugging average of .469. He is sixth all-time in career hits with 3,430, fifth in doubles with 651, third in triples with 252, and fifth in stolen bases with 722. He hit .300 or better in his first 17 seasons; he didn't fall below that mark until he was 40 years old. During most of this period, the league was batting in the .240s.

Wagner was also a great fielder. John McGraw said of him, "He was a fine catcher, as good a third baseman as I ever saw, the best shortstop I ever saw, and one of the best outfielders." His only problem was that he didn't look like a shortstop. At 5'11" and more than 200 pounds — with extreme bowlegs, long arms, and monstrous hands — Wagner didn't look like any kind of athlete. But Wagner was quick, had a rifle arm, and (much to the amazement of anyone who saw his awkward, rolling stride) he was fast.

The 1902 all-star teams (top) were pictured on a tour in the western United States. Connie Mack's 1902 Philadelphia Athletics (bottom) won the American League flag with an 83-53 record, finishing 5 games up on the St. Louis Browns. Socks Seybold, bottom row far right, led the league with 16 homers.

ing an example of him. On April 30, McGraw interrupted a game twice to vociferously protest calls by umpire Jack Sheridan. The next day, with Sheridan behind the plate, hard-throwing Boston pitcher Bill Dineen threw at McGraw and hit him five times; each time Sheridan ruled that McGraw had gotten hit on purpose and refused to allow first base. After the fifth time, McGraw sat down in the batter's box and wouldn't leave until he was ejected from the game. For this, Johnson issued McGraw another five-game suspension.

By midseason McGraw had enough, and he and New York Giants owner Andrew Freedman hatched a plot to gut the Baltimore franchise and merge its best players into the N.L. Giants. After McGraw demanded and got his release from Baltimore and signed with the Giants as manager, Freedman, Reds owner John Brush, and a few partners secretly bought a controlling interest in the Orioles. They then ordered the release of Joe Kelley, McGinnity, Dan McGann, Bresnahan, and pitcher Jack Cronin, with Kelley going to Cincinnati and the rest signing with New York. To the embarrassment of the American League, the next day the Orioles were forced to forfeit their game against St. Louis for lack of players. A furious Ban

Johnson saved the situation and cut the league's losses by stepping in, revoking the Baltimore franchise, and putting the League in charge of the team for the rest of the season. After the Orioles finished last in 1902, Johnson transferred the club to New York City under the name "Highlanders," later changed to the "Yankees." Johnson got some measure of revenge by living long enough to see the Yankees eventually win the New York fans away from McGraw's Giants in the 1920s.

Mack's Philadelphia Athletics won the 1902 A.L. pennant, finishing 83-53, 5 games ahead of St. Louis, which had replaced the Milwaukee franchise. Socks Seybold's 16 home runs and Lave Cross' 108 RBI picked up part of the slack on offense and 20-15 (3.30 ERA) Eddie Plank and 24-7 (2.05 ERA) Rube Waddell, hired away from the Cubs, anchored a pitching staff that led the A.L. in strikeouts with 455.

National League stars continued to jump to the A.L. for higher salaries, including Jesse Burkett and Bobby Wallace to St. Louis and Ed Delahanty to Washington. Delahanty won the A.L. batting title at .376 and finished first in slugging at .590 and doubles with 43.

With the addition of Nap Lajoie, who hit .366 and slugged .551 with 34 doubles in 86 games, Cleveland moved up from seventh-place to fifth, 14 games out. Lajoie was so popular that Cleveland fans renamed their team the "Naps."

The Pittsburgh Pirates completely dominated the National League in 1902 and won their second pennant, going 103-36 for a colossal winning percentage of .741, the second-best in history after the 1906 Cubs' .763. Pitts-

RUBE WADDELL

Rube Waddell's career, which stretched from 1897 to 1910, can be divided into two parts: the six years he pitched under Connie Mack in Philadelphia (from 1902 to 1907) and the rest of his career.

Waddell had a great arm, but from the shoulders up he was a kind of goofy pitching version of Mike Donlin. Like Donlin, Waddell's drinking interfered with his career; he was also very fond of women and the stage. Waddell even appeared as an actor in a melodrama titled "The Stain of Guilt." Guilt, however, was probably something Waddell was too irresponsible or perhaps too simple-minded to have experienced. He had childish fixations — such as dogs, fire engines, and kids' toys — that interested him far more than baseball, and that drove most of his managers crazy. Between 1897 and 1901, three teams gave up on him.

But Mack, who had managed him in the minors, knew how to use Waddell's eccentricities to get him to pitch. Promising him fishing trips and other indulgences, Mack coaxed four 20-win seasons out of the lefthander. Twice with the A's, Waddell had ERAs under 2.00 and six seasons in a row he led the A.L. in strikeouts. He finished his career with a 191-145 record and the sixth-best ERA in history, 2.16.

By 1908, however, even Mack couldn't control Waddell. After three seasons of decline, he was out of the major leagues for good at the age of 34.

This postcard from Panama is circa 1905.

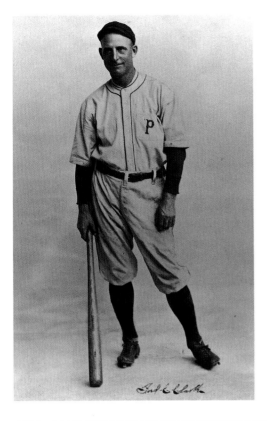

Fred Clarke (top left) was the Pittsburgh Pirates manager from 1900 to 1915 and was an outstanding outfielder for both Louisville and Pittsburgh from 1894 to 1915. He averaged more than 90 runs scored a season from 1900 to '05. He ended his 21-year career with 1,626 runs scored, 1,015 RBI, and a .325 batting average. Clarke was elected to the Hall of Fame in 1945. Wild Bill Donovan (top right) led the National League in wins with 25 in 1901 for Brooklyn; he later became an important cog in the Detroit Tiger machine from 1907 to '09. His best year was in 1907, when he went 25-4 for a league-leading .862 winning percentage. He ended his career in 1918 with 186 wins, 139 losses, and a 2.69 ERA. The entire 1903 American League (bottom) is pictured with Ban Johnson in the center. Before the '03 season, the National League reconciled for peace mainly because Johnson had built such a strong league. The A.L. was able to keep all of the players that it had signed on player raids from the N.L., and the A.L. was conceded a franchise in New York (which became the Yankees). The only compromise that Johnson had to make was to agree not to put a franchise in Pittsburgh. This peace again made the reserve clause sacrosanct.

THE 1900s

burgh finished 27½ games ahead of Brooklyn and once again suffered no personnel losses to the American League.

The Pirates had the National League batting champ, Ginger Beaumont at .357, and the home run leader, Tommy Leach with six. In his last season of utility duty, Honus Wagner led the National League in RBI (91), stolen bases (42), slugging average (.467), doubles (33), and runs scored (105). Jack Chesbro at 28-6 (2.17 ERA) led a Pirate staff that had two other 20-game winners: Phillippe at 20-9 (2.05 ERA) and lefty Jesse Tannehill at 20-6 (1.95 ERA). As a team, Wagner's juggernaut led the National League in runs, fewest runs allowed, doubles, triples, home runs, batting, slugging, stolen bases, pitchers' strikeouts, fewest walks allowed, and shutouts.

Jack Chesbro in 1904 won the most games (41) in a single season since the pitching distance was lengthened to 60 feet, six inches.

1903

In 1903, a strong Boston club that many observers felt had been the best club in 1902 finally lived up to expectations and won the American League flag with a record of 91-47. They finished a comfortable 14½ games ahead of Connie Mack's Athletics. Cy Young turned in his usual excellent performance, going 28-9 with a league-leading 34 complete games and a 2.08 ERA. An important addition was Long Tom Hughes, formerly of Baltimore, who was 20-7 with a 2.57 ERA. Big Bill Dineen had one of his best years, with a 21-13 record and a 2.26 ERA. As a team, Boston led the A.L. in ERA at 2.57 and shutouts with 20. Boston hitters recorded league-highs in runs (708), triples (113), homers (48), batting (.272), and slugging (.392). Buck Freeman hit 13 home runs and had 104 RBI, both tops in the league, and outfielder and fan favorite Patsy Dougherty hit .331 and scored a league-leading 108 runs.

Philadelphia added rookie Chief Bender to its already excellent pitching staff, but their offensive production fell off by 178 runs as the Athletics slipped to fourth in batting and third in slugging. Cleveland moved up to third place, ½ game behind Philadelphia, with Lajoie winning the batting title at .355 and first baseman "Piano Legs" Hickman hitting .330 with 97 RBI. In his second year, Addie Joss went 18-13 with a 2.15 ERA, fifth in the league, and "Crossfire" Earl Moore had his finest season, going 19-9 and winning the ERA title at 1.77.

Pittsburgh made it three straight in the National League in 1903, coasting to a 91-49 record, 6½ games ahead of the revitalized New York Giants, now under the control and tutelage of John McGraw for an entire season. Pittsburgh replaced Chesbro and Tannehill with Sam Leever, who went 25-7 with a league-leading 2.06 ERA. Leever and Deacon Phillippe combined for 11 shutouts. As usual, the Pirates offense was the most powerful in the league. Wagner hit .355 and slugged .518, and Fred Clarke hit .351 and slugged .532; they finished one-two in both categories. Ginger Beaumont hit .341 with a league-leading 137 runs scored, and the Pirates led the

JOE McGINNITY

"Iron Man" Joe McGinnity was a throwback to the 1880s in more ways than one; he carried pitching work loads that were unheard-of in his time (1899 to 1908), and he threw underhand.

In his ten-year major league career, McGinnity went 247-149 and consistently led all pitchers in the durability statistics. From 1900 through 1907, he led the league in games pitched seven times; he led in innings pitched five times in his career. Though he lacked Christy Mathewson's stuff, the combination of Matty's power-pitching and McGinnity's quality innings gave the Giants a two-man staff that equaled most teams' whole rotations. In 1904, the two gave New York its first pennant, pitching a combined 99 games, 775⅔ innings, and going 68-20 between them.

McGinnity holds a major league record for having pitched five complete-game double-headers in his career. In the 1903 pennant race, the Giants' pitching was a little short, and Iron Joe pitched and won three double-headers within a month.

Later a coach with the Brooklyn Dodgers, McGinnity gave a clue to the reason for his own success as he unsuccessfully tried to tell young Brooklyn pitchers of the late 1920s that the secret to getting out big-swinging home run hitters was "slow stuff."

When McGinnity quit coaching, he returned to the mound in his mid-50s and won 12 games and the championship for Dubuque of the minor Mississippi Valley League.

The 1903 Pittsburgh Pirates (top) won the N.L. pennant by 6½ games and were favored in the first modern World Series. Pittsburgh scored 793 runs and slugged .393, but Deacon Phillippe was their only top-line pitcher ready in the Series, and the Bucs lost to the Boston Pilgrims 5-3. In the first five seasons in the American League, Nap Lajoie (bottom middle) had a .372 batting average. The American League Two-Step (bottom left) was dedicated to the 1905 pennant winners, the Philadelphia Athletics. The Chicago Cubs won the world championship in 1907 and got their own march (bottom right).

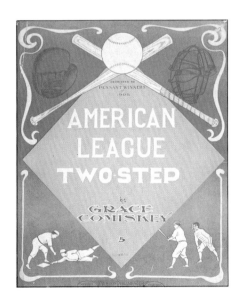

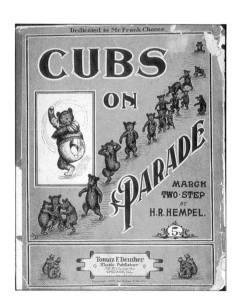

THE 1900s

National League in runs, triples, homers, and slugging.

Peace between the two major leagues in 1903 set the stage for the first 20th century World Series, although the 1903 Series, like the 1880s versions, was by informal arrangement between the two pennant winners. It was not until 1905 that postseason play came under the authority of the National Commission. In August of 1903, with both pennant races virtually over, Pittsburgh owner Barney Dreyfuss issued a public challenge for a best five of nine series to Boston Pilgrims' owner Henry Killilea, who accepted.

The 1903 Series had the inherent drama of a new league's battle to gain recognition as the equal of the National League, much like the great Chicago-St. Louis Series of the mid-1880s. But it also turned out to be the most dramatic Series of the decade on the field. When Boston came back to win 5-3, the baseball world knew that the American League was here to stay.

1904

The 1904 American League race was an exciting two-team battle that featured natural geographical rivals Boston and New York. Defending champion Boston fended off the Highlanders right up to the second to last day of the season, when Boston swept a doubleheader to go up by one half of a game, with two left to play in New York. The pennant was decided in the ninth inning of the first game, when Jack Chesbro — the A.L.'s leading winner that season with 41 wins, 12 losses, and a 1.82 ERA — threw a wild pitch that gave Boston the go-ahead run. Boston's Big Bill Dineen (23-14 with a 2.20 ERA on the year) took the mound in the bottom of the ninth. Dineen walked leadoff pinch-hitter Deacon

McGuire on four pitches. Finally, with two men on base and two out, outfielder Patsy Dougherty came to the plate. Dougherty had contributed 80 runs scored to New York in 1904, largely in the second half of the season. Throughout the 20th century, Boston fans have had the experience of watching former Red Sox stars leading other A.L. teams (more often than not the Yankees) to the pennant, but on this occasion Dougherty swung and missed at a 2-2 curve, and Boston narrowly won its second pennant in a row.

In the National League, John McGraw won the 1904 pennant easily, winning a then-record 106 games against 47 losses and finishing 13 games in front of Chicago. Even though New York once again got great pitching from McGinnity, Mathewson, and Dummy Taylor, on offense McGraw seemed to have been doing it with mirrors. No New York regular hit .300; the regular catcher, Jack Warner, hit .199. But a closer look at the Giants shows that McGraw was getting the most out of a well-matched group of fairly one-dimensional players. First baseman Dan McGann hit six home runs, third in the league. Shortstop Bill Dahlen was second in stolen bases with 47 and first in RBI with 80. Sam Mertes was second in doubles with 28, and George Browne led the league in runs scored with 99. There were not many big names in this lineup, but along with late-season addition Mike Donlin, it added up to the National League's best offense; the Giants were first as a team in runs with 744, doubles with 202, homers with 31, batting at .262, slugging at .344, and stolen bases with 283.

Dummy Taylor won 24 games for the '04 Giants.

Roger Bresnahan (top left) was four years away from making his lasting contribution to baseball when this photo was taken in 1903; he invented the padded catcher's mask and shin guards. Bresnahan played every position before settling in as a catcher on manager John McGraw's great New York Giants teams from 1903 to '08. Bresnahan batted .350 in 1903 and was regarded as the finest catcher of the 1900s. He ended his career in 1915 as the fiery player/manager of the Chicago Cubs, and he was respected by his players, feared by his opponents, and frequently suspended and fined by the league for umpire abuse. Patsy Dougherty (top middle) led the A.L. in stolen bases with 47 for the 1908 Chicago White Sox. A tobacco tin from 1908 (top right) pictures Cy Young. Fans form an outfield "wall" (bottom) during this 1904 game between Pittsburgh and New York.

THE 1900s

The second-place Cubs managed by Frank Selee were in the process of building the dynasty of 1906 to '08 with Frank Chance, young Johnny Evers, third-year man Joe Tinker, outfielder Jimmy Slagle, and catcher Johnny Kling.

Once again, in the postseason of 1904, the old animosity between John McGraw and Ban Johnson created a crisis between the two leagues. McGraw, who had not responded to World Series overtures from either A.L. contender during the season, now spitefully refused to play a World Series in 1904, claiming that as the superior league, the National League had nothing to prove by defeating the Americans. This outraged baseball fans and worried the baseball establishment in general; the last thing they wanted was another outbreak of interleague suspicion and conflict. A joint A.L. and N.L. conference was called and by 1905, it produced permanent guidelines for a yearly World Series that essentially are still in effect today.

1905

Connie Mack's A's waged an exciting two-team battle with Chicago in 1905, narrowly beating them out in the end by 2 games. The two teams were neck and neck until September, when Philadelphia's ace Rube Waddell threw 44 consecutive shutout innings to settle the matter. Waddell was the league's winningest pitcher at 26-11 and led in ERA at 1.48. The rest of the staff included Eddie Plank, 25-12 and 2.26 ERA; Chief Bender, 16-10 and 2.83 ERA; and Andy Coakley, 20-7 and 1.84 ERA. As a team, the A's led the American League in shutouts with 20 and strikeouts with 895. Philadelphia hitters led the league with 623 runs, paced by Harry Davis' league-leading eight homers, 47 doubles, and 83 RBI. They needed every one of those runs as Chicago was right behind with 612 runs scored and won the team ERA title at 1.99. Now called the White Sox, Chicago had four solid starters in Frank Owen, 21-13 and 2.40 ERA; Nick Altrock, 22-12 and 1.88 ERA; Frank Smith, 19-13 and 2.13 ERA; and Doc White, 18-14 and 1.76 ERA. Sophomore spitballer Ed Walsh — who finished his career in 1917 with the lowest lifetime ERA in history (1.82) — rounded out the Chicago staff.

McGraw's Giants did it again in the N.L., running away with the pennant on the strength of a 105-48 record. The Giants were in first place from April 23 on and never looked back. Second-place Pitts-

Joe Tinker in a 1910 collar ad.

burgh was healthy in 1905, but their offense slipped to fourth in the N.L. with only Wagner — who hit .363 with 101 RBI and 57 stolen bases — performing up to his usual standard. Deacon Phillipe came back to go 22-13 with a 2.19 ERA, and Sam Leever finished 19-6 with a 2.70 ERA.

The Giants had the major leagues' top offense, scoring 778 runs and batting .273 as a team. Donlin hit .356 and slugged .495, both third in the league, and scored 124 runs, leading the league. Bill Dahlen was third in the league in homers with seven and Sam Mertes hit .279 with 108 RBI. The Giants pitching staff led the N.L. in strikeouts and fewest walks allowed, led by Christy Mathewson at 31-8 on a league-leading 1.27 ERA, McGinnity's 21-15 (2.87 ERA), and Red Ames' 22-8 (2.74 ERA).

In the 1905 World Series, both teams put on a pitching clinic. The

CHRISTY MATHEWSON

If leading the league in ERA is the best indication of pitching dominance, then no one has ever dominated a league as completely as Christy Mathewson did the National League in the first two decades of the 20th century.

Matty was the ERA leader five times and finished with a career ERA of 2.13, fifth best in history, over a 17-year career that ended in 1916. In a five-year stretch between 1907 and 1911, his ERA was below 2.00 every year, including 1.14 in 1909; only once in 15 full seasons did his seasonal ERA rise above 3.00.

Famous for his "fade-away," or screwball, Mathewson led the N.L. in shutouts four times, with a career total of 80 — third all-time. He led in wins four times, winning 20 games 13 times and 30 games four times.

Pitching for the Giants, Mathewson won 373 games and lost

188, for a .665 winning percentage. Unlike a lot of pitchers, Mathewson's career winning percentage wasn't boosted because he played on a great team. In 1905, for example, Mathewson almost single-handedly brought his team a world championship. Finishing 31-8, he led the National League in wins, ERA, strikeouts, and shutouts. If you subtract Mathewson's personal won-lost differential of 23 from the team's record, the Giants would have finished in fourth place. And in the 1905 series, the Giants defeated Philadelphia easily, four games to one — easily, that is, with Mathewson's three complete-game shutouts and 0.00 ERA.

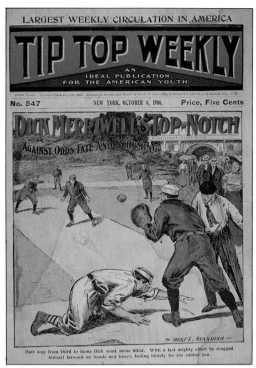

A 20-game winner in eight different seasons, Eddie Plank *(top left)* averaged 20 wins, 12 losses, and 26 complete games during his 14 seasons with the Philadelphia Athletics. His 69 shutouts rank fifth on the all-time list. This Tip Top Weekly *(top middle)* is from 1906. Shortstop Bobby Wallace *(top right)* played major league baseball for 25 years — 15 of those years with the St. Louis Browns. The 1905 world champion New York Giants *(bottom)* scored more than five runs a game, while their opponents were held to a little over three runs a game.

Champions of 1905 — McGraw's Giants. On the Club Roster Were Such Names as Bresnahan, Wiltse, "Dummy" Taylor, George Brown, Devlin, McCormick, McGinnity, McGann, Ames, Bowerman, Gilbert and Marshall

NEW YORK GIANTS
~ 1905 ~

THE 1900s

Giants hit .209 as a team and the Athletics hit .161; neither team hit a triple or a home run. It might actually have been even worse for the hitters if the A's had their ace, Rube Waddell, but Waddell hurt his shoulder after the season while horsing around on a train with Andy Coakley and was unavailable. The Giants nearly swept, winning 4-1, with three of their wins coming on Christy Mathewson shutouts. Matty won Game One 3-0, striking out six and walking none; Game Three 9-0, striking out eight and walking one; and Game Five 2-0, with four strikeouts and no walks. For the Series, Mathewson struck out 18, walked one, and allowed only 14 hits in 27 innings. McGinnity won Game Four 1-0 and Chief Bender recorded the only Philadelphia victory 3-0; every game of the 1905 Series was decided by a shutout.

1906

This was the year of the only all-Chicago World Series in history.

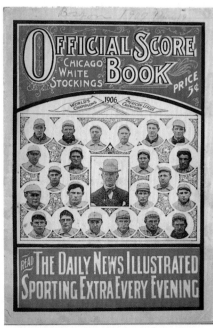

A 1906 program features the White Sox, who won the pennant despite being the only team in the A.L. with a slugging average under .300.

Fielder Jones' White Sox won in the A.L. with a team that has gone down in history as the "Hitless Wonders." It's true that the Sox depended heavily on their mighty pitching staff, which allowed a league-low 460 runs, compiled a team ERA of 2.13, and shut out the opposition in 32 games (or 34 percent of their victories). But the fact is, in the context of the dead-ball era, Chicago's offense was well above average. The White Sox had few hitters among the league leaders other than George Davis, who drove in 80 runs, and Frank Isbell, who stole 37 bases — but overall Chicago scored 570 runs, third-best in A.L. While they had mediocre power and batted only .230, the White Sox were strong in the two key elements of dead-ball offense: getting on base and running. The team had two of the top three batters in bases on balls, Fielder Jones with 83 and Ed Hahn with 72, and finished third in the A.L. in team stolen bases with 214. Chicago finished 93-58, only 3 games ahead of New York and 5 ahead of Cleveland.

In the National League, Frank Chance's Chicago Cubs started off what was to be one of baseball's great dynasties with a bang: leaving the Giants in their dust in June, the Cubs went on to win an all-time record 116 games and lost only 36, finishing 20 games ahead of second-place New York (who won 96 games) and 66½ games ahead of last-place Boston. The Cubs led the N.L. in almost everything — runs scored and fewest runs allowed (705 to 381), batting (.262), slugging (.339), fielding (.969), strikeouts (702), shutouts (31), and ERA (1.76). Chance, with 71 RBI and a league-leading 57 stolen bases, and third baseman Harry Steinfeldt, who hit .327 and drove in 83 runs, were the big guns. The Cubs' pitching was even better than the White Sox's; Three Finger Brown had a 26-6 record with a league-leading 1.04 ERA (the second-lowest seasonal ERA in history), Jack Pfiester went 20-8, and Ed Reulbach went 19-4. Five of the six Chicago pitchers finished the year with ERAs under 2.00.

The Windy City was in an uproar by October 9, when the two teams played the Series opener at the Cubs' home, West Side Park. Betting odds heavily favored the

Eddie Plank didn't consistently compile the fancy sub-2.00 ERAs that were so characteristic of the other top pitchers of the 1900s and 1910s, but he was consistently effective, going 327-193 lifetime with a career ERA of 2.34.

Pitching from 1901 to 1917, he only had two seasonal ERAs under 2.00, in 1909 (1.70) and 1917 (1.79), but Philadelphia manager Connie Mack could count on Plank for between 19 and 25 wins, 25 to 35 complete games, more than 250 innings, and an ERA in the low 2.00s.

Going to the majors directly from Gettysburg College, Plank never pitched a day in the minors. After a solid rookie season, 17-13 with a 3.31 ERA, he became the pitching mainstay of the great A's dynasty that won pennants in 1902, '05, '10, '11, '13, and '14. From 1902 to 1907, Plank won fewer than 20 games only once, winning 19 in 1906. In four World Series, he pitched seven games with a 1.32 ERA, tenth best in history, and six complete games, sixth best.

Ty Cobb picked Plank for his all-time pitching staff, not because the slight Plank had great pure stuff, but because of his consistently good control: Plank struck out 2,246 and walked only 1,072 in his career. The other secret to Plank's success was a tricky delivery. One observer described it as full of "fidgeting," with Plank pawing the mound and tugging at various parts of his uniform. Plank would delay until the batter was frustrated and then suddenly deliver the pitch.

In 1904, New York Highlanders pitcher Jack Chesbro (top left) produced one of the greatest seasons of any pitcher in the 20th century. "Happy Jack" went 41-12 with a 1.82 ERA over 454 ²/₃ innings; he completed 48 of his 51 starts. Ironically, Chesbro is remembered as much for his 12th loss that season as he is for his 41 victories. In the ninth inning of the season's final game, he fired a wild pitch that let the winning run score to give Boston the A.L. pennant. Honus Wagner (top right) hit at least .350 in seven different seasons, drove in at least 100 runs in nine different seasons, and scored at least 90 runs in 13 different seasons. Playing for both the Phillies and Cleveland, Elmer Flick (middle right) had a .319 batting average and scored 91 runs a season between 1898 and 1907. New York's Highlander Park (bottom left) in 1907. Christy Mathewson (bottom right) averaged 30 wins a season from 1903 to '08.

THE 1900s

National Leaguers, but in Game One the White Sox demonstrated the pitching form that had won 19 consecutive games in the pennant drive; they won 2-1 over Three Finger Brown behind the four-hit pitching of Nick Altrock. In Game Two, the Cubs hammered Doc White to win 7-1 behind Ed Reulbach's one-hitter, but in Game Three the surprising Sox came back to take the lead on Ed Walsh's two-hitter, 3-0. After the Cubs evened the Series the next day by winning 1-0, Brown over Altrock, it looked like a pitchers' duel to the death; in the first four games, runs had been scored in only nine of the 36 innings played.

But the White Sox had one more surprise in store. When the Cubs finally solved the Sox's pitching, scoring nine runs off Walsh and White in games Five and Six, the White Sox offense exploded. They scored eight runs on 12 hits and four Frank Isbell doubles to beat Reulbach in Game Five, and scored eight runs on 14 hits to defeat a tired Brown, who was knocked out of the second inning of the final game. In the end, the White Sox outhit the Cubs, .198 to .196 and outslugged them, .283 to .245. The real story of the Series, though, was pitching; the White Sox's 1.50 ERA against the Cubs' 3.40.

1907

The 1907 Detroit Tigers put some life into the dead-ball era. Managed by Ned Hanlon protégé Hughie Jennings, the Tigers ran, slugged, and scored like the old Orioles reincarnated. A mirror image of the 1906 pennant-winning White Sox, Detroit had only average pitching, led by Ed Killian at 25-13 (1.78 ERA) and Wild Bill Donovan at 25-4 (2.19 ERA); their next-winningest pitcher, 20-game winner George Mullin, also lost 20

and had a 2.59 ERA. But the Tiger offense was ferocious, led by Ty Cobb, who hit .350, slugged .473, drove in 116 runs, and stole 49 bases — all league highs. Sam Crawford was right behind with a .323 batting average, .460 slugging average, 34 doubles, and 17 triples. The Tigers scored 694 runs, best in the American League by a margin of 89 and 114 better than the 1906 Sox.

Jennings and his Tigers were hotly pursued all season by a resurgent Philadelphia team that included the league's two top home run hitters, Harry Davis and Socks Seybold; veteran Jimmy Collins in the infield; and a dependable pitching staff of Bender (16-8, 2.05 ERA), Eddie Plank (24-16, 2.20 ERA), and Rube Waddell (19-13, 2.15 ERA). Waddell led the majors in strikeouts with 232, averaging 7.33 per nine innings.

The Chicago Cubs had the National League race all to themselves in 1907, as they went 107-45 to finish 17 games ahead of Pittsburgh, although the Pirates had the N.L.'s best offense. Honus Wagner and Tommy Leach sparked the Pirates to 634 runs and the league's best batting (.254) and slugging (.324) averages. Wagner won yet another batting title at .350, led the league in slugging at .513, and stolen bases with 61. Leach hit .303 and scored 102 runs, second in the N.L. to New York's Spike Shannon.

The Cubs had a slightly off-year at the plate; no Cub hit .300 or drove in more than 70 runs, but the pitching staff was dominant. With their top five pitchers all

Sam Crawford, swinging in the 1907 World Series, led the A.L. in runs that year but managed only one in the Series.

ADDIE JOSS

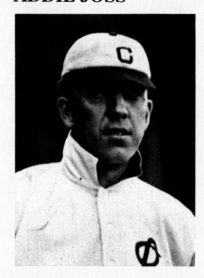

Nap Lajoie was one reason that Cleveland almost won the pennant several times between 1902 and 1910; Addie Joss was the other.

During Joss' nine-year career with Cleveland between 1902 and 1910, Joss and Lajoie were dragged down by the rest of the very thin Cleveland roster, but individually they were two of the game's brightest stars. Joss had a career record of 160-97, winning 20 games four times, with a high of 27 in 1907. He combined outstanding control (926 strikeouts to 370 walks lifetime) with a sharp curve and a hard fastball; twice Joss pitched no-hitters, one of them a perfect game at a key point in the 1908 pennant race. He led the A.L. in ERA twice, with a 1.59 mark in 1904 and 1.16 in 1908; in five of his eight full seasons, Joss had ERAs under 2.00. He finished with a career ERA of 1.88 (the second-lowest in baseball history), threw 46 shutouts, and completed 90 percent of his lifetime starts.

A converted infielder, Joss was considered the finest fielding pitcher of the 1900s and is the only pitcher in history to average three assists per game.

One of the only members of the Baseball Writers' Association to be voted into the Hall of Fame, Joss moonlighted during his career as sports editor of the Toledo *News-Bee*.

His death from meningitis in 1911 sparked an outpouring of grief and hero-worship reminiscent of the deaths of Ray Chapman, Roberto Clemente, and Thurman Munson.

With the bases loaded in the top of the sixth inning in Game Three in the 1906 World Series (top left), Cub Jack Pfiester pitches to White Sox Frank Isbell, who struck out. The next batter, George Rohe, tripled in three runs as the White Sox won the game 3-0. The White Sox beat the Cubs four games to two in the only all-Chicago Series. Sherry Magee (top right) led the N.L. in RBI in 1907, the first of four times he would top the league in RBI. He played outfield for the Philadelphia Phillies from 1904 to 1914 and ended his career in 1919. The Chicago White Sox pause at the Royal Gorge in Colorado (bottom left) while on tour in 1907. Fielder Jones (bottom right) played outfield for 15 years and managed the White Sox to a World Series in 1906.

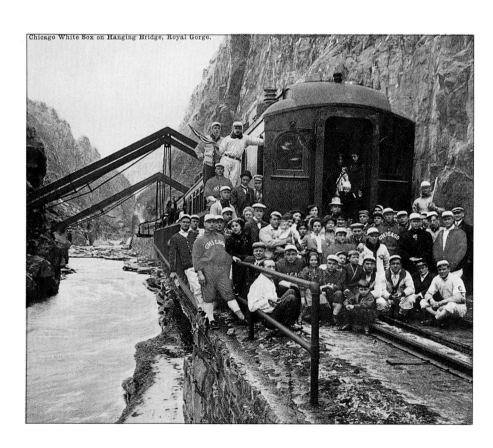

under 2.00 in ERA (led by Pfiester's league-leading 1.15), the Cubs had a team mark of 1.73 and 30 shutouts. Four of the top five pitchers in winning percentage and four of the top five in earned run average were Cubs.

In the 1907 World Series, the National League, which was still smarting from the upset defeats of 1903 and 1906, got revenge in full against Cobb and the Tigers. After an opening 3-3 tie, called on account of darkness after 12 innings, the Cubs demolished Detroit 3-1, 5-1, 6-1, and 2-0 to win the Series 4-0. The Chicago pitchers compiled an ERA of 0.75 and held the Tigers offense to a .209 batting average. Cobb and Crawford hit .200 and .238 with two extra-base hits between them. Tiger pitching held up its end, with Wild Bill Donovan leading all pitchers in the Series with 16 strikeouts while compiling a 1.71 ERA, and Mullin and Killian pitching effectively. But the Cubs hitters exploited Detroit's defensive weakness at catcher to outsteal the running Tigers 18 to seven. Chicago outfielder Jimmy Slagle led the Series with six steals; the great Cobb had none.

1908

There was a presidential election in 1908, but neither American League nor National League fans cared much. In both leagues, fans were treated to two of the greatest pennant races in history. In the A.L., Detroit's margin of victory over Cleveland in percentage points was .004, the smallest ever. The Chicago White Sox were 1½ games back and the St. Louis Browns were 6½ back. The Browns fell off the pace only in the final month. Hapless Cleveland led by 2½ games with less than two weeks to go, when the Tigers started a string of ten victories in a row to put them ½ game up. On the final day of the season, Detroit beat Chicago and Cleveland beat St. Louis to bring Cleveland's record to 90-64 and the Tigers to 90-63. Since Detroit had lost a game due to a rain-out (which under the rules of the time did not have to be made up), the Tigers won the pennant by a raindrop. As in 1907, the Tigers were primarily an offensive team, scoring a league-leading 647 runs and compiling the A.L.'s best team batting (.264) and slugging (.347) marks. Cobb and Crawford again finished one-two in batting and slugging; Cobb hit .324 and drove in 108 runs; Crawford led the league in homers with seven.

The National League race of 1908 was an equally tense, three-team affair that finished with Chicago 1 game ahead of the other two National League dynasties of the 1900s, New York and Pittsburgh, who tied for second. The three teams' ERAs were 2.14 for Chicago, 2.14 for New York, and 2.12 for Pittsburgh. Honus Wagner kept Pittsburgh in the race until the end with a near-triple crown season; he won the batting title at .354, the RBI title with 109, and finished second in home runs with ten. New York's hero was Christy Mathewson, who led the league in wins with 37, going 37-11 with a league-leading 1.43 ERA.

Late in the 1908 season, a critical game between Chicago and

THREE FINGER BROWN

Pitching for Chicago from 1904 to 1913, Mordecai Peter Centennial Brown won 239 and lost 129 games in his 14-year career, with a 2.06 lifetime ERA that is third best in history after Ed Walsh and Addie Joss. In his 13 full major league seasons, Brown's seasonal ERA was under 2.00 six times and under 3.00 six times; he led the National League in ERA with a microscopic 1.04 mark in 1906.

Brown's finest season came in 1909 when, after having led the Cubs to three consecutive pennants, he led the N.L. in games with 50, complete games with 32, and innings pitched with 342⅔. In spite of his league-leading 27 wins and nine games in relief, the Cubs finished second, 6½ behind Pittsburgh.

He is mostly remembered for his crippled right hand, the result of a boyhood accident with his father's haycutter, which gave his curveball a deceptive late movement. Ty Cobb called it "the most devastating pitch I ever faced."

Brown was also famed for his career-long rivalry with Christy Mathewson, the ace of the Cubs' nemesis, the Giants. In one game that changed the course of the 1908 pennant race, Brown came on in relief with no one out in the first inning and the Cubs down 2-0; he then beat Mathewson 4-2. Brown faced Mathewson in the final game of his career, losing 10-8 and making Brown 13-11 lifetime versus his old competitor.

The painting "Two Men Down" was done in 1908.

Ty Cobb of the Tigers steps to the plate in the 1907 World Series at Chicago's West Side Park (top left). Cub Ed Reulbach (top right) delivers a pitch during the '07 Series. A Gillette ad (left) features Bill Donovan, Frank Chance, Johnny Kling, Honus Wagner, and Hughie Jennings. Three Finger Brown (bottom left) tallied a shutout in each of the Cubs' World Series appearances from 1906 to '08. Cubs manager/first baseman Frank Chance (bottom middle) was called "The Peerless Leader." Orval Overall (bottom right) pitched only seven years but was one of baseball's most effective pitchers of the 1900s. Overall's career 2.24 ERA is eighth best in history. He was one of the stars of the incredible Cubs pitching staff — with Jack Pfiester, Ruelbach, and Brown — that led Chicago to an average of 106 wins a season between 1906 and 1910. Overall won 82 games and had three seasons with an ERA under 2.00 in helping the Cubs to four World Series. In 1907 and '08, Overall won three Series games and produced an ERA under 1.00 in 36 innings pitched.

THE 1900s

New York had ended inconclusively in a murky dispute over whether Giants first baseman Fred Merkle had legally reached second base as the winning run for New York crossed the plate in the bottom of the ninth. The matter landed in the reluctant hands of league President Harry Pulliam, who spent the rest of the 1908 season hoping that the game would have no bearing on the standings so that he could rule it a draw. However, the Giants and Cubs finished the season with identical 98-55 records, and Pulliam was forced to make a ruling; he decreed that the game should be replayed from the beginning, with the winner to take the pennant. In front of 35,000 people at the Polo Grounds on October 8, Chicago beat Mathewson behind the relief effort of Three Finger Brown to take the pennant.

The 1908 World Series was a rematch of the 1907 contest; again Chicago took on Detroit, and again the Cubs pitchers made it no contest. Detroit lost Game One in a heartbreaker when knuckleballer Ed Summers, the Tigers' ace during the regular season with 24-12 record and a 1.64 ERA, blew a 6-5 lead by giving up five runs in the ninth. For the rest of the way, except for Mullin's 8-3 win over Jack Pfeister in Game Three, the Series looked like the 1907 Series,

A fan pictures Larry Doyle.

Part II. Behind Orval Overall and Brown, the Cubs defeated Detroit 6-1 on a four-hitter, 3-0 on another four-hitter, and 2-0 on a three-hitter. Chicago pitchers held Detroit to a .203 batting average. Chicago hit .293, led by Frank Chance, who hit .421 and stole 5 bases, and Wildfire Schulte, who hit .389 and stole four bases. One difference between 1907 and 1908 was that Ty Cobb played well. The only Tiger to hit above .240, Cobb batted .368, stole two bases, and drove in four runs.

1909

Cobb started the 1909 season as though, after the disappointments of the past two World Series, he was determined to win a world championship all by himself. He wielded a hot bat all season long, finishing up with his best year in the major leagues to date. He led the American League in batting at .377 (31 points better than runner-up Nap Lajoie), slugging at .517, home runs with nine, total bases with 296, RBI with 107, stolen bases with 76, hits with 216, and runs scored with 116. Crawford hit .314 and drove in 97 runs. As in previous years, the Tigers' offense carried the team, scoring a total of 666 runs to lead the A.L., stealing a major league high 280 bases, and more than compensating for the team's no better than above-average pitching. Joining Mullin (29-8, 2.22 ERA), Summers (19-9, 2.24 ERA), and Killian (11-9, 1.71 ERA), was young Ed Willet, who won 21 and lost ten with a 2.34 ERA.

Detroit's only challenge came from a rebuilding Philadelphia team with three new names that would become very familiar to fans in the near future as three quarters of the "$100,000 infield": shortstop Jack Barry, third baseman Frank "Home Run" Baker, and second baseman Eddie Collins. With Collins hitting .346 and Baker .305, Mack's Athletics made a midsummer run at the Tigers' lead. The Tigers slumped in August, even slipping below Philadelphia into second place for a few weeks, but rallied to finish 98-54, 3½ games up. With the solid rotation of Eddie Plank, Chief Bender, Cy Morgan, and Harry Krause, all under 2.00 in ERA, the A's allowed the fewest runs as a team in the A.L. (408), and led in shutouts (27) and team ERA (1.92).

TINKER TO EVERS TO CHANCE

Joe Tinker, Johnny Evers, and Frank Chance got to the Hall of Fame the same way Abbott and Costello did — by being associated with a popular work of literature. In the case of Tinker, Evers, and Chance it was Franklin P. Adams' poem, which states in part:

"Making a Giant hit into a double,/Words that are weighty with nothing but trouble./Tinkers-to-Evers-to-Chance."

Right there in the capital "G" in "Giant" is an important clue about what this poem actually means. It is usually thought to be a tribute to a great double-play combination from the Chicago Cubs of the 1900s. And while the three did play together in the Cubs infield from 1903 to 1910, during which time Chicago won four National League pennants, they were not a particularly great double-play combination.

Adams published his poem in a New York newspaper in 1908. Chances are he was a Giants fan. And in 1908 the Giants and Cubs were locked in what many think was the greatest pennant race in history; the Giants finally lost the pennant in a one-game playoff. All this points to the conclusion that Adams' words refer to one or more *particular* double-plays that hurt the Giants.

Of the three, only Chance, who hit .300 five times in the 1900s and was the leader of one of the greatest teams in modern baseball history, would have stood much of a chance to reach Cooperstown without Adams.

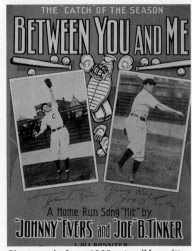

Sheet music from 1908 ostensibly written by Johnny Evers and Joe Tinker.

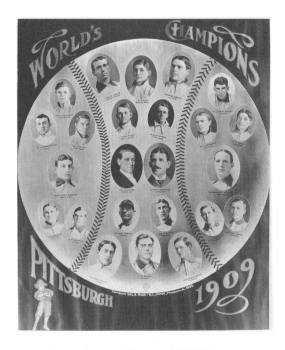

The 1909 world champion Pittsburgh Pirates (top left) led the league with 699 runs, a .260 batting average, a .353 slugging average, and a .964 fielding average. This photo of the Elysian Grove baseball team (top right) was taken sometime between 1903 and 1911. This action shot (bottom) is from Cleveland in 1908.

THE 1900s

In the National League, Chicago won 104 games, led the league in ERA (1.75) and shutouts (32), and finished second. With improved pitching and their explosive offense hitting on all cylinders, Honus Wagner and the Pittsburgh Pirates scored 699 runs, leading the N.L. in doubles, triples, batting, and slugging. Behind Howie Camnitz (25-6, 1.62 ERA) and Vic Willis (22-11, 2.24 ERA), the Pirates finished second in team ERA at 2.07. This mighty combination of offense and defense propelled the Pirates to 110 wins, 6½ games ahead of Chicago and 18½ games ahead of third-place New York.

The 1909 World Series was historic in that it matched two teams that had won three consecutive pennants in the decade, as well as the two greatest stars of the day, Honus Wagner and Ty Cobb. It was also the first time in modern World Series history that a Series went the full seven games. The surprise starter for Pittsburgh in Game One was Babe Adams, who had the team's best ERA on the season but had little major league experience and only 12 starts in 1909. Adams beat Detroit's George Mullin 4-1 on a six-hitter as Fred Clarke homered. In Game Two, Howie Camnitz was knocked out of the box in the third inning; Detroit won 7-2 on Wild Bill Donovan's five-hit pitching and Ty Cobb's electrifying third-inning steal of home. Game Three was the Honus Wagner show, as the Pirates shortstop went three for five with three RBI and three stolen bases. Nick Maddox allowed ten hits, but hung on to win 8-6. Detroit evened the Series the next day 5-0, behind Mullin's five-hit, ten-strikeout performance, but lost again in Game Five when Ed Summers fell apart in the eighth; Babe Adams won his second decision 8-4, as the Pirates ran wild on Detroit catchers Oscar Stanage and Boss Schmidt.

The Series returned to Detroit for Game Six, which Detroit won in a come-from-behind effort 5-4, thanks to a gritty nine-innings from George Mullin and four Detroit doubles off Willis and Camnitz.

Game Seven was strange in that the managers picked two starters who had a combined 20 wins during the regular season to pitch the most important game of the year. The surprise hero of the Series, Babe Adams, won the decisive seventh game, beating veteran Wild Bill Donovan 8-0 and allowing the Tigers only six hits.

Wagner thoroughly outplayed Cobb in the Series, hitting .333 with six RBI and six stolen bases to Cobb's .231, five RBI, and two stolen bases. Though the two played a combined 27 more major league seasons, neither would ever play in another World Series.

This fan (top) shows many top stars from the late 1900s. A game program (bottom) for the 1908-09 all-American baseball tour of the Orient.

THE MERKLE BLUNDER

Fred Merkle had a good 16-year big league career as a first baseman, hitting .273 lifetime and playing in five World Series. But on September 23, 1908, he was a 19-year-old rookie who was being given a rare start because of an injury to the regular first baseman, Fred Tenney. Three teams were fighting for the pennant that autumn; two of them were the New York Giants and their opponents that day, the Chicago Cubs.

In the bottom of the ninth inning the score was tied 1-1 with two out and two Giants on base — Moose McCormick on third and young Merkle on first. Suddenly, Al Bridwell singled to center field and McCormick crossed the plate; Merkle headed for the clubhouse and happy Giant fans swarmed the infield.

There was just one problem, though; Cubs manager Frank Chance, a man known to sleep with the baseball rule book, screamed for his players to retrieve the ball and tag second base. He then demanded that umpire Hank O'Day call Merkle forced-out at second for the third out of the inning, thereby nullifying McCormick's run. O'Day did so and, because the field could not be cleared, declared the game suspended and a tie. Ultimately the game was replayed after the season, the Giants lost, and Merkle's mistake cost his team the 1908 pennant.

This is the way it seems to have happened, although some say that Merkle did touch second and others claim that Chance tagged the base with a ball out of the ball-bag.

Ed Ruelbach (top left) led the N.L. in winning percentage each season from 1906 to '08. Fred Merkle (middle left) smacked at least 20 doubles in 11 consecutive seasons. The most durable pitcher in history, Cy Young (bottom left) threw 7,357 innings, 1,416 more than runner-up Pud Galvin. One of baseball history's worst teams, the 1908 St. Louis Cardinals (top right) finished last in the N.L. with a 49-105 record. In fact, the Cardinals were incredibly bad throughout the late 1900s. From 1906 to 1910, the Cards lost 90 or more games each year and never finished higher than seventh place. The '08 team scored about 300 fewer runs than league-leading New York, led the league in runs allowed, and made 348 errors during a season in which no other team made more than 300. Shortstop Patsy O'Rourke, third baseman Bobby Byrne, and catcher Bill Ludwig all batted under .200. When the Cards managed to win some games, it was thanks to pitcher "Bugs" Raymond (who led the team with 15 wins and a 2.03 ERA in '08) and outfielder Red Murray (who led the team with seven homers and 62 RBI in '08). Raymond won 18 games in 1909, and Murray led the league in homers that season; unfortunately for Cardinals fans, both players had already been traded to the New York Giants. This scene (bottom right) shows Forbes Field in Pittsburgh on July 5, 1909, during an Independence Day celebration doubleheader.

THE 1910s

Ty Cobb was one of the few hitters to succeed in the decade, as pitchers such as Walter Johnson and Grover Cleveland Alexander dominated. And baseball's growing gambling-related corruption culminated in the 1919 Black Sox scandal.

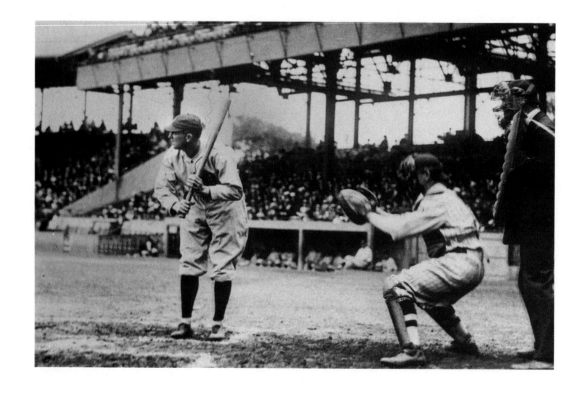

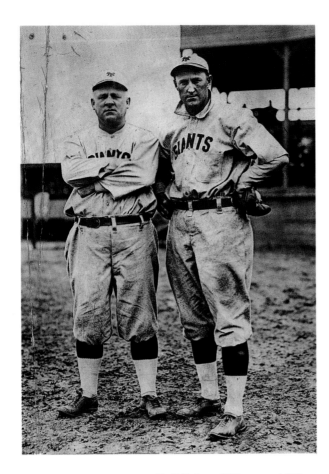

JOHNSON WASHINGTON

Ty Cobb (page 108) averaged 105 runs scored and 85 RBI a year during the 1910s. Manager John McGraw, left, and shortstop Art Fletcher (page 109, top left), shown in Jacksonville, FL, were mainstays of the New York Giants dynasty of the 1910s. The Giants won four pennants and had the highest winning percentage of the decade at .602. In the 1910s, Walter Johnson (page 109, top right) won 264 games and registered 2,219 strikeouts, leading the league in Ks nine out of the ten seasons. Brooklyn catcher Otto Miller (page 109, bottom) slides safely into third base during a 1914 game.

THE 1910s

The end of the dead-ball era coincides exactly with the end of the 1910s. After the 1919 season, baseball instituted rules changes whose impact diminished that of the foul-strike rule in the early 1900s, the lively ball experiment of 1911, or any other event in 20th-century baseball history. For the 1920 season, all pitchers (except for spitball pitchers who were "grandfathered" — allowed to use the pitch until they retired) were forbidden to throw the spitball, emery ball, shine ball, and other artificial breaking pitches or "trick" deliveries.

Before 1920, baseball on the field in the 1910s was virtually the same as in the pitching-dominated 1900s. Gavvy Cravath hit 24 home runs in 1915 and Wildfire Schulte hit 21 in 1911, the offensive peak year of the era, but for the most part, players in the 1910s led the league in home runs with totals around ten.

The greatest individual hitters of the 1910s are found not in the

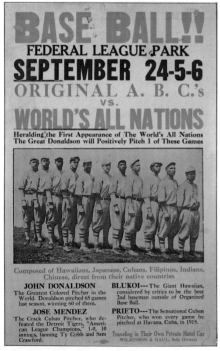

A 1914 broadside for a world team.

columns of home run leaders but among the leaders in batting averages, slugging averages, and triples. Ty Cobb hit .387 for the decade, with nine batting titles and eight slugging averages above .500, and he hit 160 triples. Cobb had only 48 home runs and never led the league. Joe Jackson hit .354 for the 1910s, slugged over .500 for the decade, and led the league in triples twice, with 26 in 1912 and 21 in 1916. He averaged slightly over four home runs per year and never led the league.

In spite of outstanding individual performances by such hitters, the 1910s (like the previous decade) were dominated by pitchers. National League ERAs were under 3.00 six times between 1910 and 1919; American League ERAs were comparable, rising above 3.00 only in 1911, 1912, and 1919. The 1910s brought a new generation of great individual pitchers as well. Replacing Christy Mathewson, Cy Young, and Three Finger Brown were Walter Johnson, who averaged a 29-15 record with a 1.59 ERA for the decade; Grover Cleveland Alexander, who averaged a 28-13 record with a 2.07 ERA; and a young lefthander named Babe Ruth, who had a 89-46 record from 1914 to 1919 and went 3-0 for Boston in two World Series, compiling the third-best World Series ERA in history.

As in the 1900s, the stolen base was considered one of the premier offensive weapons. Yearly league totals ranged from 1,000 to 2,000, as they do today. Like today, players generally led the league in stolen bases with totals ranging from 50 to 90. A look at the list of the all-time greatest individual basestealing seasons shows a strange mixture of players from before 1920 and after 1960. There is not one player from the intervening four decades in the top 50. Below the Ricky Hendersons, Vince Colemans, and Maury Willses appear Ty Cobb's 96 stolen bases in 1915, Clyde Milan's 88 in 1912, Eddie Collins' 81 in 1910, and Fritz Maisel's 74 in 1914.

So that was baseball in the 1910s: lots of singles, few home runs, and fearsome pitching. There was little the offense could do to create excitement beyond stealing bases. For the most part, the stolen base has little effect on run produc-

TY COBB

Ty Cobb was so competitive on the baseball field that it is often speculated that he was psychotic.

He was famous for sharpening his spikes (a charge he denied) and for using brute physical intimidation on the base paths. Cobb would take extra bases recklessly, even when the ball was on its way to the next base well ahead of him, with the intention of kicking the ball out of the fielder's glove or simply running him over. Senators third baseman Ossie Bluege remembered once waiting with the ball in plenty of time to tag out Cobb: "He didn't slide. He just took off and came at me in midair, spikes-first, about four or five feet off the ground." Bluege made the play but suffered a spike wound on one arm; Cobb was ejected from the game.

Cobb played 24 years, nearly all of them with Detroit. His record as a hitter is matched only by the greatest modern sluggers; in his time he had no equal. He batted .367 lifetime, the best mark in history. He is third all-time in stolen bases with 892, first in runs with 2,245, fourth in RBI with 1,961, and second in hits with 4,191. He won 12 batting titles, including nine in a row from 1907 to 1915. Though he never tried for home runs, he led the A.L. in slugging eight times; he scored or drove in 100 or more runs 18 times. In 24 years, Cobb batted under .320 only once. He hit .400 three times.

SHERWOOD N. MAGEE
Philadelphia National League

Sherry Magee (top left) led the National League in runs scored (110), RBI (123), batting average (.331), and slugging average (.507) in 1910 for Philadelphia. Magee was a hard-hitting outfielder who led the N.L. in RBI four times and slugging twice. He ended his 16-year career with a .291 batting average, a .427 slugging average, 425 doubles, 441 stolen bases, and 1,182 runs batted in. The personification of perseverance, Gavvy Cravath (top right) didn't arrive on the big league scene until 1912, at the age of 31. When he did appear, though, he made a splash. Playing for Philadelphia, he led the National League in home runs six out of seven seasons, starting in 1913. He also led the league in RBI twice and in slugging average twice. Clyde Milan (bottom left) was a good-hitting, basestealing center fielder for the Washington Senators from 1907 to 1922. He led the A.L. in stolen bases in 1912 with 88 and in 1913 with 75. He ended his career with a .285 batting average and 1,004 runs scored. John McGraw's baseball instructional (bottom right) shows Roger Bresnahan on the cover.

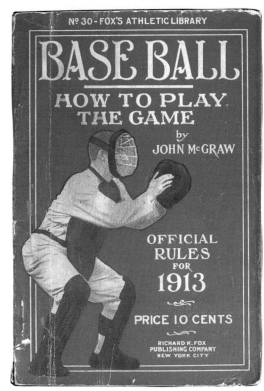

Nº 30 - FOX'S ATHLETIC LIBRARY

BASE BALL
HOW TO PLAY THE GAME
by
JOHN McGRAW

OFFICIAL RULES FOR 1913

PRICE 10 CENTS

RICHARD K. FOX
PUBLISHING COMPANY
NEW YORK CITY

tion — and whatever they may have said later when as old men they shook their heads in disapproval at the home run-happy 1920s and 1930s — the fans were bored. Total major league attendance in the 1910s never reached the 1900s record of over 7 million, which was set in 1909. For the entire decade, attendance was a little over 50 million, or just about what it had been in the previous decade, but it showed a disturbing downward trend in the late 1910s, even dropping below 5 million in some years.

Nevertheless, in some trends of the 1910s there were subtle signs that things were beginning to change. One of these was the adoption of the lively, cork-center baseball in 1911. After they experimented with it in the 1910 World Series, both leagues made the new ball official beginning with the 1911 regular season. The result was a mini-explosion of offense; ERA rose from 3.02 in 1910 to 3.39 in the N.L. and from 2.53 to 3.34 in the A.L. Then, even though the lively ball was kept in use, pitchers gradually regained their control of the game. The National League ERA declined to 3.20 in 1913 and in following years to 2.78, 2.75, and 2.61; A.L. ERAs went from 2.93 in 1913 to 2.73, 2.94, 2.81, and finally 2.66 in 1917. In 1913 there were no National League pitchers under 2.00 ERA for the season, but in 1914 there were three.

Another development that later contributed to the birth of the home run offense was the building of enclosed urban concrete-and-steel ballparks, a process that began in 1909 with the construction of Philadelphia's Shibe Park. Between Shibe and Yankee Stadium in 1923, 14 teams built concrete-and-steel parks. The new parks were intended to be perma-

nent and some even monumental. They were situated as close to the center of the city as possible. As a result, not only were all the new parks enclosed, but they were limited in size by city lots and streets. Gradually, baseball found itself with more and more parks that had home run fences that could be consistently reached by batted balls.

Another phenomenon of the 1910s that played an indirect part in the home run era was growing gambling-related corruption. This culminated in the Black Sox scandal of 1919 to 1920. In the minds of fans, baseball corruption became linked with the entire dead-ball style of play; owners promoted Babe Ruth and home run hitting as a way to sweep away the past and recapture the imagination of the public.

Baseball in the 1910s was still the nation's only major sport and (aside from horse racing) the primary object of betting interest, as it had been since the mid-19th century. Even though the major leagues had periodically cracked down on game-fixing and other abuses since the 1880s, they had never entirely disappeared. The game-throwing escapades of Hal Chase and his fellow Giant Heinie Zimmerman were far from isolated events; throughout the 1900s and 1910s there had been countless accusations and rumors of corruption.

The Black Sox scandal didn't break until the fall of 1920, but expert observers of the 1919 World Series, in which a relatively weak Cincinnati team defeated the powerful White Sox of Joe Jackson and Eddie Collins, smelled a rat. Led by Hugh Fullerton, journalists cited the poor performances of Lefty Williams, who went 0-3 with a 6.61 ERA after having a 23-11 record

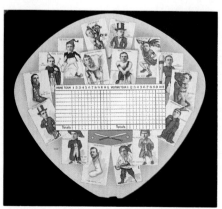

A 1913 fan with the major league managers.

EDDIE COLLINS

Lefthanded hitting Eddie Collins was the heart and soul of the Philadelphia Athletics offense during their glory years, from 1906 to 1914. When the A's decided to commit organizational suicide after the 1914 World Series loss, Connie Mack sold Collins for $50,000 in cash to Charles Comiskey's Chicago White Sox. Collins didn't get a raise of even one of the zeroes.

Batting second in the order for most of his career, Collins compiled a lifetime .333 average over 25 big league seasons; he is eighth all-time in base hits with 3,311. Collins used a big-barreled, slap-hitter's bat and tended to take pitches the other way. He didn't generate much power, but he did reach double figures in triples 12 times and managed to drive in as many as 86 runs in a season.

Collins' main specialty was getting on base and scoring runs. He had a terrific batting eye — 286 strikeouts and 1,503 walks in his career. He stole 743 bases in his career, leading the American League with 81 in 1910, 33 in 1919, 47 in 1923, and 42 in 1924. He scored 100 runs or more seven times, leading the league three times.

Consistent and durable, Collins hit .340 for a season in three different decades and played more games at second base than anyone else in history, 2,650. He has the records for career assists and total chances at his position.

One of Collins' last contributions to baseball was to sign Ted Williams, whom he saw by chance taking batting practice, and immediately optioned for the Red Sox.

House of David Baseball Team

The New York Giants purchased Rube Marquard (top left) for $11,000 in 1908, and when he struggled for the next three years, he was nicknamed the "$11,000 Lemon." In 1911, however, he was 24-7, and in 1912, he set a record by winning his first 19 starts. One of the many barnstorming teams during the era, the House of David team (top right) posed for this photo in 1912. Christy Mathewson (middle right) was nicknamed "Big Six" after a notable New York fire truck. Although he was at the end of his career, Matty averaged 25 wins a season from 1910 to 1914. Griffith Stadium (bottom), which opened in 1911, is shown during Game Six of the 1924 World Series.

THE 1910s

with a 2.64 ERA during the regular season; Swede Risberg, who hit .080 and committed four errors at short; and a number of very suspiciously timed misplays by pitcher Eddie Cicotte and others. In hindsight, a few other clues to the fix are apparent, including a last-minute shift in the World Series odds from 3-1 Sox to 8-5 Reds and a fascinating team photograph taken just before the series that shows manager Kid Gleason stationed off to one side of the team and as far away as he could get from the eight conspirators, who are grouped in a circle around the ringleader, first baseman Chick Gandil.

When the truth came out in the form of confessions by Cicotte and third baseman Buck Weaver, the baseball world was shocked to learn that eight White Sox had agreed to throw the series for promised bribes ranging as high as $20,000 for Jackson and $35,000 for Gandil. The scheme was bankrolled by New York City reputed underworld figure Arnold Rothstein through a complicated set of arrangements involving other gamblers and intermediaries such as Hal Chase. With a little help from the crooked Chicago criminal jus-

Buck Weaver hit .297 and had 75 RBI in 1919.

tice system, and possibly Charles Comiskey, the eight players (like the gamblers) avoided any legal punishment for their crimes. But the players could not escape new Commissioner Kenesaw Mountain Landis, who banned them from baseball for life.

The Black Sox case is a perfect illustration of a pattern that nearly all game-fixing scandals in the history of professional team sports have followed. Typically, there are three preconditions necessary before athletes are willing to throw a game (or manipulate a point spread) for money. First, there must be large amounts of money bet on a small number of games (as in the World Series or other championship game or games) so that the return for the gamblers justifies a large bribe; second, the players must be underpaid by their team — otherwise, the risk of losing a career's worth of income by being caught is too great; and third, there must be an atmosphere of exploitation and corruption surrounding the players. All of these conditions existed for the 1919 White Sox. They were resented and notoriously badly paid by Comiskey, who ran one of the most profitable franchises in baseball. The baseball establishment before Landis had demonstrated a great reluctance to investigate corruption. It whitewashed scandals whenever it could, as in fact Comiskey tried to do with the Black Sox scandal. Accordingly, it never occurred that the players knew of or suspected the scandal beforehand to report it. As Buck Weaver asked — after being lumped with the rest by Landis for "guilty knowledge" — who was he supposed to tell?

The dead-ball period in general was characterized by exploitation of the players and by low salaries. As time went on, baseball's labor relations grew worse, leading to two minor strikes (the first in baseball history) in 1912 and 1918. In the fall of 1912, the players made their first attempt since the brotherhood of the 1890s to form a union, the Fraternity of Professional Baseball Players of America, which concentrated on side issues like conditions for minor leaguers and small increases in salary for the lower-paid players. In 1914 the Fraternity had some

WALTER JOHNSON

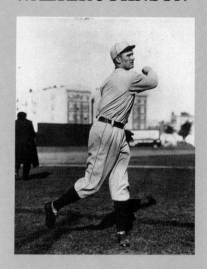

Walter Johnson pitched for 21 years with the Senators, a team that finished consistently at the bottom of the A.L. Nevertheless, Johnson won 416 games, second best in history, and lost only 279. His lifetime ERA of 2.17 is seventh-best all-time.

Johnson had the reputation of being the fastest pitcher ever. The scout who first noticed the big righthander in semipro ball in Idaho wired the Senators: "He knows where his pitches are going; otherwise, there would be dead bodies scattered all over Idaho."

Johnson — who didn't smoke, drink, or say much — never exploited the fear value of his awesome fastball. He was so reluctant to brush hitters back for fear of hurting them that Ty Cobb used to crowd the plate to throw him off. And it worked — Cobb batted .335 lifetime versus Johnson.

"The Big Train" compiled 11 ERAs under 2.00 and led the A.L. in ERA five times. He led the league in strikeouts 12 times and shutouts seven times. He led the league in wins six times, but on another team he would have won far more games; in his career he lost 27 games 1-0, and the Senators were shut out in 65 of his losses.

He had a lifetime winning percentage of .599 on teams that played .460 ball without him. This differential of .139 points is one of the greatest of any top pitcher in history. By comparison, Christy Mathewson was .106 better than his teams, Cy Young was .125 better, and Lefty Grove was .119 better.

White Sox pitchers (top, from left) Jim Scott, Ed Walsh, and Ed Cicotte in 1914. By the end of the decade, Charles Comiskey had built a championship-caliber team that had won a World Series, two pennants, and had a second-place finish in four years. Comiskey (bottom left) continued to underpay his players after the Black Sox affair; the book Total Baseball gives an example of Comiskey's cheapness: "Pitcher Dickie Kerr, one of the honest Sox in the 1919 World Series, won twice against the Reds and half his own team, then won 21 in 1920 and 19 in 1921. Comiskey paid him $4,500 and refused to give him a raise. Kerr quit. He could make $5,000 playing semipro!" Hal Chase (bottom middle), also banned from baseball in 1919 for throwing games, was the go-between for the Black Sox and the gamblers.

THE 1910s

successes, such as convincing teams to pay for players' uniforms and to provide written reasons for player suspensions, but these concessions were made with the threat of another "Monopoly War" hanging over the owners.

Though the Federal League arose out of the same causes that precipitated the Monopoly Wars of 1882 to 1903 and was backed by an impressive group of millionaires — including Robert Ward of the Ward Baking empire and oil baron Albert Sinclair — the Feds never posed the same threat to the baseball monopoly as past would-be major leagues. Since there were already two established major leagues with 16 teams in 1914, the Federal League attempted to carve out an entirely new market for major league baseball in such non-major league cities as Indianapolis, Baltimore, Buffalo, and Kansas City, as well as in big league towns like Chicago, Brooklyn, Pittsburgh, and St. Louis. But like the Union Association in 1884, the Feds discovered that the country would not support three major leagues; Federal League attendance lagged behind the break-even point for most of its franchises. In Baltimore, the Feds were even outdrawn by the minor league Orioles.

After a dry run as a minor league in 1913, the Federal League declared major league status and quickly took advantage of the low major league salary structure by luring away almost 50 National League and American League players. But by the end of the 1915 season, the most important Federal League backer, Robert Ward, was dead, and the others were ready to give up after suffering tremendous losses. In a surprisingly generous settlement, the N.L. and A.L. allowed Sinclair and Chicago Whales owner Charles Weeghman to buy the Chicago Cubs and St.

Louis owner Phil Ball to buy the Browns; two other Federal League owners were paid amounts in the hundreds of thousands of dollars for their interests, and the smaller Federal owners were paid for their players' contracts. The total cost to the two major leagues for the Federal League was about $5 million.

On the field, the 1910s were dominated by two teams, which in turn were dominated by two great personalities. One was John McGraw, who created his second New York Giants dynasty from 1911 to 1913, when the Giants won three N.L. pennants in a row. McGraw had a solid infield with second baseman Larry Doyle, who hit .310, .330, and .280 with 77, 90, and 73 RBI between 1911 and 1913; shortstop Art Fletcher, who hit .282 in 1912 and .297 in 1913; and third baseman Buck Herzog, who stole 108 bases over the three pennant winning years. Catching was Chief Meyers, who hit .332, .358, and .312. But the true strength of the Giants was the pitching of veteran Christy Mathewson — who won 74 games and lost 36 from 1911 to '13 and twice led the league in ERA: 1.99 in 1911 and 2.06 in 1913 — and young Rube Marquard, who went 73-28.

McGraw's American League counterpart, and in many ways his opposite, was Connie Mack, a dignified ex-catcher who managed the Philadelphia Athletics for the astoundingly long span of 53 years.

Mack, nicknamed "The Tall Tactician," was a sharp baseball mind, who kept the first charts on pitchers and batters and who had a great eye for talent. Between 1910 and '14, the A's won four A.L. pennants and three World Series, two of them from the New York Giants. They were built on the greatest infield in baseball: Stuffy McInnis at first, a .308 lifetime hitter who hit

A 1913 stock certificate for the Chicago Feds.

CHIEF BENDER

A big righthander, Chief Bender went 210-127 in a 16-year career, mostly with the Philadelphia Athletics' dynasty of the 1900s and 1910s. He pitched in five World Series, compiling a 6-4 record with a 2.44 ERA in ten games.

Bender's clutch pitching was one of the main reasons that Connie Mack's Athletics were able to consistently frustrate New York Giants manager John McGraw's hopes for a world championship — the A's beat the Giants twice, in 1911 and 1913. In 1911, Bender went 2-1 with a 1.04 ERA against the Giants in the Series, beating Christy Mathewson 4-2 in Game Four and Red Ames 13-2 on a four-hitter in Game Six. Bender's record for the '11 Series is 26 innings, 16 hits, eight walks, and 20 strikeouts.

In 1913, Bender went 2-0, with nine strikeouts and one walk in 18 innings; he defeated Rube Marquard 6-4 in the Series opener and won Game Four against Al Demaree 6-5.

As one third of the greatest pitching staff of three — Bender, Eddie Plank, and Rube Waddell are the only three Hall of Famers in history to pitch in the same rotation — Bender was never called upon to carry a huge workload and never led the league in games, innings, or wins. But he was the man Mack would count on to win that one important game. Bender had a lifetime ERA of 2.46 and was under 2.00 for a season four times. In his prime, 1909 to 1911, he was practically unbeatable, going 58-18 for a .763 winning percentage.

Exposition Park in Pittsburgh (middle) houses a 1914 Federal League game. The Federal League name was used for a brand of bourbon (top left). The 1915 Brooklyn Tip Tops scorecard (top right) included star outfielder Benny Kauff. Kauff led the F.L. both seasons in batting (.370 in 1914 and .342 in 1915) and stolen bases (75 in 1914 and 55 in '15). The Chicago Federal League entry (bottom left) was the most successful F.L. team, finishing in second place in 1914 and in first in 1915. The Whales were managed by former Cub Joe Tinker and starred outfielder Dutch Zwilling. As part of the settlement that led to the demise of the F.L., Whales owner Charles Weeghman was allowed to buy the Chicago Cubs in 1916. A 1914 cartoon (bottom right) celebrates the opening of the Federal League season.

.327 in 1912 and .326 in 1913; second baseman Eddie Collins, one of the first Hall of Famers, who hit .333 in 25 major league seasons and stole 743 bases; third baseman Home Run Baker, who hit .307 lifetime and led the A.L. in home runs from 1911 to 1914 and drove in 259 runs in 1912 and 1913 combined; and shortstop Jack Barry. The Mackmen were deep in starting pitching, with Jack Coombs (31-9, 1.30 ERA in 1910); Eddie Plank, who won 97 games and lost 41 between 1910 and 1914; and Chief Bender, who led the A.L. in winning percentage in 1910, 1911, and 1914.

Altogether, John McGraw and Connie Mack won eight of the 20 pennants in the 1910s.

1910

This was the last pennant-winning season for the Chicago Cubs of Frank Chance, Wildfire Schulte, and Three Finger Brown — who had won 116, 107, 99, and 104 games and three pennants over the previous four seasons. The Cubs would go on to finish second in 1911 and third in 1912 and 1913, and they didn't win another pennant until 1918, with an entirely rebuilt roster. The 1910 Cubs were the league's second-best offense, scoring three runs fewer than McGraw's Giants, who finished second, 13 games off the pace. The Cubs led the N.L. in triples with 84 and home runs with 34. They batted .268 as a team. Outfielders Schulte, who hit .301 and led the league in home runs with ten, and Solly Hoffman, who hit .325, drove in 86 runs, and had the league's second best slugging average at .461, were Chicago's big guns. Cubs pitching was at its best since 1907; the staff of Brown, Ed Reulbach, Orval Overall, and rookie King Cole — who went 20-4 with a 1.80 ERA to record a career year —

combined for a league-leading 2.51 ERA and 27 shutouts (or 24 percent of the league's 111 shutouts).

The race for first place was all but over in May and the New York Giants won the race for second, going 91-63 mainly on the back of the N.L.'s top winner Christy Mathewson, who had a 27-9 record and the league's fourth-best ERA at 1.89. But the rest of the staff, including Hooks Wiltse (14-12) and Red Ames (12-11), was no match for the Cubs' second-line pitching.

Defending champion Pittsburgh dropped all the way to third, 17½ games out of first. Honus Wagner had his worst season since the 19th century, hitting .320 and neither driving in nor scoring 100 runs. Outfielder Sherry Magee was Philadelphia's lone bright spot, leading the N.L. in batting at .331, slugging at .507, runs scored with 110, and RBI with 123.

Connie Mack's rebuilt Athletics — featuring a lineup dominated by college graduates — opened in Washington, D.C., where baseball fan and President William Howard Taft threw out the opening ball, initiating one of baseball's most sacred traditions. The A's and their famed all-star infield of Collins, Barry, and Baker fought Detroit hard all summer, finally leaving the 1909 champion Tigers and a late-charging New York Yankees team in the dust, 14½ and 18 games back. The A's offense led the A.L. with .266 batting and .356 slugging averages; Collins hit .322 and outfielder Danny Murphy slugged .436, both placing fourth in the league. But the Philadelphia pitching staff — led by Coombs, Cy Morgan (18-12, 1.55 ERA), Plank (16-10, 2.01 ERA), and Bender (23-5 1.58 ERA) — thoroughly dominated the A.L. hitters. The A's

This trolley poster advertisement featuring John McGraw is from 1910. Despite winning four pennants in the decade, McGraw's Giants did not win a World Series.

TRIS SPEAKER

Although Tris Speaker only won one batting title, hitting .386 in 1916, that was no disgrace in the era of Ty Cobb. Speaker did hit .380 or higher five times in his career. He was a prolific run-scorer, turning in seven seasons with 100 or more runs. He also had great strike-zone judgment, walking 1,381 times and striking out only 220 times in his career.

The lefty-hitting Speaker played principally for Boston from 1907 to 1915 and for Cleveland from 1916 through 1926. In his 22-year career, "Spoke" batted .344 lifetime (seventh all-time) and slugged .500. Speaker could steal bases (433 lifetime) and hit triples (223, sixth-best all-time). But his true area of expertise was the two-base hit. Speaker led the American League in doubles eight times, with a peak of 59 in 1923. He hit 20 doubles or more 20 times, 30 or more 16 times, 40 or more ten times, and 50 or more four times. His career total of 733 is the best in history.

"The Grey Eagle" was known as the greatest defensive center fielder of his time. He played very shallow, daring hitters to hit the ball over his head, and made four unassisted double plays. He led A.L. outfielders in putouts seven times, double plays six times, assists three times, and fielding average twice.

Speaker's best season was 1912 when he won the Chalmers (MVP) Award. He hit .383 with 53 doubles, 12 triples, and ten home runs. He scored 136 runs, drove in 98, and stole 52 bases to lead Boston to a world championship.

*Two Chicago Cubs (top left), Jimmie Archer, left, and Heinie Zimmerman,
pose for a photo in 1910. Before Zimmerman left baseball in 1919, he compiled
a career .295 average. Archer was a good-defense, no-hit catcher for eight
seasons with Chicago. George Gibson, left, and Bugs Raymond (top right) are
shown in an action shot in 1910. Gibson was the Pittsburgh backstop for 12
years from 1905 to 1916. Jack Coombs (bottom right) led the A.L. with 31 wins
in 1910 and 28 wins in 1911 for the Philadelphia A's.*

THE 1910s

led the league in complete games, strikeouts, shutouts, and ERA by 0.22 over fifth-placed Chicago.

With Plank unavailable because of a sore arm, Mack went with only two pitchers in the 1910 series. Coombs and Bender combined to go 4-1 with a 2.76 ERA, allowing the Cubs' hitters only 35 hits and 15 runs in 45⅔ innings. Coombs beat Brown in games Two and Five, and Bender won the opener against Overall 4-1, allowing only three Chicago hits. The vaunted Cubs pitchers had ERAs for the Series of 5.50 for Brown, 3.38 for Cole, 13.50 for Reulbach, and 9.00 for Overall. The Cubs' offense was held to a .222 batting average with one triple and no home runs. Philadelphia had four regulars over .300 for the five games, including Harry Davis, who hit .353; Collins, who led all hitters at .429; Baker, who hit .409; and Murphy, who hit .350 with three doubles and nine RBI.

1911

With the introduction of the cork-center baseball in both leagues in 1911, offense increased by almost 500 runs in the N.L. and more than 1,000 in the A.L. The New York Giants led the National League with a .279 batting average and .391 slugging average, scoring 756 runs, one fewer than the second-place Chicago Cubs. Giants catcher Chief Meyers led the team with a .332 mark, Fred Merkle hit .283 and drove in 84 runs, and Larry Doyle slugged .527 (second in the league) and led all N.L. batters with 25 triples. New York monopolized the base paths, stealing 347 bases as a team (57 more than second-best Cincinnati), on the strength of such individual totals as Josh DeVore's 61, Fred Snodgrass' 51, Merkle's 49, Buck Herzog's 48, and Red Murray's 48.

Mathewson was the only N.L. pitcher to keep his ERA below 2.00 in the live-ball year, compiling a record of 26-13 with a 1.99 ERA. He was supported by a maturing Rube Marquard, who had his first of three consecutive 20-win seasons, going 24-7 with a 2.50 ERA. As a team, New York pitchers led the league in ERA at 2.69, complete games with 95, and strikeouts with 771.

Wildfire Schulte had his finest year for Chicago in 1911, hitting .300 with 21 homers and 121 RBI, both league-leading figures. Philadelphia rookie Grover Cleveland Alexander led the N.L. in wins and went 28-13 with a 2.57 ERA. Pittsburgh finished in third place, 14½ games back, and 37-year-old Honus Wagner won his final batting title, hitting .334.

Wagner played four more years as Pittsburgh's regular shortstop but hit .300 only twice more, in 1912 and 1913.

Detroit had the American League's second-weakest pitching in 1911, compiling a team ERA of 3.73. But miraculously, the Tigers led the league early on and stayed in a two-team race with Philadelphia for most of the year. Their valiant effort is a tribute to Sam Crawford and Ty Cobb, who appeared at the top of nearly every offensive category. Cobb hit .420

This picture of the Tucson team is from 1912.

An all-star team (top left) gathered in 1911 in Cleveland for an Addie Joss benefit. Joss was a Cleveland pitcher who died of tubercular meningitis in 1911 at age 31. In the front, left to right, are Germany Schaefer, Tris Speaker, Sam Crawford, unidentified, Ty Cobb, unidentified, and Paddy Livingston; in back, left to right, are Bobby Wallace, Frank Baker, Joe Wood, Walter Johnson, Hal Chase, Clyde Milan, Russ Ford, and Eddie Collins. Philadelphia A's pitcher Chief Bender (middle left) led the A.L. in 1910 and '11 with winning percentages of .821 and .773. Bob Bescher (middle center) of the Reds led the N.L. in stolen bases in four consecutive seasons from 1909 to 1912. The 1911 Chicago Cubs (middle right) finished in second place. The 1911 world champion A's (bottom left) were 101-50 and led the league in runs scored (861), fewest opponents runs allowed (601), and fielding average (.965). Ty Cobb (bottom right) attained a .513 career slugging average, which is better than those notched by such sluggers as Harmon Killebrew, Eddie Mathews, and Jim Rice.

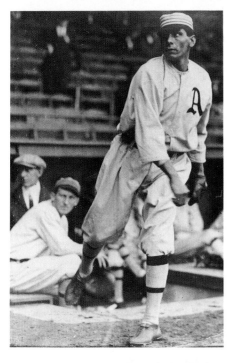

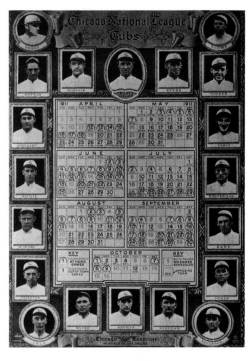

PHILADELPHIA ATHLETICS · 1911
Champions of the American League and World's Series
Copyright 1911, American B. B. Club of Philadelphia
Davis, 2. Baker, 3. Coombs, 4. Krause, 5. Thomas, 6. Bender, 7. Derrick, 8. Morgan, 9. Livingston, 10.
ng, 11. Lord, 12. Murphy, 13. Connie Mack, 14. Plank, 15. Lapp, 16. Strunk, 17. Hartsell, 18. Martin, 19.
th, 20. Van Zeldt, Mascot, 21. McInnes, 22. Collins, 23. Barry.

with 83 stolen bases, 248 hits, 147 runs scored, and 144 RBI, which were all league bests. Crawford hit .378, third in the league, and had 302 total bases, 109 runs scored, and 115 RBI. The only other significant contributions to the Tigers' offense were first baseman Jim Delahanty's .339 batting average and shortstop Donie Bush's 98 walks and 126 runs scored. Detroit hit .292 as a team and stole an A.L.-high 276 bases.

Unfortunately for Hughie Jennings and his Tigers, Philadelphia's offense was a little better; the A's scored 861 runs and led the A.L. in batting at .296 and slugging at .397. Their big guns were Collins, who hit .365, and Baker, who hit 11 homers and drove in 115 runs. And the A's pitching was a lot better: Led by Coombs (28-12, 3.53 ERA) and Plank (23-8, 2.10 ERA), the Philadelphia pitchers enabled Mack's team to run away with the race in September and finish at 101-50, 13½ games up on Detroit.

Philadelphia won its second consecutive world championship in 1911, a Series made famous by Baker's game-winning home runs in games Two and Three. Philadel-

phia outscored New York 27-13 to win the Series 4-2. The A's three starting pitchers, Bender, Coombs, and Plank, all had ERAs under 2.00 and held the powerful Giants line-up to a .175 batting average; only Doyle (.304) batted above .200.

1912

The offensive peak year of the decade for both leagues was in 1912. In the National League, batters hit .272 (a figure that would have led the league for an individual team in 1909), and the league ERA rose to 3.40. Heinie Zimmerman, third baseman for the third-place Chicago Cubs, had a triple-crown year, hitting .372 with 14 home runs and 103 RBI. He also led the N.L. in slugging at .571, total bases with 318, and doubles with 41.

The top offensive team, however, was the New York Giants, who scored 823 runs and led the N.L. in batting at .286 and stolen bases with 319. Behind Meyers, Doyle, and Merkle, the New York hitters gave McGraw his second of three consecutive pennants; the Giants went 103-48, finishing 10 games ahead of second-place Pittsburgh. Once again, New York also had the league's best pitching, with the duo of Mathewson and Marquard winning a combined 49 games and losing 23 (19 of Marquard's wins came in one winning streak) and rookie Jeff Tesreau leading the league in ERA at 1.96. The New Yorkers led the N.L. in team ERA at 2.58.

Pittsburgh's pitching staff regrouped to finish second in team ERA at 2.85 and first in shutouts with 18. The Pirates hitters led the league in slugging at .398 and were third in runs scored with 751, led by Wagner, who hit .324 with 102 RBI; Mike Donlin, who hit .316; and Owen Wilson, who set the 20th-century single-season triples record with 36.

In the American League, the Boston Red Sox celebrated the opening of Fenway Park by winning 105 games, the most up to that point in A.L. history, and winning the pennant by 14 games over Walter Johnson (32-12, 1.39 ERA) and his Washington Senators. Player/manager Jake Stahl led a Red Sox team that featured baseball's best outfield: Lewis in left (who hit

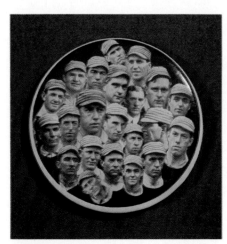

A 1911 button pictures the world champion Philadelphia Athletics.

HOME RUN BAKER

The 5'11", 175-pound Frank Baker is not exactly the modern idea of a home run hitter. In his 13-year career with the Philadelphia Athletics and the New York Yankees, Baker only hit 96 career homers and drove in 100 runs in a season only three times.

On the other hand, Baker did hit an unusually high number of home runs for the dead-ball era; he led the league with 11 in 1911, ten in 1912, 12 in 1913, and nine in 1914. The clean-up hitter for the A's and a member of the "$100,000 Infield," Baker hit .307 lifetime, with peak seasons of .347 and .336 in 1912 and '13.

Baker's nickname actually came from two particular home runs he hit in the 1911 series. The first won Game Two and came off Giants ace Rube Marquard. In a set of circumstances reminiscent of the David Cone affair during the 1988 N.L. play-offs, Giants pitcher Christy Mathewson was writing (or having ghost-written) a newspaper column that purported to give Matty's inside view of the World Series action. After Baker's game-winner, Mathewson's column the next morning criticized Marquard's pitch selection, saying that the way to pitch Baker was away.

Marquard was said to have taken some offense at this. The next day was Mathewson's turn to pitch, and with the score 0-0 in the late innings, Baker turned on an inside Mathewson fastball and sent it over the right field wall to win it for the A's, 1-0. After that, they stopped calling Baker "Frank."

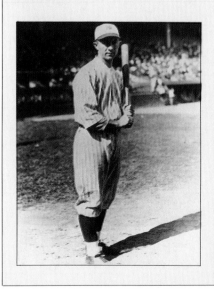

Eddie Collins of the Philadelphia Athletics won
the final Chalmers Award in the American
League and was presented with a Chalmers
Automobile. The Chalmers was the predecessor to
the Most Valuable Player award, with one hitch
— a player could only win once.

six home runs and drove in 109 runs), Hooper in right, and Speaker in center. Speaker hit .383 (third in the league behind Cobb and Jackson), slugged .567, tied for the league lead in homers with ten, led the league in doubles with 53, scored 136 runs, and stole 52 bases. In a performance that matched Johnson's great year, Smokey Joe Wood led the A.L. in wins, going 34-5 with a 1.91 ERA, second only to Johnson. Wood was second to Johnson in strikeouts with 258 to 303, but surpassed him in complete games, 35 to 24, and shutouts, ten to seven.

The 1912 World Series was a thrilling, eight-game affair (there was one tie) that was decided on a fielding mistake in Game Eight that has gone down in history as the "$30,000 muff."

The Series started in New York, where spitballer Tesreau lost 4-3 to Boston's ace Wood; Wood struck out 11 and walked only two, giving up eight hits. In Game Two, McGraw's strategy of holding back Mathewson backfired as the game ended in a 6-6 tie, called on account of darkness. But in Game Three, Marquard beat O'Brien 2-1. The Red Sox won two pitchers' duels in games Four and Five, with Wood striking out eight, walking nine, and scattering nine hits to defeat Tesreau 2-1, and Hugh Bedient beating Mathewson 2-1 on back-to-back triples by Hooper and Steve Yerkes. After Marquard beat O'Brien 5-2 in Game Six, Tesreau finally won a game, benefiting from the Giants' battering of Wood to even up the Series 3-3.

The 1912 World Series came down to one game, with Christy Mathewson once again facing Hugh Bedient. The Giants scored first, as Red Murray doubled in Josh DeVore in the third inning; the Red Sox tied it up in the seventh, when pinch-hitter Olaf Hen-

riksen doubled in Stahl with two outs. Then Wood took the mound, and he and Mathewson entered the tenth inning tied 1-1; the Giants went ahead 2-1 on Murray's double and Merkle's RBI single to center, bobbled by the always shallow Speaker long enough for Murray to come in. But the Sox pulled it out in their half of the inning, aided by two muffed fly balls, one by Snodgrass in center field and another by Merkle at first. For some reason, perhaps because Merkle had already served as scapegoat in another game, Snodgrass received most of the blame for the Giants' defeat and it was his non-catch that was called the "$30,000 muff," referring to the winner's share of the series money.

1913

Once again, National League fans had to do without a pennant race, as McGraw's team won 101 games, finishing at 101-51, 12½ games ahead of Philadelphia. It was the same old story; an offense without a dominant individual hitter managing to steal 296 bases to lead the league, bat .273, and score the third-highest total of runs in the league, 684. Left fielder George Burns came closest on the team to being a hitting star, batting .286 and finishing second in the N.L. in doubles with 37 and fourth in stolen bases with 40. On the pitching side, the Giants again led the N.L. in team ERA at 2.43; three Giants were in the top five in ERA: Mathewson at 2.06, Tesreau at 2.17, and Al Demaree at 2.21. Mathewson, Tesreau, and Marquard all won 20 games.

Gavvy Cravath of Philadelphia was the league's top slugger with

A 1913 World Series program.

Connie Mack started in baseball as a catcher in the 1880s. From 1894 to 1896 he served as player/manager for Pittsburgh and from 1901 to 1950 as manager and part-owner of the Philadelphia Athletics. While Mack was in charge of the Athletics, America fought three major wars and held 12 presidential elections.

During the early part of his career, Mack was very successful. He won six A.L. pennants between 1901 and 1914 and won three World Series. He put together the famous Philadelphia dynasty of Eddie Collins, Chief Bender, Eddie Plank, and Rube Waddell. Mack may be forgiven for thinking that it was he, and not the players, who was responsible for all this success. But after losing the 1914 World Series to the underdog Braves, a disgusted Mack sold most of his stars away over a two-year period. The A's finished in last place seven years in a row, lost 100 games five times in seven years, and went without another pennant until 1929.

Mack was able to bring out the talent in a variety of different kinds of players. He had a preference for college players including Collins, Plank, and Bender, but was also the only manager who could handle the illiterate Waddell.

After winning three straight pennants in 1929 to '31 — with the second Philadelphia dynasty of Jimmie Foxx, Al Simmons, and Lefty Grove — Mack and his A's spent most of the next two decades back in the cellar. Mack holds the records for games won (3,776) and games lost (4,025).

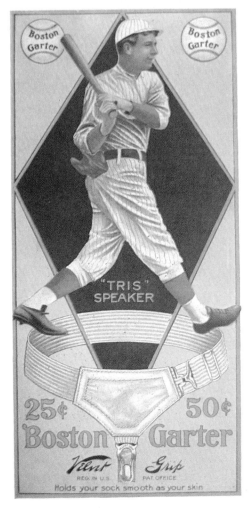

Jeff Tesreau (top left) of the New York Giants was 17-7 with a league-leading 1.96 ERA during his 1912 rookie season. He was 22-13 in 1913 and 26-10 in 1914. He led the league both seasons in games started (38 and 40). Sam Crawford (top right), an outfielder with Detroit from 1903 to 1917, is the career leader in triples with 312. He led the A.L. in triples six times, doubles once, homers twice, runs scored once, and RBI three times. Crawford batted over .300 11 times and slugged over .450 11 times. He ended his career with a .309 batting average, a .453 slugging average, 457 doubles, 1,392 runs scored, and 1,525 RBI. Tris Speaker (bottom left) and Joe Jackson (bottom right) appear in 1914 Boston Garter ads.

THE 1910s

19 home runs, 128 RBI, and 298 total bases. He and pitchers Pete Alexander (22-8, 2.79 ERA) and Tom Seaton (27-12, 2.60 ERA) were responsible for Philadelphia's improvement to second place.

The American League pennant race was also over early, as Philadelphia won more easily than the 6½-game margin might indicate. Never challenged during the last six months of the season, the A's led the A.L. in runs with 794, doubles with 223, home runs with 33, and batting and slugging at .280 and .376. Home Run Baker hit .336 with 12 homers and 126 RBI, Stuffy McInnis hit .326 with 90 RBI, and Eddie Collins batted .345, scored a league-leading 125 runs, and stole 55 bases. The pitching was merely adequate; only Chief Bender won 20 games, going 21-10 with a 2.21 ERA. Eddie Plank finished the season at 18-10 with a 2.60 ERA. Coombs was lost for the year because of illness.

Joe Jackson and Ty Cobb of also-rans Cleveland and Detroit were the league's leading hitters, with Cobb first in batting at .390 and Jackson second at .373; Jackson finished ahead of Cobb atop the slugging average list, .551 to .535.

In 1913, McGraw's Giants lost their third-straight World Series 4-1, but they had a ready and valid excuse — injuries. Merkle and Snodgrass came into the series with serious leg injuries, and catcher Chief Meyers broke his finger before Game Two. As a result, Merkle hit .231, Snodgrass missed three games, and Meyers missed all but one.

Bender easily defeated Marquard in the opener 6-4; the next day Mathewson evened things up by winning 3-0 over Plank in a 15-hit pitchers' duel that was 0-0 until the tenth inning. After that it was all the Philadelphia pitchers, as the A's won the final three games by

the combined score of 17-8. Both teams barely hit .200 for the series, but once again, Mack's workhorses, Plank and Bender, were the difference. Aside from Mathewson's 0.95 ERA in 19 innings, the Giants' pitching staff was completely ineffective, with Marquard going 0-1 with an ERA of 7.00, Tesreau going 0-1 with a 5.40 ERA, and Al Demaree going 0-1 with an ERA of 4.50.

Baseball Magazine *featured the 1914 Miracle Braves.*

1914

In the National League's most exciting pennant race of the 1910s, the Boston Braves rose from deep in the N.L. cellar not only to surpass the defending champion New York Giants but to finish 10½ games in front. Managed by George Stallings to a fifth-place finish in 1913 with roughly the same personnel, the Braves weren't expected by anyone to be within shouting distance of a pennant race. Even now, looking at their statistics, it is hard to see how they did it. Boston had a good infield defense — including former Cubs manager Johnny Evers and short-stop Rabbit Maranville — that led the N.L. in double plays, but their only slugger was Joe Connelly. He hit .306 and slugged .494, third in the league. His is the only Boston name among the leaders in any of the major offensive categories. The Braves didn't hit for average (.251) or power (.335 slugging) or steal bases (139 — last in the league), but somehow they scored 657 runs, second only to the Giants. As for their pitching — behind ace Dick Rudolph, who went 27-10 with

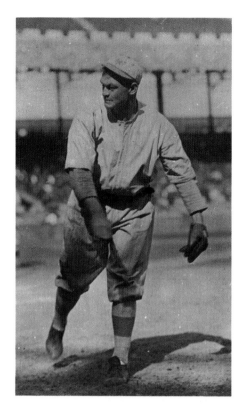

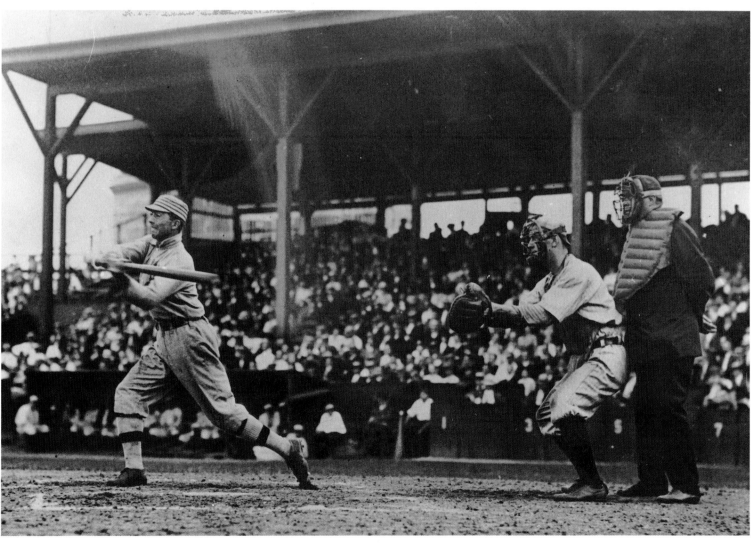

Home Run Baker, at bat (bottom), led the A.L. in homers each year from 1911 to 1913. Jeff Tesreau (top left) had a 1-3 record in the World Series. Pittsburgh hurler Babe Adams (middle top) was 22-12 in 1911 and 21-10 in 1913. Clyde Milan (middle bottom) scored 109 runs in 1911 and 105 runs in 1912. Brooklyn's Jake Daubert (top right) led the N.L. in batting in 1913 and '14.

A 1914 Boston Braves pictorial silk.

a 2.35 ERA, and Bill James, who went 26-7 with a 1.90 ERA — the Braves staff was mediocre, compiling a staff ERA of 2.74, good for fourth in the N.L.

Boston was in last place on July 18, when they suddenly started to move up in the standings. With the Giants' pitching fading and no other team stepping into the void, the Braves reached second place on August 12. Winning 34 of 44 games to end the season, they passed New York in September and ran hard to the wire; their final record was 94-59.

The Giants' main problem was their pitching. Tesreau led the staff (26-10, 2.37 ERA), but Mathewson was showing signs of wear; he went 24-13, but his ERA of 3.00 was the highest of his career. Mathewson never regained his old form after the 1914 season and won only 12 more games in his career. Marquard contributed one of his worst seasons as well, at 12-22 with a 3.06 ERA. The Giants' offense, which scored a league-leading 672 runs, couldn't pick up that much slack.

The 1914 A.L. pennant race, won with little trouble by the Philadelphia Athletics, who now had won four pennants in five years, was the last for Mack's great dynasty and his "$100,000 Infield." Disappointed with the result of the 1914 World Series and appalled by the widespread salary increases caused by Federal League competition, Mack decided that he, rather than his players, should be paid what he was worth. He auctioned off Collins, Baker, and Barry to the highest bidder, receiving several times each player's salary. The players, of course, got nothing but the right to play for their new teams at their old salaries.

The A's bowed out in style, leading the A.L. in hitting (.272), slugging (.352), and runs (749). Collins finished second in batting

(to Cobb) at .344, scored 122 runs, and stole 58 bases. Baker hit nine home runs and drove in 97. A solid pitching staff of Bender, Plank, and youngsters Bob Shawkey and Herb Pennock allowed the third-fewest runs in the league.

Second-place Boston won 91 games and the ERA title, without injured ace Wood winning more than nine games. Dutch Leonard went 19-5 with a 1.01 ERA and Ernie Shore went 10-4 with a 1.89 ERA. Shortly after the season, the Red Sox signed pitcher Babe Ruth out of the minors, a move that would pay off with three pennants in the next five seasons.

The 1914 Braves miracle kept right on going through the postseason, as Boston swept the talented Athletics 4-0, in the first complete (tie-less) Series sweep in 20th-century baseball history. Rudolph beat Bender 7-1 in the opener. Boston never looked back, winning 1-0, 5-4, and 3-1 in the remaining games to outscore the mighty A's 16-6. Catcher Hank Gowdy, a .243 regular-season hitter, was the Series hero with a .545 batting average and a 1.273 slugging average. Philadelphia hit .172 as a team with no triples or home runs.

1915

The Philadelphia Phillies, a sixth-place club only the season before, started the 1915 season with an eight-game winning streak, kept winning, and then held off the Cubs to finish in first place in the N.L. with a 90-62 record, 7 games ahead of defending champion Boston. Philadelphia already had one of the N.L.'s better offenses, with Gavvy Cravath, who led the league in 1915 with 24 home runs and 115 RBI, and Fred Luderus, who batted .315 and drove in 62 runs. But the big factor for Philadelphia was the emergence of

HAL CHASE

Everyone could see that Hal Chase had terrific talent. Signed by the New York Highlanders in 1905, "Prince Hal" hit for average, .323 in his sophomore season, and he fielded first base like no one ever had. In an era when bunting was far more important than today, Chase was famous for charging in on the batter, making plays in front of the catcher or even on the third base line, and catching runners at any base. He had style, and fans and teammates alike loved him.

It took them time, however, to discover that Chase had what one called a "corkscrew mind" — he was sneaky and dishonest. In 1910, Chase was accused by New York manager George Stallings of throwing a ballgame for gamblers. Somehow, Chase managed to survive this scandal — and even to take Stallings' job.

By 1913, Chase had worn out his welcome in New York; from then until 1919, he bounced around the majors, playing for four teams. In 1918, Reds manager Christy Mathewson suspended him for "indifferent play." The next year with the Giants, John McGraw had Chase suspended "indefinitely" — that is, for life — for attempting to fix games.

The "highlight" of Chase's criminal career was his off-field involvement in the 1919 Black Sox scandal, for which he was indicted in Illinois but never extradited from California to stand trial. Chase played the rest of his career in semi-pro leagues in the Southwest, no doubt wowing the fans with his dazzling glove.

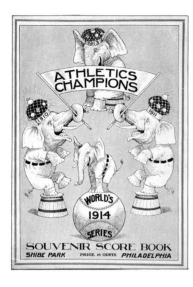

The Philadelphia Athletics (top left), as the 1914 World Series program states, had won three championships in four years; they were heavily favored to win another in '14. A Chicago Whales F.L. program in 1914 (top right) featured player/manager Joe Tinker. The 1915 opening-day Giants lineup (middle left) featured a fairly potent attack. The Giants finished third in the N.L. in runs scored. Rabbit Maranville, left, and Ernie Shore (middle right) take a break. Maranville was a key player for the 1914 Boston Braves, and played shortstop and second base for 23 years. Shore was 19-8 for the 1915 Red Sox. In Game One of the 1914 World Series (bottom left), Boston third baseman Charlie Deal tags out Eddie Murphy of the Athletics. A 1915 photo from Hot Springs, AK (bottom right), features Babe Ruth's familiar visage — Ruth is standing in the center of the picture.

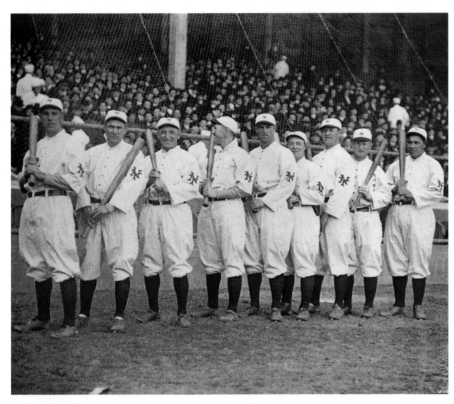

Grover Cleveland Alexander as one of the league's top pitchers. Alexander went 31-10 and led the league with a 1.22 ERA and 376 innings pitched. Alexander, Erskine Mayer (21-15, 2.36 ERA), and Al Demaree (14-11, 3.05 ERA) made the team the N.L. ERA leader at 2.17.

Boston's offensive production slipped back a notch to 582 runs, and the pitching remained average; Dick Rudolph had almost the same ERA in 1915 as in 1914 (2.37), but instead of 27-10, his record was an unmiraculous 22-19.

Brooklyn improved by a half-dozen games to take third place on the strength of the pitching of Jeff Pfeffer (19-14, 2.10 ERA) and former Athletic Jack Coombs (15-10, 2.58 ERA).

In the American League, Boston won a close victory over Detroit, which featured the A.L.'s best offense. The Red Sox, though, had a deep pitching staff, including Rube Foster, who went 19-8 with a 2.11 ERA; Ernie Shore, who went 19-8 with a 1.64 ERA; rookie Babe Ruth, who went 18-8 with a 2.44 ERA; Dutch Leonard, who went 15-7 with a 2.36 ERA; and, making a brief comeback from a shoulder injury, Smoky Joe Wood, who won the ERA title at 1.49 and pitched in pain to a 15-5 record.

The Tigers came up short, 2½ games behind. Detroit's pitching, with Harry Coveleski and Hooks Dauss, was strictly average, but their hitters almost won the pennant anyway. The Tigers led the A.L. in runs by a margin of 61, 778 to Chicago's 717; Detroit led the league in doubles with 207, batting at .268, and slugging at .358. Paced by Cobb's 96 stolen bases, Detroit led the A.L. with 241. Detroit had the majors' most powerful offensive outfield with Cobb, who hit .369; Sam Crawford, who drove in 112 runs; and Bobby Veach, who hit .313. The trio was one-two-three in the league in hits, RBI, and total bases.

In 1915, fans saw a new kind of Boston-Philadelphia Series, with the leagues switched. The Series began in Philadelphia, and Game One went according to the fans' script; Alexander held the Red Sox to eight hits and one run, winning 3-1. In the next three games, however, the Red Sox starters took over. In Game Two, Foster threw a three-hitter and won 2-1; in Boston, Leonard also allowed three hits and also won 2-1. In Game Four, Shore won again 2-1. Finally, in Game Five, the two teams played a modern-looking slug-fest, which included 19 hits and four home runs (two by Harry Hooper). With Alexander too sore to pitch, Philadelphia was forced to use Mayer and Eppa Rixey. Rixey gave up five runs and lost 6-4 to Foster, who went the distance while scattering nine hits. Boston won its second World Series of the 1910s 4-1.

1916

Manager Wilbert Robinson's Brooklyn Robins won the National League pennant in 1916, with the hitters giving their usual strong performance. Daubert was second in the N.L. in hitting at .316, and Wheat had one of his best seasons, batting .312, leading the league in slugging at .461 and total bases with 262, and hitting 32 doubles. In part-time outfield duty, Casey Stengel hit eight home runs in 462 at-bats. But it took all of Brooklyn's top five pitchers having good years at once to stave off the Phillies. Brooklyn's ace was Pfeffer, who went 25-11 with a 1.92 ERA; also below 2.00 in ERA were Larry Cheney at 1.92 (18-12 record) and a resurrected Marquard at 1.58 (13-6). Sherry Smith went 14-10 with a 2.34 ERA, and Coombs went 13-8 with a 2.66 ERA to round out the Robins staff. Brooklyn finished 94-60, 2½ games up on Philadelphia. The Phillies were led by Alexander, who went 33-12 with a league-low 1.55 ERA.

In the American League, Tris Speaker left Boston for Cleveland and Joe Jackson played his first full year as a member of the Chicago White Sox. The Speaker-less Boston offense scored 118 fewer

ZACH WHEAT

Zach Wheat was the clean-up hitter of the old Brooklyn National League club from 1909 to 1926.

Wheat batted .317 lifetime and was over .300 in 14 of his 19 major league seasons. He was incredibly consistent; looking at his stats, it would be hard to tell which years came in his 20s and which in his late 30s. He hit 36 doubles in 1910, 31 in 1921, and a career-high 42 in 1925. Wheat had decent power for an outfielder in the dead-ball era, making double figures in triples seven times before 1920 and leading the National League in slugging average at .461 in 1916. He adjusted well to the new style of play of the early 1920s; in 1923 and '24 Wheat hit .375 each year, a career-high, and in 1922 he slugged .500 for the first time at the age of 36. He then slugged over .500 the next three years in a row. He also learned how to hit home runs in the 1920s, hitting 75 homers in the six years after 1920 after hitting only 51 in the 11 years before.

Wheat was loved by the fans in Brooklyn, who forgave him his occasional mental lapses. One time the third base coach had to repeat the bunt sign so many times to a noncomprehending Wheat that the opposing pitcher read it and delivered a high fastball; Wheat, who never had got the sign, belted the ball over the fence for a home run. Baseball legend Casey Stengel once said that Zach Wheat was "the only great ballplayer who was never booed."

Heinie Zimmerman (top left) played a decade at third base for the Chicago Cubs and four years with the New York Giants. He is shown here with the Giants in 1918. Zimmerman compiled a .295 lifetime average and led the National League in RBI three times. In 1912, he led the league in homers (14), RBI (103), batting average (.372), slugging average (.571), and doubles (41). But his character, however, did not measure up to his on-field ability. His legendary temper got him thrown out of three games in five days in 1913. An anonymous fan once put up $100 if Zimmerman could go for two weeks without an ejection. An even worse problem for him, however, was his dishonesty. Like his friend Hal Chase and two dozen other players in the late 1910s to early 1920s, Zimmerman was banned from baseball for life (after the 1919 season) for fixing games. The 1916 Brooklyn Robins (top right) were National League champs. Brooklyn led the N.L. in team batting average (.261), slugging average (.345), and earned run average (2.12). Zach Wheat, middle row second from left, was the team's star and led the N.L. in slugging percentage at .461 and total bases with 262. The Robins were run over by the Boston Red Sox express in the World Series, losing 4-1. These pages (bottom) from the 1915 Reach sporting goods catalog show, left to right, chest protectors and other protective gear, catchers' masks, bats, and gloves of the day.

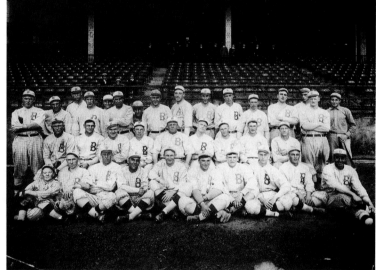

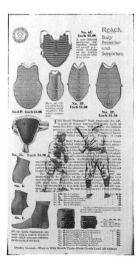

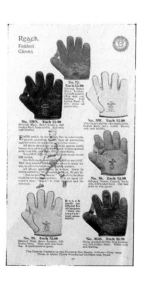

SMOKEY JOE WOOD

THE 1910s

runs than the year before, and the White Sox stayed right behind them, finishing 2 games back. But a great Boston pitching staff gave the Red Sox the pennant. Ruth came into his own, becoming the undisputed ace of the Boston staff and leading the American League in ERA at 1.75, games started with 41, and shutouts with nine. Leonard went 18-12 with a 2.36 ERA; submariner Carl Mays went 18-13 with a 2.39 ERA; and Shore won 16 and lost 10 and had an ERA of 2.63.

Chicago had a young and balanced team, including Happy Felsch, who hit .300 and drove in 70 runs; Jackson, who hit .341 and had 21 triples; and pitcher Lefty Williams who had a 13-7 record and a 2.89 ERA. The White Sox emerging ace was Cicotte, who went 15-7 with an ERA of 1.78.

In third place, 4 games out, were the always-powerful Detroit Tigers, who barely missed again because of their thin pitching. Though Cobb lost the batting title to Speaker, .371 to .386, he led in runs scored with 113 and stolen bases with 68.

Once again in the World Series, Boston's starting pitching was too much for its opponent in a short Series. Shore won Game One 6-5 over Marquard, in a game that made Boston fans nervous in the

A 1916 Baseball Magazine *with the Red Sox.*

ninth inning. Brooklyn scored five runs and had the tying run on base, when Carl Mays recorded the final out in relief. Ruth and Smith dueled for 14 innings in Game Two, Boston winning 2-1 when pinch-hitter Del Gainor batted in the deciding run with one out. The next day Mays started and suffered Boston's only loss when he bowed to Coombs, and Pfeffer in relief, 4-3. Boston then took the final two games easily, 6-2 and 4-1, behind Leonard and Shore. The Sox batted only .238 for the series, but their pitchers held Brooklyn to a .200 average.

1917

In many ways, 1917 was John McGraw's finest hour. With a makeshift lineup of veterans and youngsters, the Giants took first place from the Phillies in June and stayed on top until the end, finishing a comfortable 10 games up and winning 98 games. With an infield of light-hitting veterans Buck Herzog and Art Fletcher, the unheralded Walter Holke, and the 31-year-old Zimmerman — and an outfield of journeyman Dave Robertson, George Burns, and Benny Kauff — the Giants led the National League in runs with 635 and homers with 39. In his last good season, Zimmerman hit .297 and led the league in RBI with 102. Robertson hit .259 but led the N.L. in home runs with 12. Burns and Kauff contributed a combined 70 stolen bases.

McGraw's pitching staff wasn't very impressive on paper, either. But Ferdie Schupp went 21-7 with a 1.95 ERA, Perritt went 17-7 with a 1.88 ERA, and veteran Slim Sallee had his second-to-last effective season going 18-7 with an ERA of 2.17. All told, New York led the N.L. in team ERA at 2.27, and threw 18 shutouts.

Second-place Philadelphia was once again a one-man show put on by Alexander, who led the league in wins with 30, innings pitched with 388, and ERA at 1.86. Number-two pitcher Rixey went 16-21 with a 2.27 ERA. As for the Phillie's hitters, first baseman Fred Luderus slumped to .261 with five homers, and Gavvy Cravath hit .280 with a league-leading 12 home runs but only 83 RBI. As a team, Philadelphia hit .248, fourth in the league.

In the American League, the up-and-coming Chicago White Sox

The son of a wandering prospector, Smoky Joe Wood first attracted attention for his great right arm as a teenager in the mining town of Ouray, CO, where he played for the town team. By age 19, he was pitching for the Boston Red Sox. There he went 11-7 with a 2.21 ERA, 12-13 with a 1.68 ERA, and 23-17 with a 2.02 ERA in his first three full seasons, striking out major league hitters with a fastball that Walter Johnson always claimed was even faster than his.

Wood's greatest season, 1912, was his last as a regular starter. Leading the Sox to the pennant and a world championship, Wood went 34-5 for a winning percentage of .872. He had an ERA of 1.91 and led the American League in complete games with 35 and shutouts with ten. Boston was locked in a close fight with Washington all summer, and Wood conducted his own personal battle with Senators ace Johnson. Late in the season, Wood was threatening Johnson's record of 16 consecutive pitching victories; finally, Wood defeated Johnson to keep the streak alive and ended up tying the record.

Wood hurt his thumb and shoulder in a fielding accident in 1913 and was never the same; he could sometimes pitch with his old effectiveness, but only with considerable pain. In 1917, he gave up pitching to become an outfielder and made himself into a decent hitter. He played 417 games in the outfield, hitting .283 lifetime, with a peak of .366 in 1921.

Red Sox players (top left) Hal Janvrin, with his hands on his knees, and Ernie Shore warm up before a 1916 game. In the '16 Series, Shore was 2-0 with a 1.53 ERA. Brooklyn first baseman Jake Daubert (top right) led the N.L. in batting in 1913 and '14. The champion 1917 White Sox (bottom left) were led by Eddie Collins, who had four runs scored and two RBI in the World Series. A 1916 Phillies game program (bottom right) features catcher Bill Killefer.

COMISKEY'S CHAMPION WHITE SOX—1917

dynasty struggled most of the season against the defending champs, Boston. But at the end, Chicago finished 100-54, 9 games ahead. The Chicago pitching staff of Eddie Cicotte (28-12, 1.53 ERA), Red Faber (16-13, 1.92 ERA), and Lefty Williams (17-8, 2.97 ERA) battled the Red Sox for the team ERA title, finishing at 2.16, a shade better than Ruth and company's 2.20. Chicago had three pitchers in the league's top five in ERA and four in the top five in winning percentage.

The Chicago lineup was identical to that of the 1919 Black Sox: Chick Gandil at first; Eddie Collins, who stole 53 bases, at second; smooth-fielding Swede Risberg at shortstop; Buck Weaver at third; Nemo Leibold in right; Felsch, who hit .308 and drove in 102 runs, in center; Jackson in left; and defensive standout Ray Schalk was the catcher. The White Sox led the A.L. in stolen bases with 219 and runs scored with 656.

John McGraw lost his fourth consecutive World Series, 4-2, in 1917. Cicotte defeated Sallee in the opener 2-1 on a Felsch home run in the fourth inning. Red Faber scattered eight hits to beat four New York pitchers 7-2 in Game Two. But when the Series returned to New York, Rube Benton threw a five-hitter to beat Cicotte 2-0, and the next day, the Giants evened things up behind Schupp, who struck out seven, walked one, and defeated Faber 5-0.

But Chicago won again back home for Game Five, beating Sallee 8-5 on a gutsy relief stint by Cicotte, who relieved an ineffective Reb Russell in the first and held New York to two runs in six innings. In Game Six, the White Sox won 4-2 on three embarrassing fourth-inning runs. The frustrated McGraw, who had often seen his players make outlandish errors in important games, watched as third

baseman Zimmerman opened the inning by throwing away an easy grounder by Collins. Next, Robertson dropped Jackson's fly ball in right. Felsch then grounded to Zimmerman, who had Collins trapped in a run-down between third and home, but catcher Bill Rariden and first baseman Holke left home unattended; Zimmerman, helpless, chased Collins all the way across the plate.

1918

By 1918, America had entered World War I, and the baseball season, officially classified as a "nonessential activity," was threatened. In a compromise, the leagues shortened their seasons to an average of 126 games and were allowed to play the 1918 World Series in September.

Still, many ballplayers were drafted, and the war largely determined the outcome of both pennant

Stuffy McInnis went from the A's to Boston in 1918 and helped the BoSox win the Series.

CHARLES COMISKEY

As a first baseman in the 1880s with the old St. Louis Browns of the American Association, Charles Comiskey was known as a pioneer of defensive play at first base; some say he was the first to play far away from the bag. As the Browns manager, Comiskey was the ringleader of the bad boys of pre-Orioles baseball, leading a team famous for rowdy, and at times violent, behavior.

As a self-made millionaire and early force behind the A.L., however, Comiskey turned very conservative and very tightfisted. In an era known for its oppression of players and low salaries, Comiskey's great White Sox teams of the 1910s worked cheaper than anyone. While Honus Wagner and Ty Cobb were paid more than $10,000 a year, Joe Jackson was the highest-paid White Sox player at $6,000. The best and most profitable team in baseball in the late 1910s received the least meal money. Comiskey deserves some part of the blame for the Black Sox scandal for creating an atmosphere that made honest players very corruptible.

In the aftermath of the scandal, Comiskey, who was used to having his own way, tried to cover up his players' guilt. The confessions of Joe Jackson and others mysteriously disappeared from a Cook County, IL, prosecutor's office where Comiskey had influential friends. (Years later, Jackson's confession miraculously reappeared during Jackson's lawsuit against the White Sox for back pay.) But none of Comiskey's schemes could prevent the truth from coming out.

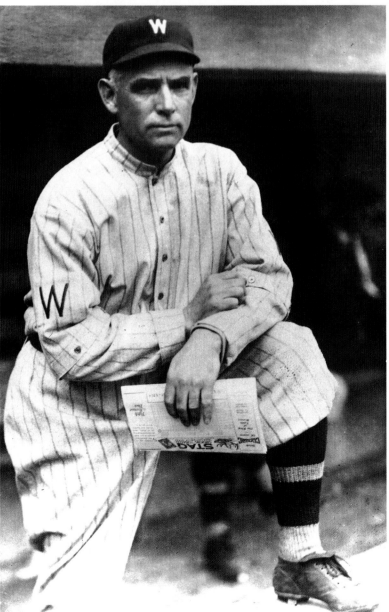

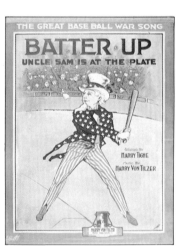

Over his three quarters of a century in baseball, Clark Griffith (bottom left) was a player, manager, executive, and owner. After a glorious pitching career with the 1890s Chicago Cubs (where he won 152 of his 237 lifetime victories), Griffith joined several of the game's biggest stars in jumping to the new American League in 1901. As a player/manager, Griffith promptly led the Chicago White Sox to the A.L.'s first pennant; he pitched his way to 24 victories, as the White Sox went 83-53. Two years later, Griffith established a New York franchise (the Highlanders) in what had been exclusively New York Giant territory. In 1912, he was hired to revive the moribund Washington Senators. By 1921, he was the team's majority owner and president. Three years later, Griffith's player acquisitions — Bucky Harris, Walter Johnson, and Goose Goslin — brought the 1924 pennant to the nation's capital. Although he hit only .214 in the 1919 World Series, Edd Roush (top right) scored six runs and had seven RBI. Nap Rucker (top left) of Brooklyn pitched three scoreless innings in the 1916 World Series. Baseball was an American symbol (bottom right), as Uncle Sam became a late-inning pinch hitter in World War I. This Partridge sporting goods catalog (bottom middle) pictures Rube Marquard.

THE 1910s

races. In the National League, Mc-Graw lost Kauff, Benton, and Jeff Tesreau to the draft and defense employment. A relatively unaffected Chicago Cubs team won the pennant by going 84-45, 10½ games ahead of the Giants. First baseman Fred Merkle hit .297 and drove in 65 runs for Chicago, and the league's top pitching staff included Hippo Vaughn, who went 22-10 with the N.L.'s best ERA, 1.74; Lefty Tyler, who went 19-9 with an ERA of 2.00; and Claude Hendrix, who was 19-7 with a 2.78 ERA.

In the American League, Boston's manager Jack Barry was drafted, so executive Ed Barrow took over the team, a move that had momentous consequences for baseball when Barrow decided to try putting pitcher Babe Ruth in the outfield on a platoon basis between starts; Ruth won 13 games, lost 7, and hit .300 with a league-leading 11 homers. It would be the first of 12 home run titles in Ruth's long career. Barrow bought Stuffy McInnis, Wally Schang, and Bullet Joe Bush from the Athletics

and managed to put together enough offense to support a solid pitching staff of Mays, Bush, Sad Sam Jones, and Ruth that led the American League in complete games with 105, shutouts with 26, and fewest runs allowed with 380. Walter Johnson went 23-13 with a league-low 1.27 ERA and led the Senators to second place.

The 1918 World Series produced baseball's second player strike (the first was a one-game strike by the 1912 Tigers), although this one lasted little more than an hour. And while both the 1918 and the 1912 incidents are often treated as comedy, they were both rooted in growing player frustration at being exploited and underpaid by the domineering baseball establishment.

With the Series standing at 3-1 in favor of the Red Sox, the players began to hear rumors that they would not receive the guaranteed prize money of $2,000 for each winning player and $1,400 for each loser. Seasonal attendance had been poor, and the owners had been criticized on patriotic grounds for putting on the Series at all. A delegation of four players, including Harry Hooper, went to the National Commission but got no answer; they then threatened to strike. At game time the crowd of 24,694 became restless as no players came out onto the field. Finally, the players were forced into giving in by public plea from Boston's Mayor Fitzgerald, who urged both sides to set aside their differences

in the name of the war effort. A proposal by the players to donate all proceeds from the Series to a war charity was ignored.

In the end, the Red Sox won the Series 4-2, with Ruth and Mays both going 2-0 to outdo Vaughn's 1.00 ERA in 27 innings and Tyler's 1.17 ERA in 23 innings. The Red Sox received a winners' share of $2208.45 each.

1919

The 1919 season is primarily remembered as the year the heavily favored White Sox threw the World Series to the underdog

Detroit right fielder Sam Crawford averaged 107 RBI from 1910 to 1915.

JOE JACKSON

Unfortunately for him, Joe Jackson's career practically coincided with Ty Cobb's.

Offensively, Jackson did most of the things that Cobb did, but

Cobb did them just a little bit better. So Jackson, who played for Cleveland from 1910 to 1912 and for Chicago from then until 1920, spent a good deal of his career hanging in there and waiting for Cobb to slump down to .350 so Jackson could have a chance to lead the A.L. in hitting.

Jackson batted .356 lifetime and never won a batting title. In fact, he hardly ever led the league in anything; he led in triples three times, doubles (with 39) in 1913, and once each in hits and slugging (even though he slugged .518 lifetime) — that's it. The height of Jackson's frustration was between 1911 and 1913. When he hit .408 in 1911, Cobb hit .420 and took the batting title;

when Jackson hit .395 in 1912, Cobb hit .410; when Jackson hit .373 in 1913, Cobb hit .390.

Jackson did have it over Cobb as a fielder. Jackson had a good arm, and his glove was nicknamed "the place where triples go to die."

His career year in 1920 — .382 batting average, .589 slugging average, 42 doubles, 20 triples, and 12 homers — raises the question of whether Jackson might have made a better adjustment to the home run era than Cobb did.

Of course, we'll never know the answer to that question. Because of the Black Sox scandal, Jackson was banished from baseball for life.

Roger Peckinpaugh (top left) was one of the greatest fielding shortstops in major league history. He was one of the cornerstones of the Yankees during the 1910s. Peckinpaugh went on to the Senators in 1922, and he was named the American League MVP in 1925. In the '25 World Series, however, he committed eight errors, including a dropped fly ball that lost the Series to the Pirates. Art Fletcher (top right) was Peckinpaugh's counterpart at shortstop for the Giants. The Philadelphia Hilldales (bottom left) included Dick Lundy, standing far left. The 1919 Cubs (bottom right) led the National League in team earned average with a 2.21 mark. Pete Alexander (1.72 ERA) and Hippo Vaughn (1.79 ERA) were ranked one-two in the league. But the Cubs were on the bottom of the league with only 454 runs scored.

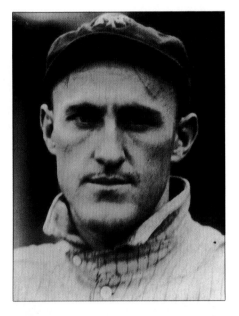

THE 1910s

Cincinnati Reds. While many observers of the time saw it that way too, it was the Reds, not the White Sox, who ran away with the pennant that year.

Bolstered by returning veterans Benny Kauff, who hit .277 with ten home runs and 67 RBI, and pitcher Jess Barnes, the N.L.'s winningest pitcher at 25-9 (2.40 ERA), New York led through August. But Cincinnati put on a charge and clinched victory by taking the final two series with the Giants. Cincinnati finished 96-44, 9 games up.

The Reds were led by hitting stars Edd Roush — who won the N.L. batting title at .321 and had 71 RBI, second in the league — and third baseman Heinie Groh, who hit .310 and tied Roush for third in slugging at .431. Greasy Neale stole 28 bases and second baseman Morrie Rath walked 64 times and scored 77 runs. The Reds' pitching staff allowed the fewest runs in the league (401) and featured two 20-game winners: Hod Eller at 20-9 with a 2.39 ERA, and Slim Sallee at 21-7 with a 2.06 ERA. Dutch Ruether won 19 and lost six with a team-low 1.82 ERA.

The American League saw an exciting three-team race between the White Sox, Indians, and Yankees, but Chicago's offense led them to first place, 3½ games ahead of Cleveland and 7½ ahead of New York. Joe Jackson hit .351 and slugged .506 with 96 RBI, and Eddie Collins stole 33 bases. The White Sox were first in the A.L. in total runs with 667, batting average with .287, and stolen bases with 150. Ace pitcher Cicotte at 29-7 (1.82 ERA) was one of two Chicago 20-game winners; Lefty Williams went 23-11 with a 2.64 ERA.

But even bigger news than the pennant race in the American League was the first pop of the coming home run explosion. In 1919, Barrow played Babe Ruth in the outfield long enough for him to get 432 at-bats, and the results were earth-shattering. Ruth hit .322 with 29 home runs, setting a modern record and exceeding the nearest player by 19. He drove in a league-leading 114 runs and slugged .657, 127 points more than runner-up George Sisler and the highest slugging average of the 20th century. Ruth's slugging average mark would stand until 1920, when he slugged .847. As a pitcher, Babe went 9-5, with a 2.97 ERA.

Cincinnati "won" the 1919 Series, which had been lengthened to eight games to celebrate the end of World War I, 5-3. The highlight for Chicago was Dickie Kerr's performance, including dramatic wins in games Three and Six by scores of 3-0 and 5-4. Joe Jackson always maintained that he had refused to go along with the plot and played his best. He is backed up by a Series-high .375 batting average and .563 slugging average, six RBI, and no errors.

The 1919 Black Sox (above) were 88-52; the Reds were 96-44.

RING LARDNER

One of the finest baseball writers of a generation that included Hugh Fullerton and Grantland Rice, Ring Lardner worked as editor of *The Sporting News* and the *Boston American*, and spent six years traveling with the Chicago White Sox for the *Chicago Tribune*. It was then that Lardner wrote his first series of short stories, works in which he tried to portray the ballplayers of the 1910s as they really were — a varied assortment of college men, rough sons of working class immigrants, and illiterate country boys.

Lardner's *You Know Me, Al* and *Alibi Ike* were shockingly realistic, showing ballplayers as often carousing, venal, and petty adolescents who were preyed upon by very unglamorous women. In *Alibi Ike*, a hilariously vain rookie named Frank X. Farrell ("the 'X' stood for excuse me") has an excuse for everything, even success. Asked what he hit in his last season in the minors, Farrell says, "I had malaria most o' the season. I wound up with .356." "Where would I have to go to get malaria?" a veteran asks.

But the later Lardner's tone grew increasingly dark, as he became personally bitter over what he saw as the corruption of the game in the home run era. When he ultimately gave up on baseball as a literary topic, Lardner somewhat unfairly blamed the Black Sox scandal and the passing of the old style of "scientific" or dead-ball play.

Harry Hooper (top left) was the Boston Red Sox right fielder in what many fans consider the greatest defensive outfield in history — Duffy Lewis and Tris Speaker were the other ballhawks. Hooper was a lifetime .281 hitter and batted over .300 five times. He played on four BoSox world champions (1912, 1915, 1916, and 1918), and his most famous moment came in the 1912 World Series. In that Series against the New York Giants, Hooper vaulted backward into the bleachers to rob Larry Doyle of a home run. When Boston owner Harry Frazee sold most of the BoSox team (including Babe Ruth) in 1920, a disgusted Hooper was dealt to the Chicago White Sox, where he finished his Hall of Fame career in 1925. Ossie Vitt (top right) was a light-hitting third baseman for the Detroit Tigers from 1912 to 1918. Ray Schalk (bottom middle), with a career batting average of .253, has the lowest lifetime batting average of any nonpitcher enshrined in Cooperstown. Schalk did not enter the Hall of Fame on his offensive ability, but defensively as a catcher he may have redefined the position. Instead of remaining stationary behind the plate, he began the now-routine practice of backing up plays behind first and third. Schalk was also the first catcher to follow the runner down to first base to protect in case of an overthrow. The World Series game program (bottom left) celebrates the 50th anniversary of the old Red Stockings, the first all-professional team. The 1919 Reds (bottom right) are pictured on the front of the champions' program for a dinner held in their honor.

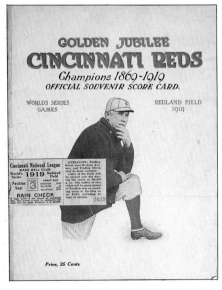

139

THE 1920s

America in the "Roaring '20s" encountered
a new chapter in baseball, emphasizing home
runs and potent offenses, authored by
Babe Ruth. The Bambino's slugging ability
and charming personality caught the public's eye
as no player ever had.

Yankee Stadium (page 140) was called "The House That Ruth Built" and opened in 1923. Lou Gehrig, left, and Babe Ruth (page 141) flank Howard Jones, USC's football coach.

THE 1920s

By 1920, postwar America was abandoning its sleepy, rural origins and becoming a dynamic, exuberant, urban-based society. Baseball emerged from the war years faced with new competition for the public's time and attention. Motion pictures and radios were to become national rages during the coming decade, and the rise of the automobile would give people added mobility and entertainment options. Baseball's stolid image needed a face lift in order to keep pace with the tempo of the "Roaring '20s." Following the example provided by a burly ex-pitcher, the game's architects tinkered with the rules and ushered in a new era in baseball, one featuring revved up offenses and a near-obsessive

Babe Ruth was the ideal sports hero for America in the "Roaring '20s."

emphasis on home runs and the sluggers blasting them. The 1920s produced an avalanche of hitting and, not coincidentally, attendance records. And fortunately for the national pastime, the public flocked to watch Babe Ruth redefine the dimensions of the game. Ruth's unique ability to hit baseballs a long distance and his magnetic personality captured the public's attention as no player ever had. He may have saved baseball from dying of a cancer that was eating away at its core.

For 1920 was not just the year Babe Ruth signed on with the Yankees. It also brought forth in September the revelation that players and gamblers had conspired to fix the 1919 World Series for personal profit. Rumors had circulated throughout the winter and summer of 1920 that members of the Chicago White Sox purposely lost the Series. Then, with two weeks left to play in the 1920 season, outfielder Joe Jackson and pitcher Eddie Cicotte confessed their roles in the fix to a Chicago grand jury, and a total of eight players were suspended by White Sox owner Charles Comiskey. In addition to Jackson and Cicotte, the eight — Chick Gandil, Swede Risberg, Buck Weaver, pitcher Lefty Williams, Happy Felsch, and Fred McMullin — were dubbed the "Black Sox."

The news of their complicity struck like a thunderbolt. So seriously did this episode undermine the public's confidence in the integrity of the game that sportswriter John Lardner wrote in 1938: "It nearly wrecked baseball for all eternity....The public came within a whisker's breadth of never seeing another box score, never heckling another umpire, never warming another hot stove. It was close — too close for comfort."

Lardner's account was not pure hyperbole. The unfolding Black Sox scandal triggered a flood of reports — accurate and otherwise — of other fixes by other players, including some of the game's brightest stars. There was talk of suspending the World Series and canceling the 1921 season. As it became obvious that this was not an isolated affair, the lords of baseball belatedly realized that they had to take quick and decisive action to save the game. As a result, in November 1920 they

BABE RUTH

Ruth was featured on the cover of a 1928 Baseball Magazine.

George Herman "Babe" Ruth dominated his sport like no athlete ever has.

Ruth began his career as a left-handed pitcher for the Red Sox, for whom he compiled a 78-40 record in four years. His $29^{2}/_{3}$ consecutive scoreless innings in World Series play was a record until 1961. But Ruth was such a good hitter that in 1919 he became a full-time outfielder and set a new home run record with 29, while also leading the league in runs, RBI, and slugging.

Ruth was sold to the Yankees that winter, and the next two seasons he hit an astounding 113 homers. His nickname became "The Sultan of Swat," and he was baseball's most beloved personality. When Yankee Stadium opened in 1923, it was called "The House That Ruth Built."

He led the league in homers three of the next four years; in 1927, as a member of the Bronx Bombers' fabled "Murderers' Row" lineup, Ruth broke his own home run record, clouting 60 round-trippers. During his 20 full seasons, Ruth led the league in homers 12 times, runs eight times, RBI six times, and slugging 13 times. His 714 lifetime homers were the record until Hank Aaron broke it in 1974. The Babe's lifetime average was .342, and he is first all time in home run percentage (8.5), walks (2,056), and slugging (.690). He is second all time in runs and RBI. Ruth hit 15 homers in 41 World Series games and ranks in the top ten in nine Series offensive categories. Ruth was one of the first five players elected to the Hall of Fame in 1936.

The Black Sox players with their lawyers in 1920
(top). Eddie Cicotte (bottom left) with a friend in
1914. Cicotte had a 208-149 career mark. Two
sluggers (bottom right), Babe Ruth, left, and
Home Run Baker; Baker had 96 career home
runs in 13 years; Ruth surpassed that mark in
533 games.

THE 1920s

turned over effective control of the game to an autocratic federal court judge named Kenesaw Mountain Landis by appointing him as the sport's first commissioner.

Judge Landis, who had presided over the 1915 Federal League antitrust suit, was able to restore the public's faith in the "National Pastime," and he did it by ruthlessly purging the game of its crooked elements. His first action was to place a lifetime ban on the eight Black Sox, even though they were acquitted in their 1921 conspiracy trial for lack of evidence. Landis knew what he was doing. Though several reports of attempts to influence the outcome of games surfaced through much of the 1920s, the rampant game-rigging of the preceding decade was eliminated. By one count, Landis banned, suspended, or blacklisted 20 players from organized ball because of their ties, or suspected connections, with gambling on the outcomes of baseball games. He also outlawed the once common practice of contending teams "rewarding" noncontenders for defeating their opponents. The owners eventually came to regret the power they ceded to the vitriolic Landis, but his puritan imprint on the game, coupled with Ruth's heroics, were greatly needed salves for baseball's festering wound.

The game, of course, survived the scandals and subsequently flourished. The 1920s became known as the "Golden Age of Sports," largely because of baseball's grip on the national consciousness. Many of the greatest players in the game's history displayed their skills during the decade, including such holdovers from the dead-ball era as Ty Cobb, Rogers Hornsby, Tris Speaker, and George Sisler. Long-time pitchers Walter Johnson, Grover Cleveland Alexander, and the last spitballer,

Burleigh Grimes, also performed in this decade. The 1920s also spawned a flock of new heroes headed by Lou Gehrig, Al Simmons, Jimmie Foxx, Paul Waner, and Mel Ott. A full 35 percent of the immortals residing in Cooperstown played during the 1920s.

Yet Ruth clearly outshined the others. Not only did he create a new style of play in 1920, he almost single-handedly prevented a widespread repudiation of the game at the turnstiles in 1921 following the Black Sox scandal. As attendance tumbled in both leagues, Ruth retained the public's interest by fashioning perhaps the greatest single season in baseball history. In 1921, the Bambino blasted 59 home runs, batted .378, knocked home a record 171 runs, and scored 177 times, the highest total in the century. En route to slugging .846 that year he also collected 204 hits, of which 44 were doubles and 16 were triples, giving

Mel Ott began his 22-year major league career in 1926 at age 17.

RAY CHAPMAN KILLED BY PITCH

In 1920, Carl Mays was a veteran New York Yankees pitcher who liked to brush hitters off the plate with fastballs. Ray Chapman was a slick-fielding, solid-hitting shortstop for the Cleveland Indians. On August 16, a tragic incident occurred that links them forever in baseball history.

From the turn of the century to the 1920s, pitchers clearly had the advantage in baseball. Unlike today, when balls are replaced for having the slightest mark on them, baseballs in those years could become as dark as an early evening sky and stay in a game. Infielders would rub balls in their tobacco and licorice-stained gloves, and pitchers would cut and spit on them.

Baseball historians theorize that Mays was using just such a discolored ball when he hit Chapman in the head with a pitch in the fifth inning, a pitch that knocked him unconscious and caused his death the following day. Chapman is the only major leaguer ever to perish from an on-field incident. Even baseball officials of the time speculated that Chapman probably didn't see the dirty ball. This led to a limited ban on spitballs in 1921. Umpires were also now required to keep clean balls in play.

The new rules had far-reaching effects. With the balls easier for hitters to see and more difficult for pitchers to control, offense, led by sluggers like Babe Ruth, became the dominant force in the game during the 1920s and 1930s.

Carl Mays (top left), whose pitch killed Ray Chapman in 1920, was one of the greatest pitchers of the late 1910s and early 1920s. Mays won 20 games five times, he led the league in complete games twice, and he ended his 15-year career with a 208-126 record and a 2.92 earned run average. His best season came in 1921, when he went 27-9 with an A.L.-leading 336⅔ innings pitched. Burleigh Grimes (top middle) won 20 games during five different seasons in the decade. According to legend, before he became a professional baseball player Grimes worked from dawn to dusk in a lumber camp for a dollar a day, and he maintained a rough-and-tumble lifestyle for 19 years in the big leagues. He always pitched with a one-day growth of beard (earning the nickname "Ol' Stubblebeard") to toughen his already intimidating appearance. Al Simmons (top right) started his career in 1924 with the Philadelphia A's. He hit .308 in his rookie season, the first of 13 seasons he batted over .300. Judge Kenesaw Mountain Landis (left) ruled baseball with an iron fist for more than two decades. He was the judge in the 1914 Federal League case, and his refusal to rule against the baseball agreement won for him a czar position in baseball five years later.

145

THE 1920s

him an all-time-high 457 total bases. That got the fannies back in the seats, to paraphrase a latter-day promoter.

The story of Ruth's arrival in New York is well-known. A brilliant pitcher early in his career, Ruth was moved to the outfield full time in 1919, after leading the league in home runs the year before as a part-time player. He proceeded to swat a record 29 home runs in 1919, an impressive feat considering that only nine blows were struck at his home field, Fenway Park, and the schedule had been shortened to 140 games. But Red Sox owner Harry Frazee abruptly sold his new drawing card to the Yankees for $125,000 prior to the 1920 season — after Frazee took a bath financing a Broadway show (*No No Nanette*) — a deal that stands as the worst decision in Red Sox (or baseball) history. Stripped of the game's greatest talent, the Sox fell into a well of mediocrity from which they did not emerge until 1946.

Once in New York, Yankees owner Jacob Ruppert doubled Ruth's salary to $20,000 for the 1920 season. The Babe repaid this generosity by doubling Yankees attendance at the Polo Grounds and nearly doubling his home run output. His 54 home runs that year must be regarded as a turning point in the game's history. While several players have since exceeded the total, at the time it was regarded as a staggering achievement. Ruth — who personally exceeded the home run totals of every other major league club that year — was the prime factor in a 40-percent jump in American League attendance, took a good deal of the sting out of the Black Sox scandal, and rewrote game strategy all in a year's work. Brash and bawdy, he emerged as the perfect hero for the Roaring '20s. The

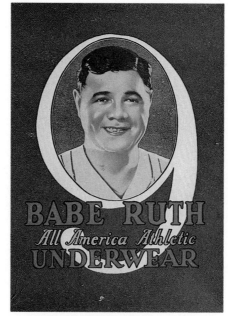

The Babe hawked athletic underwear.

Babe spent close to 15 years commanding the attention of the American public as has no other athlete in sports history, and he is still considered the greatest player to ever take the field.

The newly crowned "Sultan of Swat" made an immediate and enduring impression on the game. In the wake of his monumental 1920 season, home run production soared in both leagues. In the years preceding Ruth's full-time move to the outfield, the American League record for home runs in a season was 16, set by Socks Seybold in 1902. Gavvy Cravath, playing in Philadelphia's tiny Baker Bowl, won six National League home run crowns in the 1910s without hitting more than 24 balls out in a season. Before Ruth, seven home run titles in the 18-year history of the American League were won with fewer than ten blows.

The game's changing emphasis is further revealed by the fact that in 1919 the American League hit a record 241 home runs. The league average in the 1920s was almost twice that. National League batters fared even better. After hitting a meager 207 home runs in 1919, the senior circuit sluggers went on to average 521 four-base blows a year in the 1920s, including a high of 754 home runs in 1929. As balls started sailing out of major league parks with increasing frequency, stolen bases and sacrifices — two staples of the dead-ball era — fell dramatically and did not

GEORGE SISLER

Ask who was the best first baseman of the 1920s and fans immediately respond, "Lou Gehrig." But Gehrig's reign didn't begin until the decade's second half. During the first five years, the honor belonged to George Sisler.

Like Babe Ruth, Sisler began his career as a lefthanded pitcher. He went 4-4 with a 2.83 ERA for the St. Louis Browns in 1915, but he also hit .285 in 66 games as a first baseman and outfielder. Converted to first permanently in 1916, he hit .305 before becoming a hitting, fielding, and baserunning machine over the next 13 years of his career. He batted over .300 13 times (most of them with the Browns), winning his first A.L. batting title in 1920 with a .407 average, establishing a league record with 257 hits, and playing every inning of every game. In 1922, "Gorgeous George" batted .420, leading the league in hits, runs, triples (his third straight year with 18), and stolen bases with a career-high 51.

A debilitating sinus infection forced him to miss the entire 1923 season, and though he wasn't quite the same player upon his return in 1924, he wasn't too shabby either. He batted over .300 six of the next seven years and won his fourth stolen base crown with 27 in 1927.

Sisler still shares the A.L. record for the most seasons leading league first basemen in assists (six) and ended his career in 1930 with a .340 lifetime average. He was elected to the Hall of Fame nine years later.

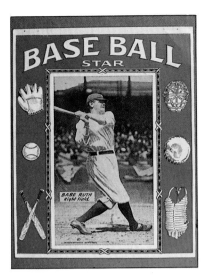

Babe Ruth enjoys a cigar while batting (middle). Ruth, featured on the cover of Strength *magazine (top right), revised the notion of a hitter. Big power hitters who could hit home runs became the norm on every team by the end of the decade. A notebook cover (top left) has Ruth as the right fielder. The Bambino lent his name to a baseball game (bottom left), Barbasol shaving cream (bottom middle), and Remington .22 cartridges (bottom right).*

THE 1920s

again become significant offensive weapons until the 1960s.

Nineteen-twenty has been christened the dawn of the so-called "lively ball" era. But what actually caused the increase in offense is a matter of considerable debate. Some historians argue that the baseball was never purposefully "juiced up" to create more offense. Instead, they argue that hitters were greatly aided by the absence of spitballs and other trick pitches, which were banned in 1920. (Only Burleigh Grimes and a handful of other pitchers under a "grandfather" clause were allowed to use such pitches.) Also, umpires began using more fresh balls in games. In baseball's leaner days, balls were kept in play indefinitely and got rubbed up, softened, darkened, and otherwise "deadened" by extensive use. The simple use of more new balls made it easier for batters to hit the ball hard and far. Furthermore, batters emulating Ruth's uppercut hitting style began swinging for the fences of the enclosed parks built in the 1910s and early 1920s, where the ball carried further. Whatever the factors,

players who batted in both eras were emphatic that the ball "had a rabbit in it" after 1920.

Actually, the increase in offensive output in the 1920s over the 1910s goes well beyond home runs and is unmatched in the game's modern history. All through the 1910s, the major league batting average hovered around .250 and pitchers allowed fewer than three runs a game. In 1919, the American League batting mark jumped to .268, then rose above .280 through the entire 1920s. The league earned run average dipped below four runs a game in only two seasons. A similar pattern prevailed in the National League. In the 1920s, outfielders began to play deeper and further apart, thus widening the alleys in which line drive hitters belted the ball.

A quick study of the record books confirms the extent to which baseball worshipped at the altar of offense in the decade. Baseball's top average hitters — Hornsby, Cobb, Sisler, and Harry Heilmann — exceeded the sacred .400 barrier seven times in the decade. Fourteen of the top 25 batting averages of this century, and 34 of the top 70, were recorded in the 1920s. Eight of the top ten slugging averages in history were posted in the decade, including six tallied by the incomparable Ruth. Six of the top ten runs-scored totals of the century, including four by the Babe, were established in the period. Existing 20th-century single-season records for batting average, slugging average, total bases, hits,

Athletics catcher Mickey Cochrane (left) and Tigers outfielder Harry Heilmann.

ROGERS HORNSBY

There's a scene in *The Winning Team,* the film biography of Pete Alexander (played by Ronald Reagan), in which the pitcher serves up a fat pitch to rookie Rogers Hornsby so the kid won't be sent to the minors. "That's the best chance I'll ever get," the movie Hornsby says. Only in America could a 1980s president save the career of a 1920s player in a 1950s movie.

Hollywood could have devoted a movie to Hornsby, especially since he is considered history's greatest righthanded hitter. Hornsby didn't reach the magical 3,000-hit mark, but he conjured up some other amazing numbers to earn the nickname "The Rajah." As a Cardinal, he led the N.L. in batting six straight years (1920 to '25), hitting over .400 three times.

Beginning in 1916 — over 16 full seasons with the Cardinals, Giants, Braves, and Cubs — Hornsby led the league four times in doubles, twice in homers, five times in runs scored, four times in RBI, and nine times in slugging percentage. He won the triple crown in 1922 and 1925, and the MVP in 1925 and '29. In 1926, he became the Cardinals' player/manager and led the team to its first pennant and world championship, an upset seven-game win over the Yankees. Hornsby won his last batting title with the Braves, batting .387 in 1928, and led the Cubs to the World Series in 1929.

Hornsby retired in 1937 with a lifetime average of .358, second on the all-time list, and was elected to the Hall of Fame in 1942.

Babe Ruth instructs a youngster on a proper grip (top left). Ruth was more than just a home run hitter. His .342 lifetime batting average is tenth on the all-time list. He hit over .300 in 17 different seasons, the first coming in 1915 and the last in 1933. Ruth batted over .350 in eight different seasons, and his highest average was .393 in 1923. His .474 career on-base average is second all time (Ted Williams has a career on-base average of .483). Ruth's .545 on-base percentage in 1923 is third all time, while his .530 on-base average in 1920 is fourth on the list. An uncut sheet of transfers (bottom left) pictures baseball players and boxers. The Hall of Famers on the sheet include Ray Schalk, Red Faber, Zach Wheat, Dave Bancroft, Tris Speaker, Grover Cleveland Alexander, Casey Stengel, Babe Ruth, and Ty Cobb. Yankee Stadium (bottom right) was filled for the 1926 World Series.

THE 1920s

runs, and walks were all posted in the Golden Age. Whatever they did or didn't do to the ball, the game changed suddenly, dramatically, and irrevocably in the 1920s.

Equipment innovations followed in short order. As players saw Ruth profit from hitting home runs, they quickly switched to thick-barreled bats with thin handles that increased bat speed and generated more force. Fielders soon realized that their existing mitts were inadequate for the faster-paced game, and the 1920s saw the introduction of a new generation of fielding gloves that were larger and better padded than their predecessors. Better gloves and more sharply hit balls led to more exciting fielding plays, as is reflected by a rise in double plays after 1920. Owners contributed to the home run frenzy in the decade by altering the dimensions of their fields as an aid to their sluggers.

All the new-found action on the field created a lot of commotion at the gate. Major league attendance topped 9 million in 1920, up from 6.5 million in the condensed 1919 season, and averaged 9.3 million a year through the 1920s. The previous decade saw only 5.6 mil-lion fans a year pass through the turnstiles. Prior to the 1920s, the National League attendance peak came in 1908 and slipped as low as 1.4 million in 1918. A.L. totals fared better in the 1910s but still showed an enormous jump from 1920 on. Baseball owners saw an immediate link between the churned up offense and rising attendance totals, and unlike in other eras, they did nothing to discourage the growing imbalance between batters and pitchers.

Ironically, the frenzy on the field lent stability to the business in the 1920s, once Judge Landis succeeded in restoring the game's integrity. No competing leagues arose to challenge the primacy of the majors as had the Federal League and even the American League in preceding decades. The same 16 franchises remained in operation in the same locations, and, with the exception of the Yankees, in the same parks. The players remained fairly docile in their relationships with the owners, and many players prospered. As salary levels rose, more players signed directly out of high school and worked their way up through the minors, so the clubs fielded fewer collegians as the decade progressed.

Teams continued to be constructed mainly by the purchasing of players from minor league clubs and other big league teams. As a result, the wealthiest teams tended to fare the best. The Yankees, under the strong ownership of brewery magnate Jacob Ruppert, spent lavishly to acquire talent while winning six pennants in the decade. They were rewarded by

The Babe signs his 1928 contract with Yankees owner Jacob Ruppert, right.

THE LONGEST GAME: BOSTON VS. BROOKLYN

Big Ed Konetchy was the Brooklyn Robins' first baseman in 1920.

The game between the Brooklyn Robins and the Boston Braves on May 1, 1920, began innocuously enough. The teams' hurlers, the Robins' Leon Cadore and the Braves' Joe Oeschger, matched zeros for four innings. Brooklyn broke through with a run in the fifth, and Boston tied it in the bottom of the sixth. Neither team would score for another 20 innings.

The Braves threatened to win it in the ninth, but a double play with the bases loaded sent the game into extra frames. The pitchers were almost unhittable for the next seven innings, when Brooklyn loaded the bases with one out. Again, a double play ended the rally. Innings were being played at a rapid rate as batters swung at everything and were getting increasingly tired doing it. When they reached the 23rd, the N.L. record for longevity set in 1917 was broken. Two innings later, the major league record set in 1906 had bitten the dust. The game was almost four hours old, darkness had set in, and, amazingly, the starting pitchers were still throwing.

With a new record established after the 26th inning, umpire Barry McCormick finally called the game. Each team had used only 11 players and just 185 batters got only 24 hits. The Robins, it turned out, didn't learn a lesson from all this. They played 13- and 19-inning games the next two days and lost both.

Switch-hitting Max Carey (top left), who played the outfield for the Pittsburgh Pirates from 1910 to 1926 and for the Brooklyn Dodgers from 1926 to 1929, was one of the National League's answers to Ty Cobb. Unfortunately, Carey spent much of his career in Cobb's long shadow. Carey batted over .300 six times, had a lifetime on-base average of .351, and scored 100 or more runs in a season five times. Carey led his league in stolen bases ten times to Cobb's six and finished with 738 thefts, fifth all time after Lou Brock, Cobb, Rickey Henderson, and Eddie Collins. An excellent center fielder, Carey retired as the all-time N.L. leader in outfield putouts and double plays. American League and National League stars toured Japan in 1920 and received prize money (bottom left). The professionals also played Japanese players. Detroit Tigers catcher Eddie Ainsmith (bottom right) tags out a player from Mieji University who tried to steal home.

THE 1920s

averaging more than one million fans a year, the highest in the majors. The Giants, Cubs, and Tigers, while lacking the Yankees' success in the standings, also flourished at the gate.

Several other franchises, however, struggled to survive. The Red Sox's Harry Frazee sold many of his best players, in addition to Ruth, thus condemning a once powerful club to seven last-place finishes in ten years. Similarly, the cross-town Braves, drawing a meager 250,000 fans a year, finished last or next to last eight times in the decade. It became increasingly apparent that some cities were unable to support two teams, even though clubs' overhead costs were minuscule by current standards. In Philadelphia, Connie Mack's A's ended a seven-year stay in the American League cellar in 1922 and gradually rose to the top by decade's end, but like the Phillies, had a rough time turning a profit.

St. Louis was the smallest of the two-team cities, and it was reflected in the clubs' payrolls. The Browns entire player outlay in 1925, including the salary of its star player Sisler, was barely $100,000, roughly one quarter of what Ruppert paid his players. To cope with St. Louis' limited revenue potential in the days before radio and television income, Cardinal manager/president Branch Rickey developed a minor league "farm system" to funnel low-cost talent to his club.

Rickey joined the Cardinals as manager in 1917 and in 1920 became club president as well. He was the leading innovator of his time and was considered a great judge of talent. His farm system was established by purchasing several "independent" minor league teams and signing "working agreements" with others, which enabled him to sign players cheaply and control them at a young age. Using this system, Rickey developed such players as Jim Bottomley, Pepper Martin, and Dizzy Dean, and Rickey won five pennants between 1926 and 1934. His system was so successful that after buying pitcher Jesse Haines in 1919, the club didn't purchase another established player for 25 years.

The Cardinals' methods, however, drew sharp criticism from Commissioner Landis and minor league operators, who said that a loss of independence would kill the minor leagues. At the time, selling young talent to the big leagues was a major source of revenue for the clubs. But Rickey and his system prevailed, and the practice became widespread in the 1930s and 1940s. By then, Rickey had unwittingly helped save the minors from bankruptcy; without the support of the big leagues, minor leagues might not have survived the Depression, World War II, and later the rise of other entertainment options (especially television). Yet in the 1920s, baseball's booming popularity provided profits for club owners at every spectrum of the professional ranks.

While the largess was not evenly distributed, the 1920s were lucrative times for baseball people. Major league attendance topped 9.5 million in 1929, and gate receipts reached $17 million. Ruth

The 1925 Kansas City Monarchs.

HARRY HEILMANN

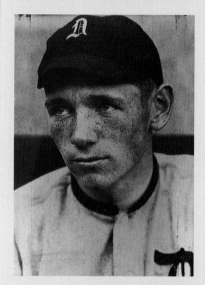

Harry Heilmann is probably the most underrated great player of the 1920s, most likely because he never played on a pennant winner and didn't hit a lot of home runs.

But "Slug" Heilmann could hit. In 1919 he first hit over .300, and then he made it a habit. During the 1920s, he won four batting titles with astronomical averages — .394 in 1921, .403 in 1923, .393 in 1925, and .398 in 1927. Heilmann won his last two batting championships on the final day of the season. In 1925, he made up almost 50 points on Tris Speaker in the final month. While Speaker sat out the last day with an injury, Heilmann went three-for-six in the first of a doubleheader to take the lead. But instead of sitting out the nightcap, he went three-for-three and won the title by four points. Two years later, he trailed Al Simmons by a point going into the last day. While Simmons went two-for-five, Heilmann went ahead with a four-for-four in the first of a double-bill. Again, he played the second game and belted three hits to win his fourth crown.

Heilmann drove in more than 100 runs eight times, scored more than 100 four times, and hit more than 40 doubles in a season seven times. He ended his 17-year career in 1932 with a .342 lifetime average. It took Heilmann 20 years to make the Hall of Fame. Today, some players with half of his numbers are getting into Cooperstown on the first ballot.

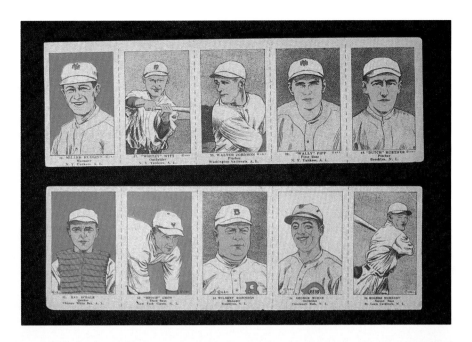

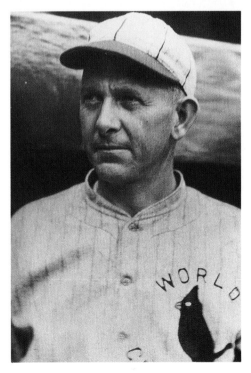

These strip cards (top) are from 1924. The 1929 Philadelphia A's (middle), with Connie Mack in the center, were 104-46. The Athletics won three pennants from 1929 to '31; Mack managed the team for 19 more years without another one. Branch Rickey (bottom left) developed the modern minor league system. Baseball commissioner Landis was against the system and forced Rickey to give up many of his signees, but the system not only endured but probably saved many minor leagues during the Depression years. Jesse Haines (bottom right) was the last player purchased from another team by Rickey.

THE 1920s

pulled down $70,000 in 1929, and the average salary for big leaguers was roughly $7,000. Though that may sound paltry by today's standards, it's not a bad sum considering that the major league average in the mid-1960s was only $14,000.

As the decade drew to a close, baseball had never had it so good. Then on October 29, 1929, Black Friday, the bottom fell out. The stock market crash not only cost many players and owners a great deal of money, it also set off the Depression, which wiped out the prosperity and good will built up throughout the country in the 1920s. Baseball, like everything else, was hit hard by the Depression, and it set off an economic retrenchment that took the game nearly ten years from which to emerge.

1920

Imagine how an American League pitcher must have felt in the summer of 1920, stripped of his trick pitches and facing a 230-pound behemoth who was making

George Sisler had 137 runs and 122 RBI in '20.

a mockery of his profession. History remembers the 54 home runs Babe Ruth blasted that year, but his offensive mastery in 1920 went far beyond that. He also batted .376 and led the league in a bushelful of other categories, including runs scored (158) and RBI (137). His slugging average that year, .847, is the highest in the history of the game.

Actually, a pitcher got very little reprieve anywhere he went that year, or in following years for that matter. Batters from every team gladly shared in the new-found offensive bounty. Home runs jumped by more than 50 percent, and the league batting average climbed by 15 points that season. Tris Speaker, the 32-year-old player/manager for the Cleveland Indians, belted .388 that year but fell 19 points short of the batting title. Joe Jackson, in his last hurrah, batted .382, and drove in 121 runners for the White Sox. Sisler, a 27-year-old first baseman with the St. Louis Browns, won the batting crown with a .407 average and rapped 257 hits, another record that stands as a monument to the new age of baseball.

But the American League wasn't only about batting feats in 1920. The season also produced one of the most dramatic pennant races in baseball history. While Brooklyn surprised everybody in the National League by coasting to an easy pennant victory, Cleveland eked out the franchise's first flag in a three-way fight that went the distance in the A.L.

The Indians boasted the league's most productive offense, featuring three hitters with more than 100 runs batted in, and a pitching staff that was anchored by 31-game winner Jim Bagby. The Tribe was clinging to a slim lead over Chicago and New York in mid-August when tragedy struck. Ray Chapman, their outstanding shortstop, was knocked unconscious by Yankees pitcher Carl Mays in a beaning incident on August 16 in the Polo Grounds. He never recovered and died the next day, the only player in big league history to be killed by an injury sustained on the field. To replace Chapman, the Indians acquired Joe Sewell, who batted .329 down the stretch.

While the Indians struggled to overcome the loss of their short-

BURLEIGH GRIMES

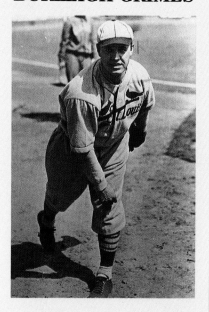

If Burleigh Grimes tried to pitch in the major leagues now, he'd probably be considered a deadly weapon. Not only did Grimes effect a mean-looking mound demeanor during his 1920s heyday, but he would regularly brush back hitters and threw the game's best spitball, which was a legal pitch for Grimes until 1934, because of a "grandfather" ruling.

Grimes' first full season (1917) was so bad that the Pittsburgh Pirates traded him to Brooklyn, where he became an instant star. He went 19-9 his first year with the Dodgers, and between 1920 and 1927 he reeled off 148 victories, including four 20-win seasons.

Grimes was traded to Pittsburgh in 1928 and, at age 35, went 25-14 for the Pirates, leading the National League in wins, starts, complete games, innings pitched, and shutouts. He helped the St. Louis Cardinals win the pennant in 1930 and 1931 and won two games in the Cards '31 Series win.

Grimes, who threw a curve, slider, changeup, and screwball along with the spitter, was also one of baseball's best fielding and hitting pitchers. He led N.L. pitchers in total chances a record seven times, and his lifetime batting average was .248 (in 1,535 at-bats).

When he retired after the '34 season, his record was 270-212, which was good enough to get him into the Hall of Fame in 1964.

In 1920, Babe Ruth hit .376, slugged an all-time best .847, scored 158 runs, drove in 137 runs, smashed 54 home runs, had an on-base average of .530, walked 148 times, and even stole 14 bases.

THE 1920s

stop, the defending champion White Sox mounted their own late-season charge despite open turmoil in the clubhouse. Led by Jackson and veteran Eddie Collins (.369 batting average) on offense and by four 20-game winners on the mound, Chicago showed signs of overtaking the Tribe, until Jackson and pitcher Eddie Cicotte confessed their involvement in the 1919 Series fix to a Chicago grand jury in mid-September. With two weeks to play, White Sox owner Charles Comiskey suspended seven Series conspirators (Gandil didn't play in 1920), and Chicago slipped to 2 games back at the end. The scandal sent the franchise skidding through a long period of decline. It fell to seventh place in 1921, did not finish in the first division again until 1936, and did not reclaim the pennant until 1959.

The Yankees landed 3 games out that season, but recorded the best record, 95-59, in the franchise's 20-year history. Ruth teamed with first baseman Wally Pipp and shortstop Roger Peckinpaugh to produce the second most runs in the league, while Mays joined with Bob Shawkey, Jack Quinn, and Rip Collins to record 78 wins. The club's attendance at the Polo Grounds rose from 620,000 to 1.3 million that season, and the franchise put the league on notice that it had become a force to contend with.

In the National League, the Brooklyn Dodgers jumped from fifth place to first and captured the flag by 7 games over John McGraw's Giants. Brooklyn was paced by spitballer Burleigh Grimes, who went 23-11 with a 2.22 ERA. The pitching staff emerged as the club's strong suit by posting a league-leading 2.62 ERA. It also turned out to be the best staff ERA of the 1920s. The league-wide earned run average in 1920 was

Casey Stengel was a part-time starting outfielder for the Phillies in 1920, hitting .292.

3.13, up slightly from 2.91 the year before. Four teams allowed less than three runs a game. Chicago's Grover Cleveland Alexander led all N.L. pitchers with 27 wins, 363 innings pitched, and a 1.91 ERA. Pittsburgh's 38-year-old right-hander Babe Adams furnished a 2.16 earned run average and had a league-high eight shutouts.

National League offensive production in 1920 was modest compared to the new standards being set in the American League. Philadelphia's Cy Williams led the N.L. with 15 home runs, and New York's George Kelly drove in 94 runs to lead the league. The best hitter in the league that year was St. Louis' Rogers Hornsby. The 24-year-old second baseman batted .370 and, like Kelly, knocked in 94 men. It was the first of Hornsby's National League record six straight batting crowns. His Cards, however, finished in sixth place.

The Giants had the most productive offense in the league, scoring 682 runs, but that total would have ranked as only sixth best in the stoked up American League. More indicative of the old style of play were the fourth-place Pirates, who batted .257 while managing a meager 16 home runs. The club, however, did lead the league in stolen bases with 181.

Several rule changes were implemented in 1920. In addition to the limited ban on spitballs and

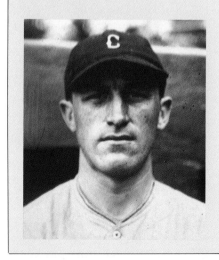

156

Red Faber (bottom left) started 39 games in 1920, which led the American League. He won 20 games three years in a row from 1920 to '22 for the White Sox. Giants lefthander Art Nehf (bottom right) was 21-12 in 1920 and 20-10 in 1921. A 1920s Spalding baseball trophy (top).

other trick pitches, it was decided that game-winning home runs would be ruled as such, rather than by the number of bases needed to score the winning run. For example, prior to that ruling, if a game was tied in the bottom of the ninth inning and the host team belted a home run with a runner on third, the blast was scored a single, and only one run was credited to the team. Also since then, a ball knocked over the fence is judged fair or foul by where the ball cleared the fence, not where it landed.

In the best-of-nine World Series matchup that year, Cleveland won five games to two, primarily on the strength of Stan Coveleski's three complete-game victories. In the seven games played, Brooklyn managed only eight runs and batted .205. Manager Speaker, who proved to be an inspirational leader following the death of Chapman, led the Tribe with six runs scored and batted .320. The Series also featured the only unassisted triple play in World Series history, turned by Indians second baseman Bill Wambsganss. Elmer Smith's

grand slam was another Series first. After this fall classic, the Dodgers entered a period of decline that lasted until 1941, while the Indians were unable to climb back on top until 1948.

1921

The 1921 season started off on a down note following Commissioner Landis' banishment of the "Black Sox," and the ensuing trial led to a decline in attendance in both leagues. However, the action on the field, especially that supplied by Ruth, may have prevented a widespread exodus from the parks.

American League hitters had now fully adjusted to the new style of play. The league batting average climbed to .292, and home runs flew out 29 percent more frequently than the previous year's inflated total. Four teams posted club batting averages above .300, and the Tigers — led by outfielders Harry Heilmann and player/manager Ty Cobb — established an A.L. record .316 team batting mark. Heilmann, who credited Cobb with his dramatic improvement in hitting, belted .393 in winning the batting title, while the 34-year-old Cobb hit .388. Only one regular player in the league, Washington shortstop Frank O'Rourke, hit below .250. The Yankees and the Indians became the first teams to go over the 900 runs scored mark, and the league ERA soared from 3.79 to 4.28.

In this volcanic offensive climate, it was only natural that Ruth's Yankees emerged on top,

FRANKIE FRISCH

You look at Frankie Frisch's statistics and wonder what all the fuss was about. While he batted over .300 13 times in his 19-year career, he never led the National League in hitting. And only once did he lead the N.L. in hits and runs. But the man known as "The Fordham Flash" was a dynamic competitor, probably the first player to make people aware of "intangibles." Frisch may not have won many awards or set many records, but he helped create winners. His teams played in the World Series eight times.

Frisch joined John McGraw's Giants in 1919 after serving as captain of the baseball, football, and basketball teams at Fordham University. Frisch became an infield triple-threat on the Giants as well, playing second, third, and shortstop. Beginning in 1921, the year he won the first of his three stolen base crowns, Frisch led the Giants to two straight world championships and four straight pennants. In those four World Series he batted .300, .471, .400, and .333.

After the 1926 season, he was traded to the Cardinals for Rogers Hornsby and made the Giants regret the deal. In '27, Frisch batted .337, led the N.L. in steals, set two fielding records, and missed winning the MVP by one vote. During Frisch's ten full seasons with St. Louis, the team won three pennants and took the World Series in 1931, the year Frisch finally won the MVP. Frisch retired in 1937 with a lifetime .316 average and was elected to the Hall of Fame in 1947.

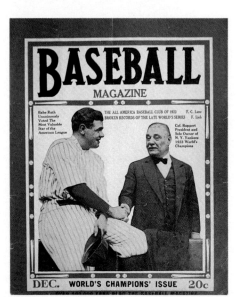

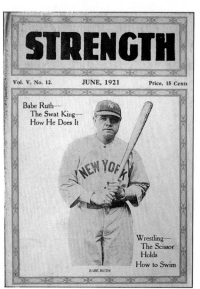

A 1923 Baseball Magazine *(left) and* Strength *magazine from 1921.*

The Chicago American Giants (top) were owned by Rube Foster, pictured in street clothes. He started the first organized league of black clubs in 1920. Foster had owned the Giants since 1911, but he figured that having a structured league would enhance his revenue. His Negro National League consisted of eight teams from midwestern cities. The 1921 Detroit Stars (middle) were part of the Negro National League. Max Flack (bottom left) was a Chicago Cubs outfielder from 1916 to 1922. He hit .302 in 1920 and scored 85 runs. Giants first baseman George Kelly (bottom right) led the National League in RBI in 1920 with 94. Kelly knocked in more than 100 runs in each of New York's pennant-winning seasons from 1921 to 1924. He was elected to the Hall of Fame in 1973.

Detroit Stars, 1921

capturing the first of the club's 33 pennants. In addition to Ruth's historic statistics, New York's cause was aided by Bob Meusel, who batted .318 with 24 home runs and 135 RBI, and by the acquisition of 19-game winner Waite Hoyt and catcher Wally Schang (who batted .316) from the Red Sox. Years later, en route to playing in six World Series with the Yankees and gaining admission to the Hall of Fame, Hoyt said of his move to the Yankees, "Thank God for Babe Ruth." Veteran shortstop Peckinpaugh scored 128 runs for the Yankees before moving over to the Senators the following year.

Cleveland mounted a strong bid to repeat until a late-season injury to Speaker caused the Tribe to limp home 4½ games back. Speaker hit .362 for the Indians, who batted .308 as a team. Larry Gardner chipped in with 115 RBI and 101 runs scored, while Cleveland also got terrific bench help from George Burns, Riggs Stephenson, and converted pitcher Smoky Joe Wood, who as an out-fielder batted .366 in 194 at-bats.

The "lively ball" style came into play in the National League in 1921, and, as expected, offensive output soared. The league batting average jumped 19 points to .289, and home runs increased by more than 75 percent. The Giants captured the first of four consecutive pennants by leading the league in runs scored. New York finished 4 games ahead of the Pittsburgh Pirates, which had the league's top pitching staff. The Giants clinched the pennant in late August by engineering a five-game sweep of the Pirates that knocked the Bucs out of first place for good.

The St. Louis Cardinals, fielding a lineup with seven starters batting over .300, finished in third place, 7 games out. Every team in the league batted over .275, and no pitching staff prevented less than three runs a game. Hornsby consolidated his position as the league's best hitter by batting .397 with 126 RBI and 131 runs scored. Kelly claimed home run honors by belting 23.

The 1921 season produced the first of 13 "subway series" pitting New York City teams against one another. Although the Yankees jumped out to a 2-0 lead in the best-of-nine format, the Giants rallied to win in eight games. The tide turned after the Giants rebounded from being shut out in the first two games by scoring 13 runs and collecting 20 hits in Game Three. The Yankees' fate was sealed when Ruth sat out the last two games with a sore arm. The Giants won both by scores of 2-1 and 1-0.

1922

Offense, particularly the kind provided by home runs, continued as the predominant theme in 1922, but for a change, the real action was taking place in the National League. Suspended for a month by Judge Landis for barnstorming in the off-season, Babe Ruth relinquished the limelight to Rogers Hornsby. As the lively ball era got into full swing in the N.L., Hornsby produced a triple-crown year. He batted .401, crushed 42 homers,

George "Specs" Toporcer, a St. Louis Cardinals utility infielder, batted .324 in 1922 and .313 in 1924.

LOU GEHRIG

Lou Gehrig was one of the few players of the 1920s and 1930s who would probably be a super-star in today's game. Gehrig was 6' and 200 pounds, powerfully built, and incredibly durable. It is the ultimate sports irony that the man called "The Iron Horse" died at age 37 of a muscular disease that now bears his name.

Fresh out of Columbia University, where he was a football and baseball star, Gehrig became a full-time Yankee in 1925 and formed with Babe Ruth the most awesome one-two punch in baseball history. Though he played in Ruth's shadow for much of his career (the Babe got a lot of great pitches to hit with Gehrig batting behind him), Columbia Lou produced some equally impressive numbers. He batted over .300 12 straight times, led the A.L. three times in homers, four times in runs, and five times in RBI. He won the triple crown in 1934 and the MVP in 1936, when he hit 49 homers, scored 167 runs, and batted .354. He ranks third all time in RBI and slugging. Gehrig also played on six World Series champions and ranks in the top ten in ten World Series categories.

But Gehrig's most impressive achievement is the record he set that may never be broken — playing in 2,130 consecutive games between 1925 and 1939. After his illness forced him out of the lineup early in the '39 season, the Hall of Fame waived its rules and immediately inducted him into Cooperstown.

Shortstop Dave "Beauty" Bancroft (top left), pictured here in 1920, didn't hit much, which explains why he played with five teams — the Phillies, Giants, Braves, Dodgers, and Giants again — during his 16-year career. Most of his contemporaries agree with Giants manager John McGraw, however, that Bancroft was "the best shortstop in baseball, without a doubt." Success seemed to follow Bancroft around. He played on Philadelphia's 1915 pennant-winning club, and later he helped the Giants to three consecutive World Series from 1921 to '23. He led N.L. shortstops in nearly every defensive category and batted over .300 in each season from 1921 to 1923. When he retired in 1930, Bancroft was the all-time major league leader in double plays by a shortstop. Rogers Hornsby (bottom left) is 17th on the all-time total bases list, beating out such power hitters as Mickey Mantle, Willie McCovey, and Ernie Banks. His .358 career batting average is the National League's best of all time. Urban Shocker (bottom right) led the A.L. with 27 wins in 1922. He won at least 20 games in four straight seasons for the Browns from 1920 to '23.

THE 1920s

and drove in 152 runs, while also leading the league in hits, doubles, and runs scored. His 450 total bases that year is the highest in National League history. It became apparent that Hornsby, who never hit higher than .327 or knocked more than eight home runs before 1920, had become a major benefactor of the new playing style.

Despite his Ruthian year in 1922, Hornsby's Cardinals could muster no better than a tie for third. Offense ruled the roost in 1922, and the Giants crowed the loudest. The top six teams in the league all batted at least .290, and the league ERA climbed to over 4.00. For the first time in league history, no qualifying pitcher compiled an ERA under 3.00. New York finished in first place with a potent attack featuring seven hitters with batting averages over .320, while the pitching staff posted the lowest ERA (3.45) in the league. Cincinnati came in second, 7 games back, though its staff ace, 31-year-old left-hander Eppa Rixey, was the league's top winner at 25-13.

In the American League, the early absence of Ruth and Meusel, who was also suspended by Landis, enabled the St. Louis Browns to climb into the pennant race. Browns first baseman George Sisler sizzled all season and wound up with a .420 batting average while winning the newly inaugurated "Most Valuable Player" award. Teammate Ken Williams hit 39 home runs and drove in 155 runs to break Ruth's stranglehold on the home run title. The Brownies hit a cumulative .313 and finished at 93-61, the best record in club history. Yet their performance was good for only second place, as the Yankees' continued raiding of talent from the cash-hungry Red Sox lifted them over St. Louis by 1 game. This time, New York acquired the services of pitchers Bullet Joe Bush

(26-7) and Sad Sam Jones (13-13, eight saves), and infielders Everett Scott and Joe Dugan. The Tigers finished a far-off third, but player/manager Cobb batted .401, marking the third time in his remarkable career he topped the .400 mark.

One of the great pitching performances of the decade was turned in by Philadelphia's Eddie Rommel, "the father of the modern knuckleball." Rommel won 19 games as a starter and eight in relief for a club that finished seventh with only 65 victories and 89 defeats. He sandwiched that season between two years in which he lost a total of 42 games. Still, Rommel's befuddling delivery enabled Connie Mack's club to escape the cellar for the first time since 1914.

The Yankees and the Giants got together again in the World Series, playing in the revised best-of-seven format. This time, the Giants took control from the beginning. Limiting Ruth to a .118 batting average and the Yankees to 11 runs, the Giants beat the American League champs in four games plus a tie. Game Five also marked the last time the two teams would

Philadelphia A's hurler Eddie Rommel led the league in wins with 27 victories in 1922 and 21 in 1925.

DAZZY VANCE

Clarence Arthur "Dazzy" Vance was the National League's premier pitcher of the 1920s, even though he didn't get to the majors until he was 31 years old. A serious elbow injury had kept him away from the mound for five years between 1916 and 1921, but when he finally made the big leagues in 1922, Dazzy was dazzling.

The big righthander with a hard fastball and a sharp curve (one that contemporary Burleigh Grimes said "came in there like a scared snake") won 18 games in each of his first two years with the Brooklyn Dodgers. Vance's greatest year came in 1924 when he went 28-6 with a 2.16 ERA, 262 strikeouts, and 30 complete games. He became the first N.L. pitcher to win the Most Valuable Player award, beating out Rogers Hornsby, who batted .424. In 1925, Vance went 22-9, struck out 17 Cardinals in a ten-inning game, and pitched a no-hitter against Philadelphia in September.

Vance still holds the N.L. record for most consecutive seasons leading the league in strikeouts, a feat he accomplished during his first seven years in the league. He also led the N.L. in ERA in 1928 and 1930. Vance ended his career in 1935 with a 197-140 record and more than 2,000 strikeouts, statistics that earned him Hall of Fame recognition in 1955.

An action shot of the 1921 World Series opener (top) shows Giants outfielder Ross Youngs hitting a pitch back to Yankees hurler Carl Mays in the fifth inning. Frankie Frisch of the Giants is heading toward second base. George Sisler (middle left) hit .420 in 1922 for the Browns. He also led the league in runs with 134, triples with 18, and stolen bases with 51. He ended his career with a .340 batting average, a .468 slugging average, 1,284 RBI, and 1,175 runs scored. Heinie Groh (middle right) was a premier third baseman first for Cincinnati and then for the Giants. He batted over .300 four times in his 16-year career, and he retired in 1927 with a .292 lifetime average. Lefthander Eppa Rixey (bottom left) led the National League with 25 wins and 313⅓ innings pitched in 1922 for the Reds. Rixey won 266 games in a 21-year career that stretched from 1912 to 1933, first for the Phillies then for Cincinnati. He was a pitcher who tried to make batters swing at bad pitches. Baseball historians say that Rixey worked more batters to three-and-two counts than any other pitcher in history, yet he only averaged two walks a game over his entire career.

THE 1920s

share the Polo Grounds. Upset by being outdrawn by their tenants, the Giants canceled the Yankees' lease, prompting Yankees owner Jacob Ruppert to begin construction on a new $2 million stadium located just across the river from the Polo Grounds in the Bronx.

1923

When Yankee Stadium opened in 1923, the sports writers quickly dubbed it "The House That Ruth Built." Ruth and the Yankees christened it by winning their third consecutive pennant. The Babe started the season by homering in the first game played at the stadium and finished the year by being named Most Valuable Player. Along the way, he hit .393 and regained his home run crown by blasting 41 long balls, while driving in 131 runs and scoring 151 runs. For good measure he established the major league record by walking 170 times, enabling him to reach base on an astonishing 54.2 percent of his at-bats.

Meanwhile, the Yankees continued to plunder the Red Sox ros-

ter. This time Boston owner Harry Frazee unloaded 29-year-old left-handed pitcher Herb Pennock, who promptly posted a 19-6 record with New York in '23. In ten major league seasons before joining the Yankees, Pennock had compiled a 76-72 lifetime mark. In 11 seasons with New York he went 162-90. He also was undefeated in World Series play and was elected to the Hall of Fame in 1948. With the addition of Pennock, Yankees business manager Ed Barrow, a former Red Sox manager, had seven front-line players, including his top three pitchers, who were once employed by Frazee.

Barrow assembled an impressive mix of offense and pitching in 1923. In addition to Ruth's ongoing drubbing of American League pitchers, the Yankees staff sported the lowest ERA in the league that year, 3.66. As a result, New York coasted to a 16-game margin of victory over Detroit. Tigers outfielders continued to serve as the most prolific trio of hitters in baseball. Harry Heilmann captured his second batting title by cranking out a .403 batting average, while Cobb and Heinie Manush hit .340 and .334, respectively. Cleveland, which mounted the most potent attack in the league, finished third, 16½ games back. Player/manager Tris Speaker led the Tribe by batting .380 with 59 doubles and 130 RBI, while shortstop Joe Sewell batted .353 and knocked in 109 runners. St. Louis, the previous year's bridesmaid, fell to fifth place after an eye injury sidelined Sisler.

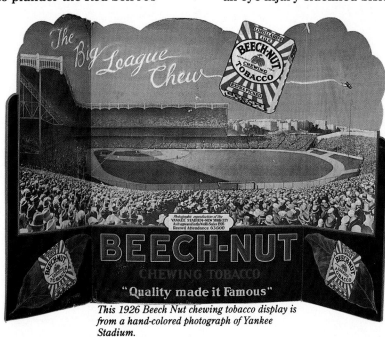

This 1926 Beech Nut chewing tobacco display is from a hand-colored photograph of Yankee Stadium.

WALTER JOHNSON WINS HIS FIRST SERIES

During his first 17 seasons, Walter Johnson had been the best pitcher the game had ever known. He had achieved everything a pitcher possibly could — except pitch in the World Series. In fact, Johnson hardly ever pitched on a winning Washington Senators team. But in 1924, at the age of 36, Johnson finally led the Senators to a pennant with his last incredible season — 23-7 record, a 2.72 ERA, 158 strikeouts, and six shutouts, all figures that led the American League.

In the Series, the Senators were facing the Giants, who had just won their fourth straight pennant. "The Big Train" pitched brilliantly in the opener. He struck out 12 but lost in the 12th inning 4-3. With the Series tied 2-2, Johnson pitched Game Five but was ineffective and lost 6-2.

The Senators won Game Six 2-1 to tie the Series. In Game Seven, Washington was down 3-1 in the eighth when they scored two to tie it. Even though Johnson had pitched eight innings just two days before, manager Bucky Harris sent his veteran to the mound in relief. Johnson held the Giants scoreless until the Senators batted in the bottom of the 12th. After a one-out double, an error on Johnson's infield bouncer put two men on base. Then Earl McNeely hit one of baseball's most famous ground balls. His roller hit a pebble and bounced over Giants third baseman Freddy Lindstrom, allowing the winning run to score. Walter Johnson and the Senators had their first world championship.

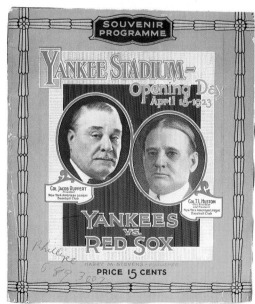

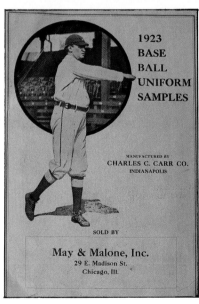

The crowds gather for opening day at monumental Yankee Stadium (top). This opening day program (bottom middle) from Yankee Stadium, April 23, 1923, features Jacob Ruppert. Stuffy McInnis (bottom left) hit .315 with 95 RBI for the Boston Braves in 1923. This 1923 uniform catalog (bottom right) features a picture of Cy Young on the cover.

THE 1920s

The Giants captured the National League crown once again by scoring the most runs in the league. New York earned its third consecutive pennant brandishing a wide array of weapons — led by Kelly, Frankie Frisch, Ross Youngs, and Irish Meusel. The Giants also received valuable contributions from reserve outfielder Casey Stengel.

The Reds again finished second, this time by 4¹/₂ games. Cincinnati compensated for a substandard offense by presenting the league's best pitching staff. Righthander Dolf Luque fashioned one of the best pitching seasons in the offensive-minded decade by posting a 27-8 record and an eye-popping 1.93 ERA that was a full two runs per game lower than the league average. Cy Williams, a 35-year-old outfielder with the Phillies, surprised the baseball world by poking 41 home runs in a

year when no one else cleared 22, but it did his team little good. Philadelphia still lost 104 games, and finished 45¹/₂ games back. It was a familiar story for the Phillies' faithful. In the 1920s, the club finished last or next to last nine times.

In their third straight World Series matchup, the Yankees finally emerged from under the Giants yoke, taking the Series four games to two. Ironically, though, the Yankees didn't fare well in their new stadium. They lost two of the three games played there, including Game One, which the Giants won 5-4 on an inside-the-park home run hit by the 32-year-old Stengel. He also homered in Game Three to beat the Yankees' ace Jones by a 1-0 score. The Yankees, however, swept the three contests at the Polo Grounds, and Ruth busted loose by hitting three home runs, helping the Yankees capture the first of their 22 world championships. The Series also was the first one to be broadcast on radio.

1924

The Yankees were poised to make it four pennant flags in a row in 1924 when they were derailed by The Big Train, pitcher Walter Johnson. The Hall of Fame hurler and his Washington Senator teammates put on a dazzling display of clutch playing down the stretch, winning 16 of their last 21 games to capture the first flag in club history by 2 games over the defending champions. The 36-year-old Johnson was the big story that year. The righthander posted a 23-7 record, struck out a league-high 158 batters, allowed only 2.72 runs per nine innings, and was selected the league's Most Valuable Player.

Washington's offense, though last in home runs due to the spaciousness of Griffith Stadium, boasted two excellent hitters. Goose Goslin hit .344 with a league-high 129 runs batted in, and Sam Rice batted .334 while scoring 106 runs. The club also had the league's top double play combination, pairing shortstop Roger Peckinpaugh with Bucky Harris. Player/manager Harris also made great use of a rookie relief specialist, Firpo Marberry, who pitched in 50 games that year and posted a record 15 saves. He was one of the first pitchers

Yankee Bob Meusel filled the void created by Babe's prolonged absence in '25 and led the A.L. in homers (33) and RBI (138).

PIE TRAYNOR

Pie Traynor is a name that invariably comes up in those arguments comparing great players of different eras. Until Brooks Robinson became hailed as the greatest fielding third baseman of all time, that title belonged to Harold Joseph Traynor.

During the 1920s and 1930s with the Pittsburgh Pirates, Traynor was just another guy who hit over .300 every year. While he accomplished that feat ten times, batting over .350 twice, he only knocked over 200 hits once and wasn't a home run hitter.

But Traynor was the best defensive third baseman of his time. He led the National League in putouts a record seven times and holds the N.L. record for lifetime putouts with 2,291. Praising his defensive skills, the saying went, "Twice Hornsby doubled down the left field line, and twice Pie threw him out."

Traynor played on his only world champion team in 1925 when he hit .320 and scored and drove in over 100 runs. He helped the Pirates win the World Series by batting .346 and fielding flawlessly. His best offensive season may have been 1930, when he had career highs in hitting (.366) and slugging (.509). While not a big power threat, Traynor drove in over 100 runs seven times and had an incredible batting eye. He struck out only 278 times in 17 years, and in 1929, he whiffed just seven times in 540 at-bats. He didn't strike out with the Hall of Fame either, being elected to Cooperstown in 1948.

The Sewell brothers (top left) Joe, left, and Luke, were two of three Sewell brothers to play in the big leagues in the 1920s and 1930s. Luke was a solid defensive catcher who played in 1,561 games behind the plate, mostly for the Cleveland Indians. Joe replaced Ray Chapman at shortstop for the Indians after Chapman was killed by a pitched ball in 1920. Joe and Luke remained teammates until 1931, when Joe went to the New York Yankees. An excellent gloveman, Joe batted .312 lifetime, drove in more than 100 runs twice, and scored 90 or more runs seven times. Amazingly, Joe struck out less than ten times in nine out of his 13 full seasons, and his 1932 performance stands alone in history: only three strikeouts in 503 at-bats. Gabby Hartnett (top right) became the Cubs regular catcher in 1924, and he responded by hitting .299 with 16 homers and 67 RBI. In 1925, Hartnett slugged 24 homers. From 1923 to 1926, Sam Rice (middle) scored 117, 106, and 111 runs for the Washington Senators. He hit .316, .334, and .350 in those years. In the '25 World Series, Rice batted .364, scored five runs, and drove in three runs. A shot from the 1923 World Series (bottom left) shows Babe Ruth in a pickle. Yankees third baseman Joe Dugan (bottom right) hit .302 and scored 105 runs in 1924.

THE 1920s

brought into games in critical situations to preserve a lead. He started 15 games in 1924, but the following year he appeared in 55 contests without making a start. In 1926, Marberry pitched in 64 games and tallied 22 saves, a record that held up until 1949.

Home runs dropped in the American League in '24, but batting averages and runs scored were once again on the upswing. The Yankees were not able to keep abreast of the league upturn in offense with the notable exception of Ruth, who won two of the three legs of the triple crown by batting .378 and swatting 46 home runs. Detroit again finished third, 6 games off the pace after getting another strong year from both Heilmann and Cobb. An exceptional individual performance was turned in by 37-year-old Eddie Collins. Playing for the last-place White Sox, Collins batted .349 and stole a league-best 42 bases.

Meanwhile in the National League, the Giants encountered stiff opposition in their effort to present manager John McGraw with his tenth pennant. A three-way battle developed between New York, Pittsburgh, and the dark-horse Brooklyn Dodgers, who only the year before finished a distant sixth. In the end, the Giants' over-powering lineup prevailed over the Dodgers' brilliant pitching by 1½ games, while Pittsburgh wound up 3 games out.

Out of the running, but not out of the limelight, was Rogers Hornsby, who recorded the highest batting average of the century that year when he hit .424. It was the Rajah's fifth consecutive batting crown, and it highlighted a five-year run, from '21 through '25, when Hornsby averaged an electrifying .401. It was also the fifth of six consecutive years in which Hornsby topped all National Leaguers in slugging, showing that his domination of the N.L. was nearly as complete as was Ruth's mastery over the American League.

The Giants fielded six regulars with batting averages over .300, including Youngs, who batted .356; Kelly, who drove home 136; and Frisch, who scored 121 runs. Brooklyn's offense was pretty well limited to Zach Wheat's .375 batting average and first baseman Jack Fournier's 27 home runs. Dodger pitching was another matter. Dazzy Vance was named the league's first Most Valuable Player, after going 28-6, with a league-low 2.16 ERA. He was paired with Burleigh Grimes, who finished with 22 wins.

Hank Gowdy was a catcher for both the Boston Braves and the New York Giants. He played in the big leagues in 17 different seasons from 1910 to 1930, and he ended his career with a .270 average.

In 1924, Vance was a 33-year-old righthander who had only recently mastered his overpowering fastball. Aside from two brief tours in 1915 and 1918, Vance didn't stick in the big leagues until 1922, when he managed an 18-12 record for the Dodgers as a 31-year-old rookie. That season he also led the league in strikeouts for the first of seven consecutive years. In '24, Vance struck out a career-high 262 batters, an astounding total considering that Grimes was the only other pitcher in the league to record more than 100 strikeouts.

The Pirates' third-place finish was spearheaded by two 24-year-olds, outfielder Kiki Cuyler and third baseman Pie Traynor, and 23-year-old shortstop Glenn Wright. Cuyler, playing in his first full season, batted .354 and stole 32 bases.

GOOSE GOSLIN

During the 1920s and 1930s, Leon Allen Goslin was the epitome of the word "clutch" and may have been baseball's first "Mr. October."

Sure, the lefthanded-hitting outfielder notched his share of over-.300 averages. He had 11 in his 18-year career and seven straight between 1922 and 1928, the year he won his only batting title, with a .379 average.

But Goslin shines when you look at his runs batted in totals. Starting in 1924 — when he led the American League (and Babe Ruth) with a career-high 129 RBI — Goslin drove in over 100 runs 11 times in 13 years, while playing with Washington, St.

Louis, and Detroit. He also scored over 100 runs seven times, led the league in triples twice, and hit a career-high 37 homers in 1930.

After Goslin led the Senators to pennants in 1924 and '25, he put on a show during the World Series, belting three homers in each Fall Classic, as Washington won the first and lost the second. Ten years later, Goose's single in the ninth inning of Game Six won the 1935 Series for Detroit.

Goslin's seven World Series homers place him tenth on the all-time list. He retired after 1938 with a .316 lifetime average, 2,735 hits, and 1,609 RBI. He entered the Hall of Fame in 1968.

EUROPEAN TOUR 1924
NEW-YORK GIANTS
CHICAGO WHITE-SOX

With the compliments of Bank Tours PARIS

Rogers Hornsby runs into the umpire after the tag was applied by Gabby Hartnett (top left) in a 1927 game. The umpire called Hornsby "safe" and then "out." Earle Mack, left, and his father confer (top right). The Giants and White Sox toured Europe in 1924 (bottom).

THE 1920s

The World Series was a tightly contested affair, with the Senators prevailing in seven games. The club was able to hoist the only world championship flag over the nation's capital by scoring a run in the bottom of the 12th inning of Game Seven when a ground ball took a bad hop over the head of Giants third baseman Fred Lindstrom. Four of the games were decided by one run. The Senators got two wins from lefthander Tom Zachary and two saves from Marberry. Walter Johnson lost the two games he started in the Series, but he nailed down a win in the decisive seventh game for the Senators by pitching four innings of scoreless relief.

1925

The Senators repeated in 1925, but the big story in baseball that year concerned Babe's bellyache. Felled in April by an intestinal abscess that required surgery, Ruth at last became a victim of his own famous appetite. Sidelined until June, Ruth struggled until September, when he was fined and suspended by manager Miller Huggins for insubordination. With and without Ruth in the lineup, the Yankees offense — with the exception of Bob Meusel and Earl Combs — disappeared, and the club tumbled all the way down to seventh place.

Despite the Yankees dismal performance, A.L. hitters turned in the league's highest batting average and runs scored total of the decade, while pitchers were saddled with a league-wide 4.39 ERA, also a high for the 1920s. The Senators, fresh off their Series win, again got strong performances from Goslin and Rice at the plate. Stan Coveleski, cast off from Cleveland, joined Walter Johnson as a 20-

game winner. Washington bested the resurgent Athletics by 8½ games.

Philadelphia, which had spent most of the past ten years serving as the league's doormat, kept pace with the defending champions until August, when it hit a 12-game skid and fell out of the race. The A's, however, did flash their potential — especially second-year man Al Simmons, who hit .384 with 24 home runs and 129 RBI. The team also debuted future Hall of Famers in catcher Mickey Cochrane and pitcher Lefty Grove, and gave a brief tryout to slugger Jimmie Foxx. But the most famous premier of all came on June 2, when Lou Gehrig became the Yankees first baseman and began a career that lasted for 2,130 consecutive performances over 15 years.

In 1923, Yankees first baseman Wally Pipp hit .304 and accumulated 108 RBI. He hit .295 in '24, with a league-leading 19 triples and 113 RBI. He had been New York's starting first baseman for a decade. According to some stories, in June 1925, Pipp asked to have his name scratched from the lineup card because he had a headache. Yankees manager Miller Huggins then put Lou Gehrig's name on the card at first base, and Gehrig proceeded to play 2,130 consecutive games.

ALEXANDER SAVES THE SERIES IN RELIEF

By 1926, most fans thought that Grover Cleveland Alexander was washed up. He was 39 years old, suffered from epilepsy, and had spent time in a sanitorium. But Cardinals player/manager Rogers Hornsby thought "Alex the Great" still had something left and signed him when he was released by the Cubs in mid-season.

It turned out to be a master stroke. Alexander won nine games, helping the Cards win their first pennant since 1888. After St. Louis lost the first game of the World Series to the mighty Yankees, Hornsby sent the cagey veteran to the mound in Game Two, and Alexander threw a four-hitter, retiring the last 21 men in a row. After the Yankees won two out of the next three, Alexander pitched a complete Game Six as the Cards won 10-2, tying the Series.

In Game Seven, St. Louis starter Jesse Haines took a 3-2 lead into the bottom of the seventh. But after getting two outs, Haines walked the bases loaded. Due up for the Yankees was the great Tony Lazzeri. Hornsby had seen Alexander strike Lazzeri out four times the previous day and brought Alexander in to pitch — a day after he'd thrown nine innings.

Alexander got Lazzeri to miss a first-pitch curve. Lazzeri belted the next pitch just foul. Then Alexander threw one more curve, and Lazzeri swung and missed. Alexander retired the Yankees in order in the eighth. The Cardinals became world champions when Ruth was caught stealing in the ninth.

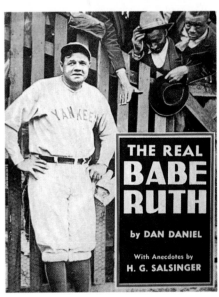

The New York Giants and the Chicago White Sox
(top) played a baseball circuit through Europe in
1924. The two keystone sackers in the 1924 World
Series (bottom left), Frankie Frisch, left, and
Bucky Harris, exchange greetings. While they both
hit .333, Harris had two homers, seven RBI, and
five runs scored to Frisch's no homers, no RBI,
and one run scored. Senators first baseman Joe
Judge (bottom middle) hit .385 in the Series and
scored four runs. Readers could discover the inside
story of Babe Ruth (bottom right).

THE 1920s

Tiger Harry Heilmann won his third batting title in dramatic fashion. He overcame nearly a 50-point deficit in September to overtake Cleveland's Tris Speaker on the last day of the season. Heilmann slashed six hits in nine at-bats in a double-header to finish at .393, while the 37-year-old Speaker closed out another sparkling season by hitting .389 in a sixth-place cause. Heilmann was joined in the Detroit outfield by Cobb, who hit .378, and Tigers newcomer Al Wingo, who batted .370. Meusel, freed from Ruth's shadow, led the league in home runs with 33 and runs batted in with 138.

In the National League, St. Louis' Rogers Hornsby replaced Branch Rickey as manager, was named the league's Most Valuable Player, and won his second triple crown all in one season. But it was the young Bucs who won the pennant, by 8½ games over the Giants. Led by Cuyler, Traynor,

and Wright, with ample help from veteran Max Carey, the Pirates fielded seven players who batted over .300 while becoming the first National League team to crack the 900-runs-scored barrier. Offense was on the rise throughout the league, as the aggregate ERA climbed from 3.87 to 4.27 and the league batting average rose nine points to .292. As usual, it was Hornsby who blazed the trail. He batted .403, hit 39 home runs, drove in 143 runs, and slugged .756, the highest in league history.

The Giants, despite the full-time addition of first baseman Bill Terry, suffered a severe drop in output from its batters and never seriously contended, relinquishing the N.L. crown they wore for four years. As for the Dodgers, the surprise team of '24, they slid back into sixth place, despite another superb effort by Vance. He won 22 games and lost only nine for a team that was 17 games below .500. He also fanned 221 batters. By comparison, Cincinnati's Dolf Luque was his runner-up with 140 strike-outs.

In the World Series, the Pirates became the first team in history to overcome a 3-1 game deficit, winning in seven games. Johnson allowed only one run in his first two starts, both Washington victories, and held a 4-0 lead in Game Seven when a heavy rain storm and 15 Pirates hits washed

Goose Goslin, running past first base, was robbed of a hit on this play in the opener of the 1924 World Series by Travis Jackson. Giants first baseman Bill Terry has the ball.

172

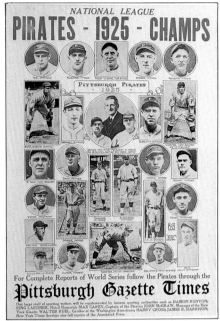

Waite "Schoolboy" Hoyt (top left) got his nickname when he was signed out of Brooklyn's Erasmus Hall High School by New York Giants manager John McGraw in 1918. Hoyt compiled a 237-182 lifetime record, including a stretch with the Yankees between 1921 and 1928 when he won 145 and lost only 87, taking advantage of a New York offense that regularly scored more than 800 runs a season. His finest year came with the 1927 "Murderer's Row" team, when Hoyt went 22-7 and led the A.L. in wins and ERA (2.63). Off the field, Hoyt was one of the leaders of the hard-living Yanks, forming along with Babe Ruth and Joe Dugan the so-called "Playboy Trio." The 1925 Pittsburgh Pirates (top right) had a team batting average of .307 and a team slugging average of .448. Shortstop Glenn Wright hit .308 with 18 homers and 121 RBI. Outfielder Clyde Barnhart hit .325 and drove in 114 runs. Outfielder Kiki Cuyler hit .357, scored 144 runs, and drove in 102. Chicago White Sox outfielder Johnny Mostil (bottom left) led the A.L. with 135 runs scored, 90 bases on balls, and 43 stolen bases in 1925. In '26, he led the league with 35 stolen bases, and he scored 120 runs. Senators outfielder Earl McNeely slides in safely at third in Game Four of the 1924 World Series (bottom right).

173

away his lead. The Pirates eventually won the game, 9-7, on a run-scoring double by Cuyler.

1926

The Pirates bid to repeat as National League champions was aided in 1926 by the arrival of rookie outfielder Paul Waner, but a significant drop in run production undermined the Bucs cause. Filling the breach was Hornsby and his St. Louis Cardinals. At the helm all season long after replacing Branch Rickey as manager in mid-1925, the cantankerous Rajah drove the Cards to the first N.L. pennant in the franchise's history, edging Cincinnati by 2 games and Pittsburgh by 4½ games.

Baseball's managerial fraternity in 1926 reads like a who's who of the game in that era. In addition to Hornsby, four National League skippers — John McGraw, Joe McCarthy, Bill McKechnie, and Dave Bancroft — and seven managers in the American League that year — Miller Huggins, Connie Mack, Bucky Harris, Eddie Collins, Ty Cobb, George Sisler, and Tris Speaker — are in the Hall of Fame. It was a short-lived assemblage, however. By the following season Hornsby and McKechnie in the National League, and Collins, Cobb, Sisler, and Speaker in the A.L., had all been ousted, proof that an absolute lack of job security is nothing new for the men occupying baseball's hot seat.

Hornsby experienced an "off-season" at the plate, hitting .317 (the only time his average dropped below .360 in the decade), but first baseman Sunny Jim Bottomley picked up the slack for the league's most potent attack by batting in 120 runners. MVP honors that year went to Redbird catcher Bob O'Farrell, who caught 146 games and batted .293. The pennant proved to be a vindication of Rick-

Lou Gehrig scored 135 runs in 1926.

ey's system of developing ballplayers through a farm system of minor league clubs.

Cincinnati's pennant chase was built around a well-distributed offense, featuring former Yankee Wally Pipp and catcher Bubbles Hargrave, whose .363 batting average made him the first receiver in league history to claim a batting crown. The league's stingiest pitching staff coupled with the acquisition of slugger Hack Wilson from the Giants (21 homers, 109 RBI) helped propel rookie skipper Joe McCarthy's Chicago Cubs from last place to a respectable fourth-place finish. The Giants plodded through an anemic sub-.500 season following the tragic loss of Ross Youngs, who fell ill during the season and later died. One bright spot for the team was the brief debut of 17-year-old outfielder Mel Ott, who batted .383 in 60 at-bats.

Babe Ruth and the Yankees rebounded from their miserable 1925 campaign with a vengeance. With the big guy in fine fettle and teamed with cleanup hitter Lou Gehrig on a full-time basis, New York reclaimed the pennant by 3 games over Cleveland. Ruth belted 47 home runs, drove in 145 runs, and scored 139 as the Yanks again displayed the most powerful offense in baseball. For his part, Columbia Lou swatted 20 round-trippers, knocked home 107 batters, and scored 135 times. It was the first of 13 consecutive seasons in which Gehrig scored and drove in at least 100 runs.

AL SIMMONS

If Rogers Hornsby was the best righthanded hitter of his era, then Al Simmons, known as "Bucketfoot Al" for his unorthodox stance, was a close second.

Simmons joined Connie Mack's Philadelphia Athletics in 1924 and batted .308. The following year, he hit .384 and led the American League with 253 hits, just four short of the record George Sisler had set five years before. In 1927, he batted .392, but just as in '25, he was aced out of the batting crown by Harry Heilmann.

Between 1929 and '32 (during which time Philadelphia won three straight pennants), Simmons was even more awesome. In '29, he led the A.L. in RBI with 157 while batting .365. In '30, Simmons led the league in runs (152), hit 36 homers, and won his first batting title with a .381 mark. He won his second successive batting crown the following year, hitting .390. And in '32, his last with Connie Mack, he led the league in hits with 216, hit 35 homers, scored 144 runs, and drove in 151. Despite this impressive production, Simmons was overshadowed by Mickey Cochrane and Jimmie Foxx and never won a Most Valuable Player award.

Simmons played for six other teams between 1933 and 1944, the year he retired. He departed with a .334 lifetime average, 307 homers, 1,827 RBI (11th all-time), and 73 hits short of 3,000. He is sixth all time in World Series home run percentage (he hit six in 19 Series games) and fourth in Series slugging. He made the Hall of Fame in 1953.

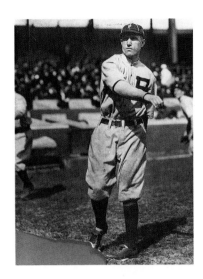

Burleigh Grimes (top left) had one of his best seasons in 1928. He led the National League in wins (25), games (48), games started (37), complete games (28), innings pitched (330⅔), and shutouts (four) for the Pirates. Dave Bancroft (top right) hit .311 in 1926. In a preview of his 1927 season, Babe Ruth hit 18 homers in 46 games on his way to 47 home runs in the season (middle left). Pirates third baseman Pie Traynor (middle right) explains how he averaged 105 runs batted in between 1923 and 1931. Traynor hit .346 in the 1925 World Series. St. Louis celebrates (bottom left) after the 1926 World Series victory over the Yankees. Philadelphia A's catcher Mickey Cochrane (bottom right) hit .338 in 1927.

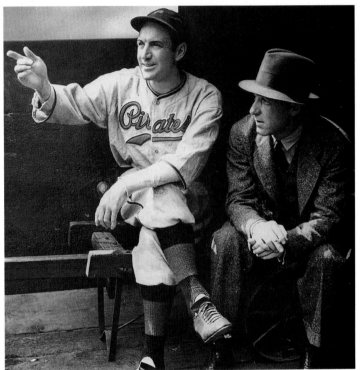

THE 1920s

The league MVP award went to Cleveland first baseman George Burns who hit 64 doubles, but otherwise couldn't match Ruth or Gehrig's output. In fact, the whole Cleveland team's attack paled in comparison to the Bronx Bombers'. Both clubs posted .289 batting averages, but whereas the Yankees clubbed 121 home runs, the Tribe managed only 27. Keeping the Indians in the race was a fine pitching staff, anchored by righthander George (The Bull) Uhle, who led the league in games started (36), complete games (32), and innings pitched (318⅓) while tallying a 27-11 record. Meanwhile, Connie Mack's young band finished 6 back, led again by "Bucketfoot Al" Simmons, so named for his unusual batting stance. And though he managed only a 13-13 record, second-year pitcher Lefty Grove led the league in earned run average for the first of a record nine times, with a 2.51 mark, more than a run and a half better than the league average.

Pitchers in both leagues regained a measure of self-respect in '26. American League pitchers tabulated an ERA of 4.02, a year after hitters battered them for a decade-high 4.39 ERA and 6,397 runs, while National League hurlers reduced their cumulative ERA from 4.27 to 3.84. In 1925, only two front-line pitchers in the American League held opposing teams to under three runs a game. The following year, the A's pitching staff had a combined ERA of 3.00. In 1926, only two N.L. staffs posted ERAs above 4.00; the previous year, only three were below four runs a game. In 1925 nine clubs in the majors recorded team batting averages of .295 or better, but none bettered that mark in '26.

Two rule changes came into effect that year. A ball was judged to be a ground-rule double if it bounced over the outfield fence in fair territory, providing the fence is less than 250 feet from home plate. In the past, such hits were ruled home runs. The sacrifice fly rule was amended to read that a batter is not charged with an official time at-bat if his fly ball is caught but advances a runner any base.

In the World Series, New York and St. Louis split the first six games, as Ruth blasted three homers for the Yanks and the Cards got an even distribution of offense, led by Bottomley. In Game Seven, St. Louis was clinging to a 3-2 lead when manager Hornsby brought in sixth-game winner, 39-year-old Grover Cleveland Alexander to snuff a Yankees rally in the seventh inning. The game ended in a bizarre fashion as Ruth was caught attempting to steal second base with two out in the ninth and Meusel at bat. The Cardinals had won the first of their nine world championships.

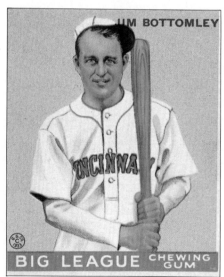

Paul Waner (top), a rookie in 1926, finished in the N.L.'s top five in six offensive categories. Jim Bottomley (bottom) led the '26 N.L. in RBI and hit .345 in the Series.

RUTH'S 60TH HOMER

Ruth on the cover of Baseball Magazine.

Had Babe Ruth smacked 60 home runs in 1922 instead of in 1927, the actual hitting of the 60th might have been a footnote in history rather than one of baseball's greatest moments. After all, Ruth had already revolutionized the game by setting home run records each year from 1919 to 1921, his 59 in '21 smashing by five the mark he had set the year before. Would another 60 in '22 have been such a surprise?

But by 1927, six years had passed and few people believed any player, including the Babe, could break Ruth's record. Though he had hit more than 40 homers three times between 1923 to '26, Ruth was 32 years old and constantly fighting to stay in shape. But a wonderful thing happened in Ruth's career: Lou Gehrig. In 1927, Gehrig was into his second full season as the Yankees cleanup hitter in "Murderers' Row." So Ruth — hitting in front of a player on his way to a record 175-RBI season — got off to one of the greatest starts of his career.

With three games left in the season, Ruth had belted numbers 58 and 59, giving him 16 for the last month. "Once he had that 59," sportswriter Paul Gallico wrote, "that number 60 was as sure as the setting sun." The next day, September 30, the Yankees and Washington were tied 2-2 in the eighth. Ruth stepped to the plate. Senators pitcher Tom Zachary threw a fastball down the middle, and the Babe parked the ball in the right field bleachers to set a record that would stand for 34 years.

Brooklyn hurler Dazzy Vance (top) led the National League in ERA in 1928 with a 2.09 mark while going 22-10. Vance led the league in strikeouts for seven consecutive seasons from 1922 to 1928. Jesse Haines (bottom left) was 24-10 for the 1927 Cardinals, with a league-leading 25 complete games. Haines won two games in the '26 World Series, compiling an ERA of 1.08. Cubs outfielder Hack Wilson (bottom middle) led the N.L. in homers from 1926 to 1928 with 21, 30, and 31. He averaged 119 RBI in those three years. Casey Stengel (bottom right) had a .284 lifetime batting average over 14 seasons.

THE 1920s

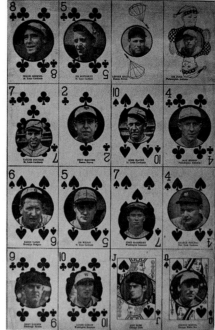
An uncut sheet of playing cards from 1927.

1927

Hornsby's position as skipper of the champion Cardinals was short-lived. Ever the strong-willed, blunt talker, the Rajah was involved in a major dispute with St. Louis owner Sam Breadon that winter, which prompted Breadon to ship Hornsby and his six batting titles to New York for the Giants outstanding second baseman Frankie Frisch. The trade marked the beginning of an odyssey that sent Hornsby to four clubs in a four-year period.

The Hornsby trade, however, was quickly obscured by events transpiring in the Bronx, as the Yankees were playing with a combination of power and precision never seen before. In what has become the accepted standard of excellence in baseball, the '27 Yankees dominated the American

League from start to finish and rewrote the record book in the process. The club's record, 110-44, stood as the league's best until 1954. The Yanks set new standards for runs scored (975) and home runs (158), and led the league in batting average, hits, triples, and walks. The club's .489 slugging average is the highest in the sport's history. To make matters worse for the opposition, the Yan-

kees also sent to the mound the toughest pitching staff in the league that season. Led by Waite Hoyt, Herb Pennock, Urban Shocker, and relief specialist Wilcy Moore, the staff posted a miserly 3.20 ERA, nearly a full run below the league average.

The pitching staff's achievements were overshadowed by the exploits of the legendary "Murderer's Row." The Yankees' sluggers propelled New York to the pennant ahead of a good Philadelphia club, led by Simmons and Grove. Ruth, in blasting his record 60 home runs, outhomered every other team in the league, as he did in 1920. He also batted .356, drove home 164, and slugged .772. Gehrig became the second man in the game's history to hit at least 47 home runs, and he also batted .373, slugged .765, and drove in a record 175 runners while being named MVP. Meusel hit .337 and drove in 103, and Tony Lazzeri hit .309 and recorded 102 RBI. The only real challenge mounted to this juggernaut was repelled on July 4 when the Yankees swept the Senators in a doubleheader by scores of 12-1 and 22-1. New York's 19-game margin of victory was the best in league history.

In the only A.L. race that went the distance, Harry Heilmann once

MICKEY COCHRANE

Without question the best catcher of his era, Mickey Cochrane is ranked among the top five catchers of all time.

Cochrane was purchased by Connie Mack's lowly Philadel-

phia Athletics in 1925 and, in 1929, he led the A's to the first of three straight pennants and two world championships. Cochrane hit .331, .357, and .349, respectively, from 1929 to '31 and established himself as the finest defensive catcher the game had ever seen.

With the depression in full force in 1933, Mack began liquidating his team and sold "Black Mike" to the Detroit Tigers, where Cochrane, just age 31, became a player/manager. His leadership skills shone again, as the Tigers won the 1934 A.L. pennant and Cochrane was named MVP. The following season, Cochrane batted .319 and scored the winning run in the last game of the World Series.

Cochrane's career abruptly ended in 1937 after he was beaned with a fastball, rendering him unconscious for ten days. Though he eventually recovered and even managed the club in 1938, his playing days were through. In 13 seasons, Cochrane batted .300 or better nine times; he is one of the few catchers with a lifetime average over .300 (.320). He was elected to the Hall of Fame in 1947.

Catcher Mickey Cochrane applies the tag.

Righthander Eddie Rommel (top left) was the first major league pitcher to exclusively feature the knuckleball. Rommel was a promising minor league spitball pitcher in 1920 when his specialty and other "trick pitches" such as the emery ball were outlawed. He turned to the knuckleball, and he quickly became one of the few hurlers who could throw the pitch consistently for strikes. Rommel compiled a 171-119 record for the Philadelphia Athletics from 1920 to 1932. In '22, Rommel went 27-13, a .675 winning percentage for a seventh-place team that played only .333 ball without him on the mound. After pitching effectively out of the bullpen for the A's 1929, 1930, and '31 pennant winners, Rommel retired to become an umpire. Lou Gehrig takes a mighty swing in the '27 World Series (bottom left). Gehrig hit .308 with five RBI in the Series. Hurlers for Game Three of the 1927 World Series (bottom right), Herb Pennock, left, and Lee Meadows, meet before the game. Meadows and the rest of the Pirates were helpless against the mighty '27 Yankees, who swept the Series. The Cherokee Base Ball Team (top right) poses for a photo.

OLSON'S CHEROKEE INDIAN BASE BALL TEAM, WATERVLIET, MICH.

179

THE 1920s

again captured a batting title on the season's last day by going six-for-eight in a doubleheader to edge out Simmons .398 to .392. Ruth and Gehrig ran neck and neck in the home run derby through early September when the Babe pulled away by blasting 20 balls over the fences in the season's last month.

In the National League, Pittsburgh, with a rejuvenated offense led by Paul "Big Poison" Waner, narrowly beat the Hornsby-less Cardinals to claim its second pennant in three years. League MVP Waner (who hit .380) spearheaded a Pirates club that batted .305 as a team. Waner's 21-year-old brother, Lloyd ("Little Poison"), playing in his first season, chipped in with a .355 batting mark and a league-high 133 runs. The Cards fell only 1½ games short thanks largely to 20-win seasons by Jesse Haines and the ageless Alexander. The Giants, with Hornsby and first baseman Bill Terry leading the way, improved by 18 games and finished 2 games back.

In the Series, the Yanks trailed the Pirates for a total of three innings en route to a four-game sweep. Most of the damage was done by the Bombers' two table-setters, center fielder Earl Combs and shortstop Mark Koenig, and Yankees pitching, which allowed only ten runs. The Babe also made his presence felt with two home runs and a .400 batting average. The defeat left a lasting impression on the Pirates, who were subsequently shut out of postseason play until 1960. Ironically, when the Bucs finally returned to the Fall Classic, they beat the Yankees in seven games.

The Yankees' sweep of '27 was a fitting finale for perhaps the greatest team ever to take the field. The season also marked the end of perhaps the greatest pitching career in history as 39-year-old

Walter Johnson called it quits after 21 seasons in a Senators uniform. While compiling a 416-279 record for a consistently poor team, Big Train led the league in strikeouts 12 times, threw a record 110 shutouts, and finished with an ERA of 2.17. The season also was the last for Ban Johnson, president of the American League since its founding in 1901. Johnson resigned, stripped of most of his authority by the appointment of Commissioner Landis and bitterly resenting the decline in prestige that his office suffered.

1928

It didn't surprise anyone that the Yankees captured their third straight flag in 1928 and sixth title of the decade. But this year's task was far tougher for New York, as

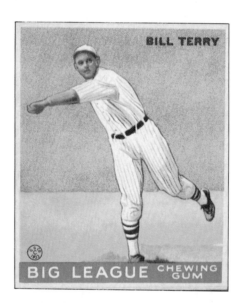

Bill Terry (top) in 1927 hit .326 with 20 homers, 121 RBI, and a .529 slugging average. Lloyd Waner (bottom) had 133 runs scored in 1927 and only 27 RBI.

PHILADELPHIA'S COMEBACK

Jimmy Dykes drove in the winning run.

In the last World Series of the 1920s, the Chicago Cubs lost the first two games to the Philadelphia Athletics in Chicago, but rebounded to win the third in Philly. In Game Four, they blasted A's pitching and took an 8-0 lead into the bottom of the seventh. A tied Series looked like a lock.

A's manager Connie Mack had decided that after his sluggers batted in the seventh he would insert his bench players. But Mack's starters decided they didn't want to leave so soon. Al Simmons led off the inning with a homer, breaking Charlie Root's shutout. Then the roof caved in on Root, as four successive singles scored two more runs. After an out, another single made it 8-4. Joe McCarthy replaced Root with lefty Art Neft to face lefty Mule Haas, who immediately sent a ball over Hack Wilson's head in center. The ball rolled to the 447-foot sign for a three-run inside-the-park homer. After a walk to Mickey Cochrane and a Simmons single, Jimmie Foxx singled to tie the game. The next batter was hit by a pitch, and a Jimmy Dykes double made it 10-8 A's.

Philadelphia sent 15 men to the plate before the inning was over. Lefty Grove pitched two scoreless relief innings to secure the unbelievable victory.

The A's heroics were more subdued the next day. Down 2-0 in the ninth, they rallied for three runs to win the Series in five games.

Babe Ruth takes a base on balls during the 1928 World Series (top). In Game Four of the sweep over St. Louis, Ruth homered three times. He batted .625 in the Series. Lu Blue (bottom left) slugged 14 homers and scored 116 runs for the 1928 Browns. He scored 111 runs for the Browns the next year. Cardinals second baseman Rogers Hornsby, left, and Pittsburgh manager Bill McKechnie flank a young fan (bottom right).

THE 1920s

Connie Mack's A's came tantalizingly close to beating out the Bronx Bombers before slipping to 2 1/2 games back at the end. Still, Philadelphia's fans were delighted with the club's showing. Built mainly from young parts assembled by Mack and sprinkled with aging stars Ty Cobb, Tris Speaker, and Eddie Collins, the 1928 A's featured seven players who are enshrined in Cooperstown. The bedrock of the team was comprised of its young stars — Al Simmons, Jimmie Foxx, and league Most Valuable Player Mickey Cochrane — plus the league's stingiest pitching staff, paced by 24-game winner Lefty Grove and 44-year-old Jack Quinn.

The A's jelled in July by tearing off a 25-8 string and remained hot through August before catching the defending champs in early September. In a showdown at Yankee Stadium on September 9, the Yankees turned back the A's in a doubleheader witnessed by more than 80,000 fans. From there, the Yanks were able to hold on. Once again, New York mounted the most fearsome attack in the league. Ruth, Gehrig, and Meusel combined for 397 RBI; Ruth's 54 homers marked the fourth time he reached that figure in the decade. Slugging second baseman Lazzeri was limited by injuries in '28, but he was capably replaced by rookie Leo Durocher. New York pitching slipped a notch in '28, but Hoyt and George Pipgras combined to win 47 games.

The A's futile chase of the Yankees marked the last hurrah for Cobb and Speaker, who both called it quits after a combined 46 seasons and 7,706 hits between them. While the Yankees and A's battled it out, another race went down to the wire. Washington's Goose Goslin edged out St. Louis' Heinie Manush to win the batting crown

Yankees pitcher Herb Pennock.

by a single hit, .379 to .378. Gehrig also stayed in the hunt till the end, finishing at .374.

The Cardinals reclaimed the top spot in the National League after withstanding a ferocious surge by the Giants, who won 25 times in September but came up 2 games short. Jim Bottomley, who batted .325 with 31 homers and 136 RBI, again provided offensive leadership for the Redbirds and was rewarded by being named the league's Most Valuable Player. The Cards also featured four players who scored more than 100 runs and received solid pitching from 20-game winners Bill Sherdel and Haines, and 16-game winner Pete Alexander.

The Giants — led by Terry and 19-year-old Mel Ott — topped the league in home runs and got 25 wins from Larry Benton, whom they acquired from the Boston Braves in mid-1927. The 31-year-old Terry batted .326, the second of ten consecutive seasons he bettered .300. The defending champion Pirates slipped to fourth, 9 games off the pace, despite the 444 hits and 263 runs contributed by the Waner brothers, and the 25 wins compiled by Burleigh Grimes, the decade's winningest pitcher. Though playing for a noncontender, Brooklyn's Dazzy Vance once again displayed his mastery over the leagues' hitters by posting a 22-10 record and a 2.09 ERA, nearly two runs a game better than the league average.

PAUL WANER

Paul Waner and his brother Lloyd began playing the outfield together with the Pittsburgh Pirates in 1927 and immediately developed a system for driving opposing pitchers crazy. Lloyd would constantly get on base and his older brother would always knock him home. In '27, Lloyd hit .355 and led the league in runs scored, while Paul led the N.L. with a .380 average and a league-leading 131 RBI. The Yankees may have murdered the opposition that year, but the Waners poisoned them. Though the Yanks beat the Bucs in the '27 World Series, Paul and Lloyd batted .367 and slugged .467.

Paul was "Big Poison," even though the lefty hitter stood just 5'8" and weighed about 150 pounds. Between 1926 and 1939, all with the Pirates, Waner hit over .300 13 of 14 seasons (hitting over .350 six of those years) and won three batting titles. He also led the N.L twice in hits, runs, triples, and doubles, setting a league record with 62 two-baggers in 1932.

Waner was known for being an intelligent man who liked his own poison — liquor. According to one story, Waner lined four hits while suffering a hangover and told a teammate he was seeing three balls. When asked how he got the hits, he said, "I swung at the one in the middle."

Waner retired in 1945 with a lifetime .333 average (third highest in N.L. history) and 3,152 hits, numbers that earned him a space in the Hall of Fame in 1952.

Sunny Jim Bottomley (top right), featured on a tobacco advertisement, averaged 121 runs batted in from 1923 to 1929. He batted over .300 nine times and slugged over .500 nine times. He ended his 16-year career with a .310 batting average, a .500 slugging average, and 1,422 runs batted in. Bottomley was elected to the Hall of Fame in 1974. Toward the end of their brilliant careers, Ty Cobb, left, and Eddie Collins (top left) were employed by Connie Mack in 1927 to help Mack's Philadelphia A's. Lou Gehrig (bottom) averaged 138 runs batted in from 1926 to 1929.

THE 1920s

In a rematch of the 1926 World Series, the Yankees exacted swift retribution by sweeping the Cards in four games. New York's pitchers again held the opposition to two runs a game, while the Bombers exploded for seven runs a game. Ruth collected ten hits — including three home runs in Game Four — in 16 at-bats, and Gehrig went six-for-11 with four home runs and nine RBI.

1929

It was like 1927 all over again, but this time the bullies of the American League were the fully matured Philadelphia Athletics. After coming so close in '28, the A's made it a no-contest race in the year of the Crash by combining a high-octane offense with the best pitching staff in baseball. The A's attack featured five players who scored more than 100 runs. Simmons batted .365 with 34 homers and 157 RBI, while Foxx rapped 33 home runs, knocked in 117 runners, and batted .354. It was the first of a record 12 consecutive seasons that "The Beast" cleared the fences at least 30 times. The A's

pitching staff posted the league's lowest ERA, and featured two 20-game winners, George Earnshaw and Grove. The combination proved almost unbeatable as Mack's White Elephants crashed to 104 wins and the club's first pennant since 1914.

The Yankees proved to be no pushovers in the slugging department, as Ruth and Gehrig again finished one-two in home runs. But new players at shortstop, third, and catcher and the late-season death of manager Miller Huggins upset the club's continuity. Despite a 12-0 record posted by newcomer Tom Zachary, the Yankees' pitching staff

A pin (top) features the 1929 Cubs. The Cubs wait before the first game of the World Series.

tailed off sharply in '29, especially perennial aces Waite Hoyt and Herb Pennock, who combined for a 19-20 record. Fourth-year man Charlie Gehringer led the league in runs scored while pacing a Tigers team that had the most prolific offense in the league, but also had the league's highest earned run average and finished in sixth place. The Boston Red Sox closed out the worst decade in franchise history by finishing last for the fifth straight year.

In the National League, pitchers were under siege once again as the circuit's batters unleashed their greatest collective barrage of the decade and gave fans a taste of the raucous output to come in 1930. In one fell swoop, the league ERA mushroomed from 3.98 to 4.71, home runs increased by 24 percent, the league batting average jumped 13 points, and runs scored ballooned by 18 percent. Four N.L. teams blasted at least 100 home runs in 1929, and a fifth (Brooklyn) knocked out 99. In 1928, only two teams managed the feat. Eleven National League players, led by Chuck Klein's new league-record 43 homers, trotted around the bases at least 20 times in '29; only five did that in '28.

In this rarefied atmosphere, it was a cinch that the club with the heaviest hitters would rise to the top. The Chicago Cubs — buoyed by the acquisition of the league's best hitter, Rogers Hornsby — grabbed their first pennant in 11 years by crossing the plate a record 982 times. Hornsby, working for his fourth employer in as

UMPIRE BILL DINNEEN

Big Bill Dinneen is the only man in baseball history to have pitched and umpired a no-hitter.

Dinneen's record after 12 years as a pitcher (between 1898 and 1909) was 171-177, but he compiled four 20-win seasons, threw his no-hitter in 1905, and won three games (including a shutout in the decisive eighth game) for the Boston Red Sox in the 1903 World Series, the first of the modern era.

But Dinneen was even more famous for the World Series games in which he served as an umpire. He was the third base ump when Bill Wambsganss pulled off his unassisted triple play in the 1920 Series. Dinneen was an arbiter in the 1924 classic when Washington Senator Walter

Johnson won the seventh game after a ground ball hit a pebble. And Dinneen worked the 1929 Series when the Philadelphia Athletics scored ten runs in the seventh to overcome an 8-0 deficit in Game Four. Dinneen eventually worked in eight World Series, a total of 45 games.

Dinneen became an umpire in 1910, the year after he retired as an active player. He immediately excelled and was partnered with the acknowledged chief umpire, Bill Klem. In 1933, Dinneen's long and distinguished service was rewarded when he was chosen as the home plate umpire for the first All-Star Game.

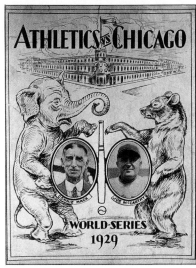

The Athletics celebrate after the final game of the 1929 World Series (top). Max Bishop scores ahead of Mule Haas (middle left) in the ninth inning of Game Five of the '29 Series. Haas hit the homer in the top of the ninth inning to tie the score 2-2. Bing Miller then doubled in Al Simmons to win the game and the Series. A scorecard (middle right) for the Series.
The 1929 National League champs, the Chicago Cubs, are pictured on a pennant (bottom).

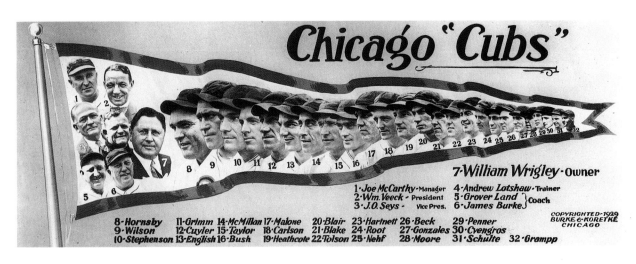

THE 1920s

many years, grabbed the league MVP honors by hitting .380, with 39 home runs, 149 RBI, and 156 runs scored. Manager Joe McCarthy had three other players who scored more than 110 runs, and four players (including Hornsby) who batted at least .345. Most of the Cubs' heavy hitters came from outside the organization. Kiki Cuyler, Riggs Stephenson, and Hack Wilson — who foretold his monstrous 1930 campaign by belting 39 home runs and driving home 159 runners — were all imported from other teams.

Pittsburgh boasted six .300 hitters, but in a year of soaring home run production, the Pirates' one-base-at-a-time approach to offense was good for only second place. The Giants received 42 home runs and 151 RBI from Ott and 18 wins from second-year screwballer Carl Hubbell, and had the only staff in the league with an ERA under 4.00, yet the team still finished a distant third. Even the Phillies got into the swing of things by batting a league high .309. Second-year player Klein, in addition to his 43 home runs, batted .356 and collected 145 RBI, while 32-year-old former pitcher Lefty O'Doul batted a league best .398, belted 32 home runs, and set a National League record for hits (254) that still stands. However, the Phillies pitching staff couldn't get anyone out and posted an astronomical earned run average of 6.13, relegating the franchise to a 12th straight second-division finish.

In the World Series, the A's pitching prevailed over the Cubs sluggers four games to one. Mack threw Chicago a curve in Game One by starting Howard Ehmke, a 35-year-old righthander who had appeared in only 11 games for the Phillies that year. He responded by allowing a harmless run in the ninth inning, while striking out a

Series record 13 batters in the A's 3-1 win. Mack also held his ace Lefty Grove in relief and he saved games Two and Four. Game Four featured the most famous comeback in Series history. With the score 8-0 in favor of the Cubs, the A's unleashed ten runs in their half of the seventh inning, and won 10-8.

The A's also scored three runs in the bottom of the ninth to win the fifth and deciding game 3-2.

Charlie Gehringer (top) led the American League with 215 base hits and 131 runs scored in 1929. Howard Ehmke (bottom) started Game One of the 1929 World Series, which he won 3-1.

EDD ROUSH

EDDIE ROUSH
OUTFIELD, CINCINNATI NATIONALS

Eddie Roush is pictured on a 1921 baseball trading card. Roush hit .352 in 1921, the first of three consecutive seasons that he hit over .350.

A lefthanded-hitting center fielder, Edd Roush played 18 years in the majors and had a lifetime batting average of .323.

Roush's prime was from 1917 to 1926; during those ten years with Cincinnati, he batted over .300 every year, with two batting titles — .341 in 1917 and .321 in 1919. From 1921 to 1923, Roush hit .352, .352, and .351 — and slugged .502, .461, and .531. He was one of the better defensive center fielders of the day and had doubles and triples power; he led the N.L. in doubles in 1923 with 41, and the next year led the league in triples with 21.

Roush was a stubborn character, known for his frequent spring hold-outs; he reported to his team late in 1921, 1922, and 1927. He sat out the entire 1930 season because he didn't like the salary he was offered. According to Roush, sometimes he held out just so he wouldn't have to go to spring training, which he considered a waste of time. "I did my *own* spring training," he once said, "hunting quail and rabbits."

The fact that Roush was able to bat .214 in a World Series, with six hits and zero homers, and still drive in seven runs and score six times may seem amazing. It is ony when one remembers that he played against the Black Sox in the 1919 fall classic that this episode becomes more believable.

Hack Wilson of the Chicago Cubs (top left) takes a big cut. He was a catalyst in the 1929 Chicago offense, batting .345 with 39 homers, 135 runs scored, and a league-leading 159 runs batted in. The Cubs offense scored 982 runs in 1929. The A's congratulate themselves after beating the mighty Cubs in the '29 World Series (top right). Slugging outfielder Chick Hafey (bottom left) played on the St. Louis Cardinals pennant winners in 1926, 1928, '30, and '31. An early product of Branch Rickey's farm system (that also developed Joe Medwick, Johnny Mize, Pepper Martin, and Terry Moore), Hafey's peak seasons came between 1928 and 1930. He hit 82 homers, scored 310 runs, and drove in 343 in those three years. In 1931, Hafey hit .349 to become the first batting champion in either league to wear glasses while playing. Hafey was such a feared line-drive hitter, Giants third baseman Freddy Lindstrom once said, "It'll sure be difficult for third basemen to get insurance while that guy is in the league."

THE 1930s

With the country enduring the torment of the Depression, baseball was knocked off its competitive balance. By 1939, however, bolstered by stars like Joe DiMaggio and Ted Williams, gate receipts reached new highs.

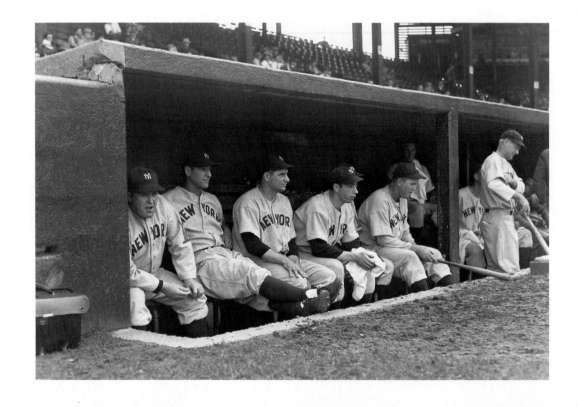

The Yankees bench (page 188) looks on while the Bronx Bombers bat in the late 1930s. Manager Joe McCarthy is far left, Lou Gehrig is second from the left, and Joe DiMaggio is fourth from the left. Jimmie Foxx (page 189) averaged 140 runs batted in during the 1930s.

THE 1930s

When the Depression altered American life in the 1930s, baseball wasn't immune from its debilitating effects. In 1930, the Depression had not yet fully taken hold, but baseball owners, anticipating a decline in attendance, allegedly had the ball juiced up to infuse more offense and action into the sport. It worked. Hits and run totals were the highest in years, particularly in the National League, where open season was declared on pitchers. The league batting average that season was .303, as five of the century's ten highest team batting averages and six of the top-20 team run totals were tallied. Home runs flew out at a record pace, and fans flocked into the parks at an unprecedented rate. Major league attendance topped the 10-million mark in 1930, a level that was unequaled until the end of World War II.

The good times were short-lived, however. After 1930, attendance dropped for four straight years, as all but two major league teams posted attendance declines. As unemployment climbed to 13 million in 1932, gate receipts for the 16 major league teams plummeted to $10.8 million from $17 million in 1929. At the same time, average player salaries sank to $4,500 from the pre-Depression high of $7,000.

By 1934, close to 40 percent of the nonfarm work force was unemployed and baseball teams suffered at the turnstiles. After peaking at 10.1 million in 1930, major league attendance sank to under 6 million in 1934, the lowest since the war-shortened 1918 season. It would be 1936 before the game's vital signs began improving, and by 1939 — buoyed by new stars such as Joe DiMaggio, Ted Williams, and Bob Feller and a strengthening economy — gate receipts would reach new highs at the close of the decade.

The Depression also had a direct bearing on what happened on the field. Success in the standings became directly linked to prosperity at the gate, and naturally, the wealthier clubs enjoyed the most success in the decade. The Yankees and Tigers won seven pennants between them in the American League, while the Cubs, Giants, and the farm system-fed Cardinals each won three flags in the N.L.

With the economy in a shambles, baseball's competitive balance was knocked askew. Connie Mack had built the Philadelphia A's into a dynasty from 1929 to 1931 with young stars like Mickey Cochrane, Al Simmons, Jimmie Foxx, and Lefty Grove. But in 1932, the A's drew only 400,000 fans to Shibe Park, the club's third consecutive year of declining attendance. Claiming imminent fiscal ruin, Mack began raising revenue by selling the club's most viable assets, its star players. In 1933, he sold Simmons, a two-time batting champion, to the White Sox, and the A's fell from second to third. In 1934, Mack divested himself of catcher Cochrane and pitching ace Grove, selling them to the Tigers and the Red Sox, respectively.

The A's Al Simmons beats the throw to first base.

JIMMIE FOXX

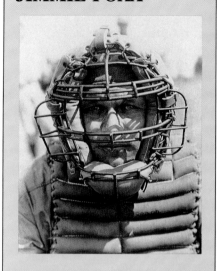

They called him "Double X" and "The Beast," but Jimmie Foxx was more adequately described in the 1930s as the righthanded-hitting Babe Ruth.

Foxx, a muscular first baseman who was famous for tape-measure home runs, began his career with Connie Mack's great Athletics teams of the late 1920s and early 1930s. Foxx first established himself as a power threat in 1929 when he hit 33 homers and batted .354. He followed that with a 37-homer, 156-RBI season in 1930 and a 30-homer, 120-RBI campaign in '31. The A's won the pennant in each of those seasons; Foxx batted .344 with four homers, 11 RBI, and a .609 slugging percentage in 18 games over the three Series.

But Foxx really became a Ruth duplicate during the 1932 season, when he threatened to break Ruth's home run record of 60. Foxx finished the year just two homers short, led the A.L. in runs (151), RBI (169), and slugging (.749), and took the MVP award. Foxx repeated as MVP in '33, this time winning the triple crown, and was MVP again in 1938, when he also won a batting title.

By the time Foxx's 20-year career ended in 1945, he had tied Ruth and Lou Gehrig for the record of most seasons with 100 or more RBI (13). He was the all-time righthanded hitting home run leader with 534 until Willie Mays passed him in 1966. He currently ranks eighth all time in homers, sixth in RBI (1,921), and fourth in slugging (.609). Foxx made the Hall of Fame in 1951, his first year of eligibility.

Lewis Robert "Hack" Wilson (top left) was the National League's Babe Ruth, both on the field and off. Wilson's career didn't take off until the New York Giants traded him to the Chicago Cubs in 1926, and Wilson immediately found Wrigley Fields' confines friendly. He led the N.L. with 21 homers, drove in 109 runs, and hit .321, his first of five straight .300-plus seasons. Wilson led the league in homers the next two seasons, and in 1929, he led the Cubs to a pennant by knocking 39 homers and a N.L.-leading 159 runs home. Though Chicago lost the Series, Wilson hit .471. Wilson generated his power from an oddly shaped body. He was 5'6" and 195 pounds and wore size-six shoes, but the man had massive arms and shoulders. Like Ruth, his homer-hitting counterpart in the A.L., Wilson also had a healthy appetite for food and alcohol. Such vices, however, didn't prevent him from achieving one of baseball's greatest records in 1930, when he belted an N.L. record 56 homers and set the all-time single-season RBI mark with 190. He played just 11 full seasons in the majors and didn't make the Hall of Fame until a Veteran's Committee elected him in 1979. The New York Giants (top right) won three pennants and a world championship in the 1930s. Babe Ruth was the idol of youngsters across the country (bottom left). Ruth, who was 35 years old in 1930, averaged 139 RBI a season in four seasons from 1930 to '33. Lou Gehrig seems amused by Babe Ruth's Universal Stars (bottom right), but The Bambino isn't too happy about it all.

"Champions get many a small boy to eat a good breakfast!"

Betty Crocker

THE 1930s

Philadelphia sank to fifth place. After falling into the cellar in 1935, the A's shipped Foxx, the game's top righthanded slugger, to Boston. In less than five years, Mack had completely dismantled his championship club, committing his team to years of dismal showings. From 1936 until his death in 1956, Mack's A's finished no higher than fourth in the A.L. and came in last 11 times.

Mack was not alone in making moves based on financial hardships. Clark Griffith made several shrewd trades in the winter of 1932 that helped his Washington Senators win the pennant in 1933. But the major factor in guiding the Nationals to the flag was player/manager Joe Cronin, who batted .309 and drove home 118 runs. Yet their success on the field didn't prevent the Senators from losing money that year, so Griffith sold former batting champ Goose Goslin to the Tigers. Then, the Senators tumbled all the way to seventh in 1934, and Griffith took an even larger loss. This time, he sold his most valuable property, Cronin, to the Red Sox for $225,000. Cronin also happened to be Griffith's son-in-law.

St. Louis' clubs may have had it toughest of all. In 1934, the Cardinals defeated the Giants by 2 games in a bitterly contested pennant race, and Dizzy Dean, the last National Leaguer to win 30 games, was the ringleader of the "Gas House Gang," one of the most popular and colorful groups of players ever assembled. Yet the Redbirds drew only 325,000 fans to Sportsman Park in 1934. The next year, the St. Louis Browns attracted a measly 81,000 fans. The club pulled in less than 1.2 million paying spectators for the entire decade, effectively crippling the franchise both competitively and financially. Except for a brief moment of glory

during World War II, the club finished no higher than sixth place from 1935 until it was sold and moved to Baltimore in 1954.

Into this have and have-not environment stepped Tom Yawkey, a Bostonian who inherited $7 million on his 30th birthday in 1933. Three days later he bought the moribund Red Sox, a club that had brought up the rear in the American League in seven of the previous eight years. Yawkey committed all his energy and resources into turning the club around. He bought respectability in the ensuing years, as he paid top dollar for the likes of Grove, Wes Ferrell, Cronin, and Foxx, but a pennant (as well as a profit) continued to elude the feckless Sox until 1946.

Detroit owner Frank Navin apparently invested more shrewdly in the 1930s. In 1934, he purchased Cochrane and Goslin to team with Charlie Gehringer and Hank Greenberg, and the Tigers won pennants in 1934 and '35. The payoff came when attendance in Detroit tripled to a league-high 919,000 in 1934, equivalent to one-third of the eight-team league's draw. The following year, the Tigers became one of the very few clubs to spin the turnstiles 1 million times in a year during the decade.

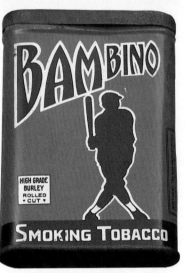

Lefty Grove on a trolley car sign (top). A Bambino tobacco tin (bottom) from the 1930s.

Former A's (top) gather before a 1935 game at Fenway Park. A's catcher Mickey Cochrane (bottom left) in 1932 hit .293 with 23 homers. Lou Gehrig, left, Bob Shawkey, and Babe Ruth (bottom right) in 1930.

THE 1930s

The Yankees also managed that feat, and ended as the sport's top draw in the decade by attracting a little over 9 million fans. Owner Jacob Ruppert saw the correlation between success in the standings with fiscal strength, and he poured money into his club to keep it stocked with talent. To that end, the Yankees followed the Cardinals lead by purchasing a minor league team, the Newark Bears, in 1934 as a cost-effective means of developing players. Ruppert was also lucky. He took what was considered a gamble in late 1934 by plunking down $35,000 and five ballplayers to acquire a young outfielder from the San Francisco Seals named Joe DiMaggio. Joe D. had been the most closely scrutinized minor leaguer in years, and it was estimated that the purchase price for him would have reached $125,000 if he hadn't suffered a knee injury in 1934. After he was hurt, other teams backed away from DiMaggio, but Ruppert was willing to risk his investment. Subsequently, DiMaggio became the major contributor in the four Yankees pennant teams of the late 1930s.

Economic factors colored most of the major developments of the period. Minor league teams had to be particularly innovative to stay afloat, and, with that in mind, 11 minor league clubs installed lights and began playing night baseball in 1930. The concept proved immediately popular in the lower leagues and may have saved many clubs from bankruptcy. However, night ball was resisted in the big leagues until 1935, when Larry MacPhail had his Cincinnati Reds play seven games under the lights that year. The practice was harshly criticized by baseball's conservative wing. *The Sporting News*, considered the weekly "Bible of Baseball," argued against the implementation of night baseball on the grounds that it would be "bad for digestion, sleep, and morale." It turned out to be good for the Reds' balance sheet, and when MacPhail left to run the Dodgers in 1938, he immediately installed lights and had "Dem Bums" playing in prime time. By 1940, six of the eight N.L. clubs played a portion of their schedules after dark.

Baseball also discovered that radio was an important revenue source in the 1930s. In use since the 1923 World Series, the clubs had never directly received income from the new broadcast medium, and originally they saw it as a threat to the gate. In 1933, a radio company paid for exclusive rights to air the World Series, and by '36 those rights cost $100,000. The lowly Boston Braves were the first team to command a fee for local rights to broadcast their games, and in '33 the club received $5,000. By decade's end, both the Yankees and the Giants took in over $100,000 a year in local broadcast rights fees.

Another lasting baseball innovation born of the Depression is the All-Star Game. Conceived by the *Chicago Tribune* as a promotional gimmick, the first game was played July 6, 1933, at Comiskey Park before 49,000 fans. The spectacle of the National League stars playing against the American League elite was an immediate hit. Fittingly enough, the game-winning blow in the first game was struck by the biggest star of them all, as 38-year-old Babe Ruth blasted a two-run homer to propel the American League to a 4-2 win.

Another large group of players, some of superstar ability, were toiling under relative obscurity during the 1930s. These players were

Red Ruffing won 175 games during the 1930s.

JOSH GIBSON

Just imagine the frustration. You are in your playing prime, and people call you the greatest ballplayer alive, yet because you are black you cannot play in the major leagues. You can't even get in during World War II to fill the void after some of the game's best players have been drafted. And when a major league team does try to sign you, the Commissioner vetoes it. For Josh Gibson, the frustration must have been so unbearable he had to drink to ease the pain. And he eased it so much that in 1947, when he was age 36, he died of a stroke—three months before Jackie Robinson broke baseball's color barrier.

But while he lived, Gibson was a Negro League legend. "The greatest hitter who ever lived," said Satchel Paige. "He hits the ball a mile and throws like a rifle," said Walter Johnson. "Once you saw him play, you knew the legends were true," said Roy Campanella.

Gibson was a catcher from 1930 to 1946, and his plaque in the Hall of Fame credits him with hitting "almost 800 home runs" and winning four batting titles. His career began in 1929 at age 17 and in 1931, he joined Satchel Paige, Judy Johnson, Oscar Charleston, and Cool Papa Bell on the Pittsburgh Crawfords, one of the greatest baseball teams ever assembled.

Had Joshua Gibson been born 20 years later, Babe Ruth might have been passed in the record books 20 years earlier.

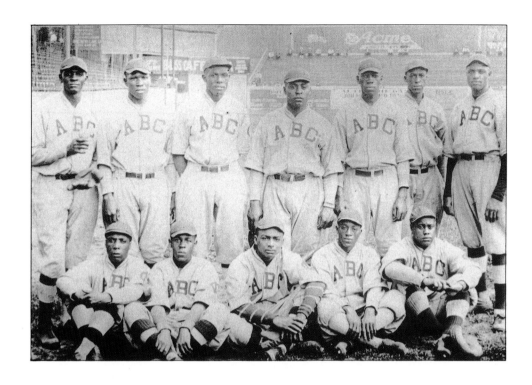

The Indianapolis ABCs (top) line up in the 1930s. Johnny Vander Meer delivers the pitch (bottom) during his second consecutive no-hitter on June 15, 1938. The game at Ebbets Field in Brooklyn was also notable for being the first night game in the East.

THE 1930s

members of the Negro Leagues that played in organized ball's shadow from 1920 until the color barrier fell in 1946.

The Negro Leagues were an outgrowth of the invisible but unbreakable barrier that slammed down on black athletes in the late 19th century to keep them out of organized baseball. As a result, black ballplayers wrote a separate history of the game in the first half of the 20th century. All-black professional teams, including the Homestead Grays, were formed in the 1910s and made money by going on barnstorming tours, taking on challengers for a percentage of the gate. The first organized league of black clubs was started in 1920 by Rube Foster, the owner of the Chicago American Giants and one of the great black players of the early part of the century. His Negro National League consisted of eight teams from midwestern cities that went through numerous franchise shifts and much financial instability before folding in 1931.

The embryonic league did spawn some outstanding ballplayers, however, including a fleet-footed outfielder for the St. Louis Stars named Cool Papa Bell. Bell joined the Stars in 1922 and played in the Negro Leagues through the 1946 season, and has often been described as the fastest man ever to play baseball. He once scored from first on a sacrifice bunt in a game against major league all-stars. Bell was clocked rounding the bases in less than 13 seconds and is said to have had a career batting average in the high .300s.

A teammate once said that Bell was "so fast he could turn off the lights and be under the covers before the room got dark." The speaker was Satchel Paige, black baseball's most famous player. Paige started pitching professionally in 1926 and was still getting paid

Cool Papa Bell entered the Hall of Fame in 1974.

to pitch 40 years later. Dizzy Dean said that Paige was the best pitcher he ever saw, a sentiment shared by many others. In his prime, Paige possessed one of the game's great fastballs. He called it his bee ball, "because it hums." There is little hard data available with which to summarize Paige's career, but he once estimated that he won 2,000 games in his life, pitched about 100 no-hitters, and played for 250 teams, mostly on a hired one-game basis. His popularity may have exceeded that of any player since Babe Ruth, and it's been said that after he joined the Cleveland Indians as a 42-year-old rookie in 1948, more than 200,000 people turned out to watch him in his first three starts.

Paige, like many black players between the wars, was a baseball nomad. If the money was there, so was he. Satchel said he pitched year-round, summer in the United States and winter in Latin America, for 30 years, and he frequently jumped contracts if a better offer arose.

One of his teammates among his many clubs was Josh Gibson, the greatest slugger in Negro League annals. Beginning in 1930, Gibson hammered balls for 16 years before he died of a stroke in early 1947. He was called the "black Babe Ruth," and his power was legendary. An eyewitness claims he saw Gibson hit a ball out of Yankee Stadium in a 1934 game, a feat no major leaguer has accomplished. A hulking 6'1", 215-pound catcher, Gibson was described by

RED RUFFING

With hitting the game's dominant force during the 1930s, only a few pitchers excelled enough to be considered in an elite class. And Charles Herbert "Red" Ruffing was up there with Dizzy Dean as the best righthanded pitcher of the era.

When Ruffing's career began in the late 1920s, however, it didn't look as though he would ever achieve such status. With the lowly Boston Red Sox between 1925 and 1930, he was a miserable 39-93, leading the A.L. twice in losses. When he lost 25 in 1928, Ruffing also led the league with 25 complete games.

Ruffing was such a good hitter — batting over .300 in 1928 and '29 — Boston was thinking of making him an outfielder. But for the second time in Red Sox history, they traded a good hitting pitcher to the Yankees. However, unlike Babe Ruth, Ruffing stayed on the mound and with the support of a great offense he did a complete turnaround. He posted only one losing season for the Yanks during the 1930s; between 1936 and '39, he notched four straight 20-win seasons. He led the A.L. in strikeouts in 1932, wins in '38, and shutouts in 1938 and '39. Ruffing's record was 7-2 in seven World Series, and he ranks in the top five in six Series pitching categories.

Ruffing was also one of baseball's greatest hitting pitchers. With a .269 career average, he is third all time for most hits by a pitcher (520) and is tied for second in pitcher's home runs (35). In 1947, Ruffing made the Hall of Fame.

The 1924 K.C. Monarchs (top) were black baseball's champions. Before Rube Foster (middle left) became an owner, he was one of the best pitchers in baseball during the 1910s. Third baseman Ray Dandridge (middle center) was one of the greatest players in the 1940s Negro Leagues. He and other black players were able to play on integrated teams in the Mexican League in the 1940s, but couldn't do the same in the United States. Dandridge eventually played in the minor leagues, but despite playing well (he was the Double-A Rookie of the Year in '49 and the league's MVP in 1950), he was never promoted to the big leagues. He was elected to the Hall of Fame in 1987. Some experienced baseball observers consider Cuban-born Martin DiHigo (middle right) the best player ever. Since many black baseball teams suffered manpower shortages, players became skilled at many positions. DiHigo excelled at every position and was elected to the Hall of Fame in 1977. Josh Gibson (bottom) rounds third base in a 1940s game at Griffith Stadium in Washington, DC. Cool Papa Bell said that Gibson slugged 72 homers in a single season.

THE 1930s

Roy Campanella, a veteran of both Negro and major league ball, as "the greatest ballplayer I ever saw." But like Paige and the others, virtually no record of Gibson's achievements exist. He was credited with hitting 75 home runs for the Homestead Grays when he was 19 years old, but it's not known how many games this encompasses.

After the first Negro Major League died in 1931, another was formed by Pittsburgh Crawfords owner Gus Greenlee in 1933. Greenlee was a wealthy numbers king in Pittsburgh and had constructed the Crawfords beginning in 1931. He counted Bell, Paige, and Gibson among his players. Greenlee pulled six teams together for the inaugural season. The ride was bumpy, but the league survived until 1948. In the latter half of the 1930s and through the war years, the league was fairly prosperous, and in 1937, a Negro American League was formed as a counterpart major league. The two held championship contests for several years in the early 1940s.

Throughout the life of all-black baseball, the teams' major revenue source came from barnstorming. This created one of the Achilles' heels of the Negro Major Leagues: a lack of strong central authority. Without a stabilizing force, club owners looked out for

themselves first, and if that meant canceling a league contest because of a better barnstorming offer, so be it. The leagues' lax attitude toward the playing schedule gave the pennant contests little legitimacy in the eyes of players and fans, and the result was little fan interest in the pennant races.

One annual event that was taken seriously was the East-West All-Star Game. The first All-Star Game was staged in 1933 — the same year as the inaugural major league All-Star Game — and was held in Comiskey Park. The early games were comprised of stars from league teams and barnstorming clubs. Each annual contest was called the most important black sporting event of the year and was always a good draw. Attendance the first year was 20,000 and reached a peak of 52,000 in 1943.

Eventually, however, the Negro Leagues went the same way as other Jim Crow institutions, such as segregated schools. Jackie Robinson's arrival in Brooklyn sharply deflected attention from the Negro Leagues, and by 1948, one year after he broke the color barrier, the Negro National League folded from lack of support. The Negro American League hung on until 1960, but its franchises were shifted out of major league cities. The league eventually became a feeder system where such players as Willie Mays, Hank Aaron, and Ernie Banks were developed for the majors.

By 1967, the only all-black professional team in existence was the Indianapolis Clowns, a sports entertainment act similar in concept to the Harlem Globetrotters. In 1971, the Hall of Fame finally recognized the contributions of the pre-integration black players to the history of the game and inducted

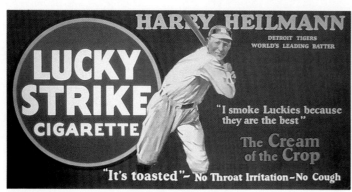

Harry Heilmann graces a Lucky Strike trolley car poster.

JOE CRONIN

The Washington Senators finished second or third each year between 1930 and 1932, but it wasn't Joe Cronin's fault they couldn't win the pennant. During that span, Cronin batted over .300 (including a career-high .346 in '30), scored more than 100 runs twice, drove in more than 100 runs three times, and led American League shortstops in putouts and double plays.

Feeling his team was ready to win a pennant in 1933, Senators owner Clark Griffith made his team's spark plug his pilot. Called the "Boy Manager," the 26-year-old Cronin led Washington to the World Series, which they lost in five games to the New York Giants. The Senators dropped to seventh in 1934, but Cronin took his mind off the disappointment by marrying the boss' daughter. While Cronin was on his honeymoon, Red Sox owner Tom Yawkey offered Griffith more than $200,000 for Cronin. After getting Cronin's approval, Griffith traded his shortstop, his manager, and his son-in-law to Boston.

Cronin had six productive years as the Red Sox player/manager, batting over .300 four times and driving in more than 100 three times, before becoming a part-time player in 1942. He led the league in pinch hits with 18 in 1943. In 1946, the Sox won their first pennant with Cronin as manager, but couldn't beat St. Louis in the Series.

Cronin continued to make his mark as a baseball executive as Red Sox general manager from 1948 to '58 and as American League President from 1959 to '73. He was elected to the Hall of Fame in 1956.

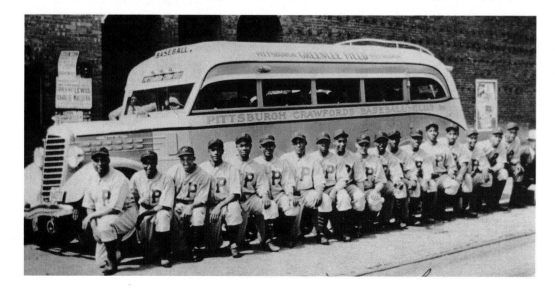

The 1906 "World's Champions" Philadelphia Giants (top left) featured Sol White, Rube Foster, and Charlie White. In 1910, it is said that George "Chappie" Johnson (top right) outhit Ty Cobb in Cuba, presumably during exhibition matches. Satchel Paige (middle right) pitched year-round. He pitched in the National Negro League during the summer, winter ball in the Caribbean, and barnstorming tours in-between. He started 29 games in one month, won five games in one week, and pitched three complete games in one day. The Homestead Grays (middle left) of Pittsburgh were one of the strongest teams in black baseball for many years. The 1943 team, shown here, starred first baseman Buck Leonard (who was inducted into the Hall of Fame in 1972), standing third from the right. The Pittsburgh Crawfords (bottom left) challenged the Grays for supremacy.

THE 1930s

Paige. In the ensuing six years, eight of his peers, including Bell and Gibson, joined him in Cooperstown.

The Hall of Fame itself is a product of the Depression. In the midst of the nation's economic gloom, organized baseball decided to celebrate itself by constructing a monument to the game and its stars. The Hall of Fame was born in 1936, and its charter members were the biggest stars of the first 35 years of the modern major leagues. The first player chosen was Ty Cobb, and he was joined by Honus Wagner, Christy Mathewson, Walter Johnson, and the man considered by many as the greatest player ever, Babe Ruth. In recognition of his enormous impact on the game's style of play, and his role in injecting the sport with a new-found excitement and popularity, the Bambino was selected for the Hall barely one year after playing his last game. The following year nine more players, managers and administrators were enshrined. By the time the National Baseball Hall of Fame and Museum at Cooperstown was opened in June 1939, 22 men whose achievements spanned the game's first 100 years had been elevated to immortality.

1930

It was the most explosive year in baseball history, and when it was over, there was a host of new records and startling statistics. Most notable were the performances of National Leaguers Hack Wilson and Bill Terry. Wilson, playing with the Chicago Cubs, hit a league record 56 home runs and established a major league standard by driving in 190 runs. The New York Giants' Terry topped the revered .400 batting mark, by hitting .401, the last National Leaguer to accomplish that deed.

The offensive madness was everywhere. Six National League teams batted over .300, and the Giants set a major league record by compiling a .319 team average. Freddy Leach, a 32-year-old Giants outfielder, hit .327, which made him only the sixth-best batter on his club.

Five of the top-ten team batting averages and six of the top-20 team runs totals of the century were recorded in 1930. The Philadelphia Phillies boasted two batters, Chuck Klein and Lefty O'Doul, who batted over .380. The team hit a cumulative .315 yet finished dead last. That's because the 1930 Phillies hold one of baseball's most dubious distinctions; the pitching staff compiled a staggering 6.71 earned run average, a modern record for ineptitude.

When the dust settled in the N.L., the St. Louis Cardinals emerged on top by 2 games over the ball crushers from Chicago. St. Louis put together a stunning stretch run by winning 21 of 25 games in September and overcoming a 12-game deficit. Every starter in St. Louis' lineup bettered .300 that year, and the team's .314 batting mark is fourth best in history. The Redbirds also became the first team in National League annals to cross the plate 1,000 times in a season. The Cards attack was remarkably well-balanced as seven regulars, led by Frankie Frisch, scored between 85 and 121 runs. The pitching staff was headed by Wild Bill Hallahan, who won 15 games,

BABE RUTH'S CALLED HOMER

Babe Ruth, while at bat in Game Three of the 1932 World Series, supposedly made some gestures toward center field. The question, then as now, is: Was Ruth waving at the Cubs dugout, which was heckling him? Was he telling Chicago pitcher Charlie Root that the next pitch would be slammed right back at him? Or was Ruth pointing at the bleachers to indicate where he would park the next pitch?

Not one sportswriter reported the so-named "Called Shot" in the next day's newspaper account of the Yankees 7-5 win. Even the players denied seeing Ruth point with such bravado.

The players admit that there was great animosity between the two teams. Yankees manager Joe McCarthy had been fired by the Cubs two years before. Former Yankee Mark Koenig, who helped the Cubs win the pennant after joining them late in the year, had been voted only a half Series share by Chicago.

When Ruth, who'd already hit a three-run homer in the game, came up with the score tied 4-4

Robert Thom's painting of Ruth's called shot.

in the fifth inning, the Cubs were taunting him from their dugout. After taking the first two pitches for strikes, Ruth supposedly smiled and held up his fingers like an umpire. Then Root fired and the Bambino sent a ball soaring over the center field fence. Later, Ruth had said that he "didn't exactly point to any spot; just sort of waved at the whole fence."

But Ruth knew that people wanted to believe the legend, and he never discouraged them.

A stand-up figure of Frankie Frisch.

The "Big Five" of the 1932 Pittsburgh Crawfords (top left) were, left to right, Oscar Charleston (elected to the Hall of Fame in 1976), Rap Dixon, Josh Gibson, Judy Johnson (elected to the Hall of Fame in 1975), and Jud Wilson. Shortstop John Henry Lloyd (top right) was often compared to Honus Wagner, which Wagner considered an honor. Bill Terry's (bottom left) total of 254 base hits (.401 average) in 1930 ranks tied for second on the all-time list. Gabby Hartnett (bottom right, arguing with the umpire), had a .630 slugging average in 1930.

THE 1930s

and the club got a major boost from the midseason acquisition of 36-year-old Burleigh Grimes, who posted a 13-6 record after joining the Cards.

The Cubs surrendered the N.L. crown in part because Rogers Hornsby was sidelined much of the season with a foot injury. In his absence, Hack Wilson was the big story in the Windy City, as he fashioned a .356 average and 146 runs scored to go with his record 56 home runs and 190 runs batted in. The return of catcher Gabby Hartnett to the lineup, following an arm injury in '29, lent extra thunder to the club. Hartnett cracked 37 home runs and drove home 122 runners, as the Cubs led the league in homers, fell two runs shy of the millennium mark in runs scored, and set the league standard for slugging average (.481).

The Giants also surpassed 900 runs scored and got solid pitching from starters Fat Freddie Fitzsimmons and King Carl Hubbell. Terry — along with his .401 batting milestone — rapped 254 hits to tie O'Doul's year-old

Kiki Cuyler scored 155 runs in 1930.

N.L. mark, batted home 129 runners, and scored 139. Third baseman Freddie Lindstrom contributed a .379 average and 127 runs, while Mel Ott popped .349 and drove home 119 runs. All that wasn't enough and the Giants finished 5 games back.

The Dodgers rose from sixth to fourth, 6 games out, led by Babe Herman's .393 batting average, 35 home runs, 130 RBI, and 143 runs scored. Dazzy Vance was one of the few pitchers in the league who could hold his head high at season's end. At age 39, he continued to dazzle for the Dodgers by posting a 2.61 earned run average in a season when the league ERA stood at 4.97. His ERA was more than a run lower than the league's next best. Pittsburgh's Ray Kremer, on the other hand, was one of two N.L. pitchers to win 20 games that year, and he did it with a 5.02 ERA. Boston Braves rookie Wally Berger walloped 38 home runs, a record for a first-year player that stood until 1987. The Phillies' Klein posted one of the best batting lines in league history — .386 batting average, 40 home runs, 170 RBI, 158 runs scored, and 250 hits — but his club still lost 102 games.

The American League campaign was saner, but just slightly. The league batting average was "only" .288, and its pitchers combined for a 4.65 earned run average. The Philadelphia A's rolled to their second straight pennant, thanks to heavy hitting by Al Simmons and Jimmie Foxx, and 50 wins tossed by Lefty Grove and George Earnshaw. Simmons captured his first batting crown by hitting .381, and he added 36 homers and 165 RBI. Foxx chipped in 37 round-trippers, 156 runs batted in, and a .335 average. Grove was masterful: 28 wins, five losses, and a 2.54 earned run average, more than two runs per nine innings below the league average.

The Washington Senators challenged for the first time since 1926, but finished 8 games back. Washington's 94 wins were fashioned by sending to the mound the only staff in either league to hold opposing batters to under four runs per game, coupled with the solid bats of 23-year-old shortstop Joe Cronin and 40-year-old outfielder Sam Rice. During the season, the club traded perennial batting

LEFTY GROVE

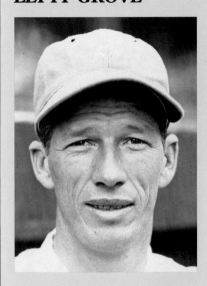

Not too long ago, a baseball writer set about explaining why Robert Moses "Lefty" Grove was not only the greatest lefthanded pitcher of all time, but the greatest all-time pitcher. He simply put Grove's lifetime record against that of Carl Hubbell. Grove's 300-141 mark is 30 games better. As the writer put it, "Grove was 30 games better than great."

Grove parlayed a blazing fastball and a tough, competitive personality into an amazing 17-year career with the Philadelphia Athletics and Boston Red Sox. His only losing season was his first in 1925. Even then, he led the A.L. in strikeouts, something he would do the next six straight years. After leading the league in ERA in '26, he reeled off seven straight 20-plus win seasons, topping the A.L. in victories and ERA four times.

Grove's masterpiece season came in 1931, when he went 31-4; led the league in ERA, strikeouts, and shutouts; and tied the A.L. record for consecutive victories with 16. He also led the A's to their third straight pennant and won two games in the World Series.

During the second half of the 1930s, Grove notched another 20-victory season and four more ERA titles (three coming when he didn't win 20 games). His nine ERA crowns are four more than Grover Alexander's and Sandy Koufax's, who are tied for second in the category. Grove retired after the 1941 season with 300 victories and an astounding .680 winning percentage, fourth on the all-time list.

Fred Lindstrom (top left) hit .379 in 1930, with 22 homers, 127 runs scored, and 106 RBI for the New York Giants. It was his last full season at third base; an injury forced him into the outfield in 1931. Hazen Shirley "Kiki" Cuyler (top right) was a multitalented outfielder who played mostly for the Pirates and Cubs in the 1920s and 1930s. A .321 lifetime batter, Kiki (his nickname came from his severe stutter) hit over .350 four times and was a prolific run-producer. He scored 100 or more runs five times and drove in 100 or more three times. Combining rare speed and power for the time, Cuyler led the N.L. in stolen bases in four seasons. His best year came with Pittsburgh in 1925, when he batted .357, slugged .593, and smacked 39 doubles, 26 triples, and 17 home runs. Cuyler also notched 41 stolen bases, 102 RBI, and 144 runs scored to propel the Pirates to the World Series against Washington. Cuyler defeated Walter Johnson's Senators almost single-handedly, winning Game Two with a late-inning two-run homer and Game Seven with a decisive two-run double off "The Big Train" in the eighth inning. New York Giants shortstop Travis "Stonewall" Jackson (middle left) had his best season batting in 1930, when he hit .339. Jackson replaced Hall of Fame shortstop Dave Bancroft in the Giants lineup, and much to John McGraw's delight, there was no drop-off in either defensive play or offensive production. Jackson was a career .291 hitter and was inducted into the Hall of Fame in 1982. Dizzy Dean (bottom left) looks serious as a young pitcher. In his rookie season for the St. Louis Cardinals in 1932, Dean was 18-15, and he led the league with 286 innings pitched and 191 strikeouts at age 21. Max "Camera Eye" Bishop (bottom right) was the Philadelphia Athletics second baseman from 1924 to 1933. He scored 117 runs in 1930 while walking 128 times. He also had 128 bases on balls in 1929, leading the league. His lifetime average of 20.42 walks per 100 at-bats is second best only to Ted Williams' walks ration of 20.76 to 100 on the all-time list.

THE 1930s

star Goose Goslin to St. Louis for Heinie Manush and pitcher General Crowder. Crowder became the ace of the Senator staff in the early 1930s. Manush batted .362 for the Senators in 88 games. Goslin hit .326 for the Brownies and blasted 30 home runs.

The Yankees finished third, 16 games back, despite batting a league-high .309, scoring 1,062 runs, and slugging .488, second highest in history. Ruth and Lou Gehrig again bombarded the league with a combined 90 home runs and 327 RBI, but the team didn't have a pitcher with more than 15 wins. The club, however, did pull another fast one on the Red Sox by snatching righthander Red Ruffing from Boston. Ruffing went 15-5 for New York and batted .374 in 99 at-bats for good measure. The previous season in Boston, Ruffing lost 22 games.

An amazing, if forgotten, performance was also turned in that year by Chicago White Sox pitcher Ted Lyons. Playing for a seventh-place club, Lyons won 22 of the club's 62 games. Lyons played only for the White Sox in his 21-year career, and he had the misfortune of joining the team in 1923, shortly after the Black Sox scandal had crippled the franchise. During his entire career, the White Sox finished as high as second only once.

The baseball world looked forward to an explosive Fall Classic as the Cards and A's fielded 13 starters who hit at least .300 that year, and the clubs had combined to score an average 12.7 runs per game during the season. But the A's pitchers were the stars of the Series; Earnshaw and Grove split Philadelphia's four wins and allowed just over one run per nine innings between them. Connie Mack's attack batted a meager .197 in the six-game set, but most of the hits counted. Mickey

Cochrane managed only four hits in the Series, but two went over the fences and another was a double. Simmons also struck two homers and hit .364. The Cardinals batted only .200 in the Series and scored just 12 runs, as Philadelphia won their second consecutive championship.

1931

The Cardinals rebounded from their World Series defeat to capture their fourth flag in six years, and they did it playing a brand of baseball vastly different from the preceding year. Following the offensive fusillade of 1930, the game's architects apparently went back to the drawing boards and deflated the helium-like ball. In 1931, the league batting average fell 26 points to .277, and runs decreased by 21 percent. Most significantly, home runs in the N.L. plummeted by 45 percent to 492. The obvious benefactors were the league's pitchers who shaved 1.11 runs off the league ERA, bringing it to a respectable 3.86.

The Cardinals again maximized their use of Branch Rickey's farm system. This year Rickey added Pepper Martin to the starting lineup and he hit .300. Chick

Ernie Lombardi's career started in Brooklyn.

CHARLIE GEHRINGER

A person in everyday life might take being called "Mechanical Man" as an insult. But to a baseball player, that term can imply consistency, durability, even flawlessness. During his 16 full seasons with the Detroit Tigers between 1926 and 1941, Charlie Gehringer typified all those characteristics and more.

Consistency — Gehringer batted over .300 13 out of 14 seasons (leading the American League with a .371 average in 1937, the year he was MVP). He hit 40 or more doubles seven times, scored more than 100 runs 12 times, and drove in more than 100 runs seven times. He averaged just 23 strikeouts per year.

Durability — He played more than 140 games ten out of 11 years between 1928 and 1938. Teammate Mickey Cochrane once said of Gehringer, "He says hello on opening day and goodbye on closing day, and in between he hits .350."

Flawlessness — He was one of the greatest fielding second basemen in baseball history. He led A.L. second sackers in fielding percentage four straight years (1934 to '37) and led the league in assists a record seven times.

Gehringer was the same efficient machine in postseason and All-Star play. He batted .379 when the Tigers lost the World Series in 1934 and hit .375 when they won it in 1935. And in 20 All-Star Game at-bats, he wound himself up and got ten hits for a record .500 All-Star average. Gehringer ranks tenth all time in doubles, retired in 1942 with a .320 lifetime average, and made the Hall of Fame in 1949.

CARDINALS VICTORY PARADE.
SATURDAY SEPT. 27, 1930. 11³⁰ A.M.

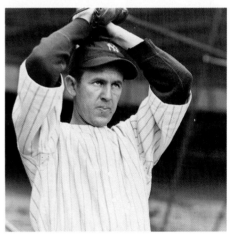

St. Louis staged a victory parade (top) for the
Cardinals after they won the N.L. pennant,
beating the Cubs out by 2 games. Tony Lazzeri
(middle center) hit .303 in 1930, with 109 runs
scored and 121 RBI. Lazzeri was the Yankees
second baseman from 1926 to 1937. "Poosh 'Em
Up" drove in more than 100 runs in seven
different seasons, and he ended his career in 1939
with 1,191 career RBI and a .292 batting
average. Lefty Gomez (middle right) was 21-9 in
his first full year as a Yankees hurler. He went on
to win 20 games in three other seasons, and his
.649 winning percentage lifetime ranks 13th on
the all-time list. Catcher Moe Berg (bottom left)
batted .243 during his 15-year career. He retired
to become one of the top intelligence officers
during World War II. Pepper Martin (bottom
right) hit .300 in his rookie year in 1931 and put
on one of the greatest displays in World Series
history that year.

205

THE 1930s

Hafey, the Cards' bespectacled right fielder, captured the batting title with a .3489 average, a fraction of a point higher than New York's Terry and Hafey's teammate Jim Bottomley. The Cards also had six pitchers who won 11 games, led by Hallahan's 19-9 mark.

John McGraw's Giants came in second, 13 games off the pace. In spite of solid contributions by Terry and Ott, the Giants suffered a sharp decline in run production, and wasted strong seasons by pitchers Fitzsimmons, Bill Walker, and Hubbell. The Cubs, also suffering from a severe power shortage, slid to third. Chicago hit 87 fewer homers in 1931, with Hack Wilson managing only 13 and Hartnett going from 37 round-trippers to eight. Among N.L. hitters, Philadelphia's Klein was the least affected by the offensive drought. He batted .337 and led the league by hitting 31 home runs and driving in 121 runners.

The Philadelphia Athletics also had little trouble repeating in the A.L., as they stormed to a 107-45 record, 13½ games ahead of the Yankees — an impressive margin considering that the Yankees fielded the most productive lineup in history. It was the A's third consecutive pennant and owner/manager Mack's ninth league title, and it was also the best won-lost record of the decade.

The strength of Mack's team was its pitching. Grove produced one of the best seasons a pitcher has ever had. He won 31 games, lost only four, and had a 2.06 earned run average in a year when the league ERA was 4.38. He led the league in shutouts, strikeouts, and complete games, and reeled off a 16-game winning streak. Two other Philadelphia pitchers, Earnshaw and Rube Walberg, won more than 20 games and another, Roy Mahaffey, went 15-4.

In the '31 World Series, Lefty Grove was 2-1 with a 2.42 ERA, 16 Ks, and only two walks.

The other side of the A's ledger was almost as impressive. Simmons defended his batting title by hitting .390 even as the league batting average tumbled ten points to .278. He also hit 22 homers and drove in 128 runs. Foxx contributed 30 home runs and 120 RBI to the cause, Cochrane hit .349, and leadoff man Max Bishop scored 115 times.

New York's lineup was more than a match for Philadelphia, but rookie manager Joe McCarthy's pitching staff was not nearly as good. The Yankees averaged almost seven runs a game and featured six players who scored at least 100 runs that season. Babe Ruth, now age 36, hit .373 with 46 home runs, 163 RBI, and a .700 slugging average. He won the home run crown for the 12th and final time in his career. It was also the 13th time he had the league's highest slugging percentage. Gehrig was equally impressive, batting .341, matching Ruth's 46 home runs, and setting an American League record with 184 RBI. Both scored well over 100 runs, as did Lyn Lary, Joe Sewell, Earle Combs, and Ben Chapman. En route to scoring a record 1,067 runs, the club led the league in home runs and stolen bases. Pitcher Lefty Gomez, in his first full year, won 21 and lost nine with a 2.63 ERA, but the rest of the staff allowed well over four runs per nine innings.

The Most Valuable Player award was reinstituted in 1931. The

MEDWICK FORCED OUT OF GAME

The 1934 World Series between the Cardinals and the Tigers was tied at three games apiece going into the last battle on October 9 in the Motor City. While the Series produced a bunch of hitting stars, the showstoppers were St. Louis' pitching Dean brothers, Dizzy and Daffy, who were one win away from making good on their prediction that they'd win four games between them.

When St. Louis scored seven runs for Dizzy in the third inning, the Series was all but won, destined to end in unsuspenseful fashion. But nothing was mundane with the "Gas House Gang" Cardinals.

In the top of the sixth, Ducky Medwick hit a triple to drive Pepper Martin home with the eighth Cardinal run. But after Medwick slid safely into the bag, he kicked at Tigers third baseman Marv Owen, who had fooled him into sliding with a phantom tag.

When Medwick returned to left field in the bottom of the inning, 18,000 Tigers fans in the bleachers began pelting him with everything from bottles to vegetables, even shoes. Four times Medwick left the field, and each time he would return to frenzied abuse.

Finally, Commissioner Kenesaw Mountain Landis questioned Medwick and Owen; after Medwick admitted to kicking Owen without much provocation, Landis removed him from the game, probably more for his own protection than for starting the ruckus. The Cardinals went on to win the game 11-0. Medwick is the only player ever suspended from a World Series game.

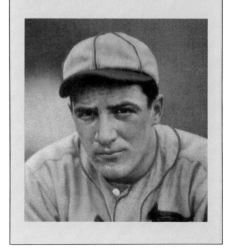

Ted Lyons (top left) pitched for the Chicago White Sox during the most dismal two decades of their history — the 1920s and 1930s. In a shambles following the 1919 Black Sox suspensions, the Sox never rose above third place and finished last three times during Lyons' career. Often overworked, Lyons completed 356 of his lifetime 484 starts. He won 20 games three times; he was 22-14 in 1927 with a team that finished 39½ games out of first and 22-15 in 1930 for a team that finished 40 games out. By 1931, Lyons' fastball was gone, and he saved his career by learning the knuckleball from a photo of Eddie Rommel's grip. The pitch was so effective that Lyons was often accused of throwing a spitball. Lyons spent his last four seasons as the White Sox's "Sunday pitcher," hurling in a rotation in which he made just one start a week. He finished his career with a 260-230 record, having pitched 21 years for the ChiSox. Lyons enlisted in the Marine Corps in 1942 and saw action in the Pacific, and he came back to pitch after the War in 1946. He was elected to the Hall of Fame in 1955. Righthander "Fat Freddie" Fitzsimmons (bottom left) combined with Carl Hubbell to give the Giants a solid righty-lefty combination. Fitzsimmons was a solid starter who won about 15 to 20 games a year and threw about 230 to 250 innings. A control pitcher, he led the league in shutouts once, in 1935, when all of his four wins were shutouts. Bill Terry scores (top right). In the six years between 1927 and 1932, Terry was an impressive run-producer; he averaged 115 runs scored and 116 RBI. The A's battery (bottom right) of Lefty Grove and Mickey Cochrane confer. In '31, Grove led the A.L. with 31 wins, a .886 winning percentage, a 2.06 ERA, 27 complete games, four shutouts, and 175 strikeouts. Cochrane hit .339 and slugged .553.

THE 1930s

Babe Ruth was a giant among men.

award was determined by a vote of the Baseball Writers Association of America, using the system in place today, and the first winners were St. Louis' Frankie Frisch and Philadelphia's Lefty Grove. The current ground-rule double interpretation was also implemented that year, along with several scoring changes — including an eight-year elimination of the sacrifice fly.

In a rematch of the 1930 World Series, Cardinal rookie Martin propelled St. Louis to the title in seven games over the favored A's. Martin collected 12 hits in 24 at-bats, stole five bases, and scored five runs.

Lefty Grove beat the Cards in Game One, 6-2, but Martin contributed three hits and a stolen base to the losing cause. In St. Louis' 2-0 second-game win Martin stretched a single into a double, stole third, and scored on a fly out in the second inning. In the seventh, he singled, stole second, advanced to third on a ground out, and scored on a squeeze play. He had two hits and two runs scored in St. Louis' 5-2 win in Game Three, and had the Cards' only two hits in

their 3-0 loss to Earnshaw that evened the Series. Martin then went three-for-four with a home run, and batted in four runs in St. Louis' 5-1 win in Game Five. Grove contained Martin in his 8-1 Game Six victory, which knotted the Series again. Martin was shut out again in Game Seven, but his teammates weren't, as St. Louis won 4-2. Martin did preserve the win by making a sparkling grab of a Max Bishop line drive in center field for the final out.

1932

While the Philadelphia A's offense remained powerful in 1932, its pitching slipped and so did they — to second place. The A's Foxx blasted 58 home runs, in the most serious challenge to Ruth's 1927 record, and wrested the home run crown from the Bambino for the first time since '25. "Double X" knocked home 169 runs and batted .364. Simmons and Cochrane also both exceeded 20 homers and 100 RBI. However, the A's team ERA soared by almost a run a game to 4.45. Grove posted a 25-10 record, giving him an 84-19 three-year mark, and he had a league-low ERA of 2.84, but the rest of the staff was woeful.

The Yankees, on the other hand, bolted from the starting gate and galloped home to a 107-47 record, 13 games ahead of the defending champs. It was the third successive season the Bronx Bombers scored more than 1,000 runs. Ruth batted .341, with 41 homers and 137 RBI. Gehrig added

34 homers, 151 RBI, and a .349 batting average; the two combined for 258 runs scored. At the top of the order, Combs scored 143 times while batting .321, and speedy outfielder Chapman contributed 101 runs scored, 107 RBI, and a league-best 38 stolen bases.

The Yankees' pitching staff jelled in '32 after several subpar seasons. It was the only team in the league to allow less than four runs per game. Gomez compiled a 24-7 record, Red Ruffing went 18-7, and newcomer Johnny Allen fashioned a 17-4 mark.

For the National League, it was a transitional season. St. Louis moved former batting champ Chick Hafey to Cincinnati, and split first baseman Jim Bottomley's playing time with Ripper Collins. Frisch was used at a variety of positions as the club sank to seventh place, despite 18 wins contributed by 21-year-old Dizzy Dean.

Chicago earned the top spot even though president Bill Veeck Sr. canned manager Rogers Horns-

---

MEL OTT

While American League monsters like Babe Ruth, Lou Gehrig, Jimmie Foxx, and Hank Greenberg were belting their 40 or 50

home runs a year during the 1930s, a 5'9", 170-pound outfielder was averaging around 30 per season and winning five N.L. home run crowns.

Mel Ott's best home run year came in 1929 when he hit 42 during his second season with the New York Giants. John McGraw's team played in the Polo Grounds and rarely have a player and a ballpark been so compatible. The right field line at the Grounds was only 250 feet away and Ott's unorthodox pull-hitting style — he lifted his front leg high and straight out as the pitcher delivered — allowed him to park many a ball into the seats.

But Ott wasn't just a cheapie home run hitter. During a 21-year career, which he started at age 17, he was one of the most consistent batters ever. Between his .383 rookie season in 1926 to his .308 in '45, Master Melvin hit over .300 11 times, and scored and drove in more than 100 runs nine times. He won the '33 World Series for the Giants by going four-for-four in Game One and hitting a game-winning homer in Game Four. Ott is one of only 14 to hit 500 home runs (511), and he ranks in the top-ten all-time list in runs, RBI, and walks. Numbers like that gained him Hall of Fame recognition in 1951.

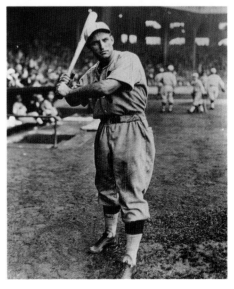

*These rival Chicago infielders (top left) include, left to right: Billy Sullivan,
Billy Herman, Jimmy Adair, and Luke Appling. Lon Warneke (top right)
hurled an N.L.-leading four shutouts for the '32 Cubs. Hack Wilson (second
row right) had 123 RBI for Brooklyn in '32. A group of 1932 Cardinals
(bottom left). Dodger Lefty O'Doul (third row right) batted an N.L.-
leading .368 in '32. Pepper Martin (bottom right) scored a league-high
122 runs in 1933.*

THE 1930s

by in August following a bitter dispute between the two men. First baseman Charlie Grimm was handed the job and guided the Cubs home 4 games ahead of Pittsburgh. The Cubs had a fairly tame attack, partly because Wilson had been shipped off to Brooklyn following a feud with Hornsby. Riggs Stephenson batted .324 and drove home 85 runs, and rookie Billy Herman scored 102 times, but it was the pitchers who sparkled for the Cubs. Rookie Lon Warneke posted a 22-6 record, Guy Bush went 19-11, and Charlie Root planted a 15-10 mark to lead the stingiest staff in the N.L. The club also benefited from the late-season acquisition of former Yankees shortstop Mark Koenig, who batted .353 and provided steady defense down the stretch.

Second-place Pittsburgh was led by the Waner brothers, Paul and Lloyd, both of whom hit over .333. The Bucs also got strong contributions from third baseman Pie Traynor and a sensational rookie shortstop named Arky Vaughan, who hit .318. Brooklyn finished third and was comprised largely of such castoffs as first baseman George Kelly, who had lost his job with the Giants to Bill Terry; shortstop Glenn Wright, displaced in Pittsburgh by Vaughan; and outfielder Hack Wilson. Lefty O'Doul, who won the batting crown with a .368 average, was formerly with the Phillies. Coming out of the bullpen was 48-year-old spitballer Jack Quinn, who had eight saves pitching for his seventh team.

The league's perennial doormats, Philadelphia and Boston, managed .500 records that year, the last time both would accomplish the feat until 1950. The Phillies, playing in the tiny Baker Bowl, topped the league in runs scored, home runs, and batting average. Chuck Klein hit .348,

slugged a league-high 38 homers, batted in 137 runs, and was voted the league's Most Valuable Player. Don Hurst batted .339, belted 24 home runs, and drove in a league-best 143 runs.

The New York Giants marked the end of an era early in the season when John McGraw, in failing health, turned over his last-place club to Bill Terry. Called "Little Napoleon," McGraw had guided the Giants to 2,658 wins and ten pennants in 30 years at the controls of the club. New York finished in sixth that year, despite fine performances turned in by Terry, who hit .350; Mel Ott, who blasted 38 homers; and Carl Hubbell, who went 18-11 with a 2.50 earned run average.

The World Series developed into a grudge match between the Yankees and the Cubs. Part of the bad blood came from Yankees manager Joe McCarthy's desire to pay back the Cubs for dumping him after the 1930 season. The Yankees players also harshly criticized the Cubs for voting their former teammate Koenig only a half-share of the Series take. In this environment of open hostility, the New York hitters unloaded on Cubs pitching for more than nine runs a game in their four-game sweep of Chicago. Lou Gehrig led the charge by slamming nine hits, including three home runs in 17 at-bats, driving in eight runs, and scoring nine. Combs averaged two runs scored a game; and Ruth hit two home runs, scored six times, and batted .333. One of his home runs was the famous "called" blast in Game Three against Charlie Root that broke a 4-4 tie. The Cubbies crumbled after that. Gehrig immediately followed with another home run; then the Yanks completed the sweep the next day by win-

A 1932 painting of Ruth's called shot.

The Yankees outfield (top left) of, left to right, Ben Chapman, Babe Ruth, and Earle Combs combined for 364 runs scored and 309 RBI during the 1932 season. They combined for 16 RBI and 15 runs scored during the '32 World Series. Red Faber, left, and Sad Sam Jones (top right) examine the ball. Jones finished his 22-year career in 1935 with a 229-217 record. Tigers second baseman Charlie Gehringer (bottom left) averaged 118 runs scored and 100 RBI a year during the 1930s. Yankee Joe Sewell (bottom right) in '32 struck out three times in 503 at-bats; his 167.7 at-bats per strikeout ranks first in the modern era of baseball.

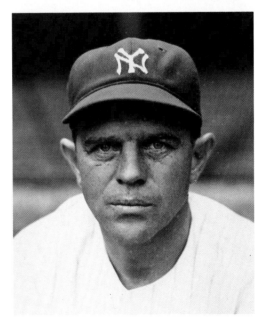

211

THE 1930s

ning 13-6 in Ruth's final World Series appearance.

1933

As the Depression drove the unemployment rate up, baseball's offense and attendance dropped — especially in the National League. The eight N.L. clubs averaged just over four runs a game in '33, and the league's most productive club, the St. Louis Cardinals, scored 4.5 runs per game. By comparison, the league norm in 1930 was 5.7 runs a game. At the gate, league attendance fell under 3.2 million fans, the lowest total since 1919. The league batting average, .266, and earned run average, 3.34, both reached their lowest levels of the lively ball era. American League averages also fell, but by a much smaller amount, and from there through the end of the decade, the junior circuit provided far more offensive clout than the N.L.

The sport received a much needed shot in the arm when the first All-Star Game was played in Comiskey Park on July 6. The game drew 49,000 fans, featured a galaxy of stars, and was won by the American Leaguers 4-2, with the help of a Babe Ruth home run.

In the regular season, the New York Giants rose back to the top of the National League for the first time since 1924. Player/manager Terry led the club with a .322 aver-

age, and slugger Ott was one of only three N.L. players to record more than 100 RBI. Hubbell paced a pitching staff that recorded a league-low 2.71 earned run average. Hubbell won 23 games that year, lost 12, and flashed a 1.66 ERA, while pitching ten shutouts and winning the Most Valuable Player award, edging out Philadelphia's Chuck Klein. Klein won the league's triple crown by batting .368, hitting 28 home runs, and driving in 120 runners. His Phillies, however, were the only team in the league whose pitching staff allowed more than four runs a game, and consequently, the club sank back into seventh place, 31 games out.

In the A.L., Clark Griffith installed his son-in-law, Joe Cronin, as manager of the Senators in 1933, and Cronin responded by leading the club to 99 wins and a 7-win pennant margin over the Yankees. Cronin led the club with 118 RBI, while first baseman Joe Kuhel chipped in with 107 RBI, and Heinie Manush batted .336 and scored 115 times. The Senators' pitching staff, led by 20-game winners General Crowder and Earl Whitehill, had the second-best ERA in the league.

New York led the league again in runs scored and home runs, but its pitching staff became very generous at a time when league scoring fell. The staff's 4.36 ERA was more than half a run a game higher than Washington's and was the main cause for the Yankees' second-place finish. Gehrig sparkled as usual, but Ruth finally showed his age, registering declines in all categories. Gehrig belted 32 home runs, drove in 139 runners, and scored 138 times, while the Bambino knocked 35 homers and drove home 103 runners. Tony Lazzeri drove home 104 runners, while

The box side (left) and box top from a 1930s Wilson "Rogers Hornsby" glove.

VANDER MEER'S TWO NO-HITTERS

Vander Meer after his second no-hitter.

Several times a season, pitchers take no-hit, no-run games into the late innings, only to have them broken up. Sometimes it is better to be lucky than good.

Johnny Vander Meer was good 'n' lucky in 1938 when he became the first and only pitcher in baseball history to hurl back-to-back no-hitters. Vander Meer was a hard-throwing but erratic 23-year-old lefthander in only his second major league season with the Reds. After working all spring to tame his wildness, Vander Meer was inserted in the rotation and won five of his first seven games.

On June 11, Vander Meer no-hit Boston, allowing only three walks in a 3-0 victory. His next start, four days later against Brooklyn, would be the first night game ever played in Ebbetts Field. Vander Meer held the Dodgers hitless for six innings while the Reds built a 4-0 lead. He walked two in the seventh but came back with two strikeouts in the eighth, leaving him an inning away from immortality.

He got the first out in the ninth, but then walked the bases loaded. Vander Meer retired the next batter on a force at the plate. Leo Durocher was the last man with a shot at altering history, but he popped out. Johnny would now forever be "Double No-Hit" Vander Meer. He never won 20 games in a season, though, and he retired in 1951 with a career 119-121 record.

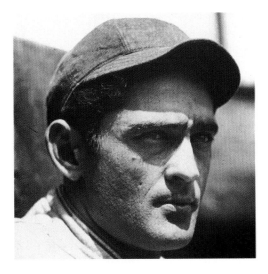

Guy Bush (top left) was 20-12 with a 2.75 ERA for the 1933 Cubs. He averaged 17 wins a season for Chicago from 1928 to '34. Pitcher Nick Altrock (top right), shown here in 1910, played in the big leagues in four different decades. He pitched 11 games for the Louisville Colonels in 1898. He was a starter for the White Sox in the mid-1900s, and saw limited action for Washington in the 1910s. He pitched one game in 1924 and had one at-bat in 1933 for the Senators. Mickey Cochrane (middle left) hit .322 and scored 104 runs in '33, his last year as an Athletic. Giants hitters (middle right), left to right, Bill Terry, Lefty O'Doul, and Mel Ott led the Giants to a world championship in 1933. Hack Wilson, left, and Chuck Klein (bottom left) pose before a game. Klein won the triple crown in '33 with a .368 average, 28 homers, and 120 RBI. A 1933 advertising display for Goudy baseball cards (bottom right).

THE 1930s

Ben Chapman brought home 98 and scored 112 times.

Connie Mack, squeezed by three years of declining attendance, implemented the first of his major cost-cutting measures by selling three veteran stars — Al Simmons, Mule Haas, and Jimmy Dykes — to the White Sox for $100,000 just after the 1932 season. The club dropped from second to third in 1933 despite Jimmie Foxx repeating as Most Valuable Player. Foxx joined fellow Philadelphian Klein in winning his league's triple crown by cracking 48 homers, batting .356, and driving home 163 runners. He also compiled 204 hits and 125 runs, and slugged .703.

Lefty Grove had another dominating season with 24 wins and eight losses, but he did surrender the ERA title he held for each of the four previous seasons. Most damaging to the A's cause was the failure of the rest of the staff, notably George Earnshaw, who after averaging 20 wins a year in the past three years compiled a 5-10 record with a 5.95 earned run average in 1933.

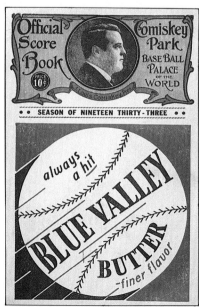

A 1933 Chicago White Sox program.

The World Series between the Giants and the Senators was a rematch of the 1924 classic, but this time the outcome was different. The Giants won Game One in the Polo Grounds behind a five-hit, ten-strikeout victory by screwballer Hubbell. King Carl allowed only two unearned runs in the opener, as Mel Ott went four-for-four with a home run and three RBI to send the Senators down to a 5-2 defeat. The teams split the next two games, but the Giants swept the remaining two games to win in five. Hubbell went the distance in the Giants 11-inning victory in Game Four, and Ott won the finale on a tenth-inning home run.

1934

The Giants were favored to repeat in '34, as once again Terry and Ott led the offense and the pitching staff was the strongest in the league. New York held the top spot for 127 days until they were chased down from behind by the resurgent St. Louis Cardinals. The Cards won 21 of 25 games in September and tied the Giants on September 28.

The Cardinals were a wild band of players, later christened the "Gas House Gang," that excelled in all phases of the game. For offense, the club called on first baseman Ripper Collins and second-year man Joe Medwick, both of whom knocked home and scored more than 100 runs. For defense, the Cards could count on the double-play combination of player/manager Frankie Frisch and Leo Durocher, obtained the previous season from Cincinnati. And for pitching, Frisch handed the ball to the Dean brothers, Dizzy and Daffy.

The Deans nailed down St. Louis' second come-from-behind pennant in the decade by combining to win the last three games against Cincinnati, two of them on shutouts by Dizzy. The Giants were knocked off by the Brooklyn Dodgers in those last two games at the Polo Grounds. Giants Manager Terry was haunted by a comment he made that spring when he derided the Dodgers by rhetorically asking, "Are they still in the league?"

Those end-of-the-season shutouts by Dizzy climaxed one of the great pitching performances in

Ossie Bluege (top), who played third base for the Washington Senators from 1922 to 1929, was a career .272 hitter with only a .350 lifetime slugging average. But Bluege was regarded as one of the finest fielding third basemen during an era when frequent bunting made the position much more important defensively than it is today. Bluege often led the American League in assists, chances per game, and double plays in a season. During World War II, Bluege managed the Senators and then ended his career as a scout, signing, among others, Hall of Fame slugger Harmon Killebrew. Work continues on the new Fenway Park (middle), which opened in 1934. The program cover of the A.L. and N.L. stars who toured Japan in the 1934 off-season (bottom left) featured Babe Ruth. Babe Ruth (bottom middle) is shown visiting blind children in Japan that same year. A poster from the Daily Record shows Ruth before his last game as a Yankee in 1934.

215

THE 1930s

N.L. history: 30 wins, only seven losses, a 2.66 ERA, and seven shutouts in 312 innings en route to winning the league's Most Valuable Player award. Daffy joined the staff as a 20-year-old and won 19 games against 11 losses.

Ott grabbed league honors in home runs (35) and RBI (135), while the Pirates' Paul Waner seized the batting title with a .362 mark and scored 122 runs. The Chicago Cubs acquired Phillies slugger Chuck Klein for three players and $65,000 one year after he won the triple crown, but he only appeared in 110 games and the Cubs finished in third. Casey Stengel surfaced to manage the Dodgers, but except for playing the role of Giants-slayer, his club only managed a sixth-place showing.

In the American League, Tigers owner Frank Navin took advantage of Connie Mack's ongoing fire sale by acquiring A's catcher Mickey Cochrane in the off-season for $100,000. He also swapped John Stone for the Senators' star outfielder Goose Goslin. Navin installed Cochrane as catcher/manager, and the Tigers roared to the pennant, winning 101 games and finishing 7 games ahead of the Yankees. It was Detroit's first pennant since 1909.

Cochrane batted .320 in 129 games, handled the pitchers and ran the club brilliantly, and was voted Most Valuable Player. Goslin stepped in and batted .305 with 100 RBI, but the real offensive fireworks came from Hank Greenberg and Charlie Gehringer. Greenberg, in his second year, batted .339, belted 26 homers, drove home 139 runs, and scored 118. Gehringer smashed 214 hits and batted .356 with 127 RBI and a league-best 134 runs scored. A fourth Tiger, shortstop Billy Rogell, also drove in and scored at least 100 runs. The Tigers lineup counted six starters with batting averages above .300.

The Tigers crossed the plate 958 times that year in support of a pitching staff headed by second-year man Schoolboy Rowe and 27-year-old righthander Tommy Bridges. Rowe chalked up a 24-8 record and 3.45 ERA. Bridges added 22 wins and 35-year-old Firpo Marberry, acquired from Washington the previous season, proved invaluable in his hybrid role as spot starter and reliever. He appeared in 38 games, started 19, and rolled up a 15-5 record.

For the second year in a row, a player compiled a triple-crown season but was denied the MVP award. This time the slighted player was Lou Gehrig, who produced a .363 average, a career-high 49 homers, and 165 runs batted in. His teammate Lefty Gomez won the pitchers' version of the triple crown by compiling a 26-5 record with 158 strikeouts and a miserly 2.33 ERA. Yet the Yankees were also riddled with injuries and limped home 7 games out. Ruth played his last season in pinstripes and completed his magnificent stay in New York by batting .288, with 22 homers and 84 RBI in 125 games. Lazzeri, Earle Combs, and Bill Dickey also missed large blocks of time. The Bombers lack of production could not adequately complement its league-best earned run average.

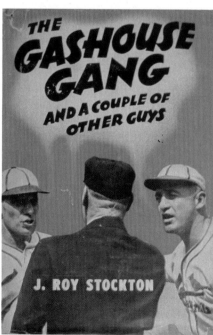

The St. Louis Cardinals' Gas House Gang led the National League with 799 runs scored, a .288 batting average, 69 stolen bases, 141 double plays, 78 complete games, and 15 shutouts en route to 95 wins.

PEPPER MARTIN

Pepper Martin takes a large hunk of chaw. The 5'8", 170-pound Martin led the National League in stolen bases three times, and he ended his 13-year career with a .298 batting average.

Pepper Martin may not have been the most prolific player of the 1930s (he played in more than 100 games only five times in his 13-year career), but he was certainly one of the most colorful. The Oklahoma-born Martin, dubbed "The Wild Hoss of the Osage," was the leader of the rambunctious St. Louis Cardinals "Gas House Gang," which, thanks to the always-hustling Martin, won world championships in 1931 and 1934.

Martin became the Cardinals center fielder in 1931 and hit a solid, if unspectacular, .300. But as a rookie in the World Series, he put on what legendary sports writer Red Smith called "The greatest one-man show baseball has ever known." In St. Louis' seven-game Series win over the Philadelphia Athletics, Martin batted .500, tying a record with 12 hits. He also stole five bases and scored five runs.

After an injury-plagued 1932 season, he came back as a third baseman in '33 and batted .316, leading the N.L. in runs and stolen bases. The Cardinals were back in the Series in '34 and again Martin made it his personal showcase. In the seven-game victory over Detroit, he banged 11 hits and scored a record eight runs. His .418 Series average is the highest in history, and he ranks in the Series top ten for doubles, stolen bases, and slugging average.

Yankees shortstop Travis Jackson (top left) had 101 RBI and 75 runs scored in 1934. Lou Gehrig (top right) was probably the greatest first baseman in the history of baseball. Only Jimmie Foxx challenges Gehrig for the honor. "The Iron Horse" averaged 39 homers, 139 runs scored, 151 runs batted in, 200 base hits, a .344 batting average, a .641 slugging average, and 36 doubles in the nine years between 1930 and 1938. Yankees manager Joe McCarthy (middle left) was a superb tactician and a stickler for fundamentals. McCarthy never played an inning of major league baseball, and he served a 15-year managing apprenticeship in the minor leagues. He won two minor league championships at Louisville. The second in a great triumvirate of Yankees managers (he succeeded Miller Huggins and preceded Casey Stengel), McCarthy managed the Bronx Bombers from 1931 to 1946. Paul "Big Poison" Waner (bottom left) ended his 18-year career with a .333 batting average, 1,626 runs scored, and 1,309 RBI. Dizzy Dean (bottom right) led the N.L. in strikeouts each year from 1932 to '35. He ended his career pitching for the Cubs.

217

THE 1930s

Senators manager Bucky Harris had a candy bar named after him in the 1930s.

The Indians moved up a notch to third place in 1934 after inserting 21-year-old first baseman Hal Trosky into the lineup. Trosky provided Earl Averill with a batting partner, and the two combined for 66 homers and 255 RBI. Boston finished as high as fourth for the first time since 1918. Owner Tom Yawkey also went shopping at the "Connie Mack Thrift Shop" and walked away with the league's best pitcher, Lefty Grove, in exchange for two players and $125,000. True to Boston's luck, however, Grove was sidelined with a sore arm and managed only an 8-8 mark with Boston. Yawkey fared better when he obtained Wes Ferrell from Cleveland early in the season for two players and $25,000. Ferrell — teamed with sibling battery mate Rick — posted a 14-5 record with Boston.

Philadelphia, now minus Simmons, Cochrane, Grove, Max Bishop, Haas, and Dykes, fell to fifth, despite another monster season by Foxx. "The Beast" slammed 44 homers, batted .334, and knocked in 130 runs. The incumbent Sena-

tors stumbled badly and tumbled all the way to seventh place.

The World Series was a raucous seven-game affair that the Cardinals won by sweeping the last two games in Detroit. The teams traded wins through the first four games before the Tigers beat Dizzy Dean in Game Five. With the Tigers ahead three games to two and the Series shifted back to Detroit, the Cardinals were kept aloft when Paul Dean singled in the go ahead run in support of his 4-3 victory. That led to the tumultuous finale, which St. Louis won handily 11-0 and which featured the sixth-inning removal of Cardinals outfielder Medwick after he was pelted with debris by Tigers fans. He had earned their wrath after scuffling with Tigers third baseman Merv Owen, and commissioner Kenesaw Mountain Landis had Medwick removed, more for Medwick's own protection than for any ruckus he helped promote.

1935

The Cardinals and the Giants restaged their pennant duel, but the Cubs crashed the party in a stunning manner. Chicago reeled off 21 consecutive wins in September and swept past St. Louis in the last three contests to win the pennant by 4 games. New York faded to 8½ games out.

Chicago finished with 100 wins by blending a potent lineup with tough pitching. Heading the attack was outfielder Augie Galan, who scored 133 runs and batted

.314, and second baseman Billy Herman, who rapped a league-high 227 hits (including 57 doubles), batted .341, and scored 113 times. Catcher Gabby Hartnett received the Most Valuable Player award by hitting .344 and handling the league's best pitching staff. Bill Lee and Lon Warneke combined to win 40 games, and the staff's earned run average was 3.26.

The Cardinals mounted a strong attack led by Medwick — who batted .353, hit 23 homers, and drove in 126 runs — and Ripper Collins, who batted .313 with 23 home runs and 122 RBI. Dizzy Dean followed his historic 1934 campaign by winning 28 games against 12 losses, and his brother Paul added 19 wins. However, both brothers were beaten by the Cubs in the last series of the season to lose the championship.

Ott belted 31 home runs, drove in 114 runs, and batted .322; Bill Terry hit .341; Hank Leiber knocked in and scored more than 100 runs; and Carl Hubbell won 23 games in New York's third-place

COOL PAPA BELL

When the Negro Leagues were in their 1930s heyday, James "Cool Papa" Bell was the game's fastest runner and one of its greatest all-around players.

Although records were not diligently kept in black baseball ("I remember," Bell once said, "getting five hits and stealing five bases, but it wasn't written down 'cause they forgot the scorebook."), Bell is credited with stealing 175 bases in 1933 (when he was 30). It is also believed that he once circled the bases in 12 seconds—that's just three seconds every 90 feet. Satchel Paige said that Bell could turn off the lights and get under the covers before the room grew dark.

Bell was a switch-hitting outfielder who played baseball in one league or another from 1922 to 1951. Major league owner Bill Veeck once said that, defensively,

Bell was "the equal of Tris Speaker, Joe DiMaggio, or Willie Mays." Another baseball man compared him with Willie Keeler as a hitter and Ty Cobb as a base runner. His lifetime batting average was somewhere between .340 and .350.

In the 1940s and 1950s, Bell worked with players like Jackie Robinson and Ernie Banks, and in the 1960s, he helped teach Lou Brock and Maury Wills how to steal bases. They just went on to become two of the game's greatest basestealers. Had Bell played in the major leagues, he might have claimed that honor, and the Hall of Fame recognized that by inducting him in 1974.

Al Lopez (top left) played catcher for a record 1,918 games, which held up for 40 years until it was finally surpassed in 1987 by Bob Boone. Lopez was a light-hitting defensive catcher for Brooklyn (1928 to '35), Boston (1936 to '40), and Pittsburgh (1940 to '46) in the N.L. and Cleveland (1947) in the American League. He had a lifetime .261 batting average and hit only 52 career homers. It was Lopez's success as a manager that got him into the Hall of Fame. In 17 seasons managing Cleveland and the Chicago White Sox, Lopez compiled a 1,422-1,026 record. While his teams finished in second place ten times (because of the Yankees dominance), Lopez was the only manager besides Casey Stengel to win an A.L. pennant in the 1950s. He won a pennant with the Indians in 1954 and another with the White Sox in 1959. The stands are filled at Navin Field (middle left) in Detroit to watch the St. Louis Cardinals and the Detroit Tigers during the 1934 World Series. Carl Hubbell (middle right) delivers the pitch. Hubbell struggled for five years in the minor leagues, and he almost quit baseball until the Giants bought his contract in 1928. Hubbell first learned and then perfected the screwball, and a year later, he became the Giants' "Meal Ticket." King Carl averaged 19 wins a season during the 1930s. Freddie Fitzsimmons (bottom left) was 18-14 in 1934 with a 3.04 ERA. Fred Lindstrom (bottom middle) was a part-time outfielder and third baseman for the 1935 pennant-winning Cubs. Managers Joe Cronin, and Walter Johnson (bottom right) confer before a game in 1935. Cronin, left, was in his first of 13 seasons as manager of the Red Sox; Johnson, right, was in his last year as manager of the Indians.

THE 1930s

finish. Shortstop Arky Vaughan batted a league-high .385 for fourth-place Pittsburgh, while Boston's Wally Berger posted league bests in home runs (34) and RBI (130). It did his club little good as the Braves lost 115 games, setting a league standard for futility that lasted until the New York Mets inaugural 1962 season. The club also signed 40-year-old Babe Ruth as a player/coach, but he hung up his spikes for good in June after hitting .181. Cincinnati also established new standards that year, light standards that is, as it became the first major league team to host night games.

The A.L. won the 1935 All-Star Game 4-1.

The Tigers repeated in the American League after a slow start, and again mounted the most ferocious attack in the league. Greenberg won the Most Valuable Player award by hitting 36 homers, driving in 170 runs, and batting .328. Gehringer, "The Mechanical Man," hit .330 while scoring and driving in more than 100 runs apiece. Outfielders Pete Fox and Goslin also made valuable contributions to the Tigers' romp, and pitchers Bridges and Rowe split 40 wins.

The Yankees, playing without Ruth for the first time in the lively ball era, finished 3 games back. The club boasted the league's low-

est earned run average, 3.60, but no pitcher managed more than 16 wins. Gomez, after winning 26 games in '34, slipped to 12-15. Gehrig had another outstanding season, and newcomers Red Rolfe and George Selkirk turned in strong performances, but the rest of the Yankees lineup lacked its usual punch.

Washington second baseman Buddy Myer went four-for-five on the season's last day and snatched the batting title from Cleveland's Joe Vosmik, .349 to .348. Foxx matched Greenberg's 36 home run output, and he also drove in 115 runners and slugged .636 for the last-place A's. Yawkey laid out $225,000 for Joe Cronin before the season, and the Sox new player/manager Cronin guided the club to another fourth-place finish. Boston's Wes Ferrell, pitching to brother Rick, led the league with 25 wins, while teammate Lefty Grove rebounded from a sore arm to win 20 games with a league-low 2.70 ERA.

In the World Series, the Tigers started on a down note by dropping the first game 3-0 to Cubs ace Warneke and losing Greenberg to a broken wrist in their Game Two victory. The Tigers pulled out Game Three in extra innings and put the Cubs in a hole by winning the fourth contest at Wrigley Field. The Cubs sent the Series back to Detroit with a 3-1 Game Five win, but the Tigers wrapped up their first championship in the bottom of the ninth in Game Six when Goslin singled home Cochrane.

1936

Frank Navin had used his checkbook to help finance two pennants for his Tigers, and took the plunge again by paying $75,000 for Al Simmons before the '36 season. Bucketfoot Al did his job by hitting .327 and driving in 112 runners, and Gehringer was magnificent in batting .354 with 116 RBI and 144 runs scored. But several pieces of bad luck undermined the Tigers bid to repeat. First, Greenberg was sidelined for the season after 12 games with another broken wrist. Then in midseason, player/manager Mickey Cochrane suffered a nervous breakdown and left the club.

The third piece of bad luck for Detroit was the revitalized New

BILL DICKEY

Bill Dickey was a splendid handler of pitchers and possessed a remarkable recall of hitters' weaknesses.

When he became the New York Yankees full-time catcher in 1929, Bill Dickey started a tradition of great Yankees backstops that would continue with Yogi Berra, Elston Howard, and Thurman Munson. Dickey's hitting was so consistent and his defense so fundamentally sound that he made the Hall of Fame in 1954, despite never leading the American League in a single offensive category.

Dickey was overshadowed during his career by Babe Ruth, Lou Gehrig, and Joe DiMaggio, but his quiet leadership was a primary force in the eight pennants the Yankees won during his 16-year career. Only Mickey Cochrane rivaled Dickey as a backstop during the 1930s. Dickey batted over .300 11 times and his .362 average in 1936 is still the highest ever for a catcher. He holds the A.L. record for playing a full season (1931) without allowing a passed ball, and he is tied with Johnny Bench for catching 100 or more games in 13 straight seasons.

Dickey's best hitting years were 1936 to 1939, when he hit more than 20 homers and drove in more than 100 runs each season. It wasn't a coincidence that the Yanks won world championships all four years. In his first World Series, in 1932, Dickey batted .438, and in his last, in 1943, he smacked the game-winning homer that beat the Cardinals in five. Dickey ranks eighth alltime for World Series RBI, with 24.

Cleveland first baseman Hal Trosky (top left) led the A.L. with 162 RBI in 1936.
Trosky slugged 30 homers a year and had 127 RBI a year from 1934 to '39. In
1935, Pirate shortstop Arky Vaughan (top right) led the N.L. in batting average
(.385), slugging average (.607), bases on balls (97), and on-base average (.491).
Braves Babe Ruth, left, and Wally Berger (bottom left) in 1935. Babe kept 'em
entertained, while Wally drove 'em home (130 RBI in '35). Ernie Lombardi
(bottom right) hit over .300 in five seasons from 1934 to '38.

THE 1930s

York Yankees. Joe McCarthy's team scored the second highest run total in history and cruised home with 102 wins and a 19½-game lead over Detroit. The Yankees had finally adapted to Babe Ruth's retirement, and his absence was compensated for by the Most Valuable Player season turned in by Lou Gehrig, a productive season from catcher Bill Dickey, and the outstanding all-around play of a rookie outfielder from California named Joe DiMaggio.

In a year that saw the American League ERA soar from 4.45 to 5.04 runs per game, the Bronx Bombers packed the most punch. The club scored 1,065 runs, just shy of its 1931 record of 1,067 runs scored, and it also recorded the third-highest team slugging average in history. Gehrig led the pack with 49 home runs, 152 RBI, a .354 batting average, and a .696 slugging average. He was one of five New Yorkers to drive home more than 100 runners, and one of seven starters to reach double-digits in home runs. DiMaggio justified the hype surrounding his arrival by batting .323 with 125 RBI and 29 home runs. Dickey launched 22 home runs, drove in 107 runs, and batted .362. To make matters worse for A.L. opponents, the Yanks pitching staff was tops in the league with a 4.17 earned run average.

The White Sox emerged in third place behind the exploits of shortstop Luke Appling. The 29-year-old infielder set a lasting standard for A.L. shortstops by posting a league-leading .388 batting average. Cleveland's Hal Trosky rivaled Gehrig as the league's top slugger by blasting 42 homers and driving in 162 runs to go with his .343 average and .644 slugging. Close behind was Jimmie Foxx, who belted 41 balls over the fences and drove in 143 runners, while batting .338. Foxx accomplished these feats for the Red Sox where he was shipped in the off-season for $150,000 by Mack. Yawkey also shelled out $75,000 to acquire Doc Cramer from Philadelphia and picked up Heinie Manush from Washington, but all this new talent brought the Sox home in only sixth place. One of the most electrifying debuts of the decade was made in August when 17-year-old Indians righthander Bob Feller whiffed 15 Brownies in his first start and followed that up three weeks later by fanning 17 A's.

The National League pennant race was a see-saw affair as three teams held the top spot for large chunks of time. St. Louis bolted to the front behind the bats of Pepper Martin, newcomer Johnny Mize, and Joe Medwick, who batted .351 with 138 RBI and 64 doubles. However, the club relinquished the lead when Paul Dean went down with an arm injury and nobody emerged to support brother Dizzy's efforts. Dizzy wound up at 24-13, plus 11 saves in a league-leading 51 appearances, but the staff's overall ERA was a full run per game over the league-leading Giants.

The Cubs ripped off 15 straight wins in midseason to capture the lead, but with the exceptions of Billy Herman and Frank Demaree, their offense was undernourished. Chicago eventually gave way to the Giants, who

Babe Herman had a .324 lifetime batting average in 13 seasons.

Outfielder Earl Averill (top) was a mainstay of the heavy-hitting Cleveland Indians of the 1930s, teams that scored a lot of runs but never were able to beat out the A's or the Yankees for the A.L. pennant. The lefthanded-hitting Averill was durable — he once played 673 straight games — and an excellent center fielder. His forte, however, was run production. A .318 lifetime batter with a .533 career slugging average and a .392 lifetime on-base average, Averill scored more than 100 runs in nine of his first ten seasons, and he drove in more than 100 runs five times. In eight of his first ten years, he batted over .300, reaching a peak of .378 in 1936, when he also hit 39 doubles, 15 triples, and 28 home runs. Averill ended his career with 238 homers, 1,224 runs scored, and 1,165 RBI. He was elected to the Hall of Fame in 1975. Jimmie Foxx (bottom left) smashed at least 30 home runs in a season a record 12 years in a row, and his 534 career round-trippers was a record for righthanded hitters until Willie Mays broke it. Wally Berger takes his cuts at the Braves training camp (bottom right). Berger averaged 27 homers and 121 RBI a year between 1930 and '36 for Boston.

THE 1930s

patched together their own 15-game winning streak and won the pennant by 5 games over both St. Louis and Chicago. New York's big weapon was Carl Hubbell, who closed the season with 16 consecutive wins and won the Most Valuable Player award for the second time. Overall, King Carl posted 26 wins, six losses, and a league-low 2.31 earned run average.

The Giants attack itself was fairly anemic, with the exception of Mel Ott. Manager Bill Terry was felled by a knee injury and missed half the season. Ott, outfielder Joe Moore, and catcher Gus Mancuso were the only regulars to bat over .300; aside from Ott's league-high 33 home runs, the Giants had no player with as many as ten homers. Pittsburgh's Paul Waner won his third batting title with a .373 mark, and the defending batting champion Vaughan scored a league-high 122 runs as the Pirates finished fourth, 8 games back.

The World Series was the first matchup between the Yankees and the Giants since 1923, the year Yankee Stadium opened. And though the faces were different, the outcome was identical — the Yankees in six games. King Carl continued his unbeaten streak by pitching the Giants to victory in Game One, but the Yankees bounced back to score a Series record 18 runs in Game Two, highlighted by a Tony Lazzeri grand slam. Yankee Bump Hadley bested Freddie Fitzsimmons in a 2-1 Game Three pitchers duel, and the Yankees handed Hubbell his first loss since midseason in the fourth game. The Giants came back to win Game Five in extra-innings, but the Yankees iced the first of four consecutive world championships by a 13-5 score in Game Six.

1937

Hank Greenberg recovered from his broken wrist well enough to blast 40 home runs and drive home 183 runs in 1937, and Charlie Gehringer claimed A.L. Most Valuable Player honors by hitting a league high .371. But the Tigers' plans to recapture the pennant were crushed when Cochrane suffered a near-fatal fractured skull in a beaning incident in late May. He recovered well enough to continue managing the Tigers, but his playing career was over. Detroit's chances were further diminished when its pitching star, Schoolboy Rowe, was limited to a handful of early season appearances by an arm injury.

Even with an intact battery, dethroning the Yankees would have been no easy chore, as the Bronx Bombers exploded for 102 wins and a 13-game bulge over the Tigers. Gehrig, DiMaggio, and Dickey each batted over .330 and drove in more than 130 runs, and DiMaggio grabbed the home run crown as well with 46 long balls. Frankie Crosetti and Rolfe, the Yankees' table-setters, benefited

THE "HOMER IN THE GLOAMIN'"

Gabby Hartnett

On a cloudy September 28, 1938, almost 35,000 fans packed into Wrigley Field to watch the Pirates, who held a ½-game lead over Chicago, play the Cubs. The Cubs went down 3-1 in the sixth inning only to come back to tie it in the seventh. After the Pirates put men on first and third with one out in the eighth, the Cubs pulled off a double play while a balk was being called on their pitcher. Umpire Dolly Stark rescinded the balk when the Cubs ran off the field.

Pittsburgh regained the lead in the eighth, 5-3, as Cubs player/manager Gabby Hartnett used three pitchers. But Chicago would not quit. As darkness began descending, the Cubs quickly scored two runs. Had Pittsburgh outfielder Paul Waner not cut a runner down at the plate after a hit, Chicago would have taken the lead. The umpires decided that if the game remained tied after one more inning, there would be a replay the next day.

Charlie Root, the Cubs' sixth pitcher, set the Bucs down in the ninth. With two outs in the bottom of the inning, Hartnett came to bat.

Pirates pitcher Mace Brown got two quick strikes on Hartnett, who could barely see the ball. On the next pitch, Hartnett flailed away and sent the ball zooming through the darkness and into the left field bleachers. The game-winning "Homer in the Gloamin' " became legend, as the Cubs won the pennant the next day 10-1.

Pepper Martin dives head-first. Martin scored 121 runs in both 1935 and '36.

Cincinnati hurler Paul Derringer (top) was 21-14 in 1938, and he led the National League with 26 complete games and 307 innings pitched. In '39, he was 25-7, and he ended his 15-season career in 1945 with a 223-212 record. In the 1936 World Series (middle), Mel Ott pulls the ball past Lou Gehrig; Jo Jo Moore and Dick Bartell scored on the play. On the 1937 All-Star Game program (bottom left), FDR gets a new deal on the ball. Lou Gehrig homered, doubled, and drove in four runs as the A.L. won 8-3. Catcher Luke Sewell (bottom middle) drove in 201 runs in three years from 1935 to '37 for the White Sox. Hal Schumacher, left, and Lefty Gomez (bottom right) meet before Game Two of the 1936 World Series. Schumaker didn't have his best stuff that day, as the Yankees set a Series record by scoring 18 runs. Schumacher was the original "Prince Hal," and he had a 23-10 record in 1934 and a 158-120 lifetime record in 13 seasons of pitching.

from the Big Three's production by scoring 270 times combined.

For the second year in a row, New York combined the most productive offense with the stingiest pitching staff, as the hurlers' combined 3.65 earned run average was nearly a full run below the league norm. The lefty-righty tandem of Lefty Gomez and Red Ruffing split 41 wins, and Johnny Murphy made 35 relief appearances and four starts, while recording a 13-4 record with ten saves.

Even in Cochrane's absence, the Tigers' claws were plenty sharp. In addition to Greenberg and Gehringer's superlative seasons, Detroit got a .335 average and 113 RBI from outfielder Gee Walker, and 35 homers and 103 RBI from replacement catcher and third baseman Rudy York. Chicago won 86 games to finish third that season, the club's best record since the Black Sox scandal broke in 1920. Cleveland's Johnny Allen overcame an early season injury to enter the season's final game with a 15-0 mark, but the former Yankee couldn't keep the streak alive. His 18-year-old teammate, Bob Feller, was limited by an arm injury to 19 starts and 26 appearances, but he still managed to average a strikeout an inning in posting a 9-7 record.

Home run production was on a sustained upswing through the decade, and the primary cause was a steady infusion of young sluggers trained to swing for the fences. DiMaggio was 22 years old when he led the circuit with 46 blasts in 1937. He was followed that year by Greenberg, who hit 40 homers at age 26. His Tiger teammate, 23-year-old Rudy York, knocked 35 home runs, while Cleveland's Hal Trosky, age 24, pounded 32 balls out of the league's parks. St. Louis' 24-year-old third baseman Harlond Clift

blasted 29 round-trippers. Among the league's top home run specialists, only Gehrig and Foxx were around in the previous decade, and Foxx was only 29 in 1937.

Bill Terry guided the Giants to their third pennant in five years, finishing the season with 95 wins and a 3-game cushion over Chicago. Ott and Hubbell again led the team. Master Melvin, playing in his 12th season with the Giants at the ripe old age of 28, again claimed the home run crown by smacking 31, while driving in 95 runs. No other player in New York's lineup drove in more than 66 runs. Hubbell made due with this limited support to win 22 games, his fifth consecutive year with more than 20 wins. He was joined in the 20-game win circle by newcomer Cliff Melton.

In 1937, Carl Hubbell was 22-8 with a 3.20 ERA. His total of 159 strikeouts that season were a career high, and '37 was the only season in which he led the league.

HANK GREENBERG

Hank Greenberg and Lou Gehrig had two things in common. They were both born in the Bronx, and they were two of the best American League sluggers of the 1930s. But had it not been for World War II, Greenberg would also have been one of the greatest sluggers of the 1940s.

Before he was drafted by the Army in May 1941, the 6'4" righthanded-hitting first baseman had been a two-time Most Valuable Player (in 1935 and 1940) for the Tigers. He led the A.L. in RBI (a career-high 183 in '37) and home runs three times, led the league twice in doubles, batted over .300 eight times, and scored more than 100 runs six times.

Though he was out of action for four-and-a-half seasons during the war, Greenberg celebrated his return in July 1945 by helping his team win a pennant. His 13 homers kept the Tigers in the race with the Senators until the last day of the season. Trailing 3-2 in the ninth, Greenberg hit a grand slam to win the pennant for Detroit. The Tigers went on to win the Series with Greenberg belting two homers.

He led the A.L. in homers (44) and RBI (127) again in 1946 but retired at the end of the '47 season. In only nine full seasons, Greenberg hit 331 homers and drove in 1,276. His 6.4 home run percentage is ninth alltime, and he is fifth alltime in slugging with a .605 average.

A "rhubarb" breaks out at Fenway Park in 1937 or 1938 (top). From the far left are Red Rolfe, George Selkirk, Joe DiMaggio, and Joe McCarthy. Frank Crosetti is at the far right. According to the book The Dickson Baseball Dictionary, the term rhubarb was popularized by Yankees broadcaster Red Barber in the late 1930s and early 1940s. Two of the game's greatest hurlers (bottom left), Lefty Grove, left, and Dizzy Dean, shake hands. Grove was inducted into the Hall of Fame in 1947, Dean in 1953. Leo "The Lip" Durocher (bottom right) was the spark plug who ignited the Cardinals' Gas House Gang in the mid-1930s.

THE 1930s

Chicago paced the league in batting average and scoring as four players crossed the plate at least 100 times. The prime run producer on the Cubs was Demaree, who batted .324 and drove home 115 runs. St. Louis slipped to fourth place, despite the triple crown performance of the league's Most Valuable Player Joe Medwick. "Ducky" capped a six-year string of steadily improving performances by batting .374 with 31 home runs and 154 RBI. He tied Ott in round-trippers, but he led the league outright in at-bats, hits, runs scored, doubles, and slugging average. The Cardinals' season, however, was torpedoed by a broken toe sustained by Dizzy Dean at the All-Star Game, which limited him to a 13-10 mark. The Braves scored the fewest runs in the league, but still managed a fifth-place finish when two 30-year-old rookies, Lou Fette and Jim Turner, combined for 40 wins, ten shutouts, and earned run averages well under 3.00.

The rematch of the 1936 World Series was decided early when the Yankees opened with twin 8-1 wins at Yankee Stadium, then won the Game Three by a 5-1 score. Hubbell rebounded from the thrashing he took in Game One to prevent a Yankees sweep, but Gomez settled matters the next day by beating Terry's crew 4-2. Lazzeri hit .400 in his last pinstripe appearance, and George Selkirk very efficiently scored five runs and drove in six with five base hits.

1938

Sluggers once again administered a pounding on American League pitchers, as the league cranked out 864 homers in 1938, the highest total of the decade. A large portion of the damage came from Greenberg, who took a long run at Ruth's record, before settling for 58 homers and 146 RBI.

Greenberg's power cost Foxx a chance to collect his second triple crown of the decade, as Double X left his mark with 50 homers, 175 RBI, and a .349 batting average while winning his third Most Valuable Player award and cementing his position as the decade's most dominant slugger.

Still, it was a collection of slightly smaller cannons who won the pennant, as the Yankees sent to the plate five hitters who cleared the fences at least 20 times that season. Gehrig, DiMaggio, and Dickey again spearheaded the attack that carried New York to its third straight flag, but this year

The N.L. won the 1938 All-Star game 4-1.

they were amply aided by rookie second baseman Joe Gordon, who belted 25 home runs, and outfielder Tommy Henrich, who chipped in with 22 homers. Overall, New York averaged 6.4 runs a game, while once again permitting the fewest scores. Ruffing and Gomez teamed for 39 wins, while Monte Pearson and Spud Chandler added 30 victories for the only staff in the league that allowed under four earned runs a game.

Boston climbed into second place, 9½ games out, and may have posed a sterner challenge if its old master, Lefty Grove, was not sidelined by a sore arm in mid-July. The 38-year-old Grove was 14-4 at the time of his injury, and he had the lowest ERA in the league. Nonetheless, Foxx led an offense in which each starter hit at least .289. Cleveland finished third, utilizing a talented group of young

JOE MEDWICK

With all the National League's great hitters — such as Rogers Hornsby, Mel Ott, Stan Musial, Willie Mays, and Hank Aaron — it's hard to believe that the last N.L. player to win the triple crown did it more than 50 years ago and his nickname was "Ducky." Tagged with the moniker because of his slight waddle, Joe Medwick had a season in 1937 players dream about.

Medwick was another one of those tough, surly, hustling characters of the St. Louis Cardinals' "Gas House Gang." During his first four full seasons, Medwick hit over .300 each year (including two over .350) and led the N.L. once each in hits, doubles (a league record 64 in '36), triples, and RBI. Then in 1937, Medwick lived up to his other nickname, "Muscles." He led the league in at-bats (633), hits (237), doubles (56), home runs (31), runs (111), RBI (154), batting average (.374), and slugging percentage (.641). For good measure, he threw in a league-leading .988 fielding percentage in the outfield.

Medwick led the N.L. in RBI again in 1938, making him one of only four players to lead the league in ribbies three straight years. He was traded by St. Louis to Brooklyn in 1940, and while he remained a solid player for another eight years, he never approached 1937 stats again. Medwick retired in 1948 with a .324 career average and made the Hall of Fame 20 years later.

Joe DiMaggio slams a home run (top left) in Game Five of the 1937 World Series; he had eight career Series homers. Lou Gehrig steps across the plate (top right) after his solo shot in Game Four of the '37 Series. Gehrig is tied for fifth (with Reggie Jackson) on the all-time World Series list with ten homers. In 1938, New York Yankee Red Ruffing (middle left) was 21-7 with a 3.31 ERA, 22 complete games, 127 strikeouts, and a league-leading four shutouts. He had two complete game victories in the '38 World Series. Ruffing was 21-7 in 1939 with a league-leading five shutouts. Lefty Gomez (middle center) was 18-12 in 1938 for the Yanks. Shortstop Frankie "The Crow" Crosetti (middle right) averaged 122 runs scored a season from 1936 to '39 for the Yankees. The 1937 San Diego Pacific Coast League team (bottom) includes, third from left, a young outfielder named Theodore Samuel Williams.

THE 1930s

sluggers and pitcher Bob Feller. The flamethrower fanned 18 Tigers in a game, setting an A.L. strikeout record that stood until 1987. Detroit couldn't find a starter to provide sufficient innings pitched and, as a result, slipped to fourth despite Greenberg's outstanding season. Chicago fell out of the first division when Luke Appling broke an ankle in the spring and missed the first half.

The National League race was a free-for-all that the Cubs pulled out in the end by 2 games over Pittsburgh. Not unlike their miraculous finish in 1935, the Cubs had to overcome a 7-game deficit at the start of September. The Pirates held a 1½-game lead heading into the final week and a three-game series in Chicago. The Cubs won the first game behind the pitching of recently acquired Dizzy Dean. The second game culminated with Gabby Hartnett's famous "Homer in the Gloamin'," a blast hit into a thick fog that snapped a ninth-inning tie in darkened Wrigley Field. The Cubs trounced Pittsburgh the next day, extending their winning streak to ten games and knocking the Bucs out of the race. Pittsburgh didn't mount another chase for the pennant until 1960.

Chicago went 21-4 in that last month, but the early part of the season wasn't so smooth. Charlie Grimm was sacked as manager midway through the season and was replaced by Hartnett, and the club lacked punch all season. Keeping them in the hunt was a solid pitching staff led by Bill Lee and Clay Bryant who combined for 41 wins. Lee also led the league with a 2.66 ERA. Dean was acquired from St. Louis in April for $185,000, but an arm injury limited him to 13 games, in which he went 7-1.

Ott won his third straight home run crown for New York, but again he had precious little support

Kiki Cuyler hit .326 in 1936.

in the lineup. When Hubbell went down with an arm injury in August, the Giants faded to third, 5 games out. Cincinnati lefthander Johnny Vander Meer thrilled the baseball world by tossing back-to-back no-hitters, the second coming in the first night game at Brooklyn's Ebbets Field. Historians frequently note that Vander Meer's remarkable achievement gave night ball a major boost in legitimacy and popularity. His battery mate, Ernie "Schnozz" Lombardi, acknowledged as the slowest man in baseball, won the batting crown that year with a .342 mark and was voted the league's Most Valuable Player.

In a rematch of the 1932 World Series, the Yankees made it eight in a row over the Cubs by combining tough pitching with timely hitting. Ruffing and company held the Cubs to nine runs in the four-game set, while the keystone combination of Gordon and Frankie Crosetti chipped in six RBI apiece to pace the Yankees to their third straight championship.

1939

Baseball celebrated its centennial in 1939 by opening the National Baseball Hall of Fame and Museum in Cooperstown, NY. Further south, the Yankees played through a bittersweet season. The club swept to its fourth straight pennant

ARKY VAUGHAN

Until Arky Vaughan was finally elected to the Hall of Fame by the Veterans Committee in 1985 (37 years after he retired), baseball historians were annually puzzled about why one of the game's greatest hitting shortstops never received his due.

After all, they reasoned, here was a player whose .318 lifetime average is the second highest among shortstops behind the great Honus Wagner. Here was a guy whose league-leading .385 average for the Pittsburgh Pirates in 1935 hasn't been surpassed by a National Leaguer since. Here was a man who still had some great seasons ahead of him, had he not been drafted into the Army in 1944 and lost three seasons.

In the 14 years Vaughan did play, he led the N.L. in just about everything, except homers and RBI. Between 1932 and 1943, he topped the league three times in triples and runs scored, three straight years in walks (a record he shares), and once in stolen bases. He batted over .300 11 out of 12 years and even led the N.L. in slugging the season he won the batting crown. No slouch in the field, Vaughan was the N.L. leader among shortstops in putouts and assists three times.

Unfortunately, Vaughan didn't live to see himself enter Cooperstown. He accidentally died by drowning in 1952 at the age of 40.

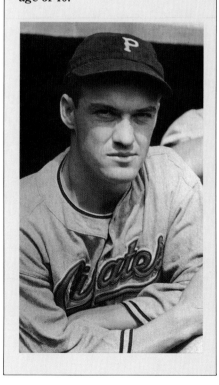

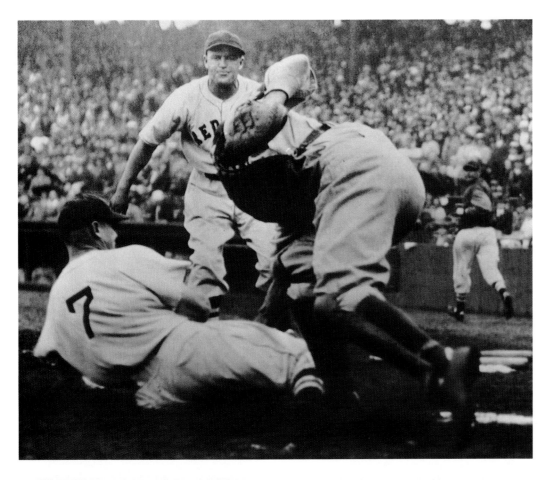

Yankees catcher Bill Dickey tags out Boston outfielder Joe Vosmik (top left) during a 1938 game, as Red Sox player/manager Joe Cronin looks on. Vosmik tried to score from first base on Jimmie Foxx's double, but the ball beat him home. Joe McCarthy (top right) was the manager who took over the Yankees in 1931, won a World Series in '32, and spent the next three seasons in second place. In those three years, the Babe Ruth era ended, and the Joe DiMaggio era began. With DiMaggio taking the post in center field in 1936, the Yankees were back on top, where they would stay for the next four seasons. The Yankees won 102 games a season in those years and were 16-3 in winning four consecutive World Series. New York slipped to third place in 1940, then returned to the peak by winning three pennants and two World Series from 1941 to '43. Before managing the Yankees, "Marse Joe" was the Chicago Cubs skipper, bringing an N.L. pennant to the Windy City in 1929. McCarthy took over the Red Sox in 1948 and led them to two straight second-place finishes. His .614 winning percentage and his .698 World Series winning percentage are all-time bests, and his 2,126 wins are fourth best all time. He was elected to the Hall of Fame in 1957. Charlie Keller (bottom left) broke into the Yankees' outfield with a flash. As a rookie in 1939, he hit .334 with 87 runs scored and 83 RBI. In the '39 World Series, he hit .438, slugged 1.188, smacked three homers, scored eight runs, and drove in six. Bill Dickey (middle top) hit .302 with 24 homers and 105 RBI in 1939; he had two homers and five RBI in the '39 World Series. Al Lopez (middle bottom) averaged 43 RBI a season for the 1930s.

THE 1930s

by winning 106 games, the fourth time in the decade New York topped 100 wins. But the club also lost its architect before the season started, when owner Jacob Ruppert died in January. A more crushing blow came on May 2, when Lou Gehrig, the team's foundation since 1925, removed himself from the lineup after a record 2,130 consecutive games. Gehrig was suffering from a degenerative muscle condition that came to bear his name. At age 36, he never played another game, cutting short one of the greatest careers in the game's history. He was voted into the Hall of Fame later that year and died in 1941.

Even with Gehrig's numbing loss, the Yankees were an irresistible force. Rookie Charlie

Keller batted .334 to pick up some of the offensive slack created by Gehrig's absence. Every Yankee starter managed at least ten home runs, and center fielder DiMaggio hit a league-high .381. Once again, New York excelled in all phases. The team scored more than a run a game above the league average and allowed 1.3 earned runs less than the A.L. norm. Ruffing paced the staff with a 21-7 record (his fourth consecutive 20-win season) and 2.94 ERA. Six other pitchers posted at least ten wins. Johnny Murphy managed only three wins, but he saved a record 19 games as manager Joe McCarthy used him primarily in a late-inning relief role.

The Red Sox challenged the Yankees until the All-Star break, then faded to second place, 17 games back. Although pitcher Lefty Grove was still brilliant — winning 15 games, losing four, and capturing his record ninth earned run average title — the staff lacked a durable pitcher who could provide 30 starts and more than 200 innings. By contrast, the Indians had three pitchers who worked over 200 frames, including league-leader Feller, who also won 24 games and fanned 246 batters.

Cleveland, however, was

A Louisville Slugger poster celebrates the opening of the Hall of Fame. The idea for the baseball shrine was born in 1936, and the structure was opened during baseball's symbolic centennial in 1939 in Cooperstown, NY.

nowhere near as productive with the bats as Boston and finished in third. The Sox owned the toughest one-two punch in baseball; 31-year-old Jimmie Foxx, who blasted a league-high 35 homers and drove home 105 runs, and 20-year-old rookie sensation Ted Williams, who provided 31 home runs and a league-leading 145 RBI. The lanky lefthanded hitter also batted .327, rapped 44 doubles, walked 107 times, and scored 131 runs.

DIZZY DEAN

Jay Hannah "Dizzy" Dean probably would have been the first to claim that if it hadn't been for a freak injury, he would have had the best statistics of any pitcher in baseball history. And he probably would have been right.

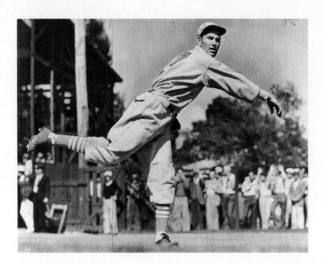

A garrulous man with boundless self-confidence and the best fastball of his day, Dean was baseball's most colorful player during the Depression years. He joined the Cardinals' "Gas House Gang" in 1932 and went 18-15, leading the N.L. in innings pitched, strikeouts, and shutouts. He topped the N.L. in strikeouts

again in '33, going 20-18. Then in 1934 he established himself as the game's best pitcher, winning 30 of 37 decisions (the N.L.'s first 30-game winner in 17 years) and leading the league in complete games, strikeouts, and shutouts. The MVP that year, he also saved seven games in relief and won two games in the World Series.

Dean won his fourth straight strikeout title in '35 and also led the N.L. in wins with 28. When he followed that with a 24-13 record and a league-leading 11 saves in '36, Dean's lifetime record at age 25 was 121-65.

Then, a line drive, hit by Earl Averill in the 1937 All-Star Game, struck Dean's small left toe and broke it. Rather than letting the injury heal, Dean compensated by altering his pitching motion and blew out his arm. He was never the same again, winning just 16 games between 1938 and '41. The Hall of Fame recognized his greatness in 1953.

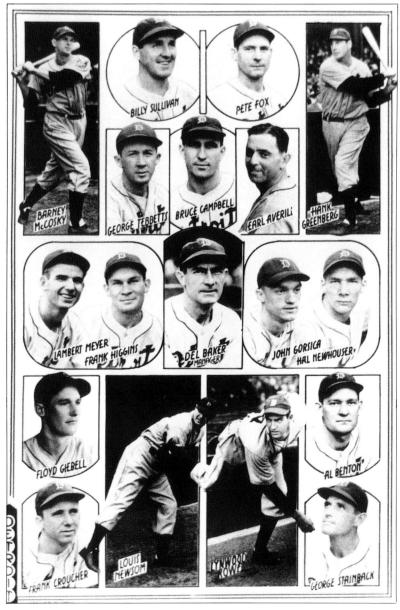

Manager/shortstop Joe Cronin (top left) of Boston hit .308 with 19 homers, 107 RBI, and 97 runs scored in 1939. It was a representative season for Cronin in the middle of his career. Yankees third baseman Red Rolfe (top right) led the A.L. with 213 base hits, 46 doubles, and 139 runs scored. Rolfe averaged 121 runs scored a years between 1935 and 1942. The 1939 Detroit Tigers (bottom) were 81-73, finishing fifth in the A.L. The Tigers, though, had the makings of a pennant-winning team, with such players as Hank Greenberg, Bobo Newsom, and Charlie Gehringer. The Tigers would win the A.L. pennant in 1940.

THE 1930s

In the National League, Cincinnati completed a remarkable two-year transformation from 1937 cellar-dweller to 1939 champs by getting outstanding pitching performances from Bucky Walters and Paul Derringer. Walters, acquired from the destitute Phillies for $50,000 midway through the 1938 season, was like a Babe Ruth in reverse. He spent his first four seasons in the big leagues as an infielder before he was converted into a pitcher in 1935. In his first full season with the Reds, he won 27 games, led the league in strikeouts and ERA, and was named Most Valuable Player. Derringer shot off 25 wins against only seven losses that year, and with Walters, they led Cincinnati home 4½ games ahead of St. Louis. Offen-

sively, the club was led by first baseman Frank McCormick, who batted .332 and drove in 128 runs. Lombardi's average dropped 55 points to .287 that year, but he still contributed 20 homers to the first Cincinnati pennant in 20 years.

St. Louis got strong offensive contributions from Joe Medwick and Johnny Mize, who led the league in home runs and batting average, but the club's cause was undermined by a lack of pitching depth. Brooklyn, under the fiery leadership of player/manager Leo Durocher, moved from sixth to third, as the club continued to rebuild under second-year general manager Larry MacPhail. Chicago slipped to fourth as both its hitting and pitching slipped several notches. Dizzy Dean, age 28 and plagued by a chronic arm problem, appeared in only 19 games.

As the decade came to a close, the Yankees administered their second consecutive sweep of the National League champions, and increased their string of world championships to four in a row, including 16 series wins against only three defeats.

The Yanks eked out a Game One win on a ninth-inning single by Bill Dickey that beat Cincinnati 2-1.

Rookie Ted Williams hit .327 with 131 runs and an A.L.-best 145 RBI in '39.

Monte Pearson took a no-hitter into the seventh inning of Game Two but had to settle for a two-hit shutout. Game Three featured four Yankee home runs, two by Keller, and the finale was won by the Yankees when they unloaded for three runs in the tenth inning to win 7-4.

GEHRIG'S FAREWELL

They are among the most immortal words ever spoken in the history of sports.

"I may have been given a bad break," Lou Gehrig told nearly 62,000 fans in Yankee Stadium on Lou Gehrig Day, July 4, 1939, "but I have an awful lot to live for. Today I consider myself the luckiest man on the face of the earth."

Only about one month before, Gehrig was told that a disease in his body—amyotrophic lateral sclerosis — would eat away at his muscles. The symptoms had begun showing during the 1938 World Series, when Gehrig batted .286. During spring training in '39, the quickness in his swing was gone, and his reflexes around first base were slow.

But this was the man who had played more than 2,100 games in 15 years, who performed with assorted aches his entire career. Yankees skipper Joe McCarthy did not sit Gehrig down. On May 2, Gehrig took a lineup card to home plate without his name. As the announcement was made that his streak of 2,130 straight games was over, he walked to the dugout with tears in his eyes.

"I went up there four times with men on base and left five stranded," Gehrig said after his last game. "It's tough to see your mates on base and not be able to do anything about it. Maybe a rest will do me some good."

Gehrig died a little more than two years later, at the age of 37.

Billy Herman (top left) was a Chicago Cubs and Brooklyn Dodgers second baseman in the 1930s and early 1940s. A career .304 hitter, Herman set some fielding records that stand to this day. He led the Cubs to three N.L. pennants in 1932, 1935, and 1938. When he was traded to Brooklyn in 1941, he made his presence immediately felt by leading the Dodgers to the pennant that year. Herman batted over .300 eight times in his 15-year career. His best season came in 1935, when he batted .341 and led the league with 227 base hits and 57 doubles. He averaged 98 runs scored a season from 1932 to '39. As a defensive player, he was perhaps the best second baseman of his day. He led the league seven times in putouts and seven times in games played. He had five seasons with 900 or more total chances — still a major league record. Cardinals catcher Mickey Owen (bottom left) takes a cut in spring training. The light-hitting Owen was the Cardinals starting catcher from 1937 to '40. The 1939 baseball centennial emblem was worn by the players that year (bottom right).

THE 1940s

Night games, televised games, and World War II
would prompt more changes in the game
during the 1940s than in any decade
since the 1880s. No other milestone matched
in importance that of Jackie Robinson
breaking the color barrier.

Bob Feller (page 236) was the dominating hurler during the 1940s, gathering a .663 winning percentage. Joe DiMaggio (page 237) averaged 120 RBI a year during the six full seasons that he played in the 1940s.

THE 1940s

By 1940, America had emerged from the Depression, which had kept many fans away from ballparks during the 1930s. The country was back at full employment, and fans were flocking to ballgames all over the land. Baseball was truly the national pastime, because in addition to the two major leagues' 16 teams, there were almost 500 minor league clubs that would attract more than 35 million spectators in 1940.

So baseball entered the new decade with high hopes — and no idea of the monumental changes that the game would undergo in the ensuing ten years. Night games, televised games, World War II, and the breaking of the color barrier (blacks would finally be permitted to play in the major leagues in 1947) would precipitate more changes in the game than in any decade since the 1880s.

In 1935, Larry MacPhail, general manager of the Cincinnati Reds, was the first man to have lights installed in his ballpark. The first night game was played at Crosley Field. MacPhail figured that since most people worked days, night games would draw more weekday spectators. He was right, as Cincinnati's weeknight games outdrew the club's weekday crowds.

The other major league ballclubs did not follow suit quickly. Baseball was run by traditionalists who maintained the game should be played in daylight. The second major league club to install lights was the Brooklyn Dodgers, who did so in 1939, because MacPhail was then the Dodgers' general manager. But by 1948, every team in the major leagues had a lighted ballpark and was playing night games except for the Chicago Cubs. Wrigley Field's switch wasn't flipped until 1988.

Although baseball commissioner Judge Kenesaw Mountain

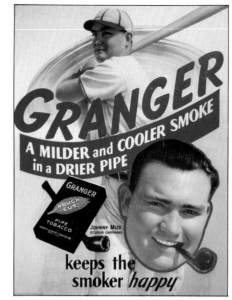

Johnny Mize was a dominant first baseman for the Cards and Giants during the 1940s, leading the N.L. in homers four times.

Landis set the teams' allotment of night games at a miserly seven, the 77 night games played in 1941 drew more than 1.5 million fans, an average of almost 20,000 per game. With the United States at war during the 1942 season, President Franklin Roosevelt wrote to Judge Landis and asked that the number of night games be doubled so that employees in defense plants would not take off afternoons to attend ballgames. It actually took a war and a presidential request to extend night baseball.

Meanwhile, attendance in the major leagues, which fell during the war, grew steadily afterward, reaching a record high of 10.8 million in 1945, then leaping to 18.5 million in 1946, when most of the servicemen had returned from battle.

If night baseball spurred attendance, television sent it soaring — and then drastically cut into the gate receipts of many ballclubs. The first ballgames to be televised were played at Ebbets Field in 1939, a doubleheader between the Dodgers and the Reds. The Cincinnati starter in the first game was Johnny Vander Meer, who had pitched a no-hitter in his previous outing. He threw a no-hitter against the Dodgers as well and became the only man in history to hold the opposition hitless in back-to-back starts. Unfortunately, few people saw the televised game simply because there were few TV sets to receive the transmission.

JOE DiMAGGIO

Joltin' Joe DiMaggio was the quintessential center fielder, a smooth, slick, effortless fielder who could go back on a fly ball at the crack of the bat, turning his back and running to a spot many yards behind him — then turn, raise his glove, and make the catch.

At the plate, DiMaggio was one of the finest righthanded hitters the game has known, a man who hit every ball hard, with power and for average. In 1933, playing with the San Francisco Seals at age 19, he hit in 61 consecutive games. Three years later he joined the Yankees and hit at a .323 clip. The next season, he led the A.L. in home runs with 46 while hitting .346. In 1939, DiMaggio led the league in batting with a .381 average and won his first of three MVPs.

The next year DiMaggio set a record that will in all likelihood never be broken, hitting in 56 consecutive games. He could hit, he could field, he could run, he could throw, and he could lead. He led the Yankees to ten pennant victories in his 13 years with the ballclub. DiMaggio hit 30 or more homers in seven seasons. He scored more than 100 runs in eight seasons. He drove in more than 100 runs in nine seasons.

A heel injury forced DiMaggio to retire early, after the '51 season, even though he was offered another $100,000 contract. His older brother Tom was asked why Joe retired. "He quit," Tom said, "because he wasn't Joe DiMaggio anymore."

Philadelphia's Shibe Park (top left) was the home for both the Phillies and the Athletics during the 1940s. Johnny Vander Meer, left, and Babe Ruth (top right) meet during the early 1940s. Vander Meer led the National League in strikeouts each year from 1941 to '43. The St. Louis Cardinals limber up (bottom left) during spring training in St. Petersburg, FL. Yankees right fielder Tommy Henrich (bottom right) slugged a career-high 31 homers in 1941. He played in four World Series and hit a home run in each.

THE 1940s

But by 1947, television sets (most with five- and seven-inch screens) were selling almost as fast as they could be produced. That was the year NBC began televising major league games and attracting a whole new audience to ballparks. People who had only casually followed baseball began going to games and enjoying themselves. The result was a major league attendance that reached a record high of 21 million in 1948.

The Boston Braves won the National League pennant that year and drew 1.45 million fans. Figuring that televised home games had fueled interest in the team, the Braves sold the television rights to all of their home games for the next two years and coverage of most of their home games through the 1952 season — all for the sum of $40,000. By the time the contract had run out, the Braves' home attendance had fallen 81 percent. Their fans preferred to watch the games on television rather than go to the ballpark. And in 1953, when baseball's attendance had shrunk to 14 million paying customers, the Braves moved to Milwaukee and refused all offers to televise home games.

That contrasts markedly with baseball's current relationship with television. In 1988, the major leagues signed a four-year contract with CBS that would pay each team almost $10 million. A separate deal with cable TV would bring each team an additional $4 million. Each team also cuts its own deal with local television. Yankees owner George Steinbrenner signed with a cable network that would pay the team $41 million annually for 12 years. Radio broadcast rights bring in additional money.

Yet in 1941, neither the Yankees nor the New York Giants could sell their radio rights for the $75,000 that the Dodgers earned from radio. Apparently, Larry MacPhail could convince companies to sponsor the broadcasts of Dodgers games announced by the old redhead, Red Barber.

By the 1942 season, no ballclub was too concerned about broadcast rights, because the United States was at war and every general manager was worried about which player he would lose to the military next. In '42, a total of 31 National League and 40 American League players who had appeared in at least one major league game were called into the armed forces. In '43, 119 A.L. players and 100 from the N.L. were drafted. In '44, the N.L. lost more players to the service, 174 to 168 from the A.L. In '45, 180 A.L. players and 204 N.L. players were called by Uncle Sam.

Connie Mack and his Athletics finished in eighth place six times in the decade.

ERNIE LOMBARDI

At 6'3" and a muscular 230 pounds, catcher Ernie Lombardi was one of the biggest and strongest players in the game from 1931 through 1947. He was also one of the most amazing hitters baseball has ever known. Lombardi hit over .300 in ten of his 17 seasons.

Yet Lombardi couldn't run a lick. He would lash a hit and come out of the batter's box like a man running in soggy sand. He was a pull hitter, driving the ball with such power that opposing shortstops always played him well back on the outfield grass. Lombardi was regularly thrown out from there.

Still, for all his strength and ability to make hard contact with pitched balls, Lombardi was not a home run hitter. In only one season did he hit as many as 20 homers. But Lombardi had a lifetime batting average of .306.

He played his first ten years with the Reds and was an excellent receiver with a great arm. He would throw out base runners trying to steal second without ever coming out of his crouch. He caught both of Johnny Vander Meer's consecutive no-hitters in 1938.

Lombardi had big years as a hitter with the Reds, batting .343 in 1935, .333 in '36, and .334 in '37. In 1938, he hit .342, which led the league. After being traded to the Braves in 1942, Lombardi again won the batting title with a .330 average. The only other catcher to lead the league in hitting was Bubbles Hargrave, who hit .353 in 1926.

As the Cooper brother battery (top left), pitcher Mort, left, and catcher Walker played together on two Cardinals world champion teams. Some of the participants at the War Bond baseball game at the Polo Grounds on August 23, 1943 (top right). The event featured the three major league teams from New York and players who had been drafted, and $800,000 was raised for war bonds. The participants are, standing left to right, Duffy Lewis, Eddie Collins, Roger Bresnahan, Connie Mack, Bill Klem, Red Murray, and George Sisler; kneeling left to right: Honus Wagner, Frankie Frisch, Babe Ruth, Walter Johnson, and Tris Speaker. The 1945 Great Lakes baseball team (middle): Ken Keltner, Bob Feller, Johnny Gorsica, and Pinky Higgins. After Feller rejoined the Indians, Higgins managed the team. A Navy team from 1944 (bottom left) included Stan Musial, top row second from the right. This painting (bottom right) pictures some of the most important members of the Yankees dynasty.

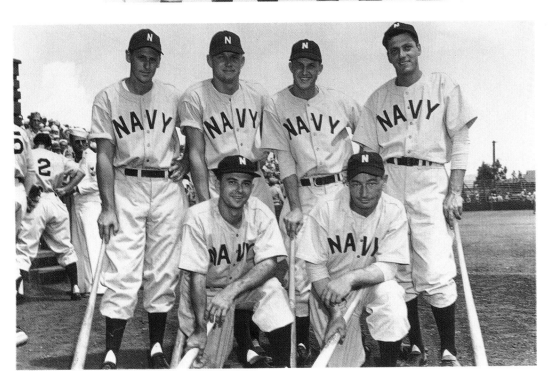

THE 1940s

Those who were drafted last received their discharges within a year and were back on the ballfield the following season. Bob Feller, Hank Greenberg, and a few others were not so fortunate, as they were among the early call-ups in 1941 and had to serve almost four years before being discharged. Feller was the best pitcher in the American League, and Greenberg was the A.L. home run champion. Both players were sorely missed by their ballclubs: Feller by the Cleveland Indians and Greenberg by the Detroit Tigers. In 1944, the Tigers certainly would have won the pennant with Greenberg in the lineup, as they finished only 1 game behind the first-place St. Louis Browns. The Tigers of '44 didn't have a player who hit more than 18 home runs. In his last full season, 1940, Greenberg had hit 41 home runs, driven in 150 runs, and led the Tigers to victory in the pennant race.

May 7, 1941, was the last day Greenberg played before reporting to duty at Camp Custer, MI. In that game he powered home runs off Ernie Bonham and Atley Donald as the Tigers beat the Yankees 7-4. Greenberg was the highest-paid player in the majors that year, and he entered the Army as a poorly paid buck private, but he didn't complain. "I'm not crying about being dropped from $55,000 a year to $21 a month," Greenberg said. "I'm just going to do my duty to this country like every other ballplayer who's drafted into the army. Winning the war against Hitler is more important to me than playing baseball."

Some owners, notably Ed Barrow of the Yankees — who was never known for his generosity with player contracts — tried to take advantage of the war to hold down salaries. Joe DiMaggio, the best center fielder in the game,

asked Barrow for a raise in the spring of '41. Barrow said he couldn't see increasing DiMaggio's salary when he might lose him to the military before the season's end. Actually, DiMaggio had a marriage exemption that kept him out of the service until 1943.

In the spring of 1942 there was talk of an impending wage freeze to aid the war effort. Ed Barrow tried to use this to keep from giving raises to DiMaggio and six other Yankees stars. They finally got a little more money out of Barrow. DiMaggio needed the salary increase as he had to help out his Italian-born father who, having never applied for U.S. citizenship, was no longer allowed on his fishing boat in San Francisco harbor for so-called "security reasons."

Joltin' Joe was finally drafted in 1943, along with a dozen of his teammates, but the Yankees still won the pennant. The teams that lost the most players to the military, the Philadelphia Athletics (36) in the A.L. and the Philadelphia Phillies (35) in the N.L., usually finished last anyway. A's owner and

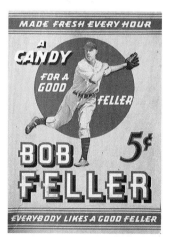

Hank Greenberg (top) had 150 RBI in 1940. Bob Feller (bottom) at age 19 struck out 15 batters during his first game in '36.

LARRY DOBY

On July 5, 1947, Larry Doby, who later said he never thought of making history, made history. He was the first black player to appear in an American League game. Playing with the Indians in a doubleheader, Doby had an infield single in five at-bats, which wasn't so bad when you consider that a number of the Indians players had refused to shake his hand.

Doby had as difficult a time of it in the A.L. as Jackie Robinson had in the National League that first season. Doby recalls, "I'd get the usual — 'nigger,' 'coon,' 'shoeshine boy.' I could understand it from some fan or some jerk sitting on the bench. But I'd get it from managers too."

But Doby battled back on the field against the racism. In his first full season (1948) Doby batted .301, then paced the team in the World Series win over the Braves by batting .318 and hitting a game-winning home run.

From 1950 through 1954, Doby was one of the best all-around players in the league, a man who could hit for average, hit with power, steal bases, and play solid center field. In 1950, he finished fourth in batting with a .326 average. In 1952, he led the league in home runs with 32. In '54, he led the league in homers (32) and RBI (126), as the Indians won the pennant.

In 1978, Doby again made history as manager of the White Sox — becoming only the second black to manage in the majors.

Pistol Pete Reiser is carried off the field (top) during a game in 1946. Brooklyn's Reiser led the National League in 1941 in batting and four other offensive categories during his rookie season, and he finished in second place in the Most Valuable Player voting. As a center fielder he was among the top five of the era. Reiser, however, was always getting hurt, snuffing out one of the most promising starts in baseball history. This scene is from Ebbets Field on June 15, 1942 (bottom left). The 1944 Great Lakes Bluejackets (bottom right) were 48-2. Managed by Mickey Cochrane, on the left, the team consisted of, lined up left to right, Schoolboy Rowe, John McCarthy, Whitey Platt, Ed Weiland, Gene Thompson, Virgil Trucks, Al Glossop, Pinky May, and Clyde McCullough. All of the players had major league experience before the war.

manager Connie Mack had grown used to that position after his earlier seasons of success.

By 1944, baseball had been stripped of most of its stars as rosters were filled by men who were, in military terms, "4-F" — very young or very old. Retired players like Paul and Lloyd Waner, Debs Garms, and Pepper Martin returned to the majors. The Reds started a 15-year-old pitcher, Joe Nuxhall, in one game. And in the following season, major league "talent" was even worse. The St. Louis Browns used a one-armed outfielder, Pete Gray. In fact, only approximately one third of the men who were regulars in 1945 played at least 100 games in '46.

Despite the wartime interruption, the 1940s proved to be the most exciting decade ever for pennant races. Eight races were decided by 2 games or less, another by 2½ games.

In the American League, the 1940 Tigers finished 1 game ahead of the Indians and 2 games ahead of the Yankees. In 1944, the St. Louis Browns finished 1 game ahead of the Tigers. In 1945, the Tigers finished 1½ games ahead of the Washington Senators. The Indians and Red Sox finished the 1948 season tied for first place, then met in a one-game playoff that Cleveland won. In 1949, the Yankees and the Red Sox played the final game of the season tied for first place, a game that New York won.

In the National League, the 1941 Dodgers finished 2½ games ahead of the Cardinals. In 1942, the Cardinals finished 2 games ahead of the Dodgers. In 1946, the Cardinals and Dodgers finished in a tie for first place, then met in the league's first playoff series. St. Louis won the first two games of the three-game set to capture the pennant. In 1949, the Dodgers finished 1 game ahead of the Cardinals.

The Dodgers-Cardinals games were wars throughout the decade. Pitchers on both sides threw at hitters, baserunners slid with their spikes high and unkind thoughts in their minds, and there were fisticuffs on the field.

In 1940, the Dodgers bought veteran slugger Joe Medwick from the Cardinals for $125,000. Medwick had been in Brooklyn only six days when the Cardinals came in for a series. He stayed in the same hotel with Dodgers manager Leo Durocher, and they happened to be joined in the elevator by Bob Bowman, the Cards pitcher who would

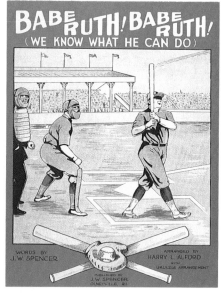

Published in 1948, this sheet music celebrates the Bambino. As the years went on, the Babe Ruth myth grew larger and larger.

start that day. Durocher made a nasty remark, and Bowman said, "There's at least one automatic out in your lineup — you." Medwick snarled, "You'll be out of there before you get to Leo."

That afternoon Bowman's first pitch to Medwick cracked him in the temple and knocked him unconscious. There were fights all over the field, and after Medwick was carried off on a stretcher, Larry MacPhail — the toughest general manager in the game — ran in front of the Cardinals' dugout and challenged the entire team. One good thing came out of the affair: The next year, MacPhail introduced plastic batting helmets to baseball.

ENOS SLAUGHTER

Enos "Country" Slaughter had two great careers in the major leagues. The first was with the Cardinals, with whom Slaughter played from 1938 through 1953 (minus three years out for the war). The second was with the Yankees, with whom he played from 1954 through 1959 (minus a season in Kansas City).

Slaughter was the original Charlie Hustle, a man who ran every place on a ballfield, who didn't mind diving after batted balls or crashing into the pivot man at second or the catcher at plate. In 1946, Slaughter won the World Series for the Cardinals when Red Sox shortstop Johnny Pesky didn't see Slaughter running all the way from first base on a single. Pesky held the ball, and Slaughter scored the winning run in Game Seven.

Slaughter batted over .300 five years in a row from 1939 to '46,

fell off to a .294 average in 1947, then hit over .300 the next two years. But after 13 years in St. Louis, the Cardinals thought Slaughter was finished at age 38 and traded him to the Yankees. He broke a wrist and didn't get going in New York until 1956, when he filled in for injured outfielders and helped the Yankees win another pennant. In the Series he batted .350.

After 19 years in the majors, Slaughter retired from the big leagues, and he took up managing in the minors. But he also played. As the 45-year-old player/manager for Raleigh in the Carolina League in 1961, he batted .341. In 1985, Slaughter was inducted into the Hall of Fame.

Paul Waner (top left) hit .279 for the Boston Braves in 1941 and .258 for them in 1942. Cardinals first baseman Johnny Mize (top right) led the National League with 43 home runs, 137 runs batted in, and a .636 slugging average. Leo Durocher (bottom right) managed the Dodgers to the World Series in 1941 but didn't get another pennant until 1951 with the Giants. Yankees shortstop Phil Rizzuto takes the throw (bottom left) as White Sox first baseman Joe Kuhel slides into second base safely for the steal. Kuhel was a fine fielder and an average hitter with little power. He knocked 27 round-trippers in 1940, 11 more than in any other season during his 18-year career. Kuhel had a .277 lifetime average with 1,236 runs scored and 1,049 RBI. Rizzuto was one of the best fielding shortstops of his time. He played 13 years and ended with a career .273 average.

THE 1940s

The 1941 season was noteworthy for another reason, as it was the year in which two baseball records were set that may never be broken. Joe DiMaggio hit in 56 consecutive games, and Ted Williams of the Red Sox batted over .400 for the season. DiMaggio's streak would have gone well beyond 56 games if Cleveland third baseman Ken Keltner hadn't made two exceptional plays on shots off Joe's bat on July 17. After going hitless in that game, DiMaggio proceeded to hit in another 17 consecutive games.

Ted Williams, age 22 in '41, would later say, "Joe DiMaggio was by far the best righthanded hitter I ever saw." But many feel that Ted Williams was the finest all-around hitter in baseball history. With a .401 average in 1930, Bill Terry had been the last man to bat over .400 in the majors. Williams went into the final doubleheader of the season with his average at .3995, which rounded off to .400. In the first game he went four-for-five, and in the second he went two-for-three, with a final average of .406.

Williams also hit 37 homers in '41, becoming the only American League player ever to hit over .400 and knock more than 20 home runs in the same season.

For all of the dramatics of the 1940s, all of the tight pennant races and all of the changes that were wrought in the game by night baseball and television, no single event matched in its implications the day in 1947 when Jackie Robinson of the Dodgers broke the color barrier and opened the doors for black players to begin entering the major leagues.

Branch Rickey, the Dodgers general manager, was the man who signed Robinson and assigned him to the organization's top farm team (Montreal) in 1946. Robinson had a great year and seemed certain to make the big club the next season. But 15 of the major league clubs voted that Robinson not be allowed in the major leagues, with Rickey casting the only affirmative vote. Still, the new baseball commissioner, Happy Chandler, had the final say in the matter. "I told Mr. Rickey," Chandler said when he was inducted into the Hall of Fame in 1982, "that someday I was going to have to meet my maker, and if He asked me why I didn't let that boy play and I said it was because he was black, that might not be a satisfactory answer. So I said, 'You bring him in, and I'll approve the transfer of his contract from Montreal to Brooklyn.' I was just doing what justice and mercy required me to do under the circumstances."

Happy Chandler (left) and Branch Rickey had the courage to break the color line.

JOE GORDON

For years, Yankees second baseman Joe Gordon was known as the man who "robbed" Ted Williams of the MVP Award in 1942. Gordon hit .322 with 18 home runs and 103 RBI and was voted the award for his "batting and fielding excellence." Two other Yankees — Joe DiMaggio and Charlie Keller — had more homers and RBI than Gordon. Williams batted .356, hit 36 homers, and had 137 RBI.

Gordon was a supremely gifted second baseman, was a power hitter for a 170-pounder, and was a very tough batter in the clutch. He led league second basemen in assists four seasons. In four of his 11 seasons in the majors he drove in more than 100 runs. His career home run total of 253 is excellent for a second baseman (Rogers Hornsby leads all second basemen with 302). Gordon also compiled 975 runs batted in, 914 runs scored, and a .466 slugging average in his career.

Gordon made major contributions to five Yankees pennant victories in the late 1930s and 1940s, and he is still regarded as the best second baseman the team has ever had. He was equally adept playing with shortstop Frank Crosetti as with Phil Rizzuto.

The Yankees traded Gordon to the Indians for pitcher Allie Reynolds in 1947 and won the pennant. But the Indians won the pennant in '48, as Gordon teamed up with shortstop Lou Boudreau. Gordon had a career year that season, batting .280, hitting 32 home runs, and driving in 124 runs.

After he retired, Gordon went on to manage in Cleveland, Detroit, and Kansas City.

Probably the greatest hitter in baseball history, Ted Williams (top) averaged 128 RBI a season during the seven seasons that he played in the 1940s. He averaged 136 runs scored a season during the decade. He led the A.L. in slugging percentage six times in those seven seasons, and he led the league in homers four times. In both 1942 and 1946, Williams won the league's triple crown. He had the highest single-season on-base average in history (.551) in 1941. The Cincinnati Reds held spring training at Indiana University (bottom).

THE 1940s

Chandler was a Southerner with an open mind. At the time, blacks were still segregated from whites in the South. Hotels, restaurants, theaters, rest rooms, and even drinking fountains that blacks could use were clearly marked "colored." Most of the Dodgers who had been born in the South were not pleased with the prospect of playing ball with a black. Dodgers manager Leo Durocher heard about the dissenting feelings and called a team meeting in spring training. "If this fellow Robinson is good enough to play on this ballclub — and from what I've seen and heard he is — he's going to play for me," Durocher said. "I'm the manager of this club, and I'm interested in one thing: winning. I'll play an elephant if he can do the job, and to make room for him, I'll send my own brother home."

Outfielder Dixie Walker had the most intolerant attitude on the Dodgers, and he requested that Rickey trade him. A deal couldn't be worked out until the following year, when Walker was sent to Pittsburgh.

Jackie Robinson was a unique individual, a graduate of UCLA (where he had been an All-America football player), and a man of great courage and patience. When he was playing his way to the N.L.'s Rookie of the Year award in 1947, he was subjected to vile racial epithets, "nigger" being the least of the taunts he heard.

Although he had never played first base (second was his natural position), Robinson was assigned there and excelled, quickly adapting to the artful footwork required around the bag. A number of players tried to land their spikes in Robinson's left Achilles' tendon as he stretched to make a catch. But Robinson proved too quick for them.

Later that season, as the Dodgers were winning the pennant, they brought up another black, pitcher Dan Bankhead. In the American League, Cleveland Indians owner Bill Veeck signed a black outfielder named Larry Doby, with whom a number of his teammates would not shake hands. The St. Louis Browns were the only other major league club to sign black players in '47, infielder Hank Thompson and outfielder Willard Brown. The Boston Red Sox in 1959 became the last team to hire a black player, Pumpsie Green.

Baseball has never been the same since that breakthrough season of 1947. Black players went on to dominate the game in many seasons since then, as would have many great black players from Negro Leagues in earlier years. Negro Leagues All-Stars such as Satchel Paige, Josh Gibson, Buck Leonard, Cool Papa Bell, Judy Johnson, Oscar Charleston, Martin DiHigo, and John Henry Lloyd certainly would have been All-Stars in the major leagues had they been given a chance. A special committee on the Negro Leagues has since inducted all of them into the Baseball Hall of Fame in Cooperstown, where they justly belong.

Judy Johnson was one of the top third sackers in baseball from 1921 to '38. He was elected to the Hall of Fame in 1975.

LOU BOUDREAU

An excellent all-around athlete who in high school starred in football, baseball, and basketball, Lou Boudreau was also one of the smartest athletes.

Though he wasn't particularly quick, Boudreau was smart enough to figure out exactly where to play hitters. The result was that in 1940 he led the league's shortstops in fielding percentage — which he would do a total of eight times — and made the All-Star team. He also batted .295.

By 1942, the 24-year-old Boudreau decided he was smart enough to not only play for but to manage the Indians. He applied for the job and got it, becoming the youngest opening-day manager in major league history. In 1946, when Ted Williams returned from the war and began destroying A.L. pitchers, the young skipper came up with the famous Boudreau Shift: He moved to the second-base side of the infield whenever the pull-hitting Williams came to bat. That enraged Williams, who nailed shots that would have been hits if three men had not been playing on the right side.

In 1948, the Indians and the Red Sox finished the season in a tie for first place. In the one-game playoff, Boudreau started rookie lefthanded knuckleball pitcher Gene Bearden, who limited the Red Sox to five hits, one a Williams' single. Boudreau pounded out four hits, including two home runs, as the Indians won the pennant. He then led his club to victory over the Boston Braves in the World Series.

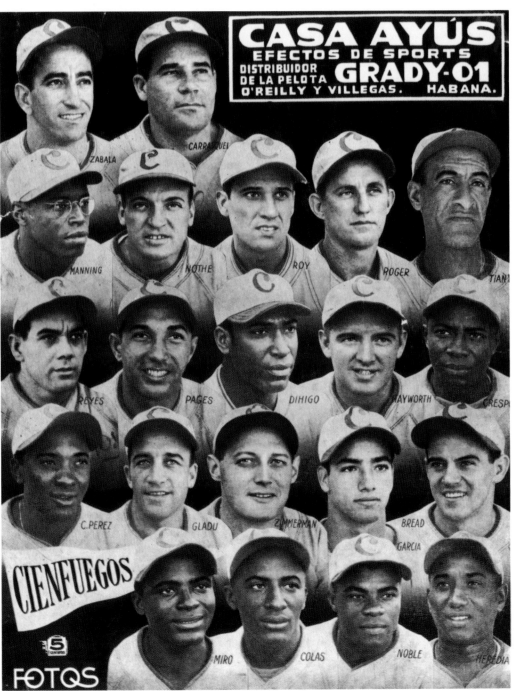

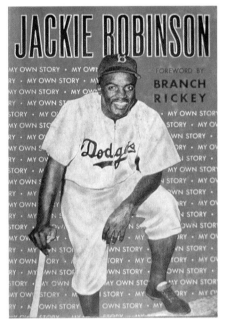

The Kansas City Monarchs (top left) won four straight Negro American League pennants from 1939 to 1943. Satchel Paige was their star hurler. Integration came too late and was too slow for outstanding black players such as Ray Dandridge (top right). While the color line was broken, by the early 1950s there were still very few blacks in the major leagues, and most organizations passed on established Negro League stars. This baseball team (bottom left) from Havana, Cuba, featured Martin DiHigo, the first Cuban player ever elected to the Hall of Fame (in 1977). My Own Story by Jackie Robinson (bottom right) tells the story of one of the most pivotal figures in baseball (and American) history.

THE 1940s

1940

The 1940 season began with a stunning performance by Cleveland's 21-year-old pitching star, Bob Feller. He became the only man ever to throw a no-hitter on opening day, as he blanked the White Sox and went on to win 27 games for the season. Joining Feller on what was probably the best pitching staff in the American League were Al Milnar (18 wins), Al Smith (15 wins), and Mel Harder (12 wins).

The Indians had a pretty fair offense too, led by rookie shortstop Lou Boudreau, who hit .295 with 101 RBI. First baseman Hal Trosky had 25 home runs and 93 RBI, second baseman Ray Mack had 12 home runs and 69 RBI, and third baseman Ken Keltner had 15 home runs and 77 RBI. Altogether, the Indians had a very hard-hitting infield that was also solid defensively.

The Yankees had been favored to win the pennant, as they had the preceding four years in a row. Joe DiMaggio led the league in hitting with a .352 average and drove in 133 runs, while second baseman Joe Gordon also topped the century mark in runners driven home with 103. But the Yankees still didn't have enough to outdo the Indians, finishing a game behind them in third place. Many felt that the Indians would have beaten the Tigers — who finished only 1 game ahead — if the Cleveland players hadn't tried to revolt against manager Ossie Vitt. They actually presented a petition to the Indians owners calling for Vitt's firing.

The Tigers had no such problem with their manager, Del Baker, who made a brilliant move to get slugger Rudy York into the lineup full time. Hank Greenberg was shifted from first base to left field. Greenberg batted .340, slugged 41

The National League won the 1940 All-Star Game held at Sportsman's Park in St. Louis by a score of 4-0. Max West of the Boston Braves slugged a three-run homer in the first inning off of Yankee Red Ruffing, scoring Arky Vaughn of Pittsburgh and Billy Herman of the Cubs. Five N.L. hurlers combined for the shutout.

home runs, and had 150 RBI to win the MVP award. York, a part-time catcher in '39, increased his homer total by 11 to 33, drove in 134 runs, and batted .316 as a first baseman.

While the A.L. pennant race was tight, the Cincinnati Reds repeated in the National League, finishing 12 games ahead of the Dodgers. The Reds were led by a pair of 20-game winners, Bucky Walters (22-10) and Paul Derringer (20-12). But they entered the World Series against Detroit with a problem behind home plate. Tragedy had struck the Reds in August, when reserve catcher Willard Hershberger grew depressed and committed suicide. In mid-September, regular catcher Ernie Lombardi was sidelined by a severely sprained ankle.

So the Reds were forced to start 40-year-old Jimmie Wilson behind the plate. Following a 15-year career in which he had batted .284 for the Phillies and Cardinals, Wilson had retired to the coaching lines. Still in good shape, he was the regular catcher right into the World Series as Lombardi limped around.

Veteran pitcher Bobo Newsome was the Tigers' ace turning in a 21-5 record, and he beat Derringer 7-2 in the Series opener. Newsome's father, who had been at

JOE PAGE

Joe Page was a fun-loving, free-spirited guy who helped the Yankees win two pennants. He joined the Yankees in 1944 and had moderate success as a starter. The big lefthander was primarily a fastball pitcher. In 1945, he was 6-3 with a 2.82 ERA, but he had only four complete games. The next year he completed six games in compiling a 9-8 record.

Early in 1947, Page was on the verge of being sent to the minors. But on May 26, trailing the Red Sox 3-1, the Yankees brought in Page with the bases loaded. He struck out Rudy York and Bobby Doerr; the Yankees went on to win 9-3. Finally, the Yankees had the relief pitcher to replace the great Johnny Murphy. That year, Page won 14 games and saved 17 as the Yankees took the pennant. In '48, the Yankees gained the pennant again as Page won seven games and saved 16.

The injury-racked Yankees would not have won the pennant in 1949 without Page. He won 13 games and saved 27 with a 2.59 ERA. His biggest win came on the next-to-last day of the season as the Yankees tied the Red Sox for first place. In the third inning, Page came in and walked in two runs to make the score 4-0, Boston. But he gave up only one hit and no runs over the last $6\frac{2}{3}$ innings as the Yankees won 5-4, then took the pennant the next day. In the World Series, Page pitched in three games and wrapped up Game Five, which won the world championship.

Dizzy Trout (top left) was outstanding during two seasons, albeit against weaker hitters. He was 20-12 with a 2.48 ERA and five shutouts in 1943 and 27-14 with a 2.12 ERA, 33 complete games, and seven shutouts in '44. The 1940 Pirates double-play combination (top right), from left, Frankie Gustine and Arky Vaughan, confers with manager Frank Frisch. Babe Dahlgren (bottom left) had the unenviable task of replacing Lou Gehrig at first base for the Yankees. Dahlgren hit .235 with 15 homers and 89 RBI in 1939, and .264 in 1940, with 12 homers and 73 RBI. He was sold to the Braves after the 1940 season. White Sox shortstop Luke Appling (bottom right) hit .348 with 96 runs scored and 79 RBI in 1940. He batted .311 in his eight full seasons in the 1940s.

THE 1940s

that game, died of a heart attack the next day. Walters tossed a three-hitter, and the Reds won 5-3. Wilson contributed two hits to the offense.

The Tigers took a one-game lead in Game Three at Detroit's Briggs Stadium, winning 7-4. Derringer evened the Series with a five-hit, 5-2 victory, but the Tigers bounced back in Game Five behind Newsome, who was all but unhittable in the 8-0 shutout of Cincinnati. Greenberg hit a three-run homer.

So the Reds returned home needing to win two straight games, which neither team had done in the Series to date. Bucky Walters earned his second victory, giving up only five hits in the 4-0 shutout and driving in two runs, one on a homer.

In Game Seven, Del Baker decided to start Newsome even though — because no travel days had been allotted that year — he'd had only one day's rest. Schoolboy Rowe, with a 16-3 record on the season, was Detroit's other outstanding pitcher, but he had just worked Game Six.

Newsom didn't look at all tired in the deciding game through six innings, as he shut out the Reds. Meanwhile, the Tigers had scored an unearned run. But in the seventh, back-to-back doubles by Frank McCormick and Jimmy Ripple tied the score. Then aging catcher Wilson sacrificed Ripple to third, where he scored the Series-winning run on a sacrifice fly. Derringer shut down the Tigers the rest of the way.

Jimmie Wilson not only handled the Reds pitchers very well, but he chipped in with a total of six hits for the series, batting .353. Not bad for a 40-year-old retiree, who the next year was hired to manage the Chicago Cubs.

1941

The Yankees, who bounced back to win a fifth pennant in the last six seasons, and the Dodgers, who brought the first pennant to Brooklyn in 21 years, were the big stories in 1941.

Dodgers general manager Larry MacPhail had begun putting together his pennant-winning ballclub by buying outfielder Joe Medwick from the Cardinals and Dolf Camilli from the Phillies. Camilli was not only the best-fielding first baseman in the league but led the circuit in home runs in '41 with 34 and RBI with 120 on his way to the MVP award. Before the season, MacPhail also brought in catcher Mickey Owen from the Cardinals and pitcher Kirby Higbe from the Phillies. Higbe won 22 games that year and lost only nine. MacPhail also acquired second baseman

Pandemonium breaks loose as the Reds win the 1940 World Series.

JACKIE ROBINSON

No one ever played with more courage or intensity and desire than Jack Roosevelt Robinson, the man who broke baseball's color barrier. When Robinson became the first black to play in the major leagues in 1947, five of his Dodgers teammates let it be known they wanted to be traded. The Cardinals voted as a team to strike rather than to play against Robinson — until N.L. president Ford Frick said they would be suspended for life if they didn't play.

But Robinson quickly won over his teammates with his fiery play on the field. Robinson batted .297 and was named Rookie of the Year at the age of 28, then led the Dodgers in batting with seven hits in the World Series.

Robinson was a superb second baseman, a great clutch hitter, and an excellent baserunner. He didn't steal a lot of bases (197), but every steal he made set up or scored a run. Teams quaked whenever Robinson was on third base. He stole home 19 times.

Robinson's best season was in 1949, when he won the batting title with a .342 average and was named MVP. He batted over .300 six times, finishing with a .311 career average in ten years, and led the Dodgers to six pennant victories.

Robinson had been a four-letter man at UCLA, averaging 12 yards a carry as a running back; he could have played pro football. But instead he played baseball, and the game has benefited from his courage ever since.

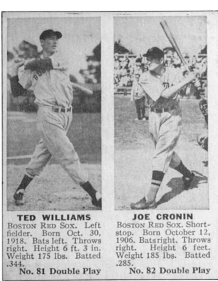

TED WILLIAMS
BOSTON RED SOX. Left fielder. Born Oct. 30, 1918. Bats left. Throws right. Height 6 ft. 3 in. Weight 175 lbs. Batted .344.

No. 81 Double Play

JOE CRONIN
BOSTON RED SOX. Shortstop. Born October 12, 1906. Bats right. Throws right. Height 6 feet. Weight 185 lbs. Batted .285.

No. 82 Double Play

"ARKY" VAUGHAN

The 1940 Reds (top left) relied on pitching; they gave up almost 100 fewer runs than second-place Brooklyn. In both 1940 and '41, Bob Feller (top right) led the A.L. in wins, strikeouts, and shutouts. Johnny Vander Meer (middle left) was 16-13 in 1941, with a league-leading 202 Ks. Ted Williams and Joe Cronin (middle center) led the BoSox to a second-place finish in '41. Arky Vaughan (middle right) scored a N.L.-best 113 runs in '40. Buddy Lewis (bottom left) in '40 hit .317 and scored 101 runs. Spud Chandler (bottom right) was 20-4 in '43.

THE 1940s

Billy Herman from the Cubs. Pitcher Whitlow Wyatt, an earlier acquisition, also won 22 games, seven of them shutouts.

Two youngsters who made major contributions to the Dodgers were shortstop Pee Wee Reese, who had played 84 games in 1940, and rookie center fielder "Pistol" Pete Reiser, who was immediately the best at his position in the league. Reiser batted .343 in his first full season in the majors to become the youngest player (age 22) to win the N.L. batting championship. He also led the league in doubles, triples, and slugging percentage.

Despite an outstanding pitching staff that included Hugh Casey (14-11) and Curt Davis (13-7), plus an excellent offense, the Dodgers engaged in a pennant race with the Cardinals in which the lead changed hands 27 times. The Dodgers didn't clinch the pennant until late September and finished 2½ games ahead of the Cards. The All-Star Game provided a thrilling moment that year when Ted Williams hit a home run with two men out and two men on base in the ninth inning to give the A.L. a 7-5 victory over the N.L.

Led by Williams' outstanding season, in which he produced a .406 average that has not been equaled since 1941, the Boston Red Sox provided the only early competition for the Yankees. Two other Boston hitters, Jimmie Foxx and Jim Tabor, joined Williams in driving in more than 100 runs. But the Yankees were a far better all-around team. They clinched the pennant early in September and finished 17 games ahead of the Red Sox.

MVP Joe DiMaggio and his 56-game hitting streak led the Yankees' attack, with able assistance from fellow outfielders Charlie Keller (.298 average, 33

homers, and 122 RBI) and Tommy Henrich (.277 average, 31 homers, and 85 RBI).

The Yankees had played in a subway World Series with the New York Giants five times, but 1941 marked the first with the Dodgers. A record crowd of 68,540 turned out at "The House That Ruth Built" for Game One. Red Ruffing of the Yankees outpitched Davis to win 3-2, but the Dodgers came back the following day as Wyatt went the distance in the 3-2 victory.

Connie Mack retired after the 1940 season with the most wins (3,776) and losses (4,025).

Ebbets Field, the bandbox with the weird angles in the outfield, was the site of Game Three. Manager Leo Durocher called on knuckleballer Fat Freddie Fitzsimmons — at age 40, the oldest pitcher ever to start a World Series game. He promptly shut out the Yankees for seven innings. But the final out of the seventh was a lined shot off the bat of Yankees pitcher Marius Russo, which popped into the glove of Pee Wee Reese after breaking Fitzsimmons' kneecap. The Yankees scored two runs in the eighth and won the game 2-1. Three successive games were decided by one run.

It looked as if Game Four would be another one-run affair as the Dodgers led 4-3 with two outs in the ninth inning. Reliever Hugh Casey, who had lost the previous day, had been working well since the fifth, and he got two strikes on Henrich for what appeared to be the upcoming final out. Casey threw a hard sinker on the inside

RALPH KINER

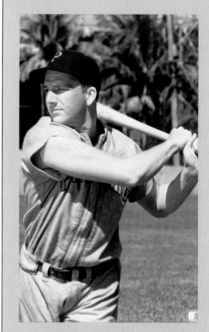

Ralph Kiner said, "Singles hitters drive Fords and such. Home run hitters drive Cadillacs."

He was the ultimate slugger. Every time Ralph Kiner stepped to the plate he was thinking home run. He started his career late, due to his service in World War II, and ended it early, due to a bad back that forced him to retire at age 33. In between he hit a lot of home runs. In fact, in every 100 at-bats, Kiner averaged 7.1 home runs, the second-highest homer percentage in history, behind Babe Ruth.

Kiner was an outfielder and a most undistinguished one. He didn't get a jump on batted balls, run well, or throw with authority. But he caught every ball he got to, and he threw to the right base …and he took his swings at the plate.

He is the only player ever to lead the league in home runs in his first seven years in the majors. He was lucky to win the homer title as a Pirates rookie in 1946 when he hit only 23. But he hit 51 home runs in 1947 and 40 dingers the next year. In 1949, Kiner reached his high in homers with 54, four of which were grand slams. He also averaged more than 100 RBI in his ten major league seasons. He became the first N.L. player to command a $100,000 salary.

When he was forced to retire early — having averaged 37 homers a year for ten seasons — he was driving a Cadillac.

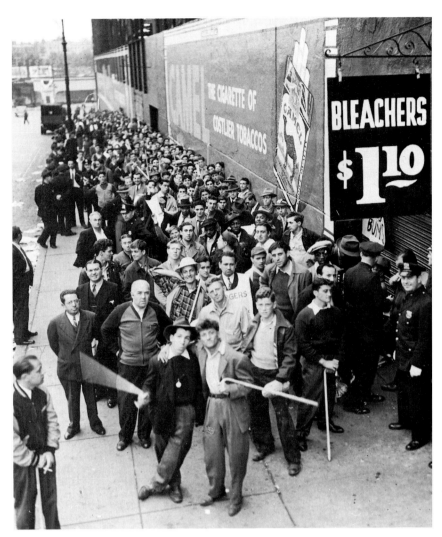

Dodgers hurler Hugh Casey (top left) won two games in relief in the 1947 World Series. Casey led the N.L. in 1942 with 13 saves and in 1947 with 18 saves. The Brooklyn Bleacher Bums line up before Game Three of the 1941 World Series (top right). Dodgers catcher Mickey Owen tags out Joe Gordon (bottom) in Game Two of the '41 Series. Yankee Johnny Sturm looks on.

THE 1940s

corner to the lefthanded hitter, and Henrich swung and missed. But the ball got away from catcher Mickey Owen and Henrich reached first safely. Next DiMaggio singled, Keller doubled in two runs, Bill Dickey walked, and Joe Gordon doubled to make the final score 7-4, Yankees. Mickey Owen, who very seldom let a pitch get past him, became the Series' dunce, even though Durocher later second-guessed himself by saying he should have relieved Casey. The loss seemed to take the heart out of the Dodgers, who lost the game and the World Series the next day.

1942

The Yankees were again favored to win the A.L. pennant and the World Series. They lost two regulars, Henrich and first baseman Johnny Sturm, to the armed services. But they still had a powerful offense, led by DiMaggio, Keller, and Gordon, each of whom would drive in more than 100 runs. They were excellent defensively, particularly up the middle, with Dickey at catcher, DiMaggio in center field, and Phil Rizzuto at shortstop. Rizzuto showed that his

rookie (1941) batting average, .307, had been no fluke, as he batted .284 and had 35 extra-base hits.

The Yankees also had the best pitching staff in the league. Ernie Bonham turned in a 21-5 record, Spud Chandler was 16-5, Hank Borowy was 15-4, Ruffing was 14-7, and Donald was 11-3. Ruffing's earned-run average was the highest in the group at 3.21. Reliever Johnny Murphy's 11 saves led the American League.

It was no surprise when the Yankees jumped off to a sizeable lead and that the Red Sox could finish no closer to them than 9 games. Williams paced a cast of good hitters, including second baseman Bobby Doerr (.290, 102 RBI), shortstop Johnny Pesky (.331) and center fielder Dom DiMaggio (.286, 58 extra-base hits). But the Boston pitching staff featured only one top individual — Tex Hughson, who won 22 games and lost six. Williams followed up his .406 season by batting .356, hitting 36 home runs, and driving in 137 runs to win the triple crown, a performance that should have earned him the MVP award. Instead, the Yankees' Joe Gordon — whose batting average was 34 points below Williams', who hit only half as many home runs, and who had 34 fewer RBI — was given the MVP. A number of baseball writers who voted for this award did not like Williams and spurned him. Had A.L. pitchers been voting for the award, the most feared hitter in the league would have won it going away.

The defending champion Dodgers were the National League

JOHNNY MIZE

Some players get menacing looks on their face when they are about to go to bat against pitchers who have knocked them down. Johnny Mize seemed to wear a menacing look on his face all the time.

Mize was 6'2" and between 220 and 240 pounds. He was so intense that he wasn't the most popular player on his team, but he was a hitter. As a rookie in 1936, Mize batted .329 and proved to be such a graceful fielder around first base that he was called "The Big Cat." At the plate his swing was compact and quick. He waited until the last instant to swing, which was why he could hit breaking balls as well as he hit fastballs.

In 1939, he led the league in batting with a .349 mark and was also the home run leader with 28. After being traded to the Giants and playing in the Polo Grounds with its cozy right field wall, Mize in 1947 hit a career-high 51 home runs, while the Giants as a team hit 221. Mize ended his career with 359 homers and 1,337 RBI. He is eighth all time in slugging average, with .562.

By 1949, Mize had won four home run titles, but he was 37 and thought to be in decline. The Yankees thought otherwise and made Mize the team's primary pinch hitter as they won five consecutive pennants and World Series. He retired with the most pinch hits in Series history.

Three Cards, left to right, in 1942: Jimmy Brown, Terry Moore, and Walker Cooper.

Phil Rizzuto, left, and Joe DiMaggio (top left) wait for their turn at batting practice. DiMaggio hit .305 with 123 runs scored and 114 RBI in 1942. Stan Musial (top right) averaged 115 runs scored and 100 RBI a season during his seven full years in the 1940s. Charlie Keller (bottom left) averaged 28 homers and 102 RBI in five years from 1940 to '43 and 1946. Braves outfielder Tommy Holmes (bottom right) led the N.L. with 28 homers, 224 base hits, 47 doubles, and a .577 slugging average in 1945.

THE 1940s

favorites, and they got off to a great start. Despite the decline in performance of Pete Reiser after he crashed into an outfield fence in July and suffered a severe concussion, the Dodgers had built a 10½-game lead over the Cardinals in mid-August. But Reiser returned to play too soon, plagued by headaches, dizzy spells, and double vision. His batting average, which was a .390 when he was hurt, fell to .310. The man many people at the time regarded as the greatest natural talent in years was never the same again.

The Dodgers were still an outstanding ballclub, with six pitchers — led by Wyatt's 19-7 record — winning ten or more games, and Dolf Camilli and Joe Medwick combining to drive in 205 runs. Brooklyn won 104 games and lost only 50 to finish 54 games over .500.

But the young Cardinals — signed by Branch Rickey and nurtured in the massive St. Louis farm system — were maturing fast. In this era, the practice was for major league clubs to buy players that had been developed by independently owned minor league teams. Rickey signed so many prospects, he had to hide them to prevent opponents from picking them off. Commissioner Landis ruled that those hidden players, most in the low minors, could sign with other organizations. That was how the Dodgers had acquired Reiser for $200.

Still, Rickey's scheme paid off as the Cardinals farm system supplied 22 of the 25 players on the big league roster and St. Louis went on to win four of the next five pennants. In 1942, the team won an amazing 42 of its last 51 games for a total of 106 victories.

The Cards' pitching staff was led by Mort Cooper — who won 22 games on a 1.78 ERA and was named MVP — and 24-year-old

Johnny Beazley, who won 21. The every-day stars were shortstop Marty Marion, third baseman Whitey Kurowski, catcher Walker Cooper, and outfielders Enos Slaughter, Terry Moore, and a rookie with a strange batting stance and a sweet stroke named Stan Musial, who would bat over .300 16 years in succession. The experts picked the veteran Yankees — who had won eight of their last nine World Series games — to beat the youthful Cardinals in the fall classic. And the experts appeared to be correct when in the opening game in St. Louis the Bronx Bombers compiled a 7-0 lead. The Cardinals didn't get a hit until the eighth inning. But then they scored four runs in the ninth, which gave them all the confidence that they needed. They roared back to win the next four games and become world champions.

1943

After the '42 season, Larry MacPhail left the Dodgers to enter the Army as a lieutenant colonel in supply services, and Rickey replaced him as the Brooklyn general manager on a five-year contract. Players in both leagues were now leaving teams for the military in bunches. The champion Cardinals lost Slaughter, Moore, Jimmy Brown, Beazley, and, after winning eight games in the first half of the

Gary Cooper played Lou Gehrig in the movie Pride of the Yankees *(top). Mel Ott (bottom) scored 118 runs in '42.*

258

Cardinals third baseman Whitey Kurowski catches Yankee Joe Gordon's pop fly (top right) in the ninth inning of Game Three of the 1942 World Series. Marty Marion slides underneath Kurowski for the rebound. Kurowski's two-run homer in the ninth inning of Game Five broke a 2-2 tie and gave the Cardinals the world championship. Augie Galan (top left) scored 1,004 runs in a 16-year career that stretched from 1934 to '49. Enos "Country" Slaughter (middle left) hit .318 in 1942 and led the National League with 188 base hits and 17 triples. Slaughter averaged 93 runs scored and 93 RBI in his seven full seasons during the 1940s. Bobby Doerr (middle right) had his career ended by a bad back after the 1951 season. But from 1937 to '51, he was one of the top-slugging and best-fielding second basemen of his time. He was a career .288 hitter, and he ended his career with a .461 slugging average. He hit 223 homers and had 1,247 RBI. He hit at least 15 homers in ten straight seasons, and he had more than 100 RBI in six seasons. Doerr led the league with a .528 slugging average in 1944. Mickey Cochrane (bottom left) was the manager of the Great Lakes naval base team from 1942 to '44.

THE 1940s

season, pitcher Howie Pollet. The Yankees lost Joe DiMaggio, Tommy Henrich, Phil Rizzuto, Buddy Hassett, and Red Ruffing.

Baseball was not only forced to scramble for players in '43; it had to scramble for areas in which to conduct spring training. The government needed to keep the train lines as free as possible for the shipment of equipment and personnel. As baseball teams all traveled by train at this time, the government ordered them not to train below the Mason-Dixon line. With traditional Florida training sites being out, the major league clubs had to prepare for the season in places like Asbury Park, NJ, and even colder West Point, NY.

But prepare they did, and despite the lineup depletions suffered by the Cardinals and Yankees, both repeated as pennant winners in runaways. The Yankees won 98 games and finished 13½ games ahead of the second-place Senators. The Cardinals were even more devastating in the National League, winning 105 games — only one less than in '42 — and coasting in 18 games ahead of the second-place Reds.

The Yankees were led by 35-year-old righthanded pitcher Spud Chandler (given name: Spurgeon Ferdinand). Chandler won 20 of 24

decisions and turned in the lowest ERA (1.64) in the American League in 24 years. No one complained when he won the MVP award. New York's offense was paced by Charlie Keller's 31 home runs and first baseman Nick Etten's 107 RBI. Etten had been acquired from the Phillies, for whom he had driven in just 41 runs in '42. And 24-year-old Billy Johnson batted .280 and had 94 RBI as a rookie.

The Cardinals, whose team batting average was a solid .279, were led on offense by Stan Musial. The man who was to become known as "The Man" batted .357 to win his first batting title and MVP award at age 22. The Cooper brothers also had big years as catcher Walker batted .318 and pitcher Mort again topped the staff with a 21-8 record on an ERA of 2.30.

The Yankees were anxious to renew battle with the team that had beaten them in the last World Series, particularly New York manager Joe McCarthy. His Yankees teams had won eight straight pennant appearances prior to 1942. In the opener at Yankee Stadium, Chandler pitched a seven-hitter and gave up only one earned run as New York won 4-2. But the Cardinals rebounded in Game Two, even though the Cooper brothers played in sorrow over the death of their father that morning. Mort pitched a six-hitter and took a 4-1 lead into the ninth inning, three of the runs scoring on homers by Marion and first baseman Ray Sanders. The Yankees scored two in their final at-bat, but then Cooper bore down and closed out the rally for the victory.

Game Three was also played in New York, with the last four games, if needed, to be played in

The N.L. won the 1943 All-Star Game 3-1. Stan Musial (right) hit .357 in '43.

Marty "Slats" Marion (top left) batted .357 and slugged .714 during the '43 World Series. The light-hitting Marion was the Cardinals shortstop throughout the 1940s. Brooklyn outfielder Augie Galan (top right) led the N.L. in walks in 1943 and '44, and he scored 98 runs a season between 1943 and '45. Spud Chandler (bottom left) led the A.L. with 20 wins, a 1.64 ERA, 20 complete games, and five shutouts in 1943. Stan Musial of the Brainbridge Naval Training Station scores (bottom right) in an exhibition match against the Giants in 1945. Giants catcher Ernie Lombardi looks on.

THE 1940s

St. Louis. The change from the usual 2-3-2 format was to limit team travel on the rails. Cardinals fans were expecting their team to win the next three games in succession as they had a year ago with the Series tied at 1-1. But this time it was the Yankees who turned the trick.

The Cardinals led 2-1 after seven innings of the third game, but in the eighth Johnson tripled home three runs to give the Yankees the lead for good. In Game Four at St. Louis, the teams were tied 1-1 in the eighth when Yankees pitcher Marius Russo led off with a double. Outfielder Tuck Stainback bunted him over to third, and Russo scored the winning run on a sacrifice fly.

Mort Cooper tried valiantly to keep the Cardinals alive in Game Five, striking out the first five Yankees batters. He gave up only two hits in seven innings, but one of them was a two-run homer to Bill Dickey. Spud Chandler gave up ten hits but no runs as the Yankees won their seventh world championship under Joe McCarthy.

1944

This was one of the worst of the war years for baseball but the best of times for the St. Louis Browns, who had not won a pennant in their 42 seasons in the American League. The humble Brownies got tough and rose from the second division, where they normally resided, to smite the big guys in New York, Detroit, and Boston.

The Browns would not have been contenders if their opponents had not been sorely drained by the war. But they opened the season showing they could play. The Browns won their first nine games, which no other A.L. team had ever done. They had three outfielders who could hit for average: Mike

Kreevich (.301), Al Zarilla (.299), and Milt Byrnes (.295). But young shortstop Vern Stephens was the only real power threat, with 20 home runs and 109 RBI.

The pitching staff had three solid workmen in Nels Potter (19-7), Jack Kramer (17-13), and Bob Muncrief (13-8), each of whom pitched more than 200 innings and had at least 12 complete games. The surprise of the staff was Sig Jakucki, age 34, who had retired in 1936 after compiling an 0-3 major league record and being sent to the minors. This season he won 13 of 22 decisions and also had 12 complete games. No one anticipated that the pennant would be decided by his right arm — and a little help from his teammates.

The pennant race proved to be one of the most exciting ever, with the Browns battling the Yankees, Tigers, and Red Sox until the latter lost their best pitcher, Tex Hughson, and second baseman Bobby Doerr to the service in August. After the Browns took a double-header from the Yankees on September 29, they were tied with the Tigers. Both teams won their next game, and on the final day of

Phil Cavaretta played for 22 seasons for the Chicago Cubs.

LUKE APPLING

In his early years with the Chicago White Sox, Luke Appling was called "Fumblefoot" because he was not a good fielder at shortstop. In fact, he would lead the league in errors four times in the 1930s. But as his fielding improved, Appling acquired another nickname: "Old Aches and Pains." He always complained that he was hurting, and he seldom took the field without a bandage or tape on some part of his body.

He regularly went to White Sox manager Jimmy Dykes and said, "Honest, Jimmy, I'm dying today."

"Well as long as you're dying," Dykes would say, "you might as well die out there at shortstop instead of cluttering up the clubhouse."

Old Aches and Pains could hit. He'd stand at the plate in his left-handed stance and foul off pitch after pitch — as many as 15 — until he got the one he wanted. Then he'd lash the ball over the infield for a hit.

During his 20 years in the major leagues, Appling hit over .300 15 times. Nine years in a row he hit over .300. In 1936, Appling set a major league record for shortstops by hitting .388. He also had 111 runs scored and 128 runs batted in. In 1943, he led the league in batting with a .328 average. He played a record 2,218 games at shortstop and retired with a career batting average of .310. He gave pitchers lots of aches and pains.

St. Louis Browns.. 1944

Photo By.. Geo Dorrill.

Top Row... WEST, p... SHIRLEY, p... MUNCRIEF, p... HAFEY, of... HAYWORTH, c... KRAMER, p... HOLLINGSWORTH, p...
GALEHOUSE, p... KREEVICH, of... JAKUCKI, p...
Center Row... C. DeWITT, Traveling Sec'y... CASTER, p... BAKER, if... POTTER, p... ZARILLA, of...
LAABS, of... McQUINN, if... CHRISTMAN, if... BYRNES, of... STEPHENS, if... BAUMAN, Trainer...
HANLEY, Property Man...
Bottom Row... PAUL, p... ZOLDAK, p... CLARY, if... HOFMAN, Coach... SEWELL, Mgr... TAYLOR, Coach...
CHARTAK, of... MANCUSO, c... MOORE, of... GUTTERIDGE, if... BOB SCANLON, Bat Boy...
© ST. LOUIS BROWNS AMERICAN LEAGUE BASEBALL CLUB

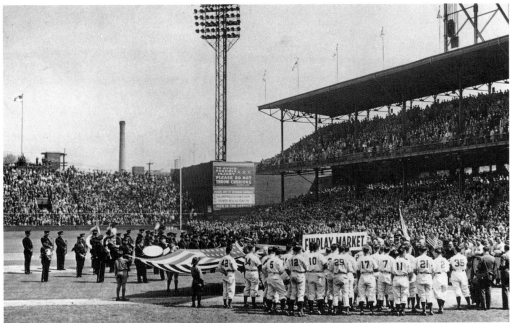

The 1944 St. Louis Browns (top left) finished at 89-65 and won the A.L. pennant by one game over the Tigers. They were managed by Luke Sewell. Cleveland manager/shortstop Lou Boudreau (top right) led the A.L. with a .327 batting average and 45 doubles in 1944. Dizzy Trout (middle right) hurled a league-leading 352 1/3 innings, 33 complete games, and seven shutouts in 1944. Opening Day ceremonies (middle left) usher in a new season in Cincinnati on April 18, 1944. Four Yankees (bottom left), Bill Steinecke, Oscar Grimes, Tuck Stainback, and Bill Bevens, at training camp in 1945. The Yankees trained in Atlantic City in 1944 and '45.

the season, while the Tigers were losing to Washington 4-1, the Browns started Jakucki. He gave up two early runs, then shut down the Yankees' bats after Kreevich singled in the fourth and scored on a home run by Chet Laabs, a part-time player who also worked in a defense plant. The next inning Kreevich again singled and Laabs again homered. The 29-9 record of Detroit's Hal Newhouser won him the MVP award by four points over fellow Tigers pitcher Dizzy Trout, who was 27-14 with a 2.12 ERA. But Jakucki won the pennant.

The Cardinals were out of first place for only four days all season and ran away with their third straight N.L. pennant, finishing 14 1/2 games ahead of the Pitts-burgh Pirates. Their 105 victories made them the first N.L. team to win more than 100 games in three consecutive seasons. The ballclub also set a major league record for fewest errors, 112, in a season. Cards shortstop Marty Marion edged Chicago Cub Bill "Swish" Nicholson (who led the league in

home runs with 33) in the MVP voting, totaling 190 points to 189.

As St. Louis was the lone city in the majors situated west of the Mississippi, 1944 became the only time the World Series was played entirely on that side of the river to this point. Neither team even had to travel within St. Louis. The Browns owned Sportsman's Park, in which the Cardinals were tenants.

The Cards were huge favorites in the Series, but the Browns shocked everyone by beating Mort Cooper in the opener 2-1. A homer by first baseman George McQuinn followed the only other hit Cooper gave up. The Cardinals had to go into the bottom of the 11th in Game Two before they could squeeze out a 3-2 win.

Cardinals manager Billy Southworth started his rookie find,

Ted Wilks — who turned in a 2.65 ERA and a 17-4 record that season — in Game Three. Browns manag-er Luke Sewell countered with Jack Kramer (17-13, 2.49 ERA), who gave up only two runs while going the distance and striking out ten. The Browns' offense cracked out five successive singles, which combined with a walk and a wild pitch to produce four runs. The 6-2 victory was the Browns' last of the Series.

The Cardinals beat Jakucki 5-1, then won the next two games by scores of 2-0 and 3-1 to win the World Series. But the St. Louis Browns in 1944 had nothing to be ashamed of.

1945

Baseball commissioner Kene-saw Mountain Landis died on November 25, 1944, soon after his

Commissioner Kenesaw Mountain Landis throws out the ceremonial first pitch.

HAL NEWHOUSER

Hal Newhouser was a tall, hard-throwing lefthander nicknamed "Prince Hal." And for 15 years, he was the prince of Detroit,

where he became one of the few players ever to be named Most Valuable Player in the league two years in succession.

Newhouser was born in Detroit on May 20, 1921, and he always said he was fortunate to play most of his career there. In 1944, he won 29 games (six of them shutouts) and lost only nine with a 2.22 ERA. He beat out teammate Dizzy Trout (who won 27 games) by four points to win MVP honors. Unfortunately, the Tigers lost out to the Browns in the pennant race.

The next year Prince Hal led the Tigers to the pennant on the final day of the season — a 3-2 win over the Browns — as they finished 1 1/2 games ahead of the

Senators. The victory was New-houser's 25th against nine losses, and he lowered his ERA to 1.81 and again was named MVP. In the '45 World Series, Newhouser was 2-1, as the Tigers had to go seven games to defeat the Cubs. Newhouser didn't have his best stuff in the finale, giving up ten hits and three runs. But he struck out ten and went the dis-tance for the win.

Prince Hal had another over-whelming season in 1946, going 26-9, and then won 56 games through the last three years of the 1940s. Overall, Newhouser won 207 games, lost only 150 — a winning percentage of .580 — and had an ERA of 3.05. As a pitcher, he was indeed a prince.

Tommy Holmes (top left) of the Braves was second in the N.L. in 1945 in batting average with a .352 batting average and 117 runs batted in. Pinky May (top middle) hit .376 at Great Lakes in 1944. Brooklyn second baseman Eddie "Muggsy" Stanky (top right) led the National League with 128 runs scored in 1945. He also led the league with 148 bases on balls. Cleveland Municipal Stadium (bottom left), shown here during a 1940 game, has the largest seating capacity (74,208) in professional baseball. Al Glossop, left, and Pee Wee Reese (bottom right) pose at Geiger Field at Guam in 1945. Glossop was a Dodgers infielder in '43.

THE 1940s

78th birthday and while in his 24th year on the job as the stern overseer of the national pastime. In April 1945, the team owners elected A.B. "Happy" Chandler as the new commissioner. Kentucky's former governor and U.S. senator, Chandler was given a seven-year contract at a salary of $50,000 annually.

Chandler was thrilled with the job — "Ah just *love* baseball," he kept saying — even though his administration began during the

Happy Chandler, a former governor and U.S. senator from Kentucky, spent only six seasons as the baseball commissioner. After he resigned in 1951, he ran for and was re-elected as governor of Kentucky.

266

season in which the quality of play was at an all-time low. There were so few stars in the majors that the All-Star Game was canceled, although the excuse given was wartime travel restrictions.

Still, there was a tight pennant race in the American League between the Tigers and Senators, with only 1½ games separating them at the end. Hank Greenberg returned to the Tigers after four years in the service and gave the team a big lift. In 78 games, he hit .311, slugged 13 home runs, and had 60 RBI. His final home run on the last game of the season against the Browns won the pennant.

The Tigers went into the ninth inning trailing 3-2 in St. Louis. But with one out, Detroit loaded the bases, and Greenberg stepped to the plate. After taking a ball and a strike, Greenberg hit the next pitch on a line into the left field bleachers. Newhouser, in relief, earned his 25th victory and his second straight MVP award.

The National League MVP was Cubs first baseman and captain Phil Cavarretta, who not only led the league in hitting with a .355 average but led his team to the pennant. Boston Braves outfielder Tommy Holmes provided the most exciting hitting of the season, connecting for at least one hit in 37 consecutive games and setting a modern (post-1900) N.L. record. His team, however, finished in sixth place.

A key to the Cubs' rise from fourth place to the league championship was its pitching staff. Hank Wyse's 22 wins were supported by the pitching of three veterans: 36-year-old Claude Passeau (17 wins), 38-year-old Paul Derringer (16 wins), and 38-year-old Ray Prim (13 wins). But the Cubs collected a major acquisition from the Yankees at midseason in Hank Borowy, who had already won ten games for New York and who proceeded to win 11 games for Chicago. Borowy completed 11 of his 14 starts and had a sparkling ERA of 2.13.

The Cardinals, who went into the season favored to win a fourth straight pennant, finished second, 3 games behind the Cubs. The Cards major personnel loss was Stan Musial to the Army.

As the Tigers and Cubs prepared to open the World Series in Detroit, Chicago sports writer War-

PETE GRAY

Pete Gray was the only one-armed ballplayer ever to perform in the major leagues. As a child, Gray lost his right arm in a farm accident in Nanticoke, PA, but he was such a good baseball player that he was signed to a minor league contract. He had an outstanding career, even leading his league in hitting just before the Browns brought him up in 1945.

Gray had good speed and was a fine base stealer. He also was an excellent fielder with a strong arm. He would catch the ball, tuck his glove under his right arm in a flash, and fire the ball into the infield. Opponents thought he would need so much time to get rid of the ball that they could run on him. After Gray threw out five of the first seven runners who tried to take an extra base on him, opponents stopped testing him.

Gray was also a good contact hitter. In 234 at-bats, he struck out only 11 times. He was so quick with the bat that he'd line shot after shot over the infield. Eight of Gray's 51 hits were doubles and triples, which shows that he could drive the ball and get around the bases quickly. He also had five stolen bases. But pitchers got wise to his quick bat and began throwing him nothing but off-speed pitches, which were his downfall. He finished his only season with the Browns batting .218.

Walker Cooper (top left) was a catcher for St. Louis Cardinals, New York Giants, and several other teams during his 18-year career. He was a career .285 hitter, and he hit .300 in three World Series from 1942 to '44 with the Cardinals. Walker's brother Mort, a pitcher, was his teammate on both the Cards and the Giants. Walker Cooper's best season came in 1947, when he hit .305 with 35 home runs and 122 runs batted in for the Giants. Hal Newhouser (bottom left) averaged 23 wins, 11 losses, and 190 strikeouts a year from 1944 to '49. Pete Gray (bottom right) was a good athlete and a surprisingly good player. Like other players before him and after him, however, he could not hit curveballs.

ren Brown was asked which team he thought would win. Replied Brown: "I don't think either of them can win."

But the Series proved to be very entertaining indeed, replete with good baseball. In Game One, Borowy shut out the Tigers on six hits, and the Cubs bombed Newhouser on the way to a 9-0 win. Wyse gave up no runs through the first four innings in Game Two; but then Greenberg tagged him for a three-run homer, and the Tigers won 4-1. Detroit pitcher Virgil Trucks, only a week out of the Navy, went the distance. In Game Three at Briggs Stadium, Passeau's sharp curve and tight control shut out the Tigers on a one-hitter as the Cubs won 3-1.

Dizzy Trout held the Cubs to a lone run in the Chicago opener, Detroit winning 4-1. Newhouser got even with Borowy the next day as the Tigers won 8-4 and were only one victory from the championship. The Cubs seemed in control of Game Six with a 7-3 lead going into the eighth inning; then the Tigers scored three runs and Greenberg homered to tie. But

Borowy threw four innings of shutout relief and picked up his second win of the Series when his teammates scored in the 12th inning.

The teams were given a day of rest. Cubs manager Charlie Grimm decided to go into Game Seven with his best arm, even though, since it belonged to Borowy, it was obviously tired. Grimm lost the gamble. Borowy was knocked out in the first inning, and Newhouser scattered ten hits as the Tigers won the game 9-3 and took the championship.

1946

World War II was over, but most players were dissatisfied with the poor salary scale still offered by the owners. A cluster of players jumped to the new Mexican League, signing for more money with millionaire Jorge Pasqual. Commissioner Chandler decreed that any player who left would be banned from the majors for five years. Chandler would stick by his decree until 1949, when Danny Gardella filed a suit against major league baseball and the blacklist was rescinded. The players who wished to return from the makeshift Mexican League finally were allowed back. Gardella was paid an out-of-court settlement to drop his suit.

In the spring of '46, Harvard lawyer Robert Murphy formed the American Baseball Guild, the forerunner of the Major League Baseball Players' Association. Hoping to keep the Guild from becoming a true union, Chandler met with player delegates to discuss their

STAN MUSIAL

Stan "The Man" Musial always seemed to have a smile on his face, and he was always friendly with the press. Even when he had a bad day at the plate, he was congenial.

"Why should I get upset if I go 0-for-four one day?" he said. "I know I'll get three hits the next day."

He was often right. The man from Donora, PA, with the strange-looking corkscrew-style lefthanded-hitting stance was a great hitter for 22 years with the Cardinals. He started off as a pitcher in the Cardinals chain and filled in as an outfielder. He had an 18-5 record in the Florida State League in 1940, when he fell making an outfield catch and damaged his left shoulder. So he became a full-time outfielder; two years later, he hit .315 in his rookie season for the Cardinals, who won the pennant and the World Series. As a sophomore, Musial batted .357 and won the first of his seven titles as batting champion. The last came in 1957, when he was 37 years old.

Musial batted over .300 18 times in 22 years and finished with a lifetime average of .331, with 475 home runs and 1,951 RBI. He led the National League in runs scored five times and led the major leagues in most extra-base hits and in total bases six times. When he retired in 1963, Musial held the N.L. records for runs, hits, doubles, and RBI.

Hugh Duffy, right, gives Ted Williams some batting tips.

The father of Walker, left, and Mort Cooper died the morning before Game Two of the 1943 World Series, which Mort won 4-3. Bob Feller (top middle) was 26-15 in 1946, with a 2.18 ERA and ten shutouts. Warren Spahn, left, and Johnny Sain (top right) each won 21 games in 1947: "Spahn and Sain and pray for rain." Ralph Kiner is at bat (bottom), while Joe Garagiola waits for the pitch.

269

grievances. In September, the owners responded to some of them, limiting salary cuts to 25 percent, establishing a players' pension fund to which teams would contribute, offering free medical benefits, and providing spring allowances of $25 per week.

Fans were less interested in the player rebellions against mistreatment by owners than they were in the return of the stars they loved. They were rewarded with fine performances. Pitcher Bob Feller returned from four years in the Navy to win 26 games for the sixth-place Indians while setting a league strikeout record of 348 and completing 36 games, the most in the league since Walter Johnson's 38 complete games in 1910.

Ted Williams, who says Feller was the best pitcher he ever faced, returned from his service as a fighter-plane pilot with a bang. His .342 batting average, 38 home runs, and 123 RBI earned him MVP honors and boosted his Red Sox team to the pennant. The last time the Red Sox had captured a pennant, Babe Ruth had pitched for them in 1918.

Musial's National League-leading .365 batting average would lead the Cardinals to the pennant, but not until they met the Dodgers in a best-of-three playoff. It was the first time in history that two teams had played an entire 154-game schedule and finished with identical records. Both the Cardinals and the Dodgers won 96 games and lost 58.

In the playoff, the Dodgers' offense missed their best base-stealer, Pete Reiser, who was sidelined with a broken ankle. Reiser, in only 122 games that season, had 34 stolen bases — seven of them steals of home. Cardinals starter Howie Pollet went all the way in the playoff opener, allowing only two runs. His teammates scored four runs to give Pollet his 21st win

of the season. The second game, in Brooklyn, wasn't as close. The Cardinals jumped off to a seven-run lead and held on to win 8-4.

The Red Sox had two other .300 hitters besides Williams in shortstop Johnny Pesky (.335) and center fielder Dom DiMaggio (.316). They also had two other run producers besides Williams who drove in more than 100 runs, first baseman Rudy York (119 RBI) and second baseman Bobby Doerr (116 RBI). And the Sox pitching staff included two 20-game winners in Boo Ferriss (25-6) and Tex Hughson (20-11), and another pair of starters, Mickey Harris and Joe Dobson, who combined to win 30 games.

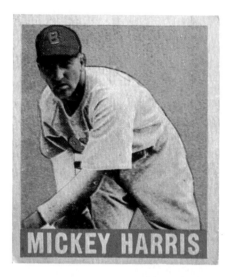

BoSox lefty Mickey Harris (top) was 17-9 in 1946. Phillies center fielder Harry "The Hat" Walker (bottom) led the N.L. with a .363 batting average in 1947. He was replaced by Richie Ashburn the next season.

BRANCH RICKEY

Branch Rickey was one of the most innovative, resourceful, and far-seeing baseball executives the game has even known.

In the 1920s, Rickey invented the batting cage and developed a spring training regimen that prepared his team for the season better than any other. Subsequently, this forced his opponents to follow his lead. In the 1930s — while other teams were buying their players from independent minor league ballclubs — Rickey signed up players for minor league clubs owned by the Cardinals. He soon developed the greatest minor league system in history, one that made St. Louis the dominant team in the National League for two decades.

But Rickey, in his 59 years as a baseball executive, made his greatest contribution to the game in the 1940s when, as a general manager of Brooklyn, he broke baseball's color line by signing black players to contracts. Jackie Robinson was the first. When Atlanta authorities refused to allow Robinson to play in a pre-season game in their city, Rickey ignored them and the game was played. Rickey became the grandfather and Jackie Robinson the father of all the superb black ballplayers who followed to the major leagues — and made baseball the great game it finally became once all citizens were eligible to play.

But Rickey wasn't finished. In the 1960s he formed the Continental League (which never played a game). It forced baseball to expand across the country and made the sport truly the national pastime.

Eddie Joost of the A's (top left) hit .263 with 23 homers and 128 runs scored in 1949. Braves second baseman Ed Miller turns two (top right) as Dodger Dolf Camilli is called out by umpire Jocko Conlan. Enos Slaughter (middle) hit .320 in the '46 World Series, with five runs scored. In Game Seven with Slaughter on first base and two outs, Harry Walker singled to center field. Slaughter, who took off with the pitch, was headed toward third by the time Red Sox center fielder Leon Culberson made his throw. Culberson threw to shortstop Johnny Pesky, while Slaughter rounded third base at full speed. When Pesky turned from taking the relay, he hesitated before throwing, off-balance, to home plate; Slaughter scored easily. While Pesky was lambasted in the press following the Series, it now is viewed that he almost certainly could not have nailed Slaughter. Brooklyn's Pete Reiser (bottom left) hit .277 in 1946 and led the N.L. with 34 stolen bases. Yankee second baseman Joe Gordon scores after slugging a home run (bottom right).

THE 1940s

The Cardinals also had three .300 hitters in Musial, Whitey Kurowski (.301), and Enos Slaughter (.300), but St. Louis went into the World Series as underdogs. The first game, though, suggested there was little difference in quality between the teams. Boston had to go ten innings before a York homer won the game 3-2. St. Louis evened the Series in Game Two at Sportsman's Park. Starter Harry Brecheen had lost as many games as he'd won (15), but that day he shut out the Red Sox and won 3-0.

In Boston, York stepped up in the first inning and belted a three-run homer, which was all Ferriss needed as he shut out the Cardinals. But they bounced right back in Game Four with 20 hits for a 12-3 victory. Then the Red Sox came back the next day with six runs while Dobson was checking the Cardinals with three runs.

The Red Sox needed only one win in St. Louis to take the championship. But once again, Brecheen excelled on the mound, and the Cardinals won 4-1. In Game Seven, Dom DiMaggio's two-run double tied the score 3-3 in the seventh. After Slaughter opened the eighth with a single and the next two Cardinals made outs, Harry Walker lined a single to left center. Slaughter was running all the way, making an unheard of attempt to score from first on a single in the last game of the World Series. Pesky hesitated in making his relay throw to the plate and, incredibly, Slaughter slid in ahead of it. Brecheen, in relief, preserved the 4-3 lead and got the win — his third of the Series. Incidentally, in his only Series appearance, Ted Williams batted .200. Stan Musial did not have a good Series either, batting .222.

1947

Over the winter, a feud developed between the year's eventual pennant winners, the Yankees and the Dodgers. Former Dodgers general manager Larry MacPhail was now one of the Yankees owners, and he hired coach Charlie Dressen away from Leo Durocher's staff; then he hired another Dodgers coach, Red Corriden. Durocher and his general manager, Branch Rickey, criticized MacPhail publicly. Then Durocher and Rickey let the press know that they had seen gamblers in MacPhail's box during an exhibition game between the Yankees and Dodgers in Havana, Cuba. MacPhail denied that he knew any gamblers and cried libel to commissioner Chandler. Saying all of the sniping in the press was bad

Jackie Robinson (sliding) hit .297 in his '47 rookie season.

LEO DUROCHER

Leo Durocher wasn't much of a hitter. In fact, Babe Ruth called him the "All-American Out." But Durocher managed to play 13 years in the major leagues and compile a .247 batting average. He was a slick-fielding shortstop who played on the late 1920s Yankees and later became the spark plug of the great 1930s Cardinals.

Branch Rickey, the Cardinals general manager, admired Durocher's intelligence and fiery demeanor and named him captain. Durocher demonstrated so much leadership ability that when Larry MacPhail of the Dodgers was looking for a new manager in 1939, he hired Durocher. That proved to be a brilliant move; in 1941, Durocher led the Dodgers to their first pennant in 21 years.

In 1947, when Rickey decided to break the color barrier by adding Jackie Robinson to the Dodgers, it was Durocher who crushed the rebellion of some of his players. The Dodgers went on to win the '47 pennant with Durocher's players, but he wasn't there because commissioner Happy Chandler had suspended him.

Midway through 1948, Durocher jumped to the Giants and, in 1951, led them to a dramatic victory over the Dodgers to win the pennant. Three years later, Durocher's Giants won another pennant and then swept the heavily favored Indians in the World Series.

Durocher retired for a few years, then coached for the Dodgers and managed the Cubs from 1966 to 1972. He then managed the Astros for two more years before finally retiring. But everywhere Durocher went, he was a feisty leader who made brilliant moves.

Red Schoendienst, left, and Marty Marion (top left) formed the Cardinal double-play combination from 1946 to 1950. Second baseman Schoendienst averaged 88 runs scored a season from 1945 to '49. The 1947 Yankees (top right) led the A.L. in batting (.271), slugging (.407), homers (115), ERA (3.39), runs (794), and opponents runs (568). Cincinnati hurler Ewell Blackwell (middle left) led the N.L. with 22 wins in 1947. Bucky Harris, left, and Lou Boudreau (bottom left) confer before a game. Harris was the Yankees manager when they won the pennant in 1947; manager Boudreau won the pennant with the Indians in 1948. The first tres amigos (bottom right) were Giants Buddy Kerr, Babe Young, and Sid Gordon at Phoenix, AZ, in 1947.

news, Chandler suspended Durocher for the entire season, citing what he called "conduct detrimental to baseball." The commissioner also fined both the Yankees and Dodgers $2,000 for "engaging in public feuding."

None of the above was of any importance compared to what some referred to as baseball's "great experiment" — the announcement that a black would play in the majors for the first time. Jackie Robinson, the Dodgers first baseman at age 28, took a lot of abuse all season, but he also played with fire all year, stealing 29 bases, batting .297, and earning the first official Rookie of the Year honors as he helped spark his team to the pennant.

Though the Dodgers, under new manager Burt Shotton, finished 5 games ahead of the Cardinals while winning 94, they were anything but a great ballclub. Robinson tied for the team home run lead with Pee Wee Reese, who also hit 12. But the Dodgers had a very competitive pitching staff, with five men winning ten or more games. Ralph Branca, age 21, was the number-one starter, winning 21 and losing 12 on a 2.67 ERA. The bullpen was headed by Hugh Casey, who had a 10-4 record and 18 saves.

The Yankees had even less competition for the A.L. pennant, finishing 12 games ahead of the Tigers, who missed the home run bat of Hank Greenberg. He hit 25 homers for the Pirates, more than anyone on the Tigers — or the Yankees, for that matter. Joe DiMaggio led the Yankees with 20 home runs, 97 RBI, and a .315 batting average. Those numbers brought him another A.L. MVP award and again showed how unpopular Ted Williams was with the writers who cast votes for the award. That year, Williams became

Yankees rookie Spec Shea (top) won two games in the '47 Series. Ralph Kiner (bottom) averaged 42 homers a year from 1946 to '49.

only the second man in baseball history to win a second triple crown, batting .343, with 32 home runs and 114 RBI.

Williams was not among the more than 73,000 people at Yankee Stadium for the World Series opener, preferring to fish rather than view a baseball game he couldn't play in. The Dodgers had a 1-0 lead, until the Yankees pounced on Branca in the fifth inning for five runs and held on to win 5-3. In Game Two, the Yankees chipped away at four Dodgers pitchers, scoring runs in the first, third, fourth, fifth, six, and seventh innings as they banged out 15 hits. The final score was 10-3. Yankees ace Allie Reynolds, who had won 19 games during the season, went the distance.

The Dodgers won their first game at home the next day, no off-day for travel being necessary,

SATCHEL PAIGE'S MAJOR LEAGUE DEBUT

In 1948, Bill Veeck, the maverick owner of the Indians, was a man who would stage publicity stunts to draw fans. Satchel Paige was a Negro Leagues pitching legend and very quotable. So it didn't surprise many people when Veeck signed Paige to a contract on July 7, Paige's 42nd birthday.

Some people were shocked by the signing. *The Sporting News* wrote that "to bring in a pitching rookie of Paige's age is to demean the standards of baseball." But while Veeck was a showman, he was also a good baseball man. His team would be in the '48 pennant race, and he thought Paige could still pitch. During his career, Paige had struck out 22 major leaguers in an exhibition game, won 21 games in a row, and beat Dizzy Dean four out of six times during a barnstorming tour.

In his first two relief outings, Paige saved one game with two scoreless innings and won the next with three scoreless innings. On August 13, he got his first start; 51,013 fans jammed Chicago's Comiskey Park to watch the game's oldest rookie shut out the White Sox 5-0 on only five hits. A week later in Cleveland, 78,382 people, the largest crowd ever to attend a night game, saw Paige shut out the Sox again 1-0 on three hits.

Paige ended the season with a 6-1 record, silencing those who scoffed at his comeback. He and Veeck both had the last laugh when the Indians won the 1948 World Series and Veeck was named Executive of the Year.

Bob Feller (left) and Satchel Paige.

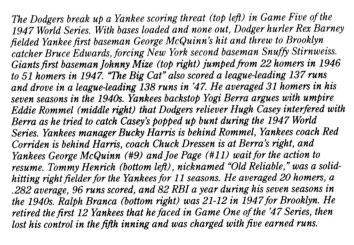

The Dodgers break up a Yankee scoring threat (top left) in Game Five of the 1947 World Series. With bases loaded and none out, Dodger hurler Rex Barney fielded Yankee first baseman George McQuinn's hit and threw to Brooklyn catcher Bruce Edwards, forcing New York second baseman Snuffy Stirnweiss. Giants first baseman Johnny Mize (top right) jumped from 22 homers in 1946 to 51 homers in 1947. "The Big Cat" also scored a league-leading 137 runs and drove in a league-leading 138 runs in '47. He averaged 31 homers in his seven seasons in the 1940s. Yankees backstop Yogi Berra argues with umpire Eddie Rommel (middle right) that Dodgers reliever Hugh Casey interfered with Berra as he tried to catch Casey's popped up bunt during the 1947 World Series. Yankees manager Bucky Harris is behind Rommel, Yankees coach Red Corriden is behind Harris, coach Chuck Dressen is at Berra's right, and Yankees George McQuinn (#9) and Joe Page (#11) wait for the action to resume. Tommy Henrich (bottom left), nicknamed "Old Reliable," was a solid-hitting right fielder for the Yankees for 11 seasons. He averaged 20 homers, a .282 average, 96 runs scored, and 82 RBI a year during his seven seasons in the 1940s. Ralph Branca (bottom right) was 21-12 in 1947 for Brooklyn. He retired the first 12 Yankees that he faced in Game One of the '47 Series, then lost his control in the fifth inning and was charged with five earned runs.

The '47 Dodgers infield was, left to right, Spider Jorgesen, Pee Wee Reese, Eddie Stanky, and Jackie Robinson.

scoring nine runs in the first four innings. The Yankees almost caught up, scoring eight runs, one coming on the first pinch-hit homer ever in the Series. It was hit by a rookie catcher and outfielder named Yogi Berra.

Game Four was a classic. The Yankees' surprise starter was Bill Bevens, who not only had a 7-13 record during the season but was given to fits of wildness. Yet he hadn't permitted a hit going into the bottom of the ninth and held a 2-1 lead. After Bevens got one out, he threw four balls to Carl Furillo, his ninth walk of the game. Following out number two, Shotton sent in a runner for Furillo, Al Gionfriddo, who promptly stole second. Reiser hit for the pitcher but was

intentionally walked. As Reiser had a bad ankle, Eddie Miksis went in to run for him. Then righthanded hitter Cookie Lavagetto was sent up to bat for Eddie Stanky. Bevens was just one out away from a no-hit Series victory, but Lavagetto changed all that by lashing a double off the right field wall that drove in the winning runs.

The Yankees won 2-1 the next day, but the Dodgers responded in Game Six with an 8-6 victory. Then the Yankees took the final game 5-2 and won the World Series. Bill

Bevens pitched 2 1/3 innings of hitless relief in the finale, yet after that he never pitched in another major league game.

1948

Two newcomers led the pennant races in both leagues this year. In the N.L., the Boston Braves, who hadn't won a pennant since 1914, finished 6 1/2 games ahead of the Cardinals and 7 1/2 games ahead of the Dodgers. Musial barely missed the triple crown, winning the batting title

JOE DiMAGGIO'S 56-GAME HITTING STREAK

On May 15, 1941, Yankees star center fielder Joe DiMaggio smacked a single during a 13-1 loss to the White Sox. He would continue to get hits in the next 55 consecutive games, a record many feel will never be broken

and is the single greatest feat in baseball history.

DiMaggio's streak reached 19 on June 2, the day Lou Gehrig died. Six days later, DiMaggio broke his personal record of 23 straight. On June 14, Joltin' Joe passed the Yankees record, set by Babe Ruth. When DiMaggio hit in his 30th straight on June 17, radio shows announced "the streak is alive." Rogers Horns-

by's National League record 33 was passed on June 21, George Sisler's 41-game A.L. mark was erased on June 29, and Wee Willie Keeler's all-time record of 44 (set in 1897) was broken on July second. That day DiMaggio belted his 15th home run during the streak.

Then on July 17, with 67,468 fans packing Cleveland's Municipal Stadium, DiMaggio was robbed of hits on his first and third at-bats by Indians third baseman Ken Keltner, who made sensational backhand stabs of hard grounders DiMaggio hit down the line. Having walked in his second at-bat in the fourth inning, DiMaggio came up in the eighth with one last chance to preserve the record, but his smash grounder to shortstop Lou Boudreau was turned into a double play.

DiMaggio didn't get upset when the streak was stopped. He just went out and hit in another 17 straight. DiMaggio batted .357 for the season, with 30 homers and 125 RBI, and won the MVP.

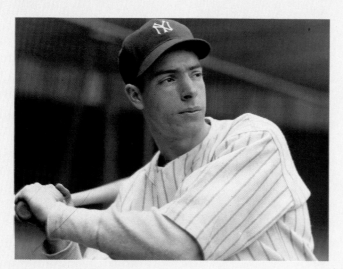

Brooklyn pinch-hitter Cookie Lavagetto (top left) doubled two runs home in the bottom of the ninth inning in Game Four of the 1947 World Series to win the game 3-2. Yankees pitcher Bill Bevens was one out away from the first Series no-hitter when Lavagetto got his hit. Substitute Dodgers outfielder Al Gionfriddo robs Joe DiMaggio of a home run in Game Six of the 1947 World Series (bottom left). This play, one of the most famous in World Series history, came during what turned out to be Gionfriddo's last major league game. In 1948, Stan Musial (top right) led the N.L. with a .376 batting average, a .702 slugging average, 131 RBI, 135 runs scored, and 230 base hits. Enos Slaughter (middle bottom) hit .321 in 1948, with 91 runs scored and 90 RBI. Ernie Lombardi (middle center) was the Pacific Coast League Oakland Oaks coach in 1948. Billy Martin (middle right and bottom right) was the Oaks third baseman. The Pacific Coast League in the 1940s and before was almost a third major league. Before most people had TV, and before the Dodgers and the Giants moved to the West Coast, the only place Californians could see high-quality organized baseball was in the PCL. The owners of these teams tried to keep their stars as long as possible; the PCL teams were not just "farm teams" in the modern sense of the word.

THE 1940s

with a .376 average and topping everyone in RBI with 131. But his 39 home runs were one less than coleaders Johnny Mize and Ralph Kiner. Still, Musial also led the league in hits (230), doubles (46), triples (18), runs scored (135), and slugging average (.702), in what many experts say was his best season at the plate.

In the A.L., the Cleveland Indians engaged in a much tougher pennant race with the Red Sox and Yankees than the Braves had with the Cardinals and Dodgers. After winning only 14 of their first 37 games, the Red Sox came on strong and beat the Yankees on the next-to-last day of the season to knock them out of contention. The Red Sox would still need a win and an Indian loss to draw even with Cleveland in the final game — and that's what happened to set up the league's first playoff game ever.

It was played in Boston, which was fine with Indians shortstop/manager Lou Boudreau, who always hit well in Fenway Park with its short poke to "The Green Monster," the left field wall. Meanwhile, Red Sox fans hoped their club, led by Williams and his league-leading .369 average, would bring Boston its first all-city World Series. But Boudreau outhit Williams in the playoff, hitting two home runs and two singles to Williams' lone single, as the Indians won 8-3.

Many felt it was fitting that Cleveland took the pennant, because the Indians had an excellent ballclub and the most colorful owner in baseball, Bill Veeck. He ran scores of promotions — such as giving away nylon stockings and later orchids from Hawaii to female fans, and providing baby care at Memorial Stadium for mothers who wanted to see the games — that attracted an all-time-high seasonal attendance of 2,260,627.

The team's stars were: Boudreau, who batted .355, scored 116 runs, drove in 106 runs, and won the MVP award; his second baseman, Joe Gordon, who hit 32 homers and drove in 124 runs; and third baseman Ken Keltner, who had 31 homers and 119 RBI. In addition, outfielder Dale Mitchell batted .336, and outfielder Larry Doby batted .301 and had 14 home runs, 66 RBI, and nine stolen bases. As the first black to play in the American League, Doby was subjected to all manner of abuse, and it was remarkable that he was able to play so well.

At midseason, Doby was joined by one of the biggest stars of the Negro Leagues, Satchel Paige, who claimed to be 42 but may have been five years older. Despite his age, Paige won six out of seven decisions — including two shutouts — on an ERA of 2.48. The

Dodger Rex Barney won 15 games in '48.

TED WILLIAMS BREAKS .400

Between 1876 and 1930, 41 major leaguers had managed to hit over .400 in a season. Since then only one player has surpassed the magical .400 mark — Ted Williams.

In 1941, Williams was a 23-year-old who had already batted .327 and .344 in his first two seasons. While Joe DiMaggio's amazing hitting streak was making all the noise that spring, Williams quietly batted .436 in June and led the A.L. in batting all summer with an average over .400. When he batted .413 in September, Williams was hitting .406 with a week left in the season.

Two months had passed since DiMaggio's streak ended at 56 games, so all the attention was on Williams' quest for the highest average since Rogers Hornsby's .424 in 1924. When Boston Red Sox manager Joe Cronin asked Williams if he wanted to sit out some games to preserve his average, the confident Williams replied: "If I'm a .400 hitter, I'm one for the entire season."

On the last day, Williams was batting .3995 when the Sox went up against the Athletics in a double-header. He insisted on playing and went four-for-five in the first game, including three singles and a home run. While a hitless game in the nightcap could have cost Williams his .400 season, he played the second game, went two-for-three, and finished the year at .406. The Splendid Splinter also drew a league-leading 145 walks. But Williams did more than just hit for average. He led the league in homers (37), runs (135), and slugging (.735).

In 1948, player/manager Lou Boudreau (top left) hit .355 with 18 home runs and 106 RBI as he led the Cleveland Indians to their first world championship in 28 years. Braves lefthander Warren Spahn (top right) led the National League with 21 wins, 25 complete games, 302 $^1/_3$ innings pitched, and 151 strikeouts. Yankees reliever Joe Page (bottom left) can't wait to get on the mound. He led the A.L. with 13 relief wins and 27 saves in 1949; in the World Series, Page pitched 5 $^2/_3$ innings of relief in Game Three to get the win and 2 $^1/_3$ innings in Game Five to get the save. In '47, he led the league with 14 relief wins and 17 saves. Yankees third baseman Sid Gordon (bottom middle) hit .299 with 30 homers, 107 RBI, and 100 runs scored in 1948. He hit .284 with 26 homers and 90 RBI in '49. In 1949, Indian outfielder Larry Doby (bottom right) hit .280 with 24 homers, 106 runs scored, and 85 RBI.

Indians staff was anchored by Bob Feller (19-15) and Bob Lemon (20-14), and bolstered by rookie knuckleballer Gene Beardon, whose 20th win came in the playoff game. Ten of Lemon's victories were shutouts.

Cleveland's World Series opponents, the Braves, weren't nearly as deep on the mound. Johnny Sain was the club's ace (24-15), followed by Warren Spahn, who would win 15 games in '48 and 363 in his career. The Braves' staff that season was known as "Spahn and Sain and two days of rain," because manager Billy Southworth, toward season's end, used his two stars every fourth day even if it meant skipping Bill Voiselle (13-13) and Vern Bickford (11-5).

Sain pitched a shutout in the Series opener, and Feller lost a heartbreaker 1-0 while giving up only two hits. Lemon gave up only

one run in Game Two, as his teammates knocked out Spahn and scored four runs to even the Series. Bearden, who had been seriously injured in the war, threw a five-hit shutout in Game Three at Cleveland before 70,306 fans, winning 2-0.

The Indians moved ahead three wins to one in Game Four, with Steve Gromek (9-3 on the season) allowing just one run on seven hits. Johnny Sain gave up only five hits, but one was an RBI double for Boudreau and another a home run to Doby that won the ballgame 2-1. The Braves bombarded Feller in Game Five and went on to score 11 runs to the Indians' five, keeping their hopes alive for a comeback in Boston the following day.

It wasn't to be, though the Braves came close. Lemon had a 4-1 lead when the Braves scored two in the eighth, but Bearden relieved Lemon and shut down the Boston bats as Cleveland won the world championship.

1949

The Yankees' fall to third place the previous year had cost manager Bucky Harris his job. His replacement, Casey Stengel, had managed the Dodgers and Braves without distinction — other than his clowning — in the 1930s. But

he had been very successful managing the Oakland Oaks of the Pacific Coast League, and he proved to be something of a genius with the Yankees.

The Bronx Bombers suffered more than 90 injuries during the season, with shortstop Phil Rizzuto being the only regular to play every game. The biggest loss was Joe DiMaggio, who would be sidelined the first half of the season with a heel injury. When he returned in June, DiMaggio batted .346 the remainder of the season. Yogi Berra was out a month with a broken finger, but he still managed to hit 20 home runs and drive in 91.

It was Stengel, though, who kept the Yankees in contention with his masterful platooning of such younger players as Hank Bauer, Bobby Brown (who later became the A.L. president), and Jerry Coleman. Stengel also had a solid pitching staff, anchored by ace Vic Raschi (21-10) and super reliever Joe Page, who won 13 games and saved 27 others.

But the Red Sox came on strong, sweeping their last three-game series with the Yankees in Boston. They were a game ahead of the Yankees when they began their final two games of the season in New York. The experts picked the Red Sox to win. Williams, who

MICKEY OWEN'S PASSED BALL

Poor Mickey Owen. Even if he didn't commit the most egregious error in World Series history, he is definitely the fall classic's most memorable goat. And all because of a passed ball.

The Brooklyn Dodgers were trailing the New York Yankees

two games to one in the 1941 World Series, but were leading 4-3 in Game Four. They were one out away from victory when the Yanks' Tommy Henrich came to bat with nobody on base. Dodgers reliever Hugh Casey got two quick strikes on "Old Reliable," and when Henrich swung at and missed the next pitch, the game appeared to be over.

But Dodgers catcher Mickey Owen dropped the third strike, and the ball got far enough away for Henrich to scamper to first, keeping the game alive. That's all the always dangerous Yankees needed. Joe DiMaggio followed with a single, and Charlie Keller smacked a two-run double, putting the Yankees ahead by one. Bill Dickey then walked, and Joe Gordon knocked in two more with another double. The demoralized Dodgers went quietly in the ninth against Yankees reliever Johnny Murphy, losing the game 7-4. The next day they lost the Series.

"Sure it was my fault," said a teary-eyed Owen after becoming the wearer of the Series' most famous goat horns. "The ball was a low curve that broke down. It hit the edge of my glove and glanced off, but I should have had him out anyway."

Cardinal catcher Del Rice prepares to tag out a baserunner after a squeeze bunt play failed (top left). The pitcher running in to help is Harry Breechen. Brooklyn's Duke Snider (top right) hit .292 in 1949, with 23 homers, 100 runs scored, and 92 RBI. Ted Williams slides under Yogi Berra (middle left). Red Schoendienst takes a high throw (middle right). He played 13 of his 19 seasons in the big leagues for the Cardinals and was widely regarded as the premier second baseman in that time. He ended his career with a .289 lifetime average and 1,223 runs scored. Bob Lemon (bottom left), was 20-14 in 1948, led the American League that year with ten shutouts, 20 complete games, and 293²/₃ innings pitched. He won both of the games that he pitched in the '48 World Series, compiling a 1.65 ERA. Dodger outfielder Carl Furillo (bottom right) hit .322 with 18 homers and 106 RBI in 1949.

would be named MVP, batted .343, hit 43 home runs, and drove in 159. Vern Stephens, who had 39 homers, also had 159 RBI. As if that wasn't enough, Bobby Doerr batted .309 and had 109 RBI. The Red Sox had over 60 more RBI than the Yankees.

But in the season's next-to-last game, the Yankees scored five runs to Boston's four to tie for first place, and in the next game the Bronx Bombers won the pennant 5-3.

The National League race was equally close between the Cardinals and the youthful Dodgers. After Leo Durocher had left the Dodgers to manage the Giants, Burt Shotton resumed command of the club and let youngsters like catcher Roy Campanella and first

baseman Gil Hodges establish themselves. This season he made rookie Duke Snider his center fielder, and Snider hit 23 home runs and drove in 92 while batting .292. Adding this trio to Carl Furillo, Pee Wee Reese, and Jackie Robinson made for a solid ballclub. Robinson, in his third season and first as a full-time second baseman, had a great year. He led the league in hitting with a .342 average, had 203 hits (66 for extra bases), scored 122 runs, drove in 124 runs, and stole 37 bases. The only other player in the majors with more than 20 steals was Reese. Robinson was the inspirational force behind the Dodgers' drive, which carried them to the

George Kell hit an A.L.-top .343 in '49.

pennant by 1 game over the Cardinals. Small wonder Robinson was voted the league's MVP.

The Dodgers' stopper was another Negro Leagues player, hard-throwing Don Newcombe, who won 17 games and shut out the Yankees in the World Series opener through eight innings. But Allie Reynolds also gave up no runs to the Dodgers, and Tommy Henrich's homer in the bottom of the ninth won the game 1-0. That same score held the next day, except the Yankees' Raschi gave up the run when Robinson doubled and Hodges singled him home in the second inning. Dodgers left-hander Preacher Roe (who was 15-6 in the season) pitched a 1-0 shutout.

In Game Three, the Dodgers got home runs from Campanella, Reese, and Luis Olmo, but the Yankees won 4-3. The next day New York jumped off to a 6-0 lead, and the Dodgers could only score four runs. In Game Five, the Yankees' lead was 10-1 before the Dodgers came back with five runs, but that was all.

The one-time clown Casey Stengel had won his first pennant managing in the major leagues. It would not be his last.

1947 WORLD SERIES — GAMES FOUR AND SIX

The Dodgers may have lost the 1947 World Series to the Yankees, but their victories in games Four and Six are among the most exciting in the fall classic's history.

When Game Four began in Brooklyn, the Dodgers were down two games to one and desperately needed a win. Things looked bleak when Yankees pitcher Bill Bevens took a 2-1 lead into the ninth inning. Bevens wasn't just winning the game, he was on his way to pitching what could've been the first Series no-hitter. After Dodger Carl Furillo drew a one-out walk, Bevens got the next batter. Pinch runner Al Gionfriddo then stole second and pinch hitter Pete Reiser was walked intentionally, despite being the winning run. Cookie Lavagetto pinch hit for Eddie Stanky, and on Bevens' second pitch,

Lavagetto belted one off the right field wall, driving in the tying and winning runs.

The Yankees rebounded the next day 2-1. Back at Yankee Stadium for Game Six, the Dodgers first blew a 4-0 lead, then went up 8-5 in the top of the sixth. But the Yanks put two on with two out, sending Joe DiMaggio to the plate as the tying run. Joltin' Joe

immediately belted a Joe Hattin pitch to deep left field that looked like it was headed for the bleachers. But Gionfriddo — inserted into the game — made a twisting one-handed catch at the 415-mark. The play became even more famous because of a film clip that caught DiMaggio, in a rare show of emotion, kicking the dirt.

Cookie Lavagetto's two RBI won Game Four of the 1947 World Series.

Dom DiMaggio (top left) was a center fielder for the Boston Red Sox, and he was one of the best center fielders in the 1940s. Unfortunately, Joe was the best center fielder in the 1940s and perhaps of all time. But Dom was a fine gloveman and a very good leadoff batter. He averaged 103 runs scored a season during the 1940s, and he was a career .298 batter. He scored 1,046 runs, hit 308 doubles, and had an on-base average of .383. Dom played in nine seasons that Joe did; Dom had more runs scored than Joe during five seasons, more RBI once, and a higher batting average three seasons. Lefthander Warren Spahn, left, and righty Johnny Sain (bottom left) were 208-156 for the Braves from 1946 until Sain was traded in 1951. Sain's best season was in 1948, when he led the league with 24 wins, 28 complete games, and 314²/₃ innings pitched. It was his third consecutive 20-win season. Sain was traded to the Yankees, who eventually put him in the bullpen. He led the A.L. in 1954 with 22 saves. He ended his 11-year career with a 139-116 record, 3.49 ERA, and 51 saves. Pee Wee Reese (bottom right) led the National League in 1949 with 132 runs scored. A leadoff hitter for the Brooklyn Dodgers, Reese batted .279 that year, but his career-high 116 bases on balls pushed his on-base average to .396.

THE 1950s

Baseball had troubles in the 1950s.
Less people went to deteriorating stadiums,
which couldn't accommodate cars and
were far away from the suburbs; fans instead
watched games on TV. The game was dominated
by a few teams, most notably the Yankees.

Willie Mays slides across the plate (page 284). He averaged 117 runs scored a year from 1954 to 1959. Mickey Mantle (page 285) averaged 120 runs scored a season from 1953 to 1959.

THE 1950s

The American popular imagination now sees the 1950s as a time of tranquility, as a time when there was little social strife, drug concern, or economic depression. And during the decade, baseball was the national game. College football was still for the few who went to college, professional basketball was still a secondary sport, and pro football was still scarcely noticed until the Colts-Giants "Sudden Death" championship game in 1958. It is remembered as a time of peace and prosperity, and baseball dominated.

There were problems with baseball in the 1950s, of course, and most were ignored. Though nobody wanted to admit it, baseball was in big trouble. Television was supposed to create vast new crowds, but instead it had the same effect on baseball that it had on boxing: Fewer people turned out to see a show they could get for free at home. In the A.L., attendance dropped from a post-World War II peak of 11 million in 1948 to just under 7 million by 1953 (it wouldn't hit over 10 million again until the 1961 expansion year). The N.L.

reached a record-high 10.4 million in 1947 and then dropped each year until '52, not surpassing the 10-million mark again until 1958.

Of course, there was another reason why fans didn't come out as often: After millions of them returned home at the end of World War II, they moved to the suburbs, far away from the inner city, where most ballparks were located. Most suburbanites had cars, and the stadiums simply couldn't accommodate the new means of transportation. The ballparks themselves were crumbling; most had been built before 1920, and renovation in declining areas was expensive and not a very good investment for team owners. Television was an immediate source of new revenue, but it also cut down on attendance.

Worse, television had a terrible side effect that became apparent a couple of years into the decade: It began to kill off attendance in minor league cities. There were many areas of the country where fans had no easy access to the major league games, and the teams from the minor leagues were their only source of organized, professional baseball. Televised big league games didn't destroy interest in the minor leagues overnight, but it cut it back enough to put a lot of teams and players out of business. The major league farm system helped some teams survive financially, but minor league franchises could not count on their major league organizations as their only revenue source. Not until the 1980s would minor league baseball face up to

Pee Wee Reese was a master at bunting for sacrifices or base hits.

WILLIE MAYS

There are those who feel Willie Mays was the finest all-around player. Certainly those who saw Mays in his early years with the Giants wouldn't argue the point.

The Giants brought Mays up in 1951, when he was barely 20 years old. Despite going 1-for-26, a tearful Mays was assured by manager Leo Durocher that he was still their center fielder. Mays went on to earn Rookie of the Year honors and lead the Giants to the pennant. Following two years in the service, Mays came back to lead the league in hitting in 1954 — with a .345 average — and led the Giants to the pennant and to the world championship. His famous catch off Vic Wertz in deepest center field of the Polo Grounds came during this Series, in which he was named MVP.

Mays hit a league-high 51 homers in 1955. In '57, he won a Gold Glove, stole 38 bases, and hit 26 doubles, 20 triples, and 35 homers to go with a .333 average. On April 30, 1961, Mays hit four home runs in one game and hit 49 the next season to lead the Giants to another pennant.

Mays led the league in home runs four times, his high coming in 1965 when he hit 52. He finished after the '73 season with 660 career homers, 1,903 RBI, a .302 batting average, and 338 stolen bases. He won Gold Gloves 11 times and set a record for career putouts in the outfield. He was twice the Most Valuable Player of the All-Star Game. He was inducted into the Hall of Fame in 1979.

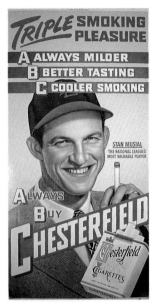

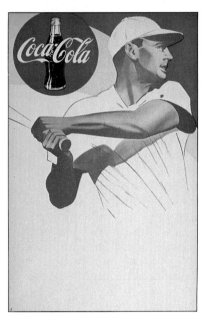

Jackie Robinson crosses the plate after homering in the 1952 All-Star Game (top left). Robinson, who was the 1949 N.L. Most Valuable Player, averaged 17 homers, a .311 average, 85 runs scored, and 68 RBI a year during his last seven seasons in the majors, from 1950 to 1956. Stan Musial appears on a cigarette advertisement in the 1950s (top right). Ted Williams is featured (middle right) on this early 1950s Coca-Cola advertisement. Bob Lemon (bottom left) led the A.L. in complete games four times during the 1950s. When Lemon was called up to the Indians in 1941 and '42, he was called up as a third baseman. A versatile performer, he didn't become a full-time major league pitcher until he was 26 years old. When his career was interrupted by three years of military service during World War II, he started pitching for post teams, and when he returned to Cleveland in '46, he was so impressive as a pitcher that the Indians kept him there. Robin Roberts (bottom right) was indefatigable, hurling at least 250 innings in ten different seasons — six times going over 300 — and completing at least 20 games in eight seasons.

THE 1950s

the ever-present threat of expanded big league TV coverage and find new ways to promote itself.

Stung with these problems, the people who ran baseball didn't always try to find solutions by working with their cities and communities. The owners took the easy way out: They moved South and, finally, West.

The first teams to move were those that were in competition with other teams in their cities. In the case of the Boston Braves, the move was probably long overdue; the Braves were a forgotten commodity in Boston, a town that wasn't even showing attendance support for the Red Sox. The Braves drew about 280,000 fans in 1952, their last year in Boston, and it can't be said that many were sad to see them go. A similar case could be made for the departure of the St. Louis Browns. A city the size of St. Louis was hard-pressed to support both the Cardinals and the Browns. So the Brownies — who, in some ways, were to the American League what the Braves were to the National League — relocated from St. Louis to Baltimore, a town that richly deserved a major league franchise.

But with the move of the Athletics from Philadelphia to Kansas City after the 1954 season, many longtime fans were jolted. The A's were one of baseball's oldest and most history-laden teams. It was the club that Connie Mack had managed for half a century, the team of Lefty Grove, Jimmie Foxx, Eddie Collins, Mickey Cochrane, and Al Simmons — more great players than the Braves and Browns had ever seen put together. Even though Philadelphia had the National League's Phillies, there were many Athletics fans in town. Probably because the A's were so steeped in history, no one had noticed how wretched their

recent performance had been, and how attendance had declined in Philadelphia's increasingly shabby inner-city area.

Precisely the same problems were bothering the league's two most famous teams, the Brooklyn Dodgers and the New York Giants, but their plans to remedy the situation were even more sensational. The improvement in air travel, or more specifically, the jet airliner, now made it possible for teams to travel to and from California, thus making it possible for baseball to cash in on the most booming economy in the United States. Dodgers owner Walter O'Malley picked the richest plum for himself, Los Angeles, and he convinced Giants owner Horace Stoneham to join him and transplant the old Dodgers-Giants rivalry to new ground by moving the Giants to San Francisco. It sounds cynical and it was, but the truth is that both O'Malley and Stoneham had legitimate gripes with the city of New York and that their grievances concerning parking, security, and declining attendance fell on deaf bureaucratic ears. The move of the Dodgers to L.A. and the Giants to

Minnie Minoso averaged 100 runs scored and 29 doubles a year from 1951 to '59.

YOGI BERRA

It is a mystery why, in his first year of eligibility for the Hall of Fame (1968), Yogi Berra was not elected.

Although he never led the league in home runs, RBI, or batting average, he was usually among the top 20 in his nearly two decades as a player for the Yankees, and he was unquestionably one of the greatest clutch hitters of all time. He was a free-swinging, bad-ball hitter who often yanked pitches out of the dirt and right out of the ballpark.

Berra's best all-around statistical season was 1954, when he batted .307, hit 22 home runs, and had 125 RBI. He was named the MVP, as he had been in '51 and as he would be for a third time in 1955. His career average was .285, and he finished with 358 home runs.

Berra led the league in putouts eight times, and three times he led the league in assists. In 1957 and '58, he caught a record 148 successive games without committing an error. Berra played in the All-Star Game 15 times. He also played in the World Series 14 times and is the only man to have played on ten winning teams in the Series. He holds the record for Series hits with 71.

When he retired, Berra managed the '64 Yankees to victory in the pennant race. In 1973, Berra managed the Mets to a pennant win — the first manager to win pennants in both leagues in nearly 40 years.

In 1972, Berra was finally elected to the Hall of Fame.

Cubs shortstop Ernie Banks (top left) averaged 38 homers a year from 1954 to '59, including four seasons with more than 40. Dodger Duke Snider (top right) hit 40 or more home runs five straight seasons from 1953 to '57. Pirate Dick Groat slides (bottom left) as Braves catcher Del Crandall takes the throw. Giant Bobby Thomson (bottom right) slugged at least 20 homers in eight seasons.

THE 1950s

the bay area can't be blamed entirely on the greed of the owners.

Beyond the off-field problems, baseball in the 1950s just wasn't as multidimensional as it would become in the 1960s. For one thing, few players stole bases in large numbers. It wasn't for lack of speed; it just wasn't in style to run. This rendered baseball a much more limited game, as skills such as running, pitchers holding runners on base, and catchers throwing them out were seldom displayed. The offensive strategy was simple: Play for the big inning, and wait for one of the big hitters to belt one out — which they frequently did in an era when so many parks, particularly Boston's

Fenway Park, Brooklyn's Ebbetts Field, and the Giants' Polo Grounds, were designed for home run hitters.

Comparing the 1950s home run and stolen base numbers to those of the 1970s helps to relate the evolution of offensive strategy. National League teams averaged 139 home runs in 1954, 158 homers in '55, and 152 homers in '56. N.L. teams averaged 107 home runs in 1974, 103 homers in '75, and 93 homers in '76. In 1954, N.L. teams averaged 42 stolen bases; in '55, 47 steals; in '56, 46 steals. In 1974, N.L. teams averaged 105 steals; in '75, 98 steals; in '76, 114 steals. The change in strategy was also evident in the American League, even though in 1974 to '76, the A.L. had an additional batter (and basestealer) with the designated hitter. A.L. teams in 1954 averaged 103 home runs; in '55, 120 home runs; in '56, 134 homers. American League teams averaged 114 home runs in 1974; 122 homers in 1975, and 94 homers in '76. American League teams averaged 45, 40, and 44 stolen bases in 1954, '55, and '56. A.L. teams averaged 103, 112, and 141 stolen bases in 1974, '75, and '76.

Richie Ashburn hit .308 in his 15-year career.

Getting on base and waiting for the big hit was more important in this era than in the 1970s.

It was also an era pretty much dominated by only a few teams, most notably by the New York Yankees. The Yanks won four of the 1950s first five World Series.

THE SHOT HEARD 'ROUND THE WORLD

The moment on October 3, 1951, has been immortalized through broadcaster Russ Hodges' frenzied, euphoric call: "The Giants win the pennant! The Giants win the pennant!" Hodges could barely get out the facts for anybody who might have missed "the shot heard 'round the world." "Bobby Thomson hits one into the lower deck of the left field stands. And they're going crazy! They're going crazy! Ohhhhhh!"

The Dodgers had just blown a 4-2 lead and the pennant after the "Miracle of Coogan's Bluff." The miracle was the embarrassing culmination of a season in which the Dodgers had led the Giants by 13 1/2 games on August 11. Beginning on August 16, New York won 16 straight games, and 37 out of their final 44. The Giants would have won the pennant without a playoff had not Dodger Jackie Robinson single-

handedly beaten the Phillies on the season's final day.

The Dodgers and Giants split the first two of the best-of-three series before Brooklyn jumped ahead 4-1 in the finale. In the bottom of the ninth, two singles and a double made it 4-2, and with two on and one out, Ralph Branca replaced Brooklyn starter Don Newcombe.

Thomson, who had made a baserunning blunder and two errors in the playoffs, was aching to redeem himself. He took a strike, and then parked the next fastball into the Polo Grounds' left field stands, becoming one of baseball's greatest heroes. Thomson was mobbed when he reached home plate. Branca sat on the clubhouse steps and cried.

The Giants go crazy after Bobby Thomson's home run.

Ted Williams (top left) led the American League in batting twice and slugging three times during the seven full seasons that he played in the 1950s. Lew Burdette (top right) of the Braves averaged 17 wins a season from 1953 to '59. He led the N.L. in shutouts twice, complete games once, ERA once, wins once, and winning percentage once. He was considered as a control pitcher, in the same class as Robin Roberts. Burdette ended his career with 203 wins and 31 saves. A vendor hawks scorecards (bottom right) as the crowd watches the action in the 1956 World Series. Braves lefthander Warren Spahn (bottom left) amassed the most victories in the decade, 203.

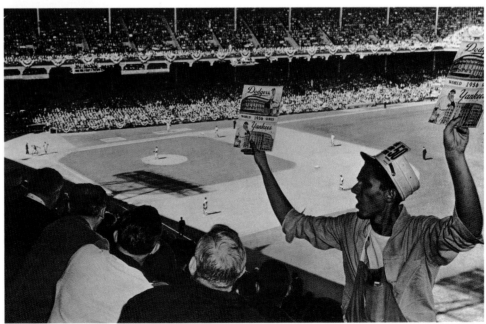

THE 1950s

Though they won only two in the last five years of the decade, their shadow seemed to hang over every season no matter who won. The Yankees' winning percentage for the 1950s was .621. In retrospect, the Yankees look just as good as they must have looked to their opponents: Mickey Mantle was the league's (and possibly both leagues') best player over the ten-year span, Yogi Berra was the best catcher, and Whitey Ford might have been the best pitcher.

But in reviewing the pennant races year-by-year, it is not at all clear that the Yanks had a top-to-bottom edge over the A.L.'s best teams (particularly Cleveland in the first half of the decade) in overall talent. Certainly not in front-line talent: The Yanks never possessed anything like the starting rotation of the Indians' Bob Lemon (perhaps the most underrated pitcher of the decade), Early Wynn, Mike Garcia, Herb Score, and Bob Feller. And the Yanks never fielded a starting lineup as solid top to bottom as the Dodgers teams they beat in three of four World Series; Brooklyn's lineup included Gil Hodges, Jackie Robinson, Pee Wee Reese, Carl Furillo, Duke Snider, Don Newcombe, and Roy Campanella. Looking back on those pennant races and World Series, it becomes more apparent that Casey Stengel was the first modern manager. He wrote the book now in use on the art of platooning, relief pitching, and pinch-hitting. The Yankees had three Hall of Fame stars in the 1950s, but the team's spectacular success was primarily due to Casey Stengel's remarkable talent for making use of what he had available.

Of course, the one enduring argument that fans, even those who are too young to remember the 1950s, still love to engage in is: Who was the greater ballplayer, Mickey Mantle or Willie Mays?

Whitey Ford (top) was 121-50 during the decade; Hank Aaron averaged 103 RBI a year.

The argument will probably endure as long as baseball, long after all those who watched them play are gone. Bill James' remarkable statistical analysis in his *Historical Baseball Abstract* reaches the conclusion that at his peak, Mantle was the better ballplayer. He hit with more power, reached base more often, and used up fewer outs. James' analysis is almost certainly correct; the real question is whether or not the evidence which shows Mantle a greater ballplayer *at his peak* justifies the conclusion that "Mickey Mantle was the greatest player of the 1950s." By James' own methods, it's clear that Mays had the better seasons in 1954 and 1955, Mantle was better in 1956 and 1957, and that the choice is about even for 1958 and 1959. Both had good rookie years in

PEE WEE REESE

Harold Henry Reese was nicknamed Pee Wee not because of his height (5'10") but because he had been a marble champion while growing up. But with the Dodgers, with whom he played from 1940 to 1958, Pee Wee was mostly called captain. Reese demonstrated so much leadership that he was the team's unofficial captain for a decade before he was officially given the designation in 1950.

Never did Reese earn more respect than in 1947 when the Dodgers signed Jackie Robinson to play with them. Reese wasn't sure he would be comfortable with a black teammate — until he met Robinson and saw the skills and desire the man brought to the team. Early in that season, Reese walked over to Robinson before a game and put his arm around Robinson's shoulders, which told everyone where he stood.

Reese was the leader of the Dodgers on the field because he did so many things to help win ballgames. As the leadoff man, he was usually successful when he bunted for a base hit. When he was called on to sacrifice to move up a base runner, he seldom failed. In 1948, he was given the sacrifice sign 14 times, and he delivered every time. Reese stole 20 to 30 bases a season and was seldom thrown out.

Reese finished his 16-year career in the majors with a .269 batting average. He led the league in putouts four times and is among the top ten in career double plays. He made the Hall of Fame in 1984.

Casey Stengel's Yankees won 955 games, six world championships, and eight pennants in the 1950s: "Good pitching always stops good hitting. And vice versa."

THE 1950s

1951. In terms of year-in, year-out value, it appears pretty much a jump ball, though there's no disputing that Mantle's 1956 and '57 seasons were the best of any player in the decade. What's often overlooked is that Mays lost two peak years to the Army; he hit 20 home runs as a rookie before he went in and 41 the year he came out. If he had hit just 30 each for 1952 and '53, he would have broken Babe Ruth's lifetime home run record before Henry Aaron did.

1950

For the American League, this season was pretty much a case of business as usual. Three aging stars for the Yankees had an average age of 35, but all were strong coming down the stretch. Joe DiMaggio, who had an uncharacteristically low average of .301, but with 32 home runs, 122 RBI, and a league-high .585 slugging average; Johnny Mize, who hit 25 home runs and was better than ever as a pinch hitter; and Phil Rizzuto, who had a career-high .324 average with 200 hits, all contributed to the Bronx Bombers narrow pennant win. When the numbers of the veteran stars were added to those of Yogi Berra, the sensational 25-year-old catcher (.322, 28 homers, 124 RBI), the Yankees had enough power to slip by Detroit, Boston, and Cleveland. All four teams won 92 games or more in a race that turned out to be tighter than most thought at the beginning of the season.

The Tigers were powered by All-Star third baseman George Kell (.340), lefthanded slugging outfielder Vic Wertz (27 home runs, 123 RBI), and outfielder Hoot Evers (.323, 103 RBI). Detroit was also sustained by the pitching of Art Houtteman and future Cincinnati manager Fred Hutchinson (the two were a combined 36-20), which kept Detroit

in the race all season long and left them just 3 games behind at the finish of the season.

The Red Sox, loaded as usual with power (Ted Williams, Dom DiMaggio, Walt Dropo, Bobby Doerr, and Vern Stephens all had 70 or more RBI), might have had a better finish if Williams hadn't fractured his elbow in the All-Star Game. Stephens and Dropo tied for the league lead in RBI with 144. Cleveland might have pulled ahead of everyone with its terrific starting rotation (Early Wynn, Bob Feller, and Bob Lemon were a combined 57-30) if it hadn't been stunned by a four-game series loss to the last-place St. Louis Browns in September. The Indians' offense was led by Al Rosen, who led the league in homers with 37.

The Indians and the Tigers were the only ballclubs in the league with lower team ERAs (3.74 for the Tribe, 4.12 for the Tigers) than the Yankees (4.15). But Yanks pitching was good enough, thanks in large part to a brash, blond lefthanded farm product by the name of Ed "Whitey" Ford. Brought up in late June, Ford bolstered the aging pitching corps, which included Vic Raschi (age 31), Eddie Lopat (age 32), and Allie Reynolds (age 35), by

Brooklyn's Duke Snider hit .321 in 1950.

RICHIE ASHBURN

Richie Ashburn started his pro career as a catcher, and if he'd stayed at that position, he would have been the most fleet-footed backstop ever.

Ashburn joined the Phillies in 1948, won the center field job from the 1947 batting champion (Harry "The Hat" Walker), and held it in Philadelphia for 12 years. He became a star his rookie year. He had a 23-game hitting streak in compiling a .333 average, and he led the league in stolen bases with 32. That season, he was the only rookie voted to the All-Star Game.

A slap hitter, Ashburn beat out lots of balls that never got out of the infield. That led some cynics to say, "He's no .300 hitter. He hits .100 and runs .200." No matter how he got them, Ashburn was usually among the league leaders in hits for a season. Three times he led the league in hits, with 221 in 1951, 205 in '53, and 215 in '58. He also won two batting titles, with a .338 average in 1955 and a career-high .350 in 1958.

Ashburn used his speed to collect 234 stolen bases in his career and to become a splendid center fielder. In four different seasons he made over 500 putouts, and he tied the record held by Max Carey by leading the league in putouts and total chances nine times.

Ashburn finished his career in 1962 with the expansion Mets. He batted .306 in his final season, becoming the Mets' first player to make the All-Star team.

Dodger Carl Furillo (top left) hit .305, drove in 106 runs, and scored 99 in 1950. He averaged 86 RBI a season during his nine full seasons in the 1950s. Tigers third sacker George Kell (top middle) had an A.L.-leading 218 hits and 56 doubles in '50. Cub Andy Pafko (top right) had 36 homers in '50. Sal "The Barber" Maglie (bottom left) was 18-4 in 1950 with an N.L.-best five shutouts and 23-6 in '51 for the Giants. Indian Bob Lemon (bottom right) won 20 games seven times in his career.

winning nine of ten decisions and making eight relief appearances.

Boston utility player Billy Goodman led the American League with a .354 batting average. Rizzuto was the league's Most Valuable Player, placing second in the A.L. in runs scored (125) and stolen bases (12), plus leading league shortstops in putouts and double plays. Lemon led the league in wins at 23, strikeouts with 170, complete games with 22, and innings pitched at 288.

But the 1950 season is largely remembered today for the accomplishments of National League youth. This was the year the miserable Phillies — which had easily the worst organization over the years in National League history — finally won the pennant. Many felt that the "Whiz Kids" didn't so much win the pennant as the Brooklyn Dodgers lost it, producing the refrain, "Wait till next year." When you look at the lineups and see that the Phillies fielded a team with such names as Mike Goliat, Eddie Waitkus, and Andy Seminick, while the Dodgers' starting lineup contained four future Hall of Famers in Jackie Robinson, Pee Wee Reese, Duke Snider, and Roy Campanella, you find it hard to resist the argument. The Dodgers hit 194 home runs to the Phillies' 125, scored 847 runs to the Phils' 722, stole 77 bases to the Phils' 33, and outslugged them by nearly 50 points.

It was great Phillies pitching that did "Dem Bums" in. Right-hander Robin Roberts was 20-11 with a 3.02 ERA, southpaw Curt Simmons was 17-8 with a 3.40 ERA, and reliever Jim Konstanty appeared in 74 games, saved 22, won 16, lost seven, and won the MVP award. Bob Miller (11-6, 3.57 ERA) was really the only other substantial Philly hurler, but those four were a combined 64-32 so depth

didn't matter (until the World Series).

The Phillies received most of their power from right fielder Del Ennis, who led the league in RBI with 126 while batting .311, slugging .551, and knocking 31 homers. The N.L. home run king in 1950 was Ralph Kiner of the last-place Pittsburgh Pirates. Kiner smacked 47 round-trippers (11 more than runner-up Andy Pafko of the Chicago Cubs). Stan Musial of the Cardinals led the league in batting (.346) and slugging (.596), and was second in total bases (331) and doubles (41). Snider led the league in total bases with 343 and hits with 199. Rookie of the Year Sam "Jet" Jethroe of Boston swiped the most bases, 35.

Warren Spahn had a great year for the Braves. He led the N.L. in wins (21) and strikeouts (191),

BoSox infielder Billy Goodman hit .354 in '50.

BILL VEECK — BASEBALL MAVERICK

On August 19, 1951, Browns owner Bill Veeck dispatched a 3'7" player, Eddie Gaedel, to pinch hit in the second game of a doubleheader. While Gaedel strolled to first base after walking on four pitches, A.L. president Will Harridge seethed.

During his 40 years in baseball, Veeck was the game's most colorful executive.

Called an iconoclast, a maverick, and an innovator, Veeck combined a flair for promotion with a deep and abiding love of the national pastime. In 1941, he bought a dying minor league franchise in Milwaukee, and a year later, they drew the most fans in the minors. He tried to buy the Phillies in 1944, intending to create a predominantly black team, but the deal was vetoed by commissioner Kenesaw Mountain Landis. Two years later, he bought the Cleveland Indians, signed the A.L.'s first black player (Larry Doby) in 1947, and signed 42-year-old Satchel Paige in 1948 (the year Veeck's Indians won the pennant).

Veeck bought the Chicago White Sox in 1959, created an exploding scoreboard, and molded a pennant winner. Years later, he would become a permanent fixture in Chicago's Wrigley Field, where he claimed to have planted the ivy on the outfield walls. Veeck would sit in the sun-drenched bleachers, smoke his cigarettes, drink his beer, regale the fans with his wit and charm, and revel in the game he loved. When he died in 1986 at 71, a campaign began to get Bill Veeck elected into the Hall of Fame.

Ewell Blackwell (top left) was 17-15 in 1950 for the Cincinnati Reds. In his last effective season, 1951, he was 16-15 for Cincinnati. The 6'6", 195-pound righthander was affectionately known as "The Whip." Sam "Jet" Jethroe (top middle) broke in like a flash as a 28-year-old for the Boston Braves in 1950. A former Negro Leagues player, Jethroe was the National League's Rookie of the Year that season, hitting .273, with 28 doubles, 18 homers, 100 runs scored, and a league-leading 35 stolen bases. Jethroe in 1951 had a similar season, hitting .280 with 29 doubles, 18 homers, 101 runs scored, and an N.L.-best 35 stolen bases. Ralph Kiner (top right) led the N.L. in homers every season from 1946 to 1952. In 1950, he slugged 47 for the Pirates. The 1950 Philadelphia "Whiz Kids" (bottom) received outstanding pitching from Jim Konstanty, Curt Simmons, and Robin Roberts. But their offense, while not the most high-powered in the league, was solid.

was second in complete games (25), and was third in innings pitched (293). Boston's Johnny Sain was tied for second in the league with 20 wins and 25 complete games. A third Boston pitcher, Vern Bickford, led the league in innings pitched with 312 and complete games with 27. Jim Hearn, who pitched with both the Giants and the Cardinals, led the league with a 2.94 ERA.

The young Phillies had struggled through an epic pennant race — losing Curt Simmons to military service coming down the stretch and losing a 7-game lead over the Dodgers over a nine-day period in September. On the final day of the

season, they had to win the pennant by beating the Dodgers at Ebbetts Field. The best pitcher that manager Eddie Sawyer could throw against Brooklyn was an exhausted Robin Roberts, who had pitched three times in seven days. But Roberts bore down and retired Carl Furillo and Gil Hodges with the bases loaded in the ninth inning to win the pennant for the spent Philadelphians. It was this game, and not the World Series, that Phillies fans would remember.

History remembers the 1950 World Series as a blowout — the Yanks won in four straight and that's the bottom line. But it wasn't the only line: The Whiz Kids lost the first three games by one run each, with Game Two going into the tenth inning. The Phillies lost Game Four by three runs, even though they were out-hit by only one, eight hits to seven. The dramatic highlight of the Series was a game-winning home run by Joe DiMaggio off Phillies ace Robin Roberts in the tenth inning of Game Two; it was one more home run than the Phils hit in four

games (Berra also had a homer for the New Yorkers). Philadelphia fans felt that the Series outcome might have been a great deal different with Simmons available.

The Yanks would, of course, continue to dominate the decade. The Whiz Kids quickly faded into "Phiz Kids" the following year when Konstanty reverted to form and Curt Simmons missed the season for military service. Roberts would continue to be a luckless star pitcher throughout the decade, and Richie Ashburn, the Phils' best every-day player, would go on to win two batting crowns and play a brand of center field that some would equate with Willie Mays. But Philadelphia fans wouldn't see a World Series game again on their home turf for three more decades.

Brooklyn's Preacher Roe was 22-3 in 1951.

1951

In one very important way the 1951 season was like the 1950 season; it's remembered now by baseball fans not because of the World Series (which was a good one) but for the National League pennant race. Also, it was another season when the Dodgers didn't win the big one and again cried, "Wait till next year."

Baseball switched commissioners in 1951, with Ford Frick taking over for Happy Chandler. St. Louis Browns' owner Bill Veeck pulled his most famous promotional stunt by having diminutive 3'7" Eddie Gaedel bat in a major league game, and Joe DiMaggio played

EARLY WYNN

Early Wynn was a hard-throwing righthander with a stinging fastball, a sharp-breaking curve, and a dancing knuckleball. But he was best known for his aggressive style on the mound. Any batter who tried to dig in on Wynn rapidly found himself dropping to the ground under a fastball.

Wynn began his career with the Senators, who were not known for their ability to score runs. He won 18 games for the Senators in 1943 and 17 in '47. In his career, his team was shut out 45 times when he was on the mound; most of those times, his team was the Senators. But in 1949, he was traded to the Indians and was on his way to a brilliant career.

Wynn won 18 games in 1950 and led the league in ERA (3.20). In '51 he won 20 games, and in '52 he won 23. In '54 he headed the Indians' staff with 23 wins as the team won the pennant. He pitched a four-hitter in his Series start against the Giants. Two years later Wynn again was a 20-game winner, and in 1959, after being traded to the White Sox, he won 22 and led the "Go-Go Sox" to the pennant.

Wynn had won 299 games by 1962. That year, the White Sox let him go. Determined to win 300, he joined the Indians in '63. He lost his first two decisions, won a final game, and retired. In 1972, he was inducted into the Hall of Fame.

Roy Campanella (top left) won the N.L.'s MVP award in 1951 both by driving in 108 runs and by leading league backstops in putouts, assists, and double plays. Gus Zernial (top right) led the A.L. with 33 homers and 129 RBI in '51. He averaged 28 home runs a year from 1950 to '57. The Giants' Monte Irvin slides safely into third (bottom left). Richie Ashburn (middle right) notched an N.L.-high 221 base hits in '51. Ford Frick (bottom right) was N.L. president from 1934 to '51 and baseball commissioner from 1951 to '68.

THE 1950s

his final game. But it was for Bobby Thomson and the "Miracle of Coogan's Bluff" that the 1951 season is remembered, and no matter how many times Brooklyn Dodgers fans replay the game it will come out the same way. It's a moment frozen in baseball time.

The American League had a pennant race, too, though most people who were around at the time didn't seem to notice the fact. Once again the Cleveland Indians mounted a challenge behind their strong starting combination of Bob Feller, Early Wynn, and Bob Lemon, but in 1951, a big right-hander named Mike Garcia helped make it the most feared rotation in baseball: The four accounted for 79 wins (against 48 losses), and very nearly brought Cleveland the pen-

Giant Al Dark had 41 doubles in 1951.

nant. The Indians hit too: Their 140 home runs tied the Yankees for the league high, with outfielder Larry Doby hitting 20, third baseman Al Rosen slugging 24, and veteran first baseman Luke Easter smacking 27. Easter had 103 RBI, and Rosen had 102; Doby was second to Ted Williams in slugging average, .512 to .556. The Indians gave the Yanks a close race, fading only in the last two weeks of the season.

The Yankees, bolstered by catcher Yogi Berra's 27 home runs and the inspired shortstop play of Phil Rizzuto (.274 with 18 stolen bases — an exceptionally high total for the nonrunning 1950s), were able to hold off Cleveland in the final month. Berra also had a .298 average and 88 RBI, and won the MVP award. The New York team suffered along with Joe DiMaggio and his bone-spurred heel; the Yankee Clipper managed only 12 home runs and turned once routine fly balls into extra base hits. Fortunately, the Yankees' farm system produced an heir at precisely the time the team needed it: Mickey Mantle. The 20-year-old hit 13 home runs in 96 games, played a flashy center field, and showed a remarkable propensity for collecting walks (43) and strikeouts (74). Gil McDougald also shined as a rookie, both at third and second, hitting 14 homers, stealing 14 bases, and batting .306 in 131 games. Stengel juggled his lineup, alternating outfielders Gene Woodling and Hank Bauer and infielders McDougald and Billy Martin. With Whitey Ford lost to the Army, Stengel established a sound starting rotation of Ed Lopat, Vic Raschi, Allie Reynolds, and a journeyman named Tom "Plowboy" Morgan, who went 9-3 in 16 starts. The trivia note of the season in the A.L. was that Dom DiMaggio drove in one more run (72) than did his brother Joe.

Philadelphia's Gus Zernial led the A.L. in homers (33) and RBI (129), while Ferris Fain of the A's won the batting crown (.344). The Athletics still finished in sixth place, 28 games out. Browns pitcher Ned Garver hurled 24 complete games, finishing 20-12 with a 3.73 ERA for a team that won 52 games and finished 46 games out.

Besides leading the A.L. in slugging average, Ted Williams had the most bases on balls with

RED SOX SCORE 17 RUNS IN AN INNING

Boston's Billy Goodman had five of Boston's 27 base hits during the game.

The 1953 season was highlighted by two bizarre individual achievements. On April 17, Yankee Mickey Mantle hit a home run in Washington that traveled over the left field wall and halfway up the scoreboard. It was measured the next day at 565 feet, one of the longest homers in recorded baseball history. On May 6, Browns pitcher Bobo Holloman threw a no-hitter in his first major league start. Holloman would be sent to the minors later in the year and never returned to the big time.

But the single weirdest team accomplishment occurred on June 18, when the Red Sox, *sans* Ted Williams (who was in Korea), produced a 17-run seventh inning during a game against the Tigers at Boston's Fenway Park. The score was 5-3 Red Sox when the onslaught started against Tigers reliever Steve Gromek. The veteran yielded nine earned runs, six hits, and three walks. Gromek said that although some of the hits were clean, most were "flukes." When the inning was over, the Red Sox had sent 23 men to the plate, knocked 11 singles, two doubles, one homer, and six walks. The final score was 23-3.

Reserve outfielder Gene Stephens set an A.L. record with three hits in the inning, which lasted 48 minutes. There were 15 other major league records or A.L. records broken or tied in front of 3,198 fans. The Tigers probably couldn't wait to get out of Boston; Detroit had also lost to the Sox the previous day 17-1.

Mickey Mantle (top left) was a 170-pound shortstop in the spring of 1951. The Yankees put him in center field, but Mantle would play seven games at shortstop in his career. Yogi Berra (top right), the 1951 A.L. MVP, had 27 homers, 92 runs, and 88 RBI that year. Yankee Eddie Lopat (bottom left) was 21-9 in 1951. Ferris Fain (bottom middle) of the A's led the A.L. with a .344 batting average in '51 and a .327 average in '52. Jackie Robinson (bottom right) makes the grab.

143 and most total bases with 295. He also had 30 homers, 126 RBI, and 109 runs scored. Minnie Minoso, who played with both the Cleveland Indians and the Chicago White Sox, led the league in stolen bases with 31 and triples with 14, and he finished second for the A.L. batting title with a .326 average and in runs scored with 112. Dom DiMaggio led the league in runs scored with 113. George Kell of Detroit led the league with 191 base hits.

The now legendary National League race, which saw the Giants close a 13½-game gap after August 12 to tie for the pennant, looks, in retrospect, like something that had a right to happen. The Giants hit nearly as well as the Dodgers — Thomson hit 32 home runs with 101 RBI, Monte Irvin had 121 RBI, and underrated shortstop Al Dark batted .303 with 14 home runs. The Giants also got help from a new source: a 20-year-old outfielder from Alabama named Willie Mays, who hit 20 home runs and batted .274 in 121 games, and had fans gasping with his one-hand "basket"

catches in center field. The Dodgers — with Most Valuable Player Roy Campanella hitting .325, with 33 homers and 108 RBI, and Gil Hodges and Duke Snider each driving in more than 100 runs — outhit the Giants a bit. But the Giants — with Sal Maglie and Larry Jansen combining for a spectacular 46-17 mark — had slightly better pitching. In the end, it was a toss-up as to which team was better. Each team finished the regular season with a 96-58 record. If Bobby Thomson hadn't hit his home run off Ralph Branca ("The Shot Heard 'Round The World") in the final inning of the three-game playoff, they might still be out there. The batter on deck for the Giants when Thomson hit his home run was Willie Mays.

Maglie and Jansen of the Giants tied for the league lead in wins (23), while Brooklyn's Preacher Roe and Boston's Warren Spahn each won 22 games. Roe had the N.L.'s best winning percentage (.880), while Spahn topped the league in complete games (26) and strikeouts (164). Don Newcombe of Brooklyn also had 164 Ks. Philadelphia's Robin Roberts had six shutouts and pitched 315 innings to lead the league, plus he won 21 games. Chet Nicholas of Boston won the ERA crown with a 2.88 mark.

Musial led the N.L. in batting for the second consecutive season by notching a .355 mark. He also slugged 32 homers, had 108 RBI, scored a league-high 124 runs (tying him with Pittsburgh's

Bobby Thomson comes home after his pennant-winning homer in 1951.

DUKE SNIDER

Edwin Donald Snider was known as the "Duke of Flatbush" during his first 11 years with the Brooklyn Dodgers. He hit prodigious home runs over Ebbets Field's right field fence, out onto Bedford Avenue. He was also an outstanding center fielder.

Snider joined the Dodgers in 1947, at age 20, but didn't become a regular until 1949, when he batted .292, hit 23 home runs, and had 92 RBI. The next season he led the league in hits with 199 and had a .321 average, 31 homers, and 107 RBI. Yet Snider didn't really find his rhythm at the plate until 1953, when he began a streak of five seasons with 40 or more homers.

From 1953 through '57, while the Dodgers were still in Brooklyn and winning three pennants and a World Series, Snider batted over .300 three times (with a high of .341 in '54), led the league in runs scored three times (with a high of 132 in '53), led the league in homers in '56 with 43, and even led the league in walks with 99 in '56.

Snider was particularly tough in the World Series. In a losing cause in 1952 against the Yankees, four of his ten hits were homers, as he set a Series record with 24 total bases. In 1955, Snider had eight hits, four of them home runs, and seven RBI, as the Dodgers finally beat their Bronx rivals.

Snider was misplaced once the Dodgers moved to Los Angeles in 1958. But he played in Los Angeles for five years and then finished with the Mets. In 1980, he was inducted into the Hall of Fame.

Dodgers left fielder Andy Pafko stands helpless as the crowd at the Polo Grounds howls its approval at Bobby Thomson's "Shot Heard 'Round the World." The score was 4-2 with two men on, first base was empty, and one out when Thomson came up. The Dodgers' skipper chose to pitch to Thomson instead of walking him to load the bases and go for the double play; the next batter was Willie Mays.

Ralph Kiner), tallied a league-high 355 total bases, and had a .614 slugging average. Kiner led the league in slugging (.627), homers (42), and bases on balls (137). He also tied Boston's Sid Gordon for second in the league with 109 RBI. Richie Ashburn was the N.L. leader in hits with 221, and he finished second in batting average (.344) and stolen bases (29).

The World Series was anticlimactic. The Giants took the first game but ended up losing to the Yanks in six games. Ed Lopat was the ace, winning two games and allowing only ten hits in 18 innings. For the Giants, the essential story was that their two aces, Maglie and Jensen, posted ERAs of 7.20 and 6.30. Irvin hit .458, and Dark hit .417; their performances were wasted. The Series produced two trivia items: Mickey Mantle, running after a fly, caught a cleat in a sprinkler at Yankee Stadium and came up with the first of a series of injuries that would plague his career. The batter who hit the fly ball was Willie Mays.

1952

This season is the best evidence that Casey Stengel supporters can point to when they argue his genius. It was Stengel's first year without Joe DiMaggio; pitchers Whitey Ford and Tom Morgan were in the service, along with infielders Bobby Brown and Jerry Coleman. Stengel always had a strategist's eye for platooning, but now he had a lot of holes to fill, and he had to fill them with guys who had once been mere role-players. Feisty Billy Martin was given the second base job and played 107 games there, batting .267. McDougald was made a fixture at third base, driving in 78 runs; and Mantle blossomed into a star, batting .311, hitting 23 home runs,

Ralph Branca was 13-12 in 1951, with a 3.26 ERA and 204 innings pitched. He also had three saves that year.

and walking 75 times. The Yanks' starting rotation of Reynolds, Raschi, Lopat, and veteran curveballer Johnny Sain averaged 34 years of age but also averaged 14 wins and just six losses apiece.

Cleveland, paced again by its remarkable pitching (Wynn, Garcia, and Lemon all won more than 20 games) and bolstered by sluggers Doby and Rosen (60 homers and 209 RBI between them), made the race close. By Labor Day, the Yanks' edge was only 2½ games, and they were faced with a three-week stretch that featured only three home games (the Indians were playing 20 of 22 at home over the same period). But the Yanks maintained the pace and beat the Indians in head-on competition to take the pennant.

Philadelphia's Bobby Shantz was the A.L. MVP, leading the league in wins with 24 and winning percentage at .774. Fain won the batting title again for the A's with a .327 average. Doby led the A.L. in homers (32) and slugging average (.541), while Rosen topped the league in RBI (105) and total bases (297).

WARREN SPAHN

In 1942, Warren Spahn began his major league pitching career with the Boston Braves, managed by Casey Stengel, and ended his career in 1965 with the New York Mets, managed by Stengel. "I played for Casey Stengel before and after he was a genius," Spahn said.

Spahn himself was a pitching genius, a man who won 363 games, more than any other left-hander in history. Only four pitchers — Cy Young, Walter Johnson, Christy Mathewson, and Grover Cleveland Alexander — won more games than Spahn.

Initially, he had a hopping fastball and was a strikeout pitcher, leading the National League in strikeouts four successive years, from 1949 through 1952. But even as he began to lose a little on his fastball, he became a smarter pitcher.

After service in World War II, in which he received a Purple Heart, Spahn had an 8-5 record in 1946, won 21 games the next year, and was on his way. He won 20 games 12 times in the next 18 seasons. Spahn won the All-Star Game in 1953, the Cy Young Award in '57, and two games in the loss to the Yankees in the '58 World Series. He led the league in wins eight times, ERA three times, complete games nine times, shutouts three times, and innings pitched four times. He didn't pitch his first no-hitter until 1960; then next year, at age 40, he pitched a second no-hitter, beating the Giants 1-0.

In 1973, Spahn entered the Hall of Fame, six years after Casey Stengel was inducted.

Athletics hurler Bobby Shantz, left, shows Mike Garcia of the Indians his MVP grip (top left). Shantz won the 1952 A.L. Most Valuable Player award by going 24-7 with a 2.48 ERA and 27 complete games. Garcia had a 124-85 record from 1950 to '57. The Brooklyn infield for 1952 (top right), left to right, Jackie Robinson, Gil Hodges, Roy Campanella, Billy Cox, and Pee Wee Reese, was the best in the National League. Cardinals outfielder Stan Musial, at bat (bottom left), led the National League with a .336 batting average, 42 doubles, and 105 runs scored in 1952. Musial scored 948 runs during the 1950s. Boston's Dom DiMaggio (bottom right), "The Little Professor," led the A.L. with 139 runs scored in 1950 and 113 in '51.

THE 1950s

Dale Mitchell and Bobby Avila both contributed to the Indians' offense. Mitchell was second in A.L. batting with a .323 mark. Avila led the league in triples (11), and was second in hits (179) and runs scored (102). Nellie Fox of the ChiSox led the league in hits with 192, while his teammate Minnie Minoso led the A.L. in swipes with 22. Reynolds led the league in strikeouts (160) and ERA (2.06). Harry Dorish of the White Sox led the circuit in saves with 11. Lemon hurled 310 innings and 28 complete games to top the league.

For the Dodgers, 1952 represented a return to the top after two years of what their fans and foes alike regarded as squandered pennants. The Dodgers once again led the league with 153 home runs; their league-high total of 90 stolen bases, though low by today's standards, was eye-catching for a 1950s team. The pitching wasn't bad either, particularly when Joe Black, a fire-balling 28-year-old relief pitcher, was on the mound. Black saved 15 games and posted a 2.15 ERA, figures that came in very handy considering that no Dodgers starter won more than 14 games. Actually, the real Dodgers MVP was Uncle Sam: Brooklyn finished only 4 games ahead of the Giants, games that could have been easily made up had Willie Mays not lost time to the service (not to mention that 1951 RBI leader Monte Irvine had an injured ankle, causing him to miss most of the year).

The Most Valuable Player award went to Cubs outfielder Hank Sauer, who slugged 37 homers and drove in 121 runs; but Chicago (at 77-77) finished in fifth place, 19½ games out. The St. Louis Cardinals threatened most of the season, thanks largely to Stan Musial's sensational season. Musial led the league in batting average (.336), slugging average

(.538), hits (194), runs scored (105), total bases (311), and doubles (42). More impressive, though, was a near-comeback by Philadelphia's Whiz Kids. Paced by a sensational performance from Robin Roberts — the righthander won a league-high 28 games, going 28-7 with an incredible 30 complete

games and 330 innings pitched — the Phils were 20 games over .500 and were perhaps one outstanding player away from winning the pennant. Oddly enough, the team's best every-day player of the decade, Richie Ashburn, had an off year, batting only .282, compared with a .344 average a year earlier.

WILLIE MAYS AND "THE CATCH"

Willie Mays hit 660 home runs. He drove in almost 2,000 runs. He banged out 3,283 hits. He was one of the most exciting baseball players ever. But if Willie Mays is forever remembered for one thing, it will be for "The Catch."

The Cleveland Indians had won 111 games in 1954 and were heavily favored to beat the New York Giants in the World Series. But the Giants, playing Game One at home in the Polo Grounds, were hanging in 2-2 when Cleveland came up in the eighth inning.

After the Indians put their first two hitters on base against Giants pitcher Sal Maglie, southpaw Don Liddle was brought in to face lefthanded hitter Vic

Wertz. Wertz sent Liddle's first pitch on a line toward the center field wall, which was over 450 feet away. Mays, who had taken off with Wertz' swing, went into overdrive with his back to the plate. Running at full speed, he reached out high in front of his body and cradled the ball in his glove about ten feet from the wall. Without hesitating, he twirled around and rifled the ball back to the infield, preventing the runner on second from scoring after the catch. If only they'd had center field cameras in those days.

After the inning, Mays received a note from Branch Rickey. "That was the finest catch I have ever seen," it read. The 53,000 other fans who saw the catch that day probably agreed.

306

Yankee Gil McDougald flips to first after forcing Nellie Fox (top left). McDougald hit 112 homers during his career. Dodger Joe Black (top right) had 14 relief wins and 15 saves in 1952. Satchel Paige (bottom left) of the Browns was 12-10 with a 3.07 ERA in 1952. He led the A.L. with eight relief wins, and he had ten saves. Paige saved 11 games in '53. Cub Hank Sauer (bottom middle) slugged .531 to go with his 37 homers and 121 RBI in 1952. Warren Spahn (bottom right) was 23-7 with a 2.10 ERA in 1953.

THE 1950s

Rookie Hoyt Wilhelm, age 29, of the New York Giants became one of the premier relief pitchers in the league in 1952. He won 15 games, all in relief, while losing only three and saving 11. His .883 winning percentage, 2.43 ERA, and 71 games pitched all were bests in the National League. Although he was 14-19 for Boston, Warren Spahn still turned in a fine season, leading the league with 183 Ks, and hurling 19 complete games and 290 innings. Al Brazle of St. Louis led the N.L. in saves with 16.

Ralph Kiner tied Sauer for the league home run crown (37), and he led the league with 110 bases on balls. Pee Wee Reese led the N.L. in stolen bases with 30. Chicago Cub Frankie Baumholtz hit .325, while Cincinnati's Ted Kluszewski

Giants reliever Hoyt Wilhelm knocked a home run in his first at-bat in 1952. In 21 seasons he never hit another one. He also pitched a no-hitter during one of his 52 career starts.

hit .320 and slugged .509. Musial's teammate, Cardinals second baseman Red Schoendienst, finished second to Stan the Man in base hits (188) and doubles (40), while Redbird Solly Hemus tied Musial for the lead in runs scored (105).

Some students of the game think that the 1952 World Series was the best of the decade. It certainly was if you were a lover of pitching: Both teams managed just 100 hits in 465 at bats — a perfect .215 batting average for each team. But amazingly, 16 of the hits were home runs, and unfortunately for the Dodgers, the Yankees had ten of them (Mantle and Yogi Berra had two apiece and, in a turn of events that was particularly galling for Dodgers fans, former Giants slugger John Mize had three). Games Five and Six were decided by a single run; games One, Three, Four, and Seven by two. The Yankees won the seventh game and the Series while making four errors.

1953

The 1953 Brooklyn Dodgers were probably the best team of the decade, the best team the Dodgers ever fielded, and the best team never to win a World Series. The Bums led the majors in runs scored, batting, homers, stolen bases, and slugging. Four players (Duke Snider, Roy Campanella, Gil Hodges, and Carl Furillo) had more than 20 home runs, with Snider and Campanella each belting more than 40. Five players had more than 90 RBI. Campy won his second MVP award by hitting .312 with 41 homers and an N.L.-best 142 RBI. The pitching wasn't the strongest in the league, but Carl Erskine was 20-6 and Russ Meyer was 15-5, while a 20-year-old southpaw named Johnny Podres went 9-4, so the Dodgers really had no serious pitching woes.

The Braves, newly arrived in Milwaukee from Boston, made a bit of noise by winning 92 games. Third baseman Eddie Mathews had a fabulous season with 47 home runs and 135 runs batted in. Mathews did more than win the N.L. home run title: He broke Ralph Kiner's seven-year hold on it and went on to hit many more career home runs than Kiner. Braves lefthander Warren Spahn won 23 of 30 decisions. But the

ROY CAMPANELLA

Roy Campanella of the Dodgers was soft-spoken but could be forthright when he needed to be. During a game against the Cubs, Chicago's Phil Cavaretta stepped in, Campanella flashed the sign, and Dodgers pitcher Carl Erskine shook it off. On the next pitch, Cavaretta singled to right. After the game, Campanella collared Erskine and said, "Don't ever shake me off again. You know I'm smarter than you are. Pitchers don't know a damn thing. That's why they have catchers."

Campanella was one of the smartest catchers and had one of the strongest arms ever. Throughout his career he threw out two of every three runners who attempted to steal a base on him.

His quick, powerful swing made him an awesome hitter. Campy played only ten years in the majors, but in three of those seasons he was named the league's MVP. His first came in 1951, when he had a .325 average, 108 RBI, and 33 home runs. His second came in 1953, when he batted .312, hit 41 homers, and had a league-leading 142 RBI. His third came in 1955, when he had a .318 average, 32 homers, and 107 RBI.

But on January 28, 1958, on an icy highway, he had an automobile accident that left him paralyzed. In 1959, before a Dodgers-Yankees exhibition game, Roy Campanella was honored. The lights were turned off in the Los Angeles Coliseum, and the 93,103 fans present each held up a lighted match. Campy tearfully said, "Thank you. Thank you from the bottom of my heart."

Phillie Robin Roberts (top) brings it home. He led the N.L. with 23 wins and 198 Ks in 1953. Dodgers hurler Carl Erskine (bottom left) struck out 14 Yankees (including Mickey Mantle four times) in Game Three of the '53 World Series to set a Series record. Braves third baseman Eddie Mathews (bottom right) drove in at least 90 runs ten different seasons.

THE 1950s

pennant race was never really close, with the Braves at 13 games behind. This year the Dodgers had no intention of letting things go down to the last day. In fact, the pennant race was all but over by the All-Star break.

Robin Roberts tied Spahn for the league lead in wins with 23. Roberts also led the league in strikeouts (198), complete games (33), and innings pitched (347). He finished second to Spahn in ERA (2.10 to 2.75) and second to St. Louis' Harvey Haddix in shutouts (six to five — Spahn also had five). Cardinal Al Brazle again led the league in saves with 18, and his teammate Red Schoendienst was second in the league with a .342 average. Musial hit .337 and slugged .609. He also led the league in doubles (53) and bases on balls (105). Richie Asburn of the Phillies topped the N.L. with 205 base hits. Bill Bruton of the Braves swiped 26 bases to best the league.

Brooklyn's Furillo won the batting crown with a .344 average. Dodger Snider finished second to Mathews in homers by belting 42. The Duke also led the league in runs scored (132), total bases (370), and slugging average (.627, tied with Mathews). Carl Erskine of the Dodgers led the league with a .769 winning percentage and was second in strikeouts with 187.

When the Dodgers got to the World Series, the Yankees were there to meet them. The Indians tried to make it a race. Cleveland was powered by 1953 A.L. MVP Al Rosen, who led the league in home runs (43) and RBI (145) while batting .336. Rosen lost the triple crown only because the Washington Senators' Mickey Vernon beat him out of the batting title on the last day of the season. Once again the Indians had fine pitching — Lemon, Garcia, and Wynn were all 17-12 or better. But the Yanks had

Cardinal Red Schoendienst hit .342 in 1953.

better pitching, thanks largely to Whitey Ford, who returned from the Army in fine style with an 18-6 record. The Yanks, though, couldn't match the Dodgers' gaudy hitting stats. Mantle (21 home runs, 92 RBI) and Yogi Berra (27 homers, 108 RBI) paced the New Yorkers to the league lead in batting, slugging, and runs scored. The Yanks won 99 games and were never really pressed.

The strangest story of the year and possibly the century was St. Louis Browns rookie Bobo Holloman. He pitched a no-hitter in his first major league start. Three months later, having lost seven of his next nine decisions and with an ERA over 5.00, he was sent back down to the minors. He never pitched in the major leagues again.

Modern fans who dislike the designated hitter will note that two future 300 game-winning pitchers, Warren Spahn of the Braves and Early Wynn of the Indians, batted for themselves and did quite well, with five homers between them. Wynn, in fact, batted .275 with three homers and ten RBI, while his pitching mate Bob Lemon also had a pair of home runs. The Korean War limited Ted Williams' playing time to 37 games and 91 at-

SANDY AMOROS' CATCH WINS 1955 SERIES

The fabled lament of Brooklyn Dodgers fans, "Wait till next year," wouldn't have had such a tragic-comic edge if "Dem Bums" hadn't made such a habit of losing the World Series to the Yankees. The Yankees beat the Dodgers in four Series between 1947 and 1953.

Although they had won the N.L. pennant by 13 1/2 games, the Dodgers dropped the first two Series games in Yankee Stadium. But the Dodgers had 23-year-old lefthanded pitcher Johnny Podres, who put the Dodgers back in it, pitching a complete-game 8-3 win in Game Three. Duke Snider took Podres' cue and hit three homers in the next two Brooklyn wins. The Bronx Bombers tied the Series 5-1 in Game Six.

It would be up to young Podres again in Game Seven; he pitched like a veteran, shutting down the Yanks for the first five innings while Brooklyn had a 1-0 lead.

In the bottom of the sixth, the Yankees put two on with none out and Yogi Berra at bat. With the Dodgers shifted toward right field, Berra lifted a long fly down the left field line. Sandy Amoros (inserted that inning for defense) raced nearly 100 feet, reached out as if trying to catch a balloon without breaking it, and snagged the drive. He then twirled, threw to Pee Wee Reese, who relayed to Gil Hodges at first base for the double play. The threat thwarted, Podres shut down the Yanks for good. Finally for Brooklyn fans, next year had arrived.

Braves hurler Lew Burdette (top left) was 15-5 in 1953. Rookie of the Year Junior Gilliam (top middle) of the Dodgers scored 125 runs in '53. Milwaukee shortstop Johnny Logan (top right) led the N.L. with 37 doubles in 1955. Bobo Holloman (bottom left), a 29-year-old rookie for the Browns who had been in the minors for ten years, became the only pitcher in modern baseball to get a no-hitter in his first major league game in 1953. In his next start, he was knocked out of the box in 1 1/3 innings and lasted only ten more weeks in the majors. Giants center fielder Willie Mays (bottom right) stole an extra-base hit from Dodger Carl Furillo by making this spectacular one-handed grab in right center during a game in 1954.

bats, but in that limited time he was awesome, with 13 home runs, a .407 average, and an incredible .901 slugging average.

Bob Porterfield of the Senators led the league with 22 wins, 24 complete games, and nine shutouts. New York's Eddie Lopat had an .800 winning percentage and a 2.42 ERA to top the league, while White Sox lefthander Billy Pierce led the A.L. with 186 strikeouts and was second in earned run average with a 2.72 mark. Lemon hurled a league-leading 287 innings while notching 21 wins and 23 complete games. Red Sox Ellis Kinder led the A.L. with 27 saves and 69 games pitched.

Philadelphia's Gus Zernial followed a 29-homer and 100-RBI 1952 by hitting .284 with 42 homers, 108 RBI, .559 slugging average, and a league-leading 7.6 home run percentage. Vernon led the league with 43 doubles, and had 205 base hits and 115 RBI. Detroit rookie Harvey Kuenn led the league with 209 base hits. Chicago's Minnie Minoso bested the A.L. with 25 stolen bases while hitting .313. Rosen also led the league in runs scored (115), slugging average (.613), and total bases (367).

The Yankees were gunning for their fifth straight world championship and a place in history, but for once the oddsmakers didn't think they could derail the Brooklyn locomotive. The Yanks took the first two games at Yankee Stadium, the second on a 4-2 decision behind "Steady" Eddie Lopat despite being outhit nine to five. The Dodgers bounced back to win the next two at Ebbetts Field, knocking out Yankees ace Ford in Game Four. The Bums looked as if they had finally taken the Bombers' measure, but the Yankees pounded out 24 hits to win the last two games, aided in no small part by four Brooklyn errors. The best team that the Dodgers ever fielded didn't just fail to win the World Series, it failed to extend it the full seven games.

The principal offender from the Dodgers fans' point of view was Billy Martin, the brash Yankees second baseman who bad-mouthed the Dodgers even before the Yanks

White Sox outfielder Minnie Minoso scores one of his 119 runs in '54.

MICKEY MANTLE

When Mickey Mantle trained with the Yankees in the spring of 1951, he was 19 years old and some 30 pounds lighter than the 200-pounder he would become. But he was already a powerful hitter. Ralph Houk said, "When he came up, all the other batting practice would stop...everyone watched Mickey hit."

Mantle was a great baseball player — a solid center fielder with a strong, accurate arm. He was probably the fastest player in baseball and a tremendous power hitter. In 1953, he hit a homer that was measured at 565 feet. Later, he hit a ball in Yankee Stadium that carried 600 feet.

It's just a shame that Mantle was healthy in only three of his 18 years in the majors. After knee surgery in 1951 and '52, Mantle was always plagued by leg problems. Despite them, he excelled.

In 1955, he led the league in homers with 37, and in '56, he won the triple crown with a .353 average, 52 home runs, and 130 RBI. He was named MVP that year and also in '57, when his batting average rose to .365. His top home run season was 1961, when he hit 54 despite being sidelined by an injury for two weeks. The next year, Mantle missed 39 games with injuries but still batted .321, hit 30 homers, and won his third MVP award.

Mantle played in 12 World Series and holds records for homers (18), runs scored (42), total bases (123), and RBI (40). He finished with 536 career homers and 1,509 RBI, but imagine what his totals would have been if Mantle had stayed healthy.

Monte Irvin (top left) of the Giants had 21 homers and 97 RBI in 1953. Hurlers (top middle) Billy Pierce (18-12 in 1953), left, and Virgil Trucks (15-6 in '53) led the ChiSox to a third-place finish. Pierce was 156-121 during the 1950s; Trucks had 157 career wins. Dodger Clem Labine (top right) had ten relief wins and seven saves in '53. Jackie Robinson steals home (bottom left), one of 19 times in his career that he stole home. Dodger Roy Campanella (bottom right) had 142 RBI in '53, an N.L. RBI record for catchers.

THE 1950s

had clinched their pennant. "We could play them ten times," said Martin after the Series, "and they'd still lose. They'd lose because they're the Dodgers." Martin, a fair hitter (.257) during the season, rapped out 12 hits in the Series for a .509 average, with two homers and eight RBI. It was one of the all-time great postseason performances, and nothing that Martin ever did in the rest of his career came close to matching it. Mantle batted only .208 but had two homers and only one less RBI than Martin.

Indians hurler Early Wynn was 23-11 in '54.

1954

The 1954 season began with a change that, like the Boston Braves move to Milwaukee the previous year, was so little noticed at the time that few realized its full implications. Unable to show a profit with the St. Louis Browns — the worst franchise in the history of the American League — Bill Veeck sold the team to a syndicate in Baltimore. The age of migration, which eventually took teams West and South, had officially begun.

It also appeared as if the age of Yankees domination had officially ended. Ironically, the Yankees had their finest team of the decade; the Bronx Bombers won 103 games and led the league in batting average, slugging average, and runs scored. The pitching was pretty good too, led by Ford's expected 16-8 (with a 2.82 ERA) season and Bob Grim's quite unexpected 20-6. Yogi Berra was the league's MVP for the second time. He had 22 home runs, 125 runs batted in, and only 29 strikeouts in 584 at-bats. He also hit .307 and slugged .488. A powerful young first baseman (and former Purdue football player) named Bill "Moose" Skowron proved an unexpected source of power, batting .340 in 87 games. Amazingly, the winningest Yankees team that Casey Stengel was ever to manage finished a distant 8 games behind Cleveland.

The Indians had the league's batting leader in second baseman Bobby Avila (.341) and the home run and RBI leader in Larry Doby (32, 126). They also got their usual powerhouse performance from Rosen (24 home runs, 102 RBI) at third. But it was pitching that brought the 1954 Indians one of the best won-lost records (111-43) in major league history, with Bob Lemon (23-7), Early Wynn (23-11), and Mike Garcia (19-8) pacing a staff that posted an amazing team ERA of 2.78 — almost one earned run a game lower than the league average. It was more than the Big Three: Bob Feller at age 35 staged a comeback with a 13-3 record, and a pair of 25-year-old relief pitchers, Don Mossi and Ray Narleski, combined for a 9-4 record with 20 saves. Like the 1953 Dodgers, the 1954 Indians seemed invincible and were odd-on favorites to beat their barely respectable World Series opponents.

CASEY STENGEL

Most people remember Casey Stengel the way he was as the first manager of New York Mets in the early 1960s; a loveable old curmudgeon, a promoter, a clown. He was "The Ol' Perfessor," a 70-year-old man who spoke his own language — Stengelese — which was kind of a nonsensical stream of consciousness. About one of his Mets players, Stengel once said, "He's only 19 years old, and in another year he's got a chance to be 20." His reasoning behind drafting a catcher as the first Met? "If you don't have a catcher, you'll have a lot of passed balls."

But Stengel was also one of the most respected and successful managers ever. During the 1950s, he directed the Yankees to eight pennants (failing only in 1954 and 1959) and six world championships (including a record five in a row), and won seven championships in ten years. Stengel is given credit for introducing spring instructional schools, making platooning a common practice, and increasing the role of late-inning relief pitchers.

As an active player from 1912 to 1925, Stengel was a speedy lefthanded hitting outfielder. In 1916, his game-winning home run off Pete Alexander helped Brooklyn win its first pennant. Stengel also compiled a World Series average of .393 and won two games of the 1923 World Series for the Giants with homers. He was elected to the Hall of Fame in 1966, a year after retiring as a manager.

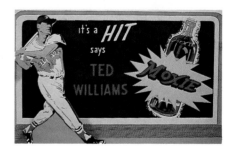

Indians slugger Larry Doby (top left) belted 32 home runs and drove in 127 runs for the Indians in 1954. Doby averaged 27 home runs, 96 runs scored, and 96 RBI from 1949 to '55. The Dodger bench congratulates Roy Campanella after a homer in 1954 (top right). Reds slugger Ted Kluszewski (bottom left) led the N.L. with 49 round-trippers and 141 RBI. Klu slammed 43 homers a year from 1953 to '56. Senators outfielder Roy Sievers (bottom middle) slammed 180 home runs from 1954 to '59. A 1950s Ted Williams Moxie counter display (bottom right).

Two Red Sox outfielders had good seasons. Ted Williams led the league with a .635 slugging average while popping 29 homers and hitting .345. Jackie Jensen led the league with 22 stolen bases while slugging 25 homers and notching 117 RBI. Minnie Minoso of the Chicago White Sox had a league-leading 304 total bases and 18 triples; he hit .320, drove in 116 runs, scored 119 runs, slugged .535, and doubled 29 times. Nellie Fox of Chicago and Detroit's Harvey Kuenn tied for the A.L. base-hit crown with 201. Mantle led the league with 129 runs scored. Baltimore's Bob Turley led the A.L. with 185 strikeouts, while Yankee Johnny Sain had the league-high 22 saves.

The Dodgers — or, specifically, owner Walter O'Malley — gave the Giants an unexpected boost when they fired manager Chuck Dressen, who, after winning consecutive pennants, was bold enough to ask for a three-year contract. The new manager, Walter Alston, would soon show his prowess. But for the 1954 season, the "wait till next year" boys were demoralized and their pitching in tatters with a 4.31 team ERA. For the Giants, on the other hand, it was an Alabama jubilee. Three native-born Alabamians made significant contributions: outfielder (and future Hall of Famer) Monte Irvin, who hit .262 with 19 homers and 64 RBI; pinch-hitter Dusty Rhodes, who hit .341 with 15 homers and 50 RBI; and outfielder Willie Mays. Mays was more like a forest fire than a spark: Returning from the Army for his first full season since 1951, Mays led the league in batting at .345, hit 41 home runs, won the Most Valuable Player award, and electrified the blasé New Yorkers with his dazzling circus catches in the Polo Grounds cavernous center field.

Giant Johnny Antonelli had a 2.30 ERA in '54.

It was, of course, precisely one of those catches for which the 1954 World Series and, in fact, the entire '54 season is best remembered: Mays' stab of a towering 460-foot shot off the bat of Cleveland's Vic Wertz during Game One, in what is probably the most talked about defensive play in baseball history. It's not often remembered that Rhodes capped Mays' performance with a tenth-inning three-run pinch-hit homer to win the game. Rhodes was a Giants Series hero; he hit .667, slugged two homers, drove in seven runs, and scored twice. The Indians, outhit by 64 points, were swept in four games by a team that had won only 97 games in the regular season. No baseball team had ever come so far to fall so fast as the 1954 Cleveland Indians.

The 1954 Giants team was a walking trivia book. It's possible that the 1954 Giants had more future managers (Whitey Lockman, Al Dark, Wes Westrum, Billy Gardner, Joe Amalfitano) than any other Series team. They also had a third-string catcher named Joe Garagiola, who was closing out his

ROBIN ROBERTS

Although Robin Roberts went to Michigan State on a basketball scholarship, he learned to pitch baseballs there. He was so successful that the Phillies signed him to a bonus contract in 1948. Without ever pitching in the minors, he won seven games as a rookie and 15 the next year, and was 20-11 with a 3.02 ERA in his third year in the majors. He would pitch 19 years in the big leagues, win 286 games, and lose 245. In the vast majority of those years he played for second-division teams, and in 44 of his losses he had no runs to work with.

In 1976, when Roberts was inducted into the Hall of Fame, he said, "I was never impressive as a pitcher. I just got batters out."

The truth was Roberts was very impressive. He had a flawless righthanded motion and threw a high, hard fastball (that shattered bats) and a biting curveball. He moved his pitches up and down, in and out. He was always more interested in wins than in preventing runs. As long as he got the victory, he didn't mind giving up a homer; in 1956, he gave up a league-leading 46 home runs.

Roberts pitched the Phillies to their first pennant in 35 years in 1950. His 20th win came on the last day of the season and prevented a playoff with the Dodgers, as he won 4-1 in ten innings. Roberts won 20 or more games six years in a row.

St. Louis' manager Eddie Stanky, left, and Cardinals outfielder Stan Musial (top left) contemplate a 1954 Real magazine article in which Musial was named "baseball's greatest player" by major league managers. Boston outfielder Ted Williams was the second choice. In 1954, Musial hit .330, with a league-leading 41 doubles and 120 runs while playing in 153 games. He also drove in 126 runs, slammed 35 homers, had a .607 slugging average, and had 103 bases on balls. Williams hit .345, with 23 doubles and 93 runs scored while playing in 117 games. He also drove in 89 runs, slammed 29 homers, had a league-leading .635 slugging average and 136 bases on balls. Willie Mays (bottom left) in 1954 batted .345, slugged .667, and had 119 runs scored and 110 RBI. Mays averaged 38 home runs and 103 RBI a season from 1954 to '59. The 1954 world champion New York Giants (top right) led the National League in fewest opponents' runs given up (550), shutouts (19), and ERA (3.09). Dodgers first baseman Gil Hodges (bottom right) hit .304 in 1954, with 42 home runs, 130 RBI, and 106 runs scored. Hodges averaged 30 home runs and 101 runs batted in from 1949 to 1959.

NEW YORK GIANTS
1954

THE 1950s

major league career with a fat World Series check. Garagiola was on two World Series teams in nine years: the '46 Cardinals and the '54 Giants. From 1947 to 1953, his childhood friend Yogi Berra played for six World Series teams. Due to repeated quirks of fate, they never got to play against each other. Garagiola would become a famous baseball humorist and television personality. Berra went to the Hall of Fame.

1955

For Brooklyn baseball fans, 1955 will always mean one thing: "Next year" had finally arrived. Not only was it next year, it was the only year that the Brooklyn Dodgers won the World Series.

It wouldn't have been the same, of course, if they hadn't been able to do it against the Yankees, and that looked doubtful at the beginning of the season. Casey Stengel was faced with the problem of finding a shortstop substitute for the aging Phil Rizzuto, as well as having to replace a pitching staff decimated by sore arms. Stengel handled the first dilemma by using the recently acquired Billy Hunter until Jerry Coleman could return from an injury. He solved the second by using 24-year-old "Bullet Bob" Turley to replace the retired Allie Reynolds and 25-year-old Don Larsen to play for sore-armed Eddie Lopat.

Once again the Indians got fine pitching: Lemon and Wynn were a combined 35-21, and a breathtaking 22-year-old lefthander named Herb Score won 16 games to cover for the ineffectiveness of Mike Garcia. But amazingly, Stengel was able to coax a major league-leading 3.23 ERA out of his ragtag pitching corps, and the Yanks finished 3 games ahead of Cleveland.

Diminutive White Sox second baseman Nellie Fox led a surprising Chicago surge (which resulted

Red Wally Post slugged 40 homers in 1955.

in 91 victories and a third-place finish) by hitting .311. Ted Williams hit .356 but lost the batting title because his 320 at-bats weren't enough to qualify (the honor went

---

DON LARSEN'S PERFECT WORLD SERIES GAME

On October 8, 1956, good luck and great pitching joined forces to turn a lifetime 30-40 pitcher into a baseball immortal.

The 1956 World Series was yet another rematch between the Dodgers and the Yankees. Brooklyn threatened to make it two straight titles when they won the first two games, but the Yankees won the next two games to tie the Series.

The Yankees sent righty Don Larsen, 11-5 on the season, to pitch the pivotal Game Five. With one out in the first, Larsen sent the count to 3-2 against Pee

Wee Reese before striking him out. It would be the only time that day Larsen would throw more than two balls to any batter. He retired Duke Snider to end the inning, and then sent the next 24 hitters back to the bench in order. Larsen needed only 97 pitches to hurl the first, and only, perfect game in Series history.

But Larsen also had good luck on his side. In the second inning, Jackie Robinson hit a line drive off third baseman Andy Carey's glove but was thrown out by shortstop Gil McDougald. In the fifth, Sandy Amoros hit a shot to right that curved just foul before reaching the seats. But the play of the Series came one batter before Amoros. Gil Hodges had belted a long drive to left center. Mickey Mantle got a great jump on the ball, raced full speed, and made a sensational backhand grab for the out.

Four innings later, Larsen struck out Dale Mitchell to become one of baseball's eternal heroes — and one of its luckiest.

Yogi Berra, left, and Don Larsen with a replica of the perfect-game glove.

Carl Furillo (top left) of the Dodgers had a .314 average, 27 homers, and 95 RBI in 1955. Detroit's Al Kaline (top right), age 20 in 1955, became the youngest player to ever win a batting crown. He batted .340, totaled 200 hits, and had a .546 slugging average, 321 total bases, 27 home runs, 102 RBI, and 24 doubles. Phillie Robin Roberts (bottom left) was 23-16 in 1955, with a league-leading 26 complete games and 305 innings pitched. The '55 Brooklyn Dodgers (bottom right) led the N.L. in runs scored (857), fewest runs allowed (650), batting average (.271), slugging average (.448), and ERA (3.68).

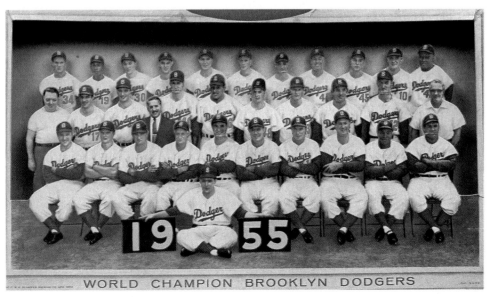

WORLD CHAMPION BROOKLYN DODGERS

THE 1950s

to Detroit's 20-year-old Al Kaline, whose .340 average made him the youngest man ever to win the crown). Former college football star Jackie Jensen drove in 116 runs for the Red Sox; Vic Power batted .319 and gave the lowly Kansas City Athletics one of the best fielding performances of any first baseman in the majors.

The Dodgers had no problems edging out anyone. They won 22 of their first 24 games for one of the fastest starts in N.L. history, and they never looked back. This was the year of the MVP catchers: Yankee Yogi Berra won his third award by hitting 27 home runs and driving in 108 runs, and Dodger Roy Campanella won his third with his best season, hitting 32 home runs and batting .318. In addition to their great catchers, the Dodgers

and Yankees had great center fielders: Mantle hit 37 home runs and batted .306, while Duke Snider hit .309 and led the N.L. in RBI with 136. Both teams had plenty of muscle — leading their leagues in home runs (171 for the Bronxers, 201 for the Brooklynites) — and outstanding pitching (Whitey Ford was 18-7 for the Yanks, while Don Newcombe went 20-6 for the Dodgers). Brooklyn seemed to have the edge on paper, but twice already in this decade they had the edge over the Yanks on paper, only to lose it on the field.

An exceptional young player began lighting up scoreboards around National League fields. Cubs shortstop Ernie Banks shattered all records for slugging at his position by hitting 44 home runs. Red Ted Kluszewski hit 47 home runs, and his teammate Wally Post hit 40. Richie Asburn hit a league-leading .338 for the fourth-place Phillies, while his teammate Robin Roberts won 23 games. Willie Mays proved his MVP in 1954 was no fluke by hitting 51 home runs and stealing 24 bases (one short of Bill Bruton's league-high total for Milwaukee). And the surprising second-place Braves featured a pair of hitters named Eddie Mathews

ERNIE BANKS

Ernie Banks was probably the most loved ballplayer — by teammates, fans, opponents, and the media — the game has ever known. Always smiling, always jovial no matter how poorly his team was playing or where the Cubs stood in the second division, Banks would greet you at Wrigley Field by saying, "What a great day for baseball. Let's play two today."

During his 19 years in the major leagues, seldom did a day pass in which Banks did not say, "I just love Wrigley Field and day baseball and the Chicago Cubs."

Banks was tall (6'1") and so skinny that he appeared much lighter than his listed weight of 180. He looked more like a player who would hit for average than one who hit home runs. But Ernie Banks, skinny body and all, was a power hitter. Five times he hit over 40 homers in a season. In two other seasons he hit over 30 homers, and in six others he hit over 20 homers. His top seasons at the plate came in 1958 (when he batted .313 and led the league in home runs with 47 and RBI with 129) and 1959 (when he batted .304, hit 45 homers and had a league-leading 143 RBI). In both 1958 and '59, Banks was named the Most Valuable Player in the league.

Banks hit 512 home runs in his career, and in 1977, the first year he was eligible for the Hall of Fame, he was voted in, on a great day for Mr. Cub, Ernie Banks.

Sandy Koufax was 28-27 from 1955 to '59.

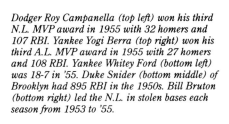

*Dodger Roy Campanella (top left) won his third
N.L. MVP award in 1955 with 32 homers and
107 RBI. Yankee Yogi Berra (top right) won his
third A.L. MVP award in 1955 with 27 homers
and 108 RBI. Yankee Whitey Ford (bottom left)
was 18-7 in '55. Duke Snider (bottom middle) of
Brooklyn had 895 RBI in the 1950s. Bill Bruton
(bottom right) led the N.L. in stolen bases each
season from 1953 to '55.*

THE 1950s

and Henry Aaron, who combined for 68 homers and 207 RBI.

It should have been a tip-off to Dodgers fans when the '55 World Series began badly. The Yankees won the first two games at New York — both of them tough, tight contests. The Dodgers rebounded to win three straight in Brooklyn, banging out 34 hits and 21 runs. Ford spun a four-hitter to cool off Dodgers bats in Game Six, and in the final game, one of the true classics in baseball history, an unknown outfielder named Sandy Amoros made a running grab of a Yogi Berra fly in left field to snuff out a potential New York rally in the sixth inning (Amoros' perfect relay to Pee Wee Reese doubled Gil McDougald off first base). Johnny Podres went all the way in a five-hit shutout, and the street cleaners of Brooklyn worked overtime for the rest of the week.

Podres won two games, pitching 18 innings with an ERA of 1.00. Snider slugged four homers, hit .320, and drove in seven runs. But in a Series and a year of great individual accomplishments, it was the ultimate success of Dem Bums that gave baseball its most significant memories of the year and the decade. Long before cable TV and advertising hype, the Brooklyn Dodgers were "America's Team." In a couple of short years, they would only be L.A.'s team.

1956

It had been a long time since the Yankees had been in the position of a team saying "wait till next year." In fact, the Yankees hadn't lost a World Series since 1942. With the memory of the 1955 World Series goading them, the Yankees won seven of their first eight games and, for the rest of the season, were never really pressed. Once again, Cleveland was put in the position of playing catch-up, and the Indians old pitching combo of Early Wynn and Bob Lemon chalked up 40 wins against just 23 losses. Young Herb Score took up the slack for the fading Mike Garcia by going 20-9. But longtime Indians sluggers Bobby Avila and Al Rosen could no longer

Mr. Cub Ernie Banks slugged 44 homers in '55.

1957 ALL-STAR VOTING FIASCO

Baseball fans now take voting for All-Star teams for granted, but between 1958 and 1970, they had lost the honor because of what Cincinnati fans did in 1957.

The National League starting lineup that year, as voted by the fans, included future Hall of Famers St. Louis' Stan Musial at first and Cincinnati's Frank Robinson in the outfield. But the rest of the starters were Robinson's Cincinnati teammates, members of a team that would finish fourth in 1957.

It seems that a Cincinnati newspaper printed ballots already filled out with Reds players' names and urged fans to mail them in. When the votes were counted, Cincinnati had placed (in addition to Robinson) second baseman Johnny Temple, shortstop Roy McMillan, third baseman Don Hoak, catcher Ed Bailey, and outfielders Wally Post and Gus Bell on the starting team. This left the N.L. with a pretty formidable bench, including Hank Aaron, Willie Mays, and Ernie Banks.

Not wanting to allow this travesty of baseball justice, commissioner Ford Frick ordered Post and Bell off the team, permitted Hoak and McMillan only one plate appearance, and got together with the baseball owners to abolish fan All-Star voting, which remained a province of the players for 13 years.

The N.L. eventually lost an exciting 6-5 game, their three-run rally falling a run short in the ninth. Maybe using the entire Reds' roster wasn't such a bad idea after all.

Johnny Temple, left, and Gus Bell were voted on the '57 N.L. All-Star team.

Berra

Amoros

Reese

Dodgers outfielder Sandy Amoros scores in the
1955 World Series (top) under New York's Yogi
Berra as the next Brooklyn batter, Pee Wee Reese,
coaches. Yankee Phil Rizzuto, sliding, turns
around to look at the ball (middle) after it hit him
in the '55 Series. Bob Lemon (bottom left) of the
Indians was 23-7 in '54 with a 2.72 ERA. He was
18-10 in 1955 with a 3.88 ERA. Lemon led the
American League in '54 and '56 with 21 complete
games each season. Dodger Johnny Podres
(bottom right) struck out ten batters, walked four,
and allowed 15 hits in 18 innings while winning
two games during the '55 World Series.

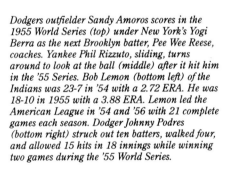

THE 1950s

supply their old sock. Although first baseman Vic Wertz hit 32 homers and drove in 106 runs, the Tribe scored 145 fewer runs than did the Yankees and finished 9 games off the pace.

Yankees pitching was, as usual, an iffy thing for most of the year, but as usual, it held up well enough to give the Yankees a pennant. Whitey Ford had perhaps his best season yet, winning 19 games and allowing less than two and a half runs per game. The rest of the staff was practically unknown before the season began: Johnny Kucks (18-9), Tom Sturdivant (16-8), and Don Larsen (11-5), pitchers who were never more than above average after the 1956 season, were brilliant that year.

But the real Yankees story wasn't the pitching; it was Mickey Charles Mantle, who turned in the finest season of any every-day player in the entire decade. In fact, most baseball experts classify Mantle's 1956 season as one of the five or six best ever by a major lea-

guer (a few say *the* best). To begin with, Mantle won the triple crown, leading the major leagues in home runs (52), batting (.353), and runs batted in (130). But amazing as it sounds, that was only the beginning. Mantle also led the majors in slugging — Ted Williams was second in the American League with a .605 and still finished 100 points behind Mantle — and walked 112 times. He led the league in runs scored (132) and had 188 base hits. Yogi Berra hit 30 homers and drove in 105 for the Yankees in '56, Bill "Moose" Skowron batted .308 with 23 home runs, and former Marine Hank Bauer hit 26 home runs. But all were overshadowed by Mantle's amazing performance.

There were six 20-game winners in the American League in 1956. In addition to the Tribe's 20-game-winning trio of Lemon, Score, and Wynn, Billy Pierce of the White Sox and Billy Hoeft of the Tigers won 20, and Frank Lary led the league with 21 wins. Williams finished second to Mantle in batting (.345) while slugging 24 homers. Al Kaline drove in 128 runs, hit .314, slugged 27 homers, and totaled 327 bases (second in the A.L.).

In the N.L., the Dodgers almost found themselves overshadowed by the performances of Cincinnati and Milwaukee. The Reds virtually had more power than the Yankees. Led by rookie Frank Robinson — who hit 38 home runs and led the league in

Willie Mays drove in 127 runs in 1955.

runs scored with 122 — Cincy had five players with 28 or more home runs and topped the majors with 221. The Braves had a formidable trio of sluggers themselves: Joe Adcock, Eddie Mathews, and Hank Aaron combined for 101 home runs, and Aaron won the batting crown as well. Adcock finished second in the National League to Cardinal Stan Musial in RBI, 109 to

LUIS APARICIO

Luis Ernesto Montiel Aparicio, Jr., was the son of Venezuela's greatest shortstop — and Little Luis, as he was called, went on to become one of the greatest shortstops in A.L. history.

In 1955, Aparicio was signed by the White Sox, who immediately traded their veteran Venezuelan shortstop, Chico Carrasquel, along with outfielder Jim Busby, to Cleveland for Larry Doby.

In 1956, Aparicio led the league in stolen bases and was such a marvel in the field that he was named Rookie of the Year. He proceeded to lead the league in steals for the next nine seasons in a row. Four times he stole over 50 bases: in 1959 (56), '60 (51), '61 (53), and '64 (57). Year after year, he and his double-play partner, second baseman Nellie Fox, turned more double plays than any other combination in the game.

Aparicio played 18 years in the majors, with the White Sox, the Orioles, and the Red Sox. He won a total of 23 fielding titles in that time, including nine Gold Gloves as the best defensive shortstop in the league. In 1959, when the "Go-Go Sox" won the pennant, they were led by Fox, who won the MVP award, and Aparicio, who finished second in the voting. Aparicio was also a key player when the Orioles won the world championship in 1966. He hit .276 and scored 97 runs.

Aparicio batted over .300 only once in his career and finished with a career mark of .262. But for his all-around play, he was inducted into the Hall of Fame in 1984.

Washington Senators slugger Roy Sievers (top left) led the American League in 1957 with 42 home runs and 114 RBI. "Squirrel" also batted .301, slugged .579, led the league with 331 total bases, and scored 99 runs. Cincinnati's Frank Robinson (top middle) was the N.L. Rookie of the Year in 1956. He hit .290, with 38 home runs, 122 runs scored, 83 RBI, a .558 slugging average, and 27 doubles. Robinson slugged 134 homers, notched 366 RBI, and tallied 415 runs scored from 1956 to '59. Billy Pierce (top right) led the A.L. in complete games each season from 1956 to '58 for the White Sox. Mickey Mantle (bottom left) is congratulated after hitting a home run. He had a triple crown season in '56 with a .353 batting average, 52 homers, and 130 RBI. He also led the league with a career-high .705 slugging percentage and a career-high 132 runs scored (he also scored 132 runs in '61). Mantle averaged 33 home runs and 97 RBI a season from 1952 to '59. Pittsburgh Pirates first baseman Dale Long (bottom right) slugs a home run in a record eighth straight game on May 28, 1956, against Dodgers righthander Carl Erskine. During the eight-game streak, Long had eight homers and batted .538 with 15 hits and 20 RBI. He ended the season with a .263 batting average, 27 home runs, and 91 runs batted in.

THE 1950s

103. Perhaps more important was the fact that the Braves had maybe the major league's best left-right pitching combo in Warren Spahn (20-11) and Lew Burdette (19-10).

The Braves probably had the best all-around team, but the Dodgers had been through pennant races before and didn't wilt down the stretch. Such Dodgers vets as 37-year-old Pee Wee Reese (.257 with 13 stolen bases), 32-year-old Gil Hodges (32 home runs), and 29-year-old Duke Snider (leading the league in home runs with 43 and slugging average at .598, and driving in 101 runs) got it together for one more big year. It was the same nucleus that had won four pennants in the previous

Yank Enos Slaughter homered in the '56 Series.

326

seven seasons. The Dodgers pitching staff wasn't overpowering, but ace Don Newcombe walked off with the N.L. MVP award and the first Cy Young Award. "Newk" was 27-7, leading the league in wins and winning percentage (.794); he pitched 268 innings, struck out 139, walked only 46, and compiled a 3.06 ERA.

The World Series started off brilliantly for the Dodgers, who won the first two games by outscoring the Yanks by eight runs. And as usual this spelled doom for Brooklyn. The Yankees won four of the next five to take the title. The most famous game of the Series was Don Larsen's perfect no-hit, no-run classic in Game Five at Yankee Stadium, which wasted a fine five-hit pitching performance from Sal Maglie. Mantle and Berra both belted three home runs apiece in the Series, but the Dodgers could have taken it all again if Newcombe had been able to continue his season-long magic. Newk lasted less than five innings in two starts, with a horrendous ERA of 21.21.

1957

The 1957 season now is regarded as a turning point in recent baseball history. The American League lost Bob Feller to retirement; the National League lost Jackie Robinson to retirement; and soon after the season was over, the city of New York was to lose two baseball teams to California. For the first time in six years, neither the Dodgers nor the Giants represented the National League in the World Series. Little did anyone suspect at the time that the team replacing them at the top, the Milwaukee Braves, was itself only a few years away from a second franchise shift.

In retrospect, the Braves' pennant and World Series triumph over the Yankees seemed inevitable. Many thought the Braves had been the league's best team the year before, and in 1957, they simply proved those people right. Certainly, they had baseball's best one-two punch in Aaron and Mathews, who would combine for 76 home runs and 226 RBI in '57. "Hammerin' Hank," the N.L.'s MVP, led the league in homers (44), RBI (132), and runs scored (118), while batting .322 and slugging .558. Milwaukee also had Cy

WHITEY FORD

The Yankees called up Whitey Ford from the farms during the 1950 season. Manager Casey Stengel used him in a relief role against Boston, and the cocky little lefthander promptly got bombed out of Fenway. That didn't hurt Ford's confidence at all. Before his first start in a night game at Yankee Stadium, he managed to scrounge up 73 passes from teammates and the front office for his friends and relatives from Queens, where he grew up. Ford won that game and eight others in succession to compile a 9-1 record. He then beat the Phillies 5-2 in Game Four of the '50 World Series to wrap up the championship.

Ford was particularly tough in the World Series. He holds the record with ten victories in the 11 Series he appeared in, as well as the records for most strikeouts and most innings pitched. In 1960, he threw two shutouts against the Pirates, then shut out the Reds in the '61 Series opener and pitched four more scoreless innings in that Series before being sidelined by injury. All told, his 32 consecutive shutout innings broke Babe Ruth's 45-year-old Series record of 29.

Ford was a 20-game winner only twice in his career, going 25-4 in 1961 and 24-7 in '63. But he was a consistent pitcher. In his 16 years with the Yankees, Ford won 236 games and lost only 106 for a winning percentage of .690 — the highest by any pitcher since 1900. In 1974, Ford was inducted into the Hall of Fame.

Yankees catcher Yogi Berra leaps into pitcher Don Larsen's arms (top right) after Larsen twirled his perfect game in the 1956 World Series. Larsen (top left), shown during the game, threw only 97 pitches and no more than 15 in any one inning. Dodger Don Newcombe (bottom left) won the first Cy Young Award in 1956 (and league MVP honors) by going 27-7 for a league-leading .794 winning percentage. He also struck out 139 batters and walked only 46 in 268 innings. "Newk" compiled a 126-73 record during the 1950s. Jackie Robinson (bottom right) retired after the 1956 season with a .311 career batting average.

THE 1950s

Young Award-winning pitcher Warren Spahn — a 21-game winner and the best National League lefthander of the decade. Righthanders Lew Burdette and Bob Buhl were 35-16, and Ernie Johnson was a bullpen star with a 7-3 record. Hard-nosed Johnny Logan was a fixture at shortstop, and 34-year-old veteran second baseman Red Schoendienst batted .310 in 93 games.

The St. Louis Cardinals, led by 36-year-old Stan Musial (who had a league-leading .351 average), kept pace till late summer, but the Milwaukee Braves ended up winning by a comfortable 8-game bulge. Ironically for the Brooklyn Dodgers, it was pitching, their one great weak spot when they were winning pennants, that turned out to be their greatest strength. The Dodgers had the National League's lowest team ERA, led by a bold 6'5" 20-year-old righthander named Don Drysdale, who won 17 games and allowed just 2.69 earned runs per game.

Willie Mays of the Giants finished second to Musial in batting average with a .333 mark, and Mays led the league with a .626 slugging percentage. He also scored 112 runs, hit 35 homers, and led the league with 38 stolen bases. Chicago's Ernie Banks tallied 102 RBI and 113 runs scored, and he finished second to Aaron in homers by slugging 43. Duke Snider of the Dodgers

Brave Warren Spahn (top) was 21-11 in '57 with 18 complete games. Tiger Jim Bunning was 20-8 in '57 with 267$^1/_3$ innings pitched.

slugged 40 homers, while Cardinal Del Ennis drove home 105 runs.

The Yankees' season was fairly similar to the Braves'. They also sustained a first-half challenge (by the Chicago White Sox) and won by 8 games. The primary question in most people's minds concerning the Yankees was not whether they'd win the pennant — most assumed they would — but whether or not Mickey Mantle could repeat his amazing '56 season. The answer was that American League pitchers had no intention of letting him try. They walked Mantle a league-leading 146 times. While the A.L. hurlers pitched away from his power, Mantle still managed 34 home runs in 474 at-bats, and his .365 average was the

HARVEY HADDIX'S PERFECT GAME LOSS

If there is one game considered to be the ultimate heartbreaker, it's the one Harvey Haddix pitched on May 26, 1959. The 33-year-old Pittsburgh Pirates lefthander threw a perfect game and lost.

It was a night game in Milwaukee, and Haddix almost begged out with a bad cold. But once he took the mound, he found his fastball-slider combination was baffling the Braves. After retiring the first 15 Milwaukee hitters in order, Haddix knew he had a no-hitter, but wasn't aware of the perfect game. When he nailed three straight batters in the eighth, Haddix was only three outs away from immortality. Only there was one problem; the Pirates hadn't scored any runs off of Lew Burdette.

Haddix took his perfect game into the tenth, 11th, and 12th innings, setting two records. He was the first pitcher ever to retire more than 27 in a row and the first to pitch a no-hitter past 11 innings. But the score was still 0-0. After the Bucs failed to reach Burdette in the 13th, Pirates manager Danny Murtaugh asked Haddix if he wanted to quit and

the pitcher said, "I want to win this thing."

The perfecto was finally ended when a throwing error put a runner on first. After an out, Hank Aaron was walked, bringing up Joe Adcock. On Haddix's second pitch, Adcock homered to end the no-hitter and the game. His masterpiece, though a loss, would be more famous than most no-hit victories.

Milwaukee's Hank Aaron (left) batted .322 with 44 homers, 132 RBI, and 118 runs scored in 1957 to win his only MVP award. He had 179 home runs, 617 RBI, and 612 runs scored from 1954 to '59. Stan Musial (bottom right) at the age of 36 won his last batting crown in 1957 by hitting .351. He also smacked 38 doubles, slugged 29 home runs, and drove 102 runs home. Musial batted .330 with 266 home runs, 972 RBI, and 356 doubles during the 1950s. Dodger Clem Labine (top right) had a 0.00 ERA in 12 innings in the '56 World Series.

THE 1950s

highest of his career. He led the league with 121 runs scored, stole 16 bases, and won his second straight MVP. The Yanks found a smart new shortstop in Tony Kubek, who batted .297, and Bill Skowron became a fixture at first base by batting .304 and driving in 88 runs. Tom Sturdivant helped take the sting out of Whitey Ford's time on the disabled list by winning 16 games. Don Larsen didn't exactly set the league on fire the year after his perfect game, but his 10-4 record was acceptable.

Ted Williams, at age 38, had one of his finest seasons, hitting .388 with 38 home runs and leading both leagues in slugging at .731. Mantle's '56 and Williams' '57 seasons stand as the best individual seasons any player enjoyed in the decade. Roy Sievers of last-

place Washington led the A.L. in homers with 42 and RBI with 114. Detroit's Jim Bunning and Chicago's Billy Pierce each won 20 games and were in the top five in strikeouts, innings pitched, and complete games.

The World Series was terrific, and because Milwaukee was participating, more fans in the West and Midwest followed the games on TV and radio than ever before. The first four games went back and forth. It was the Yanks' turn to win in Game Five, but Lew Burdette's seven-hit shutout gave the Braves a 3-2 Series lead. Bob Turley tied it up for the Yanks in Game Six, but Burdette, subbing for the ailing Spahn, came back with only two days rest to shut out the New Yorkers in the final game to complete what many feel was the finest pitching in Series history: three complete-game wins and only two runs allowed, all in eight days.

1958

There weren't too many "wait till next year's" for the old Yankees, and they made the most out of the ones they had. Never really pressed by the good-fielding, good-pitching White Sox, the Yanks won just 92 games — their lowest total

The 1958 New York Yankees, left to right, Mickey Mantle, Casey Stengel, Yogi Berra, and Hank Bauer, look relaxed as they go for their fourth pennant in a row and their ninth in ten years. The Yankees were 92-62 that season, 10 games better than second-place Chicago.

JIMMY PIERSALL

Jimmy Piersall was an outstanding baseball talent who played 17 years in the major leagues. Yet he never quite lived down the fact that some people regarded him as a little looney after he suffered a breakdown in 1951 and spent a year in a hospital. Piersall wrote a moving book about that experience, *Fear Strikes Out*, which also became a movie. Yet for years opponents rode Piersall, calling him "Gooney" and "Cuckoo."

Piersall was probably the top center fielder in the American League for some ten years. He was fast, acrobatic, sure-handed, and had a fine throwing arm. Larry Doby once said, "Jimmy's not crazy in the outfield."

In 1956, Piersall batted .293, scored 91 runs, drove in 87, and led the majors in doubles with 40. His best year at the plate was in 1961 when, playing for the Indians, he batted .322. After slumping for a couple of years, Piersall bounced back with the Angels in '64 to hit .314.

Piersall is probably best known for a stunt he pulled during a brief stay with the Mets. He was annoyed when teammate Duke Snider's 400th home run in the majors received little notice in the press. Not long thereafter when Piersall hit his 100th career home run he made sure it wasn't ignored by the media. He ran the bases backward. Although the Mets were losing almost every day, they had no sense of humor and released Piersall. But he was his own man to the end.

Boston Red Sox outfielder Ted Williams (top) turned in one of his greatest seasons in 1957 at the age of 38. "The Splendid Splinter" had a .388 batting average, a .731 slugging average, a .528 on-base percentage, and a 9.0 home run percentage, all which led the American League. He also finished in the top five in the league in home runs (38), total bases (307), and bases on balls (119). He won his last A.L. batting title in 1958 at the age of 39 by hitting .328. Williams averaged 29 homers, 92 runs batted in, 88 runs scored during his six full seasons from 1951 to 1958 to go along with a .345 batting average. Tony Kubek (bottom left) of the New York Yankees was named the Rookie of the Year for the 1957 American League. He hit .297 while playing the outfield, shortstop, third base, and second base. He averaged 22 doubles and 63 runs scored a season from 1957 to '59. Righthander Bob Friend (bottom right) of the Pittsburgh Pirates led the National League in wins in 1958. He had a 22-14 record with a 3.68 earned run average.

331

under Casey Stengel — and still won the pennant by a full 10 games. "Bullet" Bob Turley shot to the top of A.L. pitchers with 21 wins and 19 complete games, winning the Cy Young Award. Don Larsen, still flirting with respectability two years after his perfect game, was 9-6 with a 3.07 ERA. Ryne Duren led the league in saves with 20. The Yankees dominated the league in virtually every important category, led by Mantle's 42 home runs (eight Yankees had 11 or more). So evenly distributed was the Yankees' power that they led the league in RBI with 715, 50 more than the runner-up Red Sox, without having a single hitter collect more than 100.

Ted Williams won his sixth and final batting title for the Red Sox. Boston was also the beneficiary of Most Valuable Player Jackie Jensen's 35 homers and league-leading 122 RBI. Cleveland's Rocky Colavito led the American League in slugging average (.620) and was second in homers (41).

In the National League, the Braves overcame the loss of second baseman Red Schoendienst and won the pennant with relative ease. Spahn and Burdette both made the 20-win list, Mathews and Aaron both made the 30-homer list, and the Braves were never slowed. The Pirates — largely through the efforts of 22-game winner Bob Friend, wide-ranging second baseman Bill Mazeroski, and right fielder Roberto Clemente — finished a strong second. The Giants, newly settled in San Francisco and sporting an impressive rookie named Orlando Cepeda, finished a surprising third. But the Dodgers didn't immediately thrive in Los Angeles; they lost the services of Roy Campanella, who had an auto accident before the season began. The Dodgers ended up only 2 games ahead of the last-place Phillies.

Pirate Roberto Clemente hit .289 in 1958.

Phillie Richie Ashburn led the N.L. in batting, hits, triples, and walks. Ernie Banks earned the N.L. MVP award for leading the league in home runs, RBI, and slugging for the fifth-place Cubs. Willie Mays batted .347 and led the league in stolen bases and runs scored for the third-place Giants. Stan Musial batted .337 for the sixth-place Cardinals. It was a great year for first-rate performances by players on second-rate teams.

It's doubtful that two teams were ever more closely matched in a World Series than the 1958 Yankees and Braves. In fact, the similarities are amazing. Consider that both teams won 92 games and lost 62; both pitching staffs led their leagues in ERA (the Yanks with 3.22, the Braves with 3.21); the Yanks had 164 home runs and a .268 team average, while the Braves had 167 homers and batted .266; and the Yanks had a right-left pitching tandem in Turley and Ford that was 35-14, while the Braves had a right-left hitting pair in Aaron and Mathews that accounted for 61 home runs and 172 RBI.

In other words, there was no reason to believe that either team had an edge in the Series. But the

HERB SCORE

Many followers of baseball feel that Herb Score could have been one of the greatest pitchers in the history of the game.

Score was a 6'2", 185-pound lefthander who made it to the Indians in 1955. He threw the ball *hard.* He threw the ball so hard that it flew into a batter and exploded, hopping or dropping, the ball becoming nothing more than a blurry dart.

In his first season in the majors, Score's fires burned so brightly it seemed they could only soar higher. A pitcher who averages less than a hit given up per inning, combined with a strikeout per inning pitched, is usually successful in the majors. Score as a rookie gave up only 158 hits in 227 1/3 innings pitched. He also led the league in strikeouts with 245, which remains a rookie record. He was 16-10 with a 2.85 ERA.

In 1956, Score was even more overwhelming on the mound. He gave up only 162 hits in 249 1/3 innings. He struck out 263 batters. He had 16 complete games, five of them shutouts. He was 20-9 with a 2.53 ERA.

In the spring of 1957, the Red Sox offered an unheard-of $1 million for Score. The Indians turned down the offer, which they later may have regretted. Early that season Score was defenseless after throwing a pitch to Yankee Gil McDougald, who hit a liner that struck Score in the left eye. Sadly, Score was never a great pitcher again. Of his 55 wins in his seven-plus seasons, 36 came in those first two seasons.

Giants 1958 Rookie of the Year Orlando Cepeda, left, stands behind Willie Mays (top left) in a show of San Francisco's righthanded-hitting power. Cepeda led the N.L. in doubles with 38 and batted .312 with 25 homers and 96 RBI in '58. Mays led the National League with 121 runs scored and 31 stolen bases, while hitting a career-high .347 with 29 home runs and 96 runs batted in that season. He also had a career-high 208 base hits. Yankees hurler Bob Turley (top right) had 21 of his career 101 wins in 1958. Shortstop Ernie Banks (bottom left) of the Chicago Cubs led the 1958 National League with 47 home runs, 129 RBI, and a .614 slugging percentage. In 1959, Banks slugged 45 round-trippers and led the N.L. with a career-high 143 runs batted in. He averaged 109 runs batted in a season from 1954 to 1959. Lew Burdette (bottom right) secured three complete-game victories in the 1957 World Series, two of them shutouts. He ended with the Series with a 0.67 ERA. Burdette was 20-10 in 1958 for an N.L.-leading .667 winning percentage. He led the N.L. in 1959 with 21 wins and four shutouts.

THE 1950s

Braves did and didn't exploit it. They outhit the Yankees by 40 points but scored four fewer runs. The Yanks hit ten home runs to the Braves' three (Hank Bauer hit four, and Mantle had two). Lew Burdette, the hero of the previous year's Series, was completely ineffective, compiling a 5.64 ERA. Warren Spahn very nearly made up the difference by winning two out of three starts; he might have had three wins if his teammates hadn't made four errors when Spahn was locked in a duel with Art Ditmar and Duren in Game Six. The Yankees, after being down three games to one, came back to win the World Series in seven.

1959

The Yankees and the Dodgers were clearly the teams of the decade. The Yankees won eight pennants and six World Series, and the Dodgers won five pennants and two World Series, but the decade started without the Dodgers winning the pennant and ended without the Yankees in the Series.

The White Sox finally surged to the top of the league, but their league-low total of 97 home runs earned them the collective nick-name of "The Hitless Wonders." The Sox's strong suit was pitching: Early Wynn was again brilliant, winning 22 games and the Cy Young Award, and righthander Bob Shaw had his finest season at 18-6. A previously unknown reliever named Turk Lown went 9-2, saved 15 games, and had an ERA of 2.89. Chicago's 3.29 ERA was the lowest in either league. The Chicago attack wasn't entirely punchless; their home park, Comiskey, was simply too spacious for long-ball hitters, so the White Sox relied on walks (they tied for second), stolen bases (first), and the hit-and-run. Catcher Sherman Lollar led the team with 22 home runs, and outfielder Al Smith had 17 more. But the Chicago offense was typified by MVP second baseman Nellie Fox — a scrapper who batted .306 with 34 doubles — and his double-play partner Luis Aparicio. The flashy shortstop helped bring the running game back into baseball by leading the majors in stolen bases with 56.

Cleveland, powered by Rocky Colavito's 42 home runs and by a strong-armed shortstop named Woodie Held, gave the White Sox a race for most of the season, but the Indians faded down the stretch, finishing 5 games back. The Yankees, plagued by injuries to Bill Skowron and Gil McDougald, got the poorest performance ever from Mickey Mantle and Yogi Berra and were never in the race for the pennant for the first time in anyone's memory.

In truth, the Dodgers didn't hit a great deal better than the White Sox; the Dodgers had scored only 36 more runs than their American League opponents.

ChiSox shortstop Luis Aparicio led the A.L. with 56 stolen bases in 1959.

EDDIE MATHEWS

"Playing with the Hammer [Hank Aaron] definitely helped my career," says Eddie Mathews. "I usually batted behind Hank and if the pitcher got him out, he was so tired from the effort he might make a mistake with me."

Pitchers apparently made a lot of mistakes with the lefthanded-hitting Mathews, who had 512 homers in his career. Combined with Aaron's 755 total, their 1,267 tally is even more than the total of 1,207 achieved by Babe Ruth and Lou Gehrig.

Mathews is the only player to play for the Braves in Boston, Milwaukee, and Atlanta. He hit 25 homers as a rookie in 1952, then was joined by Aaron in Milwaukee in '53 and powered 47 shots over fences to win the home run crown. The next two years he also hit more than 40 homers and drove in more than 100 runs.

Mathews, a slick-fielding third baseman with a gun for an arm, also possessed a good eye at the plate. Four times he led the league in walks. In the '57 World Series in which the Braves beat the Yankees, Mathews walked eight times, and Aaron hit three homers to spark the Milwaukee offense. Mathews won Game Four in the bottom of the tenth inning with a two-run homer. In 1959, Mathews won his second homer title with 47.

All told, Mathews played 17 years in the majors, batted over .300 three times, and hit 40 or more home runs four times.

Dodgers hurler Don Drysdale (top left) led the N.L. with 242 strikeouts and four shutouts in 1959, while fashioning a 17-13 record. Yankees right fielder Hank Bauer (top right) had 147 home runs, 730 runs scored, and 600 RBI during the 1950s. Rocky Colavito (middle right) averaged 33 home runs, 99 RBI, and 83 runs scored from 1956 to 1966. Chicago White Sox second baseman Nellie Fox (bottom left) motivated the Pale Hose to a 94-60 record and an American League pennant in 1959. Fox batted .306 with 34 doubles and 84 runs scored. He also led A.L. second basemen in putouts, assists, and fielding average. Fox batted over .300 six times in his career, led the A.L. in base hits four times, and scored 80 or more runs in nine seasons. He led league second basemen in putouts ten times, assists and fielding average six times, and double plays five times. Sherm Lollar (bottom right) led the 1959 White Sox in home runs (22) and runs batted in (84).

THE 1950s

Like the Sox, the Dodgers led the league in stolen bases, though with comeback seasons from veterans Gil Hodges (25 home runs) and Duke Snider (23 home runs and a .308 average), they had a bit more power. They also had a lefthanded hitting outfielder named Wally Moon, who had an odd talent for hitting home runs the opposite way over the short left field fence at the L.A. Coliseum. The Dodgers couldn't match the Braves for muscle — Aaron and Mathews were again awesome, combining for 85 home runs and 237 RBI — but aside from of Spahn and Burdette (who won 42 games), the Braves couldn't quite match the Dodgers'

pitching arms. The Dodgers and Braves finished in a tie, and the Braves missed their third straight World Series when the Dodgers won two straight playoff games.

The Giants, who had shown such promise the year before, led for almost all of the 1959 season. But despite great years from Orlando Cepeda (.317 with 105 RBI), Willie Mays (34 homers and his fourth consecutive stolen base crown), and a powerful, sweet-swinging, lefthanded rookie slugger named Willie McCovey (who hit 13 home runs in just 192 at-bats), the Giants lost seven of their last eight games and finished 4 games out. The fifth-place Cubs finished 13 games back, but Ernie Banks won his second consecutive MVP with a .304 batting average, .596 slugging average, 45 home runs, and a league-leading 143 RBI.

The Sox shocked everyone by pounding out 11 runs to take the opener at Chicago, but that was the only offense they displayed in the Series. Except for a five-hit shutout by Shaw in Game Six (he beat a promising young lefthander named Sandy Koufax), the Sox were never really in the Series. The two teams

Cardinal Ken Boyer slammed 28 homers in 1959.

batted .261 and both had 19 RBI, but after Game One the Dodgers batted in 19 runs to the Sox' eight. Relief pitcher Larry Sherry was the hero, with two wins and an ERA of 0.71 in 12⅔ innings pitched.

But 1959 isn't remembered for anything that was done by either pennant winner so much as for two performances by pitchers on a fourth-place team. Pirate relief pitcher Elroy Face finished an amazing 18-1, and starter Harvey Haddix pitched the second most famous game of the decade (after Don Larsen's perfect Series game) when he pitched 12 perfect innings against Milwaukee — and lost.

RED BARBER, MEL ALLEN, RUSS HODGES

When the three New York teams decided in 1939 to regularly broadcast their games, they hired announcers who would be eternally linked with their respective clubs — Red Barber, the "Voice of Brooklyn"; Mel Allen, the "Voice of the Yankees";

and Russ Hodges, the "Voice of the Giants."

Hodges was Allen's radio partner in the 1940s before he became a Giants announcer in 1948. Hodges became immortalized in 1951 when he repeatedly exclaimed, "The Giants win the pennant! The Giants win the pennant!" after Bobby Thomson's home run.

Barber, known as "The Old Redhead," made two of the most

famous World Series calls in 1947. In Game Four, when Cookie Lavagetto broke up Bill Bevens' no-hitter in the ninth, Barber exclaimed, "Here comes the tying run, and here comes the winning run!" Barber also called Joe DiMaggio's blast to left that was caught by Al Gionfriddo preventing a tie of Game Six. "Back goes Gionfriddo, back...back...back...back...He makes a one-handed catch against the bullpen. Wow, ho, doctor."

In 1954, Barber left the Dodgers and joined Mel Allen in the Yankees broadcast booth. Like Barber, Allen was a southerner whose down-home drawl and easy style became popular with New York fans. Allen was famous for greeting listeners with "Hello there, everybody," and calling a home run with the famous phrase, "Going, going, gone."

Allen and Barber became the first two broadcasters honored in the Hall of Fame in 1978. Hodges joined them two years later.

Broadcasters, left to right, Russ Hodges, and Red Barber and Mel Allen.

In 1959, Roy Face (top left) of the Pittsburgh Pirates turned in one of the greatest seasons by a pitcher in baseball history. He was 18-1 for an all-time best .947 winning percentage. His 18 relief wins are also the most ever in a single season. Face also had ten saves in '59. Mickey Mantle scores (top right). He scored more than 100 runs nine times in his career, drove in more than 100 runs four times in his career, batted over .300 nine times in his career, and slugged over 30 homers nine times in his career. Harvey Kuenn (bottom left) led the American League with a .353 average in 1959 for the Tigers. Kuenn, who played both shortstop and outfielder for Detroit, averaged 192 base hits, 35 doubles, and 88 runs scored from 1953 to '59. Despite his fine play, Kuenn, the league's reigning batting champ, was traded before the 1960 season to Cleveland for Rocky Colavito, the league's reigning home run champ. Second baseman Bobby Richardson (bottom middle) of the New York Yankees batted .301 in 1959. Pittsburgh manager Danny Murtaugh, left, lends support to Harvey Haddix (bottom right) after Haddix pitched 12 perfect innings and lost the game in the 13th 1-0 on May 26, 1959.

THE 1960s

Baseball expanded in the 1960s — with more teams and more games — leading to a wider audience. Expansion brought new ballparks and Astroturf. There were more black and Hispanic players; by 1969, there were 13 blacks and Hispanics among the 18 .300 hitters.

Dodgers lefthander Sandy Koufax (page 338) averaged 273 strikeouts a season during his seven seasons in the 1960s. Mickey Mantle, left, and Roger Maris (page 339) drove in 665 runs combined from 1960 to '62.

THE 1960s

Baseball expanded in the 1960s. First, each league grew from eight teams to ten teams and then to 12 teams per league. The schedule increased from 154 to 162 games.

These changes led to a wider audience for baseball and for the network and local television that covered it, and revenues to most franchises increased appreciably. For example, local television brought the 16 major league clubs to a total net income of $2.3 million in 1950. By 1969, big league baseball had grown to 24 teams, and the net local TV revenues had leaped to $20.7 million.

Individuals and groups who wanted to start up teams in their cities had been petitioning the baseball owners for years, seeking permission to join the major leagues. But the big league owners turned down every request for expansion, until Branch Rickey and Bill Shea scared them with the

Harmon Killebrew had 393 homers in the 1960s.

announcement in 1959 that they were starting a Continental League to compete with the major leagues in two years. The new league was to have a club in New York — which lost the Dodgers and Giants after the 1957 season — as well as teams in Houston, Denver, Toronto, Minneapolis-St. Paul, Buffalo, Atlanta, and Dallas.

The major league owners did not want to compete with a new league for talent or television rights, so they agreed to allow expansion by adding two new teams in each league. New York was the plum market, with a huge potential audience of former Dodgers and Giants fans. As the American League already had a New York team in the Yankees, the National League got the new franchise; thus, the Mets were born in 1962, along with the N.L.'s other expansion team, the Houston Colt .45s.

The A.L. insisted on putting a team in Los Angeles, the nation's fastest-growing market, and the Angels were born in 1961. That year, Calvin Griffith pulled his Senators out of Washington, because he had lost many fans to the Baltimore Orioles, and moved to Bloomington, Minnesota. The team, drawing from the twin cities of Minneapolis-St. Paul, was named the Twins. Meanwhile, an expansion team, the new Senators, was installed in the nation's capital and played its games in the new D.C. Stadium. But this club fared no better than the former Senators, as the Orioles with their "Baby Birds" pitching staff continued to attract fans from the Washington area. In earlier years, the saying was that Washington "was first in war, first in peace and last in the American League." Washington finished last in the A.L. from 1961 to '63.

Expansion teams fared poorly in their early years because they were stocked with the most expendable players from the established teams. Fifteen players from each team's 40-man roster were made available to the new clubs for purchase at a fixed rate of $75,000 per man. The established teams not only picked up a nice chunk of money, they rid themselves of veterans who were on their way out and youngsters who tended to lack real skills or for whom they could find no place on the roster.

HANK AARON

Hank Aaron did not become baseball's all-time home run and RBI leader through bulging biceps or Ruthian girth. Aaron generated his power from snapping his strong, sinewy wrists the split second bat met ball. He was an extremely consistent power hitter with very good skills who piled up big numbers by staying injury-free his entire 23-year career.

"Hammerin' Henry" was just age 20 when he became the Milwaukee Braves' starting right fielder in 1954. In '56, he won the N.L. batting title. He was MVP in 1957, leading the league in homers (44, his first of eight 40-plus homer seasons), runs, and RBI. He hit a career-high .355 to win the batting crown in '59.

Aaron was underrated as an all-around player. He won the Gold Glove in 1958, '59, and '60 and between 1960 and '68, he averaged 22 stolen bases a season. He led the league in homers and RBI three times and scored over 100 runs every year of the decade except one. Just into his 30s in 1966, Aaron's power game was given a boost when the Braves moved to Atlanta, which had a great park for sluggers. At age 39 in 1973, he smacked 40 homers.

Aaron retired in '76 with numbers that take up almost a whole page of the *Baseball Encyclopedia*. Besides the all-time homer and RBI records, he is second in runs, third in games and hits, and eighth in doubles. Aaron is the only man in baseball history to drive in 1,000 runs on homers and 1,000 runs on other hits.

Bob Gibson (top) had 164 wins and 105 losses with a 2.74 ERA during the 1960s. The early 1960s Yankees power hitters (middle) were the best in baseball: left to right, Roger Maris, Yogi Berra, Mickey Mantle, Elston Howard, Moose Skowron, and Johnny Blanchard. Maris had 133 homers in three years; Berra hit 22 homers in 395 at-bats in '61; Mantle notched 94 homers in '60 and '61; Howard had 21 homers in both 1961 and '62; Skowron had 77 homers from 1960 to '62; and Blanchard had 21 homers in only 243 at-bats in '61. Maury Wills (bottom) led the N.L. in stolen bases every season from 1960 to '65.

THE 1960s

While the Senators and Twins played in new stadiums in 1961, the Los Angeles Angels played their maiden season in a ramshackle minor league ballpark. Its short outfield fences resulted in five Angels hitters — Steve Bilko, Ken Hunt, Leon Wagner, Earl Averill, and Lee Thomas — who had 20 or more home runs for the season. The Angels surprised everyone by winning 70 games and finishing eighth, only 1½ games behind the Twins, who were led by Harmon Killebrew and his 46 home runs. In 1962, the Angels became tenants of Walter O'Malley in brand new Dodger Stadium. Their home run production decreased by some 50, but they won 86 games to become a startlingly successful expansion team.

N.L. expansion gave America the New York Mets in 1962 — managed by the irrepressible Casey Stengel — who played in the decrepit Polo Grounds that had been the site of former New York Giants heroics. The Mets set a record for incompetence that prompted newspaper columnist Jimmy Breslin to write the book *Can't Anyone Here Play This Game?* as their won-lost record read 40-120. Yet the Mets truly were amazing when they moved into Shea Stadium — named for Bill Shea, the man who had fought hard to bring another ballclub into New York — for they outdrew the Yankees.

The Houston Colt .45s played their first few years in a minor league park, then, in 1965, changed their name to the Astros — in keeping with the space program headquartered in Houston — and moved into the Astrodome, baseball's first stadium with a roof over its head. It featured luxurious suites set up just under the roof, and the facility was such a so-called "wonder of the world" that millions of people paid just to tour the place. Unfortunately, though, the grass that had been planted in the Astrodome's playing field could not survive. That produced one of the greatest curses ever perpetrated on sports (according to many athletes who have played on it) — Astro-turf, and all of the other artificial playing surfaces that have followed. Initially, the surfaces consisted of a layer of macadam covered by a plastic carpet, which was not unlike concrete. Batted balls caromed off it like missiles, picking up topspin and speed as they bounced. Infielders had to play deeper, and outfielders had to be careful about charging too hard on any ball hit in front of them, since the ball might bounce 20 feet over their heads.

In addition to the Senators' shift to Minnesota, two other teams moved to new locales during the 1960s. The Braves had been in the city of Milwaukee only 13 years, after spending decades in Boston,

Hoyt Wilhelm saved 27 and won 12 games in '64.

when they accepted an offer they couldn't refuse to move to Atlanta in 1966. They were provided with a new stadium, a long-term, low-rental arrangement, and a generous television contract. Milwaukee promptly sued the American League for approving the move.

TED WILLIAMS' LAST AT-BAT

Before the 1960 season, Ted Williams decided it would be his last year as a player. Coming off a injury-plagued 1959, during which he batted under .300 for the first time in his career, Williams volunteered to take a $35,000 pay cut.

Despite constant pain, "The Splendid Splinter" batted .316, with 72 RBI in 113 games. Going into his last game in Boston, he had smacked 28 homers, giving him 520 lifetime. Williams always had a love-hate relationship with the fans and media in Boston, but before his last game he was honored at home plate with speeches and gifts, and his number "9" was retired. There were 10,454 fans packed into Fenway Park. Williams walked his first time up. In his next two at-bats, Williams hit two long flies to right center that were held up in the heavy wind and caught, the second one against the 380 sign.

When Williams came up in the eighth inning, he knew it would be his last at-bat in baseball. As soon as he reached the on-deck circle, everyone in Fenway stood and cheered. On a one-one pitch, Jack Fisher threw a fastball and again Williams hit a long one to right center. This time, however, it fought the wind and landed in the Sox bullpen. As he made his 521st and last home run trot, the fans were going wild. But Williams wouldn't tip his cap. "I had a really warm feeling," he said, "but it just wouldn't have been me."

*Bobby Richardson (top left) was the Yankees'
second baseman for ten years from 1957 to '66.
He led the American League with 209 base hits in
1962. That year he had career highs in batting
average (.302), slugging average (.406), homers
(eight), runs scored (99), and RBI (59). In the
1960 World Series, Richardson was on fire. He hit
.367, slugged .667, scored eight runs, and drove
in 12 runs. He ended his 12-year career with a
lifetime .266 average. Dick Stuart (top right)
averaged 29 homers a year from 1959 to '65. Bob
Friend (bottom left) was 18-14 in 1962 and led
the N.L. in shutouts with five. Brooks Robinson,
left, and Clete Boyer (bottom right) were two
outstanding American League third basemen
during the 1960s. Robinson plied his trade in
Baltimore for 23 years, and while not known as a
slugger, he averaged 19 homers a season. Boyer
was a good-fielding, solid-hitting player for the
Yankees for seven seasons.*

THE 1960s

Charlie Finley, who owned the Kansas City Athletics, was also angry because he had been planning to move his team to Atlanta. The A's, of course, had played for decades in Philadelphia, until 1955, when they scurried to Kansas City. They would join the Braves in becoming baseball's ping-pong-ball franchises, as Finley began negotiating with Oakland, CA, which was building a new stadium and offering a sweet deal to entice the A's to go west. The A.L. owners refused to permit the move until Finley threatened to sue his fellow owners for the right to take his team wherever he wished. Finley almost had to move after he alienated fans in Kansas City, and when the A.L. granted him permission, he opened for business in Oakland in 1968.

Fearing an antitrust action might be on the horizon from the jilted cities, baseball promised that expansion teams would be placed in Milwaukee and Kansas City. In 1969, Kansas City got another team, and Seattle got one in the American League too. The National League fielded new teams in San Diego and Montreal. Both leagues split into six-team divisions, the winners of which would meet in a three-out-of-five postseason playoff to determine the pennant winner.

While the folks in Kansas City were overjoyed to have a ballclub again, Milwaukeeans were disappointed. But the Seattle franchise went bankrupt, and the A.L. had to take over the Pilots before the '69 season's end. A year later, the team shifted to Milwaukee, which naturally precipitated a lawsuit from Seattle, so the A.L. promised that in its next expansion that city would again have a baseball team.

Expansion and the shifting of franchises brought with it the building of ten new ballparks in the 1960s, seven in the National League. All of them had virtually the same outfield dimensions, as the owners had agreed on in 1958, and they all tended to look alike. Dodger Stadium in Chavez Ravine was the lone new stadium that could be called beautiful.

In 1964, Ford Frick retired as commissioner, and for months there was speculation as to who would replace him. When the new commissioner was finally announced in 1965, it was someone whose name had not been mentioned, a man of whom seemingly no one in baseball had ever heard. He was William "Spike" Eckert, a former Army general. "My God," said New York writer Larry Fox when the general was introduced at a press conference, "they've named the Unknown Soldier." Eckert lasted only three years in the job and was replaced in 1969 by Wall Street lawyer Bowie Kuhn, who would become a strong voice for the owners.

Sluggers, from left, Harmon Killebrew, Mickey Mantle, Jim Lemon, and Roger Maris.

FRANK ROBINSON

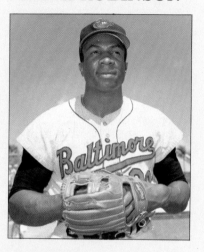

It now seems that Frank Robinson was destined for making history from the moment he put on a big league uniform.

Breaking in with the Cincinnati Reds in 1956, the righthanded-hitting Robinson was the National League's Rookie of the Year, tying the rookie home run record with 38 and scoring a league-leading 122 runs. Over his next nine seasons with Cincy, "Robby" was among the N.L.'s most consistent run producers, averaging 32 homers, 102 runs, and 102 RBI, batting over .300 five times, and leading the league in slugging three times. He was the league MVP when the Reds won the pennant in 1961.

But after the 1965 season, Cincinnati traded Robby to the Orioles. In his first A.L. season, Robinson won the triple crown, led the league in runs and slugging, became the only player ever to win the MVP in both leagues, and hit two home runs in the Orioles four-game World Series sweep of the Dodgers.

Robby was the Orioles inspirational leader until 1971 and then played for the Dodgers, the Angels, and the Indians, averaging 24 homers in three years while he was in his late 30s. Robinson became the only player to hit more than 200 homers in both leagues and holds the record for belting home runs in the most ballparks (33).

In 1975, the Indians signed him as their player/manager, making him the first black manager in baseball. Robinson is fourth on the all-time list in homers (586) and tenth in runs (1,829), and made the Hall of Fame in 1982.

Hank Aaron (top left) of the Braves during the decade smacked 40 or more home runs in five seasons and more than 30 homers in eight seasons. Harmon Killebrew (top right) of the Twins averaged 101 runs batted in and 86 runs scored during the 1960s. His 16.06 walks per 100 at-bats is 17th best all time. The Cleveland Indians outfield (middle left) of, left to right, Leon Wagner, Vic Davalillo, and Rocky Colavito combined for 250 runs scored and 227 RBI in 1965. Dodgers hurlers (bottom left) Don Drysdale, left, and Johnny Podres combined for 40 wins in 1962. Brooks Robinson (bottom right) led American League third basemen in fielding percentage nine out of ten seasons during the decade.

THE 1960s

It wasn't until 1966 that the players hired a full-time executive director of the Major League Baseball Players' Association, Marvin Miller, who had spent most of his 48 years working as a labor economist for the United Steelworkers of America. Miller proved himself to be a labor genius the next year when he negotiated a basic agreement between the owners and the association. His key victories were getting the owners to agree to contribute $4.5 million a year to the player pension fund and to increase the minimum salary — which for a decade had held at $7,000 — to $10,000. When this agreement expired two years later, Miller's negotiations raised the minimum salary to $13,500 and got the owners to permit players to be represented in contract talks by agents, who would push salaries much higher in the coming years. Another key concession in this agreement was the introduction of outside arbitrators to settle salary disputes between players and owners. Arbitration would become the means by which players scored some of their biggest salary increases.

It seems unbelievable, but the average salary of a major league player in 1964 was reportedly only $14,800 and in 1967 was only $21,000. In 1966, there were only three players who earned $100,000 salaries: Mickey Mantle, Willie Mays, and Sandy Koufax. Koufax had to stage a joint holdout with teammate Don Drysdale to get a salary increase. In '65, he had earned $70,000, while posting a 26-8 record that included eight shutouts and an astonishing 382 strikeouts. Drysdale had seven shutouts among his 23 victories.

JACKIE JENSEN
Outfield — Boston Red Sox

Jackie Jensen hit .263 in '61, his last year.

They held out in the spring, asking for salaries of $175,000 apiece, and had lawyer J. William Hayes negotiate for them. When Dodgers general manager Buzzie Bavasi mentioned the reserve clause, Hayes said that if he invoked it there would be a lawsuit in federal court. Koufax reportedly signed for $130,000 and Drysdale for $110,000. Owners feared the courts would find the reserve clause — which said that teams owned players forever — illegal.

1960 WORLD SERIES – GAME SEVEN

In the 1960 World Series, the Pittsburgh Pirates, a team which hadn't won a pennant for 33 years, faced the mighty New York Yankees, a team that had won ten pennants in 12 seasons. Everything pointed to the Yankees having the edge, and they did. The Yankees outhit the Pirates (91 to 60), outscored them (55 to 27), and outpitched them (3.54 ERA to 7.11). When the Yankees won Game Six 12-0 to tie the Series, it was their third win in which they scored ten or more runs. Pittsburgh had won its three games by the relatively sedate scores of 6-4, 3-2, and 5-2.

But on October 13 in Pittsburgh, the Bucs opened Game Seven with four runs in the first two innings. The Yanks fought back to regain the lead in the sixth inning on a Yogi Berra three-run homer and added two more in the eighth to go up 7-4.

The Pirates rallied for five runs in the bottom of the eighth, highlighted by Hal Smith's three-run blast. Down by two in their last at-bat, the Yankees fought back to tie it 9-9.

In the bottom of the ninth, the Yanks' Ralph Terry would first pitch to Bill Mazeroski. Maz, considered the game's best defensive second baseman, was having a good offensive Series. He took a ball from Terry, then rocketed the next pitch into the left field stands for a World Series winning homer. Fans poured out of the stands to run with Mazeroski around the bases and deliriously happy teammates mobbed Maz at home plate.

A crowd awaits Bill Mazeroski after his Series-winning homer in 1960.

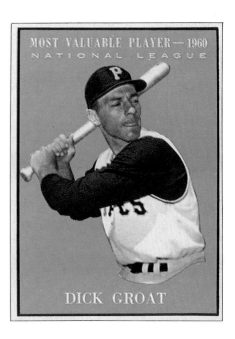

Whitey Ford (top left) was a 20-game winner in both 1961 and 1963, leading the A.L. in innings pitched in each of those seasons. Jim Lemon (top middle) slugged a career-high 38 home runs in 1960 for the Washington Senators. Pittsburgh shortstop Dick Groat (top right) was the N.L.'s MVP in 1960. Groat was a two-sport All-American in baseball and basketball at Duke, and when he graduated, he became a two-sport professional. He played 26 games with Fort Wayne of the NBA in 1952-53, averaging 11.9 points a game. Sandy Koufax (bottom) for five straight years from 1962 to '66 led the N.L. in ERA, and he won three Cy Young awards and an MVP trophy in that time.

THE 1960s

On the field in the 1960s, there were some truly remarkable performances, most notably Roger Maris' 61 home runs in 1961 (which broke the record set by Babe Ruth in 1927), Denny McLain's 31 victories in 1968 (which made him the first pitcher to win 30 games or more in the majors since Dizzy Dean did so back in 1934), and the tremendous contributions made by black and Hispanic players, as more and more minorities arrived in the major leagues during this decade and excelled.

From 1947 to 1970, black players led the league in batting 17 times, won the home run crown ten times, won the MVP award 19 times, won a triple crown, had 20 20-game-winning pitchers, and set an all-time stolen-base record when Maury Wills of the Dodgers filched 104 in 1962. In 1969, 13 of the 18 players who hit for an average of .300 or better were either black or Hispanic.

Going into the 1961 season, Roger Maris did not seem the likely candidate to approach Ruth's home run record — Mickey Mantle did. After all, Mantle had hit 52 home runs in '56. Maris' lefthanded stroke, in which he pulled most pitches down the line, was ideally suited to Yankee Stadium's nearby right field stands. But in his first year in New York (1960), Maris had won the MVP award by driving in a league-leading 112 runs while hitting 39 home runs to Mantle's 40. The 39 homers were a career high for Maris.

Both Mantle and Maris figured to have a shot at increasing their home run totals because expansion had diluted the pitching in the A.L. and the schedule had been increased by eight games. They both got off to a fine start, and by the end of May, Mantle had hit 14 home runs and Maris, 12.

During the next two months the pair really got hot, as Mantle banged out 25 more home runs and Maris topped him, hitting 28 more.

As both Maris and Mantle were on a pace to break Babe Ruth's record of 60 homers hit 34 years earlier, the media began to swarm over them for interviews. Commissioner Ford Frick announced that if the record were broken beyond the 154-game schedule that Ruth had played, there would be an asterisk next to it in the record books.

Mantle was used to the pressures in New York generated by the media and fans. But Maris had never felt such pressure, as he moved into September with 51 home runs to Mantle's 48, and it seemed as though Maris could never be left alone at the ballpark. He grew surly with the press and uncommunicative, and his crew-cut hair began to fall out in tufts under the nervous tension.

Roger Maris watches as he ties Babe Ruth's single-season mark of 60 home runs, getting the dinger off Oriole Jack Fisher.

AL KALINE

To a generation of fans, Al Kaline *was* the Detroit Tigers. He played 22 years for the Tigers and made the Hall of Fame the first year he was eligible (1980). He led the American League in hits and batting in 1955 (the youngest player in history to win the title), in slugging in 1958, in doubles in 1961, and in pinch hits in 1972.

From 1954 to 1974, Kaline was one of baseball's most consistent and reliable players (much like another Tigers immortal, Mickey Cochrane). Over that 21-year period, Kaline averaged 133 games played, 143 hits, 77 runs, and 75 RBI. He hit 20 or more homers nine times and batted over .300 nine times. And he had no peer as a right fielder. He won ten Gold Glove awards and led the league in assists and fielding percentage twice, playing an errorless outfield in 1971. Kaline had 200 hits in 1955, with 27 homers, 121 runs scored, and 102 RBI. In 1956, he had 27 homers, 128 RBI, 96 runs scored, and a .314 average. In 1966, he slugged 29 homers, with 88 RBI and a .534 slugging average. In 1967, he had 25 homers and a .308 batting average.

Kaline's only World Series came in 1968, and he led the Tigers to a seven-game victory over St. Louis by batting .379, with two homers and eight RBI. Kaline ranks 15th on the all-time hit list and is one of only 16 players to get 3,000 hits (3,007). He also had 399 career homers, 1,622 runs scored, 1,583 RBI, and a .297 average.

Roger Maris launches his 60th homer (top) into the right field stands in
Yankee Stadium in game number 158 on September 26, 1961. The catcher is
Gus Triandos and the umpire is Bill Kinnamon. Center fielder Jimmy Piersall
of the Cleveland Indians boots a Yankees fan (bottom left and right) who ran
onto the field and struck Piersall during a 1961 game. Cleveland second
baseman Johnny Temple (#16) runs to Piersall's aid.

THE 1960s

Mantle was knocked out of the home run race by troubling leg injuries and an infection. But Mantle still hit a career-high 54 home runs in '61. In the schedule's 154th game, Maris hit homer number 59, but he didn't connect with number 60 until five days later, tying Ruth's total with an asterisk. Maris went into the last game of the season looking for number 61, and he found it, hitting a blast into the right field stands at Yankee Stadium. He was happy with his accomplishment, asterisk and all. For the first time in months, Roger Maris could smile.

Meanwhile, the Yankees, who had won the pennant in 1960, were winning another one. They would extend their streak to five pennants in a row through 1964. Then the Yankees, who had dynasties that won a number of pennants from the 1920s to the 1960s, would fall on hard times. In fact, the Yankees would not win another pennant for 12 years, until 1976. During many of those years the once-proud Yankees were relegated to the second division.

No American League team managed to follow the Yankees by winning back-to-back pennants through the 1960s. But the Baltimore Orioles had been threatening for several years, building a ballclub with potential, and when they traded for Frank Robinson in 1966, they had the man who would lead them to pennants that season, in 1969, and in the first two years of the 1970s. Robinson was a true superstar, the only man to win the MVP award in both the N.L. and the A.L. Cincinnati general manager Bill DeWitt said Robinson was "an old 30" when he traded him from the Reds in '66. So all old Frank did was win the triple crown and earn MVP honors in the Orioles' World Series victory over the Dodgers.

Warren Spahn won 96 games from 1960 to '65.

In the National League, the Los Angeles Dodgers had a dynasty led by Sandy Koufax and Don Drysdale, and a manager in Walter Alston who knew how to juggle his troops and eke out runs on generally weak-hitting teams. The Dodgers won pennants in 1963, '65, and '66. The St. Louis Cardinals were the other power of the 1960s. With a pitching staff led by hard-throwing righthander Bob Gibson and an offense led by Lou Brock and Ken Boyer, the Cardinals won pennants in 1964, '67, and '68.

Pitching tended to dominate hitters after the strike zone was expanded in 1963, the authorities feeling that baseball was being overwhelmed by offense. Maris and Mantle's combining for 115 home runs in '61 — which passed the 107 hit by Ruth and Lou Gehrig in '27 — was no small factor in the owners' decision. The strike zone had been defined from the armpits to the knees, with the top of the knees being generally the lowest point where strikes were called. The new rule defined the strike zone from the shoulders to the bottom of the knees, giving the pitchers much more room to operate on batters high and low.

But what was supposed to be a blow against home runs — which decreased by 10 percent in '63 —

SANDY KOUFAX

Sandy Koufax was a manager's dream. He was young, lefthanded, and could throw fastballs past anybody. But he was also wild and he walked people. He hadn't yet come to grips with all his ability.

Brooklyn had signed the hometown boy in 1954. Koufax was only 19, and a rule on bonus players forced the Dodgers to keep Koufax on the big club. So instead of learning his craft in the minors, he sat in the bullpen and became just another mediocre starter.

After going 8-13 in 1960, Koufax nearly quit. Then Dodgers catcher Norm Sherry and scout Kenny Meyers noticed that Koufax's motion obscured his vision. With Sherry's guidance, Koufax altered his delivery. Over the next six seasons, Koufax was the most dominating pitcher ever. His record was 129-47, an amazing .733 winning percentage. He won the Cy Young Award in 1963, '65, and '66, each year leading the N.L. in wins, ERA, and strikeouts. He won two other ERA titles and led the league in shutouts three times. He retired with records of 382 strikeouts in 1965 and four no-hitters. His final no-hitter was a perfect game.

From 1964 to '66, however, Koufax was in constant pain from an increasingly arthritic left elbow. He always would pack his arm in ice after games and avoid throwing between starts. But by the end of '66, doctors warned that continued pitching could cost him use of the arm. Having not lost the use of his head, Koufax retired. Six years later he was in the Hall of Fame.

Big Don Drysdale (top left) of the Los Angeles Dodgers won the National League's Cy Young Award in 1962 when he won a league-high 25 games. Drysdale began his career with Brooklyn in 1956 and ended it with Los Angeles in 1969, when a bad shoulder forced him out of the game at age 33. During that time, he amassed 209 wins, 167 complete games, 49 shutouts, and 2,486 strikeouts. He held the record for consecutive scoreless innings pitched with 58 until Orel Hershiser broke it in 1988. Roberto Clemente (top right) was an offensive force who hit .328 during the 1960s with 916 runs scored and 862 RBI. Clemente also had the strongest and most accurate outfield arm in the game (maybe of all time). Frank Robinson (bottom) ended his 21-year career with a .294 lifetime batting average, 586 home runs, 1,812 runs batted in, and 1,829 runs scored.

THE 1960s

also reduced batting averages by 12 points. In 1968, known as "The Year of the Pitcher," Carl Yastrzemski won the A.L batting title with the lowest average ever at .301, Dennis McLain won 31 games, Bob Gibson posted a 1.12 earned run average, and Don Drysdale threw 58 consecutive innings of scoreless ball. So the owners decided in 1969 to bring the strike zone back to the area over the plate between the armpits and the knees. Another rule in '69 lowered the height of the pitcher's mound, which was also designed to give hitters a break. It's interesting that, during the years when the pitchers were supposed to have an advantage, Robinson won the triple crown and Yastrzemski won it the following year. No player in major league baseball has won the triple crown since 1967.

1960

The '59 season had been a year of discontent for Yankees general manager George Weiss, who saw his ballclub, which had played in the World Series the previous fall, in last place on May 29. While the '59 Yankees managed to climb out of the second division, they finished 15 games out of first. That winter, Weiss made a big trade with the ever-friendly Kansas City A's, sending them Hank Bauer, Norm Siebern, Don Larsen, and Marv Throneberry for a 25-year-old outfielder named Roger Maris. It was one of the best player acquisitions the Yankees had made since they purchased Babe Ruth from the Red Sox.

Maris had hit only 16 home runs the year before, but the left-handed swinger was a dead pull hitter, and right field in Yankee Stadium was a mere 301 feet down the line. In 1960, he hit 39 home runs, drove in 112 runs, and was named MVP. He also proved to be an

excellent outfielder with a very strong arm. Mickey Mantle, despite a pair of aching knees, contributed 40 home runs and had 94 RBI. First baseman Bill Skowron had 26 home runs, 91 RBI, and a .309 average. Catcher Yogi Berra hit 15 home runs, while shortstop Tony Kubek and third baseman Clete Boyer chipped in with 14 apiece.

The Yankees led the league in home runs with 193; they needed them as the pitching staff was anything but outstanding. Art Ditmar's 15 wins topped the staff. Even Whitey Ford won only 12 of 21 decisions. Yet the Yankees had enough, after a slow start, to move into the pennant race with the White Sox and Orioles in August. Then they closed the season with a blast, winning their last 15 games to finish 8 games ahead of the Orioles.

In the National League, the Pirates had to hold off threats from the Braves and Cardinals, but they led the league most of the season and won the pennant by 7 games.

Mickey Mantle of the Yankees averaged 28 home runs a season in the nine seasons that he played during the 1960s.

BROOKS ROBINSON

During his 23 years with the Orioles, Brooks Robinson was a pretty good hitter. He batted .300 twice and won an MVP in 1964 when he hit 28 homers and led the A.L. with 118 RBI. He was a terrific postseason hitter, batting .500 or better in two league play-offs (1969 and '70) and .300 or higher in two World Series (1970 and '71). While Robinson's lifetime offensive statistics — 2,848 hits, 268 home runs, and .267 average — were good, he is an immortal because he was the greatest fielding third baseman in baseball history.

Robinson was incredibly quick and had lightning reflexes at the hot corner. He caught line drives diving to his left, he backhanded unreachable balls down the line, he hustled in for slow rollers and nailed even the quickest runners with off-balance throws. Robinson won 16 straight Gold Gloves, and holds the third base records in games played, fielding percentage (.971), assists, putouts, chances, and double plays.

Robinson conducted a five-game fielding clinic against Cincinnati and was the MVP of the 1970 World Series. In Game One, he made a backhand grab of Lee May's grounder down the line. With his momentum taking him into foul territory, he managed to change direction and throw May out, keeping the score tied (Robinson then won it with a homer). In Game Three, he snared a Tony Perez line drive down the line, charged Tommy Helms' slow roller and threw him out, and leaped to catch a Johnny Bench liner. It was a personal highlight film for the ages.

Yankees shortstop Tony Kubek leaps over Indians second baseman Mike de la Hoz (bottom) to complete the double play in the early 1960s. Yankee Bobby Richardson looks on. Kubek was not an offensive force, but he was solid defensively. He ended his nine-year career in 1965 with a .266 batting average. Kubek later became a popular baseball broadcaster, sitting beside Joe Garagiola on the Game of the Week. "Doctor Strangeglove," aka Dick Stuart (top left), led his league's first basemen in errors every season from 1958 to '64. In his rookie season, Stuart tied another rookie first baseman, San Francisco's Orlando Cepeda, with 16 errors. Cepeda committed his 16 errors on 1,441 total chances; Stuart had 592 total chances. The crowds cluster outside Pittsburgh's Forbes Field (top right) before Game One of the 1960 World Series.

THE 1960s

FRANK HOWARD
Outfield-First Base — Los Angeles Dodgers

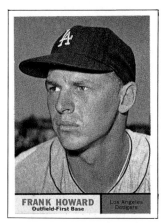

TED KLUSZEWSKI
First Base — Los Angeles Angels

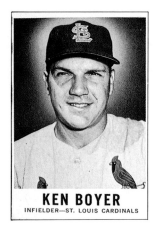

KEN BOYER
INFIELDER—ST. LOUIS CARDINALS

Sluggers Frank Howard, Ted Kluszewski, and Ken Boyer, left to right.

The Pirates were led by All-Stars right fielder Roberto Clemente and second baseman Bill Mazeroski, along with fiery third baseman Don Hoak and captain Dick Groat at shortstop. The latter won the batting championship with a .325 average, though he sat out September with a broken wrist and watched his replacement, Dick Schofield, bat .333.

The Pirates had a solid pitching staff. Vern Law was the ace with a 20-9 record, followed by Bob Friend (18-12) and lefthander Vinegar Bend Mizell, who posted a 13-5 mark after being acquired from the Cardinals in May. The bullpen ace was forkballing Elroy Face, who won ten games and had 24 saves in 68 appearances.

Roger Maris and pinch hitter Elston Howard hit homers in Game One of the World Series, but Law beat Ditmars 6-4. The Yankees had two more home runs in Game Two, both by Mantle, while Kubek and second baseman Bobby Richardson collected three hits apiece in a 16-3 victory. In the opener at Yankee Stadium, Richardson hit a first-inning grand slam, as the Yankees scored six runs in the inning and went on to win 10-0. Whitey Ford was the winning pitcher. He gave up only four hits in throwing the complete-game shutout.

The Pirates took games Four and Five by scores of 3-2 and 5-2. In Game Six, Ford tossed another shutout, giving up seven hits, but he singled and drove in two runs. Maris, Berra, and John Blanchard had three hits apiece in the 12-0 win.

ROGER MARIS BREAKS RUTH'S HOMER RECORD

The pressure on Roger Maris was so intense his hair was falling out in clumps; trying to attain one of baseball's most famous records was not fun.

In 1961, the American League expanded from eight to ten teams, and the schedule increased from 154 to 162 games. With the pitching slightly inferior, sluggers such as Maris and Mickey Mantle were having a field day. When Maris hit his 31st homer of the year on July 4, more than half what the immortal Babe Ruth smacked in 1927, the record watch was officially on. When Maris passed 50 in late August, Commissioner Ford Frick announced that if he broke Ruth's record, the mark would get an asterisk in the record books to indicate it was achieved in a longer season.

In game 154, Maris hit number 59 off Baltimore's Milt Pappas. On September 26, with five games remaining, Maris tied the record off Oriole Jack Fisher. Maris was stuck on 60 until October 1, the last day of the season.

Rookie righthanded pitcher Tracy Stallard of the Red Sox said he didn't care if he ended up as the man who gave up a record home run; he was a fastball pitcher who would challenge Maris. He did, and Maris flied out his first time up. In the fourth, Maris took two balls and then smacked Stallard's fastball into the right field bleachers to achieve immortality. Maris' teammates refused to let him in the dugout until he acknowledged the cheering fans. Years later, baseball acknowledged Maris by removing the asterisk.

Yogi Berra greets Roger Maris after Maris breaks Ruth's "unbreakable" record.

Yankees second baseman Bobby Richardson receives congratulations (top) after hitting a grand slam in Game Three of the 1960 World Series. Waiting for the shake are Gil McDougald (12), Elston Howard (32), and Bill Skowron (14). In 1961, Dodgers hurler Sandy Koufax (bottom left) was 18-13 with an N.L.-leading 269 strikeouts. Pirates lefthanded hurler Harvey Haddix (bottom middle) won two games in the 1960 World Series, with a 2.45 ERA. Yankees table-setter Bobby Richardson (bottom right) averaged 85 runs scored a season from 1961 to 1964.

THE 1960s

In Game Seven, a three-run homer by Berra in the sixth inning put the Yankees ahead 5-4. After the Yankees extended the lead to 7-4 in the eighth, Groat singled in one run.

Yankees hurler Jim Coates was too slow covering first on Clemente's infield hit in the ninth inning, and the New York lead was cut to 7-6. Reserve catcher Hal Smith then hit a three-run homer as the fans went wild. In the ninth, the Yankees opened with singles by Richardson and Dale Long. After Maris went out, Mantle singled in a run and advanced a runner to third. Berra's groundout scored him and tied the score 9-9. But Pirate Bill Mazeroski hit a homer in the bottom of the ninth to win the Series.

The Yankees had set Series records with 91 hits, 27 extra-base hits, 55 runs scored, and a team batting average of .338. But the Pirates, particularly Mazeroski, got the hits when they counted most.

1961

After winning ten pennants and seven World Series in 12 years as manager of the Yankees, Casey Stengel was fired. George Weiss suggested Stengel was too old. Ralph Houk, a successful minor league manager in the Yankees organization, became the New York skipper, taking over one of the greatest teams in history.

The '61 Yankees were a wrecking crew that slammed out a record 240 home runs. The leader, of course, was Maris with 61, which was one more than Ruth hit in a season, though Maris had eight more games in which to play. Maris won his second straight MVP. Mantle hit a career-high 54 home runs. Skowron had 28 homers, Berra had 22, and Howard and Johnny Blanchard had 21 apiece. Although the defense in left

field was unexceptional (manned by Berra and Hector Lopez), the infield play of second baseman Richardson, shortstop Kubek, and third baseman Boyer was first rate. So too was the pitching staff headed by Cy Young Award-winner Whitey Ford, who continued to flash the skills he had shown in the last Series. He won 25 games and lost only four on a 3.21 ERA. Some said that Ford, who had only 11 complete games, couldn't go the distance. But Houk used Ford wisely, keeping the "Chairman of the Board" strong all season long. Ralph Terry's ERA was lower at 3.15, and he lost just three times in 19 decisions. The starting rotation was rounded out by Bill Stafford (14-9), Jim Coates (11-5), and Rollie Sheldon (11-5). The bullpen stopper was a little lefthander named Luis Arroyo, who tantalized batters with a screwball thrown at various speeds. He won 15 games and saved 29.

The Tigers won 101 games this season, and they managed to challenge the Yankees into July. Outfielder Al Kaline had a typical year, batting .324 and hitting 19

Yankees rookie Tom Tresh in 1962 hit .286 with 20 homers, 93 RBI, and 94 runs scored while playing both shortstop and outfielder.

BILL MAZEROSKI

Submitted for your approval. Bill Mazeroski, a second baseman, was the winner of eight Gold Gloves during a 17-year career. He was the National League leader in assists nine times, total chances eight times, and putouts five times. He is the major league record-holder for double plays in a season and a career by a second sacker. Tied for second all-time in fielding percentage, he is acknowledged by his peers as the greatest defensive player at his position. The only place a player of this caliber wouldn't make the Hall of Fame is in — The Twilight Zone.

Anybody who saw Mazeroski play second base must have thought he was from another dimension. He joined the Pittsburgh Pirates in 1956 at 19, and when he made his first All-Star team two years later, he was being called "Dazzlin' Maz." All-Stars from both leagues stopped to watch him take infield practice. Players called him "No Touch" because he threw so quickly on the double play pivot that he never appeared to touch the ball. And he hung in so tough on takeout slides that teammates called him "Tree Stump."

It is ironic that Mazeroski is most remembered by fans and the media for his ninth-inning Game Seven homer that won the 1960 World Series. Lifetime, Maz hit a respectable .260, had over 150 hits five times, and belted 138 homers. But when it comes to recognizing defensive players for Cooperstown, the voters' minds enter — The Twilight Zone.

Willie Mays (top left) of the Giants led the N.L. with 129 runs scored in 1961. He also hit .308 that year, with 40 home runs and 123 RBI. He had 1,050 runs scored and 1,003 RBI during the decade. San Francisco Giant Orlando Cepeda (top middle) slugged 46 homers and drove home 142 runs in 1961 to lead the National League. During his nine full seasons in the 1960s, Cepeda averaged 28 round-trippers, 99 runs batted in, and 86 runs scored a year. Roger Maris (top right) led the league in 1961 with 132 runs scored, 142 RBI, and 366 total bases. He also had 94 bases on balls. Pirate Roberto Clemente (bottom left) led the N.L. with a .351 batting average in 1961. Whitey Ford (bottom right) was 25-4 in 1961 for an A.L.-best .774 winning percentage. He also led the league with 283 innings pitched. In Game Four of the 1961 World Series, Ford pitched six scoreless innings, extending his scoreless innings streak to 32 and breaking Babe Ruth's 43-year-old record of $29^2/_3$ innings.

THE 1960s

home runs. But fellow outfielder Rocky Colavito and first baseman Norm Cash had career years. Colavito hit 45 home runs and had 140 RBI (only two behind Maris). Cash led the league in hitting with a .361 average, and had 41 home runs and 132 RBI.

The Yankees won 109 games and went into the World Series against the Cincinnati Reds, who had a tough grind to finish 4 games ahead of the Dodgers. The Reds were figured to be a second-division club going into the season. But they traded for a number of key players, notably pitcher Joey Jay (who compiled a 21-10 record) and third baseman Gene Freese (who hit 26 homers and 87 RBI).

Frank Robinson, age 25, had another fine year, batting .323, hitting 37 home runs, driving in 124 runs, and winning the MVP. His best friend, 25-year-old Vada Pinson, cracked out 208 hits, batted .343, had 16 home runs, and drove in 87 runs. Veteran outfielder Wally Post batted .294 with 20 home runs. First baseman Gordy Coleman was the third member of the Reds to drive in at least 87 runs, and he had 26 homers to go with his .287 batting average. The Reds were masterfully managed by Fred Hutchinson, who did a lot of platooning at catcher, second base, and shortstop in bringing home a winner. But this club just wasn't a match for the Yankees lineup, which some experts said was the equal of the '27 Yankees.

The Series opened at Yankee Stadium, with Ford opposing Jim O'Toole. The Reds lefty pitched a strong game, allowing two runs. But Ford allowed only two hits and no runs. It was his third consecutive shutout in a World Series, a total of 27 scoreless innings. Cincinnati came back in Game Two as Jay pitched a four-hitter, one of which was a two-run homer by

Cubs second baseman Ken Hubbs hit .260 and scored 90 runs during his 1962 rookie season.

Berra. Coleman also hit a two-run shot as the Reds won 6-2. But the Yankees won the next game 3-2.

Ford was the hero of Game Four, which the Yankees won 7-0. He pitched five shutout innings before a foot injury forced him to leave. That brought his streak of scoreless innings in the World Series to 32, which broke Babe Ruth's record of 29⅔. The Yankees pounded the Reds 13-5 in Game Five to win the Series.

Maris had broken Ruth's homer record during the season, and Ford broke his Series pitching record. "It wasn't such a good year," Whitey said afterward, "for the Babe."

1962

Is there any way possible that the '62 Dodgers — who had the league's Most Valuable Player, the league's best pitcher, and the player who led the league in hitting and in driving in runs — could actually lose the pennant? The answer is written in the final standings. Maury Wills broke Ty Cobb's record for steals in a season by swiping 104 bases and won the MVP award. Don Drysdale won 25 games and was the Cy Young Award winner. Outfielder Tommy Davis was the batting champion with a .346 average and also led the league in RBI with 153, which was more runs than anyone had driven in since 1949.

MAURY WILLS BREAKS COBB'S STOLEN BASE RECORD

Only one year after Roger Maris broke Babe Ruth's single-season homer record, the biggest story in baseball was Maury Wills, whose 104 stolen bases in 1962 smashed another immortal's record — Ty Cobb's 96 stolen bases in 1915.

From about 1920 to 1960, offensive strategy was built around the big inning and the long ball; stolen bases were used as trick plays. With the arrival of players like White Sox Luis Aparicio (who had three straight seasons of 50-plus steals between 1959 and '61) and Dodger Wills, the stolen base again became an offensive weapon.

No one could have expected Wills to steal with such impunity in '62. After all, he had led the N.L. the previous two seasons with just 50 and 35, respectively. Before that, Willie Mays had won the stolen base crown with 40 or less for four straight years. But by 1962, the 5'11", 165-pound switch-hitting shortstop (who spent eight years in the minors) had become a student of base stealing. After three major league seasons, he had learned the pitchers and their moves and, most importantly, had become an exceptional hitter, batting .299 with a career-high 208 hits in '62. Wills didn't just assault Cobb's record; he did it with style and daring. Sixteen of his 104 steals were of third and two were of home. For his record-breaking season, Wills won a league and an All-Star MVP award. Wills' record has since been surpassed six times, but he still ranks ninth in all-time steals.

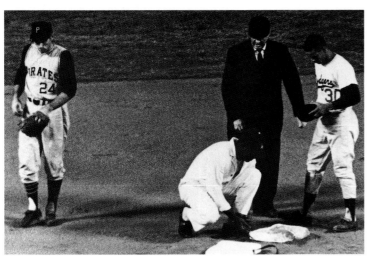

BoSox third baseman Frank Malzone can't find the handle (top right). Pirates hurler Vern Law (top left) was 20-9 in 1960. The Orioles battery of Hoyt Wilhelm, left, and Gus Triandos (middle left) pose before a game. Wilhelm was used in a relief and starting role by the Orioles; he won nine games and saved 18 in 1961, and won seven games and saved 15 in '62. Triandos averaged 21 home runs a season from 1956 to 1961. Harmon "Killer" Killebrew (middle center) led the American League with 48 homers, 126 RBI, and a .545 slugging average in 1962. He led the league with 45 homers in 1963 and 49 homers in '64. Detroit's Jim Bunning delivers the pitch (middle right). Bunning was 19-10 in 1962 with a 3.59 ERA. He led the A.L. in 1959 and '60 with 201 strikeouts each season. Maury Wills in 1962 received the stolen base (bottom) that tied him for the National League record for single-season swipes with 81, set by Bob Bescher of Cincinnati in 1911. Wills went on to steal 104.

THE 1960s

Yet the Dodgers finished in second place, a game behind the Giants. The reason the Dodgers didn't win the pennant going away was because the great lefthanded pitcher Sandy Koufax was sidelined on July 17 by a circulatory ailment in the fingers of his pitching hand. All Koufax had done to that point was strike out 216 batters in 184 1/3 innings while winning 14 of 21 decisions on an ERA of 2.54. The Dodgers still had a great season, as their stadium opened and a record 2,755,184 fans poured into the park to watch their team lead the league all summer. But as the season drew to a conclusion the Dodgers collapsed, losing all but three of their last 13 games, including their final four. Their 4-game lead disappeared as the Giants won seven of their last 13 games to deadlock the pennant race and set up a three-game playoff with the Dodgers.

The Giants also had an outstanding ballclub. Willie Mays led the league in home runs with 49, had 141 RBI, and batted .304 while playing half of his games in the worst hitter's stadium in baseball,

Candlestick Park. The wind there would catch line drives that were certain home run balls in other parks and knock them straight down for the left fielder to snare. Orlando Cepeda hit 35 home runs and had 114 RBI, and Felipe Alou hit 25 homers and had 98 RBI. In addition, San Francisco had a young lefthanded hitter named Willie McCovey, who hit 20 homers and drove in 54 runs in only 91 games.

The Giants pitching staff was also first rate. The four starters were Jack Sanford (24-7), Billy O'Dell (19-14), Juan Marichal (18-11), and Billy Pierce (16-6). The bullpen was headed by little Stu Miller, who won five games and saved 19. Miller was most famous for being blown off the mound during the All-Star Game by one of Candlestick's sudden zephyrs.

The playoff opened in Candlestick with Mays hitting two homers, Cepeda and Jim Davenport hitting one apiece, and Pierce pitching a three-hitter as the Giants won 8-0. Manager Walter Alston's gamble that Koufax could come off the injured list and exhibit his normal skills had been a failure. In Game Two, Drysdale made his fourth start in nine days and it showed. He gave up five runs in the first six innings. But the Dodgers scored seven runs in the bottom of the sixth, only to see the Giants tie the score in the eighth. In typical Dodgers scoring fashion, they manufactured the winning run in the ninth with three walks and a sacrifice fly. Game Three was a sloppy affair, as L.A.

Sandy Koufax greeted the Mets with a no-hitter June 30, 1962, his first of four.

JUAN MARICHAL

During the 1960s, righthander Juan Marichal was one of the most dominant pitchers in baseball and though he was respected, he was also very underrated. Someone else was always having a good enough year to beat him out of the Cy Young Award.

Marichal joined the Giants in 1960; two years later he was an 18-game winner, helping pitch the Giants into the World Series. He threw a fastball, slider, and screwball delivered from all angles, and his colorful motion featured an extremely high front leg kick that made it difficult for hitters to pick up the ball. In '63, he hurled a no-hitter against Houston, tied Sandy Koufax for the N.L. lead in wins with 25, and led the league in innings pitched with 321. His walks-to-innings pitched ratios (just 61 walks in '63) stamped him as one of baseball's best control pitchers.

"The Dominican Dandy" won 20 or more games five of the next six seasons, including an N.L. leading 26 in 1968. He led the league once in winning percentage and ERA, and twice in complete games and shutouts. He retired in 1975 with a 243-142 lifetime record (one of the four highest winning percentages of all time among pitchers with 200 wins), an amazing 2.89 ERA and just 709 walks in 3,509 innings. Unfortunately, Marichal was involved in a 1965 brawl in which he hit Dodgers catcher Johnny Roseboro in the head with his bat. But Marichal still made it to Cooperstown in 1983.

Tigers outfielder Al Kaline (top right) slugged 210 home runs, drove in 773 runs, and scored 811 times during the 1960s. Don Drysdale (top left) was 25-9 with a league-leading 232 strikeouts and 314¹/₃ innings pitched for the Dodgers. Los Angeles left fielder Tommy Davis (bottom left) led the N.L. with 153 RBI and a .346 batting average in 1962. He also had 230 base hits, 27 homers, and 120 runs scored. Roy Face (bottom right) displays the form that earned him 28 saves in 1962. Face was an incredible 18-1 in 1959. His .947 winning percentage that year was the highest in baseball history.

came back to bat .321, hit 30 home runs, and lead the pennant drive. Maris' home run total fell from 61 to 33, but he led the team in RBI with 100. The powerful Yankees had three other players with 20 or more home runs: Bill Skowron, Tom Tresh, and Elston Howard. Ralph Terry (23-12) anchored the pitching staff, followed by Ford, who won 17 games without a shutout among them.

Vada Pinson led the '63 N.L. with 204 hits.

committed three errors and gave up two unearned runs in a 6-4 loss that gave the Giants the pennant. The Dodgers walked in the winning run.

In the American League, the Indians headed the standings until the All-Star break, when the Yankees took first place. They were subsequently challenged by the Minnesota Twins, who were led by Harmon Killebrew's 48 home runs and pitcher Camilo Pascual's 20-win season. But the Twins finished 5 games back of New York, with the surprising Angels in third place, 10 games out.

The Yankees' sluggish start was due to the loss of Mickey Mantle for 39 games. But the A.L. MVP

But it was Whitey Ford who opened the World Series at Candlestick Park and extended his scoreless-inning streak to 33²/₃ innings before the Giants scored in the second. Ford went the distance in the 6-2 Yankees win. Jack Sanford pitched a 2-0 shutout in Game Two to even the Series.

The Yankees won Game Three in New York 3-2, and the Giants took Game Four 7-3, as their little second baseman, Chuck Hiller, hit the first N.L. grand-slam homer in a World Series. Tresh hit a three-run homer, and Terry pitched a complete game in a 5-3 win that put the Yankees ahead 3-2. But Pierce threw a three-hitter in Game Six for a 5-2 Giants win.

In Game Seven, the Yankees eked out a run on a double-play grounder, and the score was still 1-0 going into the ninth. With runners on second and third and two out, McCovey stepped up for the Giants. He hit a low liner so hard that Yankees second baseman Bobby Richardson threw up his gloved hand almost in a defensive reflex. But the ball stuck in it, and the Yankees were again champions of the world.

1962 NEW YORK METS

In 1962, the first season of their existence, the expansion New York Mets lost their first nine games. It was all downhill from there. By the end of the year, the Mets had compiled the losingest record in modern baseball history (40-120), prompting their colorful old manager, Casey Stengel, to ask: "Can't anybody here play this game?"

To the fans of New York, who'd been starved for National League baseball since the Dodgers and Giants franchises left town for the West Coast after the 1957 season, the Mets may have been losers, but they were

Casey Stengel, left, skippered the '62 Mets to a 40-120 record.

lovable ones. Almost 1 million fans packed into the Polo Grounds that first season, and "The New Breed," as the faithful were called, took Stengel's cue and supported the Mets through thin and thin.

The original Mets were made up of popular aging stars like Gil Hodges, Gus Bell, and Richie Ashburn, and young rejects from other teams. But if one player symbolized the Mets strangely appealing ineptitude, it was a player named Marv Throneberry. The 28-year-old former Yankee had a penchant for making the spectacular physical and mental mistake. Throneberry once hit a triple but was called out for missing first base. When Stengel ran out to argue, an umpire said, "I hate to tell you this, Casey, but he missed second too." Throneberry became a fan favorite known as "Marvelous Marv." Never has such a mediocre player or such a bad baseball team been as immortalized.

Willie McCovey (top left) is congratulated by
Hank Aaron (#44) and Ron Santo after homering
in the All-Star Game. McCovey led the National
League with 44 home runs in 1963. He hit 300
homers in the decade, even after sharing time with
Orlando Cepeda for the first three years.
McCovey's 18 career grand slams are the most in
N.L. history. First baseman Bill White (top right)
of the Cardinals slugged 27 home runs and drove
in 109 runs in 1963. White averaged 21 home
runs and 94 RBI a season during the first seven
years of the 1960s. He was named the National
League's president in 1988. Pittsburgh's Bob
Friend (bottom) delivers the pitch. He averaged
16 wins a season from 1960 to '64.

THE 1960s

1963

This was the last year in the major leagues for future Hall of Famers Stan Musial, age 42, and pitcher Early Wynn, age 43. In 96 games, Musial managed to hit 12 home runs for the Cardinals, and Wynn managed to win one game in three decisions (despite a 2.28 ERA) to give him a career total of 300 victories in the major leagues. Then the weary old righthander — who always said he would knock down his mother if she were batting against him — took his feisty style home to retirement in Florida.

But the big story of the year was the emergence of Sandy Koufax, after eight seasons in the majors, as the premier pitcher in baseball. He had a 25-5 record, 11 shutouts, and a minuscule ERA of 1.88 as he won both the Cy Young Award and N.L. MVP. He also became the biggest gate attraction in baseball, as record crowds turned out at ballparks every time he was scheduled to pitch. Koufax achieved his superb season with a ballclub that had fewer runs batted in than five teams that finished below them in the standings.

Not one Dodger drove in as many as 100 runs. Tommy Davis led the team with 88 RBI and a .326 batting average. Frank Howard was the only power hitter, with 28 home runs. Maury Wills was the only other .300 hitter, finishing at .302. But he led the running Dodgers with 40 stolen bases, followed by Willie Davis with 25, Jim Gilliam with 19, and Tommy Davis with 15. The Dodgers had to be daring on the basepaths to score runs. Don Drysdale (19-17) was the number-two starter for L.A., and the number-three starter was Johnny Podres (14-12). The Dodgers also had the game's best relief pitcher in lefthander Ron Perranoski, who appeared in 69 games, won 16, saved 21, and had a 1.67 ERA.

The Dodgers moved out to a substantial lead in the pennant race, trailed by the Giants and Cardinals. The Giants had a powerhouse batting order, with McCovey hitting 44 home runs and driving in 102, Mays hitting 38 homers and driving in 103, and Cepeda hitting 34 homers and driving in 97. Catchers Ed Bailey and Tom Haller combined to hit 35 homers, and Felipe Alou added another 20. But aside from Juan Marichal (25-8), the Giants' pitching staff was questionable. The Cardinals, on the other hand, had consistent pitching and a balanced lineup. In September, the team got hot and won 19 out of 20 games to pull within a game of the Dodgers on September 16. Then the teams met in a three-game series in St. Louis. Johnny Podres threw a three-hitter in the opener to win 3-1. Koufax won the second

The Yanks' infield, from left, Clete Boyer, Tony Kubek, Bobby Richardson, and Joe Pepitone.

ORLANDO CEPEDA

Orlando Cepeda had the nickname "The Baby Bull" because his father, Pedro, considered to be the Babe Ruth of Puerto Rico, was known as "The Bull." Once he got to the major leagues, Orlando set out to become the Pedro Cepeda of the United States.

Cepeda was a big, strong righthanded-hitting first baseman with line-drive power to all fields. He joined the San Francisco Giants in 1958 and was the Rookie of the Year, batting .312, hitting 25 homers, driving in 96 runs, and leading the N.L. with 38 doubles. Over the next six seasons, Cepeda averaged 33 homers and 108 RBI, and batted over .300 fives times.

A knee operation shelved him for almost all of 1965. With Willie McCovey, a first baseman out of position in the outfield available for Cepeda's job, the Giants traded him early in the '66 season to the Cardinals for pitcher Ray Sadecki. Cepeda hit .303 for the Cards. The following season, he sparked them to the world championship, hitting 25 homers, batting .325, notching a league-leading 111 RBI, and becoming the unanimous choice for MVP.

After a so-so 1968, "Cha-Cha" was again traded, this time to the Braves for Joe Torre (who would eventually win an MVP with the Cards). Cepeda hit 34 homers and had 111 RBI his first year in Atlanta, but never again produced as he had early in his career. He retired after the 1974 season with 379 homers, 1,365 RBI, and a lifetime .297 average.

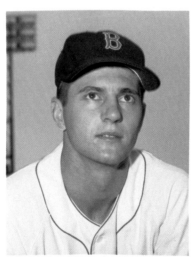

Pete Rose (top left) was the 1963 National League Rookie of the Year, hitting .273 with 101 runs scored. San Francisco's Juan Marichal (top right) was 25-8 in 1963, leading the league with 321¹/₃ innings. Marichal was the dominant righthander in the 1960s. "The Dominican Dandy" averaged 21 wins and 274¹/₃ innings pitched a season during the nine full years he pitched during the decade. His earned run average was 2.57 during the 1960s. Marichal was selected to play in ten All-Star games, winning two. Willie Stargell (bottom left) of the Pirates averaged 24 homers, 81 RBI, and 63 runs scored from 1963 to '69. Boston left fielder Carl Yastrzemski (bottom middle) led the American League with a .321 batting average, 40 doubles, 183 base hits, 95 bases on balls, and a .419 on-base average in 1963. Early Wynn (bottom right) came back to Cleveland to pitch in his 23rd season in 1963. He appeared in 20 games, started five, lost two, and then finally won a game. That victory was his 300th, and then Wynn retired.

THE 1960s

game 4-0, and the Dodgers, trailing 5-1 after seven innings of the finale, battled back to win in extra innings 6-5, locking the pennant for Los Angeles.

Other N.L. highlights this season included the play of Rookie of the Year Pete Rose, who was derisively called "Charlie Hustle" by many of his Reds teammates for his aggressiveness and was befriended only by Frank Robinson and Vada Pinson. Also, the New York Mets improved in their second season, finishing 12½ games ahead of their '62 record, only 48 games out of first place.

In the American League, the favored Yankees again won the pennant, this time by 10½ games over the White Sox. Mantle broke a bone in his foot early and injured his knee later, keeping him on the sidelines for more than 100 games. Maris was plagued by a bad back much of the season and limited to playing 86 games. Maris hit 23 home runs, Mantle only 15. The team's home run leader turned out to be Elston Howard, who hit 28, drove in 85 runs, and won the MVP. The RBI leader was a hotshot rookie first baseman, Joe Pepitone, who had 89 to go with his 27 homers. The slick-fielding 22-year-old Pepitone was such a prospect that the Yankees had traded Bill Skowron, only 32, to the Dodgers in the off-season. Despite the hitting falloff, the Yankees infield of Pepitone, Richardson, Tony Kubek, and Clete Boyer was the best in baseball. The pitching staff was deep once lefthander Al Downing was recalled from the minors in June. Downing, age 22 but pitching with the poise of a veteran, struck

out 171 batters in 176 innings and won 13 of 18 decisions on a 2.56 ERA. The staff was headed by Whitey Ford, who was 24-7 with a 2.74 ERA, and Jim Bouton, who came off a 7-7 rookie record to win 21 games and lose only seven on a 2.53 ERA.

The White Sox pitching staff led the A.L. in ERA (2.97), fewest bases on balls (440), and shutouts (19). The staff was led by A.L. Rookie of the Year Gary Peters, who was 19-8 with a league-leading 2.33 ERA. Minnesota finished in third place, with Harmon Killebrew slugging 45 homers.

Koufax opened the Series in New York and struck out 15 in beating Ford and the Yankees 5-2. The strikeouts broke the record set by Carl Erskine of the Dodgers, who had 14 in a Series game ten years previous to the day.

The Yankees and Dodgers met in the World Series for the eighth time in 1963. The former Brooklyn ballclub won only once, when in 1955 it was led by a young Johnny Podres. Podres again controlled the Yankees hitters in Game Two, with a 4-1 win that gave the Dodgers a two-game lead. Bouton pitched a fine Game Three, giving up only four hits and a lone run. But Don Drysdale allowed only three singles, a walk, and no runs while striking out nine to get the win 1-0.

HARMON KILLEBREW

If you didn't know any better, you would have thought Harmon Killebrew was the offspring of Jimmie Foxx. Like the great American League slugger of the 1930s, Killebrew was a 6', 195-pound righthanded hitter with massive arms and shoulders. And like Foxx, "Killer" played first, third, and the outfield — and could pulverize a baseball.

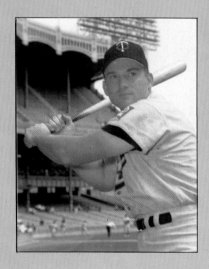

Killebrew became an everyday player in 1959, six years after the Washington Senators (later to become the Minnesota Twins) signed him at age 17. He celebrated the end of his apprenticeship on the bench by leading the A.L. with 42 homers and driving in 105 runs. Over the next 16 years of his career, Killebrew won five home run crowns (with 44 or more each time), hit more than 40 dingers two other years, and led the league in RBI three times and slugging twice. He won the MVP in 1969 by knocking 49 homers, accumulating 140 RBI, and walking 145 times.

Even though Killebrew never batted over .300, his seven seasons with more than 100 walks illustrate just how feared a slugger he was. He averaged one home run every 14.22 at-bats, a ratio better than anyone except Babe Ruth and Ralph Kiner.

Killebrew retired after the 1975 season (his last year was as a designated hitter for the Kansas City Royals). He was fifth all-time in homers with 573 and tenth in walks with 1,559. Also, he had just 14 more at-bats than Jimmie Foxx.

Sandy Koufax had 15 Ks in a '63 Series game.

Hank Aaron (top) led the National League with 44 home runs, 130 runs batted in, 121 runs scored, and a .586 slugging average in 1963. Aaron sometimes is remembered only for breaking Babe Ruth's career home run record, but he was a great all-around player. During the 1960s, he averaged 38 homers, a .308 batting average, 111 RBI, and 110 runs scored a season. Bob Allison (middle left) hit .271 with 35 homers, 91 RBI, and an A.L.-leading 91 runs scored in 1963 for the Minnesota Twins. Allison, a power-hitting outfielder, averaged 28 homers, 88 RBI, and 87 runs scored from 1959 to '65 for the Senators and the Twins. Hoyt Wilhelm (middle center) averaged 23 saves a season from 1963 to '65 for the ChiSox. Jim "Bulldog" Bouton (middle right) was 21-7 for the 1963 Yankees, with a 2.53 ERA, 12 complete games, and six shutouts. New York's Elston Howard (bottom) was the American League's MVP in 1963. He hit .287 with 28 homers, 85 RBI, and 75 runs scored that season.

THE 1960s

The next game proved to be the finale. Although Mantle homered off Koufax and Ford gave up only one earned run, Pepitone lost a throw from third in the mass of white shirts behind the bag for a three-base error. A Willie Davis sacrifice fly scored Gilliam's winning run (2-1) for the sweep. The next night in Brooklyn, a gang of Yankees fans gathered outside Pepitone's apartment and hanged him in effigy from a street lamp.

The only Yankees who seemed to benefit from the Dodgers' sweep were Ralph Houk, who was elevated to general manager, and Yogi Berra, who was named manager of the team.

1964

For some four months this season it did not look as if the Yan-

kees would win their fifth American League pennant in a row. They played a lot of listless baseball and were rumored to be wracked with disciplinary problems, which presumably would not have happened under the tough Houk. But now Berra was in charge, and that, according to some members of the press, led certain players to take advantage of the easy-going future Hall of Famer.

In addition, the Yankees had physical problems: Mantle missed 30 games with a bad knee, and Kubek sat out the last 63 games of the season with a sprained wrist. New York was also saddled with an ineffective bullpen, with the exception of Pete Mikkelsen (seven wins, 12 saves). These factors conspired to relegate the Yankees to third place in August.

Both the White Sox and the Orioles had played better ball. Chicago's strength was its pitching staff. Peters was 20-8, and Juan Pizarro was 19-9. Joel Horlen, though compiling a 13-9 won-lost record, may have been the best of the trio. Horlen gave up only 142 hits in 211 innings and had a 1.88 ERA. Behind the starters was the best relief pitcher in the league, Hoyt Wilhelm. The 40-year-old knuckleballer won 12 games and

Curt Flood led the '64 N.L. with 211 hits.

saved 27 while making 73 appearances. Baltimore was led by its All-Star third baseman, Brooks Robinson, and 22-year-old Boog Powell, who hit 39 home runs and had 99 RBI. Robinson hit 28 homers, drove in 118 runs, and batted .317, while winning MVP honors. For the third year in a row, Harmon Killebrew of the Twins won the

---

1967 ALL-STAR GAME

With its abundance of outstanding performances—Bob Gibson's 1.12 ERA, Don Drysdale's streak of 58 consecutive scoreless innings, Denny McLain's 31 wins—1968 was called the "Year of the Pitcher." Baseball fans got a preview of that unique season

at the 1967 All-Star Game in Anaheim, CA.

During a record 15 innings, 12 outstanding pitchers from the two leagues notched a record 30 strikeouts, yielded 17 hits, and walked only two batters (five American League hurlers did not yield a walk). Each pitcher (including six future Hall of

Famers) struck out at least one batter in a game that ended as a 2-1 triumph for the National League. A.L. pitchers Gary Peters and Catfish Hunter struck out four batters apiece. N.L. ace Ferguson Jenkins notched six Ks to tie an All-Star record.

All the runs scored in this superstar pitching duel came on homers. Dick Allen gave the N.L. the lead in the top of the second inning with a blast off A.L. starter Dean Chance. Brooks Robinson's homer off Jenkins tied the game in the sixth. The score remained 1-1 until the top of the 15th, when Tony Perez connected off of Catfish Hunter.

In the bottom of the inning, the N.L. called on Mets rookie Tom Seaver, who saved the game for Dodger Don Drysdale. Los Angeles manager Walter Alston, who piloted the winning squad, called the game "the best exhibition of pitching I've ever seen in All-Star competition."

Gary Peters, left, and Catfish Hunter each had four Ks.

Tony Oliva of the Twins (top left) turned in one of the greatest rookie campaigns in baseball history in 1964. He led the A.L. with a .323 average, 217 base hits, 109 runs scored, and 43 doubles. Oliva also smashed 32 homers, drove in 94 runs, and had a .557 slugging average. Cubs third baseman Ron Santo (top right) led the National League with 86 walks and 13 triples in 1964. Santo led the N.L. in bases on balls in four different seasons. He averaged 27 homers, 99 RBI, and 86 runs scored a season from 1961 to '69. Don Drysdale, left, and Jim Bouton (bottom left) confer before Game Three of the '63 World Series. Drysdale allowed only three base hits and one base on balls while striking out nine in hurling a shutout. Bouton pitched seven innings of one-run ball.

THE 1960s

home run crown, this time with 49, though his team finished sixth. For the first time, the Angels had a Cy Young Award winner, as Dean Chance was 20-9 on a 1.65 ERA.

But a strange thing happened to the Yankees on their way to third place. Berra got tough and the players got some fighting spirit again. Berra blew up on the team bus after a tough loss in August. Phil Linz, a cutup who had nevertheless done a good job in the field as Kubek's replacement, was playing a harmonica on the bus, and Berra told him to knock it off. Linz kept playing. Berra stormed back to where Linz was seated, shouting angrily all the way, and knocked the harmonica out of his hand.

Soon the Yankees were playing like they used to, particularly after Mantle returned in September and Pedro Ramos was acquired from Cleveland to shore up the bullpen. Ramos had eight saves in 13 appearances. The Yankees lost just six games while winning 22 in September. They clinched the pennant on the next-to-last day of the season, finishing 1 game ahead of the White Sox and 2 ahead of the Orioles.

The National League staged one of its wildest pennant races ever. The Philadelphia Phillies were leading the pack by 6½ games with two weeks left in the season. Then they nose-dived, losing ten games in a row. Meanwhile, the Cardinals and Reds were coming on strong. Cincinnati, led by Frank Robinson, Vada Pinson, and Deron Johnson, finished only 1 game back of the Cardinals, tied for second with the Phillies. Reds manager Fred Hutchinson was dying of cancer and had to turn over the club to coach Dick Sisler for the final 53 games of the season. But Hutch continued to sit on the bench, torn by the malignancy. Robinson says the Reds players tried too hard to win the pennant for Hutchinson; they put too much pressure on themselves and just couldn't bring it off. Hutchinson died the following spring.

The Cardinals also had distractions. Highly respected general manager Bing Devine had acquired two players who were expected to make the ballclub contenders, outfielder Lou Brock from the Cubs in June and relief pitcher Barney Schultz from the minors in August. Both would make major contributions; Brock hit .348 for the Cardinals, with 12 home runs and 44 RBI, and Schultz earned a win and 14 saves. But with the Cardinals mired in fifth place in August, Cardinals owner Gussie Busch abruptly fired Devine, and rumors had it that manager Johnny Keane would soon be gone too. Then the Cardinals got hot, and Keane was retained. They were led by third baseman Ken Boyer —

WILLIE McCOVEY

When the San Francisco Giants called up 21-year-old first baseman Willie McCovey in July 1959, the big lefthander made it clear he wanted to stay. In his first game, he went four-for-four against superstar pitcher Robin Roberts, and two of the hits were triples. McCovey eventually batted .354, hit 13 homers, and was named Rookie of the Year, despite playing only 52 games.

With 1958 Rookie of the Year Orlando Cepeda already entrenched as the Giants first sacker, McCovey averaged just 99 games played the next three years. In 1963, he was made an every-day outfielder and responded with a league-leading 44-homer season that established him as the N.L.'s most feared lefthanded power hitter. By 1965, Cepeda was gone and "Stretch" was the Giants first baseman. From 1965 to '70, McCovey never hit fewer than 31 homers or drove in less than 91 runs. He led the N.L. in homers, RBI, and slugging in '68, and in 1969, he won the MVP with a league-leading 45 homers, 126 RBI, and .656 slugging percentage.

Injuries curtailed McCovey's playing time in the early 1970s, and between 1974 and '77, he went from the Giants to San Diego to Oakland and back to San Francisco. So happy was he to be back at Candlestick Park in 1977 that, at age 39, he summoned up one more great season, hitting 28 homers and driving in 86 runs to earn Comeback Player of the Year recognition. McCovey retired in 1980 with 521 lifetime homers, tenth on the all-time list.

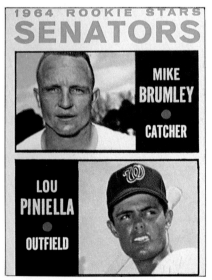

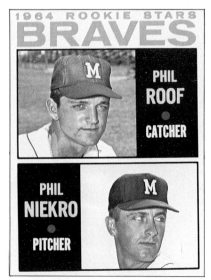

Lou Piniella, left, and Phil Niekro appeared on rookie cards in 1964.

Mickey Mantle (top left) smacked 35 homers in 1964, his last season over 30. He also hit three in the '64 World Series, bringing his total Series homers to a record 12. Orioles third baseman Brooks Robinson (top right) was the A.L. MVP in 1964. He hit .317 with 28 homers, a league-leading 118 RBI, and 82 runs scored. St. Louis third baseman Ken Boyer (bottom left) was the 1964 N.L. MVP. He hit .295 with 24 homers, a league-leading 119 RBI, and 100 runs scored. In 1964, Lou Brock (bottom right) hit .348 for the Cardinals when he came over from the Cubs. He ended the season with 43 stolen bases and 111 runs.

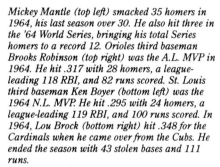

THE 1960s

who had 24 home runs and 119 RBI and was voted the league's MVP — and first baseman Bill White, who had 21 home runs and 102 RBI to go with a .303 batting average. St. Louis won the pennant for the first time since 1946.

The pitching staff featured two lefthanders, young Ray Sadecki (20-11) and veteran Curt Simmons (18-9), and righthanded power thrower Bob Gibson (19-12, 3.01 ERA), who was just coming into his own as a dominant force.

Sadecki started the World Series opener against Whitey Ford, who gave up five runs in less than six innings and was thereafter relegated to the bench with arm trouble. The Cardinals won 9-5. Gibson was beaten 8-3 in Game Two by rookie Mel Stottlemyre. In Game Three at Yankee Stadium, Curt Simmons and Jim Bouton were locked in a 1-1 pitching duel in the ninth. Schultz relieved Simmons, and Mantle hit his first pitch into the stands for the winning run. That Series home run was Mantle's 16th, breaking Babe Ruth's record.

In their initial at-bats the next day, the Yankees scored three runs, knocking out Sadecki. But in the fifth inning, Ken Boyer hit a grand-slam home run off Al Downing that won the game 4-3. Gibson had a 2-0 lead in the bottom of the ninth inning of Game Five, until Tom Tresh hit a two-run homer. But in the next inning, Cardinal Tim McCarver hit a three-run homer for a 5-2 victory.

Needing to sweep the final two games in St. Louis, the Yankees stormed back. Bouton limited the Cardinals to three runs and Pepitone hit a grand slam to win Game Six 8-3. A tired Gibson gave up five runs in Game Seven, on home runs to Mantle, Linz, and Clete Boyer, but went the distance as the Cardinals won the game 7-5 and took the World Series.

The next day the Yankees fired Yogi Berra. Johnny Keane resigned in St. Louis and was named Berra's replacement. Berra would become a coach for Casey Stengel with the Mets and have a seemingly endless career in the major leagues. Keane's tenure was short-lived, but at least he had that '64 world championship ring.

1965

The Yankees, with all their players back and healthy, were favored to win an unprecedented sixth successive American League pennant. Manager Johnny Keane, who had told off his boss in St. Louis, was looking forward to winning back-to-back pennants in the rival leagues. But the thing that nobody realized was that 1965 was to mark the sudden precipitous decline of the proud Yankees, a team that would need another dozen seasons before it found itself atop the standings at season's end.

The decline this season was aided and abetted by injuries. Roger Maris injured a hand and played in only 43 games all season, hitting eight home runs. A series of little injuries kept Mantle out of 54 games, and he hit just 19 home runs and had 46 RBI. An ailing shoulder allowed Kubek to play only 93 games at shortstop, during

Bob Gibson was 20-12 with a 3.07 ERA in 1965.

ROBERTO CLEMENTE

Originally signed by Brooklyn, Roberto Clemente was left unprotected in the 1954 draft and was purchased by the Pirates for $4,000. Clemente batted .311 in 1956, his sophomore year. Beginning in 1960, he hit over .300 12 out of 13 seasons, winning the batting title four times. His career highs of 29 homers, 105 runs, and 119 RBI earned him the MVP in 1966. He was one of the greatest fielding right fielders ever, winning 12 Gold Gloves and leading the league in assists six times.

But despite all this apparent greatness, the proud 37-year-old Clemente was anxious to display his talents to a national audience when the Pirates played the Orioles in the 1971 Series, because he believed he was unappreciated and felt he had something to prove. He proved something all right. Clemente had a hit in each game (a trick he turned in the 1960 Series) and 12 hits total, including two doubles, a triple, and two homers; the second of which was key in the Bucs' 2-1 Game Seven victory. He displayed incredible range in the outfield, cutting off balls in the gap and down the line, and dared Orioles runners to take extra bases against his powerful arm. America had discovered Clemente.

It was tragic when, three months after getting his 3,000th hit in 1972, he died in a New Year's Eve plane crash while taking food and medical supplies to victims of a Nicaraguan earthquake. The five-year waiting period was waived, and Clemente was inducted into the Hall of Fame the following year.

Smokey Burgess (top left) was a good catcher during the 1950s, but he is best remembered as a pinch hitter in the 1960s. In 1965, Burgess led the league with 20 pinch hits in 65 pinch at-bats. In '66, he went one better, gathering 21 pinch hits in 66 pinch at-bats. He again led the league in pinch at-bats in 1967, but his pinch hits went down to eight; he retired after the '67 season. Jim Bunning (top right) was 19-9 in 1965 for the Phillies. Tommy John (bottom left) was 14-7 in 1965 for the White Sox. He led the A.L. in shutouts in 1966 and '67. Atlanta's Mack "The Knife" Jones heads toward first (bottom right). Jones slugged 31 homers in 1965.

373

THE 1960s

WILLIE STARGELL

Willie Stargell, left, had 107 RBI in '65; Jim Maloney won 20 games.

which he batted .218. Elston Howard was sidelined for 60 games with continuing elbow problems. The result was that the once-fearsome Yankees lineup often included Linz at shortstop (a .207 hitter), rookie Roger Repoz in the outfield, and Ray Barker (a pickup from Cleveland) at first base. Tresh was the lone Yankee to hit over 25 home runs, and he led the team with a paltry 74 RBI. Pepitone, who didn't get along with Keane and who had additional personal problems, virtually disappeared this season, hitting just 18 home runs and batting .247.

While the Yankees were going up in smoke, the Minnesota Twins were catching fire. They had always been a tremendous long-ball club and the previous season had led the major leagues in home runs with 221. This season the power production fell off to 150 home runs, as Harmon Killebrew missed over 40 games with an elbow injury. He led the team with 25 homers and was backed by five

other regulars who could hit the ball out of the park at any time. Outfielder Bob Allison had 23 homers, first baseman Don Mincher had 22, outfielder Jimmie Hall had 20, shortstop Zoilo Versalles had 19, and outfielder Tony Oliva had 16.

Oliva led the league in hitting with a .321 average, and Versalles won the MVP award for his flawless play at shortstop, his timely hitting (.273, 77 RBI, 45 doubles), and his daring baserunning (27 steals). But the keys to the Twins improvement from 79 victories in '64 to 102 in '65 were the shift of Killebrew from first base to third, which allowed manager Sam Mele to play Mincher at first, and the sudden development of a solid pitching staff. No one suspected this club could have consistent pitching with top righthander Camilo Pascual off the mound for six weeks. But that's how long he

was sidelined with a torn shoulder muscle, though he still managed to win nine of his 12 decisions. Jim Kaat went 18-11 on a 2.83 ERA, and Jim Perry had a 12-7 record. The staff surprise, Jim Grant, was 21-7. Al Worthington headed the bullpen and did yeoman work, winning ten games and saving 21. The Twins had no trouble finishing 7 games ahead of the White Sox to win the pennant.

In the National League, the Dodgers found themselves battling the Giants, Pirates, and Reds into September. Then the Dodgers won 13 straight, and the Giants won 14 games in a row to pull away from the others.

But the Dodgers were at an advantage down the stretch as the Giants were without their 22-game winner, Juan Marichal, for the season's final nine days. During a Giants-Dodgers game in late August, Marichal felt he was

DON DRYSDALE'S CONSECUTIVE SCORELESS INNINGS STREAK

One of the most controversial umpire decisions was made on May 31, 1968, keeping alive one of baseball's most amazing records.

As he took the mound in the ninth inning of a game against the Giants, Dodgers righthander Don Drysdale was working on a consecutive scoreless innings streak that had reached 44. In going for his fifth straight shutout, Drysdale was only three innings away from Carl Hubbell's N.L. scoreless innings record and just 13 shy of Walter Johnson's major league mark of 56. But when the Giants loaded the bases with nobody out, the streak was 90 feet away from ending.

Against Dick Dietz, Drysdale threw one of his trademark inside fastballs. The pitch clipped Dietz on the left arm and the streak was over. But suddenly, umpire Harry Wendlestedt called

Dietz back to the plate, ruling he had not made an effort to avoid being hit. Drysdale then retired Dietz and the side without further damage to keep the streak intact.

It had all started on May 14, when the Dodgers 32-year-old ace shut out the Cubs 1-0. After the record was saved by the ump's call, Drysdale set a major league record with his sixth straight shutout (5-0 over Pittsburgh) and broke Hubbell's record in the process. When he faced Philadelphia on June 8, he needed only three innings to shatter Johnson's 55-year-old mark. With Roberto Pena's ground out in the third, Drysdale had a new record which he then stretched to 58⅔ innings.

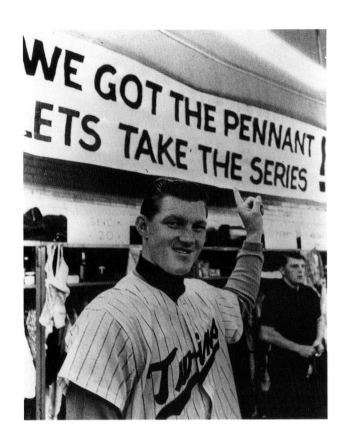

Jim Kaat (top left) points out that the Minnesota Twins won the American League pennant in 1965. Kaat was 18-11 with a 2.87 ERA in 1965. Kaat averaged 17 victories a season from 1962 to '69 for the Twins. Tony Conigliaro (top right) slugged 124 homers for Boston from 1964 to '69. Billy Williams (bottom left) slides in safely. Williams hit .315 in 1965, with 115 runs scored and 108 RBI. He averaged 27 home runs, 94 runs batted in, and 95 runs scored in his nine full seasons in the 1960s. Williams didn't miss any games between September 1963 and September 1970, a string of 1,117 straight games. He hit .300 or better five times in his career, had 14 seasons with 20 or more homers, ten seasons of 90 or more RBI, and nine seasons of at least 90 runs scored. He ended his 18-year career with a .290 batting average, 426 homers, 1,475 RBI, and 1,410 runs scored. Boog Powell (bottom right) smashed 39 homers and had a league-leading .606 slugging percentage in 1964 for the Orioles.

being thrown at while batting, and he angrily turned and bopped catcher John Roseboro on the head with his bat. The league fined Marichal $1,750 and suspended him. Thus the Giants were deprived of their pitcher, who would have made at least one if not two starts in nine days, and the Dodgers finished 2 games ahead of San Francisco at the season's end. N.L. Most Valuable Player Willie Mays hit 52 homers to lead the majors. Many experts felt that, had he played in a stadium other than Candlestick, he might have challenged Roger Maris' record for homers in a season.

Sandy Koufax was 27-9 with a 1.73 ERA, 27 complete games, five shutouts, and 317 strikeouts during his last season in 1966. Chronic arthritis forced him out of the game.

The Dodgers had no power whatsoever, as Jim Lefebvre and 30-year-old rookie Lou Johnson — who was recalled from the minors after Tommy Davis broke an ankle — led the team in homers with 12 apiece. In fact, the Dodgers didn't hit much of anything, compiling a team batting average of .245 and totaling just 548 RBI (only the expansion Mets and Astros had fewer). What the Dodgers had going for them was Maury Wills running wild again, stealing 94 bases — and Sandy Koufax and Don Drysdale becoming the most awesome pitching duo in history. Koufax won 26 games (eight of them shutouts), struck out 382 batters, and garnered the Cy Young Award. Drysdale won 23 games, seven of them shutouts, and struck out 210 batters. They had 47 — count 'em, 47 — complete games between them.

But the Twins shocked the baseball world by clubbing Drysdale for seven runs in the Series opener in Minnesota and winning 8-2. The next day Kaat won over Koufax by a final score of 5-1. Claude Osteen stopped the Twins 4-0 in L.A. Then Drysdale won 7-2, and Koufax shut out the Twins 7-0. Minnesota beat Osteen in Game Six 5-1 to even the Series. Koufax came back after only two days rest and threw another shutout, striking out ten and winning the World Series for the Dodgers.

1966

Once again the Dodgers went down to the last day of the season before securing the National League pennant, finishing 1½ games ahead of the Giants and 3 games ahead of the Pirates. Once again, the Giants seemed to be the far superior ballclub. San Francisco had three regulars with over 30 home runs in Willie McCovey (36), Willie Mays (37), and Jim Ray Hart (33); catcher Tom Haller had 27 homers. This quartet had 359 runs batted in among them. In addition, the Giants had a pitching staff led by two 20-game winners — Marichal (25-6) and Gaylord Perry (21-8). The Pirates finished the season in third, behind the leadership of MVP Roberto Clemente. He was asked to sacrifice his high batting average to supply more power to the Bucs; he finished the season with a .536 slugging average, a

As a rookie in 1961, Carl Yastrzemski was given one of the toughest jobs in baseball — replacing Ted Williams. He handled the pressure more than admirably. In his third season, "Yaz" led the league in batting, and in 1967, he took a ninth-place Boston Red Sox team to the A.L. pennant when he won the triple crown. During the last two weeks of that four-team race, Yaz batted .523, with five homers and 15 RBI. Though the Sox lost the Series in seven to the St. Louis Cardinals, Yaz batted .400 and hit three homers.

Yaz led the league in batting again in '68 with a record low .301 average, but he hit .300 only twice in his next 15 seasons. Yaz belted 40 homers in 1969 and '70, but never again won the home run title after the triple crown year, and he drove in over 100 runs just four more times. But in 1979, Yaz became the first A.L. player to compile 3,000 hits and 400 homers.

Yastrzemski was also one of the game's great outfielders, playing the difficult left field wall in Fenway Park better than anybody ever has. He had a 1.000 fielding percentage in 1977 and led A.L. outfielders in assists a record seven times. Yaz retired in 1983 after 23 seasons, ranking second all-time in games, fourth in walks, and seventh in hits and doubles. Yastrzemski was elected to the Hall of Fame in 1989, his first year of eligibility.

*Tom Tresh (top left) slugged 26 homers in 1965 and 27 homers in '66. Tresh
averaged 21 homers a season from 1962 to '67. Houston second baseman Joe
Morgan turns the double play (top right). Morgan scored 100 and led the N.L.
with 94 bases on balls as a rookie in 1965. He averaged 82 runs scored a
season during his four full seasons in the 1960s. Dick Allen (bottom left)
averaged 30 homers, 98 runs scored, and 90 RBI from 1964 to '69 for the
Phils. Jim Palmer (bottom middle) hurled a four-hit shutout in Game Two of
the 1966 World Series, beating Sandy Koufax in Koufax's last game. Joe Torre
(bottom right) in 1966 had 36 home runs and 101 RBI for Atlanta.*

THE 1960s

.317 batting average, 342 total bases, 105 runs scored, and 119 RBI to go along with his career-high 29 home runs.

The Dodgers had only one man with as many as 20 home runs (Jim Lefebvre, with 24), they had no one who drove in over 74 runs, and they had no .300 hitter. What they did have was the same style club as '65, which used the hit-and-run, stole bases, sacrificed to move baserunners, and relied on its pitching staff to keep the opposition from scoring.

Even the pitching staff wasn't what it had been the previous year. Koufax and Drysdale held out in the spring for better contracts, which they finally got after missing much of the training period. That loss of work in Florida didn't bother Koufax, who started 41 games, completed 27, won 27, lost only nine, had an ERA of 1.73, and won his third Cy Young Award. Drysdale had his problems, however, completing only 11 of 40 starts and finishing with a losing record, 13-16. Claude Osteen picked up the team by winning 17, and rookie Don Sutton (who has since gone on to win 300 games) won 12. A major acquisition for the Dodgers was Phil "The Vulture" Regan, a Tigers disaster who became a godsend. Regan won 14

games, saved 21, and had an ERA (1.62) that was even lower that Koufax's. No other Dodgers pitcher won more than six games.

The team that the Dodgers met in the 1966 World Series had an easier time of it in the American League. The Orioles, who moved to Baltimore in 1954 as the sons of the St. Louis Browns, finally won a pennant this season after years of threatening the Yankees.

The O's finished 9 games ahead of Minnesota and 10 ahead of Detroit, the only teams to offer them any real challenge. Frank Robinson was the catalyst, leading the league in batting with a .316 average, in home runs with 49, and in RBI with 122 to win the triple crown. He was also voted the A.L.'s Most Valuable Player, becoming the only man in history ever to win that award in both leagues (five years earlier he'd won the award with Cincinnati).

But the Orioles were not a one-man team, nor even a one-Robinson team, as Brooks had 23 home runs and 100 RBI. First baseman Boog Powell also hit the century mark in RBI with 109, while clouting 34 homers and batting .287. The Orioles had superb infield and outfield defense that aided a somewhat suspect pitching staff, which was led by the 15 victories of 20-year-old Jim Palmer. Don McNally won 13 games and Wally Bunker, ten. The bullpen was deep. Stu Miller had 18 saves, Eddie Fisher 13, and Dick Hall and Moe Drabowsky split 14.

The once formidable Yankees fell on the worst of times. When the Yankees won only four of their first 20 games, Keane was fired, and Houk came down from the front office to resume managing. It didn't help much. Mantle and

TONY OLIVA

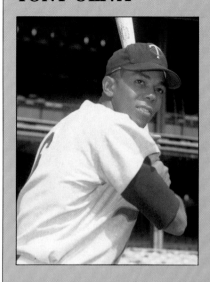

If there had been arthroscopic surgery when Tony Oliva played, the Cuban-born hitter might have a plaque in the Hall of Fame.

During a July 1971 game in Oakland, the Minnesota Twins star right fielder dove for a fly ball and ripped up his right knee, one he'd injured other times in his career. Instead of sitting out the rest of the year, Oliva hobbled through the season, led the league in slugging, and won his third batting title (.337). But at season's end, he needed tendon surgery so extensive it cost him almost the entire '72 season. Oliva played only another four years, exclusively as a designated hitter, never hit .300 again, and retired at age 36.

Before his fateful injury, Oliva was arguably the American League's best hitter. In 1964, the smooth-swinging lefthanded batter became the first rookie ever to win the hitting title, hitting .323, with a league-leading 217 hits, 43 doubles, and 109 RBI. He scoffed at the sophomore jinx by winning the batting crown again in '65. He would eventually lead the A.L. three more times in hits and doubles, and bat over .300 four of the next six seasons. He retired in 1976 with a .304 batting average, 220 homers, and 947 RBI.

Today a player can rip a knee tendon, have an arthroscopy, and be back on the field in one month. Had that procedure been around 20 years ago, it might not have been Rod Carew winning six batting titles in the 1970s, but his teammate Oliva.

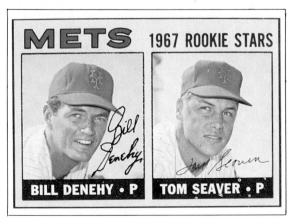

Tom Seaver was 16-13 with a 2.76 ERA during his rookie year in '67.

Orioles outfielder Frank Robinson (top) led the A.L. with 49 homers, 122 RBI, a .316 batting average, 122 runs scored, and a .637 slugging average in 1966, garnering the MVP award. Robinson averaged 32 homers, 101 RBI, and 101 runs scored a season with a .304 batting average in the 1960s. Tigers outfielder Al Kaline (bottom left) slugged 28 homers and had 88 RBI in 1966. Red Sox hurler Jim Lonborg (middle) led the A.L. in 1967 with 22 wins and 246 strikeouts, winning the Cy Young Award. Don Drysdale (bottom right) started at least 40 games for the fifth straight season in 1966.

Maris were fading, and Ford had retired. Pepitone, with 31 homers, and Tresh, with 27, were the new power threats, and the team batting average was .235. The Yankees finished in last place, ½ game behind ninth-place Boston.

Moe Drabowsky turned out to be the pitching star of the World Series opener in Los Angeles. After both Frank and Brooks Robinson homered in the first inning off Drysdale and the O's added a run in the second, McNally grew wild and gave up two runs. Manager Hank Bauer summoned Drabowsky, who allowed only one hit and struck out 11 batters in 6⅓ innings of relief. Palmer, pitching a four-hit shutout, defeated Koufax in Game Two.

When the Series resumed in Baltimore, the Orioles got only three hits, but one was a homer by Paul Blair. Wally Bunker, age 21, gave up no runs. There was a similar story in Game Four, as Frank Robinson hit his second home run, also off Drysdale, and Dave McNally pitched a shutout for another 1-0 victory and a Series sweep. Frank Robinson was named the World Series MVP, and the Orioles' dynasty had begun.

1967

Frank Robinson was severely injured early in '67 on a hard slide taking out a second baseman. He was knocked unconscious and suffered double vision the rest of the season. In addition, the entire Orioles team suffered a decline and finished in a tie for sixth place with the Senators.

While the Orioles were falling, the Red Sox were rising miraculously. Boston had finished in next-to-last place in 1966, 26 games out of first. But they finally hired a tough manager (Dick Williams), and they filled two big holes in their starting lineup with rookie second baseman Mike Andrews

Leo Durocher took the helm of the Cubs in 1966 and managed them until 1972.

and rookie center fielder Reggie Smith. They also got career performances out of team leader and left fielder Carl Yastrzemski and pitcher Jim Lonborg. Most Valuable Player Yastrzemski won the triple crown with 44 home runs, 121 RBI, and a .326 batting average. Lonborg won the Cy Young Award with a 22-9 record.

But the Red Sox scored no easy victory as the pennant race was a dogfight among four teams all season. The Twins, off to a slow start, fired manager Sam Mele in June and got hot under Cal Ermer thereafter, finishing only 1 game out of first. The favored Tigers tied them for second place, and the White Sox came in fourth, just 3 games off the pace.

The White Sox were still known as the "Hitless Wonders," having no batter with an average above .250; but they had good pitching, and manager Eddie Stanky found ways to win. The Tigers had a sound ballclub with considerable power in Norm Cash, Al Kaline, Bill Freehan, and Willie Horton. The Twins had a superb pitcher in Dean Chance (20-14) and the ever dangerous Harmon Killebrew, who hit 44 home runs.

The Twins entered the last weekend of the season in first place, 1 game ahead of the Red Sox and Tigers. Rainouts resulted in the Tigers having to play two doubleheaders with the Angels, with the Twins playing their final two games in Boston. Minnesota led in the first game until Jim Kaat was sidelined by an injury, then the Red

BILLY WILLIAMS

During the 1960s, Billy Williams established himself as one of the game's most productive players. The lefthanded-hitting outfielder joined the Chicago Cubs full time in 1961. Williams batted .278, with 25 homers and 86 RBI, and he was named the N.L. Rookie of the Year. Over his next 13 seasons with the Cubs, Williams would average 28 home runs per year, score 100 or more runs five times, average 97 RBI per season, and bat over .300 five times.

Williams waited until the 1970s to have his two greatest seasons. He led the National League in hits with 205 and runs with 137, and had a .322 batting average in 1970. In 1972, he led the league in batting (a career high .333), slugging (a career high .606), and missed winning the triple crown by three homers and three RBI—slugging 42 homers and driving 129 runs in. Both times, however, he lost the MVP award to Johnny Bench.

Williams' consistency stemmed from his durability. He played 146, 159, and 161 games his first three years. Starting with a game on September 22, 1963, Williams played in every Cubs game until September 3, 1970, a run of 1,117 consecutive games, then a N.L. record. He played his last two years (1975 and '76) as a designated hitter with Oakland. He had 2,711 career hits, 426 home runs, and a .290 average. Though he never won an MVP or played in a World Series, Williams richly deserved his Hall of Fame induction in 1987.

Carl Yastrzemski (top left) is the last player in baseball to record a triple-crown season, in 1967, one season after Oriole Frank Robinson did it. Yaz slugged 44 homers, drove in 121 runs, and batted .326 to top the league. In the 1967 World Series, Yaz slugged three homers, drove in five runs, batted .400, and slugged .840. Mickey Mantle saves an errant pickoff attempt (top right) during 1967 spring training. Hank Aaron is back at first base. Mantle played first base in 1967 and '68 because of his bad knees. Jim Bunning (bottom left) won 19 games each season from 1964 to '66 for the Phillies. Bunning was 17-15 in 1967, leading the N.L. with 253 strikeouts and $302\frac{1}{3}$ innings pitched. Maury Wills (bottom middle) hit .302 and scored 92 runs for Pittsburgh in 1967. Tom Seaver keeps an eye on Roy Face in the late 1960s (bottom right). Face helped to revolutionize the role of the relief specialist. He appeared in 848 games during his 16-year career, starting only 27 games. He led the National League in saves three times, made 821 relief appearances, saved 193 games, and recorded 96 relief wins.

THE 1960s

Sox went ahead and won 6-4 to move into a tie for first place. Fenway Park was packed for the final game on Sunday, and fans went wild when Lonborg beat Chance. The Tigers also won their first game to draw within ½ game of Boston and within reach of a tie if they won the second game. Red Sox players sat in their clubhouse listening to the game on the radio — and they went berserk, pouring champagne all over one another, as the Angels won 8-5. The Red Sox, 100-1 shots back in April, had won their first pennant since 1946.

In the National League, the Cardinals ran away from the Giants, as both Willie Mays and Juan Marichal had off years. Even though Mike McCormick won 22 games and the Cy Young Award, the Giants finished 10½ games behind St. Louis. That the Cardinals were the class of the league was clearly demonstrated after they lost their ace, Bob Gibson. Gibson's leg was broken by a lined shot off the bat of Pirates star Roberto Clemente (who would lead the league in hitting with a .357 average). The Cards won 36 of the 56 games that Gibson sat out.

They still got solid pitching from starters Dick Hughes, Nelson Briles, Ray Washburn, Al Jackson, and Larry Jaster, as well as from the bullpen duo of Joe Hoerner and Ron Willis (who combined for ten wins and 25 saves). The offense was led by first baseman Orlando Cepeda, who had been acquired in a trade from the Giants. The National League MVP had a .325 average, 25 home runs, and 111 RBI. The team's other top hitters were Curt Flood (.335), Lou Brock (.299), Tim McCarver (.295), and Julian Javier (.281). Brock also provided a big boost to the scoring by stealing 52 bases.

Gibson won the World Series opener in Boston 2-1, the only run

he allowed coming on a home run over the left field "Green Monster" wall by opposing pitcher Jose Santiago. Gibson struck out ten in going the distance. Lonborg overwhelmed the Cardinals the next day, pitching a no-hitter through 8⅔ innings. Then Javier lashed a double to left for the Cardinals' only hit, as Yastrzemski hit two home runs and Boston won 5-0.

Third baseman Mike Shannon hit a two-run homer in Game Three at St. Louis, as Briles went the distance in the 5-2 victory. The following day Gibson earned his second win of the Series, pitching a five-hitter and shutting out Boston 6-0. Lonborg came back to notch his second win in four days and keep Boston's hopes alive in Game Five. Though one of the three hits off Lonborg was a home run by Roger Maris (who had hit only nine all season), the Red Sox won 3-1. Manager Williams' pitching staff was so thin that he started Gary Waslewski, who had won all of two games during the season, in Game Six in Boston. Waslewski gave up two runs in 5⅓ innings, and reliever John Wyatt gave up two more in 1⅔ innings, but Gary

Cardinals hurler Bob Gibson was 13-7 in '67, with a 2.98 ERA and 147 strikeouts.

ROGER MARIS

Roger Maris had won his first MVP in 1960 with 39 homers, 112 RBI, and a .581 slugging average (he also won a Gold Glove in right field), a feat that should have made his record-breaking season less of a surprise than people treated it. In fact, Maris had shown a proclivity for power hitting since starting his career with the Cleveland Indians in 1957.

Early in that season, he led the American League in homers and RBI before breaking three ribs in a slide. During the '58 season, he was traded to the Kansas City Athletics and yet hit 28 homers. He was on a power roll again in '59, but an appendix operation cost him 45 games, and he ended up with 16 dingers.

Traded to the Yankees in 1960, he had slugger Mickey Mantle hitting behind him. Boom — Maris won back-to-back Most Valuable Player awards. He broke Babe Ruth's single-season home run record with 61 in 1961. But the pressure of that '61 season took such a toll on Maris that he was never the same. He managed 33 homers and 100 RBI in 1962, 23 homers in only 90 games in '63, and 26 blasts in '64. Maris was traded to the St. Louis Cardinals in 1967, where his quiet leadership and solid outfield play helped the Cards win two pennants. Ironically, though he played in five World Series for the Yankees (hitting five home runs), he had his best Series for St. Louis in '67, batting .385 with seven RBI. Maris retired after the '68 season with 275 lifetime homers.

Brooks Robinson of Baltimore scores (top left). Robinson scored 1,232 runs and drove in 1,357 runs in his career. Rod Carew (top right) of the Twins hit .292 during his 1967 rookie season. St. Louis acquired Roger Maris (bottom left) at the beginning of the 1967 season for a little run production. Maris gave them that, especially in the World Series that year. He had seven RBI, three runs scored, one homer, and a .385 average. Pirates outfielder Roberto Clemente (bottom right) followed his '66 MVP by hitting .357 with 23 homers, 110 RBI, and 103 runs scored in 1967.

THE 1960s

Bell shut out the Cardinals in the eighth and ninth. Boston got home runs from shortstop Rico Petrocelli (who hit two), Yastrzemski, and Smith to win the game 8-4.

Lonborg, starting with only two days rest, was obviously tired in the finale, giving up seven runs in six innings. Gibson allowed only three hits and two runs in winning his third game of the Series, for which he was given the Series MVP award. His chief rival in the voting was Lou Brock, whose 12 hits gave him a .414 average and who set a record by stealing seven bases for the world champion Cardinals.

1968

This was the "Year of the Pitcher." Batting averages had been falling ever since the strike zone was extended five years earlier. In '68, no American League club had a team batting average over .240 — with the pennant-winning Tigers hitting only .235 and the fifth-place Yankees batting a minuscule .214. In the National League, the first-place Cardinals batted .249, and the ninth-place Mets hit .228. The Reds were the only team

Tommy John had an A.L.-top six shutouts in '67.

in baseball that hit the ball consistently. Paced by Pete Rose's league-leading average of .335, the Reds batted .273 as a team.

In the A.L., even the batting champion barely reached .300 as Yastrzemski had to streak at the end to finish at .301. The Mets and Astros were such poor hitters that on April 15 they played a game in which it looked as though neither team would ever score. Finally, after six hours and six minutes, in the game's 24th inning, Houston managed to score a lonely run to end the marathon contest.

The Giants and the Cardinals played back-to-back games that had the Year of the Pitcher written all over them. In the first game, Gaylord Perry of the Giants threw a no-hitter at the Cardinals. The next night, the Giants couldn't manage a single hit off Ray Washburn of the Cardinals. Fans were crying out at the boring contests to which they were being subjected, but many looked forward to the annual All-Star Game, which on July 9 became the first ever played at night. Featuring the top hitters swinging away, the game figured to be exciting. The National League, as usual, won the game, which was so exciting that many fans reportedly fell asleep as it was being played. The final score was 1-0.

No pitcher had won 30 games since Dizzy Dean turned the trick in 1934. But in the Year of the Pitcher, Denny McLain of the Tigers won his 30th game of the season on September 14. He finished up with 31 wins, only six losses, 28 complete games, 280 strikeouts, and an ERA of 1.96. Naturally, McLain won the MVP and the Cy Young awards. In the National League, where the hitting was better, Bob Gibson of the Cardinals was even more unhittable than McLain, though his won-lost record was 22-9. One of the key statistics of a pitcher's effectiveness is the ratio of hits he allows per inning. McLain, for example, gave up only 241 hits in the 336 innings he pitched. But Gibson pitched over 100 innings more than the total number of hits he allowed: 198 hits in 305 innings. He started 34 games, completed 28, had 268 strikeouts, and pitched 13 shutouts. His ERA was an unheard of 1.12, a figure that had not been matched since the introduction of

DENNY McLAIN WINS 30

In 1934, a confident, colorful, outspoken young pitcher named Dizzy Dean won 30 games. Nobody would win 30 again for another 34 years, until a confident, colorful, outspoken young pitcher named Denny McLain would notch 31 victories for the Tigers.

The 24-year-old McLain had already won 53 games in three full seasons with Detroit, including 20 in 1966. In 1968, the righthander added a slider to his sidearm fastball and curve. Pitching in a four-man rotation that would allow him to start 41 games, McLain had no-decisions in his first two starts, then won 23 of his next 26. McLain won his 20th game on July 27, becoming the first pitcher since Lefty Grove to win 20 by August 1.

With the Tigers marching comfortably toward the A.L. pennant, all attention was on McLain's quest for 30. He was at 29 when he faced Oakland on September 14. The game was televised nationally and Dean was in attendance, but McLain was off his game. Behind two Reggie Jackson homers, the A's were up 4-3 in the bottom of the ninth. Al Kaline had pinch-hit for McLain and walked. Mickey Stanley singled, sending Kaline to third. When A's first baseman Danny Cater botched a throw on Jim Northrup's slow roller, the score was tied. Then Willie Horton blasted a drive over the left fielder, and McLain had made history.

McLain's spectacular season earned him the A.L. MVP and Cy Young awards, two trophies he had to sell later to pay off legal expenses when he was convicted of racketeering and drug dealing.

Reds outfielder Pete Rose (top left) led the National League with 210 base hits and a .335 batting average in '68. Rose averaged 190 base hits a season from 1963 to '69. Willie McCovey (top right) led the National League with 36 homers, 105 RBI, and a .545 slugging average in '68. He slugged 45 homers, drove in 126 runs, and had a .656 slugging average in 1969 to win the N.L. MVP award. N.L. Rookie of the Year in 1968 Johnny Bench (bottom left) hit .278 with 15 homers and 82 RBI for Cincinnati. Bench slugged 26 homers and had 90 RBI the next year. Cardinal Orlando Cepeda (bottom right) in 1967 had 25 homers, 37 doubles, 91 runs scored, and a league-leading 111 RBI to win Most Valuable Player honors.

THE 1960s

A ticket for Bob Gibson's record 17-Ks game.

the lively ball in 1920. Naturally, Gibson won the MVP award and the Cy Young Award.

It was fitting that the best pitchers in each league led their teams to victories in the pennant race, which was hardly a race in '68. The Tigers finished 12 games ahead of the Orioles, who fired Hank Bauer in July and named coach Earl Weaver manager. The Cardinals finished 12 games ahead of the Giants, who were led by Juan Marichal's 26-9 record.

Gibson and McLain started the World Series opener in St. Louis, and the Cardinals ace showed who was the better pitcher. Tigers manager Mayo Smith had benched his shortstop, Dick Tracewski — who had batted his weight, .156 — and moved outfielder Mickey Stanley to that position. This allowed Smith to use 16-year-veteran Al Kaline, who had played part time during the season, in right field. Stanley played well at short and got two of the five hits off Gibson. But the hard-throwing righthander gave up no runs and struck out 17 batters. That set a Series record, as the Cardinals won 4-0.

The next day Mickey Lolich (17-9) beat Nelson Briles (19-11), scattering six hits and hitting the first homer in his career. Willie Horton and Norm Cash also homered in the 8-1 win. The Cardinals bounced right back in Detroit, as Orlando Cepeda and Tim McCarver each hit three-run homers and Brock stole three bases in the 7-3 victory. In Game Four, Gibson allowed just five hits, struck out ten, and hit a home run as the Cardinals won a 10-1 romp. When the Cards scored three times in the first inning of the next game, the Tigers appeared to be dead cats. But Lolich didn't allow another run, and his teammates scored five for the Game Five victory.

McLain finally won a game to even the Series, going the distance and allowing only one run as the Tigers scored 13 times. In Game Seven, Lolich and Gibson pitched shutout ball for six innings, but in the seventh Curt Flood misjudged a triple to center that scored two runs. The Tigers won 4-1, as Lolich went all the way to earn his third win of the Series and MVP honors. The pudgy lefthander had outpitched the two Cy Young Award winners. It seemed almost anything was possible in the Year of the Pitcher.

1969

The strike zone was returned to its former (pre-1963) definition, covering the area from the armpits to the knees, and the mound was lowered in moves to give hitters a chance again. With both leagues now numbering 12 teams, each league was split into two six-team divisions. Teams within a division would play one another 18 times and would play teams in the other division 12 times. The winner of each division would meet in a best-of-five game playoff to determine the pennant winner.

The winner in the National League was one of the most unlikely teams ever to capture a pennant — the New York Mets. For seven years, the Mets had been doormats of the league, a team of noted players like Marvelous Marv Throneberry and Willard Hunter. They were a kind of joke perpetrated on the New York fans, who still loved

BOB GIBSON

It was called "The Year of the Pitcher," and in 1968, the St. Louis Cardinals flame-throwing righthander Bob Gibson was *the* pitcher.

Pitchers dominated the 1968 season. Denny McLain won 31 games. Carl Yastrzemski's A.L. leading average was just .301. Don Drysdale set a consecutive scoreless innings record. The top 15 pitchers in both leagues all had earned run averages under 2.75. But nobody that season measured up to Gibson, who posted a major league record 1.12 ERA, the lowest ever for a pitcher hurling more than 300 innings. In winning the Cy Young Award and the MVP, the intimidating Gibson recorded 22 wins, 28 complete games, and league leads in strikeouts (268) and shutouts (13).

"Hoot" continued his immortal season in the '68 World Series. In the opener against the Tigers and McLain, Gibson struck out a record 17 batters. His win in Game Four gave him a record seven consecutive Series victories. When he struck out eight in losing the seventh game, he established a single-Series record of 35 Ks (he's second in all-time Series strikeouts with 92).

Gibson was a fierce competitor and an incredible athlete; he once played basketball for the Harlem Globetrotters. Besides being an overpowering pitcher, Gibson posted a .206 lifetime average, with 24 home runs, and he earned Gold Gloves for defense nine straight years (1965 to '73). Gibson won his second Cy Young Award in 1970 and in July 1974 became the second pitcher to strike out more than 3,000 batters. Gibson retired in 1975 with a record of 251-174 and entered the Hall of Fame in 1981.

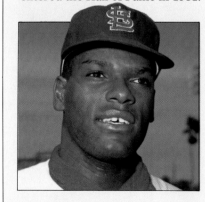

Mickey Lolich (top left) of Detroit won three games during the '68 World Series, with an ERA of 1.67. Lolich's record from 1964 to '69 was 97-65. Mickey Mantle, right, with Bobby Kennedy (top right) during Mickey Mantle Day at Yankee Stadium in '65. Cub third baseman Ron Santo (bottom left) slugged 29 homers and drove in a career-high 123 runs in 1969. Juan Marichal (bottom right) of San Francisco was 26-9 in '68, with a league-leading 30 complete games and $325^2/_3$ innings pitched. In 1969, Marichal was 21-11, and led the N.L. with a 2.10 ERA and eight shutouts.

THE 1960s

them. In seven seasons, the Mets had never finished higher than ninth place or next to last.

Of course, Mets fans looked forward to the '69 season because expansion assured that their beloved team could finish no lower than sixth place in their division. But the youthful Mets abruptly matured under the patient guidance of manager Gil Hodges. The former Dodgers first baseman had only three regulars among his fielders: outfielders Cleon Jones and Tommie Agee, and shortstop Bud Harrelson. Jones led the club in hitting, batting .340 while driving in 75 runs. Agee led the team in home runs with 26 and RBI with 76. Harrelson was a slick fielder whom Hodges sat down only against the toughest righthanded pitchers, when he used lefthanded-hitting Al Weis at short.

At every other position Hodges platooned, squeezing as much offense out of the club as he possibly could. In the latter stages of the season, the Mets picked up another big bat in righthanded-hitting Donn Clendenon. In 59 games, Clendenon hit 12 home runs and

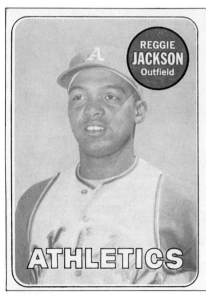

Reggie Jackson slugged .608 in 1969.

388

had 37 RBI, becoming a major force for the club's offense. The real strength of the team was its pitching staff, led by Tom Seaver, who at age 24 blossomed into the best pitcher in the league and won the Cy Young Award with a record of 25-7, including five shutouts and an ERA of 2.21. Behind Seaver was lefthander Jerry Koosman (17-9, 2.28 ERA), rookie Gary Gentry (13-12), and 22-year-old Nolan Ryan, who appeared in 25 games and won six of his nine decisions before a severe groin pull sidelined him for much of the season. The bullpen featured a solid duo in righthander Ron Taylor, who won nine games and saved 13, and left-hander Tug McGraw, who won nine games and saved 12.

In late June, the Mets trailed the favored Cubs by only 1 game; then in July, they beat Chicago two out of three in New York, and a lot of folks began to believe. Seaver won that second game on a near-perfect performance. He recorded 25 outs without giving up a walk or hit, until Jim Qualls singled with one out in the ninth. A week later, the Mets went into Chicago and again won two out of three from the Cubs — who had four players with over 20 homers for the year and two 20-game winners. The Mets' hero of the series in Chicago was infield reserve Weis, who stroked the only two homers he would hit all season.

Even an August slump that saw the Mets fall 9½ games off the pace could not deny them, as they regained first place on September 10, went on to win 100 games, and finished a full 8 games ahead of the Cubs. Then they roared into the playoffs, sweeping the favored Atlanta Braves.

The "Amazin' Mets" were also underdogs in the World Series against the Orioles, who won 109 games — playing .673 baseball — and finished 19 games ahead of the second-place Tigers. The O's had excellent hitters throughout the lineup, led by Boog Powell (37 homers, 121 RBI) and Frank Robinson (32 homers, 100 RBI). Even slick-fielding shortstop Mark Belanger had a fine year at the plate, hitting .287. The Orioles also had a pitching staff that matched the Mets'. The four primary starters were Mike Cuellar (23-11), Dave McNally (20-7, including 15

PETE ROSE

Pete Rose has been called "the least-gifted great player." The most prolific hitter of all time wasn't a remarkable athlete. After spending 1960 to '62 in the minors, he wasn't even one of Cincinnati's top prospects. A switch-hitter, Rose had little power. He could run well but didn't possess great speed. He was adequate at several positions (he played first, second, third, and left and right fields during his 24 years) but was great at none.

What Rose did have in abundance was spirit, intensity, and a burning desire to succeed. In 1963, his first year in the big leagues, his dashes to first after walks and head-first slides into bases earned him the nickname "Charlie Hustle" and the Rookie of the Year award.

Then, beginning in 1965, he batted over .300 for 14 of the next 15 seasons. He knocked over 200 hits per season a record ten times (winning three batting titles); he led the N.L. in doubles five times and runs four times. He was the MVP in 1973 and led the "Big Red Machine" to four pennants and two world championships (1975 and '76).

In the summer of 1978, Rose began an assault on the 56-game hitting streak record; he was stopped at 44, tying the N.L. mark. At the end of the 1979 season, Rose was voted by fans and sportswriters as the greatest player of the 1970s. Besides being the all-time hits leader, Rose holds the record for most games and is second all-time for doubles (746).

Oakland reliever Rollie Fingers (top left) saved 12 games in 1969. Al Oliver (top middle) of the Pirates hit .285 with 70 RBI in his '69 rookie campaign. Lou Brock (top right) averaged 96 runs scored and 48 stolen bases a season from 1962 to '69. Detroit's Denny McLain (bottom left) won his second Cy Young Award in '69, going 24-9 with 288 strikeouts. Curt Flood (bottom middle) filed suit to stop his 1969 trade from the Cards to the Phils. The case made it to the U.S. Supreme Court, which upheld baseball's exemption from antitrust laws and the reserve clause binding players to their teams. Minnesota's Harmon Killebrew (bottom right) was the '69 A.L. MVP, slugging 49 homers and tallying 140 RBI.

THE 1960s

Frank Robinson had 32 homers in '69.

wins in a row), Jim Palmer (16-4 after two years of arm miseries), and Tom Phoebus (14-7). The bullpen stoppers were Eddie Watt (five wins and 16 saves) and lefty Pete Richert (seven wins and 12 saves). The Orioles swept the Twins in the playoffs. Billy Martin won the A.L. West division title with the Twins in his first season as a manager. Then he was fired, a preview of things to come.

The Orioles won the Series opener in Baltimore handily. Don Buford hit Seaver's second pitch out of the ballpark and three innings later doubled home two runs as the O's scored three and won the game 4-1. Cuellar gave up only six hits. In Game Two, a pitching duel between McNally and

Koosman, Clendenon homered in the fourth inning, and the Orioles tied the score three innings later on the only two singles (plus a steal) that Koosman allowed. The Mets won the game in the ninth on singles by Ed Charles, Jerry Grote, and Al Weis.

In Game Three, Gary Gentry and Nolan Ryan combined for a four-hit shutout that was saved by two incredible catches by center fielder Tommie Agee, who also homered in the 5-0 victory. The next day, Clendenon homered off Cuellar in the second, and Seaver didn't give up the tying run until the ninth, when a remarkable diving catch by right fielder Ron Swoboda with the bases loaded prevented any further damage. In the bottom of the tenth, Buford misplayed Grote's fly ball into a double. J.C. Martin attempted to bunt him over, but Pete Richert fielded the bunt and then hit Martin with his throw toward first, allowing the winning run to score.

The Mets needed only one more win, but it didn't look as if they would get it when Baltimore jumped off to a 3-0 lead in Game Five. McNally was rolling along with a shutout until the sixth when

Clendenon hit a two-run homer. In the next inning, Al Weis, of all people, homered to tie the score. In the eighth, Jones and Swoboda doubled for one run, and a second scored on errors by Powell and Watt. Koosman then set down the O's — and the Amazin' Mets were world champions.

THE AMAZIN' METS

During their first seven seasons, the Mets had been the laughingstock of baseball, never finishing higher than ninth place. When the 1969 campaign began, the pundits made them 100-1 to win the World Series. The Mets went right out and lost their opening day game 11-10 to first-year Expos.

But by mid-May the Mets were playing .500 ball for the first time in their history. Manager Gil Hodges had the players believing in themselves; with a solid pitching staff anchored by Tom Seaver and Jerry Koosman, the Mets were miraculously winning close games. Mets batters struck out 19 times one evening against Steve Carlton, yet won the game. They won a doubleheader by scores of 1-0, with the starting pitcher driving in the only run in each game. After falling 9½ games behind Chicago in mid-August, the Mets won 38 of their last 49 games while the Cubs wilted. The Amazin' Mets were 100-62 and beat Atlanta three-straight in the N.L.C.S.

The Mets were given little chance of beating the mighty Orioles in the World Series, even less so after the Birds beat Seaver 4-1 in the opener. But a Koosman two-hitter won Game Two; a couple of outstanding Tommie Agee catches highlighted a 5-0 Game Three victory; a botched defense of a tenth-inning sacrifice bunt gave the Mets a win in Game Four; and home runs by Al Weis and Series MVP Donn Clendenon sparked a come-from-behind 5-3 win and an improbable world championship.

Tommie Agee (top left) hit .271 in 1969, with 26 homers, 97 runs scored, and 76 RBI. Yankees rookie Bobby Murcer (top right) slugged 26 homers and drove in 82 runs in '69. The Mets outfield (bottom) of, left to right, Cleon Jones, Tommie Agee, and Ron Swaboda accounted for 227 runs scored and 203 RBI in '69.

THE 1970s

The name of the game was speed in the 1970s.
Baseball enjoyed increased popularity
due to hustling offense, colorful superstars,
and exciting pennant races. And, in 1973,
the A.L. introduced the designated hitter.

Pete Rose (page 392) bowls over Cleveland catcher Ray Fosse at the 1970 All-Star Game; Fosse dropped the ball, and Rose scored on the play. Tom Seaver (page 393) delivers the pitch. Seaver had a 178-101 record with a 2.65 ERA and 2,304 strikeouts during the decade.

THE 1970s

The one consistent factor in baseball during the 1970s was change. New stadiums, new teams, new rules, new uniforms, new attitudes, and new legal decisions all had long-lasting repercussions on America's favorite pastime.

Stadium architecture dramatically affected the way the game was played. The new parks built between 1965 and 1977 had relatively the same dimensions — 330 feet down the foul lines — as opposed to the old stadiums, which had varied distances and their own individual personalities. All the new stadiums had artificial turf.

The new stadiums included: Three Rivers Stadium in Pittsburgh (1970), Riverfront Stadium in Cincinnati (1970), Veterans Stadium in Philadelphia (1971), Royals Stadium in Kansas City (1973), Olympic Stadium in Montreal (1977), and the Kingdome in Seattle (1977). Even Yankee Stadium had been renovated (1976), and its deep left-center and center fields were brought in by about 30 feet. By 1980, only four old parks remained: Tiger Stadium in Detroit, Fenway Park in Boston, and Chicago's Comiskey Park in the American League and Wrigley Field in the National League.

Scores of fans mourned the transformation. They insisted that baseball was meant to be played on grass and complained that going to the park was like being in a shopping mall. While purists did not like artificial turf itself, fans did like the new game that artificial turf created.

Speed, speed, and more speed was the name of the game on the new synthetic surface. Since balls hit on the "carpet" would pick up speed as they traveled and would bounce extremely high, teams placed a premium on fleet-footed infielders and outfielders who could get a quick jump on the ball.

Such skilled singles hitters as Pete Rose, Rod Carew, and Mickey Rivers punched, chopped, and sliced the ball past infielders. Road-runners Lou Brock, Rickey Henderson, and Willie Wilson changed the way pitchers pitched and the way defenses aligned themselves. Indeed, A's owner Charles O. Finley was so taken with the running game that in 1974 he hired Herb Washington, a world-class sprinter with no baseball experience, as a designated runner.

Baseball in the 1970s had gotten behind the population again. In 1972, the Washington Senators left the nation's capital, moved to Dallas-Ft. Worth and became the Texas Rangers. The American League granted expansion to Seattle and Toronto in 1977. By increasing the number of teams in each division, expansion also reduced the number of games intradivision rivals, such as the Yankees and Red Sox, played each other.

From 1969 to 1979, major league baseball enjoyed a 48 percent rise in attendance. There were

Joe Rudi makes an electrifying catch during the 1972 World Series. Rudi was the A's left fielder and an important player in a cast of characters that brought three world championships home to Oakland during the 1970s.

REGGIE JACKSON

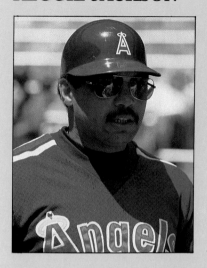

One of baseball's greatest sluggers and postseason heroes, Reggie Jackson holds 12 World Series records and ranks fifth on the all-time World Series home run list. No wonder they called him "Mr. October."

The first-round pick of the Athletics in 1966 (second overall), Jackson led the American League in runs twice, RBI once, home runs twice, and strikeouts four times during his nine years with the A's. He helped lead Oakland to three straight world championships between 1972 and '74. He won the MVP in '73 when he hit 32 homers, scored 99 runs, and knocked in 117 runs.

Jackson was traded to the Baltimore Orioles after the '75 season, played one year with the Birds, then signed a multimillion-dollar free-agent contract with George Steinbrenner's Yankees in '77. "I'm the straw that stirs the drink," Jackson said when he arrived in New York, displaying the healthy ego that clashed with manager Billy Martin's and alienated captain Thurman Munson. Then Jackson proceeded to help the Yanks win their first championship in 15 years.

Jackson won his fifth World Series ring in '78 and his third home run title in '80. When the Yanks didn't re-sign him after a poor '81, he went to California and led the A.L. in homers again with 39. When Jackson ended his 21-year career after the '87 season, he ranked sixth all-time in home runs with 563, had scored 1,551 runs and driven in 1,702, and was the all-time leader in strikeouts with 2,597.

WILLIE WILSON
OUTFIELD

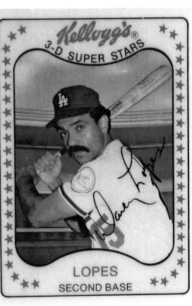

Kellogg's ®
3-D SUPER STARS

LOPES
SECOND BASE

Oakland's shortstop Bert Campaneris threw his bat at Detroit Tigers pitcher Lerrin LaGrow (top) after Campy was hit by a LaGrow pitch in the 1972 American League Championship Series. Campaneris was one of the premier shortstops in baseball during the 1970s. He stole at least 30 bases in ten consecutive seasons from 1965 to 1974. A view from "peanut heaven" in Cincinnati's Riverfront Stadium (bottom left) during the 1972 World Series. Willie Wilson (bottom middle) stole 83 bases in 1979. Los Angeles Dodgers second baseman Davey Lopes (bottom right) averaged 91 runs scored and 53 stolen bases a season from 1973 to '79.

several reasons for the dramatic growth in fan interest. The improved accessibility of the new stadiums made it easier for fans to get to the game. The split into two divisions in 1969 increased the number of teams that had a chance to win the pennant. Although the Reds, Pirates, and Phillies dominated the National League during the decade and the A's, Orioles, and Yanks became mini-dynasties in the American League, there were many competitive pennant races. The 1975 World Series, one of the greatest Series in baseball history, showed fans (61 million watched Game Six) how exciting good baseball could still be, wiping out the sentiment shared by many that the game had seen its better days. The decline of the Yankee empire in 1964 made the race for the American League title a legitimate challenge instead of a fight for second place.

Ticket prices were cheap compared to those of rival sports. Baseball had largely become a night-time event, dished up to the customer in comfy surroundings. Before the game and between innings, fans were serenaded by Top 40 tunes and on-field entertainment. (Mascots like San Diego's Chicken began strutting around the field and in the stands.) Electronic scoreboards flashed messages, led cheers, and sometimes offered replays of the game. It was almost like watching the game on the tube in your own living room.

Baseball also owed its boom in the 1970s to increased offense and colorful superstars. For the first time in years there were .350 hitters (Rico Carty, Carew, and Joe Torre) and 40-home run men (Hank Aaron and George Foster) challenging Cy Young Award winners (Tom Seaver, Jim Palmer, Steve Carlton, Catfish Hunter, and

Vida Blue). Fans were also treated to the newest superstar in baseball: the relief pitcher. The most effective and best paid were Sparky Lyle, Goose Gossage, and Rollie Fingers. The new emphasis on running saw such speedsters as Davey Lopes, Billy North, and Lou Brock challenge excellent catchers the likes of Johnny Bench, Carlton Fisk, and Thurman Munson.

Longtime stars Hank Aaron, Willie Mays, Pete Rose, Roberto Clemente, Al Kaline, Lou Brock, and Carl Yastrzemski joined the 3,000 hit club, pushing its ranks to 15 members. In 1979, Manny Mota rang up a record number of career pinch-hits (147), and that same season, Brock became baseball's all-time leader in steals with 938. (The 40-year-old star retired the same season and capped the year by batting .304 and joining the 3,000 hit club.)

This offensive explosion was due in part to some of the rule changes that were instituted in 1969 to help the hitters. One made the strike zone smaller. The other reduced the height of the pitcher's

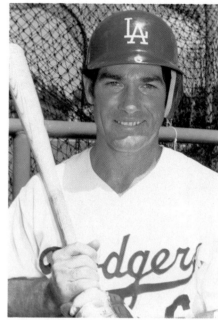

Steve Garvey averaged 104 RBI from '74 to '79.

mound. A third and even more radical change, adopted by the American League in 1973, was the introduction of the designated hitter (DH). DHs would bat in place of the pitcher but would not play the field. The rule extended the careers of great aging hitters —

JIM BOUTON'S BALL FOUR

When journeyman pitcher Jim Bouton's book *Ball Four* was published in 1970, the baseball world found out that the diary Bouton had been keeping during the 1969 season with the Seattle Pilots wasn't just about his "life and hard times throwing the knuckleball in the major leagues." He was also writing about the sex lives of players, the

greed of owners, and the vices of superstars; his book basically pulled the covers off baseball and revealed all of the game's warts.

For example, in the often hilarious kiss-and-tell tome (which would be tame by today's sensationalist standards), Bouton tarnished Mickey Mantle's image, revealing that the Yankees slugger would often play with hangovers and could be nasty to autograph-seeking kids.

The baseball establishment predictably didn't think the book was a must-read. Cubs manager Leo Durocher burned a copy in the clubhouse, players criticized Bouton in the media, baseball writer Dick Young called Bouton "a social leper," and commissioner Bowie Kuhn "censured" the book and warned Bouton against "future writings of this character."

All those actions did was stimulate enough sales to make *Ball Four* a best-seller, beget a sequel called *I'm Glad You Didn't Take It Personally*, and lead to the "Ball Four" TV situation comedy, which struck out with viewers after just a few weeks.

Vada Pinson scores as Yankee Thurman Munson awaits the ball in 1974 (top left). Munson batted .292 and averaged 12 home runs, 73 RBI, and 72 runs scored a season in his nine full seasons from 1970 to '78. Catfish Hunter (top right) had a 169-102 record with a 3.17 ERA during the 1970s. He accumulated 1,304 strikeouts, 2,398 innings pitched, 140 complete games, and 30 shutouts during the decade. Pirate Rennie Stennett flies toward Reds second baseman Joe Morgan to break up the double play in the 1972 N.L.C.S. (bottom). Stennett hit .286 in 1975, with 89 runs scored and 62 RBI. Morgan batted .282 and accumulated 1,005 runs scored, 720 RBI, 173 home runs, 1,071 walks, 518 stolen bases, and 275 doubles during the 1970s. He ended his career with 1,865 bases on balls, third on the all-time list, and 689 stolen bases, seventh on the all-time list.

THE 1970s

Orlando (The Baby Bull) Cepeda, Jim Ray Hart, Tony Oliva, and Tommy Davis are examples. In 1973, Davis helped boost the Orioles to the A.L. East title by batting .306 with 89 RBI. Not only did batting averages rise, but DHs joined the ranks of the highest paid players in the league.

Traditionalists, however, insisted that the rule would turn managers into puppets, since strategy would be reduced. The number of sacrifice bunts reduced and use of pinch-hitters would decline. Pitchers would throw too many innings because they wouldn't have to be removed for pinch-hitters. Those in favor of the rule said that the game would be more exciting having one less "automatic out" at the plate, and that a manager would still have to think on his feet. The DH is accepted in every level from high school on through the minor leagues, but the National League still hasn't adopted it.

The ballplayer of the 1970s looked stylish both on the field and on color television. Gone from all but a few clubs were the familiar baggy flannel uniforms. Bright colors marched into the game and styles swung from wide stripes to thin ones. Shirts went from button-down fronts to pullovers. The Chicago White Sox even tried shorts. In 1971, the new-look Pirates wore sexy, skin-tight threads that caught on. Charlie Finley, the most controversial owner of the era, outfitted his A's in vivid white, green, and gold uniforms of imported material that they would wear in different color schemes every game (and other teams, like the Pirates with their black and gold, soon followed suit). Finley even encouraged his players to grow long hair, sideburns, and mustaches; he paid $300 per face in an attempt to evoke a Gay '90s look.

By the late 1970s, most catchers wore fiberglass helmets, better masks, and neck flaps that were invented by Dodger Steve Yeager, who was seriously injured when a shattered bat struck him in the throat. They also donned lighter chest protectors, made possible by the advent of high-impact plastic that preserved safety and increased mobility. Baseball mitts grew even larger, which enabled players to make flashy one-handed grabs. In addition, life improved for reckless outfielders when clubs installed padded barriers.

Athletes of the 1970s were faster, bigger, stronger, more numerous (due to expansion), and better educated than they had been for decades; they also possessed a

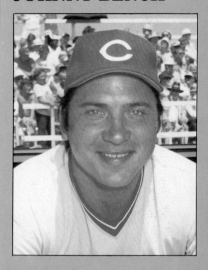

JOHNNY BENCH

"I don't want to embarrass any other catcher by comparing him with Johnny Bench," manager Sparky Anderson once said about the backstop. Though Anderson has always been famous for overstatement, his Bench comment was right on the mark.

Bench — who came from the hometown of his idol, Mickey Mantle (Oklahoma City) — joined the Reds in 1968. Displaying awesome power at the plate and a great arm and quickness behind it, he instantly became the N.L.'s premier catcher and was named Rookie of the Year, setting records for the most games (154) and most doubles by a catcher (40) in the process. Two seasons later, he led the Reds to the N.L. pennant, leading the league in homers (45) and RBI (148) and winning his first Most Valuable Player award. He took the MVP again in '72, topping the N.L. with 40 homers and 125 RBI.

Bench was the most important cog in Cincinnati's "Big Red Machine" of the 1970s, which won two successive world championships in 1975 and '76. He was the N.L. All-Star catcher for 13 straight years between 1968 and '80, and won the Gold Glove for ten successive seasons between 1968 and '77. He slugged 25 or more homers in eight seasons, and had 80 or more RBI in ten seasons. When he retired in 1983, he had caught 1,744 games, driven in 1,376 runs, and belted 389 home runs. Bench hit 327 of those homers as a catcher, another of his major league records. He was elected into the Hall of Fame in 1989.

Rusty Staub of Montreal slides into third as Cub Ron Santo takes the throw.

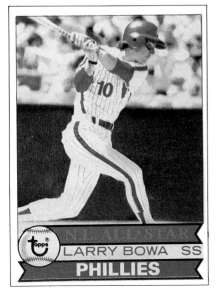

Nolan Ryan (top) tied the major league record of 19 strikeouts in a single game in 1974 against the Red Sox. The record was also held by Steve Carlton and Tom Seaver. Ryan also had a no-hitter in 1974, after getting two no-hitters in 1973. Shortstop Larry Bowa (bottom left) of the Phillies was a fine defensive player, and he scored 725 runs during the decade. Yankees reliever Sparky Lyle (bottom right) notched 200 saves.

Believe") McGraw — looked more like rock stars than role models; the players mirrored, in part, America's fascination with flamboyant, outspoken figures. They wore long hair, jewelry, batting gloves, sweatbands, and white shoes. They were also quotable, contentious, and most of all, entertaining.

In 1972, the average salary was estimated at $34,000 and 23 players earned $100,000 or more.

Rod Carew hit over .300 each year in the 1970s.

Hank Aaron reportedly earned the most, followed by Carl Yastrzemski, Willie Mays, Bob Gibson, and Roberto Clemente, each topping the $150,000 mark. A year later, 30 players broke the $100,000 barrier, with slugger Dick Allen topping the list with an annual income of $225,000. By 1978, players drew salaries that averaged more than $100,000. People compared them to Broadway entertainers, and the public's appreciation showed in better attendance at games and even higher television ratings, which became additional revenue that the Players' Association demanded and received after the strike in 1972.

While jealousy and resentment surrounded some of these I've-just-got-to-be-me characters, it only helped baseball at the box office. McGraw explained how he planned to spend his hefty contract by saying, "Ninety percent I'll spend on good times, women, and Irish whiskey. The other 10 percent I'll probably waste." Another wacky southpaw, Bill "Spaceman" Lee, openly mocked the baseball establishment by paying a fine imposed by commissioner Bowie Kuhn for his use of marijuana and then turned around and filed a grievance petition. When asked if he preferred natural grass or artifi-

different attitude toward the game, which was hard for some of the old timers to swallow. The spartan code of "playing with the small hurts" changed in the 1970s; more players admitted to injuries, refused to play hurt, demanded specialized treatment, and used their newly won rights to a guaranteed year's pay if disabled. (In July 1979, there were 127 disabled players, a figure three times higher than the entire year of 1970.)

Players of the 1970s possessed a more casual attitude toward the game, and many flaunted their personalities like never before. The volatile political climate of the 1960s that dominated the rest of the country cast a shadow over baseball. Players — such as Reggie ("I'm the straw that stirs the drink") Jackson, Ken "The Hawk" Harrelson, and Tug ("You Gotta

TOM SEAVER STRIKES OUT TEN IN A ROW

When a ballplayer's physical ability, timing, and confidence join forces to make him feel invincible, he calls it being "locked in." On April 22, 1970, Mets pitcher Tom Seaver was as locked in as any athlete has ever been.

In an afternoon game at Shea Stadium, Seaver, who had won the Cy Young Award in 1969, was pitching one of his typically efficient games against the Padres. When he struck out the side in the seventh inning, it gave him 13 for the game and four in a row. The fans were used to these "Seaver-type games" and seemed more preoccupied with the Mets

holding on to their 2-1 lead than any potential records.

But when "Tom Terrific" struck out the first two in the eighth, the scoreboard announced he had tied Nolan Ryan's club record with 15 Ks in a game. Then Seaver fanned the side for his seventh straight strikeout. Suddenly within reach was Johnny Podres' N.L. record eight consecutive strikeouts and a record-tying 19 in a game. Strikeout number eight came on three pitches to Van Kelly. In another three pitches to Cito Gaston, Podres' record was broken.

With about 20,000 screaming fans on their feet, Seaver was on automatic pilot. In another three pitches, down went Al Ferrara for the 19th strikeout of the game and tenth in a row, all coming when a pitcher is supposed to be tiring. No pitcher since has been quite so "locked in" as Seaver was that day.

Rollie Fingers (top left) was the best relief pitcher of the 1970s. Oakland's Fingers accumulated 209 saves and 79 relief wins during the decade. Boston outfielder Jim Rice (top right) led the American League with 39 home runs and a .593 slugging average in 1977. Yankees third baseman Graig Nettles (bottom left) notched 252 home runs, 831 RBI, and 773 runs scored in the 1970s. Jim Palmer (bottom right) of the Orioles won three Cy Young awards during the decade. He won at least 20 games in eight different seasons and led the league in innings pitched three times.

THE 1970s

cial turf, McGraw uttered another classic line: "I dunno. I never smoked Astroturf."

A younger, less awestruck breed of sportswriters made sure that the age of "The Ballplayer Can Do No Wrong" ended as quickly as the hula-hoop fad. Players were exposed, dissected, and analyzed in print and on television like never before. Yaz, the venerable Boston Red Sox slugger, was accused by some teammates of masterminding the dismissal of those he disliked. Dodger Steve Garvey, the clean-cut, conservative slugger, was labeled "Goody Two Shoes" and sarcastically called "The All-American Boy." Some players, such as

Phillies third baseman Mike Schmidt averaged 36 home runs a season from 1974 to '79.

Jackson and Allen, enjoyed their newfound bad-boy celebrity — it did, after all, mean more cash and glory. Others, such as Steve Carlton, Dave Kingman, and Amos Otis, treated baseball writers as social outcasts.

The 1974 A's and the 1978 Yankees had many documented arguments. Fist fights broke out among the Oakland players, who also denounced Finley as a raving lunatic and their manager, Alvin Dark, as a religious fanatic. Raging conflicts between Yankees superstar Reggie Jackson, his manager (Billy Martin), and owner George Steinbrenner made Liz Taylor and Richard Burton's liaison seem tranquil. Nevertheless, these two rocky clubs stayed together long enough to win World Series rings — three for Oakland in 1972, '73, and '74, and two for the Yankees in 1977 and '78.

In addition, former Yankees pitcher Jim Bouton's *Ball Four*, published in 1970, probably did more to demystify America's heroes than any behind-the-scene work before or since. Kuhn's attempt to suppress the book led to a humorous sequel. Other bawdy activities were reported in 1973 when Yankees pitchers Fritz Peterson and Mike Kekich engaged in a much publicized wife-swapping experiment that made great copy but (to say the least) shocked baseball's brass. At times, this "tell it like it is" style of journalism was in questionable taste.

In 1970, a record 20 blacks played in the All-Star Game. The impact of the black athlete on the game moved toward its zenith in the mid-1970s, when 26 percent of the active major leaguers were black. Some shortsighted owners (and fans) worried that blacks were taking over the game and the numbers lessened after that (from one in four to one in five), but during the decade blacks continued their offensive display, adding seven more batting titles and 12 home run titles, while often leading in stolen bases, RBI, runs scored, and total hits.

The rhetoric that had reigned years earlier on the streets of Mobile, AL, and Washington, DC, began infiltrating major league club houses. In 1974, Hank Aaron, who had accused owners of treating blacks as "trained monkeys,"

STEVE CARLTON

When Steve Carlton notched his first 20-win season in 1971, a year after leading the National League in losses with 19, the Cardinals felt it was as good a time as any to trade the hard-throwing, 6'4", 210-pound lefthander. So off he went to the Phillies for accomplished righty Rick Wise. Carlton turned in a season that made the deal the worst in Cardinal history.

What Carlton did in 1972 ranks with the greatest seasons ever by a pitcher. Hurling for the last-place 59-97 Phillies, he compiled a 27-10 record and led the N.L. in innings pitched (346), complete games (30), strikeouts (310), and ERA (1.97). Naturally, he won the Cy Young Award, the first of his major league-record four.

Carlton pitched another 13 seasons in Philadelphia. Although he refused to speak to the media during that period (which earned him the nickname "Silent Steve"), he did his talking on the mound, silencing hitters with an explosive fastball and the sharpest-breaking slider in the game. After '72, he led the N.L. in wins three more times, in complete games twice, and in strikeouts four times. He averaged a remarkable 277 innings a year for Philadelphia.

When Carlton ended his 23-year career in 1987, he was second all-time in strikeouts (4,131), ninth all-time in wins (329), and eighth all-time for innings pitched (5,207). The ten-time All-Star was one of four pitchers in history to strike out 19 batters in a game and held the major league record for most consecutive lifetime starts (544).

Johnny Bench, left, and Tony Perez were the muscle behind the Big Red Machine of the 1970s. Bench slammed 290 round-trippers during the decade, and together Bench and Perez averaged 209 RBI a season for Cincinnati from 1970 to '76.

THE 1970s

broke perhaps the most cherished record in baseball history when he belted his 715th career homer off Al Downing at Atlanta Stadium. That same year Lou Brock stole 118 bases to break Ty Cobb's old mark (Maury Wills had previously broken it in 1962). When he was passed over for MVP honors, Brock accused the voters of racism at worst and ignorance at best. Pittsburgh's Dock Ellis labeled Pirates officials as cheapskates and bigots.

That year also saw Frank Robinson, a superstar of the 1960s, become player/manager of the Cleveland Indians, making him the first black man ever to manage a major league team. (After two seasons, he became the first black manager to be fired.) Nevertheless, in 1979, there was only one black umpire among 60, few black coaches, and very few blacks in administrative posts.

Another minority, Latin Americans, continued to produce some of baseball's top stars, such as Orlando Cepeda, Tony Perez, Bert Campaneris, Luis Tiant, Dave Concepcion, Juan Marichal, and Rico Carty. Some claimed they were underpaid. Willie Montanez spoke for many when he said: "When it comes down to an American and a Latin fighting for the same spot...the Latin has gotta be twice as good. Else he don't get past April."

After the Pirates downed Baltimore in a dramatic seventh game in the 1971 World Series (the Series also featured the first World Series night game), Roberto Clemente, a native of Puerto Rico, complained to reporters of discrimination while manager Danny Murtaugh spoke to President Richard Nixon, who called to offer congratulations. At the close of the 1970s, officials at Yankee Stadium staged the first Latin American night in

baseball history to honor past Latin greats.

But more than anything else, the 1970s will be known as the decade of intense legal battles in the players' fight for freedom from owners, who could control their rights for their entire playing career. Spearheaded by a shrewd economist named Marvin Miller, the Major League Baseball Players' Association grew from a passive organization into an effective, powerful tool that earned the players increased average salaries and the right to arbitration to settle disputes between players and owners.

The players-owners war really began in 1970, when outfielder Curt Flood was traded from the St. Louis Cardinals to the Philadelphia Phillies. He likened the transaction to plantation owners trading slaves, refused to report, and filed a suit against baseball's "reserve clause," which bound a player forever to the team that held his contract. Flood insisted that he should have

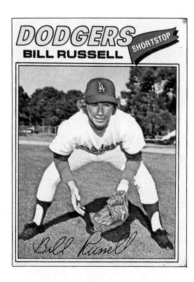

Bill Russell (top) was the Dodgers' shortstop from '72 to '83. Butch Hobson had 112 RBI in '77.

JOE MORGAN

If the trade that brought Steve Carlton to Philadelphia wasn't the biggest swindle of 1971, then the trade that brought second baseman Joe Morgan to Cincinnati from Houston was.

It had more immediate impact because the Reds were a winning team (having been to the World Series in 1970). Morgan, after seven seasons with the Astros, was a player ready to blossom. In his first Reds season, Morgan led the N.L. in walks and runs scored (two vital but underrated categories) — the first of six straight years in which he would be among the top five in the league in those departments. In '73, he began generating awesome power from his 5'7", 155-pound frame and contributed 26 homers to the "Big Red Machine." Then in 1975 and '76, he was the brightest on a team of All-Stars, batting .327 and .320, respectively, averaging 22 homers, 102 RBI, 63 stolen bases, winning the Gold Glove and Most Valuable Player awards both seasons, and leading the Reds to two world championships.

Morgan is considered by many to be the greatest all-around second baseman. The ten-time All-Star holds the major league record for the most consecutive errorless games at second (91), and the N.L. records for most games, seasons, and assists by a second baseman. He scored 100 runs in eight seasons, and he walked 100 times in eight seasons. He is second all-time for homers by a second sacker (268), third on the all-time list in walks (1,865), and seventh all-time in stolen bases (689).

Willie McCovey (top left) had 39 round-trippers and 126 RBI in 1970 for San Francisco. He also led the N.L. with a .612 slugging average, a 7.9 home run percentage, and 137 bases on balls. A's third baseman Sal Bando tries to knock the ball out of Dodgers catcher Steve Yeager's hands during the 1974 World Series (top right). Bando averaged 23 homers, 90 RBI, and 82 runs scored a season between 1969 and '76. Bubble-blowing contests spell relief for Met Tug McGraw, left, and Oakland's Rollie Fingers before the '73 World Series (bottom left). With the Twins mired in last place, some Minnesota fans (bottom right) in 1975 wanted to bring Billy Martin back.

THE 1970s

the right to sign with the team of his choice. In protest, he sat out the entire season, a move that hurt his career but helped pave the way for several significant cases that followed.

In 1972, Miller organized a players strike that wiped out spring training as well as some of the early games. The net result, however, gave players with four years of service a monthly check starting at age 50. After the 1972 strike, the owners traded 16 player reps and intimidated another 19 into resigning. Owners waged a propaganda war against Miller, citing inflated salary figures and exaggerated losses to turn the public sentiment against the players. Ironically, the players' cause was helped when owners like Finley, St. Louis' August Busch Jr., and San Diego's Ray Kroc acted like tyrants. Kroc, the owner of McDonald's hamburger chain, did little to help his brethren by calling his players "dummies" and then declaring, "I won't subsidize idiots."

The Players' Association was able to get some new concessions

for the players in a negotiated agreement with the owners at the start of the 1973 season. A system was established for arbitration of salary disputes. If a player and his team could not agree to terms, each would submit their final figures to an impartial arbitrator. The decision of the arbitrator was binding, and, for example, Jackson, Sal Bando, and Rollie Fingers were all awarded contracts that owner Finley had zealously refused to offer.

Another result of the 1973 agreement was the "ten and five" rule, which stated that a player who had ten years of major league experience, the last five with the same club, could veto a trade involving him (a ruling that would have allowed Flood to stop the 1970 trade, which led to his lawsuit).

Such provisions set the stage for Jim "Catfish" Hunter's battle with Finley after the 1974 season. Hunter (25-12 on the year) claimed that Charlie O. had failed to make certain payments under his contract and that this failure dissolved that contract and made him a free agent. The arbitration case that followed allowed him to sell his services to the highest bidder, which turned out to be George Steinbrenner's New York Yankees.

Perhaps the most significant legal change occurred in 1975 and is now known as "The Messersmith Case." Andy Messersmith of the Los Angeles Dodgers and Dave McNally of the Montreal Expos had decided to play the

Cub Bruce Sutter saved 37 games and won the Cy Young Award in 1979.

ROD CAREW

Pete Rose may be number one on the all-time hit list, but from the late 1960s to the early 1980s, nobody, not even Rose, produced better batting averages than Rod Carew.

Between 1969 and 1983, the lefthanded hit machine batted .300 or better for 15 straight seasons and won seven American League batting titles. He led the league in hits three times, had 200 or more hits four times, led the league in triples twice, and had 170 or more hits nine times. Carew was one of the greatest hitters of the last 50 years.

Although Carew was just average defensively at either first or second base, he was a great basestealer (353 lifetime) and daring runner, setting an A.L. record for steals of home with seven in 1969. And he had one glorious season when he silenced the critics who called him a "one-dimensional singles hitter." With the Minnesota Twins in 1977, he was the A.L.'s Most Valuable Player, batting .388 and leading the league in hits (239, the 14th highest season total ever), triples (16), and runs (128). He also drove in 100 runs, the only time in his career he reached the century mark in either run-production category. He had a .412 average with four runs in the 1979 League Championship Series for the Angels.

During his 19-year career — 12 with Minnesota and seven with California — Carew was named to 17 straight All-Star teams. He is 12th on the all-time hit list with 3,053, and his .328 lifetime average is the 27th highest.

Indians baserunner Leron Lee collides with BoSox catcher Carlton Fisk (top left) in 1974. Fisk suffered major ligament damage to his left knee on the play. Royals designated hitter Hal McRae (top right) hit .294 and averaged 74 RBI and 70 runs scored from 1973 to '79. Reds third baseman Denis Menke breaks up the double play by taking out A's second baseman Dick Green in 1972 (middle left). Cincinnati manager Sparky Anderson, left, gives shortstop Davey Concepcion the word (bottom right). Anderson won five division titles, four N.L. pennants, and two World Series in nine years with the Reds. He averaged 96 wins against 65 losses a season from 1970 to 1978. Al Oliver slides safely into third base as Red Denis Menke waits for the ball (bottom left).

THE 1970s

1975 season without signing contracts. As a result, they argued that they were now "free agents," free to sign with any team that they chose to bargain with. The owners understandably screamed foul, because it effectively did away with the reserve clause. The issue

went to arbitration, and arbitrator Peter Seitz ruled that a player's contract cannot be renewed indefinitely by the original owner until the player is traded, sold, released, or retired. (The owners fired Seitz and appealed his decision to the courts, which refused to change the ruling.) Although McNally retired, Messersmith signed a three-year deal with the Atlanta Braves for $1 million, a figure well above the Dodgers offer. Within two years after the decision, an annual free-agent draft sent salaries skyrocketing.

After the frenzied bidding of the first draft in 1976, 24 players (led by Jackson's five-year Yankees pact worth $2.93 million) had won a total of $25 million in contracts.

Once again, fans read of newly minted millionaires and responded by pushing attendance and television ratings sky high.

The biggest winner of the decade was Pittsburgh's Dave Parker, who in 1978 signed a five-year contract worth $900,000 a season. Jim Rice's seven-year pact with Boston averaged $700,000 a year. Vida Blue, Pete Rose, and Rod Carew also netted huge multi-year deals. As the dust settled from the latest salary explosion, 1979 (when pitcher Nolan Ryan snared the first million dollar annual salary) saw top baseball stars earning more than their counterparts in football and basketball.

This surplus of cash and glory cast players of the 1970s as a breed apart from their predecessors. In a sport as tradition-bound as baseball, this transformation was terribly disturbing to the embittered owners, who viewed Miller and the Players' Association as self-serving marauders out to destroy baseball.

As the decade closed, it seemed apparent that this bitter struggle would continue on into the 1980s, with dramatic changes in the game still to come.

HANK AARON BREAKS BABE RUTH'S RECORD

From the day in 1972 when Henry Aaron hit his 649th home run to pass Willie Mays for second place on the all-time list, it

seemed inevitable that "Hammerin' Hank" would also eclipse Babe Ruth's magic number of 714. Though he was 38, he was in great physical condition, still possessed lightning quick wrists, and was playing in one of baseball's best home run parks in Atlanta.

Aaron didn't succumb to the pressure in 1973. On the next to last day of the season, he hit his 40th homer and 713th lifetime. When the '74 season began, Braves executives wanted Aaron to sit out the first three games in Cincinnati so he could tie and break the record at home. Commissioner Bowie Kuhn ordered Atlanta to play Aaron and, in his first swing of the season, Hank tied Ruth with a homer off Jack Billingham.

The Braves lucked out when Aaron went homerless until the team arrived home on April 8 to play the Dodgers. With 53,775 fans in the stands, the largest crowd in Atlanta history, and over 30 million watching on television, Dodgers pitcher Al Downing walked Aaron his first time at bat. Boos cascaded on Downing as he threw Aaron a first-pitch ball Hank's second time up. Undoubtedly feeling the pressure to throw a strike, Downing grooved a fastball that Aaron appropriately deposited into the left field bullpen. As Aaron circled the bases as the new home run king, he smiled and said to himself, "Thank God it's over."

Braves outfielder Dale Murphy slugged 23 homers in 1978 and 21 in '79.

408

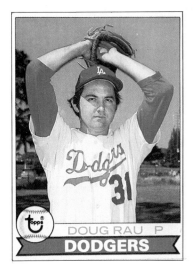

DOUG RAU P
DODGERS

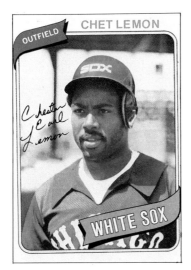

OUTFIELD
CHET LEMON
WHITE SOX

DAVE KINGMAN OF-1B
CUBS

PIRATES
BILL ROBINSON
OF-3B

3-D SUPER STARS

WATSON
FIRST BASE

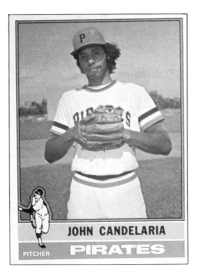

JOHN CANDELARIA
PITCHER
PIRATES

Dodgers lefthanded hurler Doug Rau (top left) averaged 15 wins a season from 1974 to '78. Chet Lemon (top middle left) of the White Sox led the A.L. with 44 doubles in '79. He averaged 16 homers and 76 runs scored from 1977 to '79. Dave Kingman (top middle right) led the National League with 48 homers in 1979. Kingman averaged 31 round-trippers a year from 1972 to '79. Bill Robinson (top right) hit .304 with 26 home runs and 104 RBI for the Pirates in 1977. Oakland shortstop Bert Campaneris (middle left) slugged 22 homers in 1970; the most homers in a season he hit after that was eight in 1972, and he ended his 19-year career with 79 total. Catcher Gary Carter (middle center) of the Montreal Expos slugged 31 homers and drove in 84 runs in 1977. Carter averaged 19 round-trippers and 67 runs batted in the five seasons from 1975 to 1979. Lefthander Jerry Koosman (middle right) ended his 19-year career with 222 wins against 209 losses and a 3.36 ERA. Astros outfielder/first baseman Bob Watson (bottom left) had 149 home runs and 822 RBI in the 1970s. Pittsburgh lefty John Candelaria (bottom right) was 20-5 with a 2.34 ERA in 1977.

THE 1970s

1970

Two-time Cy Young Award winner and former 31-game winner Denny McLain became a big-time loser. He lost his money, his reputation, and his fastball. Commissioner Bowie Kuhn suspended the reckless righthander for his involvement with underworld gamblers during the 1967 season. McLain returned in July 1970 before a standing-room-only crowd in Detroit's Tiger Stadium, but the evidence was in; one of baseball's brightest pitching stars had burned out. He was suspended again for pouring ice water on two reporters and yet again when he violated parole by carrying a pistol. At season's end, Detroit shipped him to the lowly Washington Senators.

The "On-Field Dubious Achievement Award" went to Bobby Bonds, who struck out 189 times to break his year-old record of 187.

Oakland's 20-year-old Vida Blue served notice that he had the right stuff by pitching a no-hitter. The 39-year-old Willie Mays recorded his 3,000th hit, as did 36-year-old Henry Aaron, who signed a three-year contract worth $600,000, making him, briefly, the highest-paid player in baseball.

Manager Earl Weaver led the Baltimore Orioles to a second straight A.L. East title with his same cast of veteran stars that had taken them to the 1969 World Series (with the exception of reserve outfielder Merv Rettenmund, who batted .322). The O's posted the best won-lost record of the decade (108-54, tied by the Reds in 1975). Frank Robinson and MVP Boog Powell combined for 60 homers and 192 RBI, and pitchers Mike Cuellar and Dave McNally tied for the league lead with 24 wins each. Jim Palmer, the most successful A.L. pitcher of the decade, won 20.

The Twins (without manager Billy Martin, who was fired for criticizing the owner) won 98 games and finished 9 games over the A's in the A.L. West, despite injuries to Rod Carew, Dave Boswell, and Luis Tiant. Outfielders Tony Oliva (23 homers, 107 RBI) and Cesar Tovar both hit .300, and third baseman Harmon Killebrew hit 41 homers and drove in 113 runs.

Eager to redeem themselves after last season's embarrassing loss to the Mets, Baltimore swept Minnesota in the American League Championship Series (A.L.C.S.) rematch. In the opener, pitcher Cuellar hit a grand slam to lead the O's to a 10-6 win. Frank Robinson and Davey Johnson homered in an 11-3 win the next day, and Palmer beat Jim Kaat to wrap up the Series.

The Mets, touted as likely winners of the N.L. East, fell to third. Manager Danny Murtaugh directed the Pirates to the title for the first time in a decade. The 36-year-old Roberto Clemente, considered one of the best defensive right fielders in the history of the game,

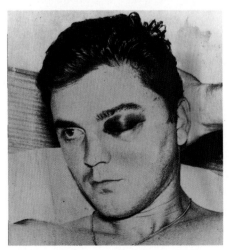

Twin Jim Perry (top) was 24-12 in '70. Tony Conigliaro (bottom) sports a shiner.

TOM SEAVER

George Thomas Seaver was not only the best pitcher of the 1970s, he is arguably the best righthanded pitcher of all time.

Seaver joined the Mets in 1967, a year after the team earned his rights in a special drawing. With his blazing fastball, exquisite delivery, and superior pitching intelligence, Seaver made an immediate impact on baseball's most inept club, going 16-13 with a 2.76 ERA to earn Rookie of the Year honors. Two years later his 25-7, Cy Young Award-winning season catapulted the "Miracle Mets" to the 1969 world championship. He was the Mets first genuine superstar and was beloved by the fans, who called him "Tom Terrific."

The future Hall of Famer was simply awesome during the 1970s, a decade in which he won two more Cy Young Awards, had four 20-win seasons, won five strikeout titles, and captured three ERA crowns. His best season was probably 1971, when he went 20-10 with a 1.76 ERA and 289 strikeouts, but lost Cy Young honors to the Cubs' Ferguson Jenkins. In '75, he was 22-9, with a 2.38 ERA and 243 strikeouts in 280 innings to win the Cy Young Award.

After a controversial trade to the Reds in 1977, Seaver remained one of the game's most effective pitchers. He finished second for the Cy Young in '81, when he won 14 games and lost only two for a .875 winning percentage. The 12-time All-Star retired in 1986 — after brief stints with the Mets, the White Sox, and the Red Sox — 15th all-time in wins (311) and third all-time in strikeouts (3,640).

Nolan Ryan (top left) had 125 strikeouts in 132 innings pitched in 1970 for the Mets. Orioles center fielder Paul Blair (top middle) in '70 had 18 homers and 79 runs scored. He had 102 runs scored in 1969. Frank Howard (top right) led the A.L. with 44 homers, 126 RBI, and 132 bases on balls in '70 for the Washington Senators. Red Sox outfielder Carl Yastrzemski (bottom left) led the American League with 125 runs scored and a .592 slugging average in 1970. Tom Seaver (bottom right) was 18-12 in 1970 for the Mets. He led the National League with a 2.81 ERA and 283 strikeouts that season. In '71, Seaver was 20-10 and led the N.L. with a 1.76 ERA and 289 Ks.

THE 1970s

hit .352 and anchored an outfield of Matty Alou and Al Oliver. Clemente and Willie Stargell set batting records en route to their 89-win season. Stargell tied a major league record with five extra base hits in a game, and Clemente set a new record with ten hits in two games.

The Cincinnati Reds led the league in homers (191) and rolled over N.L. West foes with 102 wins. Tony Perez, Pete Rose, and Bob Tolan all hit over .300. Catcher Johnny Bench led the league in homers (45) and RBI (148) and won his first MVP award.

Pitchers Don Gullett and Gary Nolan shut down Pittsburgh's big guns in the National League Championship Series (N.L.C.S.), allowing three runs in three games. Rose, Tolan, Perez, and Bench led the offense, and the Reds won by scores of 3-0, 3-1, and 3-2.

The World Series opened at the new Riverfront Stadium, the first Series game ever played on artificial turf. In Game One, the score was tied 3-3 when the human vacuum cleaner, Brooks Robinson, made the first of a series of sparkling plays at third. In the sixth inning, he backhanded a Lee May bullet down the line, preventing a sure double. In the seventh he homered, giving the Orioles a 4-3 victory. "The Big Red Machine" cruised to a 4-0 lead in the next game, but the O's rallied for five in the fifth and held on for a 6-5 win. Dave McNally held the Reds to three runs in Game Three and also hit a grand slam. This time, three fielding marvels by Robinson preserved a 9-3 win.

Thanks to Lee May's three-run homer, the Reds rallied from a 5-3 deficit in Game Four and went on to win 6-5. But it only postponed the inevitable. Cuellar settled down after a rocky first inning, and Baltimore's 15-hit

attack clinched the title with a 9-3 win. Overall, the Orioles assaulted Reds pitching for 50 hits, and proved what they were certain of the previous season: They were the best team in baseball.

Oriole Frank Robinson hit 28 homers in 1971.

1971

The pitcher of the year, in what turned out to be a big year for pitchers, was an Oakland Athletics 21-year-old southpaw named Vida Blue. Blue won nine of his first ten games, slumped somewhat in the second half of the season, and finished with a 24-8 record, 301 strikeouts, and a 1.82 ERA. He won both the Cy Young and MVP awards, despite the fact that Detroit's Mickey Lolich had won 25 games.

Blue's teammates Catfish Hunter and reliever Rollie Fingers (he of the waxed handlebar mustache) won 21 and saved 17, respectively. Baltimore boasted four 20-game winners in Mike Cuellar, Dave McNally, Jim Palmer, and newcomer Pat Dobson. Former 31-game winner Denny McLain lost 22 and won only ten for the Senators. McLain's teammate Curt Flood left the team after only 13 games while his antitrust suit was pending before the Supreme Court.

JIM PALMER

During the 1970s, the Baltimore Orioles' Jim Palmer was the outstanding pitcher in the American League. In only two years during the decade — 1974 and '79 — did he not win 20 or more games and that was because he missed parts of both seasons with arm injuries.

Palmer joined the Orioles' starting rotation in 1966 and won 15 games as Baltimore won the pennant. In the '66 World Series, just a few days short of his 21st birthday, he became the youngest pitcher to hurl a complete game Series shutout, beating the Dodgers and Sandy Koufax 6-0.

Palmer's promising career was almost ended by arm problems in 1967, and he missed most of that season and all of the following year. Fully recovered in '69, Palmer went 16-4 and anchored one of baseball's perennially great pitching staffs. His success was based on superior intelligence, a variety of pitches and outstanding control. He never led the league in strikeouts, but ERAs of 2.40 in 1973, 2.09 in '75, and 2.51 in '76 (along with the 20-plus wins) earned him the Cy Young Award in each of those seasons. He had ERAs under 3.00 in ten seasons, and he had more than 150 strikeouts in seven.

While he had a reputation for babying his arm and complaining to manager Earl Weaver, Palmer led the A.L. in innings pitched four times, hurled more than 300 innings four times, and threw almost 4,000 innings in a 19-year career. He ended his career in 1984 with a 268-152 record and a 2.86 ERA.

A's lefthander Vida Blue (top left) won the 1971 A.L. Cy Young Award. He was 24-8 that year, with a 1.82 ERA, 24 complete games, and eight shutouts. Blue averaged 17 wins a season during the 1970s. Bobby Murcer (top right) hit a career-high .331 in 1971, with 25 homers and 94 RBI. Brooks Robinson (bottom left) put on the show during the 1970 World Series. He time and again stole base hits from Reds players, and he batted .429 with two homers, six RBI, and five runs scored. Mickey Lolich, left, and Catfish Hunter (bottom right) talk before a game. Lolich was 25-14 in '71, leading the A.L. in wins, complete games (29), innings pitched (376), and strikeouts (308). Hunter was 21-7 in '71, with 16 complete games and 295 innings pitched.

YANKS

Bobby Murcer | **OUTFIELD**

413

THE 1970s

In addition, one of the most lopsided trades of the decade involved a pitcher: The Mets traded Nolan Ryan, the man who would become baseball's all-time strikeout leader, and three other players to California for third baseman Jim Fregosi.

A's owner Charles O. Finley had been through four different managers in four seasons. In Dick Williams, who would be named Manager of the Year, he found the hard-nosed skipper who would eventually direct the Athletics to 101 wins and the A.L. West title.

Oakland's offense was led by third baseman Sal Bando, outfielder Joe Rudi, and 25-year-old slugger Reginald Jackson, who led the team with 32 homers. After one shot, the ever-modest Jackson said, "God, do I love to hit that little round SOB out of the park and make 'em say 'Wow.' "

Baltimore won the A.L. East title for the third year in a row, all with 100 wins or more. The Orioles won their final 11 games of the season and soared to a 12-game lead over Detroit. The highlight of the season was 35-year-old Frank Robinson's back-to-back grand slams against Washington.

Although Pete Rose hit .304, the Cincinnati team batting average fell 29 points and the Big Red Machine sputtered to a fourth-place finish in the N.L. West. The San Francisco Giants almost squandered an 11-game lead by losing 18 of 24 during the month of September. Thanks to the clutch pitching of Juan Marichal (18-11) and Gaylord Perry (16-12), the Giants man-

aged to hold on and edge the Dodgers. Bobby Bonds led the club with a .288 average, 33 homers, and 102 RBI. The 40-year-old "Say Hey Kid," Willie Mays, finished the year hitting .271 with 18 homers.

In the East, Pittsburgh repeated as division winners. The Pirate attack was spearheaded by Clemente, Oliver, Manny Sanguillen, and Stargell, who led the N.L. with 48 home runs. Dock Ellis won 19, and Steve Blass won 15. The Cardinals finished second, led by MVP winner Joe Torre, who finished first in the league in hitting (.363) and RBI (137).

Weaver's Orioles trounced the A's in the playoffs. McNally outpitched Blue in the opener 5-3. Cuellar limited Oakland to one run in the second game, as 6'4" Boog Powell belted two homers in the 5-1 win. Jim Palmer completed the sweep with a 5-3 decision. The Pirates lost the National League Championship Series opener to the Giants in Candlestick Park, but rebounded with a 9-4 win in Game Two, thanks to Bob Robertson, who drove in five runs on three homers and a double. Robertson added another home run in Game Three, a 2-1 Bucs win. The clincher was a 9-5 slugfest,

EARL WEAVER — MANAGER

If you judge managers by who gets the most out of the players they've got, then the best manager of the 1970s was the skipper of the Baltimore Orioles, Earl Weaver.

Weaver wasn't just another journeyman minor leaguer who made good when he took over the Orioles mid-way through the 1968 season. Managing his way up the Baltimore farm system,

Weaver's teams had finished first or second seven times in eight years. The feisty, diminutive field general was a master motivator of players and one of the first to make significant use of statistics in decision-making. In his first three full seasons with the Orioles, he won three pennants and a World Series (1970), winning over 100 games each year.

When Baltimore's personnel began to change in the mid-1970s, Weaver still brought home winners. He manipulated his 25-man roster to perfection and took A.L. East division titles in '73 and '74. Then, after three straight second-place finishes and a fourth, Weaver's club won the pennant in the last year of the decade. His Baltimore teams won 90 or more games during 11 seasons. His teams finished first in their division six times and second seven times.

Overall, Weaver's .583 winning percentage is eighth all-time. His .682 winning percentage in American League Championship Series is first all-time. His philosophy for success also became the title of Weaver's autobiography, published in 1982: "It's what you learn after you know it all that counts."

Harmon Killebrew led the A.L. with 119 RBI in 1971.

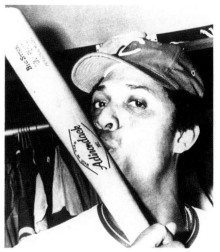

Best Wishes
Joe Torre

Cardinals third baseman Joe Torre (top left) earned MVP honors in 1971, leading the N.L. in batting average (.363), RBI (137), and base hits (230). He also had 24 homers, 97 runs scored, 34 doubles, and a .555 slugging percentage. Torre ended his 18-year career with a .297 batting average, 252 home runs, and 1,094 RBI. Catfish Hunter (top right) was 106-49 from 1970 to '74 for the Oakland A's, winning 20 games four years in a row for them. He averaged 281 innings pitched a year in those five seasons. Tony Perez (bottom right) kisses the bat that helped him drive in at least 90 runs a season for 11 years in a row for Cincinnati. Perez, who played both third base and first base for the Reds, averaged 26 home runs a season for the Reds from 1967 to '76. His best season offensively came in 1970, when he hit .317 with 40 home runs, 129 RBI, 107 runs scored, and a .589 slugging average. Perez ended his career with 379 home runs, 1,652 runs batted in, a .279 batting average, 1,272 runs scored, and 505 doubles.

THE 1970s

decided by a pair of three-run homers by Richie Hebner and Oliver.

The Pirates were distinct underdogs in the first World Series to be played at night, originally a brainchild of Oakland A's owner Charlie Finley. Baltimore boasted a 14-game win streak, including a playoff sweep, and made the odds makers look good by winning the first two games by the scores of 5-3 and 11-3. Things changed, however, when the action shifted to the artificial turf of Three Rivers Stadium.

Steve Blass, the Bucs' ace righthander, pitched a three-hitter, winning Game Three 5-1. The key blow was Robertson's three-run homer in the seventh inning. Then, before an estimated TV audience of 61 million viewers, the Pirates overcame a 3-0 deficit, as pinch hitter Milt May evened the Series by singling home the deciding run for a 4-3 win. In Game Four, 51,000 Bucs fans watched Nelson Briles pitch a two-hit shutout for a 4-0 victory.

Back in Baltimore, the O's used three of their elite starters to pull out a ten-inning 3-2 win. Blass

and Cuellar started the seventh and deciding game. Clemente, who batted safely in all seven games for a .414 average, notched the first Pirate hit, a solo homer in the fourth inning. Nursing a 2-1 lead into the ninth, Blass retired Baltimore in order to give Pittsburgh the title. Afterward, Pirates fans some 40,000 strong stormed the downtown area. Some danced nude. Windows were broken, cars were burned, people were injured, and the whole sordid affair reminded people of the war protests of the 1960s.

1972

This strike-interrupted season was further marred by the loss of three of baseball's most beloved personalities. Gil Hodges, age 47, the man who engineered the Mets Miracle in 1969, died of a heart attack during spring training. Jackie Robinson, another one of the Brooklyn Dodgers' "Boys of Summer" and perhaps the most significant athlete in baseball history, died at age 53. On New Year's Eve, Roberto Clemente, the 38-year-old Pittsburgh superstar, went down with a plane on a mercy mission for the earthquake victims of Managua, Nicaragua, just a few months after he recorded his 3,000th hit.

On September 30, Ted Williams retired after four years as the manager of the Texas Rangers franchise. Bernice Gera, a housewife from upstate New York, became the first woman to umpire a professional baseball game, ending a six-year battle for women's rights. She worked the bases in the

Roberto Clemente gets his 3,000th hit in 1972.

GAYLORD PERRY

Three hundred victories has always been considered the ultimate lifetime achievement for a pitcher. At the very least, it should get a pitcher into the Hall of Fame. But when Gaylord Perry was eligible for Cooperstown in 1989, he was ignored by the voters. It was Perry's punishment for achieving some of his success by throwing an illegal pitch.

While on the mound, Perry would touch various parts of his uniform with his pitching fingers, making everyone suspect him of using banned substances on the ball. Perry played on that suspicion to psych hitters out. Any doubt was erased when he wrote a book late in his career and admitted to throwing the spitball. "Without it," he claimed, "I'd probably been farmin' about ten years ago."

Even without the spitter, Perry would have been a successful pitcher. After notching two 20-win seasons in ten years with the Giants, Perry was traded to Cleveland in 1972 and promptly won 24 games and a Cy Young Award. Six years later, with the Padres, he went 21-6 with a 2.72 ERA and won the Cy Young again, becoming the only pitcher to win the honor in both leagues.

Perry ended his 22-year career in 1983 ranked 14th all-time in wins (314) and fifth lifetime in losses, innings pitched, and strikeouts. He won 15 or more games in 13 different seasons. He led the league in innings pitched twice, threw more than 300 innings in six seasons, and hurled 250 or more innings in 12 seasons.

416

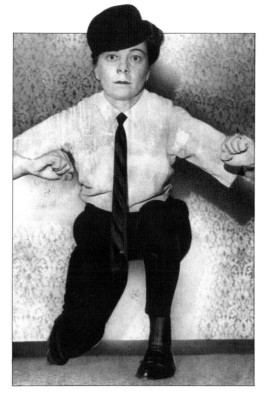

Detroit lefthander Mickey Lolich (top left) was 22-14 in 1972. Bernice Gera (top right) in '72 became the first woman to umpire a professional game. Orioles hurler Dave McNally (middle left) was 21-5 in 1971 for an A.L.-leading .808 winning percentage. McNally won 20 games in four straight years for the Birds. He ended his 14-year career in 1975 with a 184-119 record and a 3.24 ERA. Steve Blass (middle center) was 19-8 for the 1972 Pirates, with a 2.49 ERA. In the '72 World Series, Blass hurled two complete-game victories, giving up only seven hits and four walks while striking out 13 in 18 innings. Ken Holtzman (middle right) had a 77-55 record in four seasons with the Oakland A's from 1972 to '75. He compiled a 4-1 record in the three World Series that he pitched with Oakland. Holtzman's career record is 174-150 in 15 years. Dick Allen (bottom left) led the A.L. in homers (37), RBI (113), slugging percentage (.603), and bases on balls (99) for the '72 White Sox. Mets lefty John Matlack (bottom right) averaged 15 wins a year from 1972 to '76.

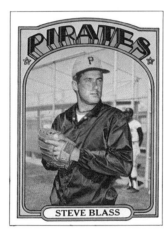

STEVE BLASS

KEN HOLTZMAN
PITCHER
Oakland A's

417

first game of a doubleheader in the New York-Pennsylvania League and quit soon after.

Willie Mays, who began his career as a New York Giant, returned to New York as a Met. Second baseman Joe Morgan was traded from Houston to Cincinnati, where he became a superstar. Frank Robinson, the only man to win MVP awards in both leagues, returned once again to the N.L. as a Dodger.

Minnesota's Rod Carew hit .318 and became the first American League batting champ not to hit a home run. Chicago's Richie Allen, in his first season with the White Sox, led the A.L. in home runs (37) and RBI (113), and walked away

Johnny Bench slugged 40 homers in '72.

with the MVP award. Cleveland newcomer Gaylord Perry, another former National Leaguer, won 24 games to nose out Detroit's Mickey Lolich (22-14) and Chicago's Wilbur Wood (24-17) for the Cy Young Award. California's Nolan Ryan (19-16) fanned 329 and pitched a league-leading nine shutouts.

In the National League, Cy Young Award winner Steve Carlton turned in the outstanding individual performance of the year. Despite playing on a Philadelphia team that finished with the worst record in the league (59-97), Carlton led the N.L. in wins (27), strikeouts (310), and ERA (1.97). Nate Colbert's 111 RBI accounted for 23 percent of San Diego's runs, setting an all-time record.

The strike forced the cancellation of 86 games and had little effect on the National League, where the Reds and Pirates romped. It did, however, have an impact on the American League East race, where Detroit edged Boston by only a 1/2 game. The Tigers, thanks to Lolich and Al Kaline, who led the team with a .313 average, finished first with an 86-70 record; the Red Sox settled for second at 85-70.

The A's coasted to the title in the A.L. West, beating the White Sox by 5 1/2 games. Finley was his old controversial self. Vida Blue, who was paid only $13,000 the year before when he won the Cy Young Award, demanded a $77,000 raise. Finley refused. Blue refused to

THE OAKLAND ATHLETICS DYNASTY

While many people argue that the Reds were the best team of the 1970s, they won only two world championships during the decade. The Oakland Athletics were the last team to win three successive titles—1972 to '74—

and in this era of free agency, its unlikely their feat will be matched.

The A's were owned by the controversial Charlie O. Finley, who allowed his independent-minded players to grow mustaches and wear multicolored uniforms. But Oakland was also known for its multitude of talent. The pitching staff was anchored

by Catfish Hunter, Vida Blue, Ken Holtzman, and reliever Rollie Fingers. The offense was powered by right fielder Reggie Jackson, third baseman Sal Bando, and left fielder Joe Rudi. With catcher/first baseman Gene Tenace and shortstop Bert Campaneris providing solid defense, the A's won five division titles between 1971 and '75.

An injured Jackson missed the 1972 Series against the Reds, but Tenace batted .348 to lead Oakland to a seven-game victory. In '73, Jackson was the Series MVP as the A's beat the Mets in seven. In '74, Alvin Dark replaced Dick Williams as manager, and the A's became notorious for feuding with Finley and amongst themselves. Still, they managed to win a third consecutive championship, beating the Dodgers in five games.

The A's won the A.L. West crown in 1975, but with Hunter gone to the Yankees, Oakland lost the pennant to Boston. By '76, Jackson was also gone; the A's 1970s dynasty was over.

Joe Rudi, left, and Sal Bando were two keys to the A's success in the 1970s.

Steve Carlton (top left) in 1972 was in the N.L.'s top five in shutouts (eight), fewest hits per game (6.68), and opponents' batting average (.206). Billy Williams (top right) led the N.L. with a .333 batting average and a .606 slugging average in 1972. Tiger Al Kaline (bottom left) hit .313 in '72. Bob Gibson (bottom right) was 19-11 with 208 Ks in '72.

419

pitch. After a bitter holdout, Blue signed for less but wasn't the same pitcher when he returned, winning only six all year.

In the American League Championship Series, the A's opened at home, winning an 11-inning thriller behind Rollie Fingers' relief work. Next, John "Blue Moon" Odom hurled a three-hitter to give the A's a 2-0 series lead. Back in Detroit, Billy Martin's revived Tigers won the next two. In the finale, second-string catcher Gene Tenace notched his only playoff hit to give the A's a 2-1 win and a pennant.

Bill Virdon replaced ailing manager Danny Murtaugh and pushed the Pirates to their third consecutive N.L. East title. Steve Blass led the staff with 19 wins. The Reds didn't have much pitching to brag about (the staff only completed 25 games all season), but the Big Red Machine boasted a powerful lineup, including Pete Rose and National League home run (40) and RBI (125) leader Johnny Bench, who won his second MVP award.

This matchup of N.L. dynasties went a full five games. In the finale, the Bucs had a 3-2 lead into the last of the ninth. After a Bench homer tied the game, a pair of singles brought in Pirates reliever Bob Moose, who threw a wild pitch that allowed the winning run to score.

The underdog A's limped into the World Series without cleanup hitter Reggie Jackson, who had injured a hamstring in the playoffs. In the first game at Cincinnati, catcher Tenace homered twice to give the A's a 3-2 win. Catfish Hunter pitched brilliantly in Game Two, and in the ninth inning, Joe Rudi made a leaping backhand catch against the left field wall to preserve a 2-1 win. The Reds won the third game 1-0. Tenace, who

hit only five home runs during the regular season, homered again and scored two runs in a 3-2 come-from-behind Oakland win to lead the Series 3-1.

The Reds won Game Five 5-4, and then romped 8-1 to push the Series to a seventh game. Game Seven was a classic. Dick Williams fended off the Reds with a star-studded pitching lineup, and Series MVP Tenace (four homers, nine RBI) drove in two runs, giving the A's a 3-2 win and their first world championship since 1931.

1973

The "Year of the Designated Hitter" raised the American League average to .259 and produced a record 12 20-game winners. Knuckleballer Wilbur Wood of the White Sox posted the most victories (24) but wound up losing 20 games. The mercurial Nolan Ryan (21-16) hurled two no-hitters and broke Sandy Koufax's single-season strikeout record (383), but he also

Wilbur Wood was a 20-game winner each season from 1971 to 1974 for the ChiSox.

ROLLIE FINGERS

By the late 1960s, the job of relief pitcher had become one of the most important roles on a team. Without a "closer," a guy who could pitch in 50, 60, even 70 games and consistently chalk up saves, a club couldn't be considered a serious pennant contender.

In Rollie Fingers, famous for his handlebar mustache and late-inning heroics, the Oakland Athletics had the king of the closers. Between 1972 and '74, Fingers averaged 68 games, nine relief wins, and 20 saves as the A's won three straight world championships.

Fingers became a free agent in '77 and signed with the San Diego Padres, where he led the National League in games (78) and saves (35). His combined wins and saves that year accounted for an amazing 62 percent of the Padres' 69 victories.

Fingers led the N.L. in saves again in '78 with a career-high 37. Two years later, he was traded to the Milwaukee Brewers and in the strike-shortened '81 season, he saved or won 34 of the Brewers' 62 victories. Although Milwaukee lost the divisional playoff to the Yankees, Fingers won the A.L.'s Most Valuable Player and Cy Young awards, the first time in history a reliever was given both honors. He led his league in relief wins three times and saves three times. He pitched in 60 or more games in nine seasons.

Fingers holds the major league record for saves (341), and he is third all-time for games pitched (944) and relief victories (107).

Dusty Baker (top left) scored 101 runs and drove in 99 for the Braves in 1973. Amos Otis (top right) batted .284, smacked 159 homers, scored 861 runs, drove in 753 runs, and stole 294 bases during the 1970s. Oakland left fielder Joe Rudi made this memorable catch against the wall in the 1972 World Series (middle) to prevent an extra-base hit. Rudi averaged 15 homers, 72 RBI, and 63 runs scored for the A's from 1970 to '76. He ended his 16-year career in 1982 with a lifetime .264 average and 179 home runs. Gene Tenace scores the winning run of Game Four in the '72 World Series (bottom left). Tenace caught and played first base for the A's, and from 1973 to '76, he averaged 25 home runs a season. Tony Perez (bottom right) scores the winning run in Game Three of the '72 World Series. Perez batted .435 in the Series.

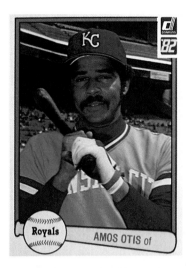

THE 1970s

led the league in walks (162) for the second straight season. Baltimore's Jim Palmer was the best of the bunch, winning 22, losing nine and posting a league-low 2.40 ERA to win the Cy Young Award for the first time.

The National League, and all of baseball, focused its attention on one of the most celebrated countdowns in baseball history: Hank Aaron's quest to eclipse Babe Ruth's lifetime home run record of 714. Aaron needed 41 four-baggers in '73 to break the record, and going into the last game of the season he had 40. Commissioner Bowie Kuhn and a horde of writers were in Atlanta to witness one of baseball's most cherished records

fall. However, Aaron could manage only three singles and would have to wait till next year. His total of 40 placed him only fourth in the league. Teammate Davey Johnson, who never hit more than 18 in the A.L., surprised everybody by belting 43, breaking the record for home runs by a second baseman set by Hall of Famer Rogers Hornsby. Third baseman Darrell Evans was second on the team in homers with 41, which gave the Braves the top three spots behind the league leader, Willie Stargell, who hit 44 for the Pirates.

Ted Simmons averaged 89 RBI from 1971 to '79.

In the N.L. West, the Reds were forced to fight back from an 11-game deficit to catch the talented Dodgers. In Tommy John, Don Sutton, Claude Osteen, and Andy Messersmith, Los Angeles had an experienced pitching staff to go with promising young hitters such as Steve Garvey, Bill Buckner, Bill Russell, and Ron Cey. Once again Cincinnati led the league in stolen bases. The spark plug was MVP Rose, who batted .338 en route to a major league-leading 230 hits. Tony Perez hit .314 with 27 homers and 101 RBI, and Bench led the club with 104 RBI.

Two noteworthy performances were turned in by the San Francisco Giants. Pitcher Ron Bryant won a league-high 24 games, and outfielder Bobby Bonds' 39 homers left him one shy of becoming the first man in major league history to hit 40 homers and steal 40 bases in a season.

Over in the East, the Mets surprised the pundits by winning a thoroughly mediocre division with a record of 82-79, the lowest percentage for a pennant winner in baseball history. It was a race in which all six teams had a chance

1975 WORLD SERIES — GAME SIX

Game Six of the 1975 World Series was so exciting that in the 11th inning, Pete Rose while at bat turned to Boston catcher Carlton Fisk and said, "Ain't this some kind of game?"

With 35,000 fans in the park and 50 million Americans watching at home, Boston jumped to a 3-0 first-inning lead. But Cincinnati scored three in the fifth, two in the seventh, and one in the eighth to go up 6-3. In the bottom of the eighth, Boston put two men on with two out. Sox pinch-hitter Bernie Carbo sent a Rawly Eastwick fastball over the center field fence to tie the game. In the ninth, Boston was 90 feet away from tying the Series when they loaded the bases with nobody out. On a foul fly to left, Denny Doyle tagged and tried to score, but George Foster's throw beat him home.

In the 11th, Sox right fielder Dwight Evans robbed Joe Mor-

gan of a home run with a leaping catch at the fence. In the 12th, Fisk dove into the stands to catch a pop foul and then led off in the bottom of the inning.

Pat Darcy was Cincinnati's eighth pitcher of the game, and his second pitch to Fisk was a

sinker. Fisk pulled the ball down the left field line. As the ball traveled for what seemed an eternity, Fisk danced toward first base, waving his arms and willing the ball fair. The ball must've heard him. It hit the foul pole for a game-winning home run.

Carlton Fisk's homer won Game Six of the '75 World Series.

Tug McGraw, left, and Jerry Koosman (top left) of the Mets take a bite out of the wood. McGraw saved 25 games in '72 and 27 in '73, while Koosman averaged 16 wins a season from 1973 to '76. Pirate Al Oliver (top right) slugged 20 homers and knocked 99 RBI in '73. Oliver averaged 81 RBI a season from 1970 to '77 for Pittsburgh. In 1975, Oriole Jim Palmer (bottom left) was 22-9 with an A.L.-best 2.09 ERA and ten shutouts. It was the first of three straight seasons that Palmer led the league in wins. Pete Rose (bottom right) led the N.L. with 230 base hits and a .338 batting average in 1973. Rose had 2,045 base hits, 1,068 runs scored, and 394 doubles in the 1970s.

THE 1970s

for the title. Trailing by 11½ games at the start of August, the weak-hitting Mets (they had the lowest team batting average in the East), won 34 of their last 53 to edge out the Cardinals and the Pirates. Tom Seaver (19-10) led the league in strikeouts (251) and ERA (2.08), and was named the Cy Young Award winner. Reliever Tug McGraw, who rallied the team with his battle cry of "You Gotta Believe," came out of the pen to save 25.

The Mets downed the favored Reds in five N.L.C.S. games behind the steady pitching of Seaver, Jerry Koosman, and McGraw, and some unexpected power supplied by Rusty Staub, who nailed three homers during the Series. Mets fans, however, remember the match most for an incident in Game Three, in which Rose, after a hard tag, body slammed shortstop Bud Harrelson into the infield dirt, leading to a brawl. Baltimore and Oakland squared off again in the American League Championship Series, which went five games. Hunter, 21-5 on the year, was mas-

terful in the deciding game, allowing no runner past second base. The A's won 3-0.

With Hunter, Ken Holtzman, and Vida Blue all 20-game winners, and MVP Jackson (.293 average, 32 homers, 117 RBI) supplying the offense, the A's were favored against the lowly Mets. Holtzman outpitched Jon Matlack in Game One for a 2-1 win. Game Two was noteworthy for two events: New York's Willie Mays, playing in his 21st season, recorded the final hit of his career, and A's second baseman Mike Andrews made two errors to give the Mets a 10-7 victory. Owner Charlie Finley said Andrews was injured and tried to replace him with another player — a move that outraged the A's players, the public, and the press. Commissioner Bowie Kuhn ordered Andrews reinstated and hit Finley with a stiff fine.

The A's won Game Three in New York 3-2 in 11 innings, but dropped the fourth game 6-1, with Staub and Matlack starring for the Mets. Koosman and McGraw combined for a three-hitter in Game Five, a 2-0 shutout. Jackson smacked three hits and two RBI off Seaver in Game Six, to force a seventh game. Once again, Jackson delivered the crushing blow, a long two-run homer to right, making the A's the first repeat champions since the Yankees of 1961 and '62. Despite the win, A's manager Dick Williams was so disgusted at the meddlesome Finley that he announced his resignation minutes after Game Seven.

Pete Rose scores a takedown on Bud Harrelson in the 1973 N.L.C.S.

LOU BROCK

During his first two seasons with the Chicago Cubs, 1962 and '63, Lou Brock was simply a good outfielder with potential. So nobody took much notice when the Cubs traded Brock the following season to the St. Louis Cardinals for pitcher Ernie Broglio. But when Brock hit .348 in the Cardinals last 103 games and ended the year with 43 stolen bases, they noticed. Then Lou Brock proceeded to make the Broglio trade the worst in Cubs history.

Until 1982, when Rickey Henderson broke Brock's single-season stolen base record of 118 (which Brock had set in 1974 by breaking Maury Wills' 104), Brock was the only player to hold both the single-season and career highs in a major category. He is still number one on the all-time steals list with 938.

Between 1965 and '77, Brock led the National League in stolen bases eight times and set a record by stealing 50 or more bases for 12 straight years. He batted over .300 eight times and ended his 19-year-career with 3,023 hits. He scored more than 100 runs in seven seasons, leading the league twice. He batted over .300 eight times and had more than 200 hits four times. Brock also made the most of his three World Series appearances (1964, '67, and '68). He holds the Series record for the highest average by a player in 20 or more games (.391) and is tied with Eddie Collins for Series steals with 14. Brock made the Hall of Fame in 1985, his first year of eligibility.

Tom Seaver (top left) led the National League with a 2.08 ERA in 1973 for the Mets. "Tom Terrific" had a 189-110 record for New York from 1967 through mid-1977, when he was traded to the Cincinnati Reds. He led the National League in strikeouts in five of those seasons. Tommy John (top middle) was 16-7 for the Dodgers in '73. He won 87 games from 1972 to '78 for L.A. Dick Williams (top right) averaged 96 wins a year during his three-year stint in Oakland. Oakland's Reggie Jackson dives for third base (bottom) while Tiger Aurelio Rodriguez tries to make the play. In '73, Jackson led the A.L. with 32 homers, 117 RBI, 99 runs scored, and a .531 slugging average. He averaged 30 homers, 89 RBI, and 83 runs scored from 1970 to '76 with the A's.

THE 1970s

1974

At the season's start, all eyes focused on Atlanta, where Hank Aaron needed just two homers to break Babe Ruth's home run record. Bill Bartholomay, the owner of the Braves, created some controversy when he opted to bench Aaron in the three-game opener against Cincinnati. Kuhn intervened and insisted that Aaron play. In his first at-bat of the season, Hammerin' Hank hit number 714 to tie the record. But it was in Atlanta on April 8 at 9:07 P.M. EST, before a packed crowd of 53,775, that the 40-year-old man with wrists of steel cracked number 715 off Al Downing of the Dodgers. By season's end he had raised his total to 733, and soon after he was traded to Milwaukee, the city where he began his career.

Lou Brock, at age 35, batted .306 and broke Maury Wills' single-season stolen base record by swiping 118 bases. St. Louis teammate Bob Gibson (11-13 but never the same after his knee injury in '73) recorded his 3,000th strikeout.

The Redbirds also featured the newly acquired Reggie Smith (.309, 100 RBI) and 24-year-old catcher Ted Simmons (103 RBI). But faulty pitching put them just 1½ games behind Pittsburgh in the N.L. East, which relied on the bats of Al Oliver (.321), Willie Stargell (25 home runs), and Richie Zisk (100 RBI).

The Dodgers won 102 games and finished 4 games ahead of the Reds in the N.L. West. Messersmith (20-6) led the league in wins, and Sutton and John won 32 games between them. Cy Young Award-winning reliever Mike Marshall appeared from the bullpen a record 106 times for 15 wins and a league-leading 21 saves. First baseman Steve Garvey hit .312, with 21 homers and 111 RBI, and won the

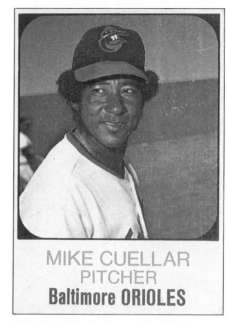

MIKE CUELLAR
PITCHER
Baltimore ORIOLES

Orioles lefty Mike Cueller was 22-10 in '74.

MVP award that many people felt Brock deserved more.

In the A.L. East, the Orioles, 8 games back on August 29, won 27 of 33, including 15 one-run games, while the Yanks floundered and the Red Sox folded, losing 21 of their last 33. Observers were hard pressed to figure out how the Orioles won it, considering that no one hit higher than .289 (Tommy Davis), hit more than 19 homers (Bobby Grich), or drove in more than 89 runs (Davis). Mike Cuellar was the only pitcher to win more than 20 games.

Oakland finished 5 games ahead of the surprising Texas Rangers in the A.L. West. The acquisition of righty Ferguson Jenkins (25-12) and the emergence of powerful Jeff Burroughs (.301, 25 homers, 118 RBI, and the league's MVP) made the difference. The A's Cy Young Award winner, Catfish Hunter (25-12), anchored a staff that included Ken Holtzman (19 wins), Vida Blue (17 wins), and Rollie Fingers, who saved 18 games in 76 appearances. Reggie Jackson hit .289 and supplied the power with 29 homers and 93 runs batted in. (Herb Washington, the world-class sprinter turned designated runner, stole 29 bases in 45 attempts.) Other A.L. highlights included Al Kaline's 3,000th hit and teammate Willie Horton's pop fly at Fenway that killed a pigeon in flight. Nolan Ryan pitched his third no-hitter, a 4-0 gem against Minnesota.

WILLIE STARGELL

Willie Stargell had been an outstanding player throughout the 1970s, but he waited until the last year of the decade, when he was 38 years old, to become a legend.

As the Pittsburgh Pirates marched to the National League pennant in 1979, their theme song was the disco hit, "We Are Family." Stargell — the team's spiritual leader since Roberto Clemente died in 1973 — boogied to the name "Pops."

Stargell wasn't just respected for his leadership off the field that year but for his performance on it as well. His 32 home runs in '79 made him a co-Most Valuable Player (with St. Louis' Keith Hernandez) for the regular season. Then he was the MVP of the League Championship Series, batting .455 with two homers in a three-game sweep of the Reds. In the World Series against the Orioles, Stargell belted two homers in the first four games. In Game Seven, the Bucs were down 1-0 in the sixth inning. Pops hit a two-run homer, the Pirates won 4-1, and Stargell was the Series MVP.

Besides '79, Stargell's two best seasons were 1971 (a league-leading 48 homers, 125 RBI) and 1973 (an N.L. best 44 homers, 119 RBI), but he lost the MVP award for both those years. He hit 20 or more homers in 13 consecutive seasons and had slugging percentages over .500 in 13 seasons. He had 90 or more RBI in nine seasons. Stargell retired in 1982 with 475 homers and 1,540 RBI, and he was elected to the Hall of Fame on the first ballot in 1988.

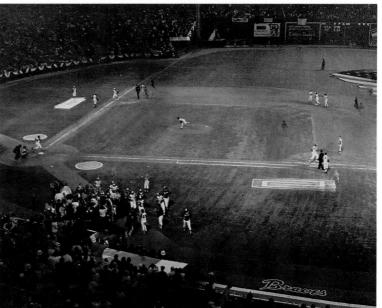

On Hank Aaron's first swing of the 1974 season (top), he hit home run number 714 against Reds hurler Jack Billingham on April 4, 1974, in Cincinnati. Cardinal Lou Brock (bottom left) stole 118 bases in 1974, breaking the single-season stolen base record set by Maury Wills (with 104) in 1962. Brock's previous high was 74 stolen bases in 1966. It was the last season he was to lead the N.L. in stolen bases; he had led the league in eight out of the previous nine seasons (Bobby Tolan led the league in '70). An overhead view (bottom right) of Aaron's 715th home run.

THE 1970s

The O's and A's met again in the A.L. Championship Series. The Orioles homered three times in the first game to win 6-3 but were shut out in the next two, first by Holtzman and then by Blue, who won 1-0 thanks to a homer by Sal Bando. The A's finished off the Series with a 2-1 win, even though they only got one hit off Cuellar. The Dodgers buried the Pirates in four to set up the first all-California World Series.

Oakland was again a team besieged by internal strife. New manager Alvin Dark, a deeply religious man, remained calm throughout the whole ordeal, comforting himself by reading passages from the Bible. In fact, during the season he told reporters: "I've tried to think of how Jesus Christ would handle ballplayers." The day before the Series opened, Hunter threatened to declare himself a free agent if owner Finley didn't come up with some back pay owed to him. Former A's second baseman Mike Andrews filed a $2 million libel suit against Finley for his actions during the 1973 World Series. Pitchers Fingers and Odom brawled in the clubhouse the day before the first game, and Jackson and Blue complained about Finley and manager Dark.

Despite all the fussin' and feudin', the A's won the first game 3-2, scoring on a Jackson homer and a double by a man who had not batted all year, pitcher Ken Holtzman. Game Two was decided by the same score, but this time the Dodgers won as L.A. reliever Mike Marshall picked off designated runner Herb Washington to halt a ninth-inning rally. Oakland won Game Three, again 3-2, thanks to two Dodger errors. In the next game, Holtzman pitched and homered the A's to a 5-2 win and a commanding 3-1 Series lead. The finale, decided again by a score of

3-2, went to the A's. Down by one in the top of the eighth inning, Dodger Bill Buckner was gunned out at third trying to stretch a double into a triple. Relief pitchers Odom and Fingers preserved the win and gave Oakland their third consecutive World Series title.

1975

"The most celebrated auction in baseball history" began after an arbitration panel released star righthander Hunter from the A's. The irate Finley went to court, lost, and received no compensation from the Yankees who paid Hunter more than $3 million. That deal, and the trade of outfielder Bobby Murcer to the Giants for outfielder Bobby Bonds, made the Yankees a strong contender in the A.L. East.

No one, not even the most fervent Boston Red Sox loyalist, could have predicted the performance of two precocious rookie outfielders named Fred Lynn and Jim Rice. The 23-year-old Lynn played superbly in center field and became the first player to win both the Rookie of the Year and MVP awards in the same season. Lynn batted .331, with 21 homers and 105 RBI. The powerfully built 22-year-old Rice, despite suffering a

Boston's Fred Lynn had 105 RBI in 1975. He also hit .331 and scored 103 runs that season.

CATFISH HUNTER

Jim Hunter was signed at age 18 by Kansas City A's owner Charlie Finley in 1964, even though Hunter had accidently shot off his right big toe the year before. When Finley asked his young phenom what his hobbies were, Hunter replied, "Fishing for catfish." A nickname was born, and a year later so was a great 15-year major league career.

In 1968, the A's first season in Oakland, Hunter hurled a perfect game against the Minnesota Twins. He notched his first 20-win season in 1971 and then led the A's to three straight world titles with 20-plus win seasons in 1972, '73, and '74. His 25-12 mark in '74 earned him the Cy Young Award. A contract dispute with Finley also earned him his freedom to sign with any team.

On New Year's Eve, 1974, Hunter signed the biggest contract to that time, a $3.75 million, five-year deal with George Steinbrenner's Yankees. Hunter went 23-14 for the Yanks in '75 and helped them win a pennant and two world championships the next three years.

Never an overpowering pitcher, Hunter relied on control, smarts, and guts. He holds the A.L. record for most home runs allowed (374), but he also had five straight 20-win seasons in the 1970s and averaged 277 innings per year for ten seasons between 1967 and '76. Hunter led the A.L. twice in wins and winning percentage, and once in ERA, complete games, and innings pitched. His lifetime 224-166 record and 3.26 ERA, along with five World Series rings, earned him induction to the Hall of Fame in 1987.

A's shortstop Bert Campaneris turns the double play to end the 1974 World Series (top left). The Oakland crowd rushes the field (top right) after the A's win their third straight world championship in 1974. The insatiable scoreboard operator was already looking to the next season. Catfish Hunter (bottom left) holds his 1974 Cy Young Award. He led the A.L. with 25 wins and a 2.49 ERA, while striking out 143 batters and walking just 46 in 318 innings pitched. Detroit's Al Kaline (bottom middle) smacked his 3,000th base hit on August 24, 1974, against Orioles hurler Dave McNally. Ferguson Jenkins (bottom right) was 25-12 for the Texas Rangers in 1975. Jenkins was the Cubs' ace from 1967 to '73; he was 141-100 during those seven seasons.

THE 1970s

broken wrist in late September, finished with a .309 average, 22 homers, and 102 RBI. Though the young duo got most of the attention, solid performances were turned in by Carlton Fisk, Carl Yastrzemski, Cecil Cooper, and eccentric righthander Luis Tiant, who won 18 games.

Neither the Orioles nor the Yankees could catch Boston, which finished 4 games in front of Baltimore. Slugger Lee May (99 RBI) and Ken Singleton (.300) revamped the O's hitting attack. Mike Torrez won 20 games, and Jim Palmer bounced back from a subpar year to win 23 (2.09 ERA) and a second Cy Young Award.

In the A.L. West, the A's fifth straight title featured a blend of power and speed. Second-place Kansas City finished 7 games back, but boasted a 22-year-old third baseman named George Brett, who batted .308 and led the league with 195 hits. After Hunter's departure (he won 23 for the Yanks) and an arm injury to rookie Mike Norris, the pitching burden fell on Blue (22-11) and Holtzman (18-14). Jackson (36 homers, 104 RBI) supplied the power, and a fleet-footed

20-year-old named Claudell Washington stole 40 bases and hit .308.

Elsewhere in baseball, Minnesota's Rod Carew (.359) won the A.L. batting title for the fourth consecutive season; the Cleveland Indians named Frank Robinson as the first black manager in major league history (he also appeared in 49 games as a DH and hit nine homers); Brewers DH Henry Aaron, age 41, upped his home run total to 745; Angel Nolan Ryan pitched his fourth no-hitter; pitching greats Juan Marichal and Bob Gibson retired; and Casey Stengel, one of baseball's most colorful characters, died at age 86.

The Big Red Machine (108-54) tied the 1970 Orioles for the best record during the decade and had the best season in the 99-year history of the franchise. Cincinnati batted .271 as a team and led the league in fielding (the club set a major league record by playing 15 straight games without an error) and stolen bases. Cincinnati finished 20 games ahead of the Dodgers in the N.L. West. Four Reds — Joe Morgan (17 home runs, 94 RBI), Pete Rose, Ken Griffey, and George Foster topped .300. Johnny Bench and Tony Perez combined to drive in 219 runs. The 5'7" Morgan led the N.L. in walks, finished second in steals (67), and became the fourth Red in six years to be named the league's MVP. Rose called him "the cog that puts the Big Red Machine in gear."

Nearly a month into the season, Sparky Anderson made a key move by shifting Rose, who had played the outfield for the past eight seasons, to third base; a

Yankees third sacker Graig Nettles dives for the ball.

THURMAN MUNSON

During the 1970s, Thurman Munson was the American League's best catcher. The fiery Yankees backstop led the Bronx Bombers to three straight pennants and two world championships between 1976 and '78. But he may never be in the Hall of Fame because of the tragic accident that cut short his life on August 2, 1979.

A flying enthusiast, Munson was practicing takeoffs and landings in a new twin-engine Cessna jet at the airport near his Canton, OH, home. On one approach to the runway, the plane hit a tree and crashed. Munson was trapped inside the burning plane and died at age 32.

But Munson packed a lot of greatness into his 11 seasons. He was A.L. Rookie of the Year in 1970 and made his first of seven All-Star teams in '71. From 1975 to '77, Munson hit better than .300 and drove in 100 or more runs each year, the first player since Al Rosen to achieve that feat in three straight seasons. A smart, quick catcher with a quick release and excellent fundamentals, Munson won three Gold Glove awards.

In 1976, Munson was named the first Yankees captain since Lou Gehrig and had the finest year of his career. He was the A.L. Most Valuable Player, hitting .302 with 105 RBI and leading the Yanks to their first World Series since 1964. In the Championship Series that year he hit .435, and followed that with a .529 World Series average, tying a record with six straight hits. Munson's .373 lifetime Series batting mark is the third highest.

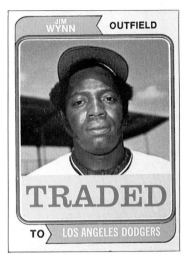

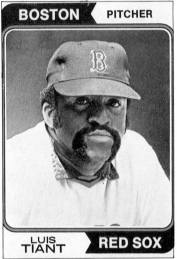

The main cogs (top left) in the Big Red Machine were, left to right, Tony Perez, Johnny Bench, Joe Morgan, and Pete Rose. Morgan (bottom left) hit .327 with 17 homers, 107 runs scored, 94 RBI, 67 stolen bases, and a league-leading 132 bases on balls in 1975. He hit .320 with 27 homers, 113 runs scored, 111 RBI, 60 stolen bases, 114 walks, and a league-leading .576 slugging average in 1976. Jim Wynn (top middle) hit 32 homers and drove in 108 runs for the Dodgers in 1975. He slugged 291 career homers in 15 seasons. Dodgers pitcher Andy Messersmith (top right) was 20-6 in 1974. Boston's Luis Tiant (middle center) was 22-13 in '74 and 18-14 in '75. He had a 229-179 career record during 19 seasons. Bobby Bonds (middle right) tallied 280 home runs, 1,020 runs scored, 856 RBI, 380 stolen bases, and 1,368 strikeouts during the 1970s. Jim Kaat (bottom right) was 20-14 for the 1975 White Sox. In 1974, he was 21-13 for Chicago. Kaat's career stretched from 1959 to 1983, and he had 11 seasons of 14 or more wins in that time. He ended his career with 283 career victories.

change that allowed the 26-year-old Foster to play every day in left. Anderson called it the best hunch he ever had. Quickly, the team jelled into one of baseball's most awesome offensive teams.

The Pirates won 92 games in the N.L. East and finished 6½ games better than the Philadelphia Phillies. Willie Stargell batted .295 and had 90 RBI; Clemente's successor in right field, 6'5" Dave Parker, led the team with a .308 average, 25 home runs, and 101 RBI.

In the N.L.C.S., Cincinnati rolled over the Bucs in three games. The series ended in Pittsburgh with a 5-3 Reds win despite a 14-strikeout effort by Bucs rookie pitcher John Candelaria. The A.L.C.S was also a 3-0 sweep. In

Carlton Fisk wins Game Six of the '75 Series.

the opener, Red Sox player Luis Tiant, known for the large Cuban cigars he smoked in the club-house after a win, pitched a three-hitter. Boston first baseman Carl Yastrzemski, who batted .455 for the series, delivered the key hits.

Cincinnati, which had failed to win the World Series in 1970 and '72, was after its first title since 1940; that must have seemed like yesterday to Red Sox fans, who last celebrated a Series win in 1918.

The '75 World Series, however, is best remembered for Carlton Fisk's dramatic 12th-inning game-winning homer in Game Six, a shot that sent the Series to a seventh game watched by a TV audience of 61 million. The finale was almost as dramatic. Boston led 3-0 after five innings, but the Reds tied it in the seventh and then won it in the ninth on Morgan's run-scoring bloop single.

1976

The 100th season of professional baseball got off to a rocky start when players found themselves locked out of spring training by the owners, who were angered by the ruling that allowed pitchers Andy Messersmith and Dave McNally to become free agents. Commissioner Bowie Kuhn intervened in time to ensure a full season of play, but baseball would never be the same. Soon after, an agreement between the owners and Players' Association gave players the right to refuse a trade after ten years in the majors and five with the same club, and to become free agents after six, thereby ending (for the time being) the court battles that filled the headlines.

Later in the season, Charlie Finley tried to sell three of his stars: Rollie Fingers and Joe Rudi to the Red Sox (for a total of $3.5 million) and Vida Blue to the Yankees. Finley had already traded Reggie Jackson and Ken Holtzman to the Orioles, but this time Kuhn stepped in and nullified the sale, stating that it would be bad for the game. Finley was incensed and filed a $3.5 million lawsuit, which he lost (along with the West Division title).

Featuring a new stadium with a waterfall behind the center field wall, a clever manager named Whitey Herzog, good pitching, a solid defense, and equally solid hit-

MARK FIDRYCH

At the Tigers' 1976 spring training camp, Mark Fidrych was an anonymous 22-year-old nonroster pitcher. Yet he impressed manager Ralph Houk enough to make a team that had finished with the major's worst record the year before — but not enough to pitch during the first five weeks. In mid-May, he was finally given a start and beat Cleveland 2-1. Two weeks later, he pitched a complete game 12-inning victory, then reeled off another seven straight victories. Fidrych had Detroit fans in a frenzy.

It wasn't just the wins that had them captivated, it was Fidrych's personality. He was an upbeat free-spirit from Worcester, MA, with long, curly blond hair. He would pace around the pitcher's mound, talk to the baseball before throwing it, and run over to congratulate teammates after good plays. He supplied sportswriters with colorful quotes. After the television networks broadcasted a couple of Fidrych's starts, he became known as "The Bird" and was the most popular rookie ever. In his 29 starts that year, Fidrych drew nearly 1 million fans, including over ½ million at home. Baseball officials estimated that half of those fans went to see Fidrych.

He ended the season at 19-9 with an A.L.-leading 2.34 ERA and 24 complete games and was named Rookie of the Year. But, tragically, The Bird hurt his arm in 1977 during a 6-4 season and was never the same again. He tried comebacks the next three seasons but couldn't make it. Fidrych reluctantly gave up in 1980 with a 29-19 lifetime record.

Dave Kingman, left, and Mike Schmidt (top left) pause before a game. Kingman smashed 36 homers in 1975 for the Mets, and 37 round-trippers in '76. He was beat out of the home run crown in those years by Philadelphia's Schmidt, however, who slugged 38 each season. Outfielder George Foster (top middle) averaged 130 runs batted in a season from 1976 to '78 for Cincinnati. Foster ended his 18-year career with 1,239 RBI. Steve Carlton (top right) of the Phillies led the National League with a .741 winning percentage in '76. He was 20-7, with a 3.13 ERA that year. Don Sutton of the Dodgers (bottom left) was 21-10 with a 3.06 ERA in 1976. Sutton had a 166-110 record for Los Angeles during the 1970s. Detroit's Willie Horton (bottom right) slugged 25 homers in 1975. Horton ended his 18-year career in 1980 with 325 home runs and 1,163 RBI.

THE 1970s

ting, the Kansas City Royals dethroned an Oakland team that ran with abandon. The A's stole 341 bases, seven short of the all-time record. But Royal George Brett led the A.L. in hits (215) and batting (.333), one point higher than team-mate Hal McRae.

Milwaukee's Hank Aaron ended his 22-year career as base-ball's all-time leading home run hitter with 755.

In the A.L. East, the revitalized Yankees, after two years of exile at the Mets' home, Shea Stadium, returned to the renovated "House

That Ruth Built" (featuring a new $3 million scoreboard) and wel-comed fans back to the Bronx with their first pennant since 1964. First baseman Chris Chambliss hit .293, with 17 home runs and 93 RBI; third baseman Graig Nettles hit 32 homers to win the home run title; and catcher Thurman Munson, the league's MVP, batted .302, with 17 homers and 105 RBI. Lefthanded stopper Sparky Lyle appeared in 64 games and topped all A.L. relievers in saves with 23.

But the team's MVP might have been Yankees general manag-er Gabe Paul, who acquired out-fielder Mickey Rivers (.312, 43 stolen bases) and pitcher Ed Figueroa (19 wins) from the Angels for Bobby Bonds; second baseman Willie Randolph and pitcher Dock Ellis (17 wins) from Pittsburgh; and pitchers Doyle Alexander (10-5), Ken Holtzman (9-7), and Grant Jackson (6-0) from the Orioles.

Jim Palmer won his second straight Cy Young Award, winning 22 and losing 13, but the pitching

Dave Concepcion hit .281 in 1976.

sensation of the year was Mark (The Bird) Fidrych, a 21-year-old rookie who spoke to the baseball while on the mound, kissed the infield, and flapped his arms all the way to a 19-9 record.

The Cincinnati Reds romped again in the N.L. West, winning 102 games and finishing 10 up on Los Angeles, who said goodbye to man-ager Walter Alston after 23 years in Dodger Blue. Mighty Joe Morgan won his second consecutive MVP award, batting .320, slugging 27 homers, driving in 111 runs, and swiping 60 bases. The Reds all-star lineup included Rose (.323, a league-leading 215 hits), Perez (91 RBI), Griffey (.336), Cesar Geroni-mo (.307), Dave Concepcion (.281), Foster (.306, a league-leading 121 RBI), and baseball's best catcher, Johnny Bench.

In the East, the Phillies (101-61), cellar-dwellers in 1972 and '73, finished 9 games up on Pittsburgh. The key moves, orchestrated by GM Paul Owens, involved the acquisitions of outfielders Bobby Tolan, Jay Johnstone (.318), and Garry Maddox (.330); pitchers Jim Lonborg (18 wins) and Tug McGraw (7-6); and second base-man Dave Cash (.284). The Phils already had a fine nucleus in home run leader Mike Schmidt (38 homers, 107 RBI), Greg Luzinski (.304, 21 homers, 95 RBI), short-stop Larry Bowa, and pitcher Steve Carlton (20-7).

Still, the Reds, who led the league in every offensive category (including attendance, 2.6 million), swept the talented Phillies in the N.L.C.S., three games to none. The Yanks were riding high from their dramatic playoff win over Kansas City. In Game Five, the score was

REGGIE JACKSON'S FOUR STRAIGHT WORLD SERIES HOMERS

On October 18, 1977, the legend of "Mr. October" was born.

Reggie Jackson had already manufactured some attractive postseason numbers before the 1977 World Series between the Yankees and the Dodgers. He had played in five Championship Series and in two World Series, and he had batted over .300 with two homers to win the MVP when Oakland won the 1973 title.

But Jackson turned the '77 Series into his own showcase. He helped put the Yankees up three games to one by hitting a homer and a double in Game Four. Though the Dodgers won Game Five 10-4, Jackson homered in his last at-bat. His first time up in Game Six, he was walked by Burt Hooton on four pitches. Jackson came up again in the fourth inning, and on Hooton's first pitch, he rocketed a two-run homer into the right field seats.

With two out and one on in the fifth, Jackson sent Elias Sosa's first pitch over the fence to put

the Yanks on top 7-3 — three swings, three homers. With the Series no longer in doubt, the drama focused on Jackson's last time at-bat in the eighth. Charlie Hough was on the mound, and Jackson sent his first knuckleball far into center field. Jackson dropped his bat and watched the ball's flight. When it landed in the stands, Jackson had set five new Series records, including most homers in a Series (five) and most consecutive homers in official times at bat (four). He was forever "Mr. October."

Mark Fidrych (top right) was 19-9 in 1976, with an A.L.-best 2.34 ERA and 24 complete games. He also had four shutouts, 97 strikeouts, and 250 innings pitched. He ended his career with a 29-19 record, 3.10 ERA, 34 complete games, five shutouts, 170 Ks, and 412 innings pitched. Nolan Ryan (bottom left) averaged 302 strikeouts with the Angels from 1972 to '79; he had a 138-121 record in those eight years. Chris Chambliss (bottom middle) averaged 82 RBI a season for the Yankees from 1975 to '79. Jose Cruz (bottom right) of the Houston Astros hit .299 with 17 homers, 87 runs scored, 87 RBI, and 44 stolen bases in 1977.

tied 6-6 in the bottom of the ninth inning when Chris Chambliss sent thousands of Yankees fans storming past police barriers with a homer to right.

However, the Billy Martin-led Yankees were a tired team going into Game One of the World Series at Cincinnati and lost 5-1. Trailing 2-0 in the Series, the Bronx Bombers returned to New York with high hopes, but the Yankees were clearly no match for the powerful Big Red Machine, the first National League team since 1922 to repeat as World Series champions.

1977

Watching his Yankees drop four straight to the Reds in the 1976 World Series galled owner George Steinbrenner. "The Boss" flexed his mighty wallet at the re-entry draft and snared Reds pitcher Don Gullett for $2 million; he doled out $3.5 million over five years for Reggie Jackson and also purchased shortstop Bucky Dent and pitcher Mike Torrez. Such lavishness pleased Yankees fans, but appalled almost everyone else and earned the Yanks the reputation as "the best team money could buy."

Jackson was probably the most important acquisition, hitting 32 homers and driving in 110 runs. However, the arrogant Jackson clashed with Martin, which only widened the gap that already existed between the embittered manager and the dictatorial Steinbrenner, who during the season fined Martin $2,500 for criticizing management. In fact, fans learned how bad the Jackson-Martin situation was when the pair almost came to blows in the dugout during a game in Boston televised to a national audience.

Martin saved his job, however, by leading the Yanks to 38 wins in the last 51 games to finish 2½ games ahead of Baltimore and

Boston. The newest Yankees star was a slender southpaw named Ron Guidry (16-7), who came out of the pen to become a starter. The bullpen belonged to Cy Young Award winner Sparky Lyle, who appeared in a league-high 72 games to register 26 saves.

The Royals had an easier time in the A.L. West. Kansas City had six players who hit 15 or more home runs, and two excellent starters in Paul Splittorff (16-6) and Dennis Leonard (20-12). The second-place Texas Rangers redefined the term "interim manager." Frank Lucchesi was assaulted by Lenny Randle during spring training and then was fired during the season. Eddie Stanky followed, decided that he was homesick, and rejoined his family after one game. Coach Connie Ryan managed six games. Billy Hunter came aboard to lead the team to a strong second-half finish (60-33). The most interesting race in the West, however, involved Minnesota's six-time batting champion, Rod Carew, who flirted with .400 for most of the season before finishing with a .388 average and an MVP award.

In the National League, the Phillies (101-61) won their second straight East title and looked forward to their first league title in 27 years. Steve Carlton (23-10) won his second Cy Young Award, and

Atlanta's Jeff Burroughs had 41 homers in 1977.

YANKEES-RED SOX 1978 PLAYOFF GAME

Bucky Dent homers in the '78 playoff.

On July 17, 1978, Boston owned a 14-game lead over the Yankees and seemed all but a lock for the pennant. Suddenly, Reggie Jackson was suspended, manager Billy Martin was fired by owner George Steinbrenner, and Bob Lemon was hired as manager. By the end of the month, the Yankees were 7½ games out; when they swept the Sox four straight, the pennant race was on. It took a last-day Boston victory and a Yankees loss to make the race a tie and force a one-game playoff on October 2.

The Sox took a 2-0 lead into the top of the seventh inning. The Yanks put two men on with one out and had relatively weak-hitting shortstop Bucky Dent at the plate. On the second pitch from Mike Torrez, Dent belted one over the Green Monster, putting the Yankees up 3-2. They scored two more by the eighth to go up 5-2, and Boston responded with two runs that inning.

With Yankees relief ace Goose Gossage hurling the ninth, Rick Burleson walked. With one out, Jerry Remy hit a liner to right field that Lou Piniella caught on one hop. His decoy of a catch, however, kept Burleson on second. Burleson could not score on Jim Rice's subsequent fly to deep right. Gossage pitched next to Carl Yastrzemski; on a 1-0 pitch, the Goose fired his best fastball, and Yaz popped it up for the final out. The Yankees went on to beat Los Angeles for their second straight world championship.

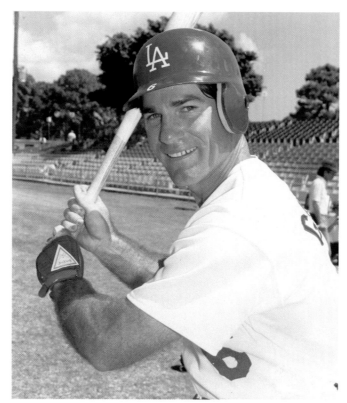

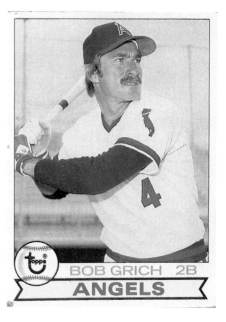

Dodgers first baseman Steve Garvey (top left) led the N.L. with 202 base hits in 1978. Ken Singleton (top right) hit .328 with 24 homers and 99 RBI in 1977 for Baltimore. Second baseman Bobby Grich (middle right) slugged 224 career homers for Baltimore and California. Twins first baseman Rod Carew (bottom left) batted .388, slugged .570, and scored 128 times in 1977 to win the A.L. MVP award. Billy Martin (bottom right) managed the Yankees to a world championship in 1977.

THE 1970s

Greg Luzinski had a career year, hitting .309, with 39 homers and 130 RBI.

The big news in the N.L. was the trading of the New York Mets "franchise," Tom Seaver, on the June 15 trade deadline, a deal that still angers Mets fans. Seaver, who had been feuding with Mets management over salary and organizational problems, went to Cincinnati for four players, none of whom became stars.

Neither the addition of Seaver nor the awesome offensive display by the soft-spoken MVP George Foster (.320, 52 homers, 149 RBI) could compensate for Cincinnati's loss of Gullett to the Yankees and Tony Perez to Montreal. The Dodgers, with rookie manager Tommy Lasorda, won 98 games, 10 games better than Cincinnati. Led by first baseman Steve Garvey (.297, 33 home runs, 115 RBI), Los Angeles' powerful lineup sported an unprecedented four hitters — Garvey, Ron Cey, Dusty Baker, and Reggie Smith — who belted 30 or more home runs.

In the N.L.C.S., the Dodgers eliminated the Phillies in four games, behind the hitting of Baker (eight RBI) and the pitching of 20-game winner Tommy John. The Yankees, however, fought another dramatic five-game war against Kansas City. This time, New York came up with three runs in the ninth inning of the final game to snatch a 5-3 win and the pennant.

The Yankees and the Dodgers met in the World Series for the ninth time in the clubs' history. Game One in New York wasn't decided until the 12th inning, when Yankee Paul Blair singled in the winning run for a 4-3 win. Catfish Hunter, who had been injured most of the year, started the next game and was shelled in a 6-1 loss. On the travel day back to L.A., Jackson, Martin, and catcher Thurman

Munson renewed their feud in the clubhouse and in the newspapers, but despite the internal strife, New York proceeded to win Game Three 5-3.

The Yanks relied on the steady pitching of Guidry and a Jackson double and homer to set down the Dodgers by a score of 4-2 in Game Four. Los Angeles refused to play dead, rocking Gullett 10-4 in Game Five, to send the Series back to New York.

The sixth and final game was produced, directed, and narrated by "Mr. October," Reggie Jackson, who launched first-pitch homers in the fourth, fifth, and eighth innings to power the Yanks to an 8-4 win. The only other player in Series history to hit three homers in one Series game was Babe Ruth, who did it twice. Jackson's five Series homers set a record and restored peace, albeit briefly, in the tumultuous Yankees clubhouse.

Yankees Ron Guidry, left, and Goose Gossage.

1978

Writers, fans, and probably the players as well started calling the Yankees clubhouse "The Bronx Zoo." Winning the World Series the previous year kept the Steinbrenner-Martin, Martin-Jackson, and Jackson-Munson feuds under wraps, but during the first half of the season there was little to celebrate. Injuries plagued the pitching staff, and Martin hoped to turn things around by juggling his lineup. He moved catcher Munson to right field and demoted Jackson to a part-time DH. By July 17, ten-

NOLAN RYAN

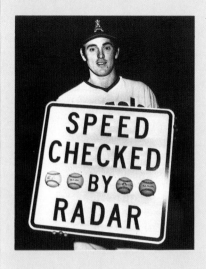

In 1988, at the age of 41, Nolan Ryan led the National League in strikeouts for the second straight year. The Texas Rangers, convinced the veteran flame-thrower still had one more big year left, signed him away from the Houston Astros as a free agent for more than $1 million. Going into the '89 season, the greatest strikeout pitcher in baseball history was at 4,775 Ks and counting.

Ryan established himself as one of baseball's most overpowering pitchers after being traded to the Angels by the Mets in 1972. Using a 100-plus mph fastball known as "Ryan's Express" and a big breaking curve, the 6' 2", 200-pound Texan notched his first 20-win season in 1973, setting the all-time record for strikeouts in a season (383) and throwing his first two no-hitters. During his eight seasons in California, Ryan led the A.L. in strikeouts seven times and threw four no-hitters. He also led the league in bases on balls six times, twice walking more than 200 batters.

After signing with the Astros as a free agent in '79, Ryan became more of a control pitcher. He threw his record fifth no-hitter in 1981, the same year he led the N.L. with a 1.69 ERA. Ryan was never a big enough winner to earn a Cy Young Award, but his amazing strikeout records — which also includes the most seasons with 300 or more Ks (five) and the most games with ten or more strikeouts (181) — should get him into the Hall of Fame.

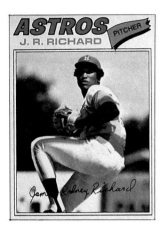

ASTROS PITCHER
J. R. RICHARD

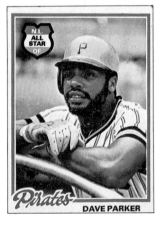

CUBS PITCHER
RICK REUSCHEL

N.L. ALL STAR OF
Pirates
DAVE PARKER

First Row Seated — BUCKY DENT, ROY WHITE, ART FOWLER, CLOYD BOYER, DICK HOWSER, BILLY MARTIN, ELSTON HOWARD, BOBBY COX, YOGI BERRA, FRED STANLEY, THURMAN MUNSON, FRAN HEALY, CATFISH HUNTER.

Second Row — GERRY MURPHY (TRAVELING SECRETARY), GENE MONAHAN (TRAINER), GRAIG NETTLES, REGGIE JACKSON, SPARKY LYLE, MICKEY KLUTTS, MIKE TORREZ, RON GUIDRY, GEORGE ZEBER, WILLIE RANDOLPH, LOU PINIELLA, DON GULLETT, KEN CLAY, GIL PATTERSON, ED FIGUEROA, CLIFF JOHNSON, PAUL BLAIR, HERMAN SCHNEIDER (TRAINER).

Third Row — CARLOS MAY, KEN HOLTZMAN, DICK TIDROW, CHRIS CHAMBLISS.

Seated on Ground — (BATBOYS) JOE D'AMBROSIO, FELIX MARTINEZ, JOHN CALDARAO.

Absent From Photo — MICKEY RIVERS, PETE SHEEHY (EQUIPMENT MANAGER).

Official Photo—New York Yankee

J.R. Richard (top left) was 84-55 for Houston from 1976 to '80. Reggie Jackson (top right) hit .286 with 32 homers and 110 RBI for the '77 Yankees. Cub Rick Reushel (second row left) was 20-10 with a 2.78 ERA in 1977. Dave Parker of the Pirates (third row left) led the N.L. with a .338 average in 1977 and a .334 average in '78. Gaylord Perry (middle center) was 21-6 with a 2.72 ERA for the 1977 Padres. George Foster (middle right) registered 52 homers and 149 RBI for the '77 Reds. The 1977 world champion Yankees (bottom) were 100-62.

THE 1970s

sions were high and the Yanks were 14 games behind the hot-hitting Red Sox. When Jackson disobeyed one of Martin's signals, Battlin' Billy suspended the slugger for five games. Steinbrenner backed Jackson, and a livid Martin complained to a reporter: "The two of them deserve each other. One's a born liar, the other's convicted."

Martin became unemployed. He was replaced by former Indian and Hall of Famer Bob Lemon, who inherited an injury-plagued team down 10½ games. But Lemon was as relaxed as Martin was fiery, and the team responded to his easy-going manner, mounting one of the greatest stretch drives since 1914.

The Red Sox, led by the exemplary playoff MVP award-winner Jim Rice (.315, 46 homers, 139 RBI), had a dangerous lineup that included Fred Lynn, Carl Yastrzemski, Dwight Evans, and Carlton Fisk. Dennis Eckersley led the staff with a 20-8 record.

Catfish Hunter regained his old Yankees form over the last two months of the '78 season. Ron Guidry — who went on to win the Cy Young Award — was unhittable (25-3, 1.74 ERA), as was bullpen ace Goose Gossage, another high-priced free agent who silenced late-inning threats with his menacing fastball. The Yankees trailed by 6½ at the end of August and ruined the Red Sox by sweeping four head-to-head games by a combined score of 42-9. The Red Sox recovered over the final two weeks, tied New York on the final day of the season, and forced a sudden-death playoff game at Fenway Park. Boston jumped out to a 2-0 lead. The Yanks rallied for four in the seventh inning, thanks to a Bucky Dent home run off former Yankee Mike Torrez that barely cleared the "Green Monster" in left field. New York added another on a blast

Ozzie Smith led National League shortstops in assists each year from 1978 to 1981 for the San Diego Padres.

by Jackson. With two out in the last of the ninth, the Red Sox, trailing 5-4, had the tying run at third with Yastremski at the plate. Red Sox fans sat stunned when their beloved Yaz popped up. Later, Yaz would call it one of his biggest disappointments in a career that lasted 23 years.

The divisional race in the A.L. West was more conventional, as the death of one of baseball's brightest talents put the game into proper perspective. The Royals won the division for the third consecutive season, finishing 5 games up on the Angels, a team that was devastated when its star outfielder Lyman Bostock, a career .311 hitter, was murdered on September 23 in Gary, IN.

The Reds collapsed down the stretch, but that didn't diminish the performances of Foster (40 homers, 120 RBI) and Pete Rose, who excited the country first with his 3,000th hit and then by hitting in 44 consecutive games to tie Wee Willie Keeler for the longest streak in N.L. history.

After a bitter struggle with Cincinnati and San Francisco, the Dodgers finished 2½ games ahead of the Reds to win the N.L. West. The close race ushered in a record 3,347,845 fans to Dodger Stadium. Garvey hit .316 with 21 home runs and 113 RBI, but had his choir-boy

MIKE SCHMIDT

Hall of Famer Brooks Robinson is unquestionably the greatest fielding third baseman ever. But Michael Jack Schmidt is the best all-around third sacker of all time.

All Schmidt has done during his 18-year career with the Philadelphia Phillies is win ten Gold Gloves for his defensive play at the hot corner and set the major league record for homers by a third baseman with 503. Entering the 1989 season, his lifetime total of 542 homers placed him seventh on the all-time list.

Beginning with his second full season in 1974, Schmidt led the National League in home runs three straight seasons, but he also led the league those years in strikeouts. Always an intense student of hitting, Schmidt eventually cut down on the Ks, while not decreasing his power output.

In 1980, he led Philadelphia to its first world championship, becoming the N.L. Most Valuable Player on the strength of a league-leading 48 homers (a record for third basemen) and 121 RBI. He repeated as MVP in 1981 by leading the league in homers (31), RBI (91), runs scored (78), and slugging (.644), all in 102 games. Schmidt won the MVP for a third time in 1986 with 37 homers and 119 RBI, both leading the league. He has hit more than 30 homers in 13 seasons. He also has more than 100 RBI in nine different seasons and has slugged over .500 in 13 seasons. The 11-time All-Star won eight home run titles, the most in N.L. history.

In 1978, Jim Rice (top left) led the American League with 46 home runs, 139 runs batted in, 213 base hits, a .600 slugging percentage, 15 triples, and 677 at-bats. He also scored 121 runs and batted .315. Rice averaged 34 homers, 114 RBI, and 102 runs scored to go with his .311 batting average from 1975 to '79. Boston catcher Carlton "Pudge" Fisk (top right) hit 26 round-trippers in 1977, with 102 RBI and 106 runs scored. Fisk averaged 18 home runs, 63 RBI, 68 runs scored, and a .284 batting average a season from 1972 to '79 for the Red Sox. Yankees reliever Goose Gossage leaps into Thurman Munson's arms (bottom left) after beating the Royals for the A.L. pennant in 1978. George Brett (bottom middle) hit .312, slugged 22 homers, and scored 105 runs for the '77 Royals. Joe Niekro of the Astros (bottom right) won 21 games in 1979; his brother Phil won 21 for the '79 Braves.

THE 1970s

image tarnished when he engaged in a clubhouse fight with pitcher Sutton.

The Phils won the East by 1½ games over the Pirates, making it their third straight East title, despite the efforts of Pittsburgh's 37-year-old "Pops" Stargell (.295, 28 homers, 97 RBI) and Dave Parker, who won the MVP award by hitting .334 with 30 home runs and 117 RBI.

After both the Yankees and the Dodgers won their respective league championship series in four games, they met in a rematch of the previous season's World Series. The Yanks lost the first two games by scores of 11-5 and 4-3. The second game ended dramatically, with Jackson swinging for the fences against fireballing rookie reliever Bob Welch. There were men on first and second with two out. Jackson ran the count to 3-2

and fouled off four straight before he struck out.

The star of Game Three was third baseman Graig Nettles, who reminded everyone of Brooks Robinson with four sterling plays that halted the Dodgers' offense. Guidry continued his brilliant pitching, and the Yanks won 5-1. The next game, a 4-3 New York win, was decided by Lou Piniella's tenth-inning single. Game Five was an 18-hit, 12-2 Yankees blow out. Munson had five RBI, and Roy White drove in three runs.

In Game Six, light-hitting infielders Dent and Brian Doyle combined for six hits and five RBI, and Jackson redeemed himself against Welch by smashing a homer in a 7-2 win. New York became the first club ever to drop the first two games of the Series and come back to win it in six games.

1979

A series of injuries, a fight, a managerial change, and the death of Munson reduced the world champion Yankees to fourth place in the A.L. East. Nagging injuries plagued Guidry, Nettles, and Jackson. Gossage was lost for 83 days when he injured his finger in a brawl with reserve Cliff Johnson. Steinbrenner canned manager Bob Lemon after a 34-30 start. On

Padre Dave Winfield is tagged out at the plate.

ROGER ANGELL — BASEBALL WRITER

His byline doesn't appear on the back pages of a daily newspaper. He's never written for one of the country's major national sports magazines. The publication he does toil for does not boast a circulation in the millions. Yet, Roger Angell may be America's best baseball writer.

For nearly three decades, Angell's articles in the literary magazine *The New Yorker* have been the among the most eagerly awaited among baseball fans. Angell writes about the game with a fan's passion, an insider's knowledge, and a poet's style. He has never failed to enhance the reader's appreciation of the national pastime. His descriptions of players become vivid word pictures, as in this perception of pitcher Tom Seaver's classic delivery:

"The motionless assessing pause on the hill while the sign is delivered, the easy, rocking shift of weight onto the back leg, the upraised arms, and then the left shoulder coming forward as the whole body drives forward and drops suddenly downward — down so low that the right knee scrapes the sloping dirt of the mound — in an immense thrusting stride, and the right arm coming over blurrily and still flailing, even as the ball, the famous fastball, flashes across the plate, chest-high on the batter and already past his low, late swing."

Angell's *New Yorker* articles have been reprinted in four hardcover anthologies — *The Summer Game, Five Seasons, Late Innings,* and *Season Ticket* — books that are considered among the classics of baseball literature.

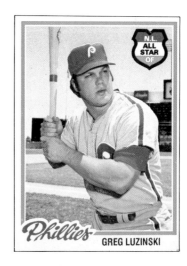

GREG LUZINSKI

DARRELL PORTER C
ROYALS

2nd BASE LOU WHITAKER
TIGERS

Alan Trammell (top left) of Detroit scored 68 runs in '79. Oriole first sacker Eddie Murray (middle left) averaged 26 homers and 94 RBI from 1977 to '79. Expo Andre Dawson (center) had 25 homers and 92 RBI in 1979. Phillie slugger Greg Luzinski (top right) averaged 29 homers a year from 1975 to '79. Kansas City catcher Darrell Porter (second row right) in 1979 hit .291 with 20 homers, 112 RBI, and a league-leading 121 walks. Lou Whitaker of the Tigers (third row right) hit .286 with 75 runs scored and 20 stolen bases in '79. Buddy Bell (bottom left) had 101 RBI for the '79 Rangers. Pirate Kent Tekulve (bottom right) appeared in 91 games in '78 and 94 games in '79.

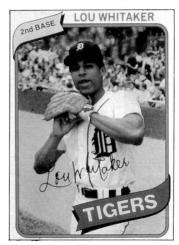

PITCHER KENT TEKULVE
PIRATES

THE 1970s

August 2, baseball lost one of its most talented catchers when Munson died in the crash of a plane he was piloting.

Six of the seven teams in the A.L. East played better than .500 ball, making it the best division in baseball. Boston watched its two star outfielders, Lynn and Rice, battle each other for the triple crown. Lynn led in average (.333) and tied with Rice in home runs with 39. Rice batted .325 and drove in 130 runs, eight more than Lynn. Though the BoSox led the league in homers, their pitchers permitted a generous four runs per game.

Baltimore won 102 games and proved that they were the most balanced team in the game and, in fact, under manager Earl Weaver, the A.L.'s winningest team in the decade with a percentage of .590. Jim Palmer faltered, winning only ten games, but Mike Flanagan (23-9) led the staff with a Cy Young Award-winning performance. Ken Singleton (.295, 35 home runs, 111 RBI) and Eddie Murray (.295, 25 homers, 99 RBI) carried the offense; catcher Rick Dempsey, center fielder Al Bumbry, and Mark Belanger anchored the defense.

The A.L. West was won by the highly compensated California Angels, who captured their first division title in the club's 19-year history. Eight Angels held multi-year contracts, each worth $1 million or more. California had a power-packed lineup that averaged 5.4 runs per game and had a team batting average of .282. Injuries cost Rod Carew (.318) his eighth batting title, but MVP Don Baylor hit 36 homers, drove in 139 runs, and batted .296. Brian Downing (.326), Dan Ford (101 RBI), and Bobby Grich (30 homers, 101 RBI) made the Angels lineup a pitcher's nightmare.

The 38-year-old Pete Rose became an instant millionaire when he left Cincinnati and signed as a free agent with Philadelphia. Cincinnati fans were furious, but the Reds still managed to win their division, beating the Houston Astros by 1½ games. The Cincinnati Reds were the 1970s winningest team, with a .592 winning percentage. Astro knuckleballer Joe Niekro led the league with 21 wins, and 6'8" J.R. Richard fanned a league-high 313 batters. Cincinnati still had ample power in George Foster (.302, 30 home runs, 98 RBI), Johnny Bench (who drove in more runs than any other N.L. player during the decade), and slick-fielding shortstop Dave Concepcion (16 home runs, 84 RBI). Rose's replacement, Ray Knight, filled in admirably, batting .318. Tom Seaver led the staff with a record of 16-6.

Rose played first base for the Phillies and finished second in the league in batting (.331) to Keith

Hernandez (.344, 105 RBI) of the Cardinals. But despite fine performances by Rose, Mike Schmidt (45 homers, 114 RBI), and Steve Carlton (18 wins), the Phils finished fourth in the East.

Pittsburgh edged Montreal by 2 games, giving them six division titles during the decade. The pitching star was lanky Kent Tekulve, who appeared in 94 games, winning ten and saving 31. Offensively, the Bucs relied on Dave Parker (.310, 25 home runs, 94 RBI) and co-MVP Stargell, who shared the N.L. honor with Keith Hernandez. Pops led the team with 32 homers, none more important than his three-run homer against the Cubs on the last day of the season that clinched first place.

The Pirates, buoyed by their rallying cry of "We Are Fam-i-ly," swept the Reds in the playoffs behind Stargell, who hit .455 with two homers and six RBI. Baltimore downed California three games to one.

In the World Series, the Orioles jumped to a three-games-to-one lead and seemed well on their way to making good on Earl Weaver's vow to avenge their bitter seven-game 1971 World Series loss to the Clemente-led Pirates. Only three teams in Series history had come back from a three-to-one deficit, but Pittsburgh romped 7-1 in Game Five, and John Candelaria and Tekulve shut out the Birds 4-0 in Game Six. The finale belonged to the Pirates spiritual leader, Stargell, who launched a game-winning two-run rocket. Pops hit .400 during the seven games and was named the Series MVP.

Left to right: Manny Mota has the most career pinch hits (150); Jack Clark had 26 homers in '79; Bill Madlock hit .309 in 1978.

Dodgers third baseman Ron Cey (top left) hit .281 in 1979 with 28 homers, 81 RBI, and 77 runs scored. Cey averaged 23 homers a year from 1973 to 1979, with 90 RBI and 75 runs scored. Billy Martin (top right) became the Yankees manager for the second time in the middle of the 1979 season. It wouldn't be the last time. Cardinal Lou Brock (middle right) hung up his spikes in 1979 with 938 stolen bases, the most in baseball history. He also had 1,610 runs scored, 900 RBI, 486 doubles, 149 RBI, a .293 batting average, a .410 slugging average, and 10,332 at-bats. Don Baylor (bottom left) led the American League with 139 runs batted in and 120 runs scored in 1979 for the California Angels. Baylor also smashed 36 homers, poked 33 doubles, and had a .296 batting average and a .530 slugging average that season. Willie "Pops" Stargell (bottom right) launches a rocket during the 1979 World Series. Stargell averaged 30 homers, 91 RBI, and 72 runs scored a season during the 1980s. He passed out "Stargell Stars" for outstanding play on the field, and he hoarded most of them for himself with his outstanding N.L.C.S. and World Series performances.

THE 1980s

In the 1980s, such words as free agent, arbitration, and collusion became a part of the lexicon. Several stars joined the million-dollar-per-year club. Improved conditioning spawned athletes who were bigger, stronger, and faster.

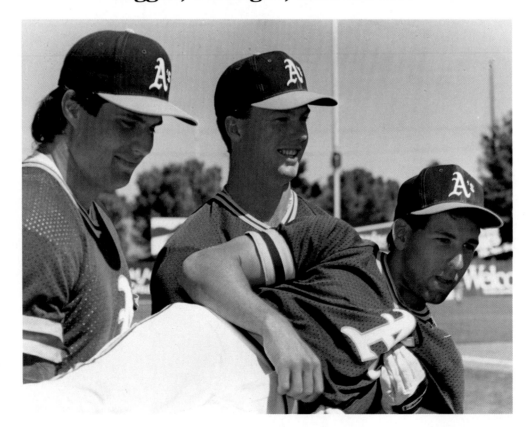

Oakland's three Rookie of the Year winners (page 446), from left, Jose Canseco (1986), Mark McGwire ('87), and Walt Weiss ('88) play around. Eddie Murray (page 447) averaged 101 RBI a season from 1980 to '88.

THE 1980s

In the 1980s, words such as free agent, arbitration, collusion, drugs, and palimony became as much a part of the baseball lexicon as hits, runs, and errors; the word "strike" took on a whole new meaning. Still, even with baseball's imperfections glaring, the game's popularity was never greater.

Red Smith, the Pulitzer Prize-winning sportswriter for the *New York Times*, called 1981 "baseball's dishonest season." A players' strike forced the cancellation of 714 games in the middle of the regular season and resulted in an estimated $98 million in lost player salaries, ticket sales, broadcast revenues, and concession receipts. Not since the "Black Sox" scandal of 1919 had baseball been so traumatized.

Although the strike, which began on June 12, was called by the players, many sportswriters and fans placed the blame on the owners. The club owners desperately wanted to win back the prerogatives over the players that they had already lost at the bargaining table and in the courts on the issue of the free-agency draft. *Sports Illustrated* magazine stated its opinion loud and clear with a cover headline that read: "STRIKE! The Walkout The Owners Provoked."

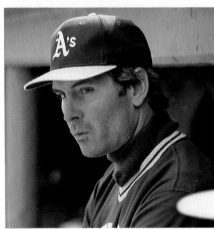

Dave Kingman slammed 442 career home runs.

So bitter were the negotiations that when the strike was finally settled seven weeks later, the players' representative Marvin Miller and the owners' negotiator Ray Grebey refused to pose with each other for the traditional "peace ceremony" picture. At issue during the negotiations was the owners' demand for compensation when losing a free-agent player to another team; the compensation would be a player selected from the signing team's roster (not including 15 "protected" players). The players maintained that any form of compensation would undermine the value of the free agent.

The stalemate ended, coincidentally, when the insurance policy that the owners had taken out with Lloyds of London expired. On July 31, a compromise was reached. The settlement gave the owners a limited victory on the compensation issue. Teams that lost a "premium" free agent could be compensated by drawing one from a pool of players left unprotected from the rosters of all the clubs, not just the signing club.

When the dust finally settled, the players had lost $4 million a week in salaries and the owners suffered a total loss of $72 million. The schedule had been cut by one third. Management came up with a split-season arrangement (with a playoff at the end) that was not popular. Despite the close second-half races in all four divisions, attendance dropped in 17 of 26 cities and television ratings slumped sharply.

There were some bright spots: Philadelphia's Pete Rose broke Stan Musial's N.L. hit record on the day the "second season" resumed; Nolan Ryan of the Houston Astros pitched a record-breaking fifth no-hitter; and Fernando Valenzuela, a 20-year-old rookie for the Los Angeles Dodgers, became Mexico's answer to Sandy Koufax.

These performances, however, were obscured by the constant complaining over the playoff format, the hostility that lingered between the players and owners, and the boos that the fans showered on the players. In one incident, St. Louis Cardinals shortstop Garry Templeton answered an obscene fan with a finger gesture of his own, earning a fine and a suspension. Cesar Cedeno of the

GEORGE BRETT

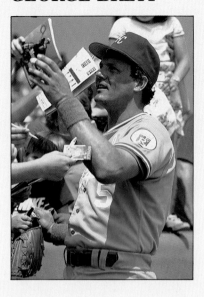

After the 1988 season, George Brett was one of only three active players with ten or more years of major league service to possess a lifetime batting average over .300. The 15-year veteran's .306 in '88 (his tenth season over .300) put his career mark at .312 and raised his lifetime hit total to 2,399. In 1976, he set a major league record for most consecutive games with three or more hits (six). When he won his second American League batting title in 1980, his .390 average was the highest since World War II.

Brett has been more than just a lefthanded-hitting singles machine. The 13-time All-Star has belted 255 homers, scored 1,233 runs, and driven in 1,231 runs. He has 446 doubles lifetime. He has also led the A.L. in triples three times and slugging percentage three times. Brett's first slugging title came in 1980, when he won the A.L. Most Valuable Player award and led the Kansas City Royals to the pennant. In 1985, he hit 30 homers, batted .335, and powered the Royals to a world championship.

Brett has been at his best in postseason play. He holds nine career League Championship Series records, including most homers in an L.C.S. (nine). He has batted .340 in 27 A.L.C.S. games. In 13 World Series games, he has batted .373 (the fourth highest Series average of all time). If all that wasn't enough, the former third baseman (now a first baseman) won a Gold Glove for his defense at the hot corner in 1985.

Houston's Nolan Ryan (top left) had one of the most unusual seasons in baseball in 1987. He led the N.L. with a 2.76 ERA and 270 strikeouts (his 11.46 strikeouts per game tops the all-time list), but he had an 8-16 record. Ryan averaged 207 strikeouts a season from 1980 to '88. Pedro Guerrero (top middle) hit .304 with 32 home runs and 100 RBI in 1982 for the Dodgers. He knocked 174 home runs and has 606 RBI from 1980 to '88 for L.A. and St. Louis. Boston's Dwight Evans (top right) led the A.L. with 22 home runs in 1981 and with 121 runs scored in 1984. "Dewey" averaged 26 home runs, 97 runs scored, 89 RBI, and 91 bases on balls a season from 1980 to '88. The Ripken family (middle), left to right Billy, Cal Sr., and Cal Jr., made baseball lore when Cal Sr. took over as the Baltimore manager in 1987 to manage his double-play combination sons. Brewer center fielder Gorman Thomas falls beneath shortstop Robin Yount (bottom left) during an otherwise routine pop fly. Thomas led the American League in homers twice, in 1979 when he smacked 45 and in '82 when he popped 39. In his 15-year career, Yount has amassed 443 doubles, 102 triples, 187 homers, 1,234 runs scored, 1,021 RBI, and 207 stolen bases to go with his .290 batting average and .436 slugging average. Julio Franco (bottom right) of Cleveland scored 501 runs from 1983 to '88.

Houston Astros took matters into his own hands and attacked a fan in the stands, and a Yankees fan assaulted an umpire.

Surprisingly enough, fans ushered in the 1982 season with renewed enthusiasm. Ticket sales matched those of baseball's best years, and it almost seemed as if the events of '81 had never occurred. In fact, the strike and its resulting agreement escalated a trend that was already taking place from 1978 to '81, when 43 players negotiated contracts worth over $1 million each. (The highest went to Dave Winfield, who in November 1980 signed a ten-year contract worth at least $13 million with the New York Yankees and a cost-of-living clause that made it worth as much as $20 million.)

Such stars as Gary Carter, George Foster, Ken Griffey, Bill Madlock, and Mike Schmidt joined the million-plus-per-year club. By 1982, the *average* salary was almost $250,000 (compared to $50,000 in 1976). One of the reasons the owners doled out such hefty contracts was that they were afraid of losing disgruntled stars in the free-agent reentry draft and paid them the new going rate to keep them at home. The Cincinnati Reds traded Griffey and Foster to the Yankees and Mets, respectively, where owners willingly paid the higher price tags. Cincinnati management figured they would lose both players to free agency anyway.

In 1988, the major league minimum salary was $62,000 and the average salary was $449,862. Ozzie Smith, the defensive magician for the St. Louis Cardinals, was the highest-paid player, earning $2.34 million. Nine other players made $2 million or more. Some sportswriters speculated that if Ted Williams or Stan Musial were free agents, owners would have to assign them half the franchise.

Cal Ripken Jr. had 183 homers from 1982 to '88.

Some justification for these huge salaries came about in 1983, when NBC and ABC television networks signed a deal that guaranteed the teams $1.1 billion over six years, which amounted to $6 million per team each season even if no fans showed up. The latest contract, signed in January 1989 with CBS, is worth $1.1 billion for three years. ESPN, a national cable sports network, paid another $400 million for a three-year package. One reason why George Steinbrenner has been tossing huge salaries to free agents is because the New York Yankees signed a $500 million deal with a local cable station in December 1988.

Free agency not only meant more money for players, but more player movement. As a result, baseball had a streak of ten different World Series champions in ten years. The only team to have won two titles in the last 11 years was the Los Angeles Dodgers. In '87, Los Angeles lost 89 games. In '88, they won 94 and the World Series. The St. Louis Cardinals went from the World Series one year to below .500 the next season three times in the decade.

The 1986 world champions, the Mets, are 488-320 since manager Davey Johnson took over in '84. The Mets franchise was the closest thing baseball has had to a dynasty during the decade. In fact, Johnson

Oakland's Rickey Henderson calls time (top left) after stealing second base. Henderson led the A.L. in stolen bases each season from 1980 to '88 except for 1987. Philadelphia's Mike Schmidt slides into third base as Dodger Ron Cey awaits the throw (middle left). Phillies reliever Tug McGraw jumps for joy (top right) after getting the third out against the Astros in Game Four of the 1980 N.L.C.S., forcing a fifth game. Dave Winfield (bottom left) had .289 batting average from 1980 to '88 and averaged 24 homers, 100 RBI, and 89 runs scored. Steve Carlton (bottom right) was 23-11 in 1982 with 295 2/3 innings pitched, 286 strikeouts, and six shutouts.

451

THE 1980s

became the first N.L. manager to win 90 or more games each of his first five seasons.

These developments did not hurt the game's image as much as the hottest topic of the decade: substance abuse. In '83, four players from the Kansas City Royals — Willie Wilson, Jerry Martin, Willie Mays Aikens, and Vida Blue — were found guilty of cocaine use. In fact, it seemed as if a different player was checking into a rehabilitation center every other day. Such established stars as Ferguson Jenkins, Keith Hernandez, Dave Parker, and Dale Berra admitted to having problems with drugs.

Commissioner Bowie Kuhn was both praised and attacked for the firm stand (including heavy fines and suspensions) that he levied against offending players. In 1982, some of the owners organized a move to push Kuhn out of office. In '83, Kuhn and his supporters made a last-ditch effort to renew his contract. They failed, but he was retained until 1984, when a successor could be found.

Kuhn's replacement was Peter Ueberroth, who had made the 1984 Summer Olympics a success as the president of the Los Angeles Olympic Organizing Committee.

Ueberroth promised to improve the financial health of baseball, and he delivered on that promise. He marketed baseball furiously, negotiated the record television deals, and urged the owners to run their teams like they ran their other businesses — more prudently. The owners responded in 1986 and '87 by drastically cutting back on signing other teams' free agents and holding the line on multiyear deals. Ueberroth took an even stronger stance on drugs, calling for what seemed a drastic measure: mandatory urine tests for all players during the season. The commissioner failed, because mandatory testing was not allowed under the Players' Association contract. During the winter of 1986-87, Ueberroth said that the game was free of drugs, but as the 1987 season was about to open, Dwight Gooden of the New York Mets failed a drug test, checked into a rehab clinic, and did not return to the rotation until mid-May. As the year ended, another promising pitcher, Floyd Youmans of the Montreal Expos, became a victim of substance abuse.

The 40th anniversary of Jackie Robinson breaking the color barrier in major league baseball was celebrated in 1987. Dodgers vice president Al Campanis appeared on ABC-TV's late-night network news show *Nightline* in what was supposed to be a tribute to the legendary Robinson. Instead, Campanis stated that blacks "lack the necessities" to become successful major league managers and executives. *Nightline* host Ted Koppel gave Campanis several opportunities to clarify his statements, but Campanis unwittingly buried himself even deeper when he began

Graig Nettles stretches to nab the line drive.

452

1980 NATIONAL LEAGUE CHAMPIONSHIP SERIES

Garry Maddox won the '80 N.L.C.S.

The decade's first N.L.C.S. pitted the Phillies (a team that hadn't won a World Series in its 79-year history) against the Astros (a team that hadn't won anything in its 28 years).

Philadelphia won Game One 3-1. Houston came back to win Game Two with a four-run tenth-inning explosion. Astro pitcher Joe Niekro hurled ten scoreless innings in Game Three before Houston won it 1-0 in the bottom of the 11th.

Game Four, won by the Phillies 5-3 in ten innings, was protested by both teams. With none out and two on in the top of the fourth, Philadelphia's Garry Maddox hit a soft line drive to the mound that pitcher Vern Ruhle caught, then threw to first for a double play. While the Phillies argued that Ruhle had trapped the ball, Houston first baseman Art Howe tagged second thinking he had made a triple play. After a 20-minute argument, a double play was called and the Astros escaped unscathed. Houston was up 2-0 when the Phillies jumped ahead with three in the eighth. The Astros tied it in the bottom of the ninth only to lose it in the tenth.

In the wild fifth game, Houston took a 5-2 lead into the top of the eighth with ace Nolan Ryan on the mound. The Phillies scored five runs to take a 7-5 lead. As was their habit all during the series, the Astros rallied to tie the game in the bottom of the eighth. Maddox, however, doubled in a tenth-inning run to end the series.

Brewers shortstop Robin Yount leaps over Orioles shortstop Cal Ripken Jr. (top left) on the front end of a double play. Reggie Jackson (top right) slammed 194 home runs from 1980 to '87. He ended his 21-year career with 563 homers, 1,702 RBI, 228 steals, a .262 batting average, and a .490 slugging average. Alan Trammell (bottom left) of the Tigers had 133 home runs, 878 runs scored, 678 RBI, and a .291 batting average from 1978 to '88. Don Mattingly of the Yankees, left, and Darryl Strawberry of the Mets (bottom right) compare tape jobs.

THE 1980s

comparing the physical attributes of whites and blacks.

During the ensuing uproar, Campanis was fired by the Dodgers, ending a 40-year association. Ueberroth responded by saying that he planned to develop an "affirmative action" plan for baseball. No blacks, however, were hired as managers or general managers during the season. In fact, only three blacks have ever managed in the big leagues, Frank Robinson (Cleveland, San Francisco, Baltimore), Larry Doby (Chicago White Sox), and Maury Wills (Seattle). In '87, there were 879 administrative positions in baseball, but only 17 of them were held by blacks. According to Ueberroth, more blacks were being hired for coaching, front-office, and minor league jobs. Robinson, baseball's first black manager in 1975, became the skipper of the Baltimore Orioles (54-107), the worst team in baseball during the '88 season. Bill White, a former player and broadcaster, was named as the

National League's president after the 1988 season, becoming the first black man to head either league.

Another minority group, women, tried to break male domination of baseball. Pam Postema almost became the first woman to call balls and strikes in the major leagues. During spring training, Postema, age 33, was invited by the N.L. to try out for two openings in the umpire ranks. She received much publicity when she worked several major league exhibition games. When the season began, though, she was back in the minors for the 12th straight year.

The tradition-bound Chicago Cubs made front page headlines across the country when the Tribune Co. (which owns the team) installed lights at Wrigley Field during the 1988 season. A horde of journalists descended on the Windy City for the Cubs' first home night game ever. On August 8, the game against the Phillies was rained out after 3½ innings of play. So the clash against the Mets the following night became the first official night game at Wrigley Field.

The most compelling story occurred in the summer when a team of U.S. college all-stars returned from Seoul, Korea, with America's first-ever gold medal. A 5-3 win over Japan, the defending gold medalist in '84, made winning pitcher Jim Abbott from the University of Michigan the best-

Kirby Puckett hit .320 from '84 to '88.

known amateur baseball player ever. Abbott, who was born without a right hand, won the Sullivan Award as the top amateur athlete in any sport.

Slow afoot, but dangerous in every other phase of the game was Yankees first baseman Don Mattingly, the A.L.'s premier fielding first baseman (four Gold Gloves). Using ten offensive categories, a statistical study determined that for the previous five seasons Mattingly was the best player in major league baseball. Mattingly has batted .332, while averaging 205 hits, 27 home runs, 115 RBI, and 100 runs scored in five full seasons. Eddie Murray, Los Angeles' new first baseman,

KEITH HERNANDEZ

There have been only a handful of players in baseball history who have "redefined the way his position is played."

At first base, a position not considered to be "important"

defensively, Keith Hernandez has been the finest fielder of all time. Between 1978 and '88, Hernandez won a record 11 Gold Gloves for defensive excellence at the initial sack, where he has been baseball's best at fielding bunts and turning the first-to-short-to-first double play. Hernandez currently holds the major league record for most lifetime assists by a first baseman (1,631 after the '88 season).

Hernandez has also been a pretty reliable offensive force over his 15-year career. A lifetime .300 hitter, he has knocked in 90 or more runs six times in his career. He has scored more than 80 runs eight times. He was

cowinner of the 1979 Most Valuable Player award (with Willie Stargell) when he hit a league-leading .344 as a member of the St. Louis Cardinals. Hernandez also led the league in doubles (48) and runs scored (116), and drove in 105 runs.

Traded to the New York Mets in 1983, he became an instant team leader and was instrumental in the club's rise to world champions in '86, when he hit .310, scored 94 runs, and walked an N.L.-leading 94 times. The only black mark on Hernandez' record occurred when he testified at the 1985 Pittsburgh drug trials that he had used cocaine while he was with the Cardinals.

Jack Morris of Detroit (top left) has a 156-105 record from 1980 to '88. Red Sox outfielder Jim Rice (top middle) had 379 homers from 1974 to '88. Fernando Valenzuela (top right) sips some bubbly after the '81 World Series. Toronto center fielder Lloyd Moseby (bottom left) had 138 homers from 1980 to '88. George Brett (bottom right) had 255 homers from 1974 to '88.

THE 1980s

finished a distant second and Boston's Wade Boggs placed third.

The new emphasis on speed, which came about in the late 1970s, gave birth to some of the greatest leadoff men in the history of the game. The two best were Rickey Henderson of the Yankees and Montreal's Tim Raines. Henderson holds the all-time single-season record for stolen bases (130 set in '82). If he stays healthy, he could break Lou Brock's lifetime record of 938 steals sometime in 1990. Like Henderson, Raines hits for average and power (he led the N.L. in batting with a .334 average in 1986), averages 60 steals a year, and sports the best lifetime steal percentage (87.5 percent). Willie Wilson, Kansas City's center fielder, is always among the stolen base leaders. Wilson has hit as high as .332 and has stolen as many as 83 bases in a season. In St. Louis, Cardinals outfielder Vince Coleman became the first player in history to steal 100 bases three years in a row. He had an "off" year in 1988 and still stole 81. Coleman has passed 400 career steals faster than any other player in history.

It used to be that scouts sought out fleet-footed jitterbug types to play shortstop, such as Baltimore's Mark Belanger and Bud Harrelson of the New York Mets. In the A.L., a new breed of "big" shortstop has redefined the way the position is supposed to be played. Cal Ripken Jr. has led A.L. shortstops in assists four times and is the third greatest home run hitting shortstop in history, behind Ernie Banks and Vern Stephens. The 6'4" Ripken has played in 1,086 consecutive games and has won a Rookie of the Year award (1982) and an MVP award (1983). Alan Trammell of Detroit has transformed himself from a slick-fielding shortstop with a decent bat to a cleanup hitter with power. In 1987, Trammell hit .343 with 28 homers

and 105 runs batted in. He has batted .300 five times in his career. Robin Yount played shortstop for the Milwaukee Brewers for 11 seasons before switching to the outfield. In 1982, Yount hit .331 with 29 home runs and 114 RBI.

In '88, Oakland A's outfielder Jose Canseco (42 home runs, 40 steals) became the charter member of the 40-40 club. In 1987, Cincinnati Reds center fielder Eric Davis (37 homers, 50 steals) just missed. That same season, New York Mets Darryl Strawberry (39 home runs, 36 steals) and Howard Johnson (36 home runs, 32 steals) became the first two teammates in history to join the 30-30 club, and Pittsburgh's Barry Bonds hit 25 home runs and stole 32 bases. (Barry's father, Bobby Bonds, was a member of the 30-30 club five times between 1969 and '79).

Improved conditioning is responsible for some of the success of this "new breed" of power-and-speed players and seems to be one of the major reasons why so many players are able to play (and play well) at an advanced age. Of course, there is added incentive to stay in shape when pulling in a six-figure salary.

Ryne Sandberg hit 109 homers from 1982 to '88.

DAVE WINFIELD

Prior to the 1989 season, Dave Winfield was receiving more publicity for his war of words with New York Yankees owner George Steinbrenner than for his exploits on the field. The off-season furor overshadowed Winfield's magnificent '88 season when, at age 36, he produced one of the best seasons of his career: a .322 average, 25 home runs, and 107 RBI.

Winfield is one of the best all-around athletes to have played the game. When he was selected as the San Diego Padres first-round draft pick in 1973, he was also selected in the National Basketball Association, American Basketball Association, and National Football League drafts. Since starting his career that same year, he has been one of the game's more consistent players, hitting for average (.287 lifetime) and power (357 homers and 1,438 RBI), stealing bases (209), and winning five Gold Gloves for defensive excellence in right field (he led the A.L. in assists in 1982). He has hit at least 20 homers in 11 seasons, and he has 100 or more RBI in seven seasons. Winfield has not dominated baseball in any specific category, but few players have excelled in so many areas.

After eight seasons with the lowly Padres, Winfield, hoping to finally play on a winner, signed a multiyear, multimillion-dollar free-agent contract with Steinbrenner's Yankees in 1981. So far, that year is the closest he has come to a world championship ring. It also produced the low point of his career, as Winfield batted .045 (1 for 22) in a Series loss to the Dodgers.

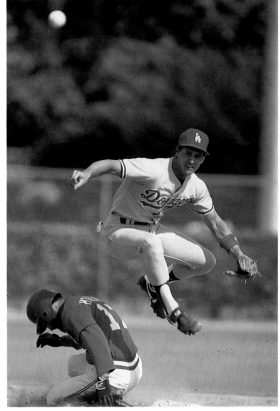

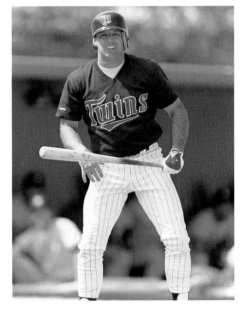

Kirk Gibson (top left) leaps with joy after his second home run in Game Five of the 1984 World Series beats San Diego four games to one. Harold Baines (top right) of the White Sox slugged 173 homers and drove in 763 runs from 1980 to '88. Los Angeles second baseman Steve Sax (middle right) completes the double play; he scored 574 runs from 1981 to '88. Philadelphia's Mike Schmidt (bottom left) had a .269 batting average, a .530 slugging average, and 1,567 RBI from 1972 to 1988. Third baseman Gary Gaetti (bottom right) of Minnesota smashed 164 homers from 1982 to '88.

THE 1980s

Steve Carlton, who won the Cy Young Award when he was 37 years old, strengthened his body by doing martial-arts exercises. He was one of the best conditioned athletes in professional sports. Hall of Famer Carl Yastrzemski, who played 23 years for the Boston Red Sox, exercised religiously in the off-season. Chicago White Sox catcher Carlton Fisk hit a career-high 37 homers at the age of 36 and credits his newfound power to the weightlifting he did throughout the season. Pitchers Jerry Koosman, Jim Kaat, Phil Niekro, Gaylord Perry, Tom Seaver, Don Sutton, and Nolan Ryan were able to pitch effectively beyond their 40th birthdays.

In addition, the advent of laser surgery has helped prolong the careers of many players, most notably pitcher Tommy John. Arthroscopic surgery has enabled players to come back from knee injuries in weeks, whereas they used to miss whole seasons.

The '88 World Series between the Los Angeles Dodgers and the Oakland Athletics highlighted another trend in baseball: the middle-inning "set-up" reliever. While both staffs had true late-inning closers in Jay Howell (Dodgers) and Dennis Eckersley (A's), they also possessed a corps of relievers who were called upon to keep games close until the bullpen could come on to save the day in the eighth or ninth inning. Almost every team in baseball now has at least one pitcher who fills this increasingly important role.

When Peter Ueberroth became commissioner in 1984, he pledged to improve the financial health of baseball, and he did just that. Major league attendance shattered records in each of the four seasons between 1984 and 1988. Many franchises are now estimated to be worth close to $100 million. For instance, in 1980, the cellar-dwelling New York Mets were sold for $40 million, but by 1989, a last-place club like the Atlanta Braves was worth more than $80 million. Because revenues are way up, the number of clubs thinking about relocating are down.

Despite the financial boom, Ueberroth announced that he planned to leave office April 1, 1989. Though his successor A. Bartlett Giamatti, the former president of the N.L., inherits an immensely popular game, he faces difficult times ahead.

The Basic Agreement between players and owners ends at the end of the 1989 season. Fierce negotiations are expected, especially now that relations between Major League Baseball and the Players' Association are at an all-time low. In 1986, the Players' Association argued that Ueberroth and the owners were conspiring to prevent

Vince Coleman gets back to first safely; Keith Hernandez tried to make the tag.

ROGER CLEMENS

"The Rocket" is a most apt nickname for Roger Clemens, a pitcher who throws a fastball in the high 90s and whose career has taken off like a missile since the mid-1980s.

Considered one of the most intense and competitive pitchers in the game, the Boston Red Sox righthander has also been the American League's most dominant since recovering from shoulder surgery in his 1985 sophomore season. Since appearing in the majors, Clemens (who turns 27 in August 1989) has compiled a 78-34 record, with an earned run average just over 3.00 and 985 strikeouts.

Clemens' 1986 season almost matched the incredible numbers that the Mets' Dwight Gooden had produced the year before. In late April, Clemens struck out a major league record 20 batters in a game against the Seattle Mariners. Clemens subsequently led the Red Sox to the A.L. pennant, going 24-4 (at one point winning 14 straight), with a 2.48 ERA and 238 strikeouts. He became the first pitcher to win a Cy Young Award, a Most Valuable Player award, and an All-Star Game MVP in the same season.

After missing the '87 spring training due to a contract dispute, Clemens started the year slowly but won 16 of his last 19 decisions to finish at 20-9. He led the league that year in complete games (18) and shutouts (seven), and became only the third pitcher in history to win a Cy Young Award in successive seasons. In 1988, Clemens led the American League in strikeouts (291), shutouts (eight), and complete games (14), while going 18-12 with a 2.93 ERA.

Eric Davis (top left) slugged 37 homers and swiped 50 bases in '87. Tony Gwynn (top middle) averaged 200 hits from 1984 to '88. Bruce Hurst (top right) was 18-6 in 1988. Orel Hershiser (bottom left) had a 2.77 ERA from 1983 to '88. Dwight Gooden (bottom middle) averaged 18 wins from 1984 to '88. Will Clark (bottom right) had 109 RBI in '88.

THE 1980s

the movement of free agents. The most prominent member of the group was Tiger Kirk Gibson, who after offering his services to the other teams in the major leagues, was forced to return to the Tigers when no other team tried to sign him. In '87, Gibson's teammate Jack Morris, the winningest pitcher of the 1980s, offered his services to the Minnesota Twins and New York Yankees. They declined, and Morris had no other choice but to re-sign with Detroit. Tim Raines, Montreal's superstar outfielder, didn't receive an offer either. Rains had to wait until May 1 to re-sign with the Expos. Rich Gedman (Red Sox), Ron Guidry (Yankees), Bob Boone (Angels), and Doyle Alexander (Braves) were also forced to re-sign with

their clubs. Bob Horner (Braves) also became a free agent, wasn't signed, and went to play in Japan instead. In fact, only two big-name free agents were signed, Andre Dawson (Chicago Cubs) and Lance Parrish (Philadelphia), both for less than their former clubs were offering. After the '87 season, with Jack Clark moving from St. Louis to the Yankees and Bob Horner returning from Japan to sign with the Cardinals, the Players' Association arbitrators again agreed with the players' charge of collusion. The players freed from their contracts after the arbitrators' decision were called "new look" free agents. These developments portend major problems in 1990.

Dan Quisenberry had 212 saves in six years.

If major league baseball faces some serious problems from drug abuse to labor negotiations to racial inequality, it is simply because baseball is an inseparable part of society. Despite the problems, a new generation of superstars — such as Wade Boggs, Don Mattingly, Roger Clemens, Darryl Strawberry, Kirby Puckett, and Dwight Gooden — assure America's pastime safe passage into the 21st century.

1980

When it came to playing in a World Series, the Philadelphia Phillies seemed to have had more near misses than James Bond. In 1980, though, the Phils put aside their century-long tradition of ineptitude, choking, and late-season collapses to usher in the new decade with a world championship.

Philadelphia was loaded with talent, including three almost certain Hall of Famers in Pete Rose, Mike Schmidt, and Steve Carlton. Rose batted .282 and led the league in doubles (42). Schmidt, a unanimous MVP selection, belted 48 homers, drove in 121 runs (including 17 game winners), slugged .624, and had 342 total bases. The best pitcher in the N.L. was the 35-

THE PINE TAR INCIDENT

Baseball has a rule saying a hitter cannot use a bat with more than 18 inches of pine tar (the sticky substance that helps players grip the bat tighter) from the knob to the barrel.

On July 24, 1983, George Brett of the Royals hit a two-out, two-

run homer in the top of the ninth inning off of Yankee Goose Gossage to put Kansas City ahead 5-4.

Yankees manager Billy Martin had known for two weeks that Brett's bat was technically illegal, but he was waiting for just the right time to protest it. So while Brett smiled in the dugout, Martin walked to the umpires, with

rule book in hand, and convinced the arbiters to declare Brett out and the game over for a Yankees win. Brett charged from the dugout and had to be physically restrained from the umpires.

The Royals protested the decision, and four days later A.L. President Lee MacPhail upheld the protest, saying that the amount of pine tar, while illegal, didn't violate "the spirit of the rules." The suspended game would be completed on August 18, but not before the Yankees announced that full regular admission would be charged for the one inning. Fans protested the proposed admission fee and, like the Royals, had that decision overturned too.

The inning was played before 1,200 fans — some admitted free with ticket stubs from the original game, others charged $1 to $2 — and took a whole nine minutes and 41 seconds. The Yankees went quietly in the bottom of the ninth inning, losing 5-4.

George Brett, left, and Billy Martin were foes in the Pine Tar Incident.

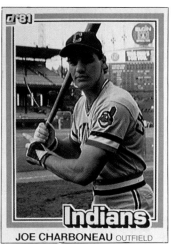

Indians

JOE CHARBONEAU OUTFIELD

Mike Schmidt (left) of the Philadelphia Phillies won two straight MVP awards in 1980 and '81. He averaged 37 home runs a year from 1980 to '87. Dodger Jerry Reuss (top right) was 18-6 in '80 and led the N.L. with six shutouts. Reggie Jackson (middle right) smashed 41 homers and drove in 111 runs for the 1980 Yankees. Indian Joe Charboneau (bottom right) in 1980 had 28 homers and 87 RBI, and was the A.L. Rookie of the Year.

461

year-old Cy Young Award-winning "Lefty" Carlton (24-9, 2.34 ERA, 286 strikeouts, and 304 innings pitched). Tug McGraw led the team with 20 saves and a 1.47 ERA, while Dick Ruthven was 17-10 with a 3.55 ERA.

The Expos, though plagued by injuries, led Philadelphia for most of the season. In former Tiger Ron LeFlore (97 stolen bases), Andre Dawson (.308, 17 homers, 87 RBI), and Ellis Valentine (.315), manager Dick Williams had perhaps the most talented outfield in baseball. Gary Carter, taking over the mantle of the best catcher in the N.L. from Johnny Bench, hit 29 homers and knocked in 101 runs. He also led the league catchers in putouts (822), assists (108), and fielding average (.993).

The Phillies and the Expos met on the next-to-last day of the regular season game to decide the winner of the N.L. East. The Phils made five errors in the game, a dismal reminder of past failures, but in the top of the 11th inning, Schmidt homered and Philadelphia held on for a 6-4 win.

The bid for the N.L. West was a three-way duel among the Astros, Reds, and Dodgers. Through July, Houston pitcher J.R. Richard was unhittable, recording ten wins and a 1.89 ERA. Later in the month he suffered a near-fatal stroke and was lost for the year. He was never able to recover after the 1980 season. The Astros led the league in team ERA with a 3.10 mark and allowed the fewest runs (589). Houston's staff included Joe Niekro (20-12, 3.55 ERA), Nolan Ryan (11-10, 3.35 ERA), Ken Forsch (12-13, 3.20 ERA), and Vern Ruhle (12-4, 2.38 ERA).

Going into their last three games of the regular season, the Astros had a three-game lead over Los Angeles, whom they would play in their final three games. The Dodgers swept Houston, forcing a one-game playoff to determine the division winner. Los Angeles was led by three players who slugged more than 25 homers — first baseman Steve Garvey (26), third baseman Ron Cey (28), and outfielder Dusty Baker (29). Houston's knuckleball specialist, Joe Niekro, responded with his 20th win of the season, giving the Astros their first N.L. West title since the team joined the league in 1962.

Bill Buckner of the last-place Cubs led the N.L. in batting with a .324 mark, beating out another first baseman, St. Louis' Keith Hernandez. Hernandez hit .321 and led the league in runs scored with 111. Chicago's Bruce Sutter saved 28 of the club's 64 victories to lead the league.

The N.L.C.S. between Houston and Philadelphia was a five-game battle that ranks with the most exciting Championship Series of all time. Four of the five games went into extra innings. In Game Five, Astros hurler Nolan Ryan fumbled a 5-2 lead in the eighth inning, and the Phillies scored a run in the tenth to grab their first pennant in 30 years.

In the A.L. East, the Yankees won 103 games, 3 games ahead of second-place Baltimore. Two key Yankees acquisitions came via the reentry draft. For $2.1 million, Yankees owner George Steinbrenner signed former Astro Bob Watson (.307) for four years and another $1 million bought lefty pitcher and former Expo Rudy May (15-5, a league-leading 2.47 ERA). Reggie Jackson enjoyed one of his finest

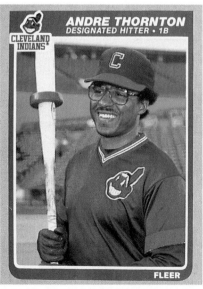

Andre Thornton had 253 homers in his career.

ROBIN YOUNT

When Robin Yount began his career with the Milwaukee Brewers in 1974 at age 18, he became the youngest regular player since 1906. Fifteen years later, Yount is still playing for the Brewers (a rarity during the days of free agency) and is considered one of the most solid players of the 1980s.

Yount was a good-hitting, slick-fielding shortstop for his first six years but didn't explode offensively until 1980, when he produced career highs in average (.293), homers (23), RBI (87), runs (121), and an American League-leading 49 doubles. Two years later, Yount produced one of the greatest seasons ever by a shortstop, leading the league in hits (210), doubles (46), and slugging (.578). He also batted .331, knocked 29 homers and 114 RBI, scored 129 runs, won the Most Valuable Player award and a Gold Glove, and led the Brewers to the A.L. pennant. Though Milwaukee lost the World Series to the St. Louis Cardinals in seven games, Yount batted .414 and set a Series record with two four-hit games.

After Yount hurt his arm in 1984, he was moved to the outfield and has continued his solid defensive play. Offensively, he has become a perennial .300 hitter, batting .312, .312, and .306 from 1986 to '88. He has had at least 80 RBI in six seasons, has hit at least 25 doubles in 11 seasons, and has had double figures in homers in eight years. After 15 seasons, he has scored 1,234 runs, hit 443 doubles, slugged 187 homers, driven in 1,021 runs, and stolen 207 bases. With 2,407 hits by the age of 33, Yount is on track to reach 3,000 by 1994.

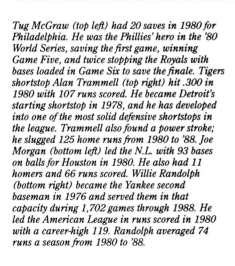

Tug McGraw (top left) had 20 saves in 1980 for Philadelphia. He was the Phillies' hero in the '80 World Series, saving the first game, winning Game Five, and twice stopping the Royals with bases loaded in Game Six to save the finale. Tigers shortstop Alan Trammell (top right) hit .300 in 1980 with 107 runs scored. He became Detroit's starting shortstop in 1978, and he has developed into one of the most solid defensive shortstops in the league. Trammell also found a power stroke; he slugged 125 home runs from 1980 to '88. Joe Morgan (bottom left) led the N.L. with 93 bases on balls for Houston in 1980. He also had 11 homers and 66 runs scored. Willie Randolph (bottom right) became the Yankee second baseman in 1976 and served them in that capacity during 1,702 games through 1988. He led the American League in runs scored in 1980 with a career-high 119. Randolph averaged 74 runs a season from 1980 to '88.

seasons, batting .300, with 41 homers (tied for the league with Milwaukee's Ben Oglivie) and 111 RBI. Tommy John led the league with six shutouts and had the winningest season (22 victories) of his 17-year career. Goose Gossage tied for the A.L. lead with 33 saves.

Baltimore was led by Cy Young Award-winning pitcher Steve Stone (25-7, 3.23 ERA), first baseman Eddie Murray (.300, 32 homers, 116 RBI), and outfielder Ken Singleton (.304, 24 homers, 104 runs batted in). Milwaukee finished third behind Cecil Cooper (.352, 25 homers, and a league-leading 122 RBI), Oglivie (a .304 average and 118 RBI to go with his 41 homers), and Gorman Thomas, who only hit .238 but slugged 38 round-trippers.

Kansas City ran away from Oakland in the A.L. West. Despite a series of nagging injuries, MVP George Brett thrilled the country by flirting with a .400 batting average all summer. Brett ended up at .390, the highest since Ted Williams hit .406 in 1941 and 25th best since 1901. He also drove in 118 runs. His performance overshadowed teammate Willie Wilson, who hit .326 (including a major league-high 230 hits) and stole 79 bases. Relief ace Dan Quisenberry led the league by pitching in 75 games and compiling 33 saves. Although Oakland had two big guns — Tony Armas (35 homers, 109 RBI) and Rickey Henderson (.303, 100 steals) — the club finished 14 games off the pace.

The Royals and Yankees met in the A.L.C.S. for the fourth time in five years. Kansas City won the first two games, and in Game Three, the Yanks built a 2-1 lead by the seventh inning when Brett stepped in against Gossage and turned one of Goose's 100-mph fastballs into a three-run home run

Dan Quisenberry compiled a 2.53 earned run average from 1979 to 1987 for the Royals.

and the first A.L. pennant for Kansas City.

Brett, the unquestioned heart of the Kansas City lineup, entered the World Series plagued by a bad case of hemorrhoids. Philadelphia and the Royals split the first four games. In the pivotal fifth game, Kansas City nursed a 3-2 lead into the eighth inning with K.C. reliever Dan Quisenberry on the mound for the third straight day. Manny Trillo's single in the ninth inning put the Phillies ahead 4-3. In the ninth, Tug McGraw walked the bases full before fanning Kansas City's Jose Cardenal to end the game.

With Carlton on the mound, the Phillies expected to wrap up the Series in Game Six. In the ninth inning, McGraw replaced Carlton with the Phils leading by the score of 4-0. Once again, the Royals loaded the bases against McGraw with only one out. First baseman Pete Rose made a diving catch on a ball that popped out of Bob Boone's glove to record the second out. The energized McGraw then fanned Wilson (4-for-26 for the Series) to end the Series and win the world championship for the Phillies.

FERNANDO VALENZUELA

Until arm problems sidetracked his career in 1988, Fernando Valenzuela had been one of baseball's most dominant pitchers of the 1980s.

During the strike-shortened season of 1981, the lefthander from Mexico was a rookie sensation. Discovered in the Mexican League at age 17 by Dodgers scouts, the 20-year-old Valenzuela was placed in the team's starting rotation after only one season of minor league ball. He hurled a complete game shutout in his first '81 start, then reeled off seven more victories in a row, including six complete games, for a 0.50 ERA. Valenzuela finished the season at 13-7, tying the record for most shutouts by a rookie (eight) and becoming the first pitcher to win the Cy Young and Rookie of the Year awards in the same season.

What made Valenzuela so effective was an excellent screwball, a hard fastball, and good curve, all thrown with pinpoint control. What made him so popular with the media and fans was his appearance and style. Although a fine athlete, Valenzuela looked like a beer-bellied Sunday softball player. Although he could barely speak English, he was fun-loving, had a great sense of humor, and was remarkably poised. During his pitching delivery, he would roll his eyeballs upward, as though he were looking for some divine guidance before releasing the ball.

He has been one of the N.L.'s workhorse pitchers, averaging more than 265 innings per year from 1982 to '87. His lifetime record stands at 118-90, with a 3.16 ERA and 1,528 strikeouts.

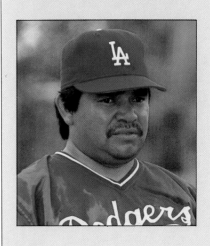

Philadelphia's Pete Rose and Houston's Joe Morgan sprawl (top) over second base during the 1980 National League Championship Series. Rose was caught stealing. Steve "Lefty" Carlton (bottom left) was 24-9 in 1980, and he led the National League in wins, innings pitched (304), and strikeouts (286). He walked only 90 batters. Carlton was 2-0 in the '80 World Series, with a 2.40 ERA and 17 strikeouts in 15 innings pitched. Jim Palmer (bottom middle) was 16-10 in 1980, with a 3.98 ERA for the Baltimore Orioles. Yankee Goose Gossage (bottom right) led the American League with a career-high 33 saves in 1980. Through 1988, Gossage has saved 302 games in his career, second on the all-time list. He also has 101 victories in relief lifetime, fourth on the all-time list.

1981

In the season of "The Big Strike," the longest strike in the history of organized sports alienated even baseball's most passionate fans. There was no major league baseball played from June 12 to August 9, as the strike wiped out 714 games.

When the season resumed, it was decided that the four teams leading their divisions when the strike started would meet the division winners from the second half of the season in a five-game playoff series to determine the division champion. No first-half winner could repeat, which meant that if a team won its division in both the first and second halves, that team still had to play the second-half second-place team in the playoffs.

The obvious flaw was that a team could have the best overall record for the entire season and still not make the playoffs because they did not win either of the mini-seasons. That happened when St. Louis (59-43) and Cincinnati (66-42, which was the best record in baseball) finished with the best overall records in the N.L. but didn't qualify for the playoffs.

Instead, the division winners in the N.L. East were Philadelphia and Montreal. The Phillies were again led by MVP third baseman Mike Schmidt, who slugged 31 homers and drove in 91 in the shortened season. Montreal countered with center fielder Andre Dawson, who powered 24 homers. The Expos downed the Phillies three games to two in the East playoff, winning the first two, dropping the next two, and then taking the fifth.

In the N.L. West, the Dodgers featured Rookie of the Year and Cy Young Award-winner Fernando Valenzuela. The pudgy 20-year-old southpaw won 13, lost seven, and led the N.L. in strikeouts (180) and

shutouts (eight). The Astros ace was Ryan, who was 11-5 with a league-low 1.69 ERA. In their play-off matchup, Los Angeles beat the Astros three games to two, but only after dropping the first two.

In the N.L.C.S., Los Angeles took the first game 5-1 behind the pitching of Burt Hooton. Montreal won the next two games 3-0 and 4-1, only to lose the next two in Montreal. In Game Four, Dodgers first baseman Steve Garvey tied the series by hitting an eighth-inning two-run homer, as L.A. won 7-1. In the finale, Rick Monday's ninth-inning blast gave the Dodgers a 2-1 win and a pennant.

In the A.L. West, first-half winner Oakland swept second-half winner Kansas City 3-0 in the West playoff. The aggressive Oakland club was led by manager Billy Martin, who had the runnin' A's playing "Billy Ball." Tony Armas tied three other players for the A.L. lead in homers with 22, while Rickey Henderson led the league with 56 stolen bases and 89 runs scored. Pitcher Steve McCatty led the league with a 2.32 ERA and had 14 victories. In the East, the ever-feuding Yankees edged the Milwaukee Brewers and Cy Young Award-winning MVP Rollie Fingers (28 saves, 1.04 ERA) in the East playoff three

Houston's Nolan Ryan led the '81 National League with a 1.69 ERA while compiling an 11-5 record.

STEVE GARVEY'S N.L. CONSECUTIVE-GAME RECORD

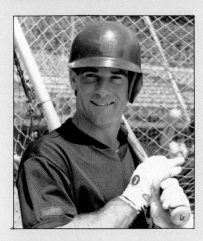

For many of today's players, a blister can mean two weeks on the disabled list. So it seems that Lou Gehrig's record of 2,130 consecutive games played is secure, but Steve Garvey — like Gehrig, a handsome, polite, muscular, solid-hitting first baseman — is a recent player who came close.

In 1975, Garvey was coming off a season during which he had been voted MVP of the National League, the All-Star Game, and the League Championship Series. On September 2, 1975, he missed only his second game of the year. From the next day until July 29, 1983, he played in every game. He broke Billy Williams' N.L. consecutive games-played record (1,117) in April 1983 and when his amazing streak finally ended, he'd seen action in a league-record 1,207 straight.

In his career, Garvey compiled some impressive numbers. He had six 200-plus hit seasons and led the league in 1978 and '80. He batted over .300 seven times, belted over 20 homers six times, and drove in over 100 runs five times. He ended his career with 272 home runs, 1,308 RBI, and a .294 average. Garvey's thick forearms were especially potent in postseason play. In 22 N.L.C.S. games he batted .356 with eight home runs (four in four games in '78) and batted .319 in five World Series. Defensively, he was as solid as they come. He had a .999 fielding average in 1981 and a record-setting 1.000 in 1984. He is currently tied with Wes Parker for the best lifetime fielding percentage (.996) by a first baseman.

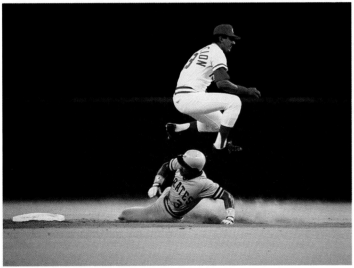

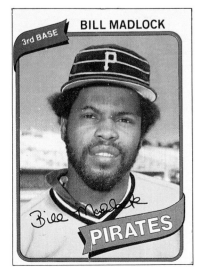

Dodgers hurler Fernando Valenzuela (top left) was 13-7 in 1981, with a 2.48 ERA, eight shutouts, 11 complete games, and 180 strikeouts and only 61 walks in 192 innings pitched. In the eight years from 1981 to '88, Valenzuela led the N.L. in complete games three times, strikeouts once, bases on balls twice, shutouts once, and innings pitched once. Jack Morris (top right) of the Detroit Tigers led the American League in wins with 14 in 1981. From 1980 to '88, Morris notched 123 complete games. Reds shortstop Dave Concepcion leaps over Pirates second baseman Johnny Ray (middle left) after throwing to first base for the double play. From 1982 to '88, Ray batted .292 and averaged 71 runs scored and 35 doubles a season. Concepcion batted .306 in 1981. Bill Madlock (bottom left) led the National League in batting in 1981 with a .341 mark. Rollie Fingers (bottom right) won the Cy Young Award in '81 with his 28 saves for the Milwaukee Brewers. He also won six games (all in relief), had a 1.04 ERA, and had 61 strikeouts and only 13 walks in 78 innings pitched.

467

THE 1980s

games to two. The Yankees pitching staff led the league with a 2.90 ERA and 606 strikeouts. In the A.L.C.S., the Yanks beat the A's three straight. New York third baseman Graig Nettles collected nine RBI. At their victory party, Nettles and Reggie Jackson made headlines in New York by engaging in a fist fight.

The '81 season wasn't all bad. Nolan Ryan recorded the fifth no-hitter of his career, one more than Sandy Koufax. Tom Seaver, who led the majors with a 14-2 record, got his 3,000th strikeout against Montreal. Philadelphia's Pete Rose stroked his 3,631st hit to break the N.L. record held by Stan Musial. A couple of third base-

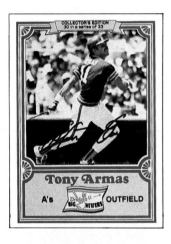

A's outfielder Tony Armas (top) smashed 22 homers in '81. Pirate Tony Pena hit .296 in '82.

468

men, Pittsburgh's Bill Madlock (.341) and Boston's Carney Lansford (.336) led their leagues in batting average. Cleveland's Len Barker pitched a perfect game against the Toronto Blue Jays — just the 11th perfect game in major league history.

In the World Series, the Yankees and Dodgers met for the 11th time in history. New York jumped out to a two-game lead and seemed well on its way to its ninth World Series win over the Dodgers. The Yankees' undoing, however, was making several crucial errors that helped the Dodgers even the series at two games each.

In Game Five, Yankees lefty Ron Guidry allowed back-to-back homers to Pedro Guerrero and Steve Yeager, and Dodger Jerry Reuss pitched a complete game, allowing five hits in a 2-1 Dodgers win. In the finale, Los Angeles scored three runs in the fifth inning and four in the sixth to close out the Series in six games. Afterward, George Steinbrenner embarrassed New Yorkers when he called a news conference to apologize to Yankees fans about the team's shoddy play, a remark that prompted Reggie Jackson to reply: "I don't have anything to apologize for. I played my best."

1982

After all the animosity, complications, and complaints of the marred 1981 season, baseball returned ready for business as usual. In fact, advance ticket sales matched those of baseball's best years. The Atlanta Braves, 13-0 in April, just sneaked into first place in the N.L. West in October, thanks in part to San Francisco second baseman Joe Morgan. His three-run homer on the last day of the season sank the Dodgers and gave the Braves the division title.

Dale Murphy, a catcher turned center fielder, played all 162 games for the Braves, hit 36 homers, led the league with 109 RBI, and walked away with the MVP award. The ace of the staff was 43-year-old pitcher Phil Niekro, who won 17 and lost 4 for new manager Joe Torre. Third baseman Bob Horner slugged 32 homers and drove in 109 runs, while Chris Chambliss (20 homers, 86 RBI) and Claudell Washington (16 homers, 80 runs batted in)

RICKEY HENDERSON

The most intimidating offensive force in baseball is the player who possesses tremendous power and extraordinary speed and uses those talents to produce runs. While Willie Mays, with his 660 homers and 338 stolen bases, was the epitome of this combination among sluggers, Rickey Henderson is not only the definitive version among the great basestealers, he is one of the greatest leadoff hitters of all time.

In 1980, his first full season in the majors, Henderson stole 100 bases (all from first base) for the Oakland Athletics and immediately became the favorite to break Lou Brock's record of 118 steals in a season. Henderson accomplished the feat easily in 1982 (against the Milwaukee Brewers on August 27), finishing the season with an amazing 130 thefts. After being traded to the New York Yankees in 1985, Henderson produced one of the greatest seasons ever by a lead-off man: .314 average, 24 homers, 99 walks, 80 steals, and 146 runs, only the second player since 1940 to score more than 145 runs in a season.

As of the '89 season, the 30-year-old Henderson had led the American League in stolen bases eight times, just two short of the all-time record. His 794 lifetime steals were just 144 behind all-time leader Lou Brock. Henderson has a .292 career average, 1,058 lifetime runs scored, and 1,455 hits. More impressive, however, are these two statistics: Henderson's runs-per-nine-innings average of 0.8 is the highest of any player in nearly 40 years, and he holds the all-time record for home runs leading off a game (36).

Robin Yount (top left) of the Milwaukee Brewers averaged 15 home runs, 95 runs scored, and 80 runs batted in from 1980 to '88. Cal Ripken Jr. (top right) of the Baltimore Orioles was the American League Rookie of the Year in 1982, with 28 home runs, 93 runs batted in, and 90 runs scored. Atlanta's Dale Murphy (bottom left) had 303 total bases and 93 bases on balls in 1982. In 1983, he had 318 total bases, 90 bases on balls, and a .396 on-base average. Pedro Guerrero (bottom right) became an offensive force for the Los Angeles Dodgers in 1982. He hit .304 that season, with 32 home runs and 100 RBI. Guerrero also had 32 home runs in 1983 with 103 runs batted in.

469

THE 1980s

rounded out an offense that led the N.L. in runs scored with 739.

In the N.L. East, the Cardinals outlasted Philadelphia and Montreal, even though St. Louis hit only 57 home runs — the lowest for any team in the majors that year. The Redbirds, though, led the N.L. in steals (200) and got timely hits from Keith Hernandez (.299, 94 RBI) and George Hendrick (104 RBI). Outfielder Lonnie Smith led the club with a .307 average, scored a league-leading 120 runs, and stole 68 bases.

Steve Garvey of the Dodgers was only the fifth major leaguer to play in at least 1,000 consecutive games. Philadelphia's Steve Carlton, the only 20-game winner in the league, won an unprecedented fourth Cy Young Award. Carlton was 23-11, and led the league in strikeouts (286), innings pitched (296), complete games (19), and shutouts (six). Another Philly, Pete Rose, notched his 3,771st hit in June to tie Hank Aaron's record for second place in the majors. Montreal's Al Oliver led the league in batting (.331), hits (204), and doubles (43), and he tied Murphy for the RBI crown (109). Met Dave Kingman slugged a league-leading 37 homers while batting just .204.

The Milwaukee Brewers were in fifth in June when they fired manager Buck Rodgers. Milwaukee responded to the easy-going manner of Harvey Kuenn and led the A.L. East by 3 games over Baltimore with four games to play — all against the O's. The Orioles responded with three straight wins and hoped 36-year-old Jim Palmer (15-5) could pitch them to a pennant before a sell-out home crowd. But Brewers veteran Don Sutton outpitched Palmer to win the game, and Orioles manager Earl Weaver called it quits after nearly 15 years.

The Brewers (nicknamed "The Harvey Wallbangers") had a power-packed lineup. MVP Robin Yount turned in one of the greatest all-around seasons ever by a shortstop, batting .331, with 29 homers and 114 RBI. Cecil Cooper (.313, 32 home runs, 121 RBI) played like an MVP, and Ben Oglivie (34 home runs, 102 RBI), Gorman Thomas (39 home runs, 112 RBI), and Ted Simmons (23 homers, 97 RBI) terrorized A.L. pitching all season. The Brewer staff relied on Cy Young Award-winner Pete Vuckovich (18-6) and reliever Rollie Fingers, who saved 29 games. Life for the '82 Yankees was chaotic as usual. Steinbrenner traded Reggie Jackson to California, had three different pilots (Bob Lemon, Gene Michael, and Clyde King), and saw his club stumble to fifth.

The addition of Reggie Jackson, who led the league with 39 homers, pushed the star-studded California Angels over the top in the A.L. West. The Angels' lineup included 23 players over the age of 30 and looked like a register of stars of the 1970s with Jackson, Don Baylor, Fred Lynn, and Rod Carew (all former MVP winners), as well as Bobby Grich, Bob Boone, Doug DeCinces, Tommy John, and Luis Tiant.

Rollie Fingers of San Diego and Milwaukee averaged 19 saves a season from 1980 to '85.

GARY CARTER

In the winter of 1984, Gary Carter was resting after his best season since becoming the Montreal Expos full-time catcher in 1975. He belted 27 homers, batted a career-high .294, and led the National League in RBI with 106. Though he had long been resented by some teammates who felt him to be too much the self-promoter, Carter was baseball's goodwill ambassador in Canada, a million-dollar player, a perennial All-Star selection, and was considered baseball's best catcher since Johnny Bench had retired. "The Kid," as he was called for his exuberant attitude and playing style, had it all — except a championship.

Suddenly, after the baseball winter meetings in December, Carter was traded to the improving New York Mets for four young players. Considered "the last piece in the Mets' puzzle," Carter belted a career-high 32 homers, drove in 100 runs, and provided solid veteran leadership to the team's talented young pitching staff during a second-place finish in '85. The next season, Carter knocked in 105 runs and finally had his World Series ring.

By the end of the '88 season, Carter had ranked fourth all time among catchers in homers (302) and seventh all time in games played (1,776). He has gathered 1,128 RBI and 1,879 hits. He holds five N.L. catching records, has won three Gold Glove awards, and has played on 11 N.L. All-Star teams, being named the Most Valuable Player in the 1981 and '84 All-Star games.

Third baseman Bob Horner (top left) slugged 32 homers and had 97 RBI for Atlanta in 1982. Reggie Jackson (top right) led the 1982 A.L. with 39 home runs for the Angels. Kansas City's George Brett (bottom) is congratulated by teammate Rance Mulliniks after slugging a home run. Brett had 21 homers in 1982.

THE 1980s

The season was a memorable one for Rickey Henderson of Oakland. Henderson broke Lou Brock's major league record of 118 stolen bases and then went on to steal a total of 130. Righthander Gaylord Perry (age 43) of the Seattle Mariners became the 15th major league pitcher to enter the 300-win club. Perry's teammate Floyd Bannister led the league in strikeouts with 209. Kansas City's Willie Wilson led the league in batting with a .332 mark, and Royal Hal McRae topped the league in runs batted in with 133. Dan Quisenberry of the Royals was again the save leader with 35.

In the A.L.C.S., the Angels beat the Brewers in the first two games. Back in Milwaukee, however, the Brewers took all three — the first time a team had come back from being down by two games to win a five-game playoff. Molitor had a .316 average, two homers, and five RBI for the Wallbangers. The Cardinals downed Atlanta three straight in the N.L.C.S., with rookie Willie McGee batting .308, hitting a homer, driving in five runs, and scoring four.

Brewer Paul Molitor scored 136 runs in 1982.

The World Series opened at Busch Stadium, where nearly 54,000 fans sat in silence and watched the St. Louis Cardinals get blanked 10-0, with Molitor getting five hits and Yount collecting four. The Cards came back in Game Two, as St. Louis reliever Bruce Sutter (who led the N.L. with 36 saves) nailed down the 5-4 win with 2⅓ innings of scoreless pitching. McGee was the hero of the Cardinals' 6-2 Game Three win, slugging two home runs, driving in four runs, and making an amazing catch at the center field wall. Down 5-1 the next day, the Milwaukee Brewers rallied for six runs in the bottom of the seventh inning for a 7-5 win. Robin Yount became the first player in World Series history to have two four-hit games, as he led the Brewers to a 6-4 Game Five win.

Down three games to two, the Cardinals rebounded in Game Six, a 13-1 runaway, behind the four-hit pitching of John Stuper. Vuckovich and Joaquin Andujar started Game Seven. Milwaukee led 3-1 in the sixth. A worn-out Vuckovich was replaced by Bob McClure. Keith Hernandez's single tied the game in the bottom of the sixth, then George Hendrick singled in the winning run. The 6-3 win gave St. Louis its first World Series title in 15 years.

PETE ROSE BREAKS TY COBB'S RECORD

When in 1973, his 11th season, Pete Rose came within a hundred hits of reaching 2,000, he said matter-of-factly: "I'm the only active guy with a legitimate chance to get 4,000 hits."

Rose wasn't quite bold enough to predict he'd break Ty Cobb's all-time hit record of 4,191, but everyone knew he was thinking it. In 1978, Rose became the 13th player ever to reach 3,000 hits and only the second N.L. player to hit in 44 straight games. Though he was 37, he was in great shape and had managed to stay injury free his entire career. The inevitable march to Cobb's record had begun.

Rose got his 3,772nd hit in 1982 to move into second place on the all-time list. In '84, Rose played in 121 games for Montreal and Cincinnati (the team he'd starred with for most of his career) and banged 107 hits, leaving him just 95 short. He became the Reds' 44-year-old player-manager in 1985, and when he got two hits on opening day, the national "Rose Watch" was on. He didn't tie Cobb's record until September 8, when he banged two singles against the Chicago Cubs. Three days later, in front of more than 50,000 fans and 300 writers in Cincinnati, Rose singled to left center in the first inning against San Diego's Eric Show. Fireworks went off, confetti came down, the Reds gave him a car on the spot — and somewhere, Ty Cobb, who got his hits in 2,334 fewer at-bats, was probably cursing "Charlie Hustle."

Pete Rose after breaking Cobb's record.

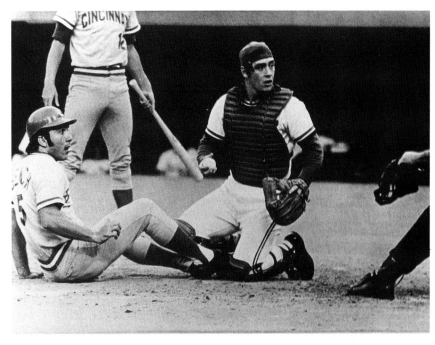

Carl Yastrzemski (top left) ended his career in '83 with 3,419 base hits and 1,844 RBI. Johnny Bench, left, and Ted Simmons (top right) wait for the umpire's call. Bench was called out after trying a double steal. A's outfielder Rickey Henderson (bottom) steals his 119th base on August 27, 1982, breaking Lou Brock's single-season stolen base record.

473

THE 1980s

1983

The Baltimore Orioles had a new manager in Joe Altobelli, a fine flock of role players, and two emerging stars in Cal Ripken Jr. (who was Rookie of the Year in '82) and first baseman Eddie Murray. The 22-year-old Ripken (.318, 27 home runs, 102 RBI) won the MVP award, although many people felt that Murray (.306, 33 home runs, 111 RBI) also deserved the honor. The Orioles led the majors in homers (168) and finished 6 games up on Sparky Anderson's Detroit Tigers in the A.L. East.

The Chicago White Sox ran away in the A.L. West. Cy Young Award-winner LaMarr Hoyt won a league-high 24 games, and Rich Dotson won 22 and lost seven. Rookie of the Year Ron Kittle (35 homers, 100 RBI), Carlton Fisk (26 home runs, 86 RBI), Harold Baines (20 homers, 90 RBI), and Greg Luzinski (32 home runs, 95 RBI) supplied the power.

Two Boston outfielders, Jim Rice and Tony Armas, battled for the league homer crown all season long. Rice won it with 39 homers; Armas was right behind him with 36. Another Red Sox player, second-year third baseman Wade Boggs, won the batting title with a .361 average. Cooper tied Rice for the A.L. lead in runs batted in with 126. Quisenberry led the league in saves (45) for the third time. Dave Righetti threw the first Yanks no-hitter in 27 years.

In the N.L. East, the Phillies were labeled the "Wheeze Kids" (they had 25 players who were over 30 years old). Former Reds Joe Morgan, Pete Rose, and Tony Perez, as well as Steve Carlton, were the fading stars. The true heroes were Mike Schmidt (40 homers, 109 RBI) and Cy Young Award-winner John Denny (19-6). On July 18, Phils general manager Paul Owens fired field manager Pat Corrales, even though the team was in first place. Owens himself took Corrales' place and led them to a 22-7 record during September. The Phillies finished 6 games ahead of the Pirates and 8 ahead of Montreal.

Atlanta Braves outfielder Dale Murphy (.302, 36 home runs, 121 runs batted in) won his second straight MVP award (making him the youngest back-to-back winner in N.L. history), but that wasn't enough to catch the first-place Los Angeles Dodgers in the N.L. West. Los Angeles had traded away the popular duo of third baseman Ron Cey (to the Cubs) and first baseman Steve Garvey (to San Diego), but third baseman Pedro Guerrero (.298, 32 home runs, 103 RBI) and pitcher Fernando Valenzuela (15-10, 3.75 ERA) led the way.

Steve Garvey's consecutive game streak ended at 1,207 games, an N.L. record. Carlton became the 16th pitcher to win 300 games, while he and Nolan Ryan of the Astros raced throughout the year to see who would break the all-time record for strikeouts (3,508) set by Walter Johnson. Ryan broke it first in April. By June, Carlton had overtaken Ryan with strikeout number 3,526. The two future Hall of Famers continued to trade the lead until 1985, when Ryan jumped ahead for good.

Royals relief ace Dan Quisenberry saved a career-high 45 games in 1983, with a 1.94 ERA. He garnered a league-high 35 saves in 1982, with nine victories.

DALE MURPHY

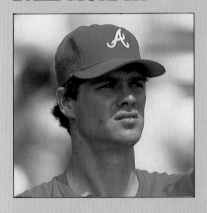

During an era when some fans have viewed baseball players as either drug addicts, money-hungry mercenaries, or publicity hounds, Dale Murphy has been around to exemplify integrity and character. His former manager, Chuck Tanner, once said that Murphy was "the epitome of the hero." He's also been a pretty fair ballplayer.

During his 13-year career, all with the Atlanta Braves, Murphy has been one of the game's most consistent sluggers. After two 20-plus homer seasons in 1978 and '79, and a 33-homer year in '80, Murphy became a genuine superstar in 1982. His 36 homers, league-leading 109 RBI, .281 batting average, .507 slugging average, 113 runs scored, and 23 stolen bases earned him the Most Valuable Player award. In 1983, he led the league with 121 RBI and a .540 slugging average. He also hit another 36 homers, scored 131 runs, batted .302, and stole 30 bases while becoming the youngest player ever (age 27) to win back-to-back MVP awards. In 1984 and '85, his 36- and 37-homer seasons led the National League. He had a superior season in 1987, attaining career highs with 44 homers and a .580 slugging average.

Originally a catcher and first baseman, Murphy had a great arm and superior speed for a man 6'5" and 215 pounds, and was switched to the outfield in 1980. He promptly won five successive Gold Gloves from 1982 to '86. Murphy has also been one of baseball's most durable players, missing just a handful of games in his last nine seasons. Said pitcher Nolan Ryan about Murphy: "I can't imagine Joe DiMaggio was a better all-around player than Dale."

ChiSox Carlton Fisk (top left) slugged 161 homers from 1981 to '88; Harold Baines (top right) had 99 RBI in 1983; Rich Dotson (bottom left) won 22 games in '83; and LaMarr Hoyt (bottom right) won 24 games in '83.

THE 1980s

The hard-throwing Lee Smith of the Chicago Cubs had the most saves in the league, notching 29, while Atlee Hammaker of the Giants had a 2.25 ERA, lowest in the league. Bill Madlock of the Pirates won the batting title with a .323 mark. Tim Raines of the Expos stole 90 bases and scored 133 runs; both marks were tops in the league. Baseball said farewell to Gaylord Perry, Carl Yastrzemski, and Johnny Bench. Perry finished his career with 314 wins; Yaz was the only A.L. player to amass both 400 homers and 3,000 hits; and Bench was arguably the best catcher of all time.

The Phillies downed Los Angeles in four games in the

Brewer first baseman Cecil Cooper hit .397 with 30 homers and 126 RBI in 1983.

476

N.L.C.S. and returned to the World Series for the fourth time in history. Schmidt hit .467 with five runs scored, and Carlton won two games with an ERA of 0.66, but the surprise hero of the Series was Gary Matthews. Matthews had a .429 batting average, four runs scored, three home runs, eight runs batted in, and a 1.071 slugging average. Baltimore lost the first A.L. Championship game to the White Sox, then came back to win three straight and the pennant. Six Orioles pitchers combined for a team ERA of 0.49 during the series.

Philadelphia started ace John Denny (a winner of 13 of his last 14 decisions) in the World Series, while Baltimore started Scott McGregor (18-7). Both pitched superbly, but Philly won 2-1. Rookie Mike Boddicker pitched a three-hitter in Game Two to even the Series.

Baltimore won the next two games by scores of 3-2 and 5-4 in Philadelphia and led three games to one. In Game Five, McGregor allowed just five hits, Eddie Murray hit two homers, and Series MVP Rick Dempsey added yet another for a 5-0 win and the coveted diamond-studded World Series ring.

1984

The Detroit Tigers opened the 1984 season with a win, as did 12 other clubs. Detroit kept on winning and winning, setting the league on its ear with a record of 35-5, including a no-hitter by righthander Jack Morris. Sparky Anderson, the first manager to lead two different teams to 100-win seasons (he did it with the Reds in the 1970s), had three solid starters in Morris (19-11), Dan Petry (18-8), and Milt Wilcox (17-8). Detroit also had an outstanding corps of relievers in Aurelio Lopez (10-1) and Willie Hernandez (9-3), the screwball specialist. The 29-year-old southpaw Hernandez appeared in a league-high 80 games, saved 32, and earned both Cy Young and MVP honors.

The Tigers were also very strong up the middle, with catcher Lance Parrish (33 homers, 98 RBI), shortstop Alan Trammell (.314, 69 RBI), second baseman Lou Whitaker (.289), and center fielder Chet Lemon (.287, 20 home runs). Kirk Gibson, a former stand-

ROGER CLEMENS STRIKES OUT 20

At the start of the 1986 season, Roger Clemens was worried. Arm injuries had already cut short the fastballing 23-year-old righthander's first two seasons with Boston. A career-threatening cartilage tear in his right arm required surgery, but Clemens had worked hard all winter to rehabilitate the arm. When he won his first two starts of '86, he was somewhat relieved.

Clemens brought a 95-mph fastball and a devilish curve out of the bullpen in front of a packed house at Fenway Park on April 29 in a game against the Seattle Mariners. He struck out the side in the first and fourth innings and had nine Ks total. While he was fanning the side again in the fifth, Red Sox rooters went into a frenzy every time Clemens reached two strikes on a hitter. The record was 19 strikeouts in a game, held by Steve Carlton, Nolan Ryan, and Tom Seaver. Clemens only needed ten more to break the record of immortals.

When he whiffed the first two Mariners in the sixth, Clemens tied the A.L. record for consecutive strikeouts at eight. He yielded a homer in the seventh, but kayoed two more that inning and in the seventh and eighth innings. In the ninth, the Red Sox were up 3-1, and Fenway was on its feet. Spike Owen went down swinging and the record was tied. Phil Bradley watched the umpire call him out for the historic number 20.

Catcher Lance Parrish (top left) slugged 33 homers in 1984 and had 114 RBI in '83 for the Tigers. He averaged 28 home runs a season from 1982 to '86 for Detroit. Kansas City's designated hitter Jorge Orta scores while Baltimore's Rick Dempsy waits for the ball (top right). Baltimore Orioles shortstop Cal Ripken Jr. (bottom left) led the A.L. with 211 base hits, 47 doubles, and 121 runs scored in 1983. Ripken averaged 102 runs scored and 93 runs batted in from 1982 to 1988.

out receiver at Michigan State, hit 27 homers, registered 91 RBI, and stole 29 bases.

Kansas City won the A.L. West by winning only 84 games. California and Minnesota finished 3 games back with .500 records. Steve Balboni provided the Royals' power by slugging 28 homers and driving in 77 runs. Bud Black won 17 and lost 12 with a 3.12 ERA to lead the Kansas City pitching staff, with Dan Quisenberry again leading the league in saves with 44.

Two Yankees, Don Mattingly and Dave Winfield, battled for the A.L. batting title, with Mattingly winning it on the final day of the season, .343 to .340. Tony Armas of Boston led the league in homers (43) and runs batted in (123). The Orioles ace Mike Boddicker was the only 20-game winner in the league, finishing at 20-11 with a league-leading 2.79 ERA. The big story in Seattle was rookie hurler Mark Langston (17-10, 3.40 ERA), who was the strikeout king with 204 Ks.

The big story in the National League was the Chicago Cubs, who trailed the Mets by 4½ games at the end of July. The Cubs battered the young Mets in the next seven out of eight times they played and finished in first place for the first time since 1945. Leon (Bull) Durham hit 23 homers and drove in 96 runs, and 24-year-old second baseman Ryne Sandberg hit 19 triples, slugged 19 homers, drove in 84 runs, stole 32 bases, and batted .314 — a performance that earned him MVP honors. The Cubs also had the Cy Young Award winner in rangy righthander Rick Sutcliffe, who won 16 and lost one. Third baseman Ron Cey slugged 25 homers and drove in 97 RBI, while catcher Jody Davis drove in 94 runs. Lee Smith saved 33 games. The Mets boasted 1983's Rookie of the Year, Darryl Straw-

Mets rookie Dwight "Dr. K" Gooden's 11.39 strikeouts per game in 1984 rank second all time.

berry (26 home runs, 97 RBI), and Keith Hernandez (.311, 94 RBI), but everyone raved about 19-year-old pitching sensation Dwight "Dr. K" Gooden (17-9), who led the league with 276 Ks and broke Tom Seaver's club record of 13 games with ten or more strikeouts. In a 1983 trade with Cincinnati, the Mets got Seaver back but forgot to add his name to a protected list and the White Sox claimed him in the free-agent compensation pool.

The San Diego Padres won their first N.L. West title, thanks in part to the acquisitions of former Yankees Goose Gossage (25 saves) and Graig Nettles (20 home runs). San Diego's lineup boasted Steve Garvey (.284, 86 RBI), N.L. batting champion Tony Gwynn (.351, 213 hits, 71 RBI), and Kevin McReynolds (20 homers, 70 RBI).

Phillie Mike Schmidt and Brave Dale Murphy tied for the league lead in homers with 36. Schmidt and Met Gary Carter tied for the RBI crown with 106, and Murphy came in third with 100. Joaquin Andujar of St. Louis won 20 games (the only 20-game winner in the league) and Cardinal Bruce Sutter led the league with 45 saves. Pete Rose (with Montreal) recorded his 4,000th hit and broke the N.L. record for career doubles (726). Rose was traded back to the Reds in August to become their player/manager; he finished the season with 4,097 hits, 94 behind Ty Cobb's all-time record.

When the Cubs downed the Padres two straight in the N.L.C.S., the Windy City shook with anticipation of the team's first pennant in 39 years. Back home the Padres

WADE BOGGS

One look at Wade Boggs' yearly batting averages and you'd think he played early in the century, when baseball stars routinely produced marks of over .350. From season to season, Boggs is the modern-day Ty Cobb.

After just seven years in the majors, Boggs held a modern-era record of six consecutive 200-or-more-hit seasons; in 1988, he won his fifth American League batting title. His .356 career average is tied for the third highest in history, behind only Cobb (.366), Rogers Hornsby (.358), and Joe Jackson (.356).

Boggs' consistently high averages and on-base percentages (.447 lifetime) were achieved thanks to a fantastic batting eye and a unique ability to wait on pitches and drive them to all fields. He is such a good contact hitter that in 1987, for instance, he batted .390 in at-bats where he was behind 0-2 in the count.

Boggs' detractors, however, have criticized his lack of run production (lifetime only 61 homers and 469 RBI), especially in a good power park like Boston's Fenway, and the fact that the Red Sox have won only one pennant in the third baseman's Beantown career. He also had a palimony suit that tarnished his reputation. But Boggs has scored at least 100 runs in every full season he has played (since 1983). He played 104 games in 1982 and hit .349. In 1983, he hit .361; in '84, he hit .325; in '85, he hit .368; in '86, he hit .357, in '87, he hit .363; in '88, he hit .366. Boggs is the only active player with an on-base average over .400.

Padres outfielder Tony Gwynn (top left) scored 88 runs and stole 33 bases in 1984. Oriole Eddie Murray (top right) averaged 28 homers, and 88 runs scored from 1980 to '88. Ryne Sandberg (bottom left) led the N.L. with 114 runs scored in 1984. He batted .368 in the '84 N.L.C.S. Tim Raines of the Expos (middle right) led the N.L. with 38 doubles and 75 stolen bases in 1984. Padre Steve Garvey (bottom right) had 27 doubles in '84.

won three in a row to take the pennant, ending many debates about the possibility of putting lights in Wrigley Field for the World Series. Garvey batted .400 with seven RBI, and former Cub Craig Lefferts won the last two games in relief. The Tigers swept the Royals in the A.L.C.S., with five Tigers pitchers compiling a 1.24 ERA and allowing the Royals to bat only .170.

The pundits said the World Series would be a mismatch and they were right. Padres outfielder Kevin McReynolds broke his wrist in the N.L.C.S., and San Diego's pitching, which wasn't that strong to begin with, was no match for Detroit's dangerous lineup.

The Tigers won the opener 3-2 behind the pitching of Jack Morris. San Diego won Game Two 5-3 on a three-run homer by utility player Kurt Bevacqua and some flawless

San Diego relief pitching. The Padres dropped the next three by the scores of 5-2, 4-2, and 8-4. Trammell slugged a pair of two-run homers in Game Four, and Gibson slammed a two-run homer and a three-run dinger to win the Series. San Diego actually outhit the Tigers 44 to 40, but the Tigers scored 23 runs to 14. Sparky Anderson received his third world championship ring, becoming the first manager to win the World Series in both leagues.

1985

Another player strike threatened the 1985 season. The players insisted that the owners were raking in the profits and that they were entitled to a greater share. Most of the owners insisted that their teams were on the verge of bankruptcy. On August 6, the deadline imposed by the Players' Association, the players walked off the job. They returned a couple of days later and all missed games were made up.

The strike was quickly forgotten, but the drug controversy was not. Curtis Strong, a former caterer in the Philadelphia Phillies clubhouse, was convicted of selling cocaine to various players in what became known as the "Pittsburgh drug trials." Stars such as Keith

Cub Ron Cey had 25 homers and 94 RBI in 1984.

Hernandez, who called cocaine "the demon," and Dave Parker testified and admitted to drug use. Commissioner Peter Ueberroth tried unsuccessfully to gain the approval of the Players' Association for mandatory urine tests in an attempt to curb any ongoing drug use by players. Ueberroth did win instant approval when he reinstated Mickey Mantle and Willie Mays. The legendary duo had been banned from major league baseball by former commissioner Bowie Kuhn because both had taken jobs as public relations "greeters" for gambling casinos in Atlantic City.

Despite its soiled reputation, baseball enjoyed new attendance records, and several elder statesmen provided the show. At center

1986 AMERICAN LEAGUE CHAMPIONSHIP SERIES — GAME FIVE

After Game Five of the 1986 A.L.C.S., Boston manager John McNamara called it the most exciting, most competitive game he had ever seen. Gene Mauch was the best manager never to win a pennant, but he came very close on October 12, 1986, when his Angels took a 5-2 lead into the ninth inning of an A.L.C.S. that they were winning three games to one.

With champagne being moved into the home clubhouse in Aneheim, Red Sox Bill Buckner singled. After Angels ace Mike Witt got the first out, Don Baylor homered, cutting the deficit to one. When Dwight Evans made the second out, Mauch replaced

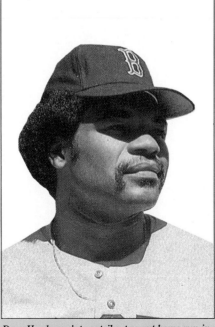

Dave Henderson's two-strike, two-out home run in Game Five of the 1986 A.L.C.S. saved Boston from elimination.

Witt with the lefthanded Gary Lucas to face lefty Rich Gedman. Lucas promptly hit Gedman with a pitch, bringing up Dave Henderson.

Henderson let a sixth-inning Bobby Grich fly pop out of his glove for a two-run homer to give California a 3-2 lead. Now Henderson would try to redeem himself against right reliever Donnie Moore. Moore hung a pitch and Henderson drove it over the left field fence, putting the Red Sox up 6-5. The Angels tied it in the ninth but blew a one-out, bases-loaded situation to send the game into extra frames. In the Red Sox's 11th, a hit batsman and two singles loaded the bases before Red Sox hero Henderson's sacrifice fly made them ship the champagne to Fenway Park.

The Sox then destroyed California in the next two games 10-4 and 8-1 to take the pennant.

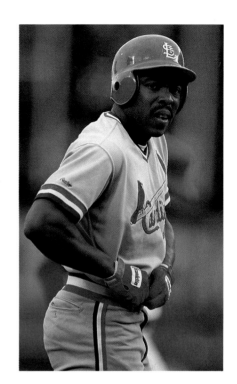

St. Louis' Willie McGee (top left) slugged a career-high .503 in 1984. Don Mattingly (top middle) had 211 base hits and 107 runs scored in 1985. Cardinal Vince Coleman (top right) averaged 102 stolen bases a season from 1985 to '88. Detroit outfielder Kirk Gibson (bottom left) hit .417 in the '84 A.L.C.S., and hit .333 with two homers and seven RBI in the '84 World Series. Gibson averaged 25 home runs, 81 runs batted in, and 85 runs scored a season from 1983 to '87 for the Tigers. Rickey Henderson (bottom right) averaged 14 home runs, 112 runs scored, and 85 stolen bases a season from 1980 to '88.

THE 1980s

stage was the 44-year-old hitting machine, Pete Rose, who set a new career record for hits, surpassing Ty Cobb on September 11 with hit number 4,192. Nolan Ryan (age 38) of the Houston Astros increased his lead as the all-time strikeout leader, finishing the season with 4,083. Darrell Evens (age 38) of Detroit slugged 40 homers. California Angels first baseman Rod Carew (age 39) reached the 3,000-hit plateau, and both 40-year-old Tom Seaver of the Chicago White Sox and 46-year-old Phil Niekro of the New York Yankees won their 300th game.

The Los Angeles Dodgers had the easiest time of any division winner, holding first in the N.L. West from mid-July to the end. After switching from third base to left field, Pedro Guerrero got hot, hitting .320, with 33 home runs and 87 runs batted in. Right fielder Mike Marshall hit 28 homers and drove in 95 runs. The Dodgers pitching duo of Orel Hershiser (19-3) and Fernando Valenzuela (17-10) helped Los Angeles finish 5½ games ahead of Cincinnati in the N.L. West. Parker was the Reds' big gun, hitting .312, with 34 home runs and a league-leading 125 RBI. Tom Browning was 20-9 with a 3.55 ERA.

The Cardinals and the Mets battled it out all summer in the N.L. East. With the exception of first baseman Jack Clark (22 home runs), the Cards relied on speed, pitching, and defense to better the Mets by 3 games. The league's MVP, Willie McGee, did it all, leading the N.L. in hits (216), triples (18), and hitting (.353). He also stole 56 bases, had 308 total bases, scored 118 times, drove in 82 runs, and played a nearly flawless center field. The "Wizard of Oz," Ozzie Smith, patrolled the infield like few shortstops in the history of the game. Tommy Herr hit .302 and

drove in 110 runs, and Rookie of the Year Vince Coleman led the majors with 110 stolen bases. Joaquin Andujar and John Tudor each won 21 games. After a 1-7 start, Tudor won 20 of his last 21 decisions and had an ERA of 1.93.

Cy Young Award-winner Dwight Gooden (24-4), the 20-year-old Mets phenom from Tampa, FL, became the youngest pitcher ever to win 20 games in a season. He also led the league in strikeouts (268), innings (277), ERA (1.53), and complete games (16). Atlanta's Dale Murphy led the league in homers (37), runs scored (118), and bases on balls (90).

The Toronto Blue Jays edged the Yankees by 2 games in the A.L. East. The outfield combination of right fielder Jesse Barfield (.289, 27 homers, 84 RBI), center fielder Lloyd Moseby (.259, 18 homers, 71 RBI), and left fielder George Bell (.275, 28 homers, 95 RBI) powered Toronto. Pitcher Dave Stieb led the league in earned run average with a 2.48 mark while going 14-13. New York first baseman Don Mattingly (.324, 35 home runs, 48 doubles, 370 total bases, a league-high 145 RBI) won the MVP and proved why many think he's the finest player in the game. Yankee Ron Guidry led the league with 22 wins against only six losses for a .786 winning percentage.

A similar race shaped up between the Kansas City Royals and California Angels in the A.L. West when the Royals won three out of four games against the Angels at the end of September, finishing 1 game up. Kansas City's George Brett returned to peak

Mark Langston fired 245 Ks in 1986.

DWIGHT GOODEN

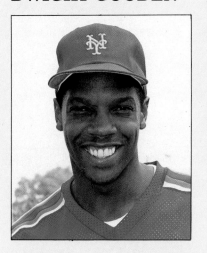

When this 19-year-old pitching phenomenon was brought to the majors by the New York Mets in 1984, he had pitched no higher than Class A ball. With a fastball clocked in the high 90s and a big breaking curve ball dubbed "Lord Charles" (average curves are merely "Uncle Charlie"), Gooden promptly produced one of the best seasons ever by a pitcher his age, going 17-9 with a 2.60 earned run average, setting the all-time rookie record for strikeouts and being named the National League's Rookie of the Year.

Gooden followed that in '85 with one of the best single-season pitching performances ever, getting a 24-4 record, a 1.53 ERA, 268 strikeouts, and the N.L. Cy Young Award. He became known throughout the country as "The Doctor."

In 1986, Gooden was 17-6, but after two poor performances in the '86 World Series, rumors began spreading about possible drug use. Then, after a highly publicized off-season scuffle with the police in his hometown, Tampa, FL, Gooden admitted to cocaine use. He entered a rehabilitation clinic and missed the first month of the '87 season. Though Gooden's absence might have cost the Mets a pennant that year, he returned, fully recovered, to produce a 15-7 record.

In '88, he helped New York win the N.L. East pennant, compiling an 18-9 mark. After his first five major league seasons, the young righty's record stood at an incredible 91-35, one of the highest winning percentages in baseball history.

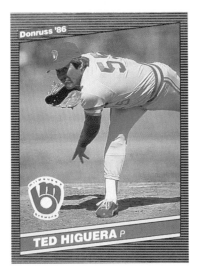

Bret Saberhagen (top left) of the Royals had a 69-55 record from 1984 to '88, with a 3.49 ERA and only 215 bases on balls in 1,066^2/$_3$ innings. Atlanta's relief ace Bruce Sutter (top right) missed the 1987 season due to elbow surgery, but he came back strongly in '88. He led the Braves in saves (14) and reached the 300-save mark before the season ended. Sutter holds the N.L. single-season record for saves with 45, and he trails only Rollie Fingers and Goose Gossage in career saves. Padres outfielders (middle left), left to right, Carmelo Martinez, Tony Gwynn, and Kevin McReynolds provided the offense for the pennant-winning Padres in 1984. Yankees lefthander Ron Guidry (middle right) was 22-6 in 1985, with a 3.27 ERA. Ted Higuera (bottom left) was 15-8 with a 3.90 ERA as a rookie for Milwaukee in 1985. Higuera had a 69-38 record for the Brewers from 1985 to '88, and he averaged 192 strikeouts and only 71 bases on balls per season.

THE 1980s

A.L. in batting with a .368 average, and he collected a league-high 240 hits. Darrell Evans' 40 homers led the league for Detroit. Yankee Ricky Henderson led the league in stolen bases (80) and runs scored (146).

For the first time, the League Championship Series were best-of-seven contests. In the A.L.C.S., the Blue Jays jumped out to a 3-1 series lead but dropped the final

Wade Boggs had a .455 on-base average in '86.

form, hitting .335 with 30 home runs and 112 runs batted in. Control pitcher Bret Saberhagen went 20-6, had a 2.87 ERA, walked the fewest batters per nine innings (1.45), and was the Cy Young Award winner. Dan Quisenberry of the Royals led the league with 37 saves. The Angels had four players with 20 or more homers (Doug DeCinces, Brian Downing, Reggie Jackson, and Ruppert Jones).

Wade Boggs of Boston led the

three games to the Royals. Brett had a .348 average, three homers, six runs scored, and five RBI in the series. Similarly, the Cards fell two behind the Dodgers before storming back with four consecutive wins. Herr continued to drive in runs, notching six RBI. The Cards, however, lost speed demon Vince Coleman, who injured his ankle when an automatic tarp rolled over his leg.

The World Series was an all-Missouri affair and was dubbed the "I-70 Series" for the interstate highway connecting the cities. St. Louis edged Kansas City in Game One 3-1 and scored four runs in the ninth inning to rebound the next day 4-2. With a two-game-to-none lead, the Cards' confidence soared. However, Saberhagen tossed a masterful six-hitter in Game Three, a 6-1 Royal victory. Game Four was all Tudor. He threw a five-hit shutout for a 3-0 win. The champagne in the Cardinal clubhouse remained unopened after games Five and Six, as Kansas City won by the scores of 6-1 and 2-1.

Tudor faced Saberhagen in the finale. The Royals chased Tudor in the third inning and Saberhagen went all the way, allowing just five hits. The final score was K.C. 11, St. Louis 0. Saberhagen won two games, posted an ERA of 0.50, struck out ten, walked only one, and was named Series MVP.

1986 NATIONAL LEAGUE CHAMPIONSHIP SERIES — GAME SIX

Three days after the Red Sox and Angels played their thrilling A.L.C.S. Game Five, another contest grabbed the fans' attention — the sixth of the 1986 N.L.C.S. between the Mets and the Astros.

The Mets were trailing 3-0 in the ninth inning and were terrified at the prospect of facing Astros ace Mike Scott in Game Seven. Scott had pitched complete game victories in games One and Four, and had held the Mets to just one run with his devilish split-finger fastball. The Mets would not go down easily. A triple, single, double, and sacrifice fly sent the game into extra innings.

Mets reliever Roger McDowell shut out the Astros for five innings, and two Astros matched him zero for zero. In the 14th, Wally Backman singled in Gary Carter with the go-ahead run. In the bottom half, Mets reliever Jesse Orosco got one out before Billy Hatcher hit a long fly ball that nicked the foul pole to tie the game.

In what had become the longest postseason game in base-

ball history, the Mets appeared to have won the pennant when they scored three runs in the top of the 16th inning. Now it was the Astros who wouldn't die. A walk and three singles off Orosco made it 7-6 with two out and two on. With the lefty Orosco running out of gas, first baseman Keith Hernandez urged him not to throw Kevin Bass any fastballs. Bass saw nothing but sliders and finally struck out to end the amazing game.

JESSE OROSCO P

Jesse Orosco got the final out.

1986

The New York Mets became the team the rest of the N.L. loved to hate. They led the league in hitting, pitching, high fives, curtain calls, bear hugs, cap-tipping, and just about every other statistical category baseball had to offer. "People were gunning for us," said Mets second baseman Wally Backman, "They didn't like the way we acted during celebrations on the field. Some of them wanted to fight us because they knew they couldn't beat us playing baseball."

At the All-Star break, the Mets (59-14) were on top by 13 games, the largest midseason N.L. edge since the start of division play in 1969. Not since the '27 Yankees had any world champion had four pitchers with 15 or more wins each and winning percentages of at least .667. The four Mets starters combined for a record of 66-23.

Dwight Gooden, left, and Darryl Strawberry led the New York Mets to the world championship in 1986. Gooden was 17-6 with a 2.84 ERA, while Strawberry had 27 homers, a .507 slugging average, and 93 RBI.

THE 1980s

Righthanders Dwight Gooden (17-6) and Ron Darling (15-6) joined forces with lefties Bob Ojeda (18-5) and Sid Fernandez (16-6). Gooden, New York's $1.3 million ace, became the only major leaguer to fan 200 batters in each of his first three seasons. Bullpen standouts Roger McDowell, a sinkerball specialist, and lefty Jesse Orosco combined for 43 saves and 22 wins. Former Montreal catcher Gary Carter (24 homers, 105 RBI), nine-time Golden Glove first baseman Keith Hernandez (.310), and Darryl Strawberry (27 home runs, 93 RBI) were the stars of the show, while Len Dykstra (.295, 31 stolen bases), Wally Backman (.320), and veteran Ray Knight (.298, 76 runs batted in) proved to be an excellent supporting cast. On September 17, the Mets clinched the N.L. East title with a 4-2 win over Chicago, which marked the earliest finish ever of a divisional race. New York (108-54) led second-place Philadelphia by 21½ games, the biggest winning margin in major league baseball since the pre-1920 period.

The Dodgers slumped to fifth in the N.L. West despite Fernando Valenzuela's first 20-win season. Steve Sax hit a career-high .332, but without Pedro Guerrero (who had a knee injury) Los Angeles was not the same team. The first-place Astros relied on sound pitching from Cy Young Award-winner Mike Scott (18-10), Nolan Ryan (12-8), and Jim Deshaies (12-5). Scott led the N.L. in strikeouts (306), innings pitched (275), ERA (2.22), and shutouts (five), baffling hitters with his split-fingered fastball. Glenn Davis powered the Astros with 31 homers and 101 RBI, and Kevin Bass had 20 homers and 79 RBI. Cincinnati manager Pete Rose led the second-place Reds to 86 wins and also recorded 51 hits in 61 games at first base. Reds right fielder Dave

Parker hit 31 homers and drove in 116 runs.

Mike Schmidt of Philadelphia won his third MVP award by leading the N.L. in homers (37), RBI (119), and slugging average (.547). Schmidt's teammate Von Hayes tied Tony Gwynn for the league's runs-scored crown with 107, and Hayes led the league in doubles (46). St. Louis' Rookie of the Year Todd Worrell led the league in saves with 36, and Cardinal Vince Coleman stole a league-high 107 bases. Montreal's Tim Raines won the batting crown with a .334 mark.

The Boston Red Sox grabbed an early lead in the A.L. East and hung on, finishing 5½ games up on the New York Yankees. BoSox third baseman Wade Boggs, the best hitter in the 1980s, led the A.L. with an average of .357 and recorded his fourth consecutive 200-hit season. Outfielder Jim Rice hit .324 with 20 homers and 110 runs batted in; Dwight Evans, a perennial Gold Glover in right field, belted 26 homers and drove in 97 runs; and Don Baylor, the designated hitter, hit 31 homers and compiled 94 runs batted in. Roger Clemens was named winner of both the Cy Young and MVP awards. The burly righthander dominated hitters, with a 24-4 record, a 2.48 ERA, 238 strikeouts, and only 67 bases on balls. Clemens was especially over-

Dodger Steve Sax batted .332 in '86.

There have been some magical defensive shortstops during baseball's recent history (Roy McMillan, Luis Aparicio, Mark Belanger, Larry Bowa, and Dave Concepcion to name a few), but only one has been called "The Wizard" — Ozzie Smith.

Now in his 12th season, Smith has been the National League's perennial All-Star shortstop since 1981. He has been an infield acrobat, combining range, quickness, leaping ability, astute positioning, a strong arm, and soft hands to make incredibly difficult plays seem routine. In 1980, his third year with the San Diego Padres, Smith won his first of eight successive National League Gold Gloves and set a single-season record for assists by a shortstop with 621.

Traded to the St. Louis Cardinals in 1982, he solidified a Redbirds' defense that was instrumental in their world championship that season and pennants in 1985 and '87. Smith also developed into an offensive force during that period, batting .283 since '85 and being an integral part of the Cardinals speed-oriented offense. In 1987, he hit .303, scored 104 runs, drove in 75 runs, and stole 43 bases. After the '88 season, he had 403 lifetime stolen bases.

Along with the Gold Gloves, Smith holds the major league record for most seasons with 500 or more assists and the N.L. record for most years (six) leading the league in fielding average. He has the fourth highest fielding average by a shortstop in a season (.987 in 1987).

Don Mattingly of the Yankees takes his lead (top) while Angel Wally Joyner holds him on. Mattingly led the A.L. with 238 base hits and a .573 slugging average in 1986. Joyner hit .290, with 22 homers and 100 RBI in '86. Jesse Barfield (bottom left) knocked 172 home runs from 1982 to '88. Don Baylor (middle top) slugged 31 homers for Boston in 1986. Tim Raines (middle bottom) averaged 67 swipes from 1981 to '88. Dave Righetti (bottom right) saved 162 games from 1984 to 1988.

powering against Seattle on April 29, when he struck out a record 20 batters.

The California Angels, a team with an average age of 33, won the A.L. West with such veterans as Don Sutton (age 41), Reggie Jackson (40), Bob Boone (38), Bobby Grich (37), and Doug DeCinces (35) as well as with young talent like rookie first baseman Wally Joyner (.290, 100 RBI), outfielder Gary Pettis (50 stolen bases), and pitcher Mike Witt (18-10). Texas finished in second place, 5 games back. The Rangers were powered by outfielder Pete Incaviglia (30 homers, 88 runs batted in), first baseman Pete O'Brien (.290, 22 home runs, 100 RBI), and designated hitter Larry Parrish (28 homers, 94 RBI).

The Kansas City Royals, the World Series winner the previous season, slumped to third. The Royals disappointed NFL scouts when they signed Heisman Trophy running back Bo Jackson of Auburn to a $7 million multiyear deal. Yankees reliever Dave Righetti set an all-time single-season record with 46 saves. Yankees first baseman Don Mattingly continued to post Hall of Fame numbers, hitting .352 with 31 homers and 113 runs batted in. He also led the league in

hits (238), total bases (388), slugging average (.573), and doubles (53). Jesse Barfield of Toronto led the league in homers with 40. Indians outfielder Joe Carter had the most RBI (121), and Tribe pitcher Tom Candiotti had the most complete games (17). New York's Rickey Henderson led the A.L. in runs (130) and stolen bases (87). Mark Langston of the Mariners was the strikeout king (245).

The A.L.C.S. was as dramatic as any in recent memory. The Angels won three of the first four games and carried a 5-2 lead into the top of the ninth inning of Game Five. There were two outs when Boston's Don Baylor belted a two-run homer to trim the lead to 5-4. Dave Henderson, who an inning earlier caught a long drive against the left-center field wall only to see it bounce out of his glove for a home run, stepped to the plate and smacked a 2-2 pitch out of the park for a 6-5 Boston lead. California tied it up in the bottom of the ninth but lost the heartbreaker 7-6 in the 11th. Boston blasted California in games Six and Seven 10-4 and 8-1, thereby denying Gene Mauch from winning his first pennant after 25 years of managing.

The Mets and the Astros played one of the greatest championship series in N.L. history. Mike Scott fanned 14 Mets in Game One, a 1-0 win over Dwight Gooden. New York won the next two games, with Dykstra ending Game Three with a two-run homer in the bottom of the ninth. Scott pitched a three-hitter in Game Four, a 3-1 Astro win. Gary Carter won Game Five 2-1 with an RBI single in the 12th inning. Game Six, one of the epic battles in N.L.C.S. history, was a 16-inning war, won 7-6 by the Mets.

The Mets bench keeps an eye on the 1986 World Series action.

TONY GWYNN

If the National League has had a version of Wade Boggs during the 1980s, it would have to be outfielder Tony Gwynn of the San Diego Padres.

In 1988, Gwynn won his second successive N.L. batting title (hitting .313) and became only the 18th player in major league history to have won three batting crowns in a career. After more than five seasons, Gwynn has compiled a .331 lifetime batting average and has averaged more than 200 base hits per year (leading the league three times) and 95 runs scored. His .370 average in 1987 was the highest in the N.L. since 1948. It was 32 points ahead of his nearest competitor, the second time Gwynn had won a title by at least a 30-point margin, making him the 15th player to accomplish that odd feat. He had 218 hits in '87, along with 56 stolen bases, 119 runs scored, and a .511 slugging average. In the 1984 League Championship Series, Gwynn had seven hits, three doubles, six runs scored, and three RBI in five games. He also had five hits in the '84 World Series.

Gwynn has also established himself as one of the game's best all-around players. He has stolen 181 career bases (he tied the N.L. record for stolen bases in a game with five) and won two Gold Glove awards for his defensive play in right field. With 1,151 hits at age 29, Gwynn has a chance for 3,000 lifetime hits.

Joe Carter (top right) of the Cleveland Indians led the 1986 American League with 121 runs batted in. He also scored 108 runs, hit .302, slugged 29 homers, and had 200 base hits. Carter was named to the All-American baseball team in 1980 and '81, and he was named the College Player of the Year in 1981. The Mets celebrate (top left) after winning the 1986 World Series. Rookie Pete Incaviglia (bottom left) of the Texas Rangers had 30 homers and 88 RBI in 1986. Boston hurler Roger Clemens (bottom middle) in 1986 was 24-4 with a 2.48 ERA. He pitched for the University of Texas, where he was the winning pitcher in the final game of the '85 College World Series. Buddy Bell (bottom right) hit .278 with 20 homers for the Reds in 1986. Bell accumulated 2,499 base hits, 421 doubles, 201 homers, 1,146 runs, and 1,103 RBI from 1972 to '88, with a career .280 batting average.

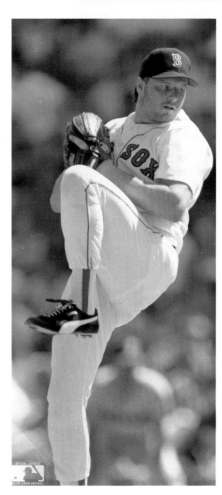

THE 1980s

The 1986 World Series left New York and New England fans drained. The Boston Red Sox stunned the Mets by winning the first two games in New York. The Mets returned the favor by winning the next two games in Boston. Red Sox southpaw Bruce Hurst outpitched Doc Gooden in Game Five, winning 4-2 to give Boston a 3-2 edge in the Series. But Game Six, a 6-5 come-from-behind victo-

ry for the Mets, will haunt Boston fans forever, as the Red Sox were leading by two runs with the Mets down to their last out (the Mets were twice down to their last strike). In the finale, the Mets came from behind to win 8-5 and lived up to the team's slogan: "Baseball like it oughta be!"

1987

"The Year of the Home Run" was the nickname for 1987. The big story of the year was the record number of home runs that soared out of ballparks. Oakland Athletics first baseman Mark McGwire set a major league rookie record with 49 home runs, which tied Andre Dawson of the Chicago Cubs for the major league title. Another first baseman, Don Mattingly of the Yankees, hit six grand slams in '87 (a single season

record), and in July, Mattingly tied Dale Long's record by homering in eight straight games. Cincinnati center fielder Eric Davis (.293, 37 home runs, 100 runs batted in, 50 stolen bases) tied a major league record with three grand slams in May. Manufacturers denied that the ball was souped up. Others claimed the bats contained cork inserts, but X rays proved that wasn't the case.

Fans turned out in record numbers, 52 million of them, shattering the old record for attendance (47.5 million, set the previous year.) It was the fifth time in six years that major league baseball set a new attendance record and the second consecutive year that all 26 teams drew at least 1 million spectators.

It was a year filled with milestones. Philadelphia's Mike Schmidt hit his 500th career homer. Bob Boone of the Angels caught his 1,919th game, breaking a major league record. Cal Ripken Jr. played in a record 8,243 consecutive innings, dating back to June 5, 1982. (He was pulled from a game in the eighth inning by his father, Baltimore skipper Cal Ripken Sr.) Cleveland's Phil Niekro, the 48-year-old knuckleballer, won against the Tigers to give himself and his brother, Joe, 530 career wins, more than any other brother tandem in history. Houston's 40-year-old righthander Nolan Ryan struck out 200 batters for a record 11th year. Ryan finished 8-16, but led the N.L. in ERA (2.76) and strikeouts (270 in 211⅔ innings). Baseball said goodbye to some of its favorite sons: Tom Seaver, Reggie Jackson, Phil Niekro, Steve Garvey, and Dick Howser. (Howser, manager of the 1985 world champion Kansas City Royals, died of cancer in July.)

In the N.L. East, the St. Louis Cardinals won 95 games to finish 3 games up on the defending world champion New York Mets. The Cards were an injury-riddled team that had just enough of whatever it took to win. Manager Whitey Herzog spoke for the team when he said, "I don't know how the hell we got here, but we're here." Jack Clark belted 35 homers and drove in 106 runs in only 131 games. Leadoff hitter Vince Coleman (.289) was caught stealing 22 times but still managed to lead the

1986 WORLD SERIES — GAME SIX

The Red Sox were leading the favored Mets three games to two in the 1986 World Series, and Boston jumped ahead twice in Game Six. But the gritty New Yorkers came back both times to send the game into extra innings.

In the top of the tenth, the Sox seemed to have clinched their first world championship in 68 agonizing years when a Dave Henderson home run, a double, and a single made it 5-3. After reliever Calvin Schiraldi retired the Mets' first two batters in the home tenth, Gary Carter singled. Then Kevin Mitchell singled. The count on Ray Knight was 0-2 when he singled Carter home and sent Mitchell to third.

This brought Mookie Wilson up to the plate and Bob Stanley

out to the mound in relief. With 55,000 fans rocking Shea Stadium, Wilson fouled off two 2-2 pitches. Stanley's next pitch was low and inside, the ball skipped past catcher Rich Gedman, and Mitchell stormed home with the tying run. With the count now 3-2, Wilson proceeded to foul off two more pitches. The next delivery was an inside sinker, and Wilson sent a slow roller down the first base line. Bill Buckner bent down to field it but came up with nothing. Somehow the ball had slithered through his legs and died just past the infield dirt. Knight danced home with the winning run that kept the Mets alive.

Two days later the Mets won the final game of the Series 8-5, and Red Sox fans replayed all winter an unforgettable tenth inning.

Mookie Wilson dribbles a slow roller down first base line in the '86 Series.

Andre Dawson of the Chicago Cubs (top left) clubbed 49 home runs and drove in 137 to earn '87 N.L. MVP honors. Dawson averaged 25 home runs, 83 runs scored, and 91 RBI from 1980 to '88. Oakland first baseman Mark McGwire (top right) broke in to the major leagues with one of the best rookie seasons ever. He smashed 49 homers, slugged .618, drove in 118 runs, scored 97 runs, batted .289, and doubled 28 times. Toronto's George Bell (bottom left) slugged 156 home runs from 1984 to '88. Dale Murphy of Atlanta (bottom right) had a career-high 44 homers in '87.

major leagues with 109 stolen bases to become the first player in history to steal 100 bases three years in a row. Willie McGee (.285, 11 homers, 105 RBI), Terry Pendleton (.286, 12 home runs, 96 runs batted in), Tommy Herr (83 RBI), and Ozzie Smith (.303, 75 RBI) also were keys to the runnin' Redbirds attack.

The Cincinnati Reds jumped out to an 18-8 start in the N.L. West and in early August led the San Francisco Giants by five games. However, San Francisco went 51-32 after the Fourth of July and finished 6 games ahead of Cincinnati. First baseman Will Clark led the offense (.308, 35 home runs, 91 RBI) and received help from outfielders Chili Davis (24 home runs, 76 RBI), Candy Maldonado (.292, 20 homers, 85 RBI), and Jeff Leonard (.280, 19 homers).

Dawson won the Most Valuable Player award by leading the league in homers (49), RBI (137), and total bases (353). Tony Gwynn of San Diego batted .370 and notched 218 hits to lead the league. Rick Sutcliffe of the Cubs won the most games with 17. Phillie Steve Bedrosian won the Cy Young Award while notching 40 saves. Tim Raines of Montreal led the league in runs scored (123), while Dodger Orel Hershiser pitched the most innings (265).

The Yankees spent more days in first place than any other team in the A.L. East, but with Willie Randolph and Rickey Henderson out of the lineup with injuries, the Yankees never recovered. The Detroit Tigers claimed first, 2 games ahead of the Toronto Blue Jays. Tigers shortstop Alan Trammell, batting cleanup for the first time in his career, collected 50 hits in the month of September and finished third in the A.L. in batting (.343), including 28 homers and 105 RBI. First baseman Darrell

Twins lefty Frank Viola was 24-7 in 1988.

Evans became the only 40-year-old to hit 30 homers in a season. Catcher Matt Nokes (32 home runs, 87 RBI), left fielder Kirk Gibson (24 homers, 79 RBI), and center fielder Chet Lemon (20 homers, 75 RBI) also contributed to the offense. Pitcher Doyle Alexander, who came over in August from Atlanta, finished the season with a 9-0 record for the Tigers with a 1.53 ERA.

The Minnesota Twins were baseball's biggest surprise. They won it all with the lowest number of wins (85) of any World Series winner in history; they won it with the highest ERA (4.63) of any first-place team in history; they won it despite winning nine road games after the All-Star break and despite being the only team to win a World Series without a win on the road. Outfielder Kirby Puckett (.332, 28 homers, 99 RBI) emerged as one of baseball's new superstars. First baseman Kent Hrbek (90 RBI), third baseman Gary Gaetti (109 RBI), and outfielder Tom Brunansky (85 RBI) each had more than 30 home runs. Southpaw Frank Viola (17-10) carried the pitching staff.

Blue Jays outfielder George Bell had a brilliant season, hitting .308 with 47 home runs, 134 runs batted in, 369 total bases, a .605 slugging average, and 111 runs scored to win MVP honors. Milwaukee Brewers DH Paul Molitor hit safely in 39 straight games, led the league in doubles with 41 and runs scored with 114, and finished with a .353 average. Wade Boggs of Boston won the batting title at .363. Red Sox pitcher Roger Clemens won his second straight Cy Young Award, going 20-9 with a 2.97 ERA, 256 strikeouts, 282 innings pitched, 18 complete games, and seven

KIRK GIBSON

The World Series can turn any player into an instant hero. The 1988 World Series turned Kirk Gibson into a legend—and he had only one at-bat.

Before 1988, Gibson was signed by Los Angeles after playing nine years for Detroit, where he hit 150 home runs and captured a World Series ring in 1984. The Dodgers had finished fifth in the National League West in 1987, and the club's management felt that Gibson would supply the intensity and lefthanded hitting power they needed to contend.

Gibson did that and more. He produced a 25-homer, 76-RBI season, winning the N.L. Most Valuable Player award and leading the Dodgers to the Western Division pennant. Then, despite nagging injuries to both his legs, he won Game Four of the Championship Series with a 12th-inning homer. Gibson's legs were in such bad shape it was announced that he would probably sit out the World Series against the powerful Athletics.

In the bottom of the ninth inning of Game One, the Dodgers were trailing 4-3 with two out and one on base. Gibson, his legs aching so badly he would barely be able to stride into a pitch, was sent to the plate to face ace Athletics reliever Dennis Eckersley. Gibson reached out, connected, and sent the ball over the right field fence for an improbable game-winning homer. Though he never appeared again in the Series, Gibson's inspirational blast catapulted the Dodgers to a five-game upset Series victory.

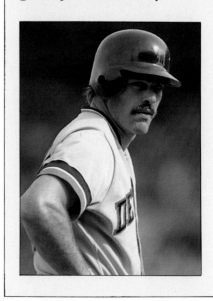

Three Minnesota Twins (top) who feel at home in the homer dome, left to right, Tom Brunansky, Kirby Puckett, and Kent Hrbek. Brunansky had at least 20 home runs a season from 1982 to '88. Puckett hit .332 in '87, with 28 homers, 96 runs scored, 99 RBI, a league-leading 207 base hits, and a .534 slugging average. Hrbek averaged 25 round-trippers from 1982 to '88. Jack Clark (bottom left) led the National League with an 8.4 home run percentage, 136 bases on balls, and a .597 slugging percentage in 1987 for St. Louis. He also slugged 35 homers, drove in 106 runs, and scored 93 runs that season. In 1988, Clark smashed 27 homers and tallied 93 RBI for the Yankees. Cardinal Ozzie Smith (bottom right) hit .303 in 1987, with 104 runs scored and 75 RBI. Smith stole 403 bases from 1978 to '88. "The Wizard of Oz" also set a major league record for most assists by a shortstop in a season, with 621 in 1980.

THE 1980s

shutouts. Tom Henke of Toronto was the save leader (34), while teammate Jimmy Key won the ERA crown (2.76). Seattle's Mark Langston was the strikeout king with 262.

Brunansky was the star for the Twins in a four-games-to-one A.L.C.S. win over the Tigers. He had two homers, four doubles, four bases on balls, five runs scored, nine RBI, a .412 batting average, and a 1.000 slugging average. In an evenly matched National League Championship Series, St. Louis won in seven games despite the loss of an injured Jack Clark. Jeffery Leonard slugged four homers for the Giants, but they resulted in only five RBI.

In the World Series, the Twins took advantage of the Cardinals inside the Metrodome, where the noise level rated on a par with that of a jet engine. Minnesota exploded for a seven-run fourth inning to win Game One 10-1 and turned a six-run fourth inning in Game Two into an 8-4 victory. The Cardinals won three straight back in St. Louis. In Game Five, a 4-2 Cardi-

nals win, the Redbirds became the fourth team in World Series history to steal five bases in a game. Back in the Metrodome, Minnesota shelled John Tudor in Game Six 11-5 to even the Series. Frank Viola held the Cardinals to two runs through eight innings before reliever Jeff Reardon finished the job, giving the franchise its first World Series championship since the Washington Senators won the title in 1924.

1988

Peter Ueberroth, perceived by many baseball insiders as a cold, distant commissioner, achieved a record level of financial success. Major league baseball, he insisted, had shattered attendance records in each of the last four seasons. However, on September 8, baseball's sixth commissioner announced that he was leaving office April 1, 1989. His replacement, former Yale University president and N.L. president A. Bartlett Giamatti, made news during the season when he fined Reds manager Pete Rose $10,000 and suspended him 30 days after Rose shoved umpire Dave Pallone. Giamatti and the rules committee instituted a stricter interpretation of the balk rule, which required pitchers to come to a discernible stop. Umpires called a record 924 balks during the season, up from 356 in '87. The old records, 219 in the N.L. and 137 in the A.L., were set in that same year.

A year after fans watched hitters pummel pitchers for a record

Met Darryl Strawberry upends stealing second base.

494

OREL HERSHISER BREAKS DON DRYSDALE'S RECORD

Don Drysdale's 58 consecutive scoreless innings streak set in 1968 was supposed to be one of those unbreakable records, like Joe DiMaggio's 56-game hitting streak and Lou Gehrig's 2,130 consecutive games played. However, another tough Dodgers righthander named Orel Hershiser knocked Drysdale's mark right out of the books 20 years later.

The 30-year-old Hershiser, one of the National League's best pitchers since joining the Dodgers in 1984, had already compiled a 17-8 record when the streak began at the end of August. Then Hershiser began doing surgery on N.L. hitters, pitching shutout after shutout in September. The scoreless string reached 49 on September 23, and five days later, Hershiser attempted to tie the record against the San Diego Padres.

Hershiser threw his nine shutout innings, but the score was 0-0. Hershiser wanted to leave the game so he could share the record with "Big D," but Dodgers manager Tom Lasorda persuaded Hershiser to go for it. "I would have gone out there and kicked him in the rear if he hadn't," said Drysdale, who witnessed the game. Hershiser set down the Padres one-two-three in the tenth to break one of the immortal records. Hershiser would go on to become the National League Championship Series and World Series MVP in '88 and would take the Cy Young Award with a 23-8 record and 2.26 ERA.

Orel "Bulldog" Hershiser of the Dodgers (top left) had an 83-49 record from 1984 to '88. He led the league with four shutouts in '84 and eight shutouts in '88, an .846 winning percentage in 1985, and 264²/₃ innings pitched in 1987 and 267 innings pitched in 1988. Will Clark (top right) of the San Francisco Giants led the 1988 National League with 109 RBI and 100 bases on balls. "The Natural" played in all 162 games that season, smacked 29 home runs, scored 102 runs, hit 31 doubles, and had a .282 batting average. Clark had 35 homers in 1987 with 91 runs batted in. Mets outfielder Kevin McReynolds (bottom left) in '88 batted .288 with 27 homers and 99 RBI.

number of home runs (4,458), pitchers fought back. The major league composite ERA dropped from 4.28 to 3.72. Tony Gwynn of the San Diego Padres led the N.L. in batting with an average of just .313, his third N.L. batting title in five years. Cincinnati Reds pitcher Tom Browning tossed the 14th perfect game in baseball history. Minnesota's Jeff Reardon saved 42 games, making him the first pitcher to save 40 games in each league. Oakland's Dennis Eckersley saved 45 games, one short of the major league record.

The pitching story of the year was Orel Hershiser of the Dodgers. Affectionately known as the Bulldog, Hershiser pitched 59 scoreless innings down the stretch (including six shutouts in a row) to break Don Drysdale's all-time record and to lead Los Angeles to the crown in the N.L. West.

Despite injuries to key players like first baseman Keith Hernandez and pitcher Bob Ojeda, the Mets (100-60) returned to their dominating form of '86, 15 games better than the Pittsburgh Pirates in the N.L. East. Home run leader Darryl Strawberry (39 home runs, 101 RBI) began living up to his awesome potential. Kevin McReynolds (.288, 27 homers, 99 RBI) was nearly as impressive. Rookie sensation Gregg Jefferies joined the team in September to hit .321, and surprising righthander Dave Cone (20-3) posted more wins than Dwight Gooden (18), Ron Darling (17), and Sid Fernandez (12).

The N.L. West became the first N.L. division in history to have five teams with winning records. Los Angeles finished 7 games ahead of Cincinnati. Outfielder Kirk Gibson (who became a "new look" free agent, being granted his freedom from Detroit after the "Collusion I" decision in the

previous year) was signed by the Dodgers and inspired his teammates with his fiery temperament and reckless style of play. He became only the third MVP in N.L. history who didn't bat .300 (.290), hit 30 home runs (25), or drive in 100 runs (76). Mike Marshall (.277, 20 homers, 82 RBI) and Steve Sax (.277, 42 stolen bases, 70 runs scored) led the offense. Cy Young Award-winner Hershiser (23-8, 2.26 ERA, 15 complete games, eight shutouts, 267 innings pitched) had a fine supporting cast in rookie Tim Belcher (12-6) and Tim Leary (17-11). Many felt that manager Tommy Lasorda did his greatest job ever, motivating his players with bear hugs, speeches, and pasta.

Nolan Ryan of the Astros led the N.L. in strikeouts (228), the eighth time in his career that he led his league in Ks. Relief ace John Franco of Cincinnati led the league with 39 saves, and Reds starter Danny Jackson tied Hershiser for the N.L. lead in wins (23) and complete games (15). Giants first baseman Will Clark led the league in RBI with 109, while Giant Brett Butler topped the league with 109 runs scored. Andres Galarraga of the Montreal Expos became the first player ever to lead the league in hits (184) and strikeouts (153).

The Red Sox were floundering in the A.L. East until long-time coach Joe Morgan replaced John McNamara as manager in the middle of July. Boston won 19 of its first 20 under Morgan, stumbled in September (they lost six of their

Atlanta's Bruce Sutter had 14 saves in '88.

JOSE CANSECO

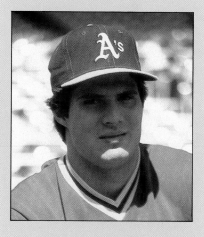

Even though he's played just three full seasons in the majors, Jose Canseco's performance has been so spectacular, he clearly deserves recognition as one of the outstanding players of the decade.

The 6'3", 210-pound Canseco wasn't selected in the 1982 draft until the 15th round by the Oakland Athletics. He moved rapidly up the A's farm system, displaying more power the higher he went. In 1985, he played in Double-A and then Triple-A, hitting a combined 36 homers and 127 RBI, and being named Minor League Player of the Year.

He continued his awesome power display with the A's in '86, winning the Rookie of the Year Award by hitting 33 homers and driving in 117 runs. Canseco also became a batting practice legend. "He'll hit the ball, and you'll say there's no way anybody can hit anything that far," said one opposing player. "Then he'll hit one farther. He really puts on a show."

In '87, Canseco defied the sophomore jinx, knocking 31 homers and 113 runs across the plate. The best was yet to come. In '88, he led Oakland to its first A.L. pennant since 1974, hitting a career-high .307 with a major league-leading 42 home runs and 124 RBI. He also scored 120 runs and stole 40 bases, becoming the first player in history to hit 40 homers and steal 40 bases in the same season. Not surprisingly, he was a unanimous choice as the league's Most Valuable Player.

It also won't be too surprising if Jose Canseco, now only 25, becomes the best player of the 1990s.

Mike Greenwell, left, and Ellis Burks (top left) of the Boston Red Sox knocked the cover off the ball in 1988. Greenwell hit .325 that season, with 22 homers, 119 RBI, 86 runs scored, 39 doubles, and a .531 slugging average. Burks hit .296 in '88, with 18 home runs, 37 doubles, 92 runs batted in, 93 runs scored, and 25 stolen bases. Frank Viola (top right) of Minnesota had a 104-81 record from 1982 to '88, with a 3.87 ERA and 1,976 strikeouts and 474 bases on balls in 1,597 innings pitched. Los Angeles Dodgers outfielder Kirk Gibson (bottom left) led the Dodgers to a world championship in 1988 with his toughness. Gibson's numbers — 25 homers, .290 average, 106 runs scored, 76 RBI, and 31 stolen bases — were not as impressive as his leadership skills. Eric Davis (bottom right) of the Reds averaged 30 home runs, 99 runs scored, 88 runs batted in, and 55 steals a season from 1986 to '88.

THE 1980s

last seven games) and won by 1 game over Detroit. Boston had an incredible .283 team batting average and scored 813 runs. Even with a $6 million palimony suit hanging over his head, Red Sox third baseman Wade Boggs (.366) led the league in hitting for the fourth straight year and 200 hits for a record sixth consecutive season. He also led the league in runs scored (128), doubles (45), and bases on balls (125, for an incredible .476 on-base average). Youngsters Mike Greenwell (.325, 22 home runs, 119 RBI) and Ellis Burks (.292, 93 runs scored, 92 RBI) joined old-timers Dwight Evans (.293, 21 home runs, 111 RBI) and Jim Rice (72 runs batted in) to provide the thump. Right-hander Roger Clemens won 18 games and led the league with 291 strikeouts.

The Oakland Athletics (104-58) claimed first place in April and stayed there for the rest of the season. MVP Jose Canseco (.307, 42 home runs, 124 runs batted in), the first player ever to hit 40 homers and steal 40 bases in the same season, also knocked in 100 runs for the third consecutive year. First baseman Mark McGwire, the Rookie of the Year in '87, hit 32 homers with 99 runs batted in. Outfielder Dave Henderson (.304,

Kirby Puckett led the '88 A.L. with 234 hits.

24 home runs, 94 RBI) had his finest season ever.

Minnesota's Kirby Puckett led the A.L. in hits (234) and total bases (358), while hitting 24 homers, driving in 121 runs, notching a .356 average, scoring 109 runs, collecting 24 doubles, and winning his third consecutive Gold Glove. Frank Viola won the Cy Young Award with a league-leading 24-win season. Rickey Henderson of the Yankees led the league in stolen bases with 93.

Belcher won two games in the N.L.C.S., and Sax scored seven runs, as the Dodgers surprised everybody by beating the favored Mets four games to three. There was no surprise in the American League, however, when Oakland swept the Red Sox 4-0.

It was an all-California World Series, matching Oakland against Los Angeles. Game One ranks as one of the all-time classics in World Series history. Trailing 4-3 with one on and two outs in the bottom of the ninth, pinch hitter Kirk Gibson hobbled to the plate. Gibson worked the count to 3-2 and, with a swing straight from Hollywood, unloaded the game-winning homer. Hershiser blanked Oakland in Game Two, allowing just three hits in a 6-0 win. McGwire's home run was the difference in Game Three, a 2-1 Oakland win. The A's managed just nine hits in Game Four (four by Dave Henderson) and lost 4-3. Hershiser proved he was human in Game Five, allowing two runs, but Los Angeles scored five, making Hershiser the first pitcher and the third player overall in 20 years of divisional play to earn MVP honors in both the playoff and World Series.

1989

After losing the two "collusion" cases. baseball owners became more liberal with checkbooks again, paying large multi-year contracts to even some mediocre players. One player who deserved the big money was the Minnesota Twins star outfielder Kirby Puckett. In January, Puckett signed a one-year $2 million contract. Orel Hershiser, Cal Ripken Jr., Dwight Gooden, Roger Clemens, Andy Van Slyke, and Tim Raines were among others who signed for multimillion dollar deals in 1989.

LEE WEYER, UMPIRE

Until he suddenly died of a heart attack during the 1988 season at age 52, Lee Weyer was one of the outstanding umpires for nearly three decades. He was also one of the most popular.

In 1961, the 6'5" Weyer became the youngest umpire (age 24) ever to call a game, and in the ensuing 27 years, he was an on-the-field witness to some of the most remarkable and historic moments in baseball history. He was umpiring third base when Hank Aaron clouted home run number 715 in Atlanta, breaking Babe Ruth's record. He was behind the plate, as he had predicted he would be three years earlier, when in 1985 Pete Rose broke Ty Cobb's all-time hit record. Weyer worked five no-hitters (not all of them behind the plate), four All-Star games, 22 Championship Series games (including the unforgettable 1986 N.L. playoff between Houston and New York), and 23 World Series games.

What made the gentle giant special was the respect he received from players and managers for his patience, his consistent judgments from behind the plate, and his willingness to admit mistakes. Weyer, who loved to play practical jokes and perform magic for friends, also enjoyed training aspiring arbiters at colleague Harry Wendelstedt's Umpire School in Florida. After his untimely death, Weyer's familiar white chest protector and other umpire paraphernalia were sent to the Hall of Fame.

After being overshadowed by A's teammate Mark McGwire and his rookie home run efforts in 1987, Jose Canseco took the baseball world by storm in '88, becoming the only player in history to hit 40 home runs and steal 40 bases in a season.

INDEX

Aaron, "Hammerin'" Henry "Hank," 142, 198, 228, 322, 324, 326, 328, 332, 334, 336, 340, 396, 400, 402, 408, 410, 422, 426, 430, 434, 470, 498
Abbott, Jim, 454
Adams, Babe, 104, 106, 156
Adcock, Joe, 324, 328
Agee, Tommie, 388, 390
Aikens, Willie Mays, 452
Alexander, Doyle, 434, 460, 492
Alexander, Grover Cleveland "Pete," 110, 120, 126, 130, 132, 144, 148, 156, 170, 176, 180, 182, 202, 304, 314
Allen, Dick "Richie" 368, 400, 402, 418
Allen, Johnny, 208, 226
Allen, Mel, 336
Allison, Bob, 374
Allison, Doug, 20
All-Star Game, 84, 184, 194, 198, 204, 212, 214, 222, 232, 254, 266, 286, 288, 294, 304, 322, 360, 368, 384, 402, 404, 430, 458, 466, 470, 498
Alou, Felipe, 360, 364
Alou, Matty, 412
Alston, Walter, 316, 350, 360, 368, 434
Altobelli, Joe, 474
Altrock, Nick, 96, 100
Amalfitano, Joe, 316
American Association, 30, 32, 34, 42, 46, 48, 50, 52, 56, 58, 60, 62, 64, 66, 78, 134
American Association war, 46, 48, 52
American Baseball Guild, 268
American League (A.L.), 38, 46, 54, 62, 74, 78, 80, 84, 86, 88, 90, 92, 94, 96, 98, 100, 102, 104, 110, 112, 116, 118, 120, 122, 124, 126, 128, 130, 132, 134, 136, 138, 146, 148, 150, 152, 154, 156, 158, 160, 162, 164, 168, 170, 172, 174, 176, 178, 180, 184, 190, 192, 194, 196, 198, 202, 206, 212, 216, 220, 222, 224, 226, 228, 230, 232, 240, 242, 244, 246, 248, 250,254, 256, 258, 260, 262, 266, 274, 276, 278, 280, 286, 288, 290, 292, 294, 296, 300, 302, 304, 306, 310, 312, 314, 316, 324, 326, 328, 330, 332, 334, 340, 344, 348, 350, 352, 384, 386, 394, 396, 398, 406, 410, 412, 414, 418, 420, 422, 426, 428, 430, 432, 434, 436, 440, 442, 444, 448, 454, 456, 458, 460, 462, 464, 468, 470, 474, 478, 482, 484, 486, 488, 492, 494, 496, 498
American League Championship Series (A.L.C.S.), 420, 424, 432, 434, 448, 464, 468, 472, 480, 484, 488, 494
Ames, Red, 96, 116, 118
Amoros, Sandy, 310, 318, 322
Anderson, Sparky, 398, 430, 432, 474, 476, 480
Andrews, Mike, 380, 424, 428
Andujar, Joaquin, 472, 478, 482
Angell, Roger, 442
Anson, Adrian "Cap," "Baby," "Pop," 32, 38, 40, 42, 46, 48, 56, 60, 62, 72
Aparicio, Luis, 324, 334, 358, 486
Appling, Luke "Fumblefoot," "Old Aches and Pains," 222, 230, 262
Arbitration, 346, 404, 406
Armas, Tony, 464, 466, 474, 478
Arroyo, Luis, 356
Ashburn, Richie, 294, 298, 304, 306, 310, 320, 332, 362
Astrodome (Houston), 342
Astroturf, 342, 402
Atlanta Braves, 334, 340, 342, 364, 388, 390, 408, 422, 426, 450, 458, 460, 468, 472, 474, 478, 492
Atlanta Stadium, 404
Atlantics (Brooklyn), 12, 14, 16, 18, 20, 24
Averill, Earl, 218, 232, 342
Avila, Bobby, 306, 314

Backman, Wally, 484, 486
Bagby, Jim, 154, 156
Bailey, Ed, 322
Baines, Harold, 474
Baker, Del, 250, 252
Baker, Dusty, 438, 462
Baker, Frank "Home Run," 104, 118, 120, 126, 128
Baker Bowl, 146, 210
Balboni, Steve, 478
Baldwin, "Lady," 64
Ball, Phil, 116
Ball Four, 396, 402
Baltimore Browns, 288, 316
Baltimore Orioles, 56, 60, 64, 68, 70, 72, 74, 80, 82, 84, 88, 90, 116, 324, 340, 344, 350, 352, 354, 368, 370, 372, 378, 380, 386, 388, 390, 394, 396, 410, 412, 414, 424, 426, 428, 430, 432, 444, 454, 456, 462, 464, 470, 474, 476, 478, 490
Bancroft, Dave, 174
Bancroft, Frank, 58
Bando, Sal, 406, 414, 418, 428
Bankhead, Dan, 248
Banks, Ernie "Mr. Cub," 198, 218, 320, 322, 336, 456
Bannister, Floyd, 472
Barber, Red, 240, 336
Barfield, Jesse, 482, 488
Barker, Len, 468
Barker, Ray, 374
Barnes, Jess, 138
Barnes, Ross, 16, 28, 32, 40
Barrow, Ed, 136, 138, 164, 242
Barry, Jack, 104, 118, 128, 136
Bartholomay, Bill, 426
Baseball Encyclopedia, 340
Baseball Writers' Association of America, 100, 208
Bass, Kevin, 484, 486
Bauer, Hank, 280, 300, 324, 334, 352, 380, 386
Baumholtz, Frankie, 308
Bavasi, Buzzie, 346
Baylor, Don, 444, 470, 480, 486, 488
Beadle's Dime Base Ball Player, 8
Bearden, Gene, 248, 280
Beaumont, Ginger, 88, 92
Beazley, Johnny, 258
Bedient, Hugh, 124
Bedrosian, Steve, 492
Belanger, Mark, 388, 444, 456, 486
Belcher, Tim, 496, 498
Bell, Gary, 382
Bell, George, 482, 492
Bell, Gus, 322, 362
Bell, James "Cool Papa," 194, 196, 198, 200, 218, 248
Bench, Johnny, 220, 352, 380, 396, 398, 412, 420, 434, 444, 462, 470, 476
Bender, Chief, 92, 96, 98, 100, 104, 116, 118, 120, 122, 126, 128
Bennett, Charlie, 40, 64, 66, 68
Benton, Larry, 182
Benton, Rube, 134, 136
Bergen, Marty, 74
Berger, Wally, 202, 220
Berra, Dale, 452
Berra, Yogi, 172, 220, 276, 280, 288, 292, 294, 298, 300, 308, 310, 314, 318, 320, 322, 324, 326, 334, 346, 352, 354, 356, 358, 368, 370, 372
Bevacqua, Kurt, 480
Bevens, Bill, 276, 282, 336
Bickford, Vern, 280, 298
Bilko, Steve, 342
Billingham, Jack, 408
Bishop, Max, 206, 208, 218
Black, Bud, 478
Black, Joe, 306
Black Sox scandal, 112, 128, 134, 136, 138, 142, 144, 146, 158, 204, 226, 448
Blair, Paul, 380, 438
Blanchard, Johnny, 354, 356
Blass, Steve, 414, 416
Blue, Vida, 396, 408, 410, 412, 414, 418, 420, 424, 426, 428, 430
Bluege, Ossie, 110
Boddicker, Mike, 476, 478
Boggs, Wade, 456, 460, 474, 478, 484, 486, 488, 492, 498
Bond, Tommy, 40
Bonds, Barry, 456
Bonds, Bobby, 410, 414, 422, 434, 456
Bonham, Ernie, 242, 256
Boone, Bob, 460, 464, 470, 488, 490
Borowy, Hank, 256, 266, 268
Bostock, Lyman, 440
Boston American, 138
Boston Beaneaters, 56, 66, 68, 70, 74, 80, 86
Boston Braves, 124, 126, 128, 148, 150, 152, 182, 202, 220, 228, 240, 248, 266, 276, 278, 280, 288, 296, 298, 302, 304, 308, 314, 334
Boston Pilgrims, 84, 86, 94
Boston Red Sox, 24, 32, 34, 36, 38, 40, 94, 112, 122, 124, 128, 132, 134, 136, 142, 146, 152, 160, 162, 164, 184, 190, 192, 196, 198, 202, 204, 222, 228, 232, 244, 246, 248, 254, 256, 270, 272, 278, 288, 294, 296, 300, 312, 316, 320, 324, 332, 342, 352, 354, 376, 380, 382, 394, 410, 418, 422, 426, 428, 432, 436, 440, 444, 456, 458, 460, 474, 476, 478, 480, 484, 486, 488, 490, 492, 496, 498
Boston Red Stockings, 10, 16
Boswell, Dave, 410
Bottomley, "Sunny" Jim, 152, 174, 176, 182, 206, 208
Boudreau, Lou, 246, 248, 250, 276, 278, 280
Bouton, Jim, 366, 372, 396, 402
Bowa, Larry, 434, 486
Bowman, Bob, 244
Boyer, Clete, 352, 356, 366, 372
Boyer, Ken, 370, 372
Bradley, Phil, 476
Brainard, Asa, 20, 22, 24
Branca, Ralph, 274, 290, 302
Brazle, Al, 308, 310
Breadon, Sam, 178
Brecheen, Harry, 272
Breslin, Jimmy, 342
Bresnahan, Roger, 88, 90
Brett, George, 430, 434, 448, 460, 464, 482
Bridges, Tommy, 216
Bridwell, Al, 106
Briggs Stadium (Detroit), 252, 268
Briles, Nelson, 382, 386, 416
Brock, Lou, 218, 370, 382, 384, 386, 394, 396, 404, 424, 426, 456, 468, 472
Broglio, Ernie, 424
Brooklyn Dodgers, 92, 154, 156, 158, 162, 168, 202, 212, 214, 216, 238, 240, 244, 246, 248, 250, 252, 254, 256, 258, 270, 272, 274, 276, 278, 280, 282, 288, 290, 292, 296, 298, 300, 302, 306, 308, 310, 312, 314, 316, 318, 320, 322, 324, 326, 328, 334, 336, 416
Brooklyn Robins, 130, 150
Brotherhood of Professional Base Ball Players, 48, 50
Brown, Bobby, 280, 304
Brown, Jimmy, 258
Brown, Mace, 224
Brown, Mordecai Peter Centennial "Three Finger," 82, 98, 100, 102, 104, 110, 118, 120
Brown, Warren, 266, 268
Brown, Willard, 248
Browne, Sam, 94
Browning, Tom, 482, 496
Brunansky, Tom, 492, 494
Brush, John, 90
Bruton, Bill, 310, 320
Bryant, Clay, 230
Bryant, Ron, 422
Buckner, Bill, 422, 428, 462, 480, 490
Buffinton, Charlie, 28, 58
Buford, Don, 390
Buhl, Bob, 328
Bulkeley, Morgan, 32
Bumbry, Al, 444
Bunker, Wally, 378, 380
Bunning, Jim, 330
Burdette, Lew, 326, 328, 330, 332, 334, 336
Burdock, Jack, 42
Burkett, Jesse, 70, 74, 88, 90
Burks, Ellis, 498
Burleson, Rick, 436
Burns, George, 124, 132, 160, 176
Burns, Oyster, 68
Burroughs, Jeff, 426
Busby, Jim, 324
Busch, Gussie, 370
Busch, Jr., August, 406
Busch Stadium (St. Louis), 472
Bush, "Bullet" Joe, 136, 162
Bush, Donie, 122
Bush, Guy, 210
Butler, Brett, 496
Byrnes, Milt, 262

Cadore, Leon, 150
California Angels, 330, 440, 444, 460, 470, 480, 482, 484, 488, 490
Camilli, Dolf, 252, 258
Camnitz, Howie, 106
Campanella, Roy, 172, 194, 198, 282, 292, 296, 302, 308, 320, 332
Campaneris, Bert, 404, 418
Campanis, Al, 452, 454
Can't Anyone Here Play This Game?, 342
Candelaria, John, 432, 444
Candiotti, Tom, 488
Candlestick Park (San Francisco), 360, 362, 370, 376, 414
Canseco, Jose, 456, 496, 498
Carbo, Bernie, 422
Cardenal, Jose, 464
Carew, Rod, 378, 394, 396, 406, 408, 410, 418, 430, 436, 444, 470, 482
Carey, Andy, 318
Carey, Max, 172, 294
Carlton, "Silent" Steve "Lefty," 390, 402, 404, 418, 434, 436, 444, 458, 460, 462, 464, 470, 474, 476
Carrasquel, Chico, 324
Carter, Gary "The Kid," 450, 462, 470, 478, 484, 486, 488, 490
Carter, Joe, 488
Cartwright, Alexander Joy, 6, 8, 10, 12, 16
Carty, Rico, 396, 404
Caruthers, "Parisian" Bob, 60, 62, 64, 66
Casey, Hugh, 254, 256, 274, 280
Cash, Dave, 434
Cash, Norm, 358, 380, 386
Cater, Danny, 384
Cavarretta, Phil, 266, 308
Cepeda, Orlando "Cha-Cha," "The Baby Bull," 332, 336, 360, 364, 370, 382, 386, 398, 404
Cey, Ron, 422, 438, 462, 474, 478
Chadwick, Henry, 6, 8, 16, 20, 30, 32
Chalmers (MVP) Award, 118
Chambliss, Chris, 434, 436, 468
Champion, Aaron, 22
Chance, Dean, 368, 370, 380
Chance, Frank, 96, 98, 104, 106, 118
Chandler, A.B. "Happy," 246, 248, 266, 268, 272, 274, 298
Chandler, Spurgeon Ferdinand "Spud," 228, 256, 260, 262
Chapman, Ben, 206, 208, 214
Chapman, Ray, 144, 154, 156, 158
Charles, Ed, 390
Charleston, Oscar, 194, 248
Chase, "Prince" Hal, 112, 114, 128
Cheney, Larry, 130
Chesbro, Jack, 88, 92, 94
Chicago American Giants, 196
Chicago Cubs, 90, 96, 98, 100, 102, 104, 106, 118, 120, 122, 128, 136, 148, 152, 172, 174, 180, 184, 186, 190, 200, 202, 206, 210, 216, 218, 220, 224, 228, 230, 238, 252, 254, 264, 266, 268, 272, 296, 306, 308, 320, 332, 336, 370, 374, 380, 388, 396, 410, 424, 450, 454, 460, 462, 472, 474, 476, 478, 480, 490, 492
Chicago Orphans, 48
Chicago *Tribune,* 138, 194
Chicago Whales, 116
Chicago White Sox, 42, 96, 98, 100, 102, 112, 114, 130, 132, 134, 136, 138, 142, 156, 168, 190, 204, 214, 222, 242, 250, 262, 274, 276, 296, 298, 302, 306, 312, 316, 324, 330, 352, 358, 366, 368, 370, 374, 380, 398, 410, 418, 420, 454, 458, 474, 476, 478, 482
Chicago White Stockings, 22, 26, 28, 32, 34, 36, 38, 40, 42, 48, 56, 60, 62
Childs, Cupid, 74
Cicotte, Eddie, 114, 132, 134, 138, 142, 156
Cincinnati Reds, 30, 90, 128, 138, 166, 194, 212, 234, 238, 240, 244, 250, 252, 320, 322, 324, 326, 344, 352, 358, 366, 370, 374, 384, 388, 396, 398, 404, 410, 412, 414, 418, 420, 422, 424, 426, 430, 432, 434, 436, 440, 444, 450, 462, 466, 472, 476, 478, 482, 486, 490, 492, 494, 496
Cincinnati Red Stockings, 10, 20, 22, 24, 26
Clark, Jack, 460, 482, 490, 494
Clark, Will, 492, 496
Clarke, Fred, 88, 92, 106
Clarkson, John, 46, 52, 60, 62, 66, 68, 70
Clemens, Roger "The Rocket," 458, 460, 476, 486, 492, 498
Clemente, Roberto, 100, 332, 356, 372, 376, 382, 396, 400, 404, 410, 412, 414, 416, 426, 432, 444
Clendenon, Donn, 388, 390
Cleveland Forest Cities, 26, 34
Cleveland Indians, "The Tribe," 138, 144, 154, 156, 158, 160, 164, 176, 196, 218, 222, 232, 242, 244, 246, 248, 250, 258, 270, 274, 276, 278, 280, 292, 294, 296, 298, 300, 302, 304, 306, 310, 314, 324, 330, 332, 334, 362, 382, 404, 430, 432, 440, 488, 490
Cleveland Spiders, 74
Clift, Harlond, 226
Coakley, Andy, 96, 98
Coates, Jim, 356
Cobb, Ty, 88, 98, 100, 102, 104, 106, 110, 114, 118, 120, 124, 126, 128, 130, 132, 134, 136, 144, 148, 158, 162, 164, 168, 172, 174, 182, 200, 218, 404, 472, 478, 482, 498
Cochrane, Mickey "Black Mike," 170, 172, 174, 178, 180, 182, 190, 192, 204, 206, 208, 216, 218, 220, 224, 226, 288, 348
Colavito, Rocky, 332, 334
Colbert, Nate, 418
Cole, King, 118
Coleman, Gordy, 358
Coleman, Jerry, 280, 304, 318
Coleman, Vince, 110, 456, 482, 484, 486, 490
Collins, Eddie, 110, 112, 118, 120, 124, 126, 128, 134, 138, 156, 168, 174, 182, 288, 424
Collins, Jimmy, 74, 80, 86, 100
Collins, Ripper, 156, 208, 214, 218
Color barrier, 194, 196
Combs, Earle, 170, 180, 206, 208, 210, 216
Comiskey, Charles, 42, 52, 60, 62, 66, 78, 86, 112, 114, 134, 142, 156
Comiskey Park (Chicago), 194, 198, 212, 274, 334, 394

Concepcion, Dave, 404, 434, 444, 486
Cone, David, 122, 496
Connolly, Joe, 126
Connor, Roger, 60, 66, 68
Coombs, Jack, 118, 120, 122, 126, 130, 132
Cooper, Cecil, 430, 464, 470
Cooper, Mort, 260, 262, 264
Cooper, Walker, 258, 260
Corcoran, Larry, 58
Corrales, Pat, 474
Corriden, Red, 272
Coveleski, Harry, 130
Coveleski, Stan, 158, 170
Cramer, Doc, 222
Crane, Ned "Cannonball," 66
Cravath, Gavvy, 110, 124, 128, 132, 146
Craver, Bill, 26, 40
Crawford, "Wahoo" Sam, 88, 100, 102, 104, 120, 122, 130
Creighton, James, 12, 14, 16, 18
Cronin, Jack, 90
Cronin, Joe "Boy Manager," 192, 198, 202, 212, 214, 220, 278
Crosetti, Frankie, 224, 230, 246
Crosley Field (Cincinnati), 238
Cross, Lave, 86, 90
Crowder, General, 204, 212
Cuellar, Mike, 388, 390, 410, 412, 414, 416, 426, 428
Cummings, William "Candy," 18, 40
Cuyler, Kiki, 168, 172, 186
Cy Young Award, 304, 326, 328, 334, 350, 356, 358, 360, 364, 370, 376, 380, 382, 384, 386, 388, 396, 400, 402, 410, 412, 416, 418, 420, 422, 424, 426, 428, 430, 434, 436, 438, 440, 444, 450, 458, 462, 464, 466, 470, 474, 476, 478, 482, 484, 486, 492, 494, 496, 498

Dahlen, Bill, 94, 96
Dalrymple, Abner, 38, 42, 60
Darcy, Pat, 422
Dark, Alvin, 302, 304, 316, 402, 418, 428
Darling, Ron, 486, 496
Daubert, Jake, 130
Dauss, Hooks, 130
Davenport, Jim, 360
Davis, Chili, 492
Davis, Curt, 254
Davis, Eric, 456, 490
Davis, George, 98
Davis, Glenn, 486
Davis, Harry, 96, 100, 120
Davis, Jody, 478
Davis, Tommy, 358, 364, 376, 398, 426
Davis, Willie, 364, 368
Dawson, Andre, 460, 462, 466, 490, 492
DC Stadium, 340
Dean, Jay Hannah "Dizzy," 152, 192, 196, 206, 208, 218, 222, 228, 230, 234, 274, 348, 384
Dean, Paul "Daffy," 206, 216, 218, 222
DeCinces, Doug, 470, 484, 488
Delahanty, Ed, 62, 66, 70, 72, 82, 90
Delahanty, Jim, 122
Demaree, Al, 116, 124, 126, 130
Demaree, Frank, 222, 228
DeMontreville, Gene, 86
Dempsey, Rick, 444
Denny, John, 474, 476
Dent, Bucky, 436, 440, 442
Derringer, Paul, 234, 250, 252, 266
Deshaies, Jim, 486
Designated hitter (DH), 290, 396, 398, 430
Detroit Tigers, 102, 104, 106, 118, 120, 122, 130, 132, 136, 152, 158, 162, 164, 172, 178, 190, 192, 204, 206, 216, 218, 220, 224, 226, 230, 242, 244, 250, 252, 262, 266, 268, 274, 294, 300, 302, 312, 316, 320, 324, 330, 348, 356, 378, 380, 382, 384, 386, 388, 410, 418, 432, 456, 460, 462, 474, 476, 480, 482, 484, 490, 492, 494, 498
Detroit Wolverines, 64
Devine, Bing, 370
Devlin, Jim, 40
DeVore, Josh, 120, 124
DeWitt, Bill, 350
Dickey, Bill, 172, 216, 220, 222, 224, 228, 234, 256, 262, 280
Dietz, Dick, 374
DiHigo, Martin, 248
DiMaggio, Dom, 270, 272, 294, 300, 302
DiMaggio, "Joltin'" Joe, 190, 194, 218, 220, 222, 224, 226, 228, 232, 242, 246, 250, 254, 256, 260, 274, 276, 278, 280, 282, 294, 298, 300, 304, 336, 474, 494
Dineen, "Big" Bill, 84, 90, 92, 94
Ditmar, Art, 334, 352, 354
Dobson, Joe, 270, 272
Dobson, Pat, 412
Doby, Larry, 242, 248, 278, 280, 296, 300, 304, 314, 324, 330, 454
Dodger Stadium (Los Angeles), 342, 344, 440
Doerr, Bobby, 256, 262, 270, 282, 294

Donald, Atley, 242, 256
Donlin, "Turkey" Mike, 88, 90, 94, 96, 122
Donovan, "Wild" Bill, 100, 102, 106
Dorish, Harry, 306
Dotson, Rich, 474
Doubleday, Abner, 6
Dougherty, Patsy, 92, 94
Downing, Brian, 444, 484
Downing, Al, 366, 372, 404, 408, 426
Doyle, Denny, 422
Doyle, "Dirty" Jack, 72
Doyle, Larry, 116, 120, 122
Drabowsky, Moe, 378, 380
Dressen, Charlie, 272, 316
Dreyfuss, Barney, 78, 94
Dropo, Walt, 294
Drysdale, Don, 328, 346, 350, 352, 358, 364, 366, 368, 374, 376, 380, 386, 494, 496
Duffy, Hugh, 56, 58, 70, 74
Dugan, Joe, 162
Dunlap, Fred, 48
Duren, Ryne, 332, 334
Durham, Leon "Bull," 478
Durocher, Leo, 182, 212, 214, 234, 244, 248, 254, 272, 274, 282, 286, 396
Dykes, Jimmy, 180, 214, 218, 262
Dykstra, Len, 486, 488

Eagles (New York), 14
Earnshaw, George, 184, 202, 204, 208, 214
Easter, Luke, 300
East-West All-Star Game, 198
Eastwick, Rawly, 422
Ebbets, Charles, 78
Ebbets Field (Brooklyn), 212, 230, 238, 254, 290, 298, 312
Eckersley, Dennis, 440, 458, 492, 496
Eckert, William "Spike," 344
Eckfords (Brooklyn), 14, 16, 18, 24
Eckfords (Greenpoint), 14
Ehmke, Howard, 186
Eller, Hod, 138
Ellis, Dock, 404, 414, 434
Elysian Fields (Hoboken, NJ), 6, 18
Empires (New York), 14, 16
Ennis, Del, 296, 328
Ermer, Cal, 380
Erskine, Carl, 308, 310, 366
Esper, Duke, 72
Esterbrook, Dude, 58
Etten, Nick, 260
Evans, Darrell, 422, 482, 484, 492
Evans, Dwight, 422, 440, 480, 486, 498
Evening Telegram, 8
Evers, Hoot, 294
Evers, Johnny, 96, 104, 126
Ewing, Buck, 54, 60, 66, 68
Excelsiors (Brooklyn), 12, 14, 16, 18, 22

Faber, Red, 134
Face, Elroy, 336, 354
Fain, Ferris, 300
Fashion Race Course, 16
Fear Strikes Out, 330
Federal League, 116, 128, 150
Federal League antitrust suit (1915), 144
Feller, Bob "Rapid Robert," 190, 222, 226, 230, 242, 250, 258, 270, 280, 292, 294, 300, 314, 326
Felsch, Happy, 132, 134, 142
Fenway Park (Boston), 122, 278, 290, 300, 326, 342, 376, 382, 394, 426, 440, 476, 478, 480
Ferguson, Bob "Death to Flying Things," 20, 28, 36
Fernandez, Sid, 486, 496
Ferrara, Al, 400
Ferrell, Rick, 218, 220
Ferrell, Wes, 192, 218, 220
Ferriss, Boo, 270, 272
Fette, Lou, 228
Fidrych, Mark "The Bird," 432, 434
$15,000 slide, 52
Figueroa, Ed, 434
Fingers, Rollie, 396, 406, 412, 418, 420, 426, 428, 432, 470
Finley, Charles O., 344, 394, 398, 403, 406, 414, 416, 418, 424, 428, 432
Fisher, Eddie, 378
Fisher, Jack, 342, 354
Fisk, Carlton, 396, 422, 430, 432, 440, 458, 474
Fitzsimmons, "Fat" Freddie, 202, 206, 224, 254
Five Seasons, 442
Flanagan, Mike, 444
Fletcher, Art, 116, 132
Flood, Curt, 382, 386, 404, 406
Forbes Field (Pittsburgh), 80
Force, Davy, 32, 38, 40
Ford, Dan, 444
Ford, Ed "Whitey," 292, 294, 300, 304, 310, 314, 320, 322, 324, 326, 330, 352, 354, 356, 358, 362, 366, 368, 372, 380

Forsch, Ken, 462
Fort Wayne (IN) Kekiongas, 26, 34
Foster, George, 396, 422, 430, 432, 434, 438, 444, 450
Foster, Rube, 130, 196
Fournier, Jack, 168
Foutz, Dave, 52, 60, 62, 64, 66, 68
Fowler, Bud, 56
Fox, Larry, 344
Fox, Nellie, 306, 316, 318, 324, 334
Fox, Pete, 220
Foxx, Jimmie "The Beast," "Double X," 124, 144, 164, 170, 174, 180, 184, 190, 192, 202, 206, 208, 214, 218, 220, 222, 226, 228, 232, 254, 288, 366
Franco, John, 496
Fraternity of Professional Baseball Players of America, 114
Frazee, Harry, 146, 152, 164
Freedman, Andrew, 70, 78, 80, 90
Freehan, Bill, 380
Freeman, Buck, 86, 92
Freese, Gene, 358
Fregosi, Jim, 414
Frick, Ford, 252, 298, 322, 344, 348, 354
Friend, Bob, 332, 354
Frisch, Frankie "The Fordham Flash," 158, 166, 168, 178, 200, 208, 214, 258
Fullerton, Hugh, 112, 138
Furillo, Carl, 276, 282, 292, 298, 308, 310

Gaedel, Eddie, 296, 298
Gaetti, Gary, 492
Gainor, Del, 132
Galan, Augie, 218
Galarraga, Andres, 496
Gallico, Paul, 176
Galvin, James "Pud," 28, 58
Gambling scandals, 24, 112, 114, 410, 480
Game-fixing, 18, 32, 36, 38, 40, 114, 128, 142, 144, 156
Gandil, Chick, 114, 134, 142
Garagiola, Joe, 316, 318
Garcia, Mike, 292, 300, 304, 310, 314, 318, 322
Gardella, Danny, 268
Gardner, Billy, 316
Gardner, Larry, 160
Garms, Debs, 244
Garver, Ned, 300
Garvey, Steve, 402, 422, 426, 438, 440, 462, 466, 470, 474, 478, 480, 490
Gas House Gang, 192, 206, 214, 216, 228, 232
Gaston, Cito, 400
Gedman, Rich, 460, 480, 490
Gehrig, "Columbia" Lou "The Iron Horse," 144, 146, 160, 170, 174, 176, 178, 180, 182, 184, 190, 204, 206, 208, 210, 212, 214, 216, 220, 222, 224, 226, 228, 232, 234, 276, 334, 350, 430, 466, 494
Gehringer, Charlie "The Mechanical Man," 184, 192, 204, 216, 220, 224, 226
Gentry, Gary, 388, 390
Gera, Bernice, 416
Geronimo, Cesar, 434
Giamatti, A. Bartlett, 458, 494
Gibson, Bob, 352, 368, 372, 382, 384, 386, 400, 426, 430
Gibson, Josh, 82, 194, 196, 198, 200, 248
Gibson, Kirk, 460, 476, 480, 492, 496, 498
Gilliam, Jim, 364
Gionfriddo, Al, 276, 282, 336
Gleason, Kid, 72, 114
Gold Glove Award, 286, 340, 348, 352, 356, 372, 382, 386, 398, 404, 430, 440, 448, 454, 456, 462, 470, 474, 486, 488
Goldsmith, Fred, 42
Goliat, Mike, 296
Gomez, Vernon Lewis "Lefty," 206, 208, 216, 220, 222, 226, 228
Gooden, Dwight "Doc," 452, 458, 460, 478, 482, 486, 488, 496, 498
Gordon, Joe, 228, 246, 250, 256, 278, 280
Gordon, Sid, 304
Gore, George, 38, 42, 60
Goslin, Leon Allen "Goose," 166, 168, 170, 182
Gossage, Goose, 396, 436, 440, 442, 460, 464, 478
Gothams (New York), 14, 18
Gould, Charlie "Bushel Basket," 22, 24, 28, 30
Gowdy, Hank, 128
Grant, Frank, 56
Grant, Jim, 374
Grant, President Ulysses S., 24
Grebey, Ray, 448
Greenberg, Hank, 226
Greenwell, Mike, 498
Grich, Bobby, 426, 444, 470, 480, 488
Griffey, Ken, 430, 434, 450
Griffith, Calvin, 340
Griffith, Clark, 86, 192
Griffith Stadium, 166

Grim, Bob, 314
Grimes, Burleigh, 144, 148, 154, 156, 162, 168, 202
Grimm, Charlie, 210, 230, 264
Groat, Dick, 354, 356
Gromek, Steve, 280, 300
Groh, Heinie, 138
Grote, Jerry, 390
Grove, Robert Moses "Lefty," 114, 124, 170, 176, 178, 180, 182, 184, 186, 190, 192, 202, 204, 206, 208, 214, 218, 220, 228, 232, 288, 384
Guerrero, Pedro, 468, 474, 482, 486
Guidry, Ron, 436, 438, 440, 442, 460, 468, 482
Gullett, Don, 412, 436, 438
Gwynn, Tony, 478, 486, 488, 492, 496

Haas, Mule, 180, 214, 218
Haddix, Harvey, 310, 328, 336
Hadley, Bump, 224
Hafey, Chick, 204, 206, 208
Hahn, Ed, 98
Haines, Jesse, 152, 180,
Hall, Dick, 378
Hall, George, 40
Hall, Jimmie, 374
Hallahan, "Wild" Bill, 200, 206
Haller, Tom, 364, 376
Hall of Fame (Cooperstown), 10, 32, 34, 94, 100, 104, 116, 118, 142, 144, 148, 152, 154, 158, 160, 162, 164, 166, 168, 170, 172, 174, 178, 182, 190, 192, 194, 196, 198, 200, 204, 208, 210, 214, 218, 220, 222, 228, 230, 232, 246, 248, 286, 288, 292, 296, 298, 302, 320, 322, 324, 326, 336, 344, 350, 356, 360, 364, 368, 372, 376, 380, 398, 410, 416, 424, 426, 428, 430, 438, 440, 458, 460, 474, 488, 498
Hamilton, "Sliding" Billy, 66, 70, 72, 74, 82
Hammaker, Atlee, 476
Hanlon, Ned, 56, 60, 70, 72, 74, 82, 84, 88, 100
Harder, Mel, 250
Hargrave, Bubbles, 174, 240
Harrelson, Bud, 388, 424, 456
Harrelson, Ken "The Hawk," 400
Harridge, Will, 296
Harris, Bucky, 164, 166, 174, 280
Harris, Mickey, 270
Hart, Jim, 78
Hart, Jim Ray, 376, 398
Hartnett, Charles Leo "Gabby," 172, 202, 206, 218, 224, 230
Harvey Wallbangers, 470, 472
Hassett, Buddy, 260
Hatcher, Billy, 484
Hatten, Joe, 282
Hayes, J. William, 346
Hayes, Von, 486
Hearn, Jim, 298
Hebner, Richie, 416
Heilmann, Harry "Slug," 148, 152, 158, 164, 168, 172, 174, 178
Held, Woodie, 324
Helms, Tommy, 352
Hemming, George, 74
Hemus, Solly, 308
Henderson, Dave, 480, 488, 490, 498
Henderson, Rickey, 110, 394, 424, 456, 464, 466, 468, 472, 484, 488, 492, 498
Hendrick, George, 470, 472
Hendrix, Claude, 136
Henke, Tom, 494
Henrich, Tommy, 228, 254, 256, 260, 280, 282
Henriksen, Olaf, 124
Herald, 8
Herman, Babe, 202
Herman, Billy, 210, 218, 222, 254
Hernandez, Keith, 426, 444, 452, 454, 470, 472, 478, 480, 484, 486, 496
Hernandez, Willie, 476
Herr, Tommy, 482, 484, 492
Herrman, Garry, 80
Hershberger, Willard, 250
Hershiser, Orel "The Bulldog," 482, 494, 496
Herzog, Buck, 116, 120, 132
Herzog, Whitey, 432, 490
Hickman, "Piano Legs," 92
Higbe, Kirby, 252
Hiller, Chuck, 362
Hines, Paul, 40
Historical Baseball Abstract, 292
Hoak, Don, 322, 354
Hodges, Gil, 282, 292, 298, 308, 310, 318, 326, 336, 362, 388, 390, 416
Hodges, Russ, 290, 336
Hoeft, Billy, 324
Hoerner, Joe, 382
Hoffer, Bill, 72, 74
Hoffman, Solly, 118
Holke, Walter, 132, 134
Holloman, Bobo, 300, 310
Holmes, Tommy, 266

501

Holtzman, Ken, 418, 424, 426, 428, 430, 432, 434
Homer in the gloamin', 224
Homestead Grays, 196, 198
Hooper, Harry, 124, 130, 136
Hooton, Burt, 434, 466
Horlen, Joel, 368
Horner, Bob, 460, 468
Hornsby, Rogers "The Rajah," 144, 148, 156, 158, 160, 162, 166, 168, 172, 174, 176, 178, 180, 184, 192, 202, 208, 210, 228, 246, 276, 278, 422, 478
Horton, Willie, 380, 384, 386, 426
Hough, Charlie, 434
Houk, Ralph, 312, 356, 368, 378
Houston Astros, 272, 342, 376, 384, 404, 438, 444, 448, 450, 452, 462, 466, 474, 482, 484, 486, 490, 496, 498
Houston Colt 45s, 340, 342
Howard, Elston, 220, 354, 356, 362, 366, 374
Howard, Frank, 364
Howe, Art, 452
Howell, Jay, 458
Howser, Dick, 490
Hoyt, LaMarr, 474
Hoyt, Waite, 160, 178, 182, 184
Hrbek, Kent, 492
Hubbell, "King" Carl, 186, 202, 206, 210, 212, 224, 226, 228, 374
Hudson, Nat, 62, 66
Huggins, Miller, 170, 174, 184
Hughes, Dick, 382
Hughes, "Long" Tom, 84, 92
Hughson, Tex, 256, 262, 270
Hulbert, William, 30, 32, 36
Hunt, Ken, 342
Hunter, Billy, 318, 436
Hunter, Jim "Catfish," 368, 396, 406, 412, 418, 420, 424, 426, 428, 430, 438, 440
Hunter, Willard, 386
Hurst, Bruce, 490
Hurst, Don, 210
Hutchinson, "Wild" Bill, 84
Hutchinson, Fred, 358, 370

I'm Glad You Didn't Take It Personally, 396
Incaviglia, Pete, 488
Indianapolis Actives, 22
Indianapolis Clowns, 198
Irvin, Monte, 302, 306, 316
Irvingtons (NJ), 18, 22, 24
Isbell, Frank, 86, 98, 100

Jackson, Al, 382
Jackson, Bo, 488
Jackson, Danny, 496
Jackson, Grant, 434
Jackson, "Shoeless" Joe, 34, 110, 124, 126, 130, 132, 134, 136, 138, 142, 478
Jackson, Reginald "Reggie," "Mr. October," 384, 394, 400, 402, 406, 408, 418, 420, 424, 426, 428, 430, 432, 434, 436, 438, 440, 442, 462, 468, 470, 484, 488, 490
Jakucki, Sig, 262, 264
James, Bill, 128, 292
Jansen, Larry, 302
Jaster, Larry, 382
Javier, Julian, 382
Jay, Joey, 358
Jefferies, Gregg, 496
Jenkins, Ferguson, 368, 410, 426, 452
Jennings, Hughie, 56, 60, 72, 74, 84, 100, 120, 122
Jensen, Jackie, 304, 316, 320, 332
Jethroe, Sam "Jet," 296
John, Tommy, 422, 426, 438, 458, 464, 470
Johnson, Ban, 78, 80, 86, 88, 90, 96, 120, 180
Johnson, Billy, 260, 262
Johnson, Cliff, 442
Johnson, Davey, 410, 422
Johnson, Deron, 370
Johnson, Ernie, 328
Johnson, Howard, 456
Johnson, Judy, 194, 248
Johnson, Lou, 378
Johnson, Walter "The Big Train," 72, 110, 114, 122, 124, 132, 136, 144, 164, 166, 170, 172, 180, 184, 194, 200, 270, 304, 374, 474
Johnstone, Jay, 434
Jolly Young Bachelors (Brooklyn), 14. *See also* Excelsiors.
Jones, Charlie, 40, 42
Jones, Cleon, 388
Jones, Fielder, 98
Jones, Ruppert, 484
Jones, "Sad" Sam, 136, 162
Joss, Addie, 92, 100, 102
Joyner, Wally, 488

Kaat, Jim, 374, 376, 380, 410, 458
Kaline, Al, 320, 324, 348, 356, 380, 384, 386, 396, 418, 426

Kansas City Athletics, 288, 320, 344, 352, 382, 428
Kansas City Royals, 366, 434, 436, 440, 448, 456, 460, 464, 466, 472, 478, 480, 482, 484, 488, 490
Kauff, Benny, 132, 136, 138
Keane, Johnny, 370, 372, 374, 378
Keefe, Tim, 58, 66, 68
Keeler, "Wee" Willie, 60, 64, 72, 74, 80, 84, 86, 218, 276, 440
Kekich, Mike, 402
Kell, George, 294, 302
Keller, Charlie, 232, 234, 246, 256, 260, 280
Kelley, Joe, 60, 72, 74, 84, 86, 90
Kelly, George, 156, 160, 166, 168, 210
Kelly, Mike "King," 26, 40, 42, 50, 52, 60, 62, 68
Kelly, Van, 400
Keltner, Ken, 246, 250, 276, 278
Kennedy, "Brickyard," 84
Kerr, Dickie, 138
Key, Jimmy, 494
Kilduff, Pete, 156
Killebrew, Harmon "Killer," 342, 362, 366, 368, 374, 380, 410
Killian, Ed, 100, 102, 104
Killilea, Henry, 94
Kinder, Ellis, 312
Kiner, Ralph, 254, 278, 296, 304, 308, 366
King, Clyde, 470
King, Silver, 62, 66
Kingdome (Seattle), 394
Kingman, Dave, 402, 470
Kitson, Frank, 86
Kittle, Ron, 474
Klein, Chuck, 184, 186, 200, 202, 206, 210, 212, 214, 216
Klem, Bill, 94, 184
Kling, Johnny, 96
Kluszewski, Ted, 308, 320
Knickerbocker Base Ball Club (New York), 6, 8, 10, 12, 18
Knickerbockers (Brooklyn), 14. *See also* Excelsiors.
Knight, Ray, 444, 486, 490
Koenig, Mark, 180, 200, 210
Konstanty, Jim, 296, 298
Koosman, Jerry, 388, 390, 424, 458
Koppel, Ted, 452
Koufax, Sandy, 82, 202, 336, 346, 350, 360, 364, 366, 368, 376, 378, 412, 420, 448, 468
Kramer, Jack, 262, 264
Krause, Harry, 104
Kreevich, Mike, 262, 264
Kremer, Ray, 202
Kroc, Ray, 406
Kubek, Tony, 330, 352, 354, 356, 366, 370, 372
Kucks, Johnny, 324
Kuenn, Harvey, 312, 316, 470
Kuhel, Joe, 212
Kuhn, Bowie, 344, 396, 400, 408, 422, 424, 426, 432, 452, 480
Kurowski, Whitey, 258, 272

Laabs, Chet, 264
Lajoie, Napoleon "Nap," "Larry," 80, 86, 88, 90, 92, 100, 104
Landis, Kenesaw Mountain, 114, 162, 206, 218, 238, 258, 264, 266, 296
Langston, Mark, 488, 494
Lansford, Carney, 468
Lardner, Ring, 138
Larsen, Don, 318, 324, 326, 330, 332, 336, 352
Lary, Lyn, 206
Lasorda, Tommy, 438, 494, 496
Late Innings, 442
Latham, Arlie "The Freshest Man on Earth," 56, 62, 64
Lavagetto, Cookie, 276, 282, 336
Law, Vern, 354
Lazzeri, Tony, 126, 212, 216, 224, 228
Leach Freddy, 200
Leach, Tommy, 88, 92, 100
League Championship Series, 448, 484, 488
League Park (Cleveland), 80
Leary, Tim, 496
Leever, Sam, 84, 92, 96
Lefebvre, Jim, 376, 378
Lefferts, Craig, 480
LeFlore, Ron, 462
Leggett, J.B., 14, 16
Leiber, Hank, 218
Leibold, Nemo, 134
Lemon, Bob, 280, 292, 294, 296, 300, 304, 306, 310, 312, 314, 318, 322, 324, 436, 440, 442, 470
Lemon, Chet, 476, 492
Leonard, Andy, 22
Leonard, Buck, 248
Leonard, Dennis, 436
Leonard, Dutch, 128, 130, 132
Leonard, Jeffery, 492, 494

Lewis, Ted, 86
Lindstrom Freddie, 202
Linz, Phil, 370, 372, 374
Lloyd, John Henry, 248
Lockman, Whitey, 316
Logan, Johnny, 328
Lolich, Mickey, 386, 412, 418
Lollar, Sherman, 334
Lombardi, Ernie "Schnozz," 230, 234, 240, 250
Lonborg, Jim, 382, 384, 434
Long, Dale, 356, 490
Long, Herman, 68, 74
Lopat, "Steady" Eddie, 294, 300, 304, 312, 318
Lopes, Davey, 396
Lopez, Aurelio, 476
Lopez, Hector, 356
Los Angeles Angels, 340, 342, 362, 370, 380, 382, 406, 430. *See also* California Angels.
Los Angeles Coliseum, 336
Los Angeles Dodgers, 288, 302, 326, 332, 334, 336, 434, 438, 440, 448, 450, 452, 456, 462, 464, 466, 468, 470, 474, 482, 486, 492, 494, 496, 498
Louisville affair (1877), 32, 40
Louisville Grays, 40
Lowe, Bobby, 74
Lown, Turk, 334
Lucas, Gary, 480
Lucas, Henry, 48
Lucchesi, Frank, 436
Luderus, Fred, 128, 132
Luzinski, Greg, 434, 438, 474
Lyle, Sparky, 396, 434, 436
Lynn, Fred, 428, 440, 470
Lyons, Ted, 204

Mack, Connie "The Tall Tactician," 86,90, 92, 96, 98, 104, 112, 116, 118, 120, 122, 124, 126, 128, 152, 162, 174, 176, 178, 180, 182, 186, 190, 192, 204, 206, 214, 216, 218, 222, 244, 288
Mack, Ray, 250
MacPhail, Larry, 194, 234, 238, 240, 244, 252, 258, 272
MacPhail, Lee, 460
Maddox, Garry, 434, 452
Maddox, Nick, 106
Madlock, Bill, 468, 476
Magee, Sherry, 118
Maglie, Sal, 302, 304, 326
Mahaffey, Roy 206
Maisel, Fritz, 110
Major League Baseball Players Association, 268, 346, 404, 458
Maldonado, Candy, 492
Mancuso, Gus, 224
Mantle, Mickey Charles, 292, 294, 300, 304, 308, 310, 312, 314, 316, 318, 320, 324, 326, 328, 330, 332, 334, 346, 348, 350, 352, 354, 356, 362, 366, 368, 370, 372, 378, 382, 396, 398, 480
Manush, Heinie, 164, 182, 204, 212, 222
Maranville, Rabbit, 126
Marberry, Firpo, 166, 168, 170, 216
Marichal, Juan "The Dominican Dandy," 82, 362, 364, 374, 376, 382, 404, 414, 430
Marion, Marty, 258, 264
Maris, Roger, 348, 350, 352, 354, 356, 358, 362, 366, 372, 376, 380, 382
Marquard, Rube, 116, 120, 122, 124, 126, 128, 130, 132
Marshall, Mike, 426, 428
Marshall, Mike, 482, 496

Martin, "Battlin'" Billy, 300, 304, 390, 394, 402, 410, 420, 436, 438, 440, 460, 466
Martin, J.C., 390
Martin, Jerry, 452
Martin, Pepper "Wild Hoss of the Osage," 152, 204, 206, 208, 216, 222
Marylebone Cricket Club, 12
Massachusetts Association of Baseball Players, 8
Mathews, Bobby, 36, 38
Mathews, Eddie, 308, 310, 320, 324, 326, 332, 334, 336
Mathewson, Christy, 82, 84, 88, 94, 98, 102, 110, 116, 118, 120, 122, 124, 126, 128, 304
Matlack, Jon, 424
Matthews, Gary, 476
Mattingly, Don, 454, 460, 478, 482, 488, 490
Mauch, Gene, 480, 488
May, Lee, 352, 412, 430
May, Rudy, 462
Mayer, Erskine, 130
Mays, Carl, 132, 136, 144, 154, 156
Mays, Willie, 190, 198, 218, 228, 286, 292, 294, 298, 302, 304, 306, 316, 320, 322, 328, 332, 336, 346, 360, 364, 376, 382, 396, 400, 408, 410, 414, 418, 424, 468, 480
Mazeroski, Bill "Dazzlin' Maz," "No Touch," "Tree Stump," 332, 346, 354, 356

McBride, Dick, 22
McCarthy, Joe, 174, 186, 200, 206, 210, 222, 232, 234, 260, 262
McCarthy, Tommy, 56, 70
McCarver, Tim, 372, 382, 386
McCatty, Steve, 466
McClure, Bob, 472
McCormick, Barry, 150
McCormick, Frank, 234, 252
McCormick, Jim, 46
McCormick, Mike, 382
McCormick, Moose, 106
McCovey, Willie, 336, 360, 362, 364, 370, 376
McDougald, Gil, 300, 304, 318, 322, 332, 334
McDowell, Roger, 484, 486
McGann, Dan, 84, 90, 94
McGee, Willie, 472, 482, 492
McGinnity, Joe "Iron Man," 86, 88, 90, 92, 94, 96, 98
McGraw, John "Little Napoleon," 56, 60, 72, 74, 80, 82, 84, 88, 90, 92, 94, 96, 116, 118, 122, 124, 126, 128, 132, 134, 156, 158, 168, 174, 192, 206, 208, 210
McGraw, Tug, 388, 400, 402, 424, 434, 462, 464
McGregor, Scott, 476
McGuire, Deacon, 94
McGwire, Mark, 490, 498
McInnis, Stuffy, 116, 126, 136
McKechnie, Bill, 174
McKnight, Denny, 42
McLain, Denny, 348, 352, 368, 384, 410, 412
McLean, Billy, 38
McMahon, Sadie, 72
McMillan, Roy, 322, 486
McNally, Dave, 380, 388, 406, 408, 410, 412, 432
McNally, Don, 378
McNamara, John, 480, 496
McPhee, Bid, 42
McQuinn, George, 264
McRae, Hal, 434, 472
McReynolds, Kevin, 478, 480, 496
McVey, Cal, 22, 32, 40
Medwick, Joe "Ducky," "Muscles," 206, 214, 218, 222, 228, 234, 244, 258
Meekin, Jouett, 72
Mele, Sam, 374
Melton, Cliff, 226
Memorial Stadium (Cleveland), 278
Mercury, 14
Merkle, Fred, 104, 106, 120, 122, 124, 126, 136
Merkle blunder, 106
Mertes, Sam, 94, 96
Messersmith, Andy, 406, 408, 422, 426, 432
Messersmith case, 406
Metrodome (Minnesota), 494
Meusel, Bob, 160, 162, 166, 170, 176, 178, 182
Meusel, Irish, 166
Meyer, Russ, 308
Meyerle, Levi, 24, 26
Meyers, Chief, 116, 120, 122, 126
Meyers, Kenny, 350
Michael, Gene, 470
Mikkelsen, Pete, 368
Miksis, Eddie, 276
Milan, Clyde, 110
Miller, Bob, 296
Miller, Marvin, 346, 404, 406, 408, 448
Miller, Otto, 156
Miller, Stu, 360, 378
Mills Commission, 6
Milnar, Al, 250
Milwaukee Braves, 240, 308, 310, 314, 320, 324, 326, 328, 330, 332, 334, 336, 340, 342
Milwaukee Brewers, 420, 430, 456, 462, 464, 466, 468, 470, 472, 492
Mincher, Don, 374
Minnesota Twins, 340, 342, 362, 366, 368, 374, 376, 378, 380, 390, 406, 410, 428, 460, 492, 494, 496, 498
Minoso, Minnie, 302, 306, 312, 316
Miracle of Coogan's Bluff, 290, 300
Mitchell, Clarence, 156
Mitchell, Dale, 278, 306, 318
Mitchell, Kevin, 490
Mize, Johnny, 222, 234, 256, 278, 294
Mizell, Vinegar Bend, 354
Molitor, Paul, 472, 492
Montanez, Willie, 404
Montreal Expos, 390, 406, 444, 452, 456, 460, 462, 466, 468, 470, 472, 474, 476, 478, 486, 492, 496
Moon, Wally, 336
Moore, Donnie, 480
Moore, Earl, 92
Moore, Joe, 224
Moore, Terry, 258
Moore, Wilcy, 178
Moose, Bob, 420
Morgan, Cy, 104, 118
Morgan, Joe, 404, 418, 422, 430, 432, 434, 468, 474

Morgan, Joe, 496
Morgan, Tom, 300, 304
Morris, Jack, 460, 476, 480
Moseby, Lloyd, 482
Mossi, Don, 314
Most Valuable Player (MVP), 148, 158, 160, 162, 164, 166, 168, 172, 174, 176, 178, 180, 182, 186, 190, 204, 206, 210, 212, 214, 216, 218, 220, 222, 224, 226, 228, 230, 232, 234, 246, 250, 252, 254, 256, 258, 260, 264, 266, 270, 274, 276, 278, 282, 286, 288, 296, 300, 302, 304, 306, 308, 310, 312, 314, 316, 320, 326, 330, 332, 334, 336, 340, 344, 348, 350, 352, 356, 358, 362, 364, 366, 372, 374, 376, 378, 380, 382, 384, 386, 388, 398, 404, 406, 410, 412, 418, 420, 426, 428, 430, 434, 436, 440, 444, 448, 454, 460, 462, 466, 468, 470, 474, 476, 478, 482, 484, 486, 492, 494, 496, 498
Mota, Manny, 396
Mullane, Tony, 72
Mullin, George, 100, 102, 104, 106
Muncrief, Bob, 262
Municipal Stadium (Cleveland), 276
Munson, Thurman, 100, 220, 394, 396, 430, 434, 438, 442, 444
Murcer, Bobby, 428
Murphy, Dale, 468, 470, 474, 478, 482
Murphy, Danny, 118, 120
Murphy, Johnny, 226, 232, 256, 280
Murphy, Robert, 268
Murray, Eddie, 444, 454, 464, 474
Murray, Red, 120, 124
Murtaugh, Danny, 328, 404, 410, 420
Musial, Stan "the Man," 228, 258, 260, 266, 268, 270, 272, 278, 296, 302, 306, 308, 310, 322, 324, 332, 364, 448, 450, 468
Mutrie, Jim, 58, 66
Myer, Buddy, 220

Narleski, Ray, 314
Nash, Billy, 56, 68
National Agreement (1883), 30, 42, 46, 80
National Association of Base Ball Players, 8, 16, 18, 20, 24, 26, 28, 34
National Association of Professional Baseball Players, "National Association," 10, 16, 22, 26, 28, 30, 32, 34, 36, 38, 48
National Commission, 80, 94, 136
National convention, 12, 16, 18
National League (N.L.), 10, 16, 18, 24, 26, 28, 30, 32, 34, 36, 38, 40, 42, 46, 48, 50, 52, 54, 56, 58, 60, 62, 64, 66, 68, 70, 72, 74, 78, 80, 82, 86, 88, 90, 92, 94, 96, 98, 100, 102, 104, 106, 110, 112, 116, 118, 120, 122, 124, 126, 128, 130, 132, 136, 138, 146, 148, 150, 154, 156, 158, 160, 162, 166, 168, 172, 174, 176, 180, 182, 184, 186, 190, 192, 194, 200, 202, 204, 206, 208, 210, 212, 216, 228, 230, 232, 234, 240, 242, 244, 250, 252, 254, 256, 260, 264, 266, 268, 270, 276, 282, 286, 290, 296, 298, 302, 304, 308, 310, 320, 322, 324, 326, 328, 332, 340, 342, 344, 350, 352, 358, 360, 362, 364, 366, 368, 370, 374, 376, 380, 384, 386, 388, 394, 396, 398, 400, 402, 404, 410, 414, 418, 420, 422, 424, 426, 430, 432, 434, 436, 438, 440, 444, 448, 450, 452, 454, 458, 460, 462, 464, 466, 468, 470, 472, 474, 476, 478, 482, 484, 486, 488, 490, 492, 494, 496, 498
National League Championship Series (N.L.C.S.), 390, 414, 424, 432, 434, 438, 452, 462, 466, 472, 476, 478, 480, 484, 488, 494, 498
Navin, Frank, 120, 192, 216, 220
Neale, Greasy, 138
Negro American League, 198
Negro Leagues, 194, 196, 198, 218, 248, 274, 278, 282
Negro National League, 196, 198
Nehf, Art, 180
Nettles, Graig, 434, 442, 468, 478
Newark Bears, 194
Newcombe, Don, 282, 290, 302, 320, 326
Newhouser, "Prince" Hal, 264, 266, 268
Newsom, Bobo, 250, 252
New York Clipper, 8, 16, 20, 22, 24
New Yorker, 442
New York Giants, 24, 48, 50, 52, 54, 60, 66, 70, 72, 80, 92, 94, 96, 98, 102, 104, 106, 116, 118, 120, 122, 124, 126, 128, 132, 134, 136, 138, 160, 162, 164, 166, 168, 170, 172, 174, 178, 180, 182, 186, 190, 192, 194, 198, 200, 202, 206, 208, 210, 212, 214, 216, 218, 222, 224, 226, 230, 240, 254, 256, 288, 290, 298, 302, 304, 306, 308, 314, 316, 318, 326, 328, 336, 418
New York Highlanders, 90, 94, 128
New York Knickerbocker Base Ball Club, 6, 8, 10, 12, 18
New York Mets, 58, 66, 68, 220, 288, 294, 302, 304, 314, 330, 340, 342, 362, 366, 368, 372, 376, 384, 388, 390, 400, 414, 416, 418, 422, 424, 434, 438, 450, 452, 454, 456, 458, 470, 478, 482, 484, 486, 488, 490, 496,498
New York Mutuals, 18, 20, 22, 24, 34, 36, 38, 40
New York Times, 8, 448
New York Tribune, 16
New York Yankees, 94, 118, 120, 122, 138, 142, 144, 146, 154, 156, 158, 160, 162, 164, 166, 168, 170, 174, 176, 178, 180, 182, 184, 190, 194, 196, 200, 204, 206, 208, 210, 212, 216, 220, 222, 224, 226, 228, 230, 232, 234, 238, 240, 242, 244, 246, 250, 252, 254, 256, 260, 262, 266, 272, 274, 276, 278, 280, 282, 288, 290, 292, 294, 298, 300, 302, 304, 308, 310, 312, 314, 316, 318, 320, 322, 324, 326, 328, 330, 332, 334, 336, 340, 342, 346, 350, 352, 354, 356, 358, 362, 366, 370, 372, 374, 378, 380, 382, 394, 396, 402, 406, 408, 418, 420, 424, 426, 428, 430, 432, 434, 436, 438, 440, 450, 454, 456, 460, 462, 464, 468, 470, 474, 478, 482, 484, 486, 488, 490, 492, 498
Nichol, Hugh, 62
Nicholas, Chet, 302
Nichols, Al, 40
Nichols, Kid, 68, 70, 74
Nicholson, Bill "Swish," 264
Niekro, Joe, 444, 462, 490
Niekro, Phil, 458, 468, 482, 490
Night games, 220, 238
Nixon, President Richard, 404
Nokes, Matt, 492
Nolan, Gary, 412
Nolan, "The Only," 40
Norris, Mike, 430
North, Billy, 396
Northrup, Jim, 384
Nuxhall, Joe, 244

Oakland Athletics, 384, 394, 396, 398, 402, 412, 414, 416, 418, 420, 424, 426, 428, 434, 456, 458, 464, 466, 468, 472, 490, 492, 496, 498
Oakland Oaks, 280
O'Brien, Billy, 64
O'Brien, Buck, 124
O'Brien, Pete, 488
O'Brien, Peter, 16
O'Day, Hank, 106
O'Dell, Billy, 360
Odom, John "Blue Moon," 420, 428
O'Doul, Lefty, 186, 200, 202, 210
Oeschger, Joe, 150
O'Farrell, Bob, 174
Oglivie, Ben, 464
Ojeda, Bob, 486, 496
Oliva, Tony, 374, 378, 398, 410
Oliver, Al, 412, 414, 416, 426, 470
Olmo, Luis, 282
Olyimpic Stadium (Montreal), 390
O'Malley, Walter, 288, 316, 342
O'Neill, Tip, 62, 64
Orosco, Jesse, 484, 486
O'Rourke, Frank, 158
O'Rourke, Jim "Orator," 24, 36, 38, 40, 66, 68
Orr, Dave, 58
Osteen, Claude, 376, 422
Otis, Amos, 402
O Toole, Jim, 358
Ott, Mel, 144, 182, 202, 206, 208, 210, 212, 214, 216, 218, 224, 226, 228, 230
Overall, Orval, 104, 118, 120
Owen, Frank, 96
Owen, Marv, 206, 218
Owen, Mickey, 252, 256, 280
Owen, Spike, 476
Owens, Paul, 434, 474

Pabor, Charlie, 18
Pafko, Andy, 296
Page, Joe, 280
Paige, Satchel, 194, 196, 198, 200, 218, 248, 274, 278, 296
Pallone, Dave, 494
Palmer, Dave, 408, 432, 442, 444, 452
Palmer, Jim, 378, 380, 390, 396, 410, 412, 414, 422, 430, 434, 444, 470
Parker, Dave, 408, 432, 442, 444, 452, 480, 482, 486
Parker, Wes, 466
Parrish, Lance, 460, 476
Parrish, Larry, 488
Pascual, Camillo, 362, 374
Pasqual, Jorge, 268
Passeau, Claude, 266, 268
Patterson, Roy, 86
Paul, Gabe, 434
Pearce, Dickey, 16, 18, 20
Pearson, Monte, 228, 234
Peckinpaugh, Roger, 156, 160, 166
Pena, Roberto, 374
Pendleton, Terry, 492
Pennock, Herb, 128, 164, 178, 184
Pepitone, Joe, 366, 372, 374, 380
Perez, Tony, 352, 368, 404, 412, 422, 434, 438, 474
Perranoski, Ron, 364
Perritt, Pol, 132
Perry, Gaylord, 376, 384, 414, 416, 418, 458, 472, 476
Perry, Jim, 374
Pesky, Johnny, 244, 256, 270, 272
Peters, Gary, 366, 368
Peterson, Fritz, 402
Peterson, Harold, 6
Petrocelli, Rico, 384
Petry, Dan, 476
Pettis, Gary, 488
Pfeffer, Fred, 60
Pfeffer, Jeff, 130, 132
Pfiester, Jack, 98, 104
Philadelphia Athletics, "A's," 18, 22, 24, 26, 28, 34, 36, 38, 86, 90, 92, 96, 98, 104, 112, 118, 120, 122, 124, 126, 128, 136, 152, 156, 170, 174, 176, 178, 180, 182, 184, 186, 190, 192, 202, 204, 206, 208, 214, 216, 220, 242, 278, 288, 300, 306, 344
Philadelphia Keystones, 24
Philadelphia Olympics, 24
Philadelphia Phillies, 86, 128, 130, 132, 152, 156, 166, 186, 200, 202, 210, 212, 216, 234, 242, 250, 252, 288, 290, 294, 296, 310, 316, 320, 326, 332, 370, 396, 402, 404, 432, 434, 436, 438, 442, 444, 452, 454, 460, 462, 464, 466, 468, 470, 474, 476, 478, 480, 486, 490, 492
Philadelphia White Stockings, 36
Phillippe, Deacon, 84, 88, 92, 96
Phinney's farm (Cooperstown, NY), 6
Phoebus, Tom, 390
Pierce, Billy, 312, 324, 330, 360, 362
Piersall, Jimmy, 330
Pine tar incident, 460
Piniella, Lou, 436, 442
Pinson, Vada, 358, 366, 370
Pipgras, George, 182
Pipp, Wally, 156
Pittsburgh Crawfords, 194, 198
Pittsburgh Pirates, "Bucs," 84, 88, 90, 92, 100, 106, 122, 154, 156, 160, 166, 172, 174, 180, 182, 186, 216, 224, 230, 264, 326, 328, 332, 346, 352, 354, 356, 372, 374, 376, 382, 396, 398, 404, 410, 414, 416, 418, 420, 422, 424, 426, 428, 432, 442, 444, 474, 476, 496
Pizarro, Juan, 368
Plank, Eddie, 90, 96, 98, 100, 104, 116, 118, 122, 126, 128
Players' Association, 400, 406, 408, 432, 452, 458, 460, 480
Players' League, 50, 52, 78
Players' League revolt (1890), 30
Players' Protective Association, 80
Podres, Johnny, 308, 310, 322, 364, 366, 400
Pollet, Howie, 260, 270
Polo Grounds (New York), 58, 104, 146, 154, 156, 164, 166, 208, 214, 286, 290, 306, 316, 342, 362
Porterfield, Bob, 312
Post, Wally, 320, 322, 358
Postema, Pam, 454
Potter, Nels, 262
Powell, Boog, 368, 378, 388, 390, 410, 414
Power, Vic, 320
Prim, Ray, 266
Providence (RI) Grays, 50, 58, 68
Puckett, Kirby, 460, 492, 498
Pulliam, Harry, 80
Putnams (Brooklyn), 14

Qualls, Jim, 388
Quinn, Jack, 156, 182, 210
Quinn, Joe, 68
Quisenberry, Dan, 464, 472, 474, 478, 484

Radbourn, Charlie "Old Hoss," 28, 42, 58, 68
Raines, Tim, 456, 460, 476, 486, 492, 498
Ramos, Pedro, 370
Randle, Lenny, 436
Randolph, Willie, 434, 492
Rariden, Bill, 134
Raschi, Vic, 280, 282, 294, 300, 304
Rath, Morrie, 138
Reach, Al, 16, 18, 24
Reagan, Ronald, 148
Reardon, Jeff, 494, 496
Reese, Harold Henry "Pee Wee," 254, 274, 282, 292, 296, 308, 310, 318, 322, 326
Regan, Phil "The Vulture," 378
Reiser, "Pistol" Pete, 254, 258, 270, 276, 282
Reitz, Heinie, 60
Relief pitchers, 396, 450
Remy, Jerry, 436
Repoz, Roger, 374
Reserve clause, 48, 50, 52, 346, 404, 408
Rettenmund, Merv, 410
Reulbach, Ed, 98, 100, 118, 120
Reuss, Jerry, 468
Reynolds, Allie, 246, 274, 282, 294, 300, 304, 306, 318
Rhodes, Dusty, 316
Rice, Grantland, 138
Rice, Jim, 408, 428, 436, 440, 444, 474, 486, 498
Rice, Sam, 166, 170, 202
Richard, J.R., 444, 462
Richardson, Bobby, 354, 356, 362, 366
Richardson, Hardy, 64, 66
Richert, Pete, 390
Rickey, Branch, 152, 174, 204, 246, 248, 258, 270, 272, 306, 340
Righetti, Dave, 474, 488
Ripken, Jr., Cal, 456, 474, 490, 498
Ripken, Sr., Cal, 490
Ripple, Jimmy, 252
Risberg, Swede, 114, 134, 142
Riverfront Stadium (Cincinnati), 394, 412
Rivers, Mickey, 394, 434
Rixey, Eppa, 130, 132, 162
Rizzuto, Phil, 256, 260, 294, 296, 300, 318
Roberts, Robin, 296, 298, 302, 306, 310, 316, 320, 370
Robertson, Bob, 414, 416
Robertson, Dave, 132, 134
Robinson, Brooks, 166, 352, 368, 378, 380, 412, 440, 442
Robinson, Frank, 322, 324, 344, 350, 358, 366, 370, 378, 380, 388, 410, 414, 418, 430, 454
Robinson, Jack Roosevelt "Jackie," 56, 198, 218, 242, 246, 248, 252, 270, 272, 274, 282, 290, 292, 296, 326, 416, 452
Robinson, Wilbert, 130
Robinson, Yank, 52
Robison, Frank, 74, 78
Robison, Stanley, 78
Rockford Forest Cities, 26, 28, 34, 36
Rodgers, Buck, 470
Roe, Preacher, 282, 302
Rogell, Billy, 216
Rolfe, Red, 220, 224
Rommel, Eddie, 162
Rookie of the Year, 252, 274, 286, 296, 324, 364, 366, 370, 380, 388, 398, 410, 428, 432, 456, 464, 466, 474, 482, 486, 496, 498
Roosevelt, President Franklin, 238
Root, Charlie, 180, 200, 210, 224
Rose, Pete "Charlie Hustle," 366, 384, 388, 394 396, 406, 408, 412, 414, 420, 422, 424, 430, 434, 440, 444, 448, 460, 464, 468, 470, 472, 474, 478, 482, 486, 494, 498
Roseboro, Johnny, 360, 376
Rosen, Al, 294, 300, 304, 310, 312, 314, 322, 430
Rothstein, Arnold, 114
Roush, Edd, 138, 186
Rowe, Jack, 30, 64
Rowe, Schoolboy, 216, 224, 252,
Royals Stadium (Kansas City), 394
Rudi, Joe, 414, 418, 420, 432
Rudolph, Dick, 126, 128, 130
Ruether, Dutch, 138
Ruffing, Charles Herbert "Red," 196, 204, 208, 222, 226, 228, 230, 232, 254, 256, 260
Ruhle, Vern, 452, 462
Ruppert, Jacob, 146, 150, 152, 164, 194, 232
Rusie, Amos "Hoosier Thunderbolt," 70, 72, 88
Russell, Bill, 422
Russell, Reb, 134
Russo, Marius, 254, 262
Ruth, George Herman "Babe," 60, 82, 88, 110, 112, 128, 130, 132, 134, 136, 138, 142, 144, 146, 150, 152, 154, 156, 158, 160, 162, 164, 166, 168, 170, 172, 174, 176, 178, 180, 182, 184, 190, 194, 196, 200, 204, 206, 208, 210, 212, 214, 216, 220, 222, 228, 234, 254, 260, 270, 276, 294, 326, 334, 348, 350, 352, 354, 356, 358, 364, 366, 372, 382, 422, 426, 438
Ruthven, Dick, 462
Ryan, Connie, 436
Ryan, Jimmy, 62
Ryan, Nolan, 70, 388, 390, 400, 408, 414, 420, 426, 430, 438, 448, 452, 458, 462, 466, 468, 474, 476, 482, 486, 490, 496

Saberhagen, Bret, 484
Sadecki, Ray, 364, 372
Sain, Johnny, 280, 298, 304, 316
St. George Cricket Club (Staten Island), 10
St. Louis Browns, 48, 52, 56, 60, 62, 64, 66, 74, 90, 116, 134, 146, 152, 154, 162, 202, 204, 222, 242, 244, 248, 264, 266, 288, 294, 296, 298, 310, 314, 378
St. Louis Cardinals, "Cards," "Redbirds," 148, 152, 154, 156, 160, 194, 200, 202, 206, 208, 212, 214, 216, 218, 228, 232, 244, 250, 252, 254, 258, 260, 262, 266, 268, 270, 272, 274, 276, 278, 282, 288, 296, 306, 308, 310, 318, 324, 328, 332, 350, 352, 354, 364, 370, 372, 376, 382, 384, 386, 402, 404, 424, 426, 456, 472, 478, 484, 488, 494

St. Louis Maroons, 48
St. Louis Stars, 196
Sallee, Slim, 132, 134, 138
Sandberg, Ryne, 478
Sanders, Ray, 260
San Diego Padres, 400, 416, 418, 420, 456, 472, 474, 478, 480, 486, 488, 492, 494, 496
Sanford, Jack, 360, 362
San Francisco Seals, 194, 238, 250
San Francisco Giants, 286, 288, 302, 304, 326, 332, 334, 336, 340, 342, 360, 364, 370, 374, 376, 382, 384, 386, 414, 416, 422, 428
Sanguillan, Manny, 414
Santiago, Jose, 382
Sauer, Hank, 308
Sawyer, Eddie, 298
Sax, Steve, 486, 496, 498
Schalk, Ray, 134
Schang, Wally, 136, 160
Schiraldi, Calvin, 490
Schmidt, Boss, 106
Schmidt, Michael Jack "Mike," 434, 440, 444, 450, 460, 462, 466, 474, 476, 478, 486, 490
Schoendienst, Red, 308, 310, 328, 332
Schofield, Dick, 354
Schulte, Wildfire, 104, 110, 118, 120
Schultz, Barney, 370, 372
Schupp, Ferdie, 132, 134
Score, Herb, 318, 322, 324, 332
Scott, Everett, 162
Scott, Mike, 484, 486, 488
Season Ticket, 442
Seaton, Tom, 126
Seattle Mariners, 458, 472, 476, 488, 494
Seattle Pilots, 344, 396
Seaver, George Thomas "Tom Terrific," 368, 388, 390, 396, 400, 410, 424, 438, 442, 458, 468, 476, 478, 482, 490
Sebring, Jimmy, 84
Seitz, Peter, 408
Selee, Frank, 68, 74, 82, 96
Selkirk, George, 220, 228
Seminick, Andy, 296
Sewell, Joe, 154, 164, 206
Sewell, Luke, 264
Seybold, Socks, 86, 90, 100, 146
Shannon, Mike, 382
Shannon, Spike, 100
Shantz, Bobby, 304
Shaw, Bob, 336
Shawkey, Bob, 128, 156
Shea, Bill, 340, 342
Shea Stadium (New York), 342, 400, 434, 490
Sheckard, Jimmy, 86
Sheldon, Rollie, 356
Sherdel, Bill, 182
Sheridan, Jack, 90
Sherry, Larry, 336
Sherry, Norm, 350
Shibe Park (Philadelphia), 80, 112, 190
Shocker, Urban, 178
Shore, Ernie, 128, 130, 132
"The Shot Heard 'Round the World," 290, 300, 302
Shotton, Burt, 274, 276, 282
Show, Eric, 472
Siebern, Norm, 352
Sievers, Roy, 330
Simmons, "Bucketfoot" Al, 144, 152, 170, 174, 176, 178, 180, 182, 184, 190, 206, 208, 214, 218, 220, 288
Simmons, Curt, 296, 298
Simmons, Ted, 426, 470
Singleton, Ken, 430, 444, 464
Sisler, Dick, 370
Sisler, "Gorgeous" George, 138, 144, 146, 148, 152, 154, 162, 164, 174, 276
Skowron, Bill "Moose," 314, 324, 330, 334, 352, 356, 362, 366
Slagle, Jimmy, 96, 102
Slaughter, Enos "Country," 244, 258, 272
Smith, Al, 250, 334
Smith, Charles, 20
Smith, Elmer, 156, 158
Smith, Frank, 96
Smith, Hal, 346, 356
Smith, Lee, 476, 478
Smith, Lonnie, 470
Smith, Mayo, 384, 386
Smith, Ozzie "Wizard of Oz," 450, 482, 486, 492
Smith, Red, 216, 448
Smith, Reggie, 380, 426, 438
Smith, Sherry, 130, 132
Snider, Edwin Donald "Duke of Flatbush," 282, 292, 296, 302, 308, 310, 318, 320, 322, 326, 328, 330, 336
Snodgrass, Fred, 120, 124, 126
Soden, Arthur, 78
Sosa, Elias, 434
Southworth, Billy, 264, 280

Spahn, Warren, 280, 296, 302, 304, 308, 310, 326, 328, 330, 332, 334, 336
Spalding, Albert, 6, 28, 32, 36, 38, 40, 48, 50, 52, 62, 78, 80
Spalding Guides, 8
Spalding Sporting Goods Company, 36
Speaker, Tris "The Grey Eagle," "Spoke," 118, 124, 130, 132, 144, 152, 154, 158, 160, 164, 172, 174, 182, 218
Splittorff, Paul, 436
Sporting Life, 50
Sporting News, 50, 138, 194, 274
Sports Illustrated, 448
Sportsman's Park (St. Louis), 80, 264, 272
Stafford, Bill, 356
Stahl, Chick, 74, 86
Stahl, Jake, 122, 124
Stainback, Tuck, 262
Stallard, Tracy, 354
Stallings, George, 126, 128
Stanage, Oscar, 106
Stanky, Eddie, 276, 282, 380, 436
Stanley, Bob, 490
Stanley, Mickey, 384
Stargell, Willie "Pops," 412, 422, 426, 432, 442, 444, 454
Stark, Dolly, 224
Start, Joe, 18, 20
Staub, Rusty, 424
Steinbrenner, George "The Boss," 240, 394, 402, 406, 428, 436, 440, 442, 450, 456, 462, 468, 470
Steinfeldt, Harry, 98
Stengel, Casey "The Ol' Perfessor," 130, 166, 216, 280, 282, 292, 304, 314, 318, 326, 332, 342, 356, 362, 372, 430
Stephens, Gene, 300
Stephens, Vern, 262, 282, 294, 456
Stephenson, Riggs, 160, 186, 210
Stewart, Dave, 498
Stieb, Dave, 482
Stivetts, Jack, 70, 74
Stone, John, 216
Stone, Steve, 464
Stoneham, Horace, 288
Stottlemyre, Mel, 372
Stovey, George, 56
Stovey, Harry, 42, 60, 68
Strawberry, Darryl, 456, 460, 478, 486, 496
Strikes, 114, 120, 136, 416, 448, 450, 466, 480
Strike zone, 350, 352, 386, 396
Strong, Curtis, 480
Stuper, John, 472
Sturdivant, Tom, 324, 330
Sturm, Johnny, 256
Sullivan, Dan, 60
Summer Game, The, 442
Summers, Ed, 104, 106
Sunday, Billy, 38, 60
Sutcliffe, Rick, 478, 492
Sutter, Bruce, 450, 462, 472, 478
Sutton, Don, 422, 426, 442, 458, 470, 488
Sutton, Ezra, 42
Sweasy, Charlie, 22
Sweeney, Charlie, 48, 58
Swoboda, Ron, 390
Syndicated baseball, 74

Tabor, Jim, 254
Taft, President William Howard, 118
Tannehill, Jesse, 92
Tanner, Chuck, 474
Taylor, Dummy, 94
Taylor, Ron, 388
Tebeau, Patsy, 74
Tekulve, Kent, 444
Television, 238, 240, 286, 288, 340, 450
Temple, Johnny, 322
Temple Cup, 72
Templeton, Garry, 448
Tenace, Gene, 418, 420
Tenney, Fred, 74, 106
Terry, "Memphis" Bill, 172, 180, 182, 192, 200, 202, 206, 210, 212, 214, 218, 224, 226, 228, 246, 260
Terry, Ralph, 346, 356, 362
Tesreau, Jeff, 122, 124, 126, 128, 136
Texas Rangers, 394, 416, 426, 436
$30,000 muff, 124
Thomas, Gorman, 464, 470
Thomas, Lee, 342
Thompson, Hank, 248
Thompson, Sam, 64, 66, 70, 72
Thomson, Bobby, 290, 300, 302, 336
Three Rivers Stadium (Pittsburgh), 394, 416
Throneberry, Marv, 352, 362
Tiant, Luis, 404, 410, 430, 432, 470
Tiernan, Mike, 66
Tiger Stadium (Detroit), 394, 410
Tinker, Joe, 96, 104

Tolan, Bobby, 412, 434
Toledo News-Bee, 100
Toronto Blue Jays, 468, 482, 484, 488, 492, 494
Torre, Joe, 364, 396, 414, 468
Torrez, Mike, 430, 436, 440
Tovar, Cesar, 410
Tracewski, Dick, 386
Trammell, Alan, 456, 476, 480, 492
Travers, Al, 120
Traynor, Harold Joseph "Pie," 166, 168, 172, 210
Tresh, Tom, 362, 372, 380
Tribune Co., 454
Trillo, Manny, 464
Triple Crown, 148, 160, 168, 172, 190, 210, 212, 214, 216, 222, 228, 310, 324
Trosky, Hal, 218, 222, 226, 250
Trout, Dizzy, 264, 268
Troy (NY) Haymakers, 26, 28
Trucks, Virgil, 268
Tucker, Tommy, 68
Tudor, John, 482, 484, 494
Turley, "Bullet" Bob, 316, 318, 330, 332
Turner, Jim, 228
Tyler, Lefty, 136

Ueberroth, Peter, 452, 454, 458, 480, 494
Uhle, George "the Bull," 176
Union Association, 28, 34, 46, 48, 50, 52, 58, 60, 178, 116
Union grounds (Brooklyn), 18, 20, 24
Unions (Morrisania), 14, 18, 22

Valentine, Ellis, 462
Valenzuela, Fernando, 448, 464, 466, 474, 482, 486
Vance, Clarence Arthur "Dazzy," 162, 168, 172, 182, 202
Vander Meer, Johnny, 212, 230, 238
Van Slyke, Andy, 498
Vaughan, Arky, 210, 220, 224, 230
Vaughn, Hippo, 136
Veach, Bobby, 130
Veeck, Bill, 248, 274, 278, 296, 298, 314
Veeck, Sr., Bill, 208
Vernon, Mickey, 310, 312
Versalles, Zoilo, 374
Veterans Stadium (Philadelphia), 394
Viola, Frank, 492, 494, 498
Virdon, Bill, 420
Vitt, Ossie, 250
Voiselle, Bill, 280
Von der Ahe, Chris, 48, 56, 64, 74
Vosmik, Joe, 220
Vuckovich, Pete, 470, 472

Waddell, Rube, 86, 90, 96, 98, 100, 116, 124
Wagner, Honus, 82, 84, 86, 88, 92, 96, 100, 102, 106, 118, 120, 122, 134, 200, 230
Wagner, Leon, 342
Waitkus, Eddie, 296
Walberg, Rube, 206
Walker, Bill, 206
Walker, Dixie, 248
Walker, Gee, 226
Walker, Harry "The Hat," 272, 294
Walker, Moses, 56
Walker, Welday, 56
Wallace, Bobby, 74, 90
Walsh, Ed, 96, 100, 102
Walters, Bucky, 234, 250, 252
Wambsganss, Bill "Wamby," 156, 158, 184
Waner, Lloyd "Little Poison," 180, 182, 210, 244
Waner, Paul "Big Poison," 174, 180, 182, 210, 216, 224, 244
Ward, John Montgomery "Monte," 40, 50, 58, 66, 68
Ward, Robert, 116
Warneke, Lon, 210, 218, 220
Warner, Jack, 94
Washburn, Ray, 382, 384
Washington, Claudell, 430, 468
Washington, Herb, 394, 426
Washington Nationals, 18, 22, 24, 36
Washington Olympics, 24, 26
Washington Senators, 110, 114, 122, 132, 136, 160, 164, 166, 168, 170, 176, 178, 180, 184, 192, 198, 202, 204, 212, 214, 216, 218, 226, 244, 260, 298, 310, 312, 330, 340, 342, 366, 394, 412, 494
Waslewski, Gary, 382
Waterman, Fred, 20, 22
Watson, Bob, 462
Watt, Eddie, 390
Weaver, Buck, 114, 134, 142
Weaver, Earl, 386, 410, 412, 414, 444, 470
Weeghman, Charles, 116
Weis, Al, 388, 390
Weiss, George, 352, 356
Welch, Bob, 442

Welch, Curt, 52, 64
Welch, Mickey, 28, 60, 66
Wendlestedt, Harry, 374, 498
Wertz, Vic, 286, 294, 316, 324
Westrum, Wes, 316
West Side Park (Chicago), 98
Weyer, Lee, 498
Wheat, Zack, 130, 168
Whitaker, Lou, 476
White, Bill, 372, 454
White, Doc, 96, 100
White, Jim "Deacon," 30, 32, 34, 36, 40, 64
White, Roy, 372
White, Will, 42
Whitehill, Earl, 212
Whitney, "Jumbo" Jim, 42, 68
Whiz Kids, 296, 298
Wilcox, Milt, 476
Wilhelm, Hoyt, 308, 368
Wilks, Ted, 264
Willett, Ed, 104
Williams, Billy, 380, 382, 466
Williams, Cy, 156, 166
Williams, Dick, 380, 414, 418, 420, 424, 462
Williams, Ken, 162
Williams, Lefty, 112, 132, 134, 138, 142
Williams, Theodore Samuel "Splendid Splinter," "Ted," 112, 190, 232, 246, 248, 254, 256, 260, 270, 272, 274, 278, 280, 294, 300, 316, 318, 324, 330, 332, 342, 376, 416, 450, 464
Williamson, Ed, 38
Willis, Ron, 382
Willis, Vic, 106
Wills, Maury, 110, 218, 348, 358, 364, 376, 404, 424, 426, 454
Wilson, Hack, 174, 180, 186, 200, 202, 206, 210
Wilson, Jimmie, 250, 252
Wilson, Mookie, 490
Wilson, Owen, 122
Wilson, Reverend, 8
Wilson, Willie, 394, 452, 456, 464, 472
Wiltse, Hooks, 118
Winfield, Dave, 450, 456, 478
Wingo, Al, 172
Winning Team, 148
Witt, Mike, 480, 488
Wood, "Smoky" Joe, 124, 128, 130, 132, 160
Wood, Wilbur, 418
Woodling, Gene, 300
World, 8
World Series, 30, 46, 52, 58, 60, 62, 64, 66, 68, 78, 80, 84, 142, 148, 156, 158, 194, 196, 206, 208, 216, 218, 220, 230, 234, 250, 252, 254, 256, 258, 260, 264, 272, 276, 278, 290, 292, 296, 298, 302, 304, 306, 308, 310, 312, 314, 316, 318, 322, 326, 330, 332, 334, 336, 344, 346, 350, 352, 356, 366, 372, 378, 380, 382, 394, 396, 402, 410, 412, 422, 424, 428, 432, 434, 436, 438, 442, 444, 450, 452, 458, 464, 466, 468, 470, 472, 476, 480, 484, 488, 490, 492, 494, 498
Worrell, Todd, 486
Worthington, Al, 374
Wright, George, 10, 16, 20, 22, 28, 38, 40
Wright, Glenn, 168, 172, 210
Wright, Harry, 10, 16, 20, 22, 24, 28, 32, 38, 40
Wright, Sam, 10
Wrigley Field (Chicago), 220, 224, 230, 296, 320, 394, 454, 480
Wyatt, John, 254, 258, 382
Wynn, Early, 292, 294, 298, 300, 304, 310, 314, 318, 322, 324, 334, 364
Wyse, Hank, 266

Yankee Stadium, 112, 142, 164, 182, 196, 228, 234, 260, 274, 282, 348, 350, 352, 254, 304, 310, 312, 326, 358, 372, 394
Yastrzemski, Carl "Yaz," 352, 376, 380, 382, 384, 386, 400, 402, 430, 432, 436, 440 458, 476
Yawkey, Tom, 192, 218, 220, 222
Yeager, Steve, 398, 468
Yerkes, Steve, 124
York, Rudy, 226, 238, 250, 270, 272
You Know Me, Al, 138
Youmans, Floyd, 452
Young, Denton True "Cy," 28, 42, 70, 72, 74, 82, 84, 86, 92, 110, 114, 304
Young, Dick, 396
Young, Nick, 78
Youngs, Ross, 166, 174
Yount, Robin, 456, 462, 470, 472

Zachary, Tom, 170, 176, 184
Zarilla, Al, 262
Zernial, Gus, 300, 312
Zettlein, George, 20, 36
Zimmerman, Heinie, 112, 122, 132, 134
Zisk, Richie, 426